A History of War Resistance in America

A History of War Resistance
in America

James M. Volo

GREENWOOD

AN IMPRINT OF ABC-CLIO, LLC
Santa Barbara, California • Denver, Colorado • Oxford, England

Library of Congress Cataloging-in-Publication Data
Volo, James M., 1947–
  A history of war resistance in America / James M. Volo.
      p. cm.
  Includes bibliographical references and index.
  ISBN 978-0-313-37624-5 (hard copy : alk. paper) — ISBN 978-0-313-37625-2 (ebook)
1. Peace movements—United States—History. 2. Pacifism—United States—History.
3. War—Prevention—History. I. Title.
  JZ5584.U6V65 2010
  303.6′6—dc22   2010000929

ISBN: 978-0-313-37624-5
EISBN: 978-0-313-37625-2

14   13   12   11   10   1   2   3   4   5

This book is also available on the World Wide Web as an eBook.
Visit www.abc-clio.com for details.

Greenwood
An Imprint of ABC-CLIO, LLC

ABC-CLIO, LLC
130 Cremona Drive, P.O. Box 1911
Santa Barbara, California 93116-1911

This book is printed on acid-free paper ∞

Manufactured in the United States of America

Contents

Introduction: The Antiwar Tradition in America

Battles over history—dry, old history—and whose history gets to be told can become heated and emotional because the ways we behaved then say so much about the kind of people, society, or nation we have become.

—Colin G. Calloway, historian

Farewell to treaties, now war must be our judge.
—Marcus Lucanus, on Caesar crossing the Rubicon, 49 B.C.

The race is not to the swift nor the battle to the strong, but the God of Israel is He that giveth strength and power unto his people.

—Abigail Adams, 1775

The continued series of wars and the threats of war that form the background to much of American history have inevitably divided society in the United States into prowar and antiwar factions. Few subjects in U.S. history—with perhaps independence, slavery, and abortion excepted—have proven to be as polarizing of U.S. public opinion or as long-lasting as a nexus of public discourse. Religious pacifists, peace proponents, conscientious objectors, war resisters, anti-imperial isolationists, disarmament proponents, and global supernationalists have all expressed some form of antiwar sentiment at one time or another over the last two and a half centuries of American history.

Although most people alive in the early 21st century regard the Vietnam antiwar movement of the 1960s and 1970s as the pinnacle of war resistance in the United States, pacifists and war resisters have been present throughout the history of the nation. Among these have been religious pacifists during the French and Indian War (1754–1763); political moderates during the American Revolution (1775–1783); Francophile Republicans in the quasi-war with revolutionary France (1798–1800); Anglophile Federalists during the War of 1812; Transcendentalist writers, academics, and abolitionists in the War with Mexico (1846–1848); Northern Copperheads and Southern anti-Confederates in the Civil War (1861–1865); the Anti-Imperialist League of the Spanish-American War (1898); the Fellowship of Reconciliation and the Women's Peace Party of the World War I era (1914–1918); the United World Federalists of the post–World War II decades; and the mass of antiwar protestors and almost innumerable alphabetically designated organizations (acronyms) from the Vietnam War era. Today those who would foster global governance, collective security, and social progressivism make up the bulk of war resisters. Each of these groups has opposed the military policy of the government of the United States in some fashion, and each individual war resister and antiwar group has been important in forming or reforming government policy with respect to war and peace throughout American history.[1]

While numbering only a minority of its citizens, these groups traditionally have expressed antiwar feelings in the United States. Significantly, rarely has a corresponding tradition among the majority of its citizens concerned the legitimacy of U.S. policies regarding the prosecution of war. As the historic record shows, however, warfare seems to be tolerated by the majority of Americans when four factors regarding war are present. Acceptable warfare must be quick, decisive, cheap, and relatively bloodless. As soon as one or more of these factors fails, support for continued combat is quickly undermined among the population. Long wars like Vietnam, bloody wars like the Civil War, and wars without decisive outcomes like the Korean conflict produce the most virulent antiwar sentiment.

The guardian of civil liberties in America has always been the press. In *The Artillery of the Press,* author and journalist James Reston noted that the press has been obligated to oversee for the public just what it is that U.S. government officials and the diplomatic corps are doing. The book—with a title borrowed in part from a phrase uttered by Thomas Jefferson in his second inaugural address—was based on the Elihu Root Series of foreign policy lectures given in 1966. Reston noted,

> The old tradition of the American press was that anything a government hides, except during open and declared war, was wrong, probably wicked, and therefore should be exposed; but a press demanding unlimited freedom for this principle today [1966] could in many cases risk the nation's security. Yet the problem cannot be solved simply by saying that the operations . . . of the government are none of the public's business.[2]

The nature of war-making and peace-making has changed since the founding of the nation. It is now a clandestine war or a peace of self-interest; an economic war of sanctions or a peace adorned with financial inducements; an intelligence war or a peace filled with unmitigated propaganda, all pursued at some level among every people and nation on every continent on the earth. In this morass, the legitimate rights of the government to secure the nation and the civil liberties of those who protest against war or preparations for war are inextricably enmeshed. Responsible officials, civil libertarians, and media pundits have not been able to resolve this problem.

Throughout American history, the free press has been no less unrestrained and partisan than at present. Nonetheless, newspapers, radio, television, and the Internet are no longer catering to a small national audience, they have become part of the strategy used to prepare the battleground of war or turn world opinion toward peace. Press reports generally travel faster than official reports. They also usually are filled with inaccuracies, anecdotal reports, and unsubstantiated opinions. When official reports arrive, those in opposition to the government tend to see any differences as damage control (spin, if you will). This is an unfortunate surmise because the official reports are often more accurate.

An inaccuracy about foreign affairs in the American press might have been overlooked before World War II, but in the 21st century, it becomes a significant issue on the Internet in a matter of minutes, in foreign capitals in an hour, in the presidential briefing room before the beginning of the nightly news cycle, and in the White House press briefing room the next day. The personal dimension of opinion-making also has become overpowering with the advent of Internet blogs and Web sites that deprofessionalize news reporting, and individuals of all political persuasions driving the direction of national policy in an unrestrained and undisciplined manner. Peace proponents whose goal in the 19th century was once to influence the legitimate war-making policies of their government, in the 21st century are more focused on changing the fundamental underpinnings of their government. Uninformed beliefs have been conflated with uncontested truths to the detriment of America and have, in the words of the noted journalist Eric Severeid, "elevated the influence of fools to that of wise men; the ignorant to the level of the learned; [and] the evil to the level of the good."[3]

Most Americans believe that the recent high level of partisanship in the conduct of the U.S. government is a recent development attributable somehow to the concept of a politics of personal destruction. Yet the lack of bipartisanship on the foreign policy front has been astonishing throughout American history. Since the Jay Treaty of 1794, political parties in America have consistently used disagreements over such important matters as foreign relations, military appropriations, and force levels simply to pry one another out of office. Even within the military establishment, the proper course of action often has led to charges of malfeasance and incompetence. Serious disagreements concerning the powers of government and the rights of the governed have been contested in the antiwar arena. Those outside the process are likely to conclude that the United States has been governed by a persistently confused set of officials elected by an inherently unstable people. "Discordant voices are raised on every side. The debates seem to proceed in a series of vast and unregulated explosions. It is a process that encourages extremes, and, as public opinion slowly forms, the extreme voices are those most loudly and frequently heard."[4] These disputes have often been bitter ones involving war and peace, and they have led some Americans to distrust those in government regardless of their party.[5]

The topic of *peace-seeking* is intimately tied to that of *war-making*. The two are ideological adversaries—a dichotomy of human nature (or of human frailty, if you will) continually at odds. The two positions regarding war and peace are mutually exclusive with the center ground of compromise untenable for dedicated adherents of either side. Yet one can not be considered without equal consideration of the other, for they have little meaning out of context. In this no-man's land no wars are so small as to allow peace to exist with them simultaneously, and no peace so solemnly entered into that it could not be broken at a moments notice. Consequently, peace-making requires as much preparedness as war-making, and in many ways, the preparations for peace have proven the more difficult task. One of the unfortunate outcomes of a virtually uninterrupted history of successful war-making was that *Americans came to believe that war worked*—that it could be used to resolve seemingly insoluble problems, work out thorny issues, and bring lasting peace. By comparison, America's relationship with peace-making has traveled a rocky road. This dichotomy provides a major theme for this work. Although reality teaches that some conflict will always exist between nations and peoples, lofty aims and high ideals are necessary starting points to establish a lasting peace. The vital question is how well-intentioned aims and ideals toward peace can be made to work in a dangerous world.

Certain dynamic forces between nations seemingly make either war or peace the natural state of their relations, and the nations of the world have had vast and bitter experience with both types. In the 17th and 18th centuries, for instance, Britain and France were implacable enemies, yet in the 20th century, they have several times been allies. To divorce the state of war from the state of peace is to skew their relationship beyond recognition. This volume is, therefore, as much concerned with the military, the preparations for war, and its justifiable prosecution as it is with pacifism, the legitimate resistance to war, and the appropriate and free exercise of civil liberties. It describes, hopefully in a balanced manner, the reasons for conflict among peoples, the prosecution of war among nations, the role of the media in forming public opinion, the role of the courts in protecting or limiting civil liberties, and the development of loyal war resistance movements. Readers who hope to find in this volume an excoriation of the American military establishment or the actions of the U.S. government in pursuing its legitimate foreign policy goals will be just as disappointed as those who are looking for a similar condemnation of sincere pacifists or of the peace movement in general. Almost every definable segment of the American population has held prowar or antiwar positions at some time in American history, and their beliefs often have changed over time or according to circumstance.

The American nation was founded on the lofty goals and self-evident liberties listed in the Declaration of Independence, but the terms of governance were established under the more practical structural paradigms and limiting details of the U.S. Constitution. The two must be made to work in concert for the nation and its people to succeed. The ability to appeal foreign policy decisions and methods of diplomacy "to the Supreme Judge of the world for the rectitude of our intentions" as stated in the Declaration of Independence or to know what's right "as God gives us to know the right" as suggested by Abraham Lincoln in his second inaugural address is open to the moral judgment of the individual reader. At some point, individuals inevitably will disagree over the legitimacy of some policy initiative or critical war decision. American society has therefore vested in the U.S. Supreme Court the function of determining right and wrong as a function of law and constitutionality rather than one based on ethics and morality. Hopefully, the two sets of criteria are not too divergent. Many of the precedent-setting decisions and opinions of the justices and associate justices of the court regarding the civil liberties of protestors and the constitutionality of war policies are referenced within the chronologically arranged chapters of this work.

For the historian, writing about the past means thinking in the present and conveying ideas about bygone events and ideas using modern rather than arcane terms. Herein lies a great difficulty with regard to describing the history of the peace movement in America. Antiwar traditions in America have had many faces that are not immediately recognizable as movements. Each is the product of hindsight expressed in the modern vernacular. Moreover, in modern times, many terms concerning the prosecution of peace have been conflated or used interchangeably with little regard to their discrete usage in the past. To write the history of war resistance only in terms common to the Vietnam-era antiwar movement, for example, is to misrepresent a long tradition of American peace-seeking that was largely as individual and apolitical as the peace movement of the 1960s and 1970s was collective and partisan. It is also impossible to include in the text every war-resisting group or person, author, or politician—many of whom exhibited their own form of unwarranted self-importance at the time. Consequently, only those who made the most significant contributions to the antiwar movement over time are included.

Not all the war resisters of the past couched their objections to war in so-called *antiestablishment* terms nor did they all participate in mass marches, protests, and sit-ins. Many grounded their personal resistance to war solely in religious, economic, or constitutional terms, and some combined their antiwar objections under many headings unfamiliar to the protestors of the 20th century. Moreover, words and phrases like *pacifism, isolationism, draft evasion,* and *conscientious objection* were not in common usage until the beginning of the 20th century. Americans living in the 18th and 19th centuries probably would have understood the underlying meaning of such words and phrases, but they also would have found them novel and not completely appropriate when used to describe themselves.

Before the Spanish American War, for example, *isolation* was a physical reality for the United States, a barrier of oceans, space, and time as well as of available supplies of food, water, and human endurance aboard vessels at sea that effectively limited America's active involvement in the affairs of other nations to its contiguous international boundaries with British, French, and Spanish North America—essentially Canada, Mexico, or the islands of the Caribbean. The successful prosecution of U.S. naval operations in the Pacific against a major European power (Spain) in the far away Philippines in 1898 and the expansion of U.S. military influence in faraway China in 1900 converted *isolationism* from a geographic barrier to be overcome into an antiwar ideal to be pursued. It is from this period that the term *isolationist* enters the common vocabulary of Americans as a descriptor of the nation's long-standing tradition of noninvolvement in overseas affairs as a means of safeguarding its own distinctive way of life.

Before World War I, peace proponents rarely numbered more than a handful of persons in any community, and they would not be counted in the thousands nationwide for decades. Pacifists were conspicuous, therefore, because of their rarity in the general population. Among these, the largest and most consistent identifiable group was found among those who professed an absolute dedication to pacifist religious principles like the Quakers (Society of Friends). So profound and steadfast was Quaker resistance to war that Quakers have sometimes been construed incorrectly as the sole group in America dedicated to absolute pacifism.

Absolute pacifism has never been a majority position among Americans. Yet other people, not so easily recognized or categorized by their religious scruples, held a general antipathy toward the profession of arms and military expenditures, a selective opposition to a particular war or foreign policy initiative, or a nonsectarian (that is, not religion-based) opposition to war in general. Nonetheless, it has been the sum of antiwar, pacifist, isolationist, and antimilitarist sentiments rather than any particular war-resistance rationale that has informed American policy regarding war and peace from the founding of America into the 21st century.

A central theme of all recorded history has been the use or abuse of power—how it lurks in the shadows behind the professed idealism of politicians and the compelling reasons they expound when they bring their nations to war. Such words are often used to cloak those who wield political power and redistribute it among themselves as a consequence of success or failure on the battlefield. The ancient Greek historian of the Peloponnesian Wars (fourth century B.C.), Thucydides, urged historians to embrace skepticism in their analysis of great events and to look to personal or national self-interest rather than publicized grievances and high-sounding intentions when writing of warfare. Whenever a conflict breaks out in American history, its own generation of historians often rushes forward to record it with preconceived theories that often require for their support facts that are not in evidence while ignoring some of the so-called "realities on the ground" that might confound their pet hypotheses.

Armies exist to exert power. They have no other legitimate purpose. When Americans entered the Revolution, they did so as military amateurs, and they left it eight years later in much the same condition. Throughout the crisis the revolutionary army and navy were tightly controlled by the civilian authority of Congress. The obvious impracticality of relying on a citizen-force for the defense of the nation-state during the War of 1812 had led the population to tolerate a leadership monopoly among its professional military officers not only on the battlefield, but also in the halls of government. Moreover, the inherent inefficiency of a citizen-army was thought to be an effective brake on any politician who wished to misuse such a force to establish a despotic nation-state. Consequently, both Federal and Confederate forces entered the American Civil War with a "martial tradition that had glorified the civic and military virtue of the studiously unprofessional citizen-soldier." Yet both ended the war in 1865 with veteran armies that were "as professional as any other Western military in the world." Military officers—North and South—were given access to and influence over political policy-making "entirely out of proportion to either antebellum precedent or wartime preference . . . [yet]

civilian political leaders still saw themselves as the undisputed masters of both war efforts." The balance between the realms of military necessity and civilian control remains imperfectly understood and a topic of controversy in the United States to this day.[6]

Much has been written concerning the antiwar movement of the Vietnam era, and the modern antiwar case against foreign intervention, nation-building, and unbounded militarism remains forceful and relevant. Yet this work will focus on the lesser-known and largely unreported instances of religious pacifism, antiwar sentiment, and isolationist politics from Anglo-colonial times to the Vietnam era, while making historical connections to the more recent wars, such as in Somalia, Bosnia, Iraq, and Afghanistan. Antiwar movements have affected the prosecution of many wars, and sentiments similar to those of pacifists and isolationists from America's past were present in a large segment of American opinion as the United States entered the 21st century. Regretfully, the history of these earlier movements is poorly documented, widely misunderstood, and repeatedly misrepresented as to its character.

Although formally organized peace societies began to appear around 1815, they did not take on the characteristics of an *antiwar movement* in America until the 20th century. Regardless of the terminology used in this volume, however, it is the position of its author that the core beliefs underpinning antiwar sentiment, war resistance, and pacifism were well formed, sincerely founded, and deeply rooted in a historical tradition characteristic of America since colonial times.

A History of War Resistance in America sheds light on the largely unrecorded historical tradition of antiwar, pacifist, and isolationist sentiments among Americans and the sometimes-visceral response to them. It will attempt to draw historical boundaries among genuine disloyalty, self-serving pretensions, and political posturing, and the legitimate expressions of free speech, national concern, and real patriotism. The volume is arranged in two parts. Part I is composed of three chapters that delineate the ideologies of peace and war, and separate wide-ranging historical overviews of war-making and peace-making. Part II includes several chapters arranged chronologically exposing the detailed give and take of militarists and antiwar proponents during pivotal periods of American history, including the colonial period, the Civil War, the world wars, Korea, and Vietnam. From the very nature of these topics, this work is as much about making war as it is about resisting it. Hopefully, the reader will find the text neither radically militaristic nor rabidly antiwar in its presentation. This attempt at fairness may be off-putting for some less-than-open-minded readers, but the contents will highlight in a fair and balanced manner the illegitimate attempts that were made by government agencies to suppress criticism and interfere with basic American liberties in times of war, as well as the effect of antiwar and isolationist sentiment in thwarting legitimate foreign policy initiatives and obstructing necessary military preparedness.

Notes

1. Derogatory and disparaging racial terms have been removed from all period sources in this text. Unwarranted controversy continues to surround the use of the term *Indian* for Native Americans, however. Even Native Americans disagreed in this regard. However, *Indian* was the term used during the periods under scrutiny, and the author has chosen to use it where appropriate in this volume.

2. James Reston, *The Artillery of the Press: Its Influence on American Foreign Policy* (New York: Harper and Row, 1966), 20.

3. Reston, 17.

4. Reston, 22.

5. George C. Herring, *From Colony to Superpower: U.S. Foreign Relations Since 1776* (New York: Oxford University Press, 2008), 427.

6. Wayne Wei-Siang Hsieh, *West Pointers and the Civil War: The Old Army in War and Peace* (Chapel Hill: University of North Carolina Press, 2009) 4–5.

Part I

Chapter I

An Overview of Peace Principles

The vital question in peacemaking is how our aims and ideals are to be made to work. That is, by what means, what powers, what machinery, is peace to be made to prevail. It takes little imagination to picture the results, if, instead of elaborating the details of a constitutional government, the Founding Fathers had endeavored to govern this country under the ideals of the Declaration of Independence.

—Herbert Hoover, 1943

Peace without Victory

Both the Old and New Testaments look forward to a time at the so-called *end of days* when all peoples "will beat their swords into plowshares and their spears into pruning hooks. Nations shall not lift up against Nation, neither shall they learn war anymore" (Isaiah 2:4). The prophet Isaiah envisioned a time when each and every person would enjoy peace, *shalom*, and this word itself was used no less than thirty times in the Hebrew Bible that has come down to us, and peace as a condition is referred to more than 240 times in most English versions. God himself "shall command peace unto the nations . . . from sea even to sea and from river even to the end of the earth" (Zechariah 9:10). The birth of the Christ in the New Testament was quickly visited with the exclamation "Peace on earth and good will to men!" (Luke 2:14). Yet the references to war and warfare—especially in the early books of the Old Testament—are more numerous (more than 350) than those espousing peace.

The more secularized generalization that peace is good and war is bad is somewhat oversimplified. Dedicated peace-seeking is complex. War resisters have assembled the underpinnings of the antiwar movement from a surprisingly wide spectrum of sources and ideas: religious, political, social, intellectual, constitutional, and even simply obstructive and reactionary. They have not only relied on certain religious tenets found in the Bible, but also have formed their core beliefs from many nonreligious sources and historical precedents. Americans have often expressed moral indignation at the seeming depravity of Europe and the *balance of power* system that has informed European diplomacy and war-making for centuries,

3

but they also have "observed it closely, understood it workings, and sought to exploit it."[1] For example, President George Washington in his Farewell Address (1796) warned the nation to avoid permanent alliances, foreign entanglements, and wars outside the United States. These are the same ideas that serve as the basic principles of American isolationism to this day. Almost two centuries later (1961), in his farewell as president, Dwight David Eisenhower warned his countrymen of the growing domestic threat to civil liberties and democracy posed by an unbridled military-industrial complex—a common target of Vietnam War era anti-war activists.

The response by some proponents of military intervention to pacifism and isolationism as a solution for challenges to American self-interests suggests that warfare brings out the best in those who engage in it: courage, determination, cooperation, inventiveness, and an ability to cope with changing conditions. Peace proponents, on the other hand, point out that these same laudable personal qualities and outcomes could be applied to those who engage in peace with equal fervor before the outbreak of any armed conflict. In this way, peace might be established without the need for one nation to overwhelm another on the battlefield. Such an outcome would eliminate the loser's quest for revenge and ensure a more enduring peace. *Peace without victory* could be construed as a bilateral victory.

The Glorious Triumph of Arbitration

President Theodore Roosevelt, the first American to win a Nobel Prize in any of its categories, apparently understood the balance inherent in the concepts of war-making and peace-seeking. Although famed for his military leadership in Cuba during the Spanish-American War less than a decade earlier, Roosevelt was awarded the Nobel Peace Prize in 1906 for his work in negotiating the Treaty of Portsmouth (New Hampshire) that ended the Russo-Japanese War of 1905—by all accounts a gruesome and inhumane affair. A Quaker peace proponent at the time, unaware of the major conflagrations that would grip the world in the 20th century, wrote of the negotiations chaired by Roosevelt,

> There is nothing more gratifying and significant in the signs of the times, than the increase of peace principles among enlightened men and nations, and the ever-widening conviction that war is the most selfish, brutal, wasteful and ineffectual means of settling differences among men. . . . The substitution of reason for force in the settlement of differences between nations . . . [is] the glorious triumph of arbitration."[2]

The idea of attaining peace through means other than warfare, like negotiation and coercive diplomacy, is not new. "When you march up to attack a city, make its people an offer of peace. If they accept and open their gates, all the people in it shall be subject to forced labor and shall work for you. If they refuse to make peace and they engage you in battle, lay siege to that city" (Deuteronomy 20:10–12). And "the people of Gibeon had made a treaty of peace with Israel and were living near them" (Joshua 10:3). Treaties, like wars, are as old as the history of human kind, as is the need to seek their acceptance by an authorizing body (ratification). "Then Joshua made a treaty of peace with them to let them live, and the leaders of the assembly ratified it by oath" (Joshua 9:14–16). Even the treatment of prisoners can be gleaned from the ancient texts.

> When the king of Israel saw them [the captives], he asked Elisha, "Shall I kill them, my father? Shall I kill them?" "Do not kill them," Elisha answered. "Would you kill men you have captured with your own sword or bow? Set food and water before them so that they may eat and drink and then go back to their master." So he prepared a great feast for them, and after they had finished eating and drinking, he sent them away, and they returned to their master. So the bands from Aram stopped raiding Israel's territory. (2 Kings 6:21–23)

It should be noted here at the beginning of this discussion on the ideology of peace that the way of war resistance has not always been clear, and that some of the players—certainly a minority—were less than admirable in their sentiments. Although the substitution of reason (diplomacy) for force (armed conflict) has been a consistent underlying theme among war resisters, the core beliefs of many antiwar groups have exhibited a changing character over the more than two centuries since the founding of the United States. Certainly, Roosevelt's public utterances concerning peace-seeking, peace-keeping, military preparedness, and war-making in 1900 would be almost unrecognizable and not wholly acceptable to religious pacifists a century earlier or to political activists a century later.

Arms and Force Limitations

Arms limitations have long served as a foundation of the peace-seeking doctrine. From the inception of the American nation in the late 18th century, the majority of its residents have evidenced a strong apprehension of maintaining large standing armies and navies. Armies have long been considered tools for the suppression of the domestic population, while navies were thought to be the mechanism for entangling the nation in foreign affairs. Yet these professional forces were composed of men armed with generally inaccurate muskets fixed with bayonets and wooden ships that relied on the wind to move them about the oceans of the world. In the past—before the advent of airplanes, armored vehicles, machine guns, and other force projectors—it was reasonable to expect that people could maintain their liberties by overcoming the power of even the best armed forces through their own numbers. A powerful navy was much harder for the citizen to resist, but it was less capable of projecting its force beyond the immediate coastline. Modern war resisters have added to the inventory of objectionable weapons negative appraisals of atomic-powered aircraft carriers and submarines, cruise missiles, inter-continental ballistic missiles (ICBMs) and antimissile defense systems, land mines, spy satellites, strategic bombing, radio-controlled drones, and all biological, chemical, and nuclear weapons technologies.

Critics of U.S. militarism at the turn of the 20th century recognized the need to deter the growth of military technologies such as steel-plated battleships (dreadnaughts) and long-range artillery. The first effort to reduce worldwide naval armaments, for instance, came in 1922 at the Washington Conference that resulted in the Five Power Naval Treaty, which sought to maintain a fixed ratio of warships among the United States, Great Britain, Japan, France, and Italy. Under this highly praised treaty, the United States dismantled or sank more than 1 million tons of its own naval vessels from 1923 to 1933. The agreement failed—and U.S. and world naval rearmament revived in anticipation of growing world tensions—when Japan, France, and Italy refused to extend the naval-building "holiday" in 1935. At the end of World War II (1946), the United Nations unanimously agreed on a similar form of naval disarmament for all its member nations.

Historically, defense spending in the United States reached annual peaks of 38 percent of the gross national product (GNP) during World War II, 14 percent during the Korean War, 9.4 percent during Vietnam, 6.2 percent during the Cold War following Vietnam, a post–World War II low of 3 percent during Bosnia, and 3.6 percent since the fall of the Soviet Union. If taken by decade, defense spending has consistently placed an increasingly smaller burden on the U.S. economy than during any decade since the pre–World War II isolationist spending of the 1930s (1.5 percent). The recent conflicts in Iraq and Afghanistan, and the war on terrorism have raised the portion of GNP dedicated to security by a historical small amount that is less than the 4.9 percent level of the Carter years when no active military conflicts were in progress. By comparison, Medicare, Medicaid, and Social Security easily could drive federal spending dedicated to social programs from 20 percent of GNP in 2008 to around 24 percent of GDP by 2015, 34 percent by 2030, and more than 45 percent by 2040. The United States can almost certainly afford all of the national security it needs if it can manage other aspects of social programs and defense spending.[3]

Absolute versus Partisan Protest

While many war resisters eschew warfare in all its forms, some antiwar protestors, for their own reasons, choose to resist not war in general but rather a particular conflict or type of warfare—explicitly exempting, for instance, wars of national independence or popular struggles against imperial, dictatorial, or colonial powers. Conversely, absolute pacifists and conscientious objectors, among them colonial era Quakers and members of other pacifist religious groups to this day, argue that simply preparing for a war—whether offensive or defensive in nature—is immoral and un-Christian. "According to the convictions of our consciences [we] pray that we may be required to perform no military duty; for we consider the throwing up of a battery, or the driving of an ammunition or other team [wagon], as much an act of war as fighting in the ranks."[4]

These absolutist war critics based their pacifist sentiments on beliefs firmly rooted in their interpretation of the Bible, and the sincerity of their position as war resisters is generally beyond question. One of these wrote, "God's love in sending his Son [the Prince of Peace] into the world was an overture of peace."[5] Many Revolutionary and Civil War era moralists openly based their political beliefs on religious convictions similar to these.

Still other opponents of war assumed anti-administration or antimilitary positions simply as rhetorical expedients that allow them to be critical of their political adversaries, only to revert to their own form of strident militarism once they gained power. This observation may be regarded by some as cynical when applied to important topics such as war and peace. On the other hand, over the decades, many politicians and would-be popular leaders have attired themselves in the garments of antiwar sentiment or the "bloody shirt" of revenge as pragmatic responses to the immediate temper of the voters to keep or gain their seat in the halls of government. The phrase *situational hypocrisy* best seems to describe these changes in position due to political advantage.

Isolation versus Constitution

Antiwar sentiment has a long record in America beyond religiosity, and its historical roots are deeply set in both conservatism and nonintervention. Initially, religious absolutists were well separated as a pacifist group from other types, such as the *America-first* war resisters, who eschewed foreign wars for political, economic, or ethnic reasons, and the *constitutionalists*, who considered the deployment of American forces outside the United States unlawful and outside the powers granted to the federal government under the U.S. Constitution. Late in the 19th century, the latter group generally considered the preparation for war in terms of military expenditures a wasteful form of American imperialism, while the former thought foreign alliances and foreigners dangerous to the continuation of the republic.

The founders of this nation generally understood that principled opposition to warfare was neither disloyal nor subversive. George Mason, father of the Bill of Rights, detested the concept of unfettered militarism, believing that it was a danger to a republican (small "r") form of government; and George Washington warned the nation in 1796 that "real patriots . . . are liable to become suspected and odious, while . . . dupes usurp the applause and confidence of the people, to surrender their interests." Yet Mason and Washington were no pacifists as some commentators have suggested, and they believed that military preparedness and warfare were legitimate methods of pursuing the interests of the country as long as there was a consensus among Americans that the nation was pursuing a just cause. "If we remain one people," wrote Washington, "we may choose peace or war, as our interest—guided by justice—shall counsel."[6]

A Loyal Opposition

Many war resisters believed that a principled and constitutional opposition to the policies of their government—*a loyal opposition*—was one of the fundamental characteristics of a free people. Most of the founders would have agreed with this proposition. They themselves had been the opposition in the fight for American liberties in 1775. Yet during the colonial period, the individual colonies had the right to wage war as separate entities, and it was only through their agreement to work together in the Revolution that a united front was able to oppose the British. Under the Articles of Confederation and the Constitution,[7] the states gave up the right to wage individual wars outside their boundaries, placing all such authority under the federal government. In this regard, however, the singular power of the president (and the executive branch of the federal government, in general) to utilize the military or to prosecute war in the name of the nation has presented a problem that is a favorite target of the peace movement.

Francis Biddle, attorney general during the presidency of Franklin Delano Roosevelt (one of America's greatest wartime leaders), made the following insightful observation concerning the historical character of the war powers as exercised by the executive. "The Constitution has not greatly bothered any wartime President," he wrote. The executive branch of government must often get on with the fighting. Through inaction, the president often faces the potential loss of his prerogatives within the tripartite federal government or his ability to affect international negotiations at the peace table. For Biddle, and others, the constitutionality of the wartime actions of the executive branch was "a question of law" ultimately to be decided by the Supreme Court at a later date.[8]

Unlike the antiwar constitutionalists who view foreign wars as violations of law, isolationists in America often have fueled their antiwar sentiment through the disgust engendered by the results of wars fought elsewhere. Isolationists in the interwar period between World War I and World War II (1918–1939), for instance, pointed to the massive human carnage on the battlefields of France from 1914 to 1918, the wrecking of some budding democracies in central Europe, the continued existence despite a negotiated peace of several inhumane empires, and the appalling failure of Old World Europe to repair its aristocratic power structure and dispense with its endless interfamily feuding as reasons to oppose U.S. entry into World War II.

It was not surprising to find large isolationist minorities among the immigrant population of the United States. America has been a land composed of foreign immigrants and the children of immigrants—British, Irish, German, Italian, Hispanic, eastern European, Asians, and others arriving in waves over time. No nation on earth has had such a diverse and interlaced population since the time of the Roman Empire. Many foreign-born and first-generation (hyphenated) Americans with relations remaining in foreign places feared for their countries of origin and considered U.S. foreign policy unfriendly to their former homelands. Most of these, however, had come to America to escape the seemingly endless warfare, economic upheaval, and the continued threat of life-altering military conscription in the "old country." Consequently, only a minority of immigrants actively spurned U.S. involvement in foreign wars, while most held antiwar sentiments that were not inherently disloyal to America. As will be seen, many immigrant and hyphenated Americans loyally volunteered to serve in American wars (particularly in the Civil War); however, many others simply did not want to see the worst excesses of unremitting warfare in Europe repeated on the continent.

For both constitutionalists and isolationists, however, opposition to war was generally rooted in a political conservatism and an antimilitarism that was uniquely American. The necessary preparations for war—especially those not directly defensive in

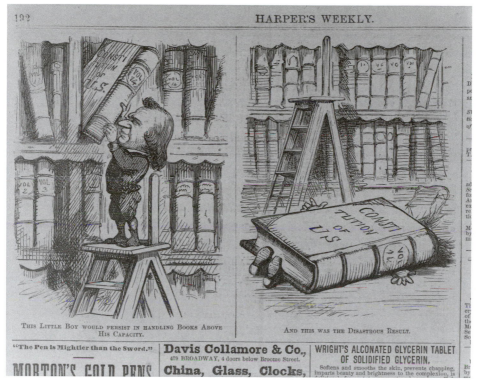

Thaddeus Stevens is standing on the top step of a step-ladder and lifting a large, heavy book from a high bookshelf. As he falls off the ladder, he is crushed by the book, the "Constitution of U.S.," 1868. (Library of Congress Prints and Photographs Division, LC-USZ62-131563)

nature—were often viewed as expensive, redundant, and generally unpopular with voters. Many persons over the last 200-plus years of U.S. history have expressed the belief that a continuous and unremitting reliance on military force, aggressive posturing, and open warfare as tools of government policy and pawns of coercive diplomacy presaged a dangerous consolidation of military power in the hands of just a few men outside the representative legislature—particularly those in the executive branch of government.

President John Tyler, for example, was widely accused of desiring war with Mexico during the 1840s, and he spent much of his tenure in office engineering several political and military maneuvers to get Texas annexed to the United States. He considered this goal a great benefit to the United States, but he left the prosecution of the war in Mexico that followed to his successor, James K. Polk. During the American Civil War, Abraham Lincoln was simultaneously greeted as both the savior of his country and denounced as the invader of a peace-loving Confederacy. President (Thomas) Woodrow Wilson, a strong believer in the "peace without victory" concept, led the United States into World War I to make the world safe for democracy, but none of the belligerents would accept the type of peace that he proposed. Ironically, the conclusion of World War I led to the creation of two European dictatorships—Fascist Italy and Nazi Germany—that would foment a second world

The United States is portrayed as Death wrapped in the American flag supplying munitions and death-dealing armaments to the nations of the developing world in this detail from a 1915 antiwar cartoon. (Library of Congress Prints and Photographs Division, LC-USZ62-22598)

confrontation. Two decades later, Franklin D. Roosevelt led the nation into World War II in the same democratic cause and realized peace only after devastating his enemies. No more complete victory and level of devastation could be imagined than that inflicted on Japan and Germany in 1945. Yet the peace at the end of World War II surrendered one-third of Europe to the Communist slavery of Soviet Russia and presaged a decades-long Cold War. In many of these cases, those opposed to wartime policies of the government were silenced, called reactionaries and anti-Americans, or prosecuted for exercising their civil liberties.

A Fickle Electorate

In this regard, a large segment of the American electorate seems equally fickle when supporting or opposing the war-making apparatus of their nation. Only the most dedicated among war resisters have been unswerving in their attitudes. Both antiwar sentiment and military interventionism, as expressed in the hallways of government, are easily affected by the attitudes of the general electorate, which has swung wildly over the decades. The majority of the electorate in early 1942, for instance, viewed U.S. entry into World War II with particular favor, yet before the Japanese attack on Pearl Harbor in December 1941, antiwar sentiment and isolationism seemed to have prevailed. On the other hand, the Vietnam War was seemingly detested by a large and vocal segment of the population from its inception, yet prowar political posturing endured for the better part of a decade. Only as the war dragged on and antiwar candidates gained attention at the ballot box did resistance to government policies increase in Congress. Moreover, many wars that started with overwhelming popular support, or even euphoria in the case of the Civil War, produced in just a short time an equally overwhelming atmosphere of war weariness that resulted in negative political consequences for the incumbent party, even in the presence of military success on the battlefield. The most recent iteration of this phenomenon can be seen in the success of the 2007–2008 surge of troops in Iraq and the concurrent collapse in the national elections of the incumbent Republican Party, which received little credit for the strategic victory.

The notion that the United States must play a military role in sustaining peace after victory, first advanced by President Wilson in 1918, seemingly remains unacceptable to many Americans in the early 21st century.[9] In this manner, President George H. W. Bush failed to win reelection in 1992 after a successful war with Iraq (Iraq I), and the Republican Party lost control of the Congress in the elections of 2006, although the incumbent administration had displaced the Saddam Hussein government (Iraq II). Many brave young Americans have responded to the call to arms when the nation was obviously in danger, but even so-called peacekeeping missions seemly require the deployment of thousands of men, guns, bombs, tanks, planes, and other "infernal machines" of warfare. American public opinion has seemingly rejected all but the most brief and bloodless of U.S. military efforts at playing the role of global police.

Generational Warfare

Americans have not been at war only during very few periods in history, and major conflicts have dominated the U.S. historical record up to the 21st century. The interwar decades, however, as few as there have been without major combat, have also evidenced an almost continuous series of small wars against Native Americans, Barbary pirates, and Mexican border bandits; a series of undeclared cold wars and quasi-wars; and numerous international interventions and police actions. Each succeeding generation of young Americans seems to have been challenged by its own encounter with warfare, and if no legitimate cause for war developed on its own, one might seemingly be found or even manufactured by willing politicians. As stated by an 18th-century American anti-nationalist, "they have severally laid their foundations in the blood and slaughter of three, four, and sometimes, ten successive generations."[10]

In response to these operations, each generation has produced a cadre of sincere antiwar protestors, peace advocates, and war resisters. Although the Vietnam War era presently serves as a watershed moment in the history of American pacifism, antiwar sentiments have been expressed by both the politically conservative and the politically liberal, and pacifism has been represented by a number of vastly diverse political parties. Peace-minded conservatives generally have responded to a combination of a fear of an evolving social order, a growing militarism on the international front, and the threat of an expanding executive power at the expense of a duly elected congress. On the other hand, the roots of liberal peace advocacy are more widely set in preoccupations with more intangible concepts like social justice, the establishment of international law or global government, or a more practical belief in the efficacy of arbitration and mediation over military force. All groups—whether politically conservative, liberal, moderate, or radical—were highly moralistic in their rhetorical tone and shared a common antiwar purpose, yet each tended to be largely dismissive of the other's underlying arguments and tactical paradigms. This feature of American opposition to war has had the effect of making the antiwar movement a fragile instrument for peace with its component parts sometimes fractured and set at cross purposes.[11]

In many cases, the peace movements undertaken before the 20th century were uncoordinated—initiated by small groups of like-minded individuals around a specific issue of war and aligned only long enough to mushroom and metamorphose for a decade before losing momentum and fading away. Before the Vietnam War, few groups attracted more than 2,000 adherents at the height of their activity. The flash point for the expansion of antiwar sentiment usually has been the threat of an imminent intervention in a foreign war, particularly those conflicts that arose in Europe, or the deployment of American troops outside the borders of the nation as in Mexico, Cuba, or Iraq. Once the conflict or crisis was concluded, the interest in continuing the struggle for an enduring peace or a system of global arbitration often waned among all but the most committed absolute pacifists and antiwar internationalists.[12]

Peace advocates often can be identified by those issues to which they look for inspiration. Conservative antiwar voices often repeat the founding principles as voiced by Washington, Adams, or Madison. Moral pacifists repudiate war and military service based largely on religious concepts, and liberal pacifists—like those active in the late 19th and early 20th centuries—are often brought together based on the need to extend a particular social reform within the nation such as abolition, temperance, women's issues, poverty, or civil rights.

Before the Vietnam War, only rarely did antiwar protests take the form of widespread civil disobedience, direct action, or mass violence. In this regard, the Civil War era draft riots were a notable exception. Antiwar advocates from previous decades were not revolutionaries or anarchists. They were largely "inner-directed persons" who had little use for highly charismatic leaders, formal organizations, or grand demonstrations. They generally repudiated violence as a tactic, and the level of their personal activism was restrained and often kept within self-imposed limits.[13]

This characteristic restraint slowly evaporated during the 20th century. The four major conflicts of the century, two world wars followed close by conflicts in Korea and Southeast Asia, were entered into by progressive American leaders: Woodrow Wilson, Franklin Roosevelt, Harry Truman, and John F. Kennedy, respectively. Each was a foreign war ostensibly undertaken to protect democracy, and each was resisted initially by the "old Right" composed of conservative voices who doubted, like the antiexpansionists and anti-imperialists of earlier eras, the wisdom of becoming

Members of a U.S. Marine veterans group carry placards as they heckle some 10,000 marchers in New York, 1965. Police barricades separated the veterans from the demonstrators who paraded down New York's Fifth Avenue to protest U.S. involvement in the Vietnam War. (AP Photo)

embroiled in foreign conflicts. This war resistance was often apolitical with members of both parties taking part in making antiwar and prowar statements.[14]

Globalist Thought

Emeric Crucé, a 17th-century French political theorist, was among the first to envision an international body to maintain peace much like the League of Nations, World Court, or the United Nations. He felt that this body should be a permanent gathering of princes, or their representatives, in session at some prominent city. Crucé, a Frenchmen, suggested that it be located at Versailles, then the most gloriously appointed of European capitals. The Palace at Versailles, now in a wealthy suburb of Paris, was often the unofficial seat of French government. After 1879, Versailles was never again used as a capital, but the presence of the French Parliament there in the 1870s left a vast hall built in one aisle of the palace, which is still used by the French Parliament when it meets in Congress to amend the French constitution. Versailles has hosted many of the most significant peace negotiations held in Europe. The transfer from Versailles to The Hague (the Netherlands) as the international city of peace and seat of global justice was initially based on the formation of the Permanent Court of Arbitration at the first Hague Peace Conference (1899)—largely the work of Tobias Asser, a Dutch jurist and Nobel Prize Laureate (1911).

John Bellers, like his friend William Penn, was a Quaker pacifist. He was first and foremost an advocate for the poor and downtrodden. The commercial growth and the expanding incomes of the proprietary classes in Britain in the latter part of the 17th century brought only slender benefits to a small section of the working classes, while the situation of the greater part of the citizenry changed for the worse. Bellers suggested a generally utopian remedy for this condition, the formation of communities of workers who would sidestep the need for capital and management. Nonetheless, these communities were not quite the communes suggested by 19th-century socialists as not everything deemed a tool of industry was to be held in common. Bellers called these communities Colleges of Industry, which suggested the idea of a voluntary system in opposition to the involuntary workhouses or almshouses characteristic of the prevalent British system of poverty reform. Bellers may have been the first to try to put socialist ideas like these into practice, that is to say, to justify the antagonism toward capitalists and industrialists that he shared with later Communist theorists.

Bellers derived an argument in favor of an international confederation of states that might terminate long wars like the War of the Spanish Succession (1701–1714), which had been raging among several European powers, including Britain, since the opening of the century. Bellers noted that the war had involved great sacrifices in money and blood. A decade of warfare had passed, yet no end seemed to be near. In response, Bellers suggested the establishment of an international league, or European State, cobbled together from among the existing powers on the continent. The title of his pamphlet best summarizes the intent of his proposal: *Some Reasons for an European State proposed to the Powers of Europe, by an universal guarantee and an Annual Congress, Senate, Dyet or Parliament, To settle any Disputes about the Bounds and Rights of Princes and States hereafter*.[15] He also proposed a General Council or Convocation of all the different Christian sects to settle the general principles and religious doctrines on which they might agree. This council would prevent further sectarian wars within the so-called European State once all the political disputes had been adjudicated.

As with many of his proposals, Bellers's call for a super-state was well in advance of other political theorists, yet he was careful to make allowances for existing circumstances and outstanding monarchies. In a dedication addressed to Britain's Queen Anne at the end of the war in 1714, Bellers pointed out the sacrifices incurred over more than a dozen years of warfare and the treaties concluded (with Holland, Austria, and Prussia) to secure peace with Britain's main adversary, France. He emphasized how few were the guarantees these treaties afforded, how many contingencies needed to be met for their maintenance, and how each one of the allied states had the right to take its own conditions and circumstances into account before acting to preserve the peace. He further calculated the expenditure in men, money, ships, and damage to the economy incurred throughout the war. This method of calculating the costs of war by including its collateral cost to the economy was thoroughly original for the period. Finally, Bellers unfolded his proposal for a European super-government.

Bellers planned for Europe to be divided into a number of districts of equal size (to be called cantons or provinces), and each European power was to send one member per canton to a Parliament of States, that is, each power would be represented in proportion to its size and population. This Parliament of States, having 100 or more representatives, would deal exclusively with the external relations of the powers to each other, without interfering with their internal affairs. It also would have an arms control function determining how many soldiers, cavalry, and naval vessels each member power might have and how much military financing each power might provide per canton. The various powers would have the number of their votes in the joint Parliament proportioned, so that in addition to their geographic extent, their military capabilities would be taken into account. The Parliament of States would then arrange for the reduction of standing armies and navies and set the number of men per canton to be kept under arms in times of peace.[16]

The modern British political theorist, Bertrand Russell was never a complete globalist, but he held views similar to that of Bellers with regard to nation-states even though they lived 250 years apart. Russell resisted specific conflicts like both world wars, Korea, and Vietnam protesting against them on the grounds that they were contrary to the interests of civilization, and thus immoral. Ironically, in 1915, he had written an article defending the wars of colonization in Africa and India on utilitarian grounds, suggesting the more advanced civilizations could put the land to better use than their less technologically equipped indigenous populations. In this, his perspective was clearly Victorian and elitist. Yet Russell opposed nearly all wars between modern nations in the 20th century. He was branded a traitor in Britain for his opposition to World War I, and was arrested for interfering with British foreign policy. In World War II, he favored appeasement, but ultimately he admitted that Hitler had gone too far and the Nazi's needed to be defeated. Russell initially expressed great hope for Communism, but in the postwar period, he became disillusioned by the stark utilitarianism and overt corruption of Soviet-style government. He later embraced a less strident form of socialism.

Russell is best known as an opponent of the nuclear arms race and later the war in Vietnam. The Russell-Einstein Manifesto was issued in London on July 9, 1955, by Russell in the middle of the ban-the-bomb protests of the Cold War. It highlighted the dangers posed by nuclear weapons and called for world leaders to seek peaceful resolutions to international conflicts, especially the growing disputes between the United States and Soviet Union. The signatories included eleven preeminent intellectuals and international scientists, most notably the popular figure Albert Einstein, who had signed the document just days before his death (April 18, 1955). At the time of his death, Einstein was considered the premier intellectual and most advanced thinker of his day, and his inclusion among the signatories gave the statement not only weight and authority, but also a reason for popular interest.

The manifesto—also signed by Max Born, Percy Bridgman, Leopold Infeld, Frederic Joliot-Curie, Herman Muller, Linus Pauling, Cecil Powell, Joseph Rotblat, and Hideki Yukawa—called for an conference where *scientists*, rather than politicians, would assess the dangers posed to the survival of humanity by weapons of mass destruction (then considered only to be nuclear weapons). The idea was not an entirely new one. Horrified by the use of atomic bombs at Hiroshima and Nagasaki, the Federation of American Scientists (FAS) was formed in 1946 to resist the proliferation of nuclear weapons technologies. The emphasis of the Russell-Einstein signers was on the conference being *politically neutral* and *international*, thereby extending the question of global nuclear weapons proliferation to all nationalities and governments. The signers of the manifesto made it clear in their statement, however, that the abolition of war would demand limitations on the sovereignty of the nation-states.

Incredibly, four years before the Russell-Einstein Manifesto, Hollywood moviemakers had created *The Day the Earth Stood Still* (1951), a critically acclaimed black-and-white science fiction film that told the story of a humanoid space alien who comes to earth to warn its leaders not to take their nuclear conflicts into space, or they will face devastating consequences imposed by a universal league of planets. The alien (played by Michael Rennie) suggests to an Einstein-like mathematician (played by Sam Jaffe) the convocation of an international conference of earth scientists eerily similar to that called for by the Russell-Einstein Manifesto. Produced in the aftermath of the development and aboveground testing of the first hydrogen bombs in the Pacific, the film strongly addressed issues of violence, national politics, the fear of nuclear annihilation, and the need for global government. The moviemakers included in the film a large alien robot called Gort, which steps out of a flying saucer and melts all the weapons present without harming the soldiers, an obvious metaphor to the wisdom of conventional weapons limitations as well as a general nuclear disarmament. The relative timing of the film to the manifesto also suggests that rather than being the genesis of an idea constructed by a group of elite intellectuals, the thought that the nuclear arms race between nations already had gone too far toward endangering the planet had been percolating through society—and the scientific community in particular—for some time.

Peace at a Pace with History

The year 1948 was a watershed in the history of peace-seeking. It was a year in which America's concept of the structure of the world changed. In many respects, the worldwide conflicts of the first half of the 20th century spawned serious changes in global politics and the concept of an international balance of power. Peace advocates had instead pinned their hopes on the concept of *collective security* in the form of a United Nations. The establishment of the United Nations in 1945 to replace the ineffective League of Nations seemed to portend an era of peaceful cooperation and diplomacy among the nation-states. Yet under a U.N. mandate, the State of Israel was established in 1948 and British governance in Palestine was terminated, leading to the first Arab-Israeli War. Also in 1948, Pakistan (then two political regions: East Pakistan—as of 1971 the People's Republic Bangladesh—and West Pakistan—formally the Islamic Republic of Pakistan—was partitioned from India along traditional religious lines, and all three entities eventually were made independent of British governance. The attempt to dissemble the worst consequences of the colonialism of the previous century had led instead to heightened religious tension in both regions.

Also in 1948 many of the major global antagonisms active for the remainder of the century matured into serious international rivalries, and the division among the Communist (Soviet and Chinese) spheres of influence in the East and the Euro-American sphere of influence in the West became consolidated. Berlin became a divided city requiring a humanitarian airlift, and Germany became two political entities: East and West Germany, respectively. A Communist-inspired civil war wracked Greece, and Czechoslovakia declared a people's republic—a preliminary step toward the formation of its Communist government.

The foreign policy makers in America were particularly affected by these events. The struggle with global Communism came to define all conflicts anywhere in the world. Each nationalist struggle assumed the complexion of a Communist versus non-Communist conflict rather than one between a colonial imperium and a subjugate indigenous population intent on their independence. The formation of a Soviet-dominated Communist bloc among the nation-states of Eastern Europe seemed to confirm American suspicions, and the United States and its NATO (North Atlantic Treaty Organization formed in 1949) allies began to plan for a third major ground war in Europe. Meanwhile, China (excepting Taiwan) seemingly betrayed America after the United States helped to free it from Japanese imperialism in World War II. The Communist-Chinese bamboo curtain in Asia came to be viewed as great a threat as the Soviet iron curtain in Europe. Asian nationalist movements, even if remotely connected with Moscow or Beijing, immediately became suspect to policy makers in Washington, D.C., as parts of a worldwide anti-Western conspiracy.

In fact, American policy makers ultimately came to believe that all nationalist movements—including those in Africa, the Caribbean, and South America—were part of a Communist threat that would replace democratically inspired independence with the totalitarian imperialism of a world Communist movement. The strategic and economic prizes were thought to be so great as to warrant open conflict between the Eastern and Western hemispheres. It is with this backdrop in mind that many of the foreign policy initiatives undertaken by the United States—especially in Southeast Asia, in the Middle East, and in Central and South America—must be viewed.

Since the establishment of the United Nations at the end of World War II, American officials have been dealing with more problems in more places than ever before in history. All over the world, from the finest government offices in Europe to the tiniest developing world consulates, in the 1950s and 1960s a "swollen diplomatic corps" was established and supported by a Central Intelligence Agency more than willing to perform covert operations (black ops), support undercover agents, and play the real-life role of a James Bond or a Napoleon Solo. There were more ambassadors, more diplomatic aids, more embassy dinners, more conferences, more intelligence estimates, more black ops, and more demands from committees of Congress for more explanations of decisions and actions that were often beyond the pale of explanation. Yet, the United States did not have time to adjust its attitudes or tune its national institutions to new global responsibilities. It was in "a race with the pace of history" with government decision makers thinking in terms of future generations and global threats, while the postwar American public was thinking in terms of the next year, the next months, or even the next week. As Henry David Thoreau said in the 19th century of the first railroad locomotive that he saw, it was "wickedness going faster."[17]

Under the post–World War II administrations of presidents Harry Truman and Dwight Eisenhower, in particular, foreign policy became increasingly militarized and diplomatically entangled in a worldwide set of alliances opposing the so-called Communist threat, which by 1949 included the People's Republic of China (Red China). While this does not justify American foreign policy decisions, the presence of Soviet troops in Hungary in 1949 was formalized by a mutual assistance treaty, which granted the Soviet Union rights to a continued military presence. This ensured ultimate political control by the Communists. The American global presence included membership in NATO and later in a parallel organization known as SEATO (South East Asia Treaty Organization), which was formed in 1954. The Korean War (1950) had galvanized the member states of NATO into a large military and anti-Communist force under the direction of a U.S. supreme commander, rather than into the diplomatic instrument its establishment had initially envisioned. The Soviets countered with its own alliance called the Warsaw Pact, establishing a virtual iron curtain in Eastern Europe and a physical concrete and barbed wire wall separating East and West Berlin.

Although a Non-Aligned Movement (NAM) of states considering themselves outside the influence of any major power bloc was founded in 1955, the developing world nations—especially the former colonies of European powers—were thought to be fated eventually to be aligned with either the East or the West. Although the NAM was intended to be as close an alliance as NATO, SEATO, or the Warsaw Pact, it had little actual cohesion, and many of its members were quite closely aligned with one or another of the great powers.

Many pacifists and antiwar activists in America saw Western posturing against a supposed Communism threat as unnecessary. SEATO, in particular, seemingly reflected a sinister mid-1950's reliance on "out of area" European powers and "in area" pro-Western Asian dictators and warlords acting under U.S. leadership and direction. Such posturing implied that the contest with Soviet and Chinese Communism was to be waged on a global scale, and it threatened to change the United Nations from a place of mediation, arbitration, and hope into a tool with which the West might check Sino-Soviet expansion.

"Progress toward [these] noble goals," wrote Dwight David Eisenhower in 1961, "is persistently threatened by the conflict now engulfing the world. It commands our whole attention, absorbs our very beings." Nonetheless, Eisenhower believed in the policy of *containment*, which was developed in opposition to the increasing influence of Communism in the world. During the ensuing Cold War, the U.S. military-industrial complex (MIC) would account for close to half of the world's total arms expenditures. Nonetheless, on leaving office Eisenhower observed,

The potential for the disastrous rise of misplaced power exists and will persist. We must never let the weight of this combination endanger our liberties or democratic processes. We should take nothing for granted. Only an alert and knowledgeable citizenry can compel the proper meshing of the huge industrial and military machinery of defense with our peaceful methods and goals so that security and liberty may prosper together.[18]

Social Conscience

As the Cold War developed through the latter half of the 20th century with its ICBMs and theories of *mutually assured nuclear destruction*, pacifism became more radical than formerly and more closely identified with a liberal agenda. The peace advocates of this later period generally believed that peace required a process of social justice, economic change, and military retrenchment that was best promoted through their support of international agencies, multilateral agreements, and world government. "Drawn to the defense of the powerless, radical pacifists believed that peace required individual acts of resistance to challenge arbitrary authority based on violent force and open the way for physical and spiritual liberation. Peace meant saying 'No to power' and 'action now.'"[19]

The founding of the journal *Liberation* in 1956 signaled a new turn in the antiwar movement toward a more radical pacifism. It gave pacifism a more revolutionary and activist wing. The editorial board of the publication included several individuals who would play significant roles in the peace and antiwar movements of the post-1956 period. Among these was Dave Dellinger who "was poised to become the William Lloyd Garrison of the antiwar movement in the 1960s," and whose journal recalled Garrison's own antislavery *Liberator*. The movement founded around Dellinger and others like him considered the U.S. government as culpable as any other power for inequality and injustice in the world. They stressed the liberation and empowerment of disadvantaged peoples, and called for "the transformation of the very structure of wealth and power in America and the world." The most fundamental change in their pacifist and antiwar sentiment was their intention to "transform America's core ideals and governing consciousness."[20] For these new radicals, questions of war and peace were intimately connected to shifts in existing political institutions and the displacement of ruling groups.

In the 21st century, political conservatives, social liberals, and libertarians; interventionists, antiwar activists, and isolationists; Hawks, Doves, and neutrals; Republicans, Democrats, and third parties have largely forgotten the history of peace-minded nonintervention and passive antiwar protest in America, and they incorrectly speak of each other as misdirected, dishonest, or unpatriotic.[21] In the 1960s, it was common for activists to express distrust of anyone over the age of thirty. In the 21st century, those under the age of thirty generally have no clear idea of any form of antiwar sentiment that does not reflect the unrestrained rhetoric, the emotional activism, and the graphic images of the Vietnam era. They are generally under the

With the U.S. Capitol in the background, demonstrators march along Pennsylvania Avenue in an anti–Vietnam War protest in Washington, on Moratorium Day, November 15, 1969. (AP Photo)

misapprehension that the antiwar movement found its birth rather than its maturity during the era of the Vietnam War.

Notes

1. George C. Herring, *From Colony to Superpower: U.S. Foreign Relations Since 1776* (New York: Oxford University Press, 2008), 15.

2. S. F. Sanger and D. Hays, *The Olive Branch of Peace and Good Will to Men: The Antiwar History of the Brethren and Mennonites, the People of the South during the Civil War, 1861–1865* (Elgin, IL: Brethren Publishing House, 1907), 190.

3. Anthony H. Cordesman and William D. Sullivan, "US Defense Planning, The Challenge of Resources," pp. ii-iii, http://www.csis.org/media/csis/pubs/060707_defense_resource_challenges.pdf (accessed March 2009).

4. Sanger and Hays, 231.

5. Sanger and Hays, 24.

6. George Washington, *Washington's Farewell Address of 1796,* http://www.yale.edu/lawweb/avalon/washing.htm (accessed October 2008).

7. ABC-CLIO editorial style guidelines require that the official titles of government documents such as declarations, treaties, and constitutions should be placed in neither italics nor quotation marks.

8. William H. Rehnquist, *All the Laws But One Civil Liberties in Wartime* (New York: Vintage Books, 1998), 191–192.

9. Herring, 408.

10. John Dewitt (possible pseudonym), "John Dewitt I," *The Anti-federalist Papers*, http://www.constitution.org/afp/dewitt01.htm (accessed June 18, 2008).

11. Charles DeBenedetti, *An American Ordeal: The Antiwar Movement of the Vietnam Era* (Syracuse, NY: Syracuse University Press, 1990), 13.

12. DeBenedetti, 13.

13. DeBenedetti, 18–19.

14. Examples might be found in Henry A. Wallace, Democratic vice president under Franklin D. Roosevelt, or Lyndon B. Johnson, vice president under John F. Kennedy.

15. John Bellers, *Some Reasons for an European State proposed to the Powers of Europe, by an universal guarantee and an Annual Congress, Senate, Dyet or Parliament, To settle any Disputes about the Bounds and Rights of Princes and States hereafter* (London: n.p., 1710).

16. Eduard Bernstein, "John Bellers, Champion of the Poor and Advocate of a League of Nations," *Cromwell and Communism Socialism And Democracy in the Great English Revolution* (London: George Allen & Unwin, 1895), http://www.marxists.org/reference/archive/bernstein/works/1895/cromwell/17-bellers.htm#top (accessed July 10, 2008).

17. James Reston, *The Artillery of the Press: Its Influence on American Foreign Policy* (New York: Harper and Row, 1966), 9, 22.

18. See Dwight David Eisenhower, *Farewell Speech to the Nation*, January 17, 1961, http://mcadams.posc.mu.edu/ike.htm (accessed October 2008).

19. DeBenedetti, 23.

20. DeBenedetti, 24–25.

21. Bill Kaufman, *Ain't My America: The Long, Noble History of Antiwar Conservatism and Middle-American Anti-Imperialism* (New York: Henry Holt, 2008), 8.

Chapter 2

To Learn the Ways of War

The Lord . . . wanted to teach the men in Israel who had never been in battle before to learn the ways of war.

—Judges 3:1–2

War is an ugly thing, but not the ugliest of things. The decayed and degraded state of moral and patriotic feeling, which thinks that nothing is worth war, is much worse.

—John Stuart Mill, 19th-century philosopher

Diplomacy is the extension of warfare by other means.

—Carl von Clausewitz, 1832

What must be done to defend the country must be done.

—U.S. Attorney General Francis Biddle, 1942

Peace Founded on Victory

War is older than recorded human history, and if conflict is an innate part of human nature as some psychologists suggest, it will be difficult, if not impossible to escape it. Yet it is not battlefield victory and widespread human carnage that wins wars. Although it is possible to drag an opponent to the peace table by the force of arms, social, religious, and political considerations carry much more weight. An army is power. Its entire purpose is to coerce others, yet it is almost impossible to win a war in a free society without the backing of the people. In the introduction to the 1854 edition of his *The Fifteen Decisive Battles of the World*, Sir Edward S. Creasy noted:

> It is an honorable characteristic of the spirit of this age, that projects of violence and warfare are regarded among civilized states with gradually increasing aversion. The Universal Peace Society certainly does not, and probably never will, enroll the majority of statesmen among its members. But even those who look upon the appeal of battle as occasionally unavoidable in international controversies, concur in thinking it a deplorable necessity, only to be resorted to when all

peaceful modes of arrangement have been vainly tried, and when the law of self-defense justifies a state, like an individual, in using force to protect itself from imminent and serious injury.[1]

The 17th-century English philosopher John Locke—author of much of the conceptual foundation upon which the U.S. Constitution was based—noted the contrast between the state of nature and the state of war. The *state of nature* involved people living peacefully together, governed by reason, without a common superior, whereas the *state of war* occurred when people made designs of force upon one another without the authority of their consent. Locke defined war as a state of enmity and destruction brought about by one person's (or one group's) premeditated attempts upon another's life, liberty, or property. The law of self-preservation, integral to Locke's state of nature, allows that those attacked may kill the attackers in *self-defense*. A state of war can exist without actual combat taking place, however. Locke's definition rests on the presumption that any aggression by the first party constitutes a challenge to the freedom of the second party. In this case, the aggrieved party has a justifiable right to make war on its oppressor. When the will of one group does not threaten the existence or *vital interests* of another rival group, compromise through diplomacy, or *peaceful coexistence*, may result. When rival groups are unable to resolve the issues that separate them through diplomacy, but no active conflict ensues, a *cold war* may exist.

Americans have a short political history when compared with other peoples, but they have a long familiarity with war. Anglo-colonials came to North America armed to the teeth and prepared to make war on Native Americans or other Europeans who might threaten them. Evidences of lances, crossbows, firelocks, body armor, and helmets reminiscent of the Middle Ages have been found in even remote colonial settlements. Although each of the thirteen colonies devised its own defensive system—generally around a militia formed of the entire free male population—these organizations were remarkably similar. "The story of the military institutions of the American colonies is an account of efforts to keep as much of the population as possible armed and prepared on short notice."[2] Only the peace-seeking Quakers of Pennsylvania expressed doubts about the need for an active military defense.[3]

Military Doctrine

Every profession has its own language, and the profession of arms is no exception. The bulk of modern military terminology can be traced back to the works written by two 19th-century men of war: Carl von Clausewitz (*On War*, c.1832) and Antoine-Henri Jomini (*The Art of War*, c.1838). The precepts gleaned on the Napoleonic battlefields of Europe by these men concerning infantry, cavalry, and artillery were taught at West Point and other military schools in the United States and Europe. Much of the naval doctrine used since the beginning of the 20th century was proposed by U.S. Adm. Alfred Thayer Mahan in *The Influence of Sea Power upon History, 1660–1783* (1890). Mahan's arguments influenced the naval policies of governments around the world for decades.

As with any set of military concepts proposed in an environment of budget constraints, radically new ideas often were met with reluctant disbelief by traditional military leaders. Nonetheless, in the 20th century, the intellectual leadership of British military theorists such as John F. C. Fuller and Basil Liddell Hart helped pioneer the use of tanks, and the complete mechanization of the U.S. Army received aid from an unlikely source, that is, former cavalry officer George S. Patton. Not until August 1918 did any major Allied operation of World War I coordinating armor, artillery, infantry, and air reconnaissance take place. Nonetheless, it was German theorist Heinz Guderian who developed the tactical use of tanks in large formations and combined them with air power into the *blitzkrieg* that made the operations of other nations look like child's play two decades later. The concepts of warfare in the air, visualized as early as the 18th century, became a reality during World War I with the introduction of dirigibles, fighter planes, and fixed-wing bombers. American General Billy Mitchell endangered his military career in the period between the world wars advocating the feasibility of a modern air arm (particularly the use of bombers and carrier-based aircraft against naval vessels) to a military hierarchy firmly rooted in traditional operations, and the Soviet Marshal M. N. Tukhachevsky took the lead in developing the concept of vertical warfare in 1928 with the introduction of paratroops, gliders, drop-platforms for artillery, and bombers converted to troop transports. U.S. airborne theory, tactics, and basic rules of engagement used in World War II were developed slowly by Col. James M. Gavin and Lt. Gen. Matthew B. Ridgway in combination with other Allied officers, and the development of German airborne theory usually is attributed to Gen. Kurt Student who commanded the airborne arm of the Luftwaffe from its inception to the end of the war. Throughout the period, these ideas were incorporated into a worldwide concept of modern conventional (non-nuclear) war.

Before the publication of the *Field Service Regulation of the U.S. Army* in 1904, American military doctrine was promulgated through the use of numerous general orders and regulations, such as the U.S. Army Regulations of 1861, or through authorized commercial publications authored by serving or retired military officers. The war-making doctrines of many nations can be found in works similar to those of the United States, and many of America's North Atlantic Treaty Organization (NATO) allies use translations of U.S. publications as their principal texts.

In the literature of military history, modern concepts are often used to describe events from long ago, and some long-established concepts of war that no longer appear among modern *military doctrines* may still be well-suited for use during current events. From the rise of rival city-states in antiquity to the development of nuclear armed superpowers in the last century, significant changes have taken place in the nature and attitudes of soldiers, the organization of fighting forces, the technologies brought to the battlefield, the conduct of battle, and the means by which peace is sought. Between the world wars, Rudyard Kipling, war correspondent and author, was asked what he thought of modern war. He responded that it "smelled like a garage and looked like a circus."[4] One can only guess what Kipling would have thought of pilotless drones, smart bombs, and real-time satellite surveillance of the battlespace. Yet over the ensuing millennia, warfare on the most basic level has remained more as it was than as it has changed. The paradigms of victory have remained unchanged: physical confrontation, the destruction of assets, the occupation of positions, and the bending of the enemy's will to force on him an unequal and disadvantageous peace.

The professional military recognizes a wide compendium of discrete offensive and defensive strategies and tactics. They recognize—better perhaps than the general public—that military operations require the convergence of several extremely favorable conditions to succeed as planned. Few military plans meet all these criteria and rethinking and adjustment are always part of the operation. Solid militarists continue to believe in the need for dynamic action generally rejecting diplomatic passivity and wait-and-see strategies. They believe that, as in antiquity, glory can be won in war and that the ultimate test of leadership at all levels can be found on the battlefield not at the conference table. Furthermore, because war and the deterrence of war are human events that continue to persist, military and naval forces will necessarily persist along with them.

Major powers can fight *limited wars* because the consequences for failure are relatively minor at the national or international level, but when survival is at stake, a *general war* ensues. This latter type of warfare jeopardizes the fundamental social, economic, or cultural interests of the participants. Finally, a general war may evolve into a *total war* in which all the resources of the opposing societies become involved. A total war is waged in an all-embracing manner, by all means possible, not only against the armed forces of the opponent but also against the entire population of a rival with a view toward their complete destruction. Sherman's march to the sea in 1864 is often considered the first example of total war in America. *Asymmetrical warfare* ensues when the weak encounter the mighty. If done correctly, such operations can succeed against daunting odds. The revolutionary American militias of 1775, for example, seemingly had no chance to stand toe to toe with the might of Great Britain; the Apache had no chance against the U.S. Cavalry; and the Viet Cong had no chance against either France or the United States.[5]

Military theorists have observed that "the sanction of force lies at the root of [all] social organizations."[6] Orchestrated as the situation demands, the use of force has continued to persist ever since humans formed the first tribal groups to ensure order, combat enemies, and correct wrongs. A society without such means of policing or defending itself quickly decays into lawlessness and chaos. With regard to these duties, *preparedness* has evolved as an important concept. The state of preparedness requires that political and military leaders be attuned to all of the elements within their realms of responsibility and also be responsive to unforeseen developments and changes in the increasingly complex global environment. A careful reading of history reveals that physical force, or the threat of it, has been applied successfully to a wide range of social and political problems since antiquity, yet in the 21st century, a greater value must be derived from the profession of arms than the simple pride in victory that satisfied our ancestors. The understanding of this future role is bound to the past, and a review of the "threads of continuity" that link the two may provide evidence of where and how the use of force should be directed in the future.

The Way of War

Warfare—sometimes total, brutal, and inhumane—is a common historical occurrence, set down in ancient cuneiform, hieroglyphics, and biblical texts. The term *limited warfare* is often used to describe the military campaigns of antiquity, yet some ancient conflicts claim our attention because of their enduring consequences on our own politics, culture, and social order. Others stand out because of the level of the cataclysm, the carnage left on the battlefield, or the lessons to be gleaned by studying them.

Some historians tend to discount the records of events that happened in antiquity as having gone through too many revisions with the addition of possibly spurious details. Yet as researchers widen the scope of their studies, they often find a more accurate record of what happened in the past than would be expected. They have found it extremely interesting to dissect the social and military histories of unique peoples as they remembered and reconstructed the pasts of their ancestors to uncover their collective ethnic consciousness. One would hope that those with interest in the patterns of human behavior will recognize in military history more than just an inevitable series of violent phenomena fated to be repeated during the long course of human affairs.

The moral (religious) basis for war seemingly has led to a particularly violent form of conflict. Fueled by ideology and supported by a political structure, religious wars have been conducted on a larger scale with more casualties and against more noncombatants than other wars. At times such warfare has had as its main objective the complete elimination of entire peoples or rival religious groups. Genocide, as practiced by the Nazis on the Jews or by Serb forces on Bosnian Muslims, has become a tactic used to fulfill the goal of religious purification.

Yet religious warfare is not a modern derivative. It seems certain that the Egyptian pharaoh Akhenaten (ca. 1375 B.C.E.), a man dedicated to his particular brand of monotheism, intended to exterminate all traces of the old Egyptian religious order and replace it with a single god and a new theology. So radical and violent was Akhenaten's program of religious reform that his successors attempted to eradicate any memories of him after his death. In similar fashion, the early Roman emperors attempted to persecute Christianity out of existence, Muslims made war on the Infidel, Crusaders made war on Islam, and Protestants made war on Catholics and vise versa.

In 570 A.D., for example, with the tacit approval of Christian Byzantium the Coptic Christians of Ethiopia advanced against present-day Yemen with the goal of planting Christianity deep within the Arabian Peninsula. The Ethiopians amassed an army supplied with war elephants, the first such to be introduced to the Arabian desert. The people of Mecca, which was directly in the line of march, "quaked behind their flimsy wattle fortifications as sand clouds on the horizon trailed the advancing Ethiopian host." The Ethiopians were warded off by the arrival of an Iranian (Sassasian) fleet carrying an army that quickly routed them. That day and that operation—viewed as a miracle that saved the city—are recorded in the Koran (Qur'an) as a symbol of the very moment of Mohammed's birth within its clay walls. According to the British historian Edward Gibbon, "If Christian power had been maintained [in the Middle East] Mahomet [Mohammed] must have been crushed in his cradle, and Ethiopia would have prevented a revolution which has changed the civil and religious state of the world."[7]

Religious dedication cannot, by itself, sustain a war footing, however. In *God's Battalions* (2009), historian Rodney Stark noted that as long as the human and financial costs of the wars against the Muslims—a period generally considered to be two centuries long (ca. 1095–1291)—were born by the actual crusaders, their families, or their estates, few Europeans objected to the loss of life and expenditure of treasure in the Levant. Yet when the rulers of Europe began to impose the expense of religious war on the general population at home in the form of war taxes, the people began to grumble. In 1166 the first income tax of any kind imposed in Europe (ranging from 10 percent in France to one penny per pound sterling in England) was established to pay for the effort. Crusading—although supported by the Papacy and promulgated as a religious duty—had become too expensive. Even the church fathers railed at being forced to melt down the silver and gold furnishings on their altars in order to raise the sums demanded, and the aristocratic rulers were openly described as tyrants who had taken up the Cross "more . . . out of greed than faith." Most persons of faith ultimately decided to leave the Muslims alone unless they again invaded Europe. As bloody campaigns became directed at Cathars, Waldensians, and other European pacifists rather than the more militant Saracens, "a medieval version of an antiwar movement eventually prevailed; after two centuries of support, the [Crusader] kingdoms in the Holy Land were abandoned." Nonetheless, the war to drive Islam from Spain continued until its objective was attained at the end of the 15th century.[8]

In an effort to demonize the Papacy, Protestant intellectuals and enlightenment writers of the 17th and 18th centuries condemned the Crusades "in order to glorify themselves and vilify the Catholic Church." Today there remains a widespread—and not wholly unwarranted—conviction that crusading was an expression of "Catholic bigotry and cruelty" during its long campaign to deprive Muslims of their "lawful" occupation of Palestine. Moreover, current Muslim "memories" of the Crusades are often cited as a cause of the present continuing unrest in the Middle East, yet no Muslim history of the Crusades appeared before 1899.[9] These anti-Crusader themes have been adopted by a number of present-day Muslim nationalists, Islamic extremists, and antiwar activists. "Eventually, the image of the brutal, colonizing crusader proved to have such polemical power that it drowned out nearly everything else in the ideological lexicon of Muslin antagonism toward the West." Yet self-serving, selective, and unrelenting Muslim support for imperialism, fascism, Nazism, and anti-Semitism during the 20th century is often ignored by these same critics, who continue to entertain the idea of a Jewish–Western Powers conspiracy against them.[10]

War by Proxy

Important wars among empires (or great powers) are sometimes fought by *proxy*. Smaller states, tribes, or groups often take up battles for their giant allies. War by proxy also has a long history and many advantages. The proxy force receives arms and technical or financial support for its own objectives that it could hardly hope to amass on its own, and the sponsoring power receives any laurels associated with victory and plausible deniability in the case of catastrophe or mishap.

In this fashion, 18th-century France had supported the American revolutionaries of 1775 as a proxy force with arms and munitions to diminish the power of their rival, Britain (who used many of the Native American tribes in similar fashion). Through overt and clandestine efforts, Charles Gravier Vergennes, French minister of state, planned to weaken Britain economically through the loss of its colonies and to reestablish the balance of power in Europe that had been lost in the Seven Years' War. Initially, he had hoped to sustain the American war effort solely with military supplies and money. In 1776, he secretly arranged for the rebels to receive aid through the services of Hortalez, Rodriquez, and Company, a front for the French government managed by the playwright Beaumarchais. The American victory at Saratoga, New York, in late 1777 traditionally has been cited as the impetus needed to establish an open alliance with France in 1778. However, the French Council of State had faced the necessity of entering the war on the side of the Americans from the opening of hostilities in Boston three years earlier.[11]

The Judeo-Christian Bible has had a disproportionate effect on the development of war-making doctrines throughout Europe and America largely because so-called Western civilizations have adopted the precepts contained in it among the foundation stones of their traditions, laws, morals, and culture. Even John Locke firmly based his 17th-century political premises in scripture. The Old Testament, in particular, rather than being the document dedicated to the pathways of absolute peace as some would imagine from the themes contained in its companion New Testament, is almost a manual on how to wage *total war*—conflicts of extermination and utter ruthlessness that used fear, terror, and unwarranted bloodshed as weapons.

Anthropologists have noted that desert-dwelling peoples like the ancient Hebrews tend to exhibit particularly insular social structures generally antagonistic to outsiders. Perhaps this explains the ongoing friction between Jews and Muslims in the modern Middle East. Nonetheless, Joshua, one of the great Hebrew generals of early biblical times, paused in his war of conquest and destruction in Canaan to review and make copies of the "Treaty-Teachings of Moses," and he willingly formed military alliances with local peoples if it served the self-interests of his people. "Here we see Joshua's brilliant strategic mind at work as he utilized skilled diplomacy and religious ideology to increase Israelite military power, sufficient proof, even in ancient times, of the accuracy of Clausewitz's dictum that diplomacy is the conduct of war by other means."[12] It is remarkable that an ancient people could exhibit such military and diplomatic sophistication. Yet the Old Testament as a military history and as a source of Western military doctrine has been largely overlooked until recent times.[13]

Many tactical and strategic lessons are contained in the biblical accounts of warfare. Empires, or highly centralized forms of governance, seemed conducive to aggression and repression in antiquity as can be seen among the Egyptians, Babylonians, Assyrians, and other empires whose histories are recorded (in part) in the Bible. Only successful corporate states—such as kingdoms, empires, or consolidated theocracies—could hope to sustain a military or naval force capable of a meaningful offensive. Given the narrow cultivated zones of ancient times, the generally open and unsecured tribal borders, and the limited populations of antiquity, most people lived under the constant threat of war or military intervention by the great powers of the day. Small tribes living peacefully in pastoral settings were generally incapable of providing even a respectable defense to such forces, and it is remarkable that the Hebrews were so successful in waging war with the empires of their day.

Exodus 17:12–13 tells of Rephidim, the first battle waged in the Bible by the Israelites after leaving Egypt. After being outflanked and ambushed by the Amalekites shortly after crossing out of Egyptian territory, the Hebrews turned in retaliation for the unprovoked attack. Moses sent a unit of soldiers under the command of Joshua—the Bible's first great military commander—to fall on the camel-riding Amalekite archers in uneven and narrow terrain, thereby putting the enemy at a tactical disadvantage. The text records that the Battle at Rephidim lasted until sunset and that Joshua overwhelmed the enemy "with the edge of the sword." It is clear from the success of this *strategic defense* that Joshua and his men were not only brave and resourceful warriors but also men with some previous form of military structure, organization, and knowledge of weapons and tactics. Nonetheless, the most important quality of any soldier in antiquity was the willingness to kill.[14]

Killing is always difficult, but it was a very nasty business in antiquity when compared with modern warfare where death-dealing is more impersonal and somewhat removed from the machine gun operator, the rifleman, or the pilot of an unmanned drone. In antiquity, death was wielded up close with instruments more closely related to those found in a butcher's shop than in a modern arsenal. Herein "the pain, suffering, fear, and gore were apparent to the slayer."[15] Even from a nonsectarian point of view, it was through the adoption of the Old Testament as part of its own history that Western civilization first came to know many of the parameters for future warfare and diplomacy. The Bible and other texts from antiquity provide the historian with an opportunity to compare the efficacy of different battle formations, tactics, and military technologies in a period when the only *weapon of mass destruction* was fire.

Cross-Cultural Warfare

The New Testament is widely regarded as the book of peace and reconciliation. Yet, in the New Testament, the biblical promise of global peace concludes with the ultimate battle at Armageddon. Thought to be the flat plain in the shadow of strategically important Mount Megiddo in Central Israel, Armageddon is proposed by many biblical scholars as the site of the final battle between God and Satan at the end of days as predicted in the book of Revelation 16:16. "And he gathered them together into a place called in the Hebrew tongue Armageddon." In other words, Armageddon is an ancient image of conflict based on several millennia of warfare in the region, and it embodies the essence of the struggles waged by men—and women—from time immemorial. Given the present state of relations between Israel and Iran (both soon to be nuclear armed), the Bible may be more predictive of the end of the world than we presently fear.

Religiosity and nationalism are often condemned as causes for war, and no doubt throughout history disagreements over fundamental belief systems rank high among the discrete reasons for going to war. The compendium of wars inspired by religious causes is seemingly endless. In early Christianity membership was restricted to those of Jewish heritage—a sect within Judaism closed to Gentiles until expanded by St. Paul. In a similar fashion early Islam "appears to have been perceived by many at the time [seventh century] as a badge of Arabian identity."[16] Of course, both Christianity and Islam went on to conquer many unrelated peoples who either chose or were forced to accept the orthodoxy of their conquerors. Richard I (Coeur de Leon) and Saladin (Salah al-Din), for instance, were both military men of the 12th-century Crusader era driven by religious undercurrents set in motion centuries before their births, and both used violence not only to defeat the enemy but also to establish a social order among those they conquered based on a radically different ideological view of the world. Yet there was war before the Bible or Koran were written, and even before there was Judaism, Islam, Christianity, or any other religious sect or political entity. To blame warfare on religion alone is to misread history. Peace, too, can be found in the historical record of many religions. Usually rooted in grand global ambitions, at times peace seemed to need only the application of imperial willpower (sometimes fortified by annual subsidies and outright bribes) to take hold. Yet the competition among empires for glory, territory, slaves, and riches has often devolved into ideological conflicts for a monopoly on revealed truth and the right to determine just whose divine order would emerge to dominate the earth.

Warfare arose in antiquity for many modern-sounding reasons outside of religion, including the desire for wealth, the control of rivers and land routes for transportation, the settlement of boundaries, the need to acquire goods and materials such as timber, stone, and metal, and the need to secure the homeland. Even small tribal groups fought to fend off raiders or to acquire or keep additional arable lands and pastures to raise their standard of living above that of mere subsistence. Many of these reasons for war remain relevant in the 21st century.

The oldest surviving records of human warfare are older than the pyramids. Around 4000 B.C.E. (6,000 years ago) city-states began to develop in the Tigris and Euphrates valleys of ancient Mesopotamia in what would become the Sumerian Empire. Mud-brick villages evolved into walled urban centers and fortress cities—a seemingly natural evolution toward centralization throughout human history that is largely ignored by the "it takes a village" supporters of peace movements. With the growth of towns and cities, conflicts developed among them for control of limited resources such as agricultural lands, pastures, or water rights. The almost constant occurrence of war among the city-states of ancient Sumer over the next two millennia spurred the development of military technologies and tactical techniques far beyond those found elsewhere at the time. Bronze weapons and armor, for instance, appeared in the Tigris and Euphrates valleys more than 300 years earlier than they appeared anywhere else in the world.

Although not the earliest recorded conflict, the first Sumerian war for which there is detailed evidence occurred between Lagash and Umma, two cities located just eighteen miles apart, fighting over a disputed land boundary in 2525 B.C.E. On a stone fragment found in Egypt from the Second Dynasty (ca. 2500 B.C.E.) is recorded an early political war centered on control of the city of Nekhet. This was a major and dramatic conflict between the kingdoms of Upper and Lower Egypt in which some 47,000 persons were reported killed—a huge number under any circumstance made more significant by the relatively small population of Egypt during the early dynastic periods.

War Profits

War was good business. In early tribal societies, it was the practice to kill defeated enemies on the battlefield. Enslaving rather than killing prisoners is considered by some historians to have been a step forward in the development of an advanced civilization—ironically the first faltering steps toward prisoner-of-war (POW) rights. When city-states or empires required more labor than residents could provide, they let it be known that they were interested in purchasing slaves. The neighboring tribes, who might be warring among themselves, quickly put all the captives that they could not use on the auction block as human merchandise. In this way, men, women, and children from many regions became enslaved in far away places, and the slave traders became richer.

Stone fragments from the Second Dynasty in Egypt describe organized military expeditions to foreign lands such as a campaign to Nubia that resulted in the capture of 7,000 slaves and 200,000 head of cattle in a single operation. War (itself a source of slaves in the form of prisoners of war) increased the domestic demand for and value of slave labor. The constant fighting created a steady demand for war materials and the handicraft industries that produced weapons, armor, and projectiles (especially consumable items like arrows). Yet, as war continued, more and more citizens were conscripted to fight, and the shrinking labor supply of freemen was most easily supported through the use of slave craftsmen and artisans. In this manner, the military-industrial complex of ancient time was fueled in part by slavery.[17]

Weapons Systems

The Battle of Kadesh (1274 B.C.E.) more than 1,000 years before the appearance of Christianity is one of the better documented Egyptian military campaigns in history because it is the earliest battle that can be reliably reconstructed in detail from various records on both sides of the conflict. Fought between the Hittites of the upper Euphrates Valley under King Muwatalli II and Ramses II, one of Egypt's best-known fighting pharaohs, Kadesh was a battle fought for control of territory in present-day Syria that recently had been ravaged by plague. The widespread illness (that also took the life of the former Hittite king and may be related to the angel of death that smote the first born of the Egyptians in Exodus) created a power vacuum in the region that Ramses II may have tried to exploit with questionable success.

More important, in the aftermath of the battle, the Egyptians and their former Hittite opponents formulated the first-known treaty of alliance (1264 B.C.E.) against a third party (in this case, Assyria). This temporary state of peace and imperial weakness may have precipitated the flight of the Hebrew people. Fragments of a stone tablet recording the terms of the treaty agreed to by Muwatalli II and Ramses II are on display at the United Nations.

Kadesh has received considerable attention from many military analysts over the years because of the extensive use of heavy (Hittite) and light (Egyptian) chariots. Such chariots were the mobile *force multipliers* (like modern tanks) of the ancient world, with the Hittites relying on the lumbering power of their chariot-borne spear throwers and the Egyptians firing arrows from their fleet weapons platforms with composite bows. The Egyptians won an important phase of the battle. Once back in Egypt, Ramses proclaimed that he had won a great victory, but in reality, all he had managed to do was to rescue a small part of his army from a well-planned ambush. Modern historians conclude the campaign was a draw, but it was also a great victory for Egyptian military preparedness. New technologies had been developed, and the army had been rearmed before pushing back against the potential threat posed by the Hittites.

The Egyptian chariot, like many modern technological advances in weaponry, lent a novel lethality, mobility, and shock to warfare. These were great advantages against massed formations of infantry in open terrain especially when coupled with the firepower of the composite bow, but as with the modern tank, the most dangerous enemy of the chariot was the individual infantryman who might move in close and strike a single disabling blow. The Roman legions more than a thousand years later were frustrated by Britons in light wicker chariots pulled by large ponies, once again authenticating the legitimacy of the technology.

In World War II, German and American light tanks were similarly designed to act in conjunction with infantry to overcome obstacles and to exploit breakthroughs by rapid advances. More often than not they were used against enemy infantry and not against other tanks. "Encounters with enemy tanks, while not rare, were not a daily occurrence except in major campaigns." The German light tanks [Panthers] had formidable firepower (the 75 mm gun), but studies suggest that the primary factor in deciding the victor in tank-on-tank encounters was "who spotted the enemy tank first, who engaged first, and who hit first."[18] The German light tanks developed a fearsome reputation among those who faced them, but their overall combat effectiveness was relatively low because of their tactical misuse, especially in the Russian campaign. Moreover, as Germany's battlefield prospects shifted to the defense in late 1942, the premium on speed and mobility shifted also. German tanks from the second half of the war were slower and more heavily armored and gunned than earlier models, emphasizing their defensive rather than their offensive role.

Arms Technology

The development and dispersal of advanced arms technologies is often thought to be a modern diplomatic problem involving nuclear arms and biological or chemical weapons, but these facets of militarism also are documented in ancient texts. The use of the horse and the chariot seems to have spread across the Middle East from the northern reaches of Mesopotamia to the south and southwest and into Egypt. The bronze socket axe and sickle sword, throwing javelins, compound bows, and the changes from bronze to less expensive and stronger weapons and armor made of iron followed the same route. Horsemen, whether mounted individuals or charioteers, helped to reshape the time, the place, and the pace of battle. These were generally mounted archers. Although the use of iron weapons spread slowly through the ancient world, the compound bow and iron-tipped arrow made a more remarkable advance—a situation with tactical and strategic implications very much like the American development of the rifle over the musket in the Revolution. Archers using this system could reach out to 200 or more yards with their armor-piercing arrows and make a quick retreat to show up suddenly elsewhere on the battlefield (the so-called Parthian Shot made famous in the Middle Eastern wars against Imperial Rome).

Chariots and charioteers were expensive to maintain, but they and the mounted men associated with them allowed the nation fielding such a force to erect a *strategic defense in depth* that utilized mobility to ambush the enemy, harass his supply lines, and range far from one's base while securing the homeland from insult. While light cavalry firing arrows from horseback had existed almost since the domestication of the horse, it was only with the development of sturdier horses that heavy cavalry assumed many of the tactical roles played by chariots. The stereotypical example of this development was the medieval knight with his protective plate armor similar to that used in flak jackets in more recent wars.

Terrain

Nothing compels the conduct of warfare quite as much as terrain. Take as recent examples the difficulty of Soviet and NATO operations in the mountainous regions of Afghanistan or Pakistan, or of French and American operations in the jungles of southeast Asia. Until the advent of steam-powered military transportation during the American Civil War, the speed of an army over good roads was limited to that of a marching column of infantryman (3–4 mph) or, over longer periods, to the speed of the supply carts drawn by animals that carried his provisions and extra weapons. Chariots and cavalry could move more quickly for short periods, but no ancient commander wanted to go into a mounted attack without his infantry support and logistics in place. Bad terrain, hills and mountains, tangled undergrowth, river crossings, muddy roads, flooded rice paddies, and desert sands slowed everyone down, but they were particularly difficult for chariots, wagons, and horsemen to negotiate when pressed by the enemy.[19]

A number of geopolitical factors (such as land-bridges, hills and mountains, natural ports, marshes and waterways, and mountain passes) have in the past brought war to many otherwise-remote places. *Strategic positions* like the islands of Gibraltar, Malta, and Sicily in the Mediterranean, the Isthmuses of Corinth, Panama, and Suez, the Khyber Pass between Central and South Asia and the pass at Thermopile in Greece, the Straits of Artemesium, the English Channel, the Lake

Champlain Corridor, and the escarpment upon which the city fortress of Quebec sits are all examples of places that, by their unique character, have become the focus of war. Many of these geopolitical hotspots have been known since antiquity even if the wars fought over them have faded into memory.

The biblical land of Canaan, known since the time of the Roman Empire as Palestine (the Levant), for instance, contained the only practical land-bridge between Asia and Africa, a passage through Gaza that skirts the Mediterranean Sea on one side and the desert of Shur on the other. As with other land routes like the later Silk Road out of China, the passage through Gaza was an international pathway through a region over which trade items and *strategic materials* were transported. Tin, copper, and iron were among the *strategic metals* necessary in antiquity for the production of weapons and armor. Ingots of tin from the present-day Iran-Iraq border in the east were particularly important to the large emerging empires of the region, because when mixed with local copper they produced bronze. Soft iron weapons and armor did not appear until late 12th century B.C.E. The fortress city of Hazor was a major transshipment point for tin ingots in the north of Palestine while copper came from the Sinai, eastern Anatolia, and from the island of Cyprus, the greatest copper producer of the Bronze Age (3300–1200 B.C.E.). Yet tin was the rarer metal by far, making its shipment through Palestine a strategic necessity.[20]

Gaza remains the focus for continuing conflict into the 21st century for different reasons. Yet "long before there was an Exodus . . . the Palestine land-bridge was the cockpit for war and great power conflict."[21] According to inscriptions from the Sixth Dynasty of Ancient Egypt, the Pharaoh Pepi I (ca. 2350 B.C.E.) moved an army out of Egypt following the coastal road to put down a rebellion among the "sand dwellers" of Gaza. His main force proceeded in the enemy's front to the northeast, while a smaller force landed from transport barges on the seacoast in the enemy rear and took the rebel army by surprise while their attention was directed elsewhere. This tactic—utilized by Pepi a thousand years before the birth of Moses—would be used again and again in more recent times as at Anzio and Salerno in Italy during World War II and at Inchon during the Korean War.

Command and Control

The first definite description of a system of *command and control* was recorded 3000 years ago in the Book of Numbers delineating the arrangement of the Hebrew camp, the procedures for assembling, the order of march, and a series of signals for communications. These arrangements were pragmatic and very much like those found in use among American forces during the Civil War. Being a far less numerous people than their enemies, the Hebrews practiced a form of asymmetric warfare pitting their light troops and hit-and-run tactics against their more organized and heavily armed opponents, much in the same manner that the Viet Cong fought their wars of national independence in Southeast Asia three millennia later. The light infantry—possibly the most common type of Hebrew soldier before the reign of Solomon—was arranged into tactical units of 600, subdivided into three or four combat units of either 200 (Canaanite or Philistine Style) or 150 (Egyptian style), respectively. It seems that these tactical units were further divided into more intimate groups of thirty men. The biblical texts are unclear which system the Hebrews favored, but the results are eerily similar to the arrangements of platoons, companies, battalions, and regiments used in modern armies. In addition, although almost every warrior carried a sword or long dagger, certain of the tribes seem to have specialized in the manufacture, maintenance, and use of certain weapons—slings, light javelins, thrusting spears, or bow and arrow—as do specially armed 21st-century troops, such as airborne, heavy weapons, or antitank units.[22]

During biblical times, a wide-ranging *military conscription* was established that could call up *levies* from among the twelve tribes of Israel suggesting a politico-military plan to carry out a coherent intertribal defense policy. Men became eligible for military service at age twenty, but no upper-age limit is found in the biblical texts. As with American colonial militias three millennia later, there was no permanent professional officer corps, and leadership in battle was largely based on consensus with men of good reputation being chosen as leaders from among those to be led. Such a system was regarded as the natural way to fight, because each man knew the quality of both his comrades and his officers.[23] The Biblical text implies, however, that some tribal assembly had to decide to mobilize for war, and in the traditional practice of the Hebrews since Exodus, representatives of the assembly sought out divine sanction of God through the judges or the prophets. Also found in the Bible is the first *exemption* from military service applied to the tribe of Levites. This was a religious exemption for those who were to provide the priests to Israel and guard the Ark of the Covenant with force of arms, if necessary.

Armies like these were common in antiquity and had the same decentralized form and social interactions as those recorded in early literary sources as in the *Iliad* or in *Beowulf*. The number of Hebrew troops that actually took the field under the conscription provisions dictated in the Bible was disappointing, however. The fact that only four of the twelve tribes regularly contributed troops to the common defense force suggests a weakness in their alliance in the absence of self-interest, oddly similar to that found in America under both British colonial rule and the Articles of Confederation.[24]

Standing Forces

A successful armed force—whether an ancient or more recent one—needed to systematically use reconnaissance, judge terrain, make forced marches, fight night battles, besiege cities, make feints and diversions, and follow up a beaten foe with lethal purpose. The cultivated fringe of the biblical desert with its stores of grain and flocks of goats and sheep was always a tempting target for hit-and-run desert raiders in the Middle East. Then as now, Israel was accosted by outside forces and threats to its existence that could not be ignored. The constant presence of enemy forces on Israel's borders emphasized the need for a standing army domestically—a lesson that American strategic planners were slow to appreciate before the War of

1812. It was the inability of the Hebrew levies to defend their agriculturally abundant regions that had led to the popular demand for a more centralized government and a standing army.

Under Israel's first king, Saul, a centralized national army was built, and the king was empowered to levy conscripts from all twelve tribes for one month's service annually. This system also provided the king with a standing force of 3,000 "professional" warriors arranged in two unequal *divisions*. One of these—probably the smaller—may have been commanded by Saul's nemesis and ultimate successor, David. Nonetheless, a successful leader also had to know when and how to make peace, and David's son, Solomon, built or reinforced several cities that controlled important roadways, passes, or river crossings to better maintain the peace in much the same way that Benjamin Franklin did with his string of frontier forts in Pennsylvania in 1755.

Combined Operations

One of the necessary characteristics of a successful and long-lived empire is the development of a navy. Although bordering on the Mediterranean, the Israelites never established a meaningful naval presence in antiquity. As with the Americans of the Revolutionary and Federalists Periods, whose forte was light infantry not warships, the Israeli national strategy was to draw their enemies into the rugged and mountainous hinterland where light troops were at an advantage. Coastal Israel in Biblical times was, therefore, open to attack from the sea, and the Philistines, and later the Phoenicians, were seagoing peoples who found the vulnerability of the Israeli coastline attractive. The Romans and Carthaginians developed formidable warships during the Punic Wars of the second century B.C.E., but these were designed for ramming and served as fighting platforms for land troops to fight much as they did ashore rather than in the naval fashion of the 17th or 18th centuries.

Yet a navy can not operate on an unfriendly coast for an extended period. The need for fresh water alone limits its ability to maintain its station. Land forces often were required to establish themselves ashore to secure the supply of water for their ships, who in turn supplied the land forces with food and munitions. The island of Britain was remarkable in that it provided a nearby base for British warships patrolling the coast of Europe. The British strategy for the American War of Independence was to secure or otherwise blockade America's port cities, thereby starving the colonial economies into submission while preventing the import of the necessary materials of war for the Patriot army. Initially, their plans contemplated only a police action to restore order among a small fraction of their own subjects in New England. No plan was formed to pursue a general conflict along a 1,500-mile coastline populated by hostile inhabitants who might deny the Crown forces all the necessities of war, including food and water. It was thought that the British North American Squadron alone could handle this operation. However, no previous navy in history had attempted to support its armies from the distance of 4,000 miles with munitions, reinforcements, and food. It actually took three times their number to maintain a naval presence in American waters. Moreover, ordnance vessels and troop transports, without escort, made easy targets for America's miniature warships whose bases were nearby. Yet, the ministers in London should not be regarded too harshly for their strategic naiveté with respect to the colonies. The American Revolution was the first major conflict waged for the purpose of political independence, and many of its deeper aspects were unknown or misunderstood.[25]

Historians have been forced to admit that many of the most famous battles of the Bible stand in isolation. Although some of the details are noted, little is known of the causes of the wars and nothing of their consequences for the victors or for the vanquished beyond the initiation of a general and short-lived peace.[26] The Bible also includes useful references to alliances, treaties, compromises, arbitrations, and diplomatic ploys aimed at peace-seeking. In this regard, the Bible is also a virtual textbook of foreign policy protocols. "The Old Testament provides the military historian with a rich human context through which to study the armies and wars of the Bible, a dimension of human understanding that is all too frequently absent in more modern and technical accounts of warfare."[27]

Generations

Among those familiar with the Bible, some have noted that the reign of Biblical kings in the Old Testament is repeatedly reported as being forty years. No forty-year term limits, of course, were imposed on these rulers. The authors of the Bible were simply using the forty-year duration as a practical determinant of a generation—a lifetime as an active adult. There are also recorded a number of reigns of twenty years' duration (half a lifetime) as well as extended periods of peace (twenty, forty, and eighty years).

Many of the major wars in American history also can be deemed generational—their cause, duration, or aftermath taking up the attention of an entire adult generation during the most productive years of their lives (approximately age twenty to sixty). Many of the men who served as officers during the American Revolution in 1775, for instance, served in two wars—fighting alongside the British and against the French in the 1740s and 1750s as young men and then leading other young men against the redcoats as older men in the Revolution. John Adams wrote in a letter to his wife, Abigail, in 1777, "Posterity! You will never know how much it cost the present generation to preserve your freedom! I hope you will make a good use of it. If you do not, I shall repent in Heaven that I ever took half the pains to preserve it."[28]

Those Americans who went to war against Britain in 1812 or against Mexico in 1846 were, with a few exceptions, each a new generation of warriors. While many of the general officers of the Civil War were young men during the campaign in Mexico, most of the soldiers who fought from 1861 to 1865 had traded only rhetorical bullets concerning slavery and secession before taking up arms. Three decades later, another generation of men, initially innocent of warfare, gleefully went to Cuba and the Philippines in the Spanish-American War.

The young Americans who went to Europe in 1917 during World War I initially thought in terms of weeks or months of conflict and were shocked to find the war bogged down in indecisive trench warfare. Nonetheless, it was Europe rather than America that lost an entire generation of young men to warfare from 1914 to 1918. Moreover, the imperfect peace that ended World War I created an incubator for Fascism and Nazism, and provided the raison d'être for World War II, in which many of the men who had survived in the trenches were now leading armies composed of the next generation of boys and young men.

In much the same way, the conflict in the Pacific Rim in the 20th century—beginning in the 1930s with Japanese aggression in China and ending in the 1970s with an American defeat in Vietnam—seemingly crossed from one generation to the next, that of the Great Depression to that of the post–World War II Baby Boom. This period encompassed five major confrontations in the region: the Sino-Japanese War, World War II, Korea, and the two phases of the war in Indochina (French and American). Meanwhile, Arabs and Israelis in the Middle East, as well as Muslins and Hindus in the Indian subcontinent, have been in conflict since their independence in 1948, seemingly fighting from one generation, to the next, and to the next again with no near end in sight.

All the Land Rent Asunder

As one of humanity's most terrible self-imposed afflictions, the continuous reappearance of war and the almost sacrificial commitment of American youth to its prosecution requires an attempt to find some fundamental answer to why conflict continues to exist even in the presence of almost unanimous agreement that the state of peace is better than the state of war for all concerned.

Why do nations continue to go to war? The conventional wisdom suggests that the nature of human beings, and of national leaders in particular, is fundamentally corrupt. Yet as a proximate cause of war, the personal dimension eludes simple quantification even when comparing well-documented war leaders such as Lincoln and Davis, George Washington and George III, Hitler and FDR, LBJ and Ho Chi Minh, or Hussein and both Bushes. It can be argued that in most cases the war decision makers were not people with a conscious design bent on global destruction. Personality and human frailty also fail to answer two further crucial questions. Given the known horrors and terrible ferocity that accompany warfare of any kind, why do so many otherwise peace-loving citizens praise their politicians for their leadership in wartime, and why do so many young men voluntarily follow their generals to their doom?

The causes of war and the resolution of conflicts between nations are always rooted in the political sphere, but they often are fought for high-sounding causes like independence, nationhood, or the defense of democracy or are attributed to more nebulous forces like militarism, imperialism, racism, or other bloodless abstractions that distract the view from the awful and horrible spectacle of armed conflict, destruction, and death. The cause of war has been assigned to negative quantities, such as a lack of diplomacy, a dearth of communication between nations, and a general absence of good will among human kind. Warfare seems at times an irrational and illogical aberration created by devious, evil, or cunning creatures, yet

most world leaders bring their nations to war with great care and serious consideration of the possible consequences, doing so in a seemingly logical and purposeful
manner. So strange is this characteristic of warfare that Gen. Maxwell D. Taylor,
chairmen of the U.S. Joint Chiefs of Staff (JCS) in the 1960s, could rationally discuss with President John Fitzgerald Kennedy a so-called flexible response to world
conflict that ranged from the "mutual assured destruction" of waging tactical nuclear war in Europe to preventing the minor infiltrations of peasant insurgents
across national borders in the jungles of Southeast Asia or Central America.[29]

For reasonable people, who believe at some instinctual level that peace rather
than violence is the natural condition of human society, these observations are
remarkably distressing and chillingly disheartening. On the other hand, peace seems
illusive. Any prolonged period of history during which a generation has not been
involved in a major conflict (and there are few) can be viewed as an astonishingly
gratifying and uniquely satisfying occurrence, because the state of war in the world
has remained almost uninterrupted.

Yet even young readers will remember that America's most recent foreign war
(Iraq II) was greeted at some level with martial grandeur and public rejoicing at the
outset. Only with time and increased civilian and military casualties did the initial
euphoria for the second Iraq war vanish. In this case, distance—once a major factor
in muting the anguish, horror, and reality of warfare and thereby subduing domestic
resistance to war—has given way to a close-up view of warfare provided by an
expanded international news media, Internet access, embedded reporters, and
twenty-four-hour television coverage. This aspect of modern communications—
sometimes monitored by the government—has largely rendered inoperative the
insulating barrier between war and the noncombatant citizen. In some ways, it may
bring us back to some simulation of the daily dread of war that overshadowed the
lives of our ancestors. This factor alone may portend a possible change of historical
proportions in public attitudes toward war-making. "A slow dawning of compassion
and of global consciousness" may be taking place with respect to the public
response to war as a tool of foreign policy.[30] Yet in an era of asymmetrical warfare,
terrorism, and roadside bombs, images that governments would have schemed to
conceal from the public in the past, are now featured on the evening news or posted
on terrorist Web sites as tools for recruitment and financial support.

Coercive Diplomacy

At first the idea of coercive diplomacy seems an oxymoron because most people,
unfamiliar with the intricacies of the diplomatic process, believe coercion and diplomacy to be mutually exclusive and on opposite ends of the spectrum of international relations. Yet both are commonly used devices of foreign policy. The general
idea of coercive diplomacy, however, is "to back one's demand on an adversary
with a threat of punishment for noncompliance that he will consider credible and
potent enough to persuade him to comply with the demand."[31] In many cases, coercive diplomacy serves as a more appropriate response to international disputes than
force or diplomacy alone. The presence of several conditions for maintaining the

peace and avoiding war seems to make coercive diplomacy more likely to be successful than not. These include a number of factors determined by the context of the crisis event that include but are not limited to the following:

- the potential of the dispute to become an armed conflict in any case
- the presence or absence of allies for each party and the level of their commitment as allies
- the cost of any subsequent war in terms of lives, money, or lost prestige
- the perception of urgency on the part of the parties
- the attitudes of the nation's own citizens and those of the wider international community

Some of these factors are psychological in nature and their outcome is difficult to predict or to guarantee in any case. No single factor seems sufficient for predicting the successful employment of coercive diplomacy in resolving a crisis without resorting to war, but the support of one's own population is essential. Nonetheless, clear and consistent demands at the conference table, adequate motivation, the ability to instill a sense of urgency in the opponent, and the opponent's fear of escalation to open warfare seem to be key factors in influencing the success of coercive diplomacy.

Embarking on a course of coercion requires a toughness of national will and a steadfastness of purpose while negotiating a sometimes confusing menu of diplomatic strategies. For example, if the other side of the table wants something badly, it is advisable for the diplomat to seem almost intractable on that subject, thus increasing the possibility that the opponent will seek mollification on a different issue that is, perhaps secretly, the more important issue to the diplomat and the actual object of the diplomacy. Coercive diplomacy, according to Helmut Sonnenfelt, counselor for the U.S. State Department in 1975, is

> an attempt to evolve a balance of incentives for positive behavior and penalties for belligerence; the objective being to instill in the minds of . . . potential adversaries an appreciation of the benefits of cooperation rather than conflict and thus lessen the threat of war. . . . [National self interests] will be respected only if it is clear that they can be defended. Restraint will prevail only if its absence is known to carry heavy risks.[32]

The concept of using diplomacy backed by the threat of force is not new. Although Napoleon Bonaparte did not invent the concept of coercive diplomacy, he used it to greater effect than anyone previously had. Although the reader may wonder at the inclusion of Napoleon in a work concerning the history of the American antiwar movement, his diplomatic strategies—taught at the U.S. Military Academy (USMA) at West Point in tandem with Bonaparte's many military maxims—were a bulwark of 19th-century diplomacy and warfare throughout the Western world. Sylvanus Thayer (superintendent of West Point during its formative decades) had a long-standing admiration for Napoleon, and James Renwick, sent to acquire books, instruments, and models of education for the nascent USMA in 1816, wrote of "the terrific splendor" of the Napoleonic wars, which had "paled the lustre of all former European battles."[33] Students of the process have observed, "American officers fully participated in a larger European profession of arms and drew Old World practice for the New World Army they were trying to create."[34] Napoleon seemingly thought faster and acted faster than any of his contemporaries, both on the battlefield and at the conference table, and his skills have added importance to the discussion of America's war-making doctrine as instructional examples for the reader.

At the beginning of the 19th century, Napoleon undertook to revolutionize the political aspects of international relations, overturning many formerly established diplomatic and military conventions in the process, and setting the tone for much of the warfare that followed. Thereafter, defeat meant more than losing isolated positions on a battlefield or signing an unfavorable treaty. Napoleon would redraw the boundaries of Europe, and war would come to involve the future prospects of whole nations, all their people, all their resources, and their very form of governance. It is recorded that Napoleon at the height of his power sat astride his white horse amid the ruins of battle in Central Europe, anxiously awaiting not the casualty reports of his commanders, but rather his daily courier's report on the mood of the mob in Paris. Napoleon had come to prominence in 1796 by sweeping the royalist mob from the streets of Paris with artillery fire, a form of crowd control not before used in France, but he feared them and respected their power nonetheless. It is difficult to assess the level of Napoleon's influence over the people, but it is certain that he had the devotion of the army—an instructive example for antimilitarists in the nascent Untied States.[35]

Napoleon's chief diplomatic advisor was the devious Foreign Minister Prince Charles Maurice de Talleyrand, who would serve six French governments and betray four of them. Talleyrand was the consummate diplomat and propagandist being equally duplicitous and talented. Napoleon and Talleyrand shared a dream of establishing a French-led global government, by force if necessary, and extended their war as far as the pyramids of Egypt. The original plan was undoubtedly to seize Egypt as a colony, thereby replacing some of the economic value lost to France in the West Indies, and move on to the Middle East and India as had Alexander the Great. The French expected the Egyptian population, suffering under the Mamelukes of the Ottoman Empire, to welcome them as liberators—a common delusion shared by many empire makers. Although the Egyptian campaign and occupation were more difficult than either Napoleon or Talleyrand had expected, Napoleon used the prestige gained in the victory to invade the halls of government in Paris with armed troops and raise himself to First Consul of France.

Napoleon and Talleyrand used coercive diplomacy to brilliant affect, especially in negotiating the Peace of Amiens (1803), an armistice that was probably more advantageous to the French than to the British. Nonetheless, the public welcomed the peace on both sides of the English Channel. Towns were illuminated with fireworks, feasts were held, and congratulatory addresses and sermons were given celebrating the return of peace after nine long years of European conflict. If Napoleon had wished after the Peace of Amiens, he might have convinced British diplomats to allow him to keep all that he had conquered on the Continent, but this was not to be. His diplomacy was a tissue of lies, and his desire to conquer all of Europe including Britain was pathological. He managed his own propaganda (spin, if you will) printing and distributing favorable newssheets throughout France. For almost twenty years, through victory and defeat, the people of France answered his every call to arms. No modern political or military leader has ever been better served.[36]

With the Peace of Amiens going into effect as of January 1, 1803, Paris was filled once again with expectant internationals—businessmen, expatriates, and casual visitors planning for a peaceful Christmas. Amiens was, nevertheless, a phony peace, a bad peace, if one can imagine even the brief cessation of killing and mayhem as bad, on the level of the Munich Agreement signed by Adolf Hitler and Neville Chamberlain in 1938. In the case of Amiens, neither France nor Britain considered the terms of the treaty conclusive of the issues that had precipitated war. It was viewed only as a temporary respite before the fighting was to be renewed—a convenient interlude used by historians to mark the end of the French Revolution and the beginning of ten years of Napoleonic Wars. Bonaparte, the penultimate war monger of the early 19th century, had used coercive diplomacy on Britain with great skill to win a breathing space in which to rearm and recollect his armies, build a larger navy, confirm his domestic political position, and crown himself Emperor of the French (1804). Like Alexander or Caesar before him, Napoleon embodied both the general and the head of state in a single being.

In 1805, war broke out again and Britain convinced Austria and Russia to join a Third Coalition against France. On December 2, the first anniversary of his self-coronation, Napoleon defeated Austria and Russia at Austerlitz—ending the Third Coalition and signing another peace treaty (Peace of Pressburg). And so it went with fourth, fifth, and sixth coalitions forming and each signing a disadvantageous peace treaty when it was defeated by Napoleon's almost flawless tactics. Invasions occurred over increasingly broader fronts, and in many places simultaneously. The landscape of Europe was rent asunder.

This series of events introduced strategic and diplomatic outcomes that made future wars costlier than formerly in terms of lives lost, treasure expended, and political consequences to be sustained. In addition to his military and diplomatic strategy, Napoleon waged an economic war against his most implacable and relentless enemy (Britain), attempting to enforce a Europe-wide commercial boycott on the island nation as part of his Continental System and sweeping America into the fray in 1812 largely by accident. Napoleon brought a new emphasis in warfare toward destroying, not just outmaneuvering, his enemies, and he then attempted to change the politics, economy, and culture of his victims to better reflect French interests. After Napoleon, warfare was never again the same. It is not surprising, therefore, that it was at the end of the Napoleonic Wars (1815) that serious organized war resistance had its beginning in the form of the first international antiwar societies and peace committees.

Coercive diplomacy is often confused with blatant militarism because, when it fails, it usually yields to the explicit use of force. This is an error. Both the threat and the ability to bring force to bear in these situations must be creditable for the diplomacy to work in the first place. The coercive ploy can be rendered impotent if its target recognizes any weakness in the public will of the aggressor nation(s) to follow through with the threat. The logic behind coercive diplomacy assumes that the target of the negotiations will behave rationally—a factor on which Napoleon relied repeatedly. However, an adversary's motivation and commitment to a particular behavior, and his assessment of the credibility and potency of the threat, play a significant role in determining the success or failure of such a strategy.

If success is defined as the avoidance of war, the recent use of coercive diplomacy by the United States has had a varied record of limited successes and abysmal failures. This record may be due to a characteristic American willingness to fight when its diplomacy is the least bit frustrated—seemingly part of its national temperament. In July 1941, for instance, the United States threatened Japan with an oil embargo unless Japan withdrew from China where its had been fighting intermittently since 1931, horrifying the world with its barbaric methods of suppressing the civilian population. Chief among these was the Rape of Nanking (December 1937), an infamous series of war crimes committed against the civilian residents in what was then the capital of the Republic of China. Using phrases like "Asia for Asians," Japan justified its China policy by stressing the need to liberate Asian countries from imperialist European powers.

At the time, the developing Japanese economy was totally dependent on foreign petroleum imports, and President Franklin D. Roosevelt backed his threat of an oil embargo with the concentration of U.S. naval forces at Pearl Harbor, Hawaii—not too close to Japan to seem aggressive (as it would have been if stationed in the Philippines or at Guam) but close enough to pose a convincing threat of coercive action. This coercive form of diplomacy not only failed, but it may have actually provoked Japanese attacks on both the Philippines and Hawaii.

The Roosevelt administration, and the nations of the British Commonwealth, who also were targeted by Japan, had seriously misread the commitment of Foreign Minister Shigenori Togo to the concept of a Greater East Asia Co-Prosperity Sphere—considered in the 21st century to be a front for Japanese imperialism. They also failed to acknowledge in their diplomatic strategy the effect of an active and concurrent war with Germany and Italy (Japanese allies) on the continent of Europe. This led the Japanese leaders to believe the Western powers incapable of mounting a significant response to their first strike strategy; and they were almost correct. The United States and its allies were able to win World War II only through a strategy of winning first in Europe while attempting a series of holding actions in the Pacific. Moreover, it is uncertain whether they would have succeeded in this stratagem without the entry of the Soviets into the European theater of the war.

In 1961, President John F. Kennedy employed coercive diplomacy while defending the royalist forces in Laos against Communist incursions. For Kennedy, the Laotian crisis was among the first of his administration. He went on national television to declare that a Communist takeover in Laos would affect the security of the United States, a clear implication that the United States would not stand for any such takeover. Kennedy was, in fact, trying some scare tactics on the Laotians that did not work completely, and he was eventually forced to accept the

The Russian Embassy burns after the Japanese occupation of Nanking, the capital of the Republic of China during the Second Sino-Japanese War. The destruction of Nanking was also known as the rape of Nanking, following its capture by the Japanese Imperial Army on December 29, 1937. (AP Photo)

compromise of a coalition government that would include some Communist leaders. In the short run, the new president was attempting to orchestrate some persuasive military move that would make his ultimate commitment to go to war in Southeast Asia credible and underpin his authority as a world leader. Unfortunately in April 1961, he gave the green light to the failed Bay of Pigs invasion of Cuba—to which the United States gave only lackluster support—and he thereby seriously damaged the diplomatic credibility of his administration. The capitulation in Laos and the Cuban fiasco raised serious doubts about Kennedy's leadership abilities among both foreign and domestic sources.[37]

In 1962, Kennedy again attempted to employ coercive diplomacy to compel the Soviet Union to remove missiles from Fidel Castro's Cuba in one of the most compelling eyeball-to-eyeball standoff's in modern history. In this case, Kennedy threatened a naval blockade of the island and added urgency to his demands by setting a date certain for the Russians to remove their weapons. The crisis continued unabated for some time, and in an exchange of telegrams between Soviet Premier Nikita Khrushchev and the antiwar activist Bertrand Russell, Khrushchev utilized some back-channel coercive diplomacy of his own by warning that the U.S. action could lead to thermonuclear war. Kennedy's diplomatic ploy ultimately worked in removing the missiles because Khrushchev decided on October 28, 1962, that he was unwilling to go to war for Cuba. Kennedy immediately responded, issuing a presidential statement calling the Soviet change in position with regard to Cuba an important and constructive contribution to world peace. The practical effect of the Kennedy-Khrushchev Pact of 1962, however, was the sharpening of U.S.-Soviet hostility elsewhere in the world and the strengthening of Fidel Castro's position in Cuba in that it removed the practical threat of a future invasion by the United States.

The failure of the U.S.-supported Diem government in South Vietnam in 1963—a military coup carried out just weeks before the Kennedy assassination—further damaged the diplomatic posture of the United States on the international scene. Fearing that the Central Intelligence Agency (CIA) or some other secret agency of the U.S. government was plotting a similar overturn of the Cambodian government, Prince Norodom Sihanouk of Cambodia severed all economic and military ties with America the day after the coup, and the Kennedy administration aids scrambled to reassure the Cambodians of their continued support. In addition, both the secretary of state (Dean Rusk) and the secretary of defense (Robert S. McNamara) under Kennedy warned the president that a failure to actively defend South Vietnam from communism might be "seized upon by extreme elements" in America "to divide the country [the United States]." Ironically, it was the continued prosecution of the war in Southeast Asia during the Johnson and Nixon administrations, rather than the failure to do so, that produced this unwanted domestic effect.[38]

Conflict Resolution

In the 1970s, the administration of President James E. "Jimmy" Carter abandoned the use of coercive diplomacy, making its primary diplomatic strategy that of *conflict resolution*—a stratagem that generally had produced little in the way of fruitful results during the 20th century up to that time. Successful conflict resolution has several characteristics:

- communication and continuing dialogue between parties
- providing opportunities to meet the needs of all parties
- addressing the interests of all parties so that each is satisfied with the outcome
- finding win-win outcomes as opposed to win-lose dynamics
- preventing conflicts before they start or before they lead to open violence

Conflict resolution can be affected using many approaches, but no single characteristic has emerged as most effective in terms of avoiding destructive action, violence, or the use of force. However, all approaches have some tactics in common: talking about the issues, focusing on areas of agreement in the initial stages of discussion, negotiating concessions on each side, and arranging for continuing dialogue. Proponents of conflict resolution tend to focus solely on this need for *continuing dialogue* (while ignoring other fundamental factors) as if some magic words might be intoned during one of the numerous diplomatic sessions that would cause the parties to change their positions. Of the many organizations involved in international conflict resolution, the United Nation is foremost.

To many liberal American legislators coming out of the era of the Vietnam War, reliance on coercive diplomacy had made the United States a partner in aggression and killing around the world. Candidate Carter interjected the issues of coercion, intervention, and arms sales to developing nations into his presidential campaign in 1976 to attract a war-weary electorate to the Democratic Party. He attempted specifically to influence an improved opinion of U.S. foreign policy among European governments. Congress passed laws giving itself the power to veto arms sales to foreign entities approved by the executive branch and to mandate a reduction in U.S. military advisors and their deployment overseas. Antiwar legislators considered advisors like these the gateway instrument to involvement in Southeast Asia, and they were pledged not to repeat the strategy. To many conservative observers, this method of diplomacy was naïve, and it proved an unmitigated disaster when U.S. diplomats were held hostage by an Iranian Revolutionary government that valued the propaganda value of the conflict higher than its resolution. President Carter found that talking alone produced no positive outcome. An added unanticipated consequence of the ban on military advisors was later discovered when it was noted that the military men who had composed the advisor groups were being replaced with so-called *civilian contractors*—usually former military men or covert (black) operatives—who proved to be more difficult to control and discipline than active service military personnel.

In the 1980s, Ronald W. Reagan largely abandoned the strategy of conflict resolution and successfully reapplied coercive diplomacy as president-elect with the Iranian government, which had been holding U.S. embassy personnel for more than 400 days. Just the credible threat of military action secured the release of the hostages on the day of his inauguration. The Beirut bombing of the U.S. Marine barracks in October 1983 was a major diplomatic setback effecting the Reagan presidency. Two truck bombs struck separate buildings in Beirut that housed U.S. and French military forces—members of the Multinational Peacekeeping Force in Lebanon—killing 299 servicemen, including 220 U.S. Marines. In fact, the United States made no serious retaliation for the Beirut bombing. In December 1983, U.S. aircraft from the USS *Enterprise* (CVN-65) battle group attacked Syrian targets in Lebanon, but this action was in response to Syrian missile attacks on planes overflying the region, not the barracks bombings. Reagan moved the Marines offshore where they could not be targeted, and in February 1984, he ordered the Marines to begin a complete withdrawal from Lebanon. The rest of the Multinational Peacekeeping Force was withdrawn by April. The attack on the barrack and the subsequent withdrawal of U.S. forces gave a boost to the growth of the Shi'ite organization Hezbollah. Hezbollah denied involvement in the attacks but was considered as involved nonetheless. The bombing was one of the first categorized by the United States as an act of Islamic terrorism.

Reagan had limited success in Nicaragua in his effort to derail the influence of Marxist revolutionaries called Sandinistas. The United States conducted a "not-very-covert war" against the revolutionary government, and many Americans greatly feared that Nicaragua might become a Latin American version of the Vietnam disaster. Forces unfriendly to Reagan viewed the Sandinista revolution as an indigenous attempt to build "a new, more humanistic society in Nicaragua that combined socialist economic and political theory with religious ideals."[39] The flagging antiwar movement in the United States, having reached its pinnacle during Vietnam, protested Reagan's use of so-called terrorism against the Sandinistas to undermine what they considered an acceptable war—a war fought for what they deemed the right reasons. Proponents of the revolution portrayed it as fulfilling the "social justice" promised in the Bible. The Roman Catholic clergy operating out of its missions and churches and the University of Central America, the major Roman Catholic institution in the capital city of Managua, actively supported the Sandinistas claiming that the "authentic nature of religion is the liberation of people."[40] Anti-Reagan forces portrayed the president's counter-revolutionary strategy and the administration's claims of widespread anti-Semitism among the Sandinistas as "an attempt to alienate the [influential] American Jewish community" from supporting the antiwar movement in the United States.[41]

In 1984, there were elections in Nicaragua, and the Marxists won the majority of the votes. The United States was virtually alone in the world in disputing the fairness of these elections, which were widely observed and almost universally declared to be free and fair by international referees. In late 1985, Lt. Col. Oliver North was at the center of national attention during the Iran-Contra Affair, a political scandal tangentially involving Nicaragua. North was a National Security Council member under Reagan involved in the clandestine sale of weapons to Iran, which served to encourage the release of American hostages from Lebanon. North formulated the second part of the plan: diverting proceeds from the arms sales to support the anti-Sandinista Contra Rebel group in Nicaragua in direct opposition to the dictates of Congress. Although clinging to his executive prerogative to pursue foreign policy as an equal branch of the government, the president, nonetheless, claimed no knowledge of this particular operation—a form of so-called *plausible deniability*. North was charged with several felonies in 1987, but the charges were dismissed in 1991. The Democrat-controlled Congress issued a report in 1987, stating that if the president did not know what his national security advisers were doing, he should have. The report was seen as a devastating indictment of Reagan's style of government.[42]

In 1986, Reagan used coercive diplomacy against Libya in an attempt to end Libyan support for terrorism—specifically airline hijacking and bombing. After several days of diplomatic talks with European and Arab partners, Reagan ordered limited air strikes on Libya directed against the Libyan leader Omar Khadafi (Muammar Abu Minyar al-Gaddafi) killing 45 Libyan military and government personnel as well as fifteen civilians in Tripoli and Benghazi. Khadafi's adopted daughter, Hannah, was also killed in the raids. Several predetermined targets were hit and destroyed, but some civilian and diplomatic sites in Tripoli were struck as well, notably the French embassy. The operations were justified as a response to the killing of several American servicemen in a restaurant bombing but were undertaken more to fix the credibility of the Reagan administration with the rest of the terror-supporting world leaders than to achieve the goal of assassinating Khadafi. Nonetheless, the Libyan leader seemingly got the message, and ceased any open support of terrorists. Khadafi also attempted to improve his image in the West. Two years before the terrorist attacks of September 11, 2001, Libya pledged its commitment to fighting al-Qaeda and offered to open up its own weapons program to international inspection.

In the 1990s, Saddam Hussein of Iraq decided to attack neighboring Kuwait, which he accused of stealing Iraqi oil by a method called slant drilling. The invasion decision was taken while the Hussein regime was under severe pressure from the international community, but the Iraqis may have misread the diplomatic signals coming from the United States thinking that their aggression would be tolerated. A U.S.-led international coalition under President George H. W. Bush attempted to use coercive diplomacy to compel Iraq to withdraw from Kuwait. Initially, the coalition used a progressive embargo on Iraqi imports and exports under U.N. auspices, but the strategy quickly shifted to an ultimatum backed by the threat of military force. War broke out shortly thereafter. The U.S.-led invasion (January 1991) ended when Iraqi forces were quickly ejected from Kuwait. By March 1991, coalition troops were beginning their withdrawal.

The War in Bosnia and Herzegovina, commonly known as the Bosnian War, was an international armed conflict that took place between March 1992 and November 1995. The war involved several separate and competing parties. The involvement of NATO and U.S. forces under President Clinton, during the 1995 Operation Deliberate Force against the positions of the Army of Republika Srpska internationalized the conflict, but only in its final stages. The Bosnian government lobbied to have the embargo lifted, but this was opposed by Britain, France, and Russia. The U.S. Congress passed two resolutions calling for the embargo to be lifted, but both resolutions were vetoed by President Clinton for fear of creating a rift between the United States and the aforementioned countries. Although airstrikes were countenanced, no U.S. ground troops took part in this war. Nonetheless, the United States used both "black" C-130 air transports and back-channel diplomacy, including that with Islamist groups, to smuggle weapons to the Bosnian government forces via Croatia. Although misdirected bombing by U.S. forces killed and wounded numerous civilians, a popular president and the absolute lack of U.S. military casualties essentially muzzled American antiwar sentiment during these operations.

In 2002, a less popular U.S. president, George W. Bush, attempted to diplomatically coerce Saddam Hussein with regard to his supposed development and stockpiling of weapons of mass destruction (WMDs). U.S.- and U.N.-sponsored sanctions had been laid after the first Gulf War, and no-fly zones in the north and south of the country were established and patrolled by U.S. and coalition aircraft to protect the regional minorities (Kurds and Shi'ites) in Iraq from the Sunni-dominated Bath government. Again Hussein called the bluff of the coalition firing surface-to-air missiles at the aircraft and refusing to allow the inspections of his military facilities by U.N. officials agreed to under the 1991 treaty. This time (2003) coercive diplomacy ended in the preemptive invasion and occupation of Iraq by U.S.-led coalition forces, the toppling of the Sunni-controlled Bath government, and the execution of Hussein and many of his ministers by order of an Iraqi court. Saddam Hussein had seriously misread the temperament of President George W. Bush as well as the fragile psychology of an American people looking for a martial victory in the months after the September 11 terrorist attacks in New York and Washington in 2001. Nonetheless, a virulent and prolonged insurgency plagued U.S. operations and turned American popular opinion against the war. Additional troops (the so-called Surge) were required to calm things down in 2008.

War: Diplomacy by Other Means

There is no contradiction in the idea that military doctrines at times aim at avoiding wars rather than fighting them.[43] War often provides the essential interface between domestic politics and the realm of foreign policy through which diplomatic efforts are driven to completion. Carl von Clausewitz, a Prussian officer during the Napoleonic Wars and a theorist on war in general, published *On War* in 1832. This work remains the most important general treatment of the subject of warfare yet produced. Herein Von Clausewitz wrote to the effect that *war was the extension of diplomacy by other means*, a dictum concerning the nature of both war and diplomacy that seems cynical at first glance. The conventional and legal definitions of warfare reflect the fact that in many circumstances organized violence is a legally acceptable or even a preferable option when dealing with unresolved disputes between governments. Violence sometimes clears the air and resolves the otherwise-irresolvable disagreements between parties. Clausewitz also suggested that most aggressor nations want to avoid war because they would rather achieve their objectives without having to fight for them, whereas weaker nations often have to fight to win their point or otherwise capitulate.

Reliance on these particular doctrines to maintain peace misses two points. The first is that capitulation to the demands of an aggressor is generally too high a price for most free and independent nations to pay to simply avoid a war. The second is that high-quality deterrence in terms of modern arms and sufficient armies, not unilateral restraint to the point of eroding deterrence, has historically proven the surest way to avoid war.

Since the adoption of nuclear weapons after World War II, for instance, there have been no further world-consuming conflicts. There have been few other 60-plus-year periods of relative peace since the Pax Romana in the first millennium of the current era. The Peace of Rome was a long period of relative peace and minimal expansion experienced by the Roman Empire for approximately 200 years

(27 B.C.E. to 180 A.D.) when its military force was all but unquestioned. Given the prominence of the concept of Pax Romana, historians have coined variants of the term to describe eras of relative peace that have been established, attempted, or argued to have existed, usually under the hegemony of a single great power or group of allied powers. These include the Pax Britannica, Pax Europeana, Pax Germanica, Pax Hispanica, and the present Pax Americana, among others.[44]

The advocates of warfare often present the reasons that lead countries into armed conflict as affecting the *vital self-interests* of the whole nation (or even of the whole world) and not merely those applicable to the special interests of a segment of society or a single nation. Conversely, the opponents of warfare, those with pacifist or antiwar sentiments based on conviction and not merely on political expediency, usually insist that the proponents of war and militarism have not demonstrated that the vital interests of society are at stake, or they argue that the burdens on the population of going to war, maintaining a war footing, or supporting military industries are too heavy to justify the risks of opening an armed confrontation in the first place.

Some people probably will choose warfare over other courses of action such as diplomacy, compromise, or nonlethal coercive measures like resolutions of censure, economic isolation, or financial and trade sanctions. They will make the decision to go to war rationally and attempt to justify their choice in the courts of domestic or world opinion through a compendium of premises and logical conclusions based on the accepted *rules of war*. For others, every decision to go to war is believed to be unwarranted or blatantly immoral, even when an enemy has struck the first blow. Sometimes these antiwar factions represent a small and ineffectual minority of society who make but a feeble objection to warfare; at other times, the war resistance is more widespread and "strong enough to reverse the momentum toward war or to compel the government to enter war-termination negotiations rapidly." Ironically, modern democracies, with their expanded and widely accessible news media, usually find it harder to go to war than did their predecessors with their history of rule by the elite; however, once involved in warfare, democratically elected governments also may find it harder to satisfactorily terminate wars without committing political suicide.[45]

Many of the wars between nations were triggered by unanticipated circumstances, such as assassinations (Archduke Franz Ferdinand in 1914), surprise attacks (Pearl Harbor in 1941), or unexpected actions on the part of an adversary (British troops firing on the Lexington militia in 1775). In cases like these, the decision to prosecute a war is often thrust on the nation by a sudden shift in public opinion, rather than through a conscious decision of national leaders taken in the abstract. This shift in opinion is often reactionary and may be made in an atmosphere of public embarrassment at having been caught unprepared, or (if prepared) unaware of the threat level, as was the case for the United States at Pearl Harbor in 1941. *Reactionary wars* are often characterized by retaliation and revenge, rather than rationale decision making or political expediency; and emotion, rather than reason or self-interest, is often the primary impulse for going forward in these cases.

Most war resisters grant that limited violence is sometimes necessary for self-defense—that is, when retaliatory violence is used for the purpose of personal or societal survival with the goal of disabling the attacker. *Defensive war* might also be justified when the primary motivation is the prevention of a second attack. Absolute pacifists often claim that violent means—limited to deterring the aggressor—are only rational or morally justifiable under such circumstances.[46]

Preemptive warfare—opening an armed conflict by striking first in anticipation of an attack or to eliminate an overwhelming threat—is never justified in the pacifist philosophy. They believe that most disputes can be resolved through a combination of positive bargaining and diplomatic good will rather than through coercive threats and armed conflict.

Disaster has sometimes followed a stubborn and unconditional adherence to such an ideology, especially if based on a miscalculation or misappraisal of the purposes and determination of a potential opponent. The preamble for many major conflicts has included a promising series of peace conferences, diplomatic advances, and interim agreements such as with Napoleonic France in 1803 (Peace of Amiens), Hitler's Germany in 1938 (the Munich Dictate), or the Palestinian-Israeli agreement (Oslo Accords) of 1993. Similar negative outcomes, however, have ensued through a blind reliance on the use of coercive force where miscalculations of the enemy on the battlefield have provided an equal number of remarkable martial disasters. Take as examples the overconfidence of the British as they repeatedly assaulted the rebel trenches on Bunker (Breeds) Hill in 1775, the misplaced exuberance of the federal army as it took the field against the Confederacy at the first battle of Bull Run in 1861, or the debacle of the ten-year-long U.S. war in Vietnam.

The Function of Public Opinion

It is safe to say that no war in history has been fought with the unqualified backing of the entire population. Realistically, opposition by a minority of the population—if disorganized, uncommitted, or silent—poses no obstacle to a government intent on going to war, whereas that same minority—organized, decisive, and outspoken—poses an almost insurmountable impediment to the willingness of even a popular government to open an armed conflict that the minority does not want.

The mind-set of the individuals who make up the society-at-large often goes beyond a simple contemplation of the human costs and economic risks of war, or of the reasons and justifications for maintaining a war footing. This mind-set, while unique to the individual, produces a collective sense—a public opinion—that reflects the sum of the cognitive predispositions of the general population toward war or peace. As stated earlier, Americans like their wars quick, decisive, cheap, and relatively bloodless. While not statistically precise, the answers to several questions can better determine the public's opinion concerning a nation's war policy:

- Do they regard the actions of their government (or of a potential enemy) as generally benign or hostile?
- Do they favor a national strategy based on the threat of force or on continued diplomacy?

- Is a multilateral, multinational response (a coalition) more justified in their opinion than a unilateral one when responding to a threat or attack?

- Once at war, do they agree with the overall strategy or the tactics that are used by their own government or that of the enemy?

- Is their primary response to extended warfare (months or years of combat and rising death tolls) focused on ultimately attaining a decisive victory, or is it a simple desire to end the fighting as quickly as possible?

- Do they have a comprehensive appreciation of the extended nature of negotiations, the necessity of compromise, and the catalog of diplomatic devices employed in the peace-making process?

- Do they have the ability to make an educated assessment of the quality of the peace that will inevitably follow even the hardest fought of wars?

- Finally, do they trust or mistrust their national leaders?

The answers to these questions often determine the points of contention between the proponents of militarism and those that resist war-making. Unfortunately many war resisters avoid educating themselves with regard to the principles of war, and many militarists equally eschew a comprehensive study of peace-making and diplomacy.

Nonetheless, even when all the public relations factors are satisfied in favor of war, resorting to force and violence is not always inevitable. It is the crucial role of leaders and decision makers in government to sidestep avoidable wars or to control the level of bloodshed and destruction in those conflicts they cannot circumvent. Since World War II, however, antiwar Americans tend to express absolute distrust of the executive branch while ascribing to the enemy leadership an unquestioned integrity. Many U.S. presidents (Truman, Lyndon B. Johnson, Nixon, Reagan, George W. Bush) since that time have been portrayed as liars, deceivers, and distorters of constitutional liberties, while their opposite numbers (Mao Tse Tung, Ho Chi Minh, Fidel Castro, and Ernesto "Che" Guevara) have been endowed with almost saintly qualities of understanding, compassion, and near-utopian social insight.

This tendency to demonize the president of the United States was particularly obvious during the tenure of Richard M. Nixon. The personality of Nixon was perceived by a large portion of the public as "thoroughly unattractive." Elected by a mere plurality of the electorate in 1968, he took office in a country divided as it had not been for a century over social issues and the war in Vietnam. The diplomatic masterstrokes of his first term—the opening of China, détente with Russia, even his initial policy regarding a political solution in Vietnam—were washed away during his second term by his grating personality even though he had won reelection in a landslide. "Even his admirers conceded that Nixon had a mean streak . . . brooding over the stings and scars of a long embattled career, he compiled his lists of enemies with the obsessive precision of an accountant, moving with vindictive glee at every opportunity to avenge old wrongs."[47] The growing mistrust of the public stemmed from Nixon's own mistrustful side. He could never achieve the careless ease of a Kennedy or the sparkling personal aura of a Reagan. Nixon's tenure in the White House—ending in resignation over the Watergate break-in—seriously damaged both the power and the reputation of the executive. More recently, the judgments concerning the Nixon presidency have been somewhat revised, but the negative caricatures drawn of him by orthodox liberals and the antiwar establishment continue with an enduring force because of their basis in truth.

Culture of War

In the absence of truly eccentric leaders like a Napoleon or a Hitler, who turned to warfare as an alternative to diplomacy, nations themselves may have an inherent corporate inclination toward war. Such nations may exhibit a *culture of war*—a belief system, shared communal environment, or economic infrastructure that makes the use of military force relatively easy. It is not uncommon, for instance, to describe certain nations as having a war culture, especially when their government is based on a warrior tradition, such as the *Bushido* (way of the warrior) of Japan's ruling Samurai class in the 1930s or the warrior traditions of many tribal societies.

Yet such a war culture is thought to be an aberration in a democratically elected government. These attitudes are often rooted in a warped form of cross-cultural snobbery, which suggests that certain nations have wisely abandoned and evolved beyond their own cultural roots, while other "less developed" countries have stagnated among their archaic traditions or have failed to see the light of a more refined diplomacy. Of course, many of these assessments are made against a historic background (which lends no reliability to them) such as the anecdotal judgments that France was more warlike in the 17th century, Germany more aggressive in the 20th century, or the United States more belligerent in the 21st century than at other times. Several U.S. presidents have been tagged as having a "cowboy gun-slinger" attitude, including Teddy Roosevelt, Ronald Reagan, and George W. Bush.

The culture of war can affect the wider global community, featuring "patterns of attitudes and behavior conditioned by the anarchic structure of the world polity."[48] These global characteristics persist not only within nations, but also among them—often reinforced by a superstructure of diplomatic agreements, interconnecting alliances, and time-honored treaties—with each nation playing its role in international relations as if in a scripted Shakespearean tragedy that ends in war. Herein, the pacifist argument for increased diplomacy, conferences, and talks finds its principal flaw—not in its conception, which is laudable, but rather in its reliance on the sincerity of diplomats, the reliability of governments, and the integrity of national leaders.

War as Peacekeeping

The U.N. Charter gives the U.N. Security Council the power and responsibility to take collective action to maintain international peace and security. Armed peacekeepers are charged with monitoring and observing peace processes in postconflict areas and with helping ex-combatants implement the peace agreements they may have signed. Such assistance comes in many forms, including confidence-building measures, power-sharing arrangements, electoral support, strengthening the rule of law, economic and social development, and humanitarian endeavors. Coalitions of willing member countries deploy troops under U.N. command to undertake peace-keeping or peace-enforcement tasks. Accordingly U.N. peacekeepers (often referred to as Blue Berries because of their light blue berets or helmets) can include soldiers, civilian police officers, and other civilian personnel from many nations.

Peacekeeping and humanitarian operations can be difficult or even counterproductive. The first peacekeeping mission of the U.N. era was launched in 1948. This mission, the United Nations Truce Supervision Organization (UNTSO), was sent to the newly created State of Israel, where a conflict between the Israelis and the Arab states over the creation of Israel had just reached a ceasefire. The mission failed, but the UNTSO remains in operation to this day, although the Israeli-Palestinian Conflict has certainly not abated. UNTSO troops have proven ineffective in suppressing conflict between the Israelis and Palestinian irregulars such as Hamas and Hezbollah.

When North Korea invaded South Korea in 1950, the United States responded by leading a U.N. force aimed at reestablishing the former boundaries of the two nations, but ultimately it attempted the retaking all of the Korean Peninsula to reunite the country. The U.N. forces initially pushed the North Koreans out of the south, and made it to the Chinese border at the Yalu River before the Chinese Army intervened and pushed the U.N. forces back to the 38th parallel. U.N. peacekeeping forces (mainly U.S. troops) remain deployed along the DMZ (demilitarized zone) to this day.

Since 1991, the involvement of the United Nations in such operations has become larger and more complex. U.N. peacekeeping missions, often launched to help implement comprehensive peace agreements between protagonists in intrastate conflicts and civil wars, have come to involve more nonmilitary elements to ensure the proper functioning of civic functions, such as elections. The U.N. Department of Peacekeeping Operations was created in 1992 to support this increased demand for such missions.

One of the last official actions of President George H. W. Bush, for instance, was to send 1,800 U.S. Marines to Somalia in a humanitarian operation called Operation Restore Hope in December 1992. The U.N. troops landed in Mogadishu (the capital) with the purpose of ensuring that emergency food supplies delivered to the nation reached the Somali people rather than remaining in the hands of the local warlords. The intervention followed years of famine and civil strife. The Marine landing was unopposed, and unlike any other military operation in U.S. history, it was a media event. The landing craft were met by the press, with television cameras and blaring lights, and by many Somalis who eagerly sought to touch the Marines and to offer their thanks.

Historian Peter B. Levy has noted of the operation in Somalia that the warm reception and the ease of entry presented the greatest threat to the endeavor—*mission creep*:

> Many Somalis hoped that the troops might do more than simply open a corridor
> through which the United Nations (U.N.) and other groups could provide medical

supplies and food to the famine-stricken populace. In addition, they wanted US forces (and their allies) to stabilize the nation, restore peace, and even initiate a new Marshall Plan, which had helped rebuild Europe after World War II. . . . [But] the cease-fire did not force the warlords to surrender their weapons. . . . As long as Bush was in office [he had lost reelection in November to Bill Clinton], support for the operation in Somalia and the United States remained strong. . . . In the long run, however, support was tempered by sporadic gunfights between American (or French) troops and Somali gunmen. . . . By the time American troops left and relinquished control to [other] U.N. troops in 1993, support for the effort had virtually eroded in the United States.[49]

To make matters worse, gunmen under the control of Somali warlord Mohammed Farrah Aidid had ambushed the U.S. Marines in the infamous Blackhawk Down incident, in which eighteen Americans were killed and some of the bodies mutilated and dragged through the streets. Although the assault and withdrawal occurred under Clinton, the operation did not add to Bush's formerly considerable reputation as a strong world leader, nor did it stand as a shining example of the new world order espoused by Clinton. It was clear that mission creep had frustrated the U.S. attempt to establish a permanent peace and a new more democratic government in Somalia, and decreased respect for U.S. military force may have promoted the rise of world terrorism and engender the attacks of September 11.

The Wages of War

The principal promoters of warfare as a tool of government are commonly thought to be imperialists, capitalists, or advocates of national self-sufficiency. Ethnic hostilities, opposing political systems, and long-held religious antagonisms, however, often lead to warfare regardless of any material differences, territorial ambiguities, or desires to gain control over the geographic, economic, or technical assets of neighbors. Certainly, tangible things like access to fresh water, fertile land, fishing grounds, or raw materials such as timber, coal, oil, or metallic ores have led to intense political confrontations as nations attempt to gather scarce resources under their control or to deny them to their adversaries, but ideological differences between and among peoples can also whet an appetite for conflict. Take, for instance, the dispute over the holy city of Jerusalem that has festered for a thousand years.

Ideas can sometimes better galvanize popular support for warfare than material things. War has often served as a decisive determiner of otherwise vexing and seemingly insoluble disputes involving religion, independence, liberty, or morality. Unfortunately, improved arms technologies, entangled alliances, and third-party interventions have largely removed the decisive aspect of warfare. This indecisiveness has left modern disputes unresolved as opponents continue to expend the lives of their soldiers and the gold in their coffers over many years of pointless fighting.

Warfare in medieval Europe was more decisive than in more recent times. Medieval war was like an interpersonal duel fought between feudal princes and their retainers. Armies were largely composed of professional soldiers or mercenaries rather than conscripts or draftees. Castles were taken, battlefield prisoners redeemed, and the land laid waste by foragers, but the majority of the population was ignored unless they were in the direct path of enemy operations. Certain weapons were deemed to be unfair. The crossbow, for instance, was so effective against armored noblemen that the pope declared its use illegal in warfare against other Christians. It could be used with a clear conscience, however, against heretics, heathens, and other non-Christians such as the Muslim armies in Spain and Jerusalem or the Christian Albigencian heretics in Languedoc, France.

In the 16th century, Catholic-on-Protestant fighting fractured Europe in a series of religiously inspired wars that were so distressing as to eliminate any hope of maintaining the rules of martial conduct. Whole populations of coreligionists aligned to fight against one another, and the population of much of Europe was intimately involved in the combat either as active participants, or collaterally, as potential enemy resources to be put to the sword. This included the massacre of men, women, and children by both sides. During the worst of these outbreaks, the Thirty Years' War (1618–1648), nearly one-half of the residents of central Europe (generally present-day Germany and Austria) were killed and everywhere the countryside was devastated and stripped of its resources with no clear winner emerging from either side. Ironically, a generation of almost unlimited and indecisive warfare produced the realization among the states of Europe that some limit must be placed on their warlike propensities.

Blueprint for Peace

The Peace of Westphalia (1648) that ended the Thirty Years' War was a watershed event in the history of warfare. It was the first blueprint for a lasting peace in Europe. The Peace of Westphalia resulted from what is considered the first modern diplomatic congress, and it initiated a new order in central Europe based on the concept of national sovereignty rather than on feudal or monarchial rights. The agreement—actually a series of treaties taken voluntarily by the warring parties—ended the worst of the fighting by declaring those regions to be Protestant that were held by Protestant princes and those to be Catholic that were held by Catholics. An enduring legacy of the treaty was the division of the numerous German states into fairly distinct regions of religious practice. Roman Catholicism remained the preeminent faith in the south and west (surrounding Austria), while Protestantism became firmly established in the northeastern and central regions (Prussia). Nonetheless, pockets of Catholicism existed in Oldenburg in the north and in areas of Hesse, and Protestant congregations could be found in north Baden and northeastern Bavaria. The Habsburg rulers of Austria were the leading political representatives of Roman Catholicism in the conflict, and Austria has remained a predominantly Roman Catholic country.

The Peace of Westphalia also established two principles of international law that continue to be pertinent in the 21st century. The government of a state was recognized as the *unequivocal sovereign* of the territory and people within that state, and other countries were not to interfere with the *internal domestic affairs* of other states. These principles relieved the need for open warfare regarding religious predominance, but they had the unintended consequence of opening the population of any particular region to internal religious persecution and domestic governmental intolerance. Christians (but not Jews, Muslims, Gypsies, or groups considered cults) living in principalities where their denomination was not that of the established church were guaranteed the right to practice their faith in public during allotted hours or in private at their will. The Dutch extended this form of limited religious tolerance to their American colony of New Amsterdam (New York).

Those Czech-speaking Pietists following the teachings of Jan Huss (John Huss) known as the Brethren, for example, were abandoned and betrayed by the local nobility of Moravia and Bohemia, who previously had tolerated or supported them. The Brethren were forced to operate underground and eventually dispersed across Northern Europe as far as Holland and Belgium, where they attempted a resurgence. A small group of Bohemian Brethren (no more than a dozen family groups) lived as an underground remnant in Moravia for nearly 100 years on the estate of Count Nikolaus von Zinzendorf, a nobleman who had been brought up in the traditions of Pietism, before removing to America in the 18th century where they represented a formidable antiwar minority.

The unification of Germany in 1871 under Prussian leadership led to the strengthening of Protestantism. The Jesuit order of the Catholic Church was prohibited in Germany, and its members were expelled from the country. Although active persecution was rare, Catholics distrusted their government and its officials. Before World War II, about two-thirds of the German population was Protestant and the remainder Roman Catholic. Bavaria was a Roman Catholic stronghold. Although raised a Roman Catholic, Adolf Hitler respected only the power and organization of the Roman Catholic Church, not its religious tenets. In 1933, shortly after coming to power, the Nazis scored their first diplomatic success by concluding a concordat with the Vatican, regulating church-state relations and allowing free practice of religion as long as the Catholic clergy refrained from political activity.

With respect to a wider significance of the religious wars of the 17th century, the terms agreed upon in the Peace of Westphalia were instrumental in laying the foundations for the development of the *sovereign nation-state*. Aside from establishing fixed territorial boundaries for many of the modern countries of Europe, the treaty changed the fundamental relationship of subjects to their rulers making the citizenry of a respective nation subject first and foremost to the laws of their respective governments rather than to those of any other religious or other secular power. The monarchs and autocrats of the 17th century generally respected these principles, but the rise of the nation-state in the 19th century was seemingly incompatible with the "culture of moderate statecraft and rule-contained warfare" that the signers of the Peace of Westphalia had envisioned. The origins of the principle of religious toleration and the development of the rights of states, prominent in the constitutional law of the United States, can be found among the provisions in the Peace of Westphalia.[50]

The Concept of a Just War

It was the Roman Catholic Church that first defined certain types of warfare as being morally acceptable. The so-called *just war,* one in which the criteria for opening an armed conflict are deemed to be founded on ethical principle (*jus ad bellum*), is often the conflict most difficult to avoid. Even if the majority of the public considers warfare morally wrong, the concept of a just war often makes conflict permissible, and nations and leaders will go to great lengths to cloak their own behaviors in the *just cause* mantle of self-defense, opposition to aggression, or the defeat of evil. Thus, Jefferson Davis, seeking justification, put the Confederacy on a war footing in 1861 to withstand the threat of northern aggression, while Lincoln invaded the South to defend the sovereignty of the Union. During the Vietnam War, Hanoi justified its operations and support of the Viet Cong in South Vietnam as a defense of the entire country against foreign imperialism, while the United States considered its actions part of a mutual self-defense agreement with the government in Saigon. In similar fashion, when Ronald Reagan declared the Soviet Union the "Evil Empire," his was no unscripted comment but a deliberate attempt at justification for the steps he planned to take to win the Cold War.

In 1974, a special committee of the United Nations established a series of standards that defined aggression so that "just" nations might apply them to the lawful use of force. These were adopted by the General Assembly. They included invasion, bombardment, blockade, attack on a military contingent or installation, and the sending of armed bands, groups, irregulars, or mercenaries to carry out aggressive acts against another state. Attacks on ships at sea and aircraft were later added to the list. Even so, the list of *just provocations* to war was not exhaustive, but in defining aggression, the United Nations may have made the opening of armed conflict easier for national leaders by making self-righteous military actions so readily definable. Under this definition, missile attacks by Saddam Hussein on U.S. aircraft patrolling in U.N.-designated "no fly" zones in 2001 and 2002 seemingly would have been enough to warrant an attack on Iraq. Of course, national leaders have found that the weight of any response to aggression needs to be commensurate with the level of provocation, or the world community will criticize it nonetheless.

Add to these standard provocations other just war realities such as support for popular efforts toward independence or national liberation; counterintervention to relieve the effects of an unwarranted intervention by another foreign power; and cases of enslavement, massacre, or genocide (the *cause de jour* of recent decades). Ironically, the definitions of aggression adopted by the United Nations were so diverse that, given the historical readiness of states to open armed conflicts with each other, war could not be construed as justified only under few circumstances.

The Nation-State

The old state system that typified Western Europe in the 16th and 17th centuries rested on the idea of concentrating power in a single sovereign head (king, queen, prince, elector, and so on), who would manage the basic functions of the state, fight wars, and form alliances with other monarchs that often reflected only temporary coalitions of personal self-interest. The first powerful nation-states were monarchies, advocates of the divine right of kings dedicated to centralized authority and absolute power—for example, Philip II of Spain, Elizabeth I of England, Louis XIV of France, Catherine (II) the Great of Russia, and Frederick the Great of Prussia. After a series of revolutions in the 18th and 19th centuries, rooted in the political philosophies of Hobbes, Spinoza, Locke, Rousseau, and others, absolute monarchs like these were generally stripped of their exclusive powers, and new nation-states were formed, presumably based on the popular consent of the people to be governed. Even those that remained kingdoms featured limited constitutional monarchies and parliamentary governance.

One of the earliest nation-states—so early (late 16th century) as to be considered unique—was the Dutch Republic (the Netherlands, or United Provinces) composed of seven Protestant provinces governed by the *städtholders* of the States General (seated in The Hague). The Dutch declared their independence from Catholic Spain under the Union of Utrecht in 1579. In theory, the *städtholders* were freely appointed by and subordinate to the legislators of each province. In practice, however, the Princes of Orange-Nassau were always chosen as *städtholders* for most of the provinces, and Zeeland, Utrecht, and Holland all had the same *städtholder*. This gave Holland great influence among the provinces. Under the domination of Holland during its decades-long struggle with Spain, the republican form of governance passed into practical disuse by 1672 to be replaced by the virtual monarchial rule of William of Orange. In 1688, William and his wife Mary (Stuart) became king and queen of Britain. Thereafter, the states-general were under the effective politico-economic control of the Dutch East India Company and Dutch West India Company. As can be seen, the chronological history of this first nation-state is generally confused and roundabout. Nonetheless, the United Provinces was officially recognized in the Peace of Westphalia in 1648 as a republic, and it lasted until French revolutionary forces invaded in 1795. Thereafter, it was briefly called the Batavian Republic, which in turn would be replaced by the French-controlled Kingdom of Holland under the control of the Napoleon, emperor of the French. The Dutch Republic (now known as The Netherlands) regained its independent republican sovereignty at the end of the Napoleonic wars in 1815.

The Dutch Republic was neither a true nation-state nor an absolute autocracy like its traditional opponent, Spain. In fact, the early nation-states wielded the same centralized powers as kings, queens, and emperors, but these were now vested in representative assemblies, executive officers, and administrative councils. In a few cases, as with the United States, these powers were fixed in a constitution, and republican forms of federalism were established that combined national supremacy—at least for purposes of foreign relations and national defense—with the real power over citizens reserved to the constituent states.

Nation-states often are regarded as particularly susceptible to fomenting and engaging in international war. A long line of prominent intellectuals have either implicitly suggested such an association or made the outright claim that nation-states are "continually preparing for, actively engaged in, or recovering from organized violence in the form of war."[51] These thinkers include Niccolo Machiavelli, Thomas Hobbes, Emeric Crucé, William Penn, John Bellers, Bertrand Russell, Albert Einstein, and many others. According to these intellectuals, the nation-state system is essentially a war-based system, which for the continuation of peace needs to be placed under the control of a nonpartisan world body such as a world court or replaced by a wider republican form such as a super-state or global government.

Civil Strife

Not only wars between governments, but also internal civil and revolutionary conflicts, may collectively engage the general population in warfare whether or not they agree with their raison d'être. Internal conflicts often set the common interests of diverse groups from the same population against one another. Collective action and mutual agreement in these cases is often impossible, and coordination, communication, and solidarity of sentiment often form along strongly exclusive lines. This is especially true when the extremes make war on one another and leave those in the uncommitted middle to fall victim to both sides, as in the American Civil War.

Civil wars are particularly gruesome because the contending parties often hold highly principled positions regarding religion, culture, or morality that exhibit themselves as hatred and loathing of the opposition among individuals. Revolutions sometimes engender violent repression by the government, or equally violent intimidation by antigovernment forces. It is not unusual under these circumstances for large unconvinced segments of the population to form who simply refuse to participate in the violence or to perform the roles assigned to them by the opposing parties. This may have been the case during the American Revolution when a large portion of the population fell victim to the contending rebel and Loyalist extremes. It was among the uncommitted middle that opposition to the war was the strongest.

Among the first authors to produce a profound theoretical work concerning a government in crisis was Thomas Hobbes, the famous philosopher of state absolutism. This work was the *Leviathan*, which appeared in 1651 at the end of the English Civil War (1641–1649), which supplanted the Stuart dynasty in Britain with a republican theocracy. Hobbes was clearly in sympathy with the Royalist point of view, and it is not surprising that the first important work to deal with the essence and legitimacy of monarchial government should be hostile to the idea of revolution. The Roundhead partisans—largely Puritan followers of Oliver Cromwell—were far too busy meditating on practical measures (like executing their king and forming a practical republican government) to have any spare time to pen theories concerning society and the foundations of the state. Those who seized the pen did so to justify the republican cause or criticize that of the Royalists, as the case might be. Hobbes's writings exercised great influence on the sociological literature of the next (18th) century and influenced many socialists in the 19th century. Oddly nothing was further from the author's intentions than a socialistic application of his arguments.[52]

As a precursor of the American Revolution 125 years later, the English Civil War was an important part of U.S. history. Although Puritan religious principles seemingly dominated the war, the issues in dispute were largely focused on the relationship between the executive branch of British government in the person of the king (Charles I Stuart) and the legislative branch represented by the Parliament. Chief among these was the issue of military finances in the form of "ship money," considered one of the king's prerogatives. The king received an income from ports on the English Channel coast known as the Cinque Ports (Hastings, Romney, Hythe, Sandwich, and Dover). This income was free from parliamentary control and was supposed to be used by the king to provide ships and sailors for the Royal Navy. The first Stuart king, James I (James VI of Scotland) minimized the need for a navy and thought it expensive to maintain. Charles I, James's brother and successor, as the Duke of York had been lord high admiral of the fleet, and he demanded the income from these ports and came into conflict with the Parliament more than once over his utilization of this "ship money." It is difficult to say how much influence such disputes had in costing Charles his throne (and ultimately his head), but they left the executive and legislative branches of British government overwhelming contemptuous of each other. This cynicism was transferred, by way of a common history and a shared set of political mechanisms, to the relationship between the colonial legislature and governors of the colonies and ultimately to the Congress and president of the United States.

Since the end of the 18th century, the examples of the American and French revolutions have inspired many aggrieved ethnic communities to undertake war as a legitimate tool for political autonomy and national self-determination. Europe experienced such a spat of nationalistic wars in the mid-19th century, and the mid-20th century saw the number of recognized nation-states on the globe triple from 50 to 150 as former colonial possessions fought for independence under concepts generated by the American Declaration of Independence, the French Declaration of the Rights of Man, and a hybrid collection of ideas based on Marx, Lenin, Ho Chi Minh, and Mao Se Tung. This sudden transformation left the world first with a Cold War between Capitalism and Communism and then with a virtual epidemic of ethnic violence in Africa, eastern Europe, and East Asia as the unintended consequences of the end of the eyeball-to-eyeball confrontation between the United States and the USSR.[53]

Wars of Self-Determination

Self-determination conflicts, like the warfare among Serbs, Croats, and other ethnic minorities in the former Yugoslavia, evidence a high potential for violence. This is especially true when ethno-cultural or religious disputes are mixed into the political questions as with the Christian-Muslim dichotomy in Bosnia. Similar conflicts between the Palestinians and the government of Israel, the Christian Armenians and Muslim Azerbaijan, the Kurds and Turkey, or Catholics and Protestants in Northern Ireland—some of which seem resolved and others seemingly chronic and insoluble—are often regarded as conflicts between ways of life wherein the community mobilizes behind a campaign of extreme violence in the conviction that their entire culture is at stake.[54]

Historically, national governments claim the right to possess military forces more powerful than the combined abilities of their constituents. Herein the well-being of the state is at stake. The manner in which this power is utilized often affects the stability of the state and the determination of just who will hold high office. No government freely admits that it maintains power by controlling the means of mass coercion and utilizing force on its people to suppress illegal activity, subversion, or domestic violence. It is not unusual for a regime to become established through a violent revolution against an older order that seems to favor one particular class or ethnic group. Weak states bordering on anarchy are often the victims of recurring violence and internecine warfare. By way of contrast, strong states tolerate a good deal of legal and nonviolent protest. "The more undemocratic a political system is, the more prone it is to engender . . . violent inclinations in aggrieved groups." Nonetheless, "even groups constituting numerical majorities in democratic systems sometimes conclude that the normal political system works against them when the more affluent minorities appear to be able to control government policy."[55] An eruption of violence in these cases is sometimes cathartic. The ensuing warfare need not have a rational objective, nor must it produce a winner. The violence itself sometimes serves to release the pent-up emotional needs of the populace with the government and its officers serving as convenient targets.

Terrorism involves a series of violent acts or threats of violence directed against individuals who are not in direct opposition to those acting violently. It is often the hope of terrorists to bring their grievances to the attention of the public by fighting an asymmetrical war, which they could not hope to win through conventional means. Insurgent and revolutionary groups become terrorists when they attack or threaten to attack unarmed government officials, supporters of the government, or civilian targets. Terrorists often use violence to disrupt civic life: commerce, culture, religion, or communications. "Some degree of terrorism in one form of another has always been an element of acts of political violence."[56] Increased terrorism in recent years has focused on highly exposed transportation systems, hijackings, airport and subway bombings, suicide bombings in the streets, and flying aircraft into buildings. It is altogether possible that as the effect of global government takes hold and decreases the likelihood of international warfare, terrorism (covertly supported by nation-states) will increase.

Notes

1. Edward S. Creasy, *The Fifteen Decisive Battles of the World* (New York: Heritage Press, 1969), 3.

2. Daniel J. Boorstin, *The Americans: The Colonial Experience* (New York: Vantage Books, 1958), 353.

3. Dorothy Denneen Volo and James M. Volo, *Daily Life on the Old Colonial Frontier* (Westport, CT: Greenwood Press, 2002), 189–190.

4. Stephen Bull and Gordon L. Rottman, *Infantry Tactics of the Second World War* (Westminster, MD: Osprey Publishing, 2008), 215.

5. Thomas E. Griess, ed., *Definitions and Doctrine of the Military Art: The West Point Military History Series* (Wayne, NJ: Avery Publishing Group, 1985), 2.

6. Griess, 193–194.

7. David Levering Lewis, *God's Crucible: Islam and the Making of Europe, 570–1215* (New York: W. W. Norton, 2008) 24–25.

8. Rodney Stark, *God's Battalion: The Case for the Crusades* (New York: Harper Collins, 2009) 238–239.

9. Stark, 247.

10. Stark, 245–246.

11. Jonathan Dull, *The French Navy and American Independence: A Study of Arms and Diplomacy, 1774–1787* (Princeton, NJ: Princeton University Press, 1975), 33.

12. Richard A. Gabriel, *The Military History of Ancient Israel* (Westport, CT: Praeger, 2003), 139.

13. Gabriel, 60.

14. Gabriel, 86.

15. Gabriel, 125.

16. James E. Lindsay, *Daily Life in the Medieval Islamic World* (Indianapolis: Hackett Publishing Company, 2008) 11.

17. Milton Meltzer, *Slavery I: From the Rise of Western Civilization to the Renaissance* (Chicago: Cowles Book Company, 1971), 61–62.

18. Steven J. Zaloga, *Panther vs. Sherman: Battle of the Bulge, 1944* (New York: Osprey Publishing, 2008), 4–5.

19. Gabriel, 2.

20. Gabriel, 116.

21. Gabriel, 2.

22. Gabriel, 29–30.

23. Gabriel, 83.

24. Gabriel, 178.

25. For a wider discussion of this period see James M. Volo, *Blue Water Patriots: The American Revolution Afloat* (Westport, CT: Greenwood Press, 2007).

26. Gabriel, 177.

27. Gabriel, 17.

28. John Adams letter to Abigail Adams, 26 April 1777. *Letters of John Adams, Addressed to His Wife. Edited by His Grandson, Charles Francis Adams, Volume I, 1841.* Accessed November, 2009. URL: http://www.familytales.org/dbDisplay.php?id=ltr_jod2912.

29. William J. Rust, *Kennedy in Vietnam: American Vietnam Policy, 1960–1963* (New York: Da Capo Press, 1985), 43.

30. John G. Stoessinger, *Why Nations Go to War* (New York: St. Martin's Press, 1993), 227.

31. Alexander George, *Forceful Persuasion: Coercive Diplomacy as an Alternative to War* (Washington, DC: United States Institute of Peace Press, 1991), 4.

32. Helmut Sonnefelt, "The Meaning of Détente," *Naval War College Review* (July-August 1975), 3–8: 3.

33. Wayne Wei-Siang Hsieh, *West Pointers and the Civil War: The Old Army in War and Peace* (Chapel Hill: University of North Carolina Press, 2009), 22.

34. Hsieh, 23.

35. Henry Seidel Canby, *Prefaces to Peace: A Symposium* (New York: Columbia University Press, 1943), 124.

36. He worked successfully from the regime of Louis XVI, through the French Republic and then under Napoleon I, Kings Louis XVIII, Charles X, and Louis-Philippe.

37. Rust, 33.

38. Rust, 51.

39. Karl Grossman, *Nicaragua: America's New Vietnam?* (New York: The Permanent Press, 1984), 113.

40. Grossman, 113.

41. Grossman, 126–127.

42. "Reagan's mixed White House legacy," *BBC News* (June, 2004), http://news.bbc.co.uk/2/hi/americas/213195.stm (accessed May 2009).

43. Harald Müller, "Multinational Security Cooperation and Military Doctrines in the OSCE Area," *Disarmament Diplomacy* 60 (September 2001), http://www.acronym.org.uk/dd/dd60/60op2.htm (accessed July 2008).

44. Paul H. Nitze, "Assuring Strategic Stability in an Era of Détente," in *Arms Control and Security: Current Issues,* ed. Wolfram H. Hanrieder (Boulder, CO: Westview Press, 1979), 42–43.

45. Seyom Brown, *The Causes and Prevention of War* (New York; St. Martin's Press, 1994), 48–49.

46. Brown, 17.

47. Charles R. Morris, *A Time of Passion: America, 1960–1980* (New York: Harper & Row, 1984), 131–132.

48. Morris, 100.

49. Peter B. Levy, *Encyclopedia of the Reagan-Bush Years* (Westport, CT: Greenwood Press, 1996), 332–333.

50. Brown, 107.

51. Brown, 66.

52. Eduard Bernstein, "John Bellers, Champion of the Poor and Advocate of a League of Nations," in *Cromwell and Communism: Socialism and Democracy in the Great English Revolution* (London: George Allen & Unwin, 1895), http://www.marxists.org/reference/archive/bernstein/works/1895/cromwell/17-bellers.htm#top (accessed July 2008).

53. Brown, 36.

54. Brown, 39.

55. Brown, 41.

56. Brown, 43.

Chapter 3

Peace Societies

When Elijah was fleeing the wrath of war, the Lord commanded him to stand upon a mountain. And as he stood there a mighty whirlwind swept by him, and thereafter came an earthquake, and then an all-consuming fire. And all the land was rent asunder. But God was not in the wind, nor in the earthquake, nor in the fire. Nor is God in the ironclads that sweep the oceans with their guns, nor in the armies that shake the earth with their tread, nor in the fire of musketry; but in the still small voice of world justice.

—S. F. Sanger

Nations can blunder into war. They cannot blunder into peace.

—Herbert Hoover and Hugh Gibson

The Year of Global Peace: 1815

Signed in 1802 and taking effect in 1803, the Peace of Amiens marked the end of the French Revolutionary War. For the British and their allies, it brought only a brief respite from conflict. With the final defeat of Napoleon at Waterloo in June 1815, Europe began a century of relative peace after almost a century and a quarter of almost constant warfare. This peace was greeted with a giant celebration featuring balls, concerts, and masquerades attended by the victors and called the Congress of Vienna. The ostensible purpose of this meeting of European diplomats was to settle the issues remaining after the most recent outbreak of fighting and to redraw the continent's political map after the final defeat of Napoleon.

Beginning at the end of the 17th century (1688), Europe had been plagued by a number of all-encompassing conflicts involving most of the major powers and petty kingdoms of Europe: three wars of succession (English, Spanish, and Austrian), the Seven Years' War, the Wars against the French Republic, and finally the Napoleonic Wars. Interposed among these was the War of American Independence that ultimately had involved Britain, France, Spain, and Holland. Each of these 18th-century wars had been "world wars" in their own way with battles being fought in Europe, the Americas, the West Indies, the East Indies, Egypt, and India. Not until 1914 would the globe again erupt in such widespread warfare.

Notwithstanding the celebration and glorification of arms that took place among the luminaries in attendance, the Congress of Vienna was fundamentally a peace conference charged with correcting the political and economic ills that had kept the world at war for more than a generation. However, wartime unity quickly dissolved into a peacetime pursuit of national self-interest and political power. The work went slowly during the ten-month span of the meeting. The leaders who gathered at Vienna—Lord Castlereagh of Great Britain, Count von Hardenberg of Prussia, Prince Klemens von Metternich of Austria, Tsar Alexander I of Russia, and Prince Charles Maurice de Talleyrand[1] of France—met to decide the future of Europe. Yet the vision they fashioned for Europe frequently has been criticized as too reactionary—ignoring the democratic and liberal impulses spreading across Europe at the time and imposing a stifling political conservatism on the continent. The peace settlement in 1815 failed to digest the political and social transformations that had taken place in the previous quarter-century or anticipate the new demands created by the changes Napoleon had wrought in politics, economics, diplomacy, and the military. The liberties and civil rights associated with the American and French Revolutions were deemphasized (if not ignored) at Vienna, and a return to royal hierarchy, imperial stability, and class-based social order were emphasized instead. The major powers generally isolated the lesser European states during their deliberations, meeting in small conclaves where the voice of individual minor states could be drowned out by the great powers rather than in a general assembly where the foundations of a supposed *perpetual peace* might be more fully debated.

The desire to construct an effective balance of power among the victors remained the center of attention at Vienna. In November 1815, Austria, Britain, Prussia, and Russia signed the Quadruple Alliance—to become the Quintuple Alliance when a reconstituted France joined in 1818. Under this agreement, the powers pursued their goals through what came to be known as the Congress System, or the Concert of Europe, a continent-wide network devoted to maintaining order, peace, and stability through a *balance of power*. This is often considered the first truly functional experiment in collective security and global peacekeeping, and it worked fairly well until it became stale and outdated.

While the product of the Congress of Vienna avoided any major continental war for almost a century, this was not a period of universal peace. Instead, conflicts in the 19th century were a constant series of small wars such as the nationalistic and liberal revolts in the "German" states, Greece, Spain, Italy, and Latin America in 1820 and 1821; the "wars of national liberation" in 1848; the wars of national unification, such as in Italy (1859–1861) and Germany (1863–1871); and the small colonial and imperial conflicts around the globe such as the Opium War (1842), the Sepoy Mutiny in India (1857), the Franco-Vietnamese War (1861–1862), the Zulu Wars (1879), the Franco-Siamese War (1893), the Boxer Rebellion (1899–1901), or the two Boer Wars (1880–1881, 1899–1902), to mention but a few.

Occasionally, two or three major powers would face off. In 1854, for instance, several world powers focused on the Crimea, as the French and British allied against Turkey and Russia in what some historians consider the first modern war. Yet no long-lasting general conflagrations were evident. The world entered an era during which many nations turned their focus inward, and the United States, an ocean away, passed through a long period of internecine brawling over Indian removal, tariff nullification, states' rights, the extension of slavery, and abolition, which ultimately led to the American Civil War (1861–1865).

Common Purposes of Mind

The year 1815 also marks the formal emergence of the peace (antiwar or war resistance) movement. It is significant that the movement began in the United States because Americans (at least some of them) had maintained a long and often ignored tradition of seeking peace and resisting warfare. This had changed with the nation's hotly contested (at least in New England) and widely protested entry into the War of 1812 against Britain. A Swiss journalist and peace activist living in the United States, Élie Ducommun is commonly credited with the establishment of the world's first peace society in 1815 founded in New York as a means to promote peaceful relations between governments. Immediately thereafter, many small conclaves of like-minded peace advocates formed local peace societies across the United States, especially in New England and the northeast. Among these peace-seekers were persons sharing common understandings of the purposes of diplomacy as well as a common hope for a lasting peace. They resolved, each in their own way, to find instrumentalities and methods for cooperation among nations that might ensure that war need not happen again.

In the 1820s, another American citizen, William Ladd suggested to the Maine Peace Society that the many regional peace societies that had formed in the United States since 1815, become associated in a national organization to increase their effectiveness. As a result, the peace societies of Maine, New Hampshire, Massachusetts, New York, and Pennsylvania merged in May 1828 to form the American Peace Society (APS). By 1835, many other local peace societies also became affiliated with the national APS office in Hartford, Connecticut. The stated purpose of the APS was to "promote permanent international peace through justice; and to advance in every proper way the general use of conciliation, arbitration, judicial methods, and other peaceful means of avoiding and adjusting differences among nations, to the end that right shall rule might in a law-governed world."[2]

The pacifist philosophy of the APS, however, was never as radical or political as some of its members would have liked. Over the years, many of those who were disaffected by the seeming conservatism of the APS broke away to form new organizations led by more radical activists, such as William Lloyd Garrison's New England Non-Resistance Society in 1838, and the Universal Peace Union formed by Alfred H. Love, Lucretia Mott, and other social reformers in 1866. These organizations were less well focused on maintaining world peace, and attempted to affect a wider range of social goals, including education and prison reforms, economic relief for the poverty stricken, and the abolition of slavery.

Although many of its breakaway members considered the APS too willing to accept compromise, APS founder, William Ladd, who died in 1841, had been among the first to propose the radical ideas of forming a Congress of Nations and a World Court that would have jurisdiction over the countries of the world. This makes the idea of establishing some form of global governance for the purpose of maintaining peace an American one.

Although a politically focused antiwar movement failed to coalesce in America during most of the 19th century, the concept of a peace organization or peace society quickly spread to Europe. There followed a long list of important peace meetings focused largely in Europe. The British convened the first Congress of Peace in London in 1843, and Elihu Burritt, an American, founded the first International Peace Congress (IPC) in Brussels in 1848. Here, proposals were made for a league of nations and for the arbitration of international disputes by that body. The IPC urged the use of peace propaganda and advocated the control of the manufacture and sale of arms and munitions. The 1848 meeting of the IPC, commonly known as the Universal Peace Congress, was followed by a series of such meetings in Paris, 1849; Frankfurt, 1850; and London, 1851. Ironically, international peace activity was interrupted first by the Crimean War (1854) and then by the American Civil War (1861–1865) because the IPC members deemed it unseemly to actively propose peace while one's nation was at war.

In 1867, Charles Lemonnier convened the next significant peace congress in Geneva known as the International League of Peace and Liberty (ILPL). In 1872, U.S. congress member David Dudley Field prepared the *Draft Outlines of an International Code*, the submission of which to the ILPL resulted in the organization of the International Association for the Reform and Codification of the Laws of Nations, of which he became president in 1872. Field's proposals for a unified international code of law—an en masse revision, resolution, and codification of the laws of all nations—formed the basis for future discussion of this extremely contentious facet of international concern. After suspending its meetings during the Franco-Prussian War (1870–1871), the ILPL reconvened (1873) in Brussels.

Meanwhile, Frenchman Frédéric Passy had founded in 1867 the International Peace League (IPL) and in 1889 the French Peace Society (FPS). In 1889, Passy co-founded with Britain's William Randal Cremer the Inter-Parliamentary Union for Arbitration and Peace (IPUAP). A longtime supporter of the APS, Passy shared the first Nobel Peace laureate (1901) with Henry Dunant, a Swiss. It was Dunant who helped to inspire the creation of the International Committee of the Red Cross (ICRC) in 1863 and to promote the Geneva Peace Convention of 1864.

Dunant had witnessed in 1859 the Battle of Solferino, a small Italian town in Lombardy. On the evening of the battle, Dunant noted that thousands (it proved to be 38,000) of injured, dying, and dead soldiers remained largely unattended on the battlefield. There appeared to be little attempt to provide care for the wounded or to bury the dead. Military commanders often took drastic steps—the threats of punishment, flogging, or even execution—to discourage unwounded soldiers from leaving the battle line to help their fallen comrades, and few medical services were proved beyond assigning the drummers and flag carriers to duty as stretcher bearers and burial details. Shocked by the seeming lack of compassion, Dunant took the initiative of organizing the civilian population of the town, especially the women and girls, to provide assistance to the wounded. Because they lacked medical supplies, Dunant arranged for the purchase of the needed materials and helped to erect makeshift field hospitals. He convinced the population to help the injured without regard to their sympathies in the conflict.

Due to this experience, Dunant sought to promote the International Conference in Geneva in 1864 to develop possible measures to improve medical services on the battlefield. The so-called "international" meeting was actually attended by only thirty-six individuals: eighteen official delegates from national governments, six delegates from nongovernmental organizations, seven nonofficial foreign delegates, and the five members of the ICRC. Given the popular ignorance of the peace movement at the time, this was not unusual, but it helps emphasize the relatively small size of the peace movement during the 19th century. Nonetheless, the representatives at Geneva adopted a number of meaningful proposals:

- The foundation of national relief societies for wounded soldiers worldwide
- The legal cover of neutrality for medical personnel and physical protection for wounded soldiers
- The utilization of noncombatant volunteers for assistance of the wounded on the battlefield
- The introduction of a common distinctive protection symbol for medical personnel in the field, namely, a white arm band or flag bearing a red block cross
- The incorporation of these concepts in legally binding international treaties

In 1869, Clara Barton, formerly a nursing aid in America's Civil War, went to Europe for a restful vacation. There, she saw and became involved in the work of the ICRC during the Franco-Prussian War (1870–1871), and she determined to bring the organization home with her to America. Like many other peace proponents, she began her organizational work with only a handful of like-minded persons (fifteen in all) in the front parlor of the home of U.S. Sen. Omar Conger of Michigan in 1873. The inclusion of Conger gave the meeting and its proposal for the formation of an American Red Cross (ARC) some political weight. Few in government favored the proposal, however, because at the time they thought it unlikely that the country would ever again face as grim an experience as that of the American Civil War. Barton was not one to lose hope in the face of bureaucrats, and after ten years of badgering and pleading, she finally succeeded in 1881 in launching the ARC. A meaningful part of Barton's proposal to President Chester A. Arthur—possibly the single overriding item that led to its adoption—was the promise that the new ARC would be available to respond to other types of medical crises outside those associated with warfare, especially domestic crises produced by such natural disasters as epidemics, storms, and floods.

The APS, more than fifty years old and consistently moderate in its tactics, was instrumental in bringing about a number of further developments in relation to the wider peace movement in the second half of the 19th century, including the Pan American Congress of 1889–1890, arranged by Secretary of State James G. Blaine. The Pan American Union (PAU) founded in 1910 grew out of the latter organization. The PAU was an organization made up of eighteen North and South American republics joined for the purpose of promoting peace, cooperation, and good will in the Western Hemisphere. As the PAU grew it became the present Organization of American States (OAS). This organization, under U.S. leadership, adopted the American Declaration of the Rights and Duties of Man (1948) that some consider the world's first international human rights instrument, predating by more than six months the Universal Declaration of Human Rights (1948) adopted by the United Nations.

Religious Pacifism

From colonial times, there had been religious pacifists in America. Most were *absolute pacifists* belonging to the so-called peace denominations. They generally considered themselves *conscientious objectors* who refused to swear allegiance to any nation or serve in the military on the basis of their faith: "Do not swear at all" (Matthew 5:34), and "Do not resist one who is evil" (Matthew 5:39). The *peace churches* in America were Christian denominations explicitly advocating pacifism and denouncing warfare in any form as part of their doctrine. "It is . . . upon the democracy of the heart that the hope of arbitration and permanent peace must rest," wrote a Mennonite member of the General Missionary and Tract Committee in 1907. "The conscience is the most potent force of which man has personal knowledge, and . . . its gentle promptings are more imperative than statute laws."[3]

The term *historic peace churches* refers specifically to certain Anabaptist traditions: the Brethren, Mennonites, Amish, and Hutterites, as well as the members of the Religious Society of Friends called Quakers. The historic peace churches have, from their origins as far back as the 16th century, always taken the position that Jesus was himself a pacifist who explicitly taught and practiced pacifism, and that his followers must do likewise. Pacifist churches varied on whether physical force could ever be justified even in cases of self-defense or protecting others, but many adhered strictly to nonresistance when confronted by violence (turning the other cheek). However, all the peace denominations agreed in principle that violence on behalf of a country or a government was prohibited for their observant Christian followers. Although many other religious denominations eschewed warfare and violence as a general tenet, the peace denominations exhibited a sharpened sense of dedication to absolute pacifism and to their antiwar mission. They often viewed themselves as crusaders not only in terms of their political aspirations, but as unwavering dissenters and as people with a special mission to resist war in the name of God. "In these days," wrote Rev. W. H. McIntosh in preparation for the requiem of a fallen soldier, "some entertain the wicked delusion that he who dies for his country will [save his soul] by virtue of his patriotism."[4]

Most of the peace denominations had old European roots. The Brethren movement, for example, began as a melding of Pietist and Anabaptist ideas in the unconsolidated 16th-century German states of central Europe before the Peace of

Westphalia. These religious pacifists became commonly known in America as the German Baptist Brethren. The Brethren were more colloquially known as Dunkers (from a German term for their practice of whole-body immersion during baptism). The first Dunker church in America was established in 1723.

The Mennonites were a group of Christian Anabaptist denominations named after Menno Simons (1496–1561), though his teachings had a relatively minor influence on the religious tenets of the U.S. groups. As one of America's earliest historic peace churches, Mennonites were committed to general nonviolence, nonviolent war resistance, reconciliation, and absolute pacifism. The largest population of 21st-century Mennonites live in just a few conclaves in the United States—the best known of which is centered around the city of Lancaster, Pennsylvania; however, they also can be found in tight-knit communities in at least fifty-one countries on six continents. The sometimes picturesque Amish, or Amish Mennonites, were a constituency within Anabaptist Christianity that had broken from the so-called Old Order Amish of the Mennonite faith, but they resisted absorption into a wider Mennonite constituency. Many 21st-century Amish identify themselves as Conservative Mennonites.

Hutterites were a communal branch of Anabaptists who traced their roots to their founder Jakob Hutter who died in 1536. The beliefs of the Hutterites, including absolute pacifism, had developed during hundreds of years of wandering and persecution through many of the countries of Europe. Among these beliefs was a form of utopian communalism that separated them from other Anabaptists. Common ownership, especially for those living in a *community of goods* (a form of communitarianism), referred to joint or collective ownership by all individuals in the religious society, not a wider political Communism.

Begun in 17th-century England by George Fox and Margaret Fell, Quakerism, or the Religious Society of Friends, was the religion most closely identified with pacifism in America. Quakers had founded Pennsylvania, one of the original thirteen colonies, as a sanctuary against intolerance for the practitioners of their faith. American Quakers made extraordinary efforts to develop the agriculture and economy of the lower Delaware River valley and southeastern Pennsylvania during the colonial period. Considered a radical religion because of its pacifist sentiments and the religious authority it allowed for women within the meeting house discipline, in the 17th century, religious conservatives had driven Quakers from much of New England. The Massachusetts Assembly had gone so far to pass a law announcing the punishment of death on all Quakers returning to the colony after banishment. Besides a sizable presence in Pennsylvania, enclaves of Quakers also existed in Rhode Island, North Carolina, and western New Jersey.

Quakers resisted becoming involved in the wars of the colonial period—best characterized by their resistance in the Quaker-dominated Pennsylvania Assembly during the French and Indian War in America (1754–1763) and during the War of Independence (1775–1783). Often during these times of crisis, the Quakers and other religious pacifist groups were accused of caring too much for the Indians, of being indifferent to the sufferings of the frontier settlers or to the cause of independence, or even of being complicit in the deaths of whites through their neglect of basic military necessities. "[I]t is remarkable how many of the bitterest arguments between groups came to depend on tying enemies to Indians—a linkage by which even what had once been the bumbling, almost benign figure of the Pennsylvania Quaker could be remade as something ominous."[5] Although considered dissenters by the British Crown, Quakers were widely accused of serving as spies for the British during the revolution. Quakers again suffered the scrutiny of the wider public when they resisted service in the American Civil War (1861–1865).

After the American Revolution, the Quakers in particular concentrated on a wide variety of reform activities anathema to more conservative American thinkers: Native American (Indian) rights, antislavery, prison reform, temperance, freedmen's (Negro) rights, black education, and the women's movement. Yet in a conflict over theology, the Religious Society of Friends underwent a series of schisms beginning in the early decades of the 19th century that ended with the formation of three major subgroups of Quaker adherents separated by doctrine. These were, in descending order by membership, Orthodox (evangelical, called Wilburites after their leader John Wilbur), Hicksites (liberal followers of Elias Hicks), and Conservative (so-called Quietists, a mystical form of Quakerism seeking inner perfection that became popular in Europe). Since that time, however, the distinct divisions among the Quakers have attempted to heal their differences. Many groups have merged for their yearly meetings, and many Quaker subgroups have cooperated in organizations such as the Friends World Committee for Consultation and the Friends World Conferences. The founding of the religion in England; its development in America; its rapid growth of pastoral Quakerism in Africa, South America, and India; and its silent meetings (Quietists) in Europe made the Religious Society of Friends one of the largest of international antiwar organizations.

Arbitration and Collective Security

When two groups disagree over ethereal things that they feel are important, like the ideals surrounding pacifism and the need for national defense, they will almost always attempt to strengthen the status of their arguments by turning the other group into cultural villains and driving up negative feelings toward them. They also try to focus their idealism on more tangible aspects of the question so that the public might better visualize the concepts involved. Disarmament—or rather the huge visually moving stockpiles of weapons and munitions; the fleets of tanks, ships, and aircraft; and the other machines of destruction—was among these concepts.

The earliest American pacifists raised a significant and logical question concerning war that was difficult for the militarists and interventionists to answer. If peace commissions and conferences were necessary at the close of a conflict to determine the conditions of peace, why not submit the questions at issue to arbitration at once and thereby avoid the bloodshed?[6] This concept was to become a cornerstone of the arguments posed by many peace societies and antiwar activists, and it was thinking along these lines that was the genesis of the League of Nations, the World Court (called after 1946 the International Court of Justice), and the present United Nations.

The attempt to form an apparatus for the eradication of war through a system of collective security and limited armament rather than through state-to-state diplomacy and nation-by-nation arms races has a long and checkered history, which in modern times goes back to the work of political theorists like Emeric Crucé and John Bellers. The idea requires that member countries renounce the use or threatened use of war as an instrument of foreign policy and make provision to restrain or even punish, through cooperative and coordinated action, any country that attacks another for any reason other than self-defense. Under such a system of collective security, the member nations surrender some of their sovereignty, and war remains legitimate only if waged on behalf of the principles set by the members of a global body. Such systems—the League of Nations and the United Nations being the most notable—did not change the fundamental rules of war, but they did attempt to alter the decentralized nature of international law enforcement. "Arms races, alliances, and provocative threats of war . . . would no longer be necessary, since deterrence would now be provided by the prospect of concerted international response to any aggressor."[7]

Absolute pacifists sought to combat militarism by sharing information and engaging public opinion in the cause of peace. "Governments are helpless in the hands of an enlightened people," noted one pacifist tract written by S. F. Sanger and D. Hays in 1907. "The leavening of peace must be infused among the people. . . . The only remedy is for each one to become an advocate of peace, each society a peace society, each church a peace church."[8] Many of the champions of peace advocated mediation and arbitration between hostile parties to solve outstanding disputes rather than deciding issues through the force of arms. As chroniclers of sectarian conscientious objection during the American Civil War, Sanger and Hays wrote, "The cause of war often hinges upon a single point, and after two nations have exhausted their resources in devastating war, the question at issue is as much undecided as before the war began."[9] These men failed, however, to address the fact that in their lifetimes both slavery and secession—which they abhorred—had been eradicated only through warlike means after decades of argument, litigation, and compromise had failed to resolve the issues.

In the later part of the 19th century, Quakers and other pacifists became associated with the annual religious conferences at Lake Mohonk in the Shawangunk Mountains near New Paltz, New York. Although called to deal with the problems confronted by the Protestant religious missions to the Native tribes in the American West, these conferences also attempted to find solutions to other difficult social problems in terms of both world peace and race relations. The continued influence of the Mohonk Conferences as part of the peace initiative can be directly attributed to their founder (and the owner of Mohonk Lake House), Albert Smiley, a Quaker who was a member of the Board of Indian Commissioners. By the turn of the 20th century, the Mohonk meetings had effectively superseded nearly all the functions of the Board of Indian Commissioners, which had audited the accounts and inspected the supplies on the Native American reservations supervised by the Office of Indian Affairs of the federal government.

International Peace Societies

Frédéric Passy, a French economist and politician, was an ardent pacifist who founded the International Peace League in 1867. However, world peace congresses did not begin to meet on a regular basis until 1889 beginning with the meeting held in Paris and followed consecutively by meetings in Washington, D.C., in 1890, and in The Hague in 1899. The delegates again met in The Hague in 1907, at the invitation of President Theodore Roosevelt, to deal with voluntary arbitration, debt collection, the rights of neutral states, and the rules of war. The 1907 conference, administered by U.S. Secretary of State Elihu Root, marked the high–water mark of the pre–World War I international peace movement. However, as a former secretary of war under President William McKinley, Root was no antiwar isolationist, and he had sought "a peace made secure by the organized major force of mankind," along the lines of President Woodrow Wilson's League of Nations.[10] Strong antiwar sentiment only retarded American entrance into World War I, and it was an even stronger isolationist sentiment that prevented the United States from joining the postwar League of Nations.

Although the U.S. Senate refused to endorse the league system, the organization initially worked fairly well—settling, for example, the border disputes between Albania and Yugoslavia in 1921 and between Greece and Bulgaria in 1925. Yet the organization seemed impotent when trying to deal with the aggressive tendencies of the major powers. When Italy bombed the Greek island of Corfu in 1923, the pressure from Italian diplomats prevented the league from assuming jurisdiction in the matter. In 1935, Italy's open aggression in Ethiopia resulted in economic sanctions and an arms embargo, but it was recognized by only a portion of the league members and proved porous to strategically important items such as oil. When China brought charges of aggression against Japan in 1931, the league took a more determined stand by refusing to recognize the Japanese-imposed government in Manchuria. In response, Japan's delegates dramatically walked out of the session and resigned from the league in anger. Japan remained in control of Manchuria and followed with a full-scale invasion of China in 1937.

The aggression of both Italy and Japan remained unchecked because "no country of any weight was prepared to go to war to defend the status quo, let alone to defend the concept of world order."[11] This reality regarding the league did not escape Adolf Hitler, who formed his own collective security agreement with Italy and Japan. In response, Britain and France formed their own network of international security alliances, much as they had before World War I. The inability to deal with some of the most powerful nations among the world polity made the league not only irrelevant but also superfluous. The lack of moral support from the United States did not change the situation at the time. The league had failed to keep the peace largely due to its absolute refusal to use righteous warfare as a coercive tool against member states that violated it precepts.

Although absolute pacifists generally did not define themselves in terms of organizations, several important and active antiwar groups were founded in the first half of the 20th century. Among these were the Fellowship of Reconciliation

(1915), the Women's Peace Party (1915), the American Friends Service Committee (1917), the Women's International League for Peace and Freedom (1919), the War Resisters League (1923), the Catholic Worker Movement (1933), and the America First Committee (1940). These organizations, while not uniform in their core beliefs, all eschewed involvement in warfare, some for religious reasons and some based on social priorities or isolationist principles.

The Fellowship of Reconciliation (FOR) was begun in 1915 in opposition to World War I, and it served as a community of support for conscientious objectors (COs) while promoting social justice and internationalism as stopgaps to future world conflict. The American Friends Service Committee (AFSC) originated in response to the needs of COs during World War I. The group was founded in 1917 by American members of the Religious Society of Friends to assist civilian victims of the war. It was largely Quaker oriented and hoped to establish a legal alternative service for COs.

Several women, who had tried in vain to check the conflict while World War I was raging, founded the Women's International League for Peace and Freedom (WILPF) in 1919, thereby combining their efforts for peace. In that year, the WILPF established a single office in Geneva, Switzerland. Among the leaders were Jane Addams, best known for her social work at Hull House, and Emily Green Balch, both of whom would receive Nobel Peace Prize laureates in 1931 and 1946, respectively. By 1955, the WILPF had chapters in sixteen countries and was expanding its work into the developing world.

The War Resisters League (WRL) was founded in 1923 as the American branch of War Resisters International (WRI). The purpose of both groups was to move pacifist principles based on sectarian conscientious objection to a wider and more comprehensive nonreligious foundation of collective and public resistance to war. Among the founders of WRL and WRI were a number of Americans who rejected the seemingly violent and manipulative strategies used by politicians in the United States, but a few democratic socialists and believers in European-style anarchism quickly came to dominate the activities of the organizations. The WRL, the oldest purely secular antiwar organization in America, held no meetings or mass conclaves, instead choosing to communicate through the mail or in small interpersonal settings. This left the U.S. organization and its American members open to charges of conspiracy, deception, and un-American activity.

Although the Roman Catholic Church does not list absolute pacifism among its religious tenets—as do many other churches—it generally upholds the right of individuals to their conscientious objection to serve in wartime. The Catholic Worker Movement (CWM)—founded largely on principles of social justice—had an effect on the antiwar movement much larger than its small membership should have warranted. Founded in 1933 at the height of the Great Depression by a French-émigré to Canada, Peter Maurin, and an American journalist and activist, Dorothy Day, the organization reached out to COs from its social service center on Manhattan's East Side.

Meanwhile, midwestern isolationists and antiwar activists formed the backbone of the America First Committee (AFC), dedicated to the simple proposition that neither private financial interests nor foreign governmental influences should come before the welfare of America. The issue that spawned the group in 1940 was the prevention of the U.S. entry into another world war for another nation's benefit, specifically that of Great Britain. The founders of the AFC were chiefly Robert E. Wood, chairman of the board of Sears Roebuck & Company, and R. Douglas Stewart, Jr., of the Quaker Oats Company. Its most effective spokesman was the famous transatlantic flyer Charles A. Lindbergh, and his support attracted many prominent Americans. Among these were the actress Lillian Gish; World War I fighter-ace and racecar driver Eddie Rickenbacker; Chicago publisher William H. Regnery; journalist and consistent antimilitarist John T. Flynn; auto industrialist Henry Ford; and social reformers Father Charles Coughlin and Rev. Gerald L. K. Smith.

The AFC was exceptional among antiwar groups for the radicalism of its right-wing positions. Although considered by its detractors a racist, anti-Semitic, anti-Communist, and pro-German (or even pro-Nazi) organization, rather than simply being antiwar, the AFC drew on many of the prejudices of Middle America for its support. It grew to become one of the largest antiwar membership organizations in America, with more than 850,000 dues-paying members in 450 chapters across the nation. Among the core beliefs espoused by the organization were racial and genetic integrity, the preservation of traditional white American culture, and right of the United States to determine and assert its foreign policy without submission to any foreign states, alliances, or international bodies. Claiming that the Franklin D. Roosevelt administration was using lies and deceptions in an attempt to involve the nation in European affairs, AFC mounted campaigns against Lend Lease, the Selective Service, and many New Deal initiatives that it considered degenerate forms of socialism. The AFC organizations helped to keep America from entering World War II before the attack on Pearl Harbor in late 1941, after which it disbanded for the duration of the conflict. A totally new group using the same name and espousing many of the same policies was created in 1980.

Apprehensions concerning the survival of a post–World War II world with nuclear weapons generated a novel set of peace organizations dedicated to disarmament. Horrified by the use of atomic bombs at Hiroshima and Nagasaki, the Federation of American Scientists (FAS) was formed in 1946 to resist the proliferation of nuclear weapons. At the same time, a number of smaller and less coherent groups, which supported the federation of Western democracies into a single supernation, coalesced to form the United World Federalists in 1947. Americans for Democratic Action (ADA) was also formed in 1947. ADA members endorsed the containment of Communism and a new type of social justice for areas of the world just emerging from colonial rule.

Taking their name from the location of the first meeting, in the village of Pugwash, Nova Scotia, and stimulated by the Russell-Einstein Manifesto of 1955, a group of scientists and intellectuals established a series of peace conferences known as the Pugwash Conferences. Twenty-two eminent scientists attended the 1957 meeting (seven from the United States, three each from the USSR and Japan, two each from Britain and Canada, and one each from Australia, Austria, China, France, and Poland). The purpose of the Pugwash Conferences was to bring together influential scholars and public figures from around the world concerned with reducing the danger of armed conflict and nuclear war, and seeking cooperative solutions for global problems. Among the principles of the manifesto was the following statement:

> The abolition of war will demand distasteful limitations of national sovereignty. But what perhaps impedes understanding of the situation more than anything else is that the term "mankind" feels vague and abstract. People scarcely realize in imagination that the danger [of nuclear weapons] is to themselves and their children and their grandchildren, and not only to a dimly apprehended humanity. They can scarcely bring themselves to grasp that they, individually, and those whom they love are in imminent danger of perishing agonizingly. And so they hope that perhaps war may be allowed to continue provided modern [nuclear] weapons are prohibited. . . . If the issues between East and West are to be decided in any manner that can give any possible satisfaction to anybody, whether Communist or anti-Communist, whether Asian or European or American, whether White or Black, then these issues must not be decided by war.[12]

Meeting in private as individuals, rather than as representatives of governments or institutions, the Pugwash participants exchanged views and explored alternative approaches to arms control and tension reduction with a combination of candor, continuity, and flexibility seldom attained in official international discussions and negotiations. By late 2002, more than 10,000 people had attended more than 275 Pugwash Conferences, Symposia, or Workshops.

By the mid-1950s, however, public support for the Cold War and a membership shaken by Red Scare McCarthyism had left organized internationalism in disarray, and many of its adherents turned their focus to preventing a nuclear arms race. Membership in pacifist and antiwar groups plummeted during the 1950s. Some pacifists like journalist I. F. Stone questioned if any peace movement remained in America. In 1952 Norman Cousins, editor of the *Saturday Review of Literature* and founding member of the United World Federalists (UWF), looked back to the end of World War II trying to rally the faithful to the new cause, "Seven years ago, when world law was mentioned, people said it was too soon . . . now they say it is too late."[13]

Organizations like the ADA of the 1950s were closely associated with the left wing of the Democratic Party. ADA members were prominent persons who were trying to reprise the progressive policies of the Franklin Roosevelt era like intellectuals John Kenneth Galbraith and Arthur M. Schlesinger, Jr., and politicians like Adlai Stevenson. This movement was not made without opposition. The John Birch Society was founded in 1958 by Robert H. Welch, Jr., and eleven other prominent businessmen to combat communism and promote conservative causes. It was named for an American missionary and army intelligence officer killed by Chinese communists in 1945 who was considered by the society the first hero of the Cold War. Society membership may have reached 100,000, and the group enlisted hundreds of influential persons who sat on school boards and library committees or held other civic offices. The society quickly emerged as one of the best-known and most-influential conservative groups in the United States, reserving its election year imprimaturs only for clearly anticommunist and antisocialist candidates from both parties. Successive domestic and international crises in 1956 put a premium on safe politics rather than radical protest, and the peace concerns and liberal leanings of progressives proved problematic in producing positive results at the polls. Subsequently, many liberal activists and war resisters reentered politics by supporting moderate attempts to relax superpower tensions rather than trying to eradicate war.

The radical peace movement of the late 1950s had been a disappointment. Membership numbers in America had withered to only a few thousand adherents, mainly shopworn Marxist-Leninists left over from the depression years. These activists were generally members of the American Communist Party, the Socialist Workers Party (SWP), and the socialist-democrat League for Industrial Democracy (LID). Their continued popularity during the late 1930s had been eclipsed by a world war that had found justification in the eyes of the American public through the attack on Pearl Harbor and an after-the-fact validation of war found in the Nazi concentration camps at Auschwitz, Buchenwald, Dachau, and other places. The membership in war resistance organizations continued to evaporate under the heat of a second round of Red Scare politics and McCarthyism.

The lessening of world tensions in the wake of World War II had briefly opened fresh opportunities for pacifists in the area of nuclear disarmament, however. Americans of both major parties generally feared the atomic weapons that only they had ever used in anger. Robert Pinkus, a member of AFSC, organized a program called Acts for Peace coordinating the activities of more than a dozen antiwar groups in reaching out to chambers of commerce and parent-teacher associations in the United States to explain their nuclear disarmament principles. In England, the Campaign for Nuclear Disarmament (CND) was established. In the United States, the Committee for Non-Violent Action (CNVA) and the National Committee for a Sane Nuclear Policy (known simply as SANE) were begun.

A large number of prewar antiwar advocates turned their interests to the growing civil rights struggle through their support of the Congress of Racial Equality (CORE) that had been formed in 1943. In 1955, when Rosa Parks's arrest for refusing to ride in the rear of a public bus brought Martin Luther King, Jr. to prominence, advisors from both CORE and the pacifist group FOR were at his side. King openly proclaimed that racism, poverty, and militarism were the major obstacles to peace, reestablishing the link among social reformers, civil rights activists, and war resisters. Inextricably linked, peace was impossible as long as these three ills existed. Thereafter there formed an unquestioned, if informal, coalition of antiwar, disarmament, civil rights, and other social reform organizations.

The New Left

The new radicals of the 1960s generally abandoned both the old leftism of the Soviet model and the rightist capitalism of the military-industrial complex for a so-called Third Camp. Many of these new radicals were college-age students—as were the anti-Soviet members of the Young People's Socialist League (YPSL) and the so-called Student SANE. Most believed that "Marxist modes of analysis," freed of the dogmatic evil of Soviet-style Communism, could provide "direction to change" in American society. The fundamental cry of the New Left was "change." This included the following:

- Change in the tactics of engagement for protestors
- Change in the stratified structure of American society
- Change in the conduct of international affairs[14]

One of the earliest organizations to proceed from this New Left thinking was commonly called SLATE (1958), a coalition of young activists developed at the University of the State of California at Berkeley. SLATE was not an acronym, but referred to the candidates for student government at USC Berkeley endorsed by the group. SLATE was never very large in terms of membership and remained active only until the late 1960s. Another coalition of undergraduate collegians, the Student Peace Union (SPU), was founded at the University of Chicago by Kenneth and Ele Calkins, a young Quaker couple—presently members of the Socialist Party and formerly involved in a number of pacifists groups including FOR, AFSC, and CNVA. In 1959, SPU had 120 members based in twelve chapters in midwestern schools, with its strongest affiliates at the historic reform sanctuaries of Oberlin and Antioch Colleges. Most of the members were religious pacifists, ban-the-bomb liberals, spillovers from the anti-Soviet YPSL, and dropouts from Student SANE. The SPU was active only briefly, largely a victim of its own moderation. Riding the rising tide of civil rights agitation, 200 students at Shaw University in North Carolina in June 1960 formed the Student Nonviolent Coordinating Committee (SNCC) with the purpose of bringing increased militancy to the drive for minority equality. SNCC was spontaneous and individualistic in character; committed to fundamental social and political change as a moral duty, and generally indifferent to the ideological quarrels of the past.

By the end of 1960, several more student-oriented New Left organizations were popping up on college campuses nationwide. Among these were the Young Socialists Alliance (YSA) and the Student League for Industrial Democracy (SLID), both offshoots of older parent organizations, and a reconstituted form of Students for a Democratic Society (SDS) all of which had war resistance and a fundamental belief in the primacy of socialism among their core principles.

A mass meeting of pacifists and antiwar intellectuals was held at Bear Mountain Lodge in New York in 1960. The conferees were responding to the same fundamental principles and sense of urgency as the student unions, and they also formed the same type of understandings regarding the need for cooperation and coordination regarding their activities. Those present agreed to establish a Committee of Correspondence that would allow for the exchange of ideas regarding antiwar tactics and progressive strategies. The agreement formed something less than a coalition and somewhat more than a polite assurance among friends. The rhetorical use of the phrase committees of correspondence made popular during the American Revolution was not lost on those in attendance.

The peace movements of the New Left—pacifist, student, and intellectual—had largely secularized the concept of war resistance and conscientious objection of religion-based groups of earlier centuries into a political movement that would combine to protest the Vietnam War. SANE would be one of the first to organize against the war in Southeast Asia calling for the United States to end its limited involvement as early as September 1963. At the time, John F. Kennedy had not yet been assassinated (November 1963), and only a few thousand U.S. advisors to the Ngo Dinh Diem government were in theater. In 1964, Lyndon B. Johnson, president since the death of Kennedy, won his own term in office as a "peace candidate" against the more aggressive Sen. Barry Goldwater. In April 1965 SDS organized the first mass march (in excess of 25,000 persons) *against* the war, imperialism, and racism, and *for* women's liberation and the so-called counterculture of long hair, love beads, bra burning, tinted granny glasses, and ragged blue jeans. "They claimed a different set of beliefs and values from the *establishment* as they called the political and social systems created by the generations before theirs."[15]

The Vietnam era antiwar movement left a legacy of political activism for 21st-century pacifists. These include liberal internationalists and global reformers who identify the peace movement more closely with social justice and the extension of economic aid to disadvantaged people in the developing world. Committed to both peace and social justice, these antiwar activists and war resisters are rarely radical revolutionaries, but rather devotees of selective reforms in areas such as the environment, civil rights, feminism, reproductive choice, and animal rights. All have reaped the benefits of the experiences of antiwar protestors of the past.[16]

Shared Assumptions

Antiwar and peace organizations have shared a number of assumptions that resound throughout the historic period and resonate with modern movements. There is evidence in the historical record that some of these assumptions have merit and that some do not. Many pacifist and antiwar groups adhere to a majority of the same core principles, few accept all of them. The European Green Party, for instance, lists the decentralization of nation-states and the establishment of communal cooperatives or minimalist village leaderships among their Ten Key Values.[17] Few other antiwar organizations so openly call for the establishment of such a combination of socialist politics, civil and gender rights initiatives, and environmental principles.

The common ideological strands found among the major antiwar organizations can be listed in a generally complete, if not exhaustive summary of fundamental attitudes:

- War is immoral and is to be avoided at all costs; but the needs of self-defense and the defense of others, who are in helpless situations, are sometimes recognized.

- Dedication to religious beliefs (conscientious objection) supersedes obligations to political institutions such as paying war-related taxes, personal service in the military, or the active support of war industries.

- Nonviolent resistance and civil disobedience are effective methods of attaining antiwar and social objectives.

- Mediation and arbitration, rather than confrontation and force of arms, should be used to resolve issues between hostile parties.

- Disarmament, whether unilateral or multilateral, ultimately will eradicate war or limit the tendency to go to war.

- Negotiations and international dialog are necessary for peace. National isolation will not alone prevent entanglement in foreign wars.

- Military preparedness generally fails to prevent the outbreak of warfare and makes conflict more likely.

- The resources spent on military preparedness are better spent on social reforms, such as the eradication of homelessness and poverty, the extension of free public education and universal health care, the improvement of environmental quality, or other recognized social problems.

- Nation-states with industrial economies and corporate oligarchies are particularly prone to being warlike.

- Centralization of wealth and power in the hands of a few persons or a detached ruling class contributes to militarism and thereby the threat of war.

- The creation of new types of global political organizations dedicated to a process of social justice and economic change lessens the likelihood of war.

- Global peace is best promoted through collective security as administered through international agencies, multilateral cooperation, and the development of world government (the so-called super-nation or global village).

Antiwar and pacifist political parties seeking to win elections in the 21st century often moderate their demands, calling for de-escalation or arms reductions rather than the outright disarmament that was advocated by many absolute pacifists in the past or simply enunciating the unspecified need for "change" or "transformation." Furthermore, once in power, as with the case of the Bolshevik-Soviet revolutions, these parties have been known to wander somewhat from their antiwar leanings. One common justification for the change in policy is the concept of using the violence of repression to prevent further acts of violence, thereby limiting the "net-sum" of violence, as in sending armed forces into Rwanda, Lebanon, or Bosnia as peacekeepers under U.N. auspices.

The controversial *democratic peace theory* holds that liberal democracies have never (or rarely) made war on one another and that lesser conflicts and internal violence are rare between and within liberal democracies. It also argues that the growth in the number of progressive democratic states will, in the not so distant future, end warfare. Some pacifists and multilateralists are in favor of the establishment of a world government as a means to prevent and control international aggression. While some unions, like the European Union, have been brought together peacefully, most large nation-states have been united through warfare and held together only by the force of military action. It is questionable, therefore, whether a world government devoted to peace could be formed without years of ensuing internecine conflict.

Notes

1. Talleyrand would serve as a diplomat for six regimes, and he would betray four of them.

2. Lyra Trueblood Wolkins, "The American Peace Society," Swarthmore College Peace Collection, http://www.swarthmore.edu/Library/peace/DG001-025/DG003APS.html (accessed July, 11, 2008).

3. S. F. Sanger and D. Hays, *The Olive Branch of Peace and Good Will to Men: The Antiwar History of the Brethren and Mennonites, the People of the South during the Civil War, 1861–1865* (Elgin, IL: Brethren Publishing House, 1907), 210.

4. W. H. McIntosh, "James C. Sumner, the Young Soldier Ready for Death," Rare Book Collection, University of North Carolina at Chapel Hill, http://docsouth.unc.edu/imls/mcintosh/mcintosh.html (accessed April 2008).

5. Peter Silver, *Our Savage Neighbors: How the Indian War Transformed Early America* (New York; W. W. Norton, 2008), xxii.

6. Sanger and Hays, xvi

7. Seyom Brown, *The Causes and Prevention of War* (New York; St. Martin's Press, 1994), 180.

8. Sanger and Hays, xiv.

9. Sanger and Hays, xvi.

10. Elihu Root, Speech before the International League for Peace, January, 25, 1917.

11. Brown, 181.

12. Bertrand Russell, "The Russell-Einstein Manifesto," http://www.pugwash.org/about/manifesto.htm (accessed July 11, 2008).

13. Charles DeBenedetti, *An American Ordeal: The Antiwar Movement of the Vietnam Era* (Syracuse, NY: Syracuse University Press, 1990), 27.

14. DeBeneditti, 40.

15. Anita Louise McCormick, *The Vietnam Antiwar Movement in American History* (Berkeley Heights, NJ: Enslow Publishers, 2000), 45–46.

16. McCormick, 110.

17. "Ten Key Values of the Green Party," http://www.gp.org/tenkey.shtml (accessed June 2009).

Part II

Chapter 4

The Colonial and Revolutionary Period

Let us look to the most high who blessed our fathers with peace.
—Caption on a Quaker peace medal given to the Indians

Independence will permit America to shake hands with the world—live in peace with the world—and trade to any market.
—Thomas Paine, *Common Sense,* 1775

How easily do men pass from loving, to hating and cursing one another!
—Hector St. John de Crévecoeur, 1782

First in war, first in peace, first in the hearts of his countrymen.
—Henry Lee, on Washington's death

The Peaceful People: 1755

From a historical perspective, the Quakers stand out as a group with regard to the development of antiwar sentiment in America. The greatest concentration of these Quakers in the colonial period were in Pennsylvania where William Penn had recruited the settlers for his colony from among the Cheshire and Welsh farmers who had lived on the fringe of Britain's cultural, economic, and social mainstream. Here they had learned to scrape out a living in a harsh agricultural environment. In Pennsylvania, with its rich soils and well-watered landscape, Quaker farmers succeeded beyond their own imaginings in making the colony the richest among all those in British North America.

Penn's personal dedication to religious tolerance also attracted a wide collection of non-Quakers to the middle colonies, including German-speaking Moravian and Mennonite Pietists, Scotch-Irish Presbyterians, dissidents from the Church of England, and a few Catholics who spilled over from Maryland. Philadelphia—the major center of population, seat of government, and city of brotherly love—was described as a world "unsettled and overwhelmingly alien—with sects, cults, and bizarre religious splinter factions, many of which were there precisely because they had been scourged as subversives out of Europe."[1] Despite the diversity of its citizenry, the Quakers ruled Pennsylvania politics in the days of colonial proprietors forming "an almost imaginary state, with no taxes, no military establishment, very little public spending, a scant smattering of officials outside Philadelphia, and, in many years, no laws passed at all."[2]

This form of governance closely followed the way that Quakers—as well as Moravians, Mennonites, and other Pietist groups—applied their unique principles to everyday life, relying heavily on a number of religious and spiritual forms of human relations to inform their decisions. Among these principles, absolute pacifism was only one of the many that distinguished them from other colonials. The burden of producing, sustaining, and incorporating moral, civic, and economic virtues into the community was taken on by the entire family and supported by the whole body of brethren (a form of religious communitarianism). Everything in the individual household was subjected to a familial order based in this morality.

Quakers and other Pietists tended to separate themselves from other less morally focused Pennsylvanians. They considered authorities outside their unique religious disciplines such as an intolerant established priesthood, an authoritarian governing class, or even a pedantic university system "not only unnecessary but even pernicious."[3] This feeling characterized their relationship with government; however, even among the Pietist groups, few interconnecting bonds were formed among distinct sects. Quakers tended to bond with Quakers, Mennonites with Mennonites, and so on. Some of this exclusionary activity was a function of language or ethnic origin; but all the Pietist groups in Pennsylvania tended to exhibit certain common characteristics such as simplicity in the manner of living and dressing, encouraging the role of women in the ministry, spiritual democracy within the meeting house discipline, absolute adherence to truth, and universal peace and brotherhood regardless of sex, class, nation, or race.[4]

Under increased pressure from non-Pietist German, Scotch-Irish, Welsh, and English immigrants in the 1730s and 1740s, the Pietists, and the Quakers in particular, adjusted the level of their orthodoxy to combat the growth of outside influences, often disowning members of their own communities at disturbingly high rates for breaches of moral behavior like drunkenness, the selling of liquor to Native Americans, the ownership of slaves, Sabbath breaking, war-related acts, supposed sexual promiscuity, prenuptial pregnancy, and deviations from religious norms of plain dress and speech. The prosecution of members for marrying outside the meeting house discipline, for example, put such a severe brake on the growth of Quakerism in Pennsylvania that the Quaker population, which had doubled every twenty years since the founding of the colony, simply stagnated under the severity of internal attrition by the middle of the 18th century. The population of other Pietist groups—mere minorities when compared with the number of Quakers—experienced similar negative outcomes until reinforced by German-speaking immigrants late in the century.[5]

The Quakers had, nonetheless, maintained an absolute majority in the Pennsylvania Assembly from its founding until 1755, and they remained a potent political force in the colony thereafter by allying themselves with political splinter groups representative of the other pacifist sects. By the beginning of the American Revolution, however, their continued pacifism—especially with respect to defending the colony against attack by Indians—had so tainted their patriotic reputations that they lost their position of control.

The Friendly Association

During the Seven Years' War in Europe, known as the French and Indian War (1754–1763) in America, Quakers cemented their position as America's earliest antiwar activists as they attempted to impose their pacifism on the Pennsylvania colony by refusing to allow the raising of a colonial militia or the appropriation of funds for warlike operations. These activities included an almost total ban on practical provisions that might be taken for the defense of the colony from frontier raids by French-allied Indians. As the frontier war began, the Quakers founded the Friendly Association for Regaining and Preserving Peace with the Indians by Pacific Means, a high-sounding effort at promoting interracial justice for the tribes, particularly the Delaware and the Shawnee nations, with whom they had long-standing ties. The formation of this organization (known simply as the Friendly Association) was widely unpopular with the non-Pietist, Indian-fearing residents of the colony.

Like other societies founded in the colony in the 1750s, the Friendly Association was a charitable organization devoted to easing the misfortunes of those adversely affected by frontier war. If not the very first peace organization in America, it was among the first. Other associations with members drawn from a single religion or a particular national origin also existed for the purpose of war relief. Among these were the St. Andrew's Society in Philadelphia, which served those of Scottish origin; Deutsche Gesellschaft su Philadelphia, established by the German speakers; the Society of the Friendly Sons of St. Patrick set up by the Irish; and the Corporation for the Relief of Presbyterian Ministers, Their Widows, and Children. When war refugees flooded the city of Philadelphia, these associations came to their aid, directing funds largely to those of their own religion or common national origin. The Friendly Association, however, spent its funds on Indians as well as whites, and it is hard to overstate the resentment that its activities produced among those who ascribed every evil perpetrated by Native Americans on the frontier to the background manipulations of Quaker pacifists. Moreover, the Quakers meant their actions with regard to the Native Americans to be as conspicuous as possible to better demonstrate how intercultural negotiations should be conducted, and to illustrate as forcefully as possible that it was *they* who should be chosen to conduct any diplomacy with the tribes.[6]

The Friendly Association was formed around a core of dedicated evangelical activists like John Woolman, and antislavery and racial justice advocates like the writer Anthony Benezet. These activists were all led by Israel Pemberton, Jr., the organization's fantastically rich and conspicuous public figurehead. Outsiders often accused Pemberton, who was committed to Quaker principles, of self-aggrandizement. He often assumed an air of being more important than the colony's actual governor and was often addressed as "Governor Pemberton" by his acquaintances in public. His airs were somewhat understandable because it had been Quakers who had founded the Pennsylvania colony and who had made many of the initial treaties with the Native Americans in the time of William Penn. In some cases, however, the Native leaders may have misunderstood the actual status of representatives of the Friendly Association. In the new scheme of government, Penn's heirs, Thomas and Richard Penn, had become Anglicans and the colonial government had been restructured to include a governor, a provincial council, and an elected assembly.

Both the Quakers and their detractors acknowledged the continued existence of a special Quaker–Native American relationship, but each drew from its existence widely different conclusions. The Quakers reveled in the existence of their special relationship with the tribes sitting side by side with Native leaders at religious services and inviting Indians to attend the Quakers' Greater Meetinghouse in the heart of Philadelphia. They meant through these outward actions to retrieve the tradition of Quaker–Native American diplomacy that had been lost over the decades to the representatives and agents of the Crown or of the Board of Trade in London. Members of other pacifist sectarian groups in the colony respected the influence that the Quakers had with the tribes and wrote repeatedly to Philadelphia asking them for advice on how to ready the Indians for religious instruction, ameliorate their supposed natural tendency for violence, or best accomplish the redemption of white captives.

This impression of a special relationship was further supported by the Quakers' own determined and public efforts to appear open to the Indians—holding worship services at diplomatic meetings while sitting around Native campfires from dawn to dusk—all the while pinning their hopes for peace on Indians and whites "being melted down together before God." For members of the Friendly Association, Indians and whites were spiritually the same in the eyes of God—a concept that put them at odds with many other Euro-Americans who viewed Native Americans as somehow fundamentally different from other humans, if not inferior to them. Benezet continually urged that "erroneous ideas" and "superficial prejudices" based on skin color be abandoned in favor of a brotherly unity under God, and Woolman made extraordinary trips into the hinterland to hold religious prayer meetings with Native Americans in their villages even at the height of a crisis.[7]

The fear of Indians was a powerful and pervasive feature shared by much of the population of British North America, and it was widespread enough throughout the colonies to determine what many colonial governments did diplomatically, militarily, and politically throughout the 17th and 18th centuries. Although Pennsylvania refused to raise a defensive force or even to appropriate funds to build forts, Virginia, the Carolinas (officially one colony until 1710), Connecticut, and Massachusetts had raised thousands of provincial militiamen to fend off unfriendly tribes and French-allied Indians. The Connecticut colony, for example, built a string of fortified villages and trading posts up the Connecticut River far into the interior of

Vermont reaching well north of the rather nebulous boundary between New England and New France.

Although fearful of large standing forces, the New England colonies in times of crisis were able to raise upward of 1,000 men to take the field, prosecute, and win major wars against the Native populations. As early as 1672, Virginia alone supported twenty troops of horse (thirty mounted men each) and an equal number of companies of infantry (each composed of thirty musketmen and thirty pikemen). Virginia also established a system of paid, mounted rangers numbering almost 1,000 men who patrolled the frontiers, held down depredations, and tried to keep abreast of the attitudes of the various tribal groups.

Carolinians on the frontiers were forced to defend themselves from both Spanish aggression directed from Florida and the Gulf Coast and the possibility of Indian outrages from the interior almost without aid of any kind. Ultimately, the militia of South Carolina became so scattered by the rapid expansion of the frontier settlements as to be incapable of any effective defense. The defensive system became so poor that most of the outlying settlements in South Carolina had to be abandoned with settlers fleeing east to avoid the raids and attacks brought on by the French and Indian War. With the introduction of a regiment of British regulars into the buffer colony of Georgia in 1732, the South Carolina militia system evolved from a military force poised to withstand outward aggression into a simple slave patrol.

Almost all the colonies used rangers. By 1760, North Carolina's rangers were spread out over 150 miles of frontier. Only Pennsylvania and New York seem to have neglected the establishment of a formal corps of these paid frontiersmen to watch their outlying borders. New Yorkers relied on their ubiquitous Iroquois allies to guard the frontier, but the pacifists in Pennsylvania absolutely refused to take any steps toward creating military units, even defensive ones.

The pacifist Quakers in the Pennsylvania Assembly—almost alone among colonial governments—had steadfastly refused to establish any permanent military force or to provide funds for weapons and ammunition to defend against attack. When the Crown determined to eject the French from the forks of the Ohio by force, the Quakers had resisted Gen. Edward Braddock's call for wagons and horses to carry his provisions and for funds to pay the militia as being a contradiction of their religious beliefs. Individual Quakers not only refused to enlist in a defense force, but also protested against its formation. For these acts, they were strongly criticized both by British military officers and by colonial representatives like Benjamin Franklin, who—though noted for his humorous jibbing—sometimes spoke of Quaker intransigence with uncharacteristic vitriol and impatience. Ultimately, the non-Quaker settlers of Pennsylvania paid the price of pacifism with their blood on the western frontiers.

Braddock's defeat in July 1755 on the Monongahela River in the western portion of the Pennsylvania colony had been a major setback for the British in the early stages of their latest war with France. This disaster—thought at the time to have occurred in the jurisdiction of Virginia—was the most significant event in British colonial history in North America to that time, and it was clear that Delaware and

Shawnee warriors—supposed friends and sometimes protégées of the Quakers, Moravians, and other pacifist sects—had fought on the side of the French. The entire frontier region was placed in a state of terror as rumors of an invasion of 1,500 French allied Indians and Canadien troops swirled through the settlements. Although such a force never materialized, in October 1755 there was an Indian attack on white settlers at Penns Creek. Two weeks later, Delaware and Shawnee warriors nearly wiped out the Scotch-Irish settlements on the Pennsylvania-Maryland border. Shortly thereafter a group of Delaware warriors killed or captured more than a dozen settlers in Lebanon and Berks counties (Pennsylvania).

The threat reached the pacifist Moravian community at Nazareth, Pennsylvania, on November 21, and that evening a breeze from the northwest carried the distinct odor of smoke from burning frontier cabins. "Late in the night came an express messenger from Bethlehem with the order, that in all places good guards should be put out, because the rumor of Indian uprising has come to us worse than before," wrote an unidentified Moravian minister in what was called the *Nazareth Diary*. "To-day marched constantly men with guns on the street and passed here on the road to Bethlehem. . . . Several brethren and sisters from here and from the other places had a foreboding in the night of the hard circumstances, which had come over our brethren and sisters . . . and one did smell even the burning here because the wind was coming from that direction."[8]

These raids came at a time of political crisis for Pennsylvanians. For months, Gov. Robert Hunter Morris, former governor James Hamilton, Benjamin Franklin, and others on the provincial council had wrestled with the Quaker-controlled Assembly over the question of how to protect a frontier virtually devoid of regular troops. The "backcountry" settlers of Pennsylvania, who found themselves without professional military protection due to Braddock's defeat, scrambled to organize a rudimentary defense. Col. James Innes, protecting Braddock's supply lines at Cumberland, Maryland, then the westernmost outpost of the British North American Empire, noted upon learning of Braddock's defeat, "Please God, I intend to make a stand here. It's highly necessary to raise the militia everywhere to defend the frontiers."[9] A colonial newspaper reporting on the battle noted, "In consequence of this shameful defeat the frontiers of several southwestern provinces lay exposed to the enemy and how much innocent blood may be inhumanly sacrificed . . . we have the highest reason to fear the worst."[10] Small groups of frontier residents vowed to engage the enemy until "others of our brethren should come up and do the same" or to die together in the defense.[11]

Quakers, Moravians, Mennonites, and other pacifist groups were quickly chosen as scapegoats for this series of tragedies. Pacifists were largely detested simply because they were pacifists and held strangely different attitudes toward Native Americans than other Euro-Americans. Moreover, many Euro-Americans saw an unbridgeable chasm between whites and Indians that simply did not exist for Quakers who saw any difference as political or cultural rather than racial. The idea of Native Americans versus whites as naturally occurring opponents was as yet a relative novelty, and same-race-based coalitions even in times of war had not yet become self-evident. Surely, the Frenchmen and Canadiens with whom the British were at war were also "white," and the English also had a solid military alliance with the Iroquois who were certainly "Indian." Yet race-based words at this point in American history were far less useful as identifiers and framers of political and military coalitions than other characteristics such as national origin, religious affiliation, or social class. The Native American's opinions concerning human differences were often more racially and culturally exclusive than those of Euro-Americans.

The best proof of loyalty to the "white people" of Pennsylvania was to have been the victim of an Indian attack. Those who had been attacked (and survived) often had their political opinions imbued with added authority. Those who had not suffered at the hands of the Indians might be excluded from the colonial polity. The doctrine-based hostility that many mainstream religions held toward Quakers, Moravians, and other pacifist sects often prevailed over any race-based solidarity that may have existed during the crisis. Exclusion of such persons was deemed essential in the face of crisis, and the politics of the Indian wars shoved many Euro-Americans—including the Quakers and other pacifists—out of the political surround of being considered "white." Their sympathies were questioned and their pacifism was seen as secret collusion with outside attackers.[12]

Over the continued Quaker objections, Franklin had tried for eight years to establish volunteer militia companies in Philadelphia (called *associators* so that the word "militia" would not offend any pacifist sentiments). He even penning a pamphlet—*Plain Truth*—printed in 1747 in both English and German to reach the widest audience. This pamphlet was filled with Old Testament references to the Divine approbation of making a military defense when the need arose. Franklin argued his case from the events of the bible as readily as military proponents argue from the attack on Pearl Harbor or the events of September 11. "May . . . the Lord of the Armies of Israel . . . unite the Hearts and Counsels of all of us, of whatever Sect or Nation, in one . . . generous Publick Spirit."[13]

In the autumn of 1755, the violence that militarists and pacifists alike dreaded took on the form of an unremitting terror of Indian attack. With armed colonists displaying the mutilated bodies of victims on the capital steps and frontier families huddling together in their homes in the face of imminent capture, torture, or death, the assembly finally gave in to Franklin's long-standing proposal for an unpaid volunteer force in the form of the colony's first Militia Act. This became law on November 25, 1755. Two days later, the assembly created a "fund for public safety" made possible by a compromise brokered by Franklin and his assembly colleague and opposition leader, Joseph Galloway. The deal exempted William Penn's sons from taxes on their land in return for their contribution to the defense fund along with the founding of a number of hospitals and the establishment of several philanthropies. The colonists would be taxed only to pay for their share of the cost of replenishing the fund. At the same time, the Quakers imposed on themselves and on those who followed their discipline a stricter standard of pacifism that hardened their positions against paying war-related taxes, raising provisions for provincial troops, and serving in the military.[14]

The 1755 law named Franklin, Morris, Hamilton, and four others to an independent commission in charge of public safety, and the members of the assembly salved the consciences of their pacifist constituents by emphasizing the public safety and philanthropic aspects of the deal. Franklin thought it a great accomplishment, nonetheless, to get even a grudging approval for the establishment of a string of frontier refuge forts from the assembly.

Governor Morris, with the cooperation or acquiescence of the other commissioners, used the money appropriated for public safety not only to initiate a military building program but also to quickly replace the proposed volunteer militia with paid regularly enlisted provincial troops. This duplicity angered the Quakers. A law passed during the subsequent year (1756) subjected the commonwealth's troops to British-style military discipline, and in the next year another law made militia service compulsory for all male residents of the colony between sixteen and sixty years of age. The last requirement wrecked havoc among the antiwar pacifists in the colony who generally resisted efforts to force them to serve.

Meanwhile, Franklin undertook the direction of establishing the lightly stockaded refuge forts—about fifteen miles apart with a wall of saplings and planks built around one or more log blockhouses or fortified homes along the low lying hills known as the Blue Mountains between the Susquehanna and Delaware River frontiers. These would serve as temporary shelters for settlers under threat of attack. At this time, the Blue Mountains marked the natural geographic limit of white settlement, and "it was along this range that the storm burst in all its fury."[15] The forts were strategically placed on the prominent trails through the mountain gaps chiefly on the south side of the mountains. But depending on the needs and disposition of the local settlements, the forts sometimes repeated on the north. Chief among these were Fort Harris (Harrisburg) and Fort Hamilton (Stroudsburg) that anchored the ends of the Blue Mountain defense line. In addition to these were the series of strong houses and minor forts that stretched along the Delaware River from the Water Gap to the New York border.

During January 1756, Franklin personally directed the construction of Fort Allen (at present-day Allenton, Pennsylvania) and inspected Fort Hamilton at Stroudsburg that spring. "This kind of fort," Franklin declared, "is a sufficient defense against Indians, who have no cannon."[16] The militia could patrol in the gaps between the forts to discourage incursions. Nonetheless, the enemy could, and did, slip through the cordon in small groups, but it was hoped that the presence of troops who could cut off their withdrawal would prevent large groups from penetrating too deeply into the settlements. The soldiers who garrisoned the forts were provincial troops, which almost without exception were detailed from the 1st Battalion of the Pennsylvania Regiment under the command of Lt. Col. Conrad Weiser, the colonial Indian agent. Between thirty and sixty soldiers were commonly deployed at a major post, but they often numbered as few as six men at some of the lesser forts.[17]

Consequently, ordinary people took to "forting up" in houses, taverns, and churches, rebuilding or building strong-points and stockades for themselves and their neighbors with newly cut gun slits, boarded over windows, and heaps of arms and ammunition. Unfortunately, these generally insecure and undermanned refuges could serve like "honeypots" for attackers providing tempting targets of small groups of country people who, being untrained at arms, could be killed or captured by as few as a half dozen warriors. A single householder had little chance of making a defense alone, but these makeshift strong-points almost always did as badly when holding off a determined attack, and they provided the enemy with arms and munitions when they fell. Nonetheless, fear proved a community adhesive, and many settlers flocked to them because "all their neighbors were going and they would not stay alone."[18]

Throughout the following year, only a small number of settlers were killed or captured, usually lone farmers in their fields or women and children traveling between settlements. The corpses of victims—often mutilated and scalped—were sometimes dragged to the center of a road or byway or propped in a tree in grotesque postures and set as "tableaus of devastation" so that the enemy might announce his presence and increase the terror of the inhabitants. More often, the first indication of trouble might be an abandoned cart on the road, slaughtered livestock, or a sudden scarcity or movement of forest game. Franklin noted, "[T]he Indians . . . lurk about for opportunities of attacking single houses, and small weak neighborhoods. . . . We have now 1500 men on the frontier, and yet people are sometimes scalped between fort and fort, and very near the forts themselves."[19]

Ironically, the forts and strong-houses often added to the frustration of the people, making the refugees inside feel not so much sheltered as surrounded and hemmed in by faceless enemies who never materialized. These circumstances left the frontier communities with much to fear but no one to fight. Unfortunately, large numbers of neutral and British-allied Indians could be found close to the forts, trading posts, and towns innocently negotiating deals for their furs and venison. Many Native American nations tried to maintain neutrality in the white man's war (that is, France versus Britain), but the frontier inhabitants exhibited a peculiar disability for determining who among the Native population were enemies and who were simply trying to remain neutral. Throughout the war, many Native Americans attempted to cling to a neutrality that would cost them dearly. The frustration of hearing of reported attacks by Indians, who rarely were ever identified with any specificity, made many whites decide that it was simply impossible to discern Native friend from Native foe and to abandon any attempt to draw distinctions among their Native American neighbors. Consequently, groundless anxieties and unfounded rumors caused some frontier settlers to kill Native Americans without cause simply because they were passing through a region under alarm (an early form of racial profiling).

Quaker Diplomacy

Although no major attacks composed of hundreds of warriors were made on the Pennsylvania frontier settlements during the French and Indian War (as they would during Pontiac's Rebellion and the Revolution), pacifist elements in the colonial assembly pointed to the continued series of atrocities perpetrated by small bands as proof that the military steps forced on the assembly by the committee of public safety were ineffective or unnecessary. They noted correctly that Quaker diplomacy and their policy of friendship toward the Native Americans had kept the Pennsylvania frontier generally peaceful for more than seventy-five years since the days of King Philip's War in New England (1675) and Bacon's Rebellion in Virginia

(1676). Any minor disruptions since that time could be attributed to the overly aggressive policies of neighboring governments in Virginia, Maryland, or New York, all of whom then had competing claims on lands in present-day Pennsylvania. The pacifists pointed to "the Emotion and unreasonable Panick, which [had] lately possessed great Numbers of the People [through] Ignorance and Fear" as the true source of the present breakdown in relations with the Indians.[20]

In fact, diplomatic overtures to the Native nations, begun by Quaker agents in the Ohio country, set in motion a series of diplomatic exchanges and negotiations that ended in a durable peace with the Delaware and Shawnee nations signed in Easton, Pennsylvania, in 1758. Nonetheless, these treaty meetings proved to be chaotic events where feasting and drinking exposed some of the Native representatives as drunken and out of control. Government officials feared that the Quakers would "tamper" with the Indians, thus making businesslike negotiations with the tribes into public ordeals full of humiliating Native demands sparked by Quaker interference. Previous peace treaties—and hundreds of agreements had been negotiated with the tribes—had proved inconclusive and uncertain with regard to the behavior of the supposedly aligned and neutral tribes who seemingly needed an endless series of diplomatic efforts and bribes to keep them on the Anglo-colonial side.

The loosely supervised crowds of white onlookers often did all they could to derail the peace process. They called out insults and threats directed at the Native American diplomats, Quakers, and anyone willing to treat with them as legitimate negotiators. "Might we not," wrote one peace opponent, "before we have intelligence of a Peace being concluded, send a party from this garrison . . . and cut them off [kill them] . . . preventing the ratification of a Peace, from its nature, odious to almost every man?"[21] So serious were the threats to the lives of the peace delegates that several such conferences were forced to relocate to neighborhoods that seemed "safe." Native American diplomats were urged to avoid passing through places where threats had been made against them and to gather for safety at the Moravian settlement in Bethlehem while waiting for the peace conferences to begin in Easton.

The rhetoric appearing in colonial newspapers and in the anecdotal accounts of these meetings seldom included a straightforward indictment of the Indians or of the sometimes lethargic government ministers. Moreover, critics of the peace process excluded from the ranks of "white people" all Quakers and antiwar groups because of their supposed spineless pacifist attitudes. Meanwhile, a virtual army of armchair hardliners, who could indulge vicariously in anti-Indian hatred from the safety of their city dwellings, was growing. These shared the sharp partisanship of the frontier settlers without having experienced the actual terror of Native warfare, and they became pivotal in forming the character of anti-Quaker sentiment throughout the region.

High emotions and growing anti-Indian sentiment led provincial observers, editors, and journalists to sweep away any attempt to discover the causes of Native American unrest. Pacifists believed that someone in power must have been at fault for the Indian outbursts to have taken place, but they also found that mutilated corpses and tales of scalping, capture, and torture were simply unanswerable in such a highly charged environment. The paper war among anti-Indian forces, Quakers, and other politicians in the assembly (who backed the wartime powers of the proprietary governors) would continue for more than a decade.

William Smith, a college provost and political writer, produced an antipacifist (anti-Quaker) pamphlet that painted the attempt of the Friendly Association to learn the causes of Native American dissatisfaction and belligerence as blatantly ridiculous and possibly even malicious and disloyal. Franklin had chosen Smith provost of the College of Philadelphia in 1753, and Smith had set many of the distinctive features of the antipacifist sentiment that appeared in print. The attraction of this propaganda rested largely in the immediacy with which it surfaced after the report of a frontier attack. In an age during which the concept of a "twenty-four-hour news cycle" was unimaginable, Smith was able to have speeches recorded in the newspapers, printed in pamphlets, and made available to the public before the inflammatory effects of the attacks had cooled. His unbridled rhetoric was a tool used to unleash overpowering sympathies for those unfortunate whites who were victims of Indian warfare and to trigger a political reaction against the Quakers' political machinations, the Moravian missionaries, and the colony's few Roman Catholics. Acts that Quakers and Moravians saw as open, unbigoted, and filled with Christian kindness toward Native Americans were decried as collusion with killers, rapists, and kidnappers. Anti-Catholic rhetoric was not isolated to Pennsylvania, and the black-robed Jesuit missionaries living among the tribes generally were held suspect everywhere with regard to inciting the French-allied Indians to war on the English.

Writers produced themes, pamphlets, verses, and plays based on the fundamental concepts of dehumanizing and demonizing the Indians, and many cartoons—including some by Franklin—attacked the so-called flat-hat Quaker party and their German-speaking sectarian allies for coddling the enemy as the life-blood of their victims flowed into the rich Pennsylvania soil and turned its streams and creeks red. According to their detractors, Quaker-dictated toleration of non-English and Native American cultures had left the colony prey to foreign agents and savage invaders, respectively. Many of these writers saw themselves as the guardians of Anglo-American liberty and security, and they hoped to reshape the politics of the colony through the weight of a frightened public eager to see something definite done against the Indian attackers and their pacifist supporters.

Among the stratagem employed in these pieces, the frontier dead were given lines to speak describing how they had been abused by their tormentors, mocked by missionaries, and abandoned by the Indian pacifist abettors. Quakers were shown as kneeling at the throne of Satan, and their policies were termed demonic. One anti-Quaker poet noted:

Go on good Christians never spare
To give your Indians clothes to wear:
Send 'em good beef, and pork, and bread,
Guns, powder, flints and store of lead,
To shoot your neighbors through the head.[22]

Many Quakers were hounded out of government in Pennsylvania by the mastery of their political opponents' rhetoric of war—yelling negligence and insensibility in print and filling the minds of the people with indignation and resentment against anyone who would negotiate with Indians. Each time the Quakers tried to defend themselves against charges of guilt by association, they seemed to sink ever deeper into the morass of antipacifist sentiment, and all their efforts to bring about peace with the tribes through negotiations and diplomacy were increasingly presented as acts of treachery. The picture of Native Americans being cared for by "a particular set of men [Quakers], deeply concerned in the government . . . holding treaties from time to time with Indians, without prospect of advantage to the province" exasperated the minds of many colonials.[23] The gruesome images of Indian massacre, mutilation, and scalping were so strongly presented as the fault of Quaker intervention that even an arch-pacifist like Israel Pemberton, Jr., head of the Friendly Association, had to recognize the innate evil of Native American actions publicly so that denunciation of the Indians did not turn to open persecution of Quakers.

Nonetheless, the colonies soon seethed with anti-Quaker and antipacifist sentiment, and any who held moderate positions concerning relations with the Native Americans were placed under suspicion. Grief and fear were quickly turned into political demands for greater executive authority, the establishment of standing forces, and the extension of the war against the Indians. The attacks made possible a politics of opposition to everything and everyone who could be brought under suspicion. A column of French infantry entering Philadelphia unopposed could not have caused a more virulent reaction. Even the colonial Indian agent Conrad Weiser, conspicuous as a government go-between with the Indians, was called a traitor and betrayer, and threatened with death because he had attempted to deal with the Native Americans in a diplomatic fashion.[24]

In fact, the diplomatic process that had led to peace with the Delaware and Shawnee had been greatly aided by the appearance of Gen. James Forbes, with a force of 5,000 provincial soldiers and 1,500 Scots Highlander regulars, moving across Pennsylvania toward the valley of the Ohio. The establishment of Fort Pitt at the forks of the Ohio with a series of fortified and well-garrisoned posts on a new military road stretching east-west across the colony caused the Shawnee, the Delaware, and many lesser Native nations to virtually abandon their alliances with the French. This in turn forced the French to withdraw.

In 1759, the French and their remaining allies among the Algonquian nations of the Great Lakes region suffered a number of defeats at the hands of the British regulars, the provincial forces (under Sir William Johnson), and the British Native allies (primarily the Iroquois). The fall of French outposts at Ticonderoga, Crown Point, Frontenac, Louisburg, Montreal, and Quebec effectively cut out the heart of France's Native American allies. The fall of Niagara at the head of Lake Ontario, in particular, isolated the French-allied Indians residing in the Great Lakes region from weapons, ammunition, and contact with the French government in Canada. By 1763, Britain controlled much of North America east of the Mississippi River and throughout the Great Lakes region into Canada.

Unremitting fear during the French and Indian War had caused a cascade of reverse migration from the farthest outposts of Anglo-American settlement on the frontier to the larger towns and cities in the east, some to the very precincts of Philadelphia. The crush of refugees had found a common cause in blaming Quakers, Moravians, and Catholics for their situation, an agreement that was unprecedented among such a diverse population. The population of cities and towns swelled with unemployed and fearful refugees—English, Welsh, German, and Scotch-Irish—and the sense of intolerance for pacifists made each person feel included in the common bond of pioneers from which their lack of common language or ethnic background had formerly excluded them. In this manner, persons formerly viewed with suspicion came to be seen as neighbors, Pennsylvanians, and fellow Americans because they had withstood the same threats and had identified a common set of enemies— Indians and Quakers.

Moreover, the sudden unsettling of the frontier during the French and Indian War acted like a giant compressed spring of humanity that flew forward suddenly and uncontrollably when peace ended the Native American threat in 1763. Hundreds of new arrivals to America and hundreds more former residents of the backcountry flooded the military roads cut through the forests to the west by the Braddock and Forbes expeditions.

Proclamation of 1763

A large part of the friction between Anglo-colonials and the British Crown can be traced back to the desire of the Americans to expand the boundaries of English settlement to the west. To limit friction between the Native nations and these pioneers, King George III signed the Proclamation of 1763, which prohibited any white settlement west of the Appalachians and which required those already settled there to return to the east immediately. Yet, the line drafted in London between the Native American lands and the new limits of white settlement was so hastily adopted that it took no account of the farmsteads already made, nor of the royal lands granted to certain colonies and land companies in their charters.

In April 1763, the Indian threat reappeared in the form of a multitribal force under the leadership of an Ottawa chief named Pontiac. This uprising against British rule was a final attempt to rid the Native American landscape of white interlopers. The Indians struck at Fort Detroit first. Although the British garrison was able to drive them from the fort and withstand a prolonged siege, the spark set at Detroit set other posts aflame. The British post at Venango—including men, women, and children—was totally wiped out even though the garrison had surrendered. At this point, the revolt collapsed because several western tribes chose to defend the remaining British in the westernmost garrisons or to escort them to safety in Montreal. Although the Ojibwas at Michilimackinac took the British post at the Straits of Mackinaw, they nonetheless denounced Pontiac for the needless cruelties he had allowed elsewhere. The most dedicated among Pontiac's remaining followers thereafter returned to the frontiers where scores of traders and settlers were either killed or taken captive. By autumn, Pennsylvania alone had sustained almost 600 scattered killings. Nonetheless, Pontiac's Rebellion—a genuine pan-tribal uprising of the Native nations—had collapsed from within and faltered. Yet, Pontiac's War was neither the first nor the last effort made by Native Americans to form a confederacy that would prevent whites, and particularly the British, from occupying their lands.

The real problem illustrated by the failure of the Proclamation of 1763 was that, given the reality of the colonial frontier at the time, the gradual elimination of the Native American population was as inevitable in the trans-Appalachian country as it had been on the Atlantic seaboard in the east a century and a half earlier. Many Anglo-Americans had invested both their labor and their scant capital in recently cleared fields, newly planted crops, and recently erected homes, barns, and fences. The potential economic hardship that they faced if they obeyed the proclamation and abandoned these holdings was staggering. British policies that aspired to control the Native Americans were doomed to fail largely because of their inability to control the settlers, some of whom thought it was their God-given right to take the land from the Indians. "On the frontier, the Scotch-Irish were hewing their way through the woods, killing Indians when it suited them, and developing a righteous indignation against the restraining orders which came from the government." Increased regulation "only aggravated the tensions, alienated backcountry settlers and ensured that many of them would throw in their lot with the rebels once the Revolution began."[25]

During the winter of 1763–1764, a sensational series of anti-Indian and anti-Quaker riots broke out backed by a furious population of indignant backcountry settlers. In 1764, Matthew Smith and James Gibson wrote an open letter to Parliament. Called "A Remonstrance from the Pennsylvania Frontier," the letter was published and widely read in the colonies. It stated in part, "It grieves us to the very heart to see such of our frontier inhabitants as have escaped savage fury with the loss of their parents, their children, their wives or relatives, left destitute by the public, and exposed to the most cruel poverty and wretchedness [by the government]."[26]

A group of Native Americans residing on an island in the Delaware River near Trenton, New Jersey—all converts to the Moravian faith—were alarmed by the threats being made against them in the wake of Pontiac's Rebellion. They soon became targets for a protest over public spending on Indian welfare. Groups of white insurgents appeared in Philadelphia numbering in the thousands and quickly spinning out of control and milling about without purpose. Companies of frontier volunteers were galloping and trumpeting their way through the city. Sometimes these undisciplined groups would shoot at one another in their excitement. So violent were the volunteers that the Quakers feared for the lives of the Moravian converts. A definitive report from Lancaster told of 1500 to 5000 men gathering in the surrounding townships to kill the Moravian Indians, and in a rising panic the assembly promulgated the Riot Act.

Consequently, about 200 Quakers of the Philadelphia Monthly Meeting appeared in public armed with guns ostensibly to take charge of the Moravian Indians in the city and conduct them to safety outside the colony of Pennsylvania. Whole troops of young boys followed the armed Quakers through the street amazed at the sight of pacifists carrying firearms. Since both the governors of New York and New Jersey rejected the idea that the Moravians find refuge in their colonies, the Native Americans were quietly moved into abandoned military barracks in Philadelphia where they were cared for under government expense. The marchers evaporated with the winter snows and pitiless rains of February, and the immediate crisis ended. The Moravian Indians remained in the barracks receiving food and supplies from the government for more than a year.[27]

A "disquietude" concerning the government support of the Moravian Indians remained however, and the Quakers and Israel Pemberton, in particular, were singled out as targets for public enmity everywhere in the colony that they had once controlled. Quakers were attacked rhetorically as if they were carriers of the plague. "Who shall gather up the blood that has been spilt upon our borders," wrote William Smith, "Quakers . . . are the bloodiest people in our land; and the blood of those murdered through their default, cries to heaven against them."[28]

Colonial confidence in British government was severely shaken by the events of the Native American rebellion in 1764. The effectiveness of the Indian attacks had humiliated the British regulars and embarrassed the bureaucracy in London. Anglo-Americans soon began to realize that their own best interests were not always those espoused by the Crown. James Otis, soon to voice independence from the Crown and writing from the perspective of the colonials, noted, "The late acquisitions [from the French] in America, as glorious as they have been, and as beneficial as they are to Great Britain, are only a security to these colonies against the ravages of the French and Indians. Our trade upon the whole is not, I believe, benefited by them one groat."[29]

Rules of War

One of the unique characteristics of Native American warfare that whites dwelled on was its lack of "proper violence." The Indians seemed to act in a savage, barbarous, and excessively cruel manner contrary to the accepted rules of European warfare, which were considered systematic, controlled, and honorable. A great many gruesome things were allowed under the accepted rules of European war, but the destruction of property, burning of crops, or even the means of taking the life of legitimate combatants were of little concern. It was considered legitimate to shoot, hack, stab, explode, or burn the enemy to death in formal battle. But the cruel process of torturing prisoners, the waging of war against those who would not fight like the frontier pacifists, or those who could not resist like women, children, babes in arms, and the aged as practiced by the Indians was prohibited by accepted European standards. For these reasons, the Indian nations were often regarded as the 18th-century equivalent of war criminals and terrorists marking them as inappropriate or illegitimate partners in the diplomacy of peace. In this manner the nature of Native American warfare—traditional in its manner and culturally acceptable to them—was often counterproductive and incapable of producing a fair and reasonable peace settlement with whites. The attitude of Anglo-Americans in this regard was generally dismissive of any of the legitimate differences in traditional or cultural method of waging war, and a similar attitude can be identified in American dealings with indigenous cultures throughout a number of historical conflicts.

The Quaker Peace Medal

Throughout the French and Indian War, the British government issued peace medals to the various chiefs of its allied tribes. These medals had the image of George II on the front and a scene of a white man and an Indian in peaceful conference beneath a tree on the back with the dictum "Let us look to the most high who blessed our fathers with peace."[30] During the American Revolution, and for some time thereafter, the United States copied the British medals exactly in silver, bronze, and pewter for distribution among the tribes of western Pennsylvania. The engraver Edward Duffield included the 1757 date and the likeness of George II to symbolize the continuity of Anglo-American relationships with the Indians. Called Quaker Peace Medals, they were among the first items struck by the U.S. Mint, and they continued to be distributed among Native American tribes until the dies failed in 1878.

Divided Loyalties: 1775

The British won a great worldwide empire in the French and Indian War (Seven Years' War in Europe), but their grip on much of North America was a tenuous one. The accumulated effects of almost a century of colonial neglect, widespread prejudice against the Indians, and a growing hatred of British regulars would cause the Anglo-American colonists to attempt to sever their ties with Britain in 1775. Political independence would require some Americans to acquire new modes of thinking not only about the structure of their government but also about their national and personal identity. Many believed that their future ties with Europe should be restricted to commercial ones, and through their experience as members of the British Empire, they had embraced the idea of freedom of trade. They wished to replace the corrupt and oppressive features of mercantilism and the restrictive politics of power with free trade, harmony among nations, and a more peaceful world. Others saw revolution as an opportunity to expand domestic borders into Canada and some of the lands they recently had helped to take from France. Once mighty, Spain was a feeble shadow of itself hardly capable of making a vigorous defense of its North American holdings in Mexico, Florida, and Louisiana.[31]

In 1774, as the revolutionary crisis approached, John Adams wrote to a friend saying that about one-third of Anglo-Americans were loyal to the British Crown, one-third in favor of the cause of independence, and one-third undecided or too "timid" to take a stance. The characterization of timidity made by Adams was patently unfair. Most Anglo-Americans were deeply conscious of their British roots. Some, like the radicals who pursued independence, were anxious to remove the "Anglo" from their Anglo-American identity. Many more simply could not countenance the traumatic loss of any part of their British being and were willing to take up arms as Loyalists.[32] Others—including many political moderates and pacifists—were uneasy about giving up their traditional roots. For many submission to a traditional authority, restrained by British law and custom, seemed preferable to submission to a new and untested American authority supported by violence and underwritten by foreign agents and recent former enemies like France and Spain. It was this middle group—caught between the fire of zealots on both extremes—that suffered most for their antiwar sentiments.

In New England, the Revolution was a vastly popular movement springing from the rocky soil of Massachusetts with ideas of independency taking root among the populace from the first. Timothy Ruggles, a Loyalist known for his service in the militia in the French wars of the 1750s, sought to promote a Loyalist Association as a counter to the Continental Association of the radicals, but he had little success in attracting allies to his position and had to flee to the British army in Boston to avoid the furor of the radical mobs. In Connecticut, the only colony for which anything like an exact estimate of the resistance to the Revolution has been made, hard-core Loyalists (those willing to actively take up arms for the Crown) made up as little as 6 percent of the population. By 1776, what remained of Loyalism in New England had been driven underground, but a significant portion of the moderates were unwilling to fight for independence and tried to remain aloof from the conflict.

Many outside the group of revolutionary radicals in New England complained that the Crown had allowed the colonies to drift into "the lowest and most imperfect of all political systems, a tumultuous, seditious, and inert democracy" during the previous decades simply to garner colonial support and manpower against the French and their Native American allies. A majority of these radicals felt that the present crisis was a product of British liberality and colonial irresponsibility. "The whole has been guided by deception," wrote one moderate American. Another wrote that the Revolution was built on "the natural human love of liberty" and on the readiness of the people to be led to war by "ambitious, mad, or fractious men."[33]

Historians have fixed upon Adams's tripartite estimate of support for the Revolution as evidence that it was a minority movement, and that a majority of the residents of British America outside New England either attempted to stand aloof from the rebellion or actively resisted it. As such, this majority—although fragmented and largely undirected—represents the first antiwar movement in U.S. history and shares many of the characteristics and sentiments of later war resistance groups. "Rouse, America!" a Patriot newspaper editor warned against such persons, "Your danger is great—great from a quarter where you least expect it. [They] . . . will yet be the ruin of you! 'Tis high time they were separated from among you. They are now just engaged in undermining your liberties."[34]

Men of property generally resisted the radicals everywhere. In parts of Maryland, Loyalists clearly outnumbered radicals, and the Chesapeake peninsula had the highest proportion of active Loyalists in the colonies. White Loyalists in the South were in constant fear of slave insurrections and Indian attacks, and those from the back country of Georgia and North and South Carolina were highly disaffected from the Revolution because of the isolation of their holdings from the support of other whites. Those who were active in the Loyalist Party and willing to take up arms to fight for Britain, however, were limited to just a few marauding bands. New Jersey residents, led by their "tenacious champion" Gov. William Franklin (son of Benjamin Franklin), generally resisted the Revolution, preferring neutrality to insurrection in greater proportion than the total populations of any other colony except New York and Georgia. William Franklin proved himself an unbending proponent of negotiation and conciliation stiffly holding his ground even after being arrested and confined by the New Jersey Provincial Congress. Quakers and the members of many religious groups dedicated to nonviolence throughout the Middle Colonies recommended nonparticipation in all measures concerning the rebellion as an indispensable duty. "It is not our business to set up governments," a session of the Philadelphia Friends Meeting of 1775 decided, "much less to plot and contrive the ruin or overturn of any of them."[35]

The radical revolutionaries and hard-core Loyalists had a simplicity of purpose that gave each group a level of cohesion and direction. The moderates, pacifists, and neutrals of the revolutionary period, however, followed a thousand individual and personal principles of behavior that often gave way like a foundation built on sand. Even those who tolerated the war thought of it as a means to reconciliation with Britain rather than a path to complete independence. In trying to stand uncommitted in an oppressive political environment, many colonial moderates shifted positions between radical and Loyalist sentiments depending on who was asking. Many of these recantations were forced, and the pressure on moderates and pacifists to conform to the wishes of their tormentors was great. The British authorities, for their part, considered almost all Anglo-colonials suspect in their loyalty, thereby making the situation far worse for most undecided Americans than it needed to be.

The situation that Adams described, however, should not be surprising. In 1774, most of the residents of the Atlantic-facing colonies between Florida and Newfoundland were British subjects endowed with the traditional rights of Englishmen, and both those loyal to the king and those determined to be independent of him considered themselves to be "patriotic Americans." Both groups, those in rebellion and those actively loyal to the government, were decidedly American in their character, patriotic with regard to their country, and loyal, in their own way, to their core beliefs. Historians need to be mindful when differentiating between these two groups not to strip the so-called *Loyalist* population of the colonies of their genuine patriotism by pitting them grammatically against those so-called *Patriots* who had rebelled against their lawful monarch. Nor should the final so-called timid third of Adams's tripartite analysis be ignored. These were often moderates in their political leanings or persons trying to maintain precarious neutrality between two parties warring over ideology. The hard-core Loyalists, in one way or another, may have been more afraid of the independent America envisioned by the radicals than they were of a repressive Britain. The great mass of passive citizens had no such clear point of view, hoping perhaps that one side or the other would quickly dominate and end the disturbance, but mostly wanting to be left to live their lives as they always had.

Indeed, for the great majority of Anglo-Americans, loyalty to the king, Parliament, and the traditions of British colonial government was the "normal condition" of political life. Some historians believe that the so-called Patriot Party in America aspired to make changes in this social order and attempted to convert these otherwise loyal or neutral Anglo-American citizens into revolutionaries. However, the principles expounded by the rebels were not really novel, and commitment to local governance rather than imperial authority was not at all unusual. It had been practiced in most colonies since their inception. The concepts of individual and property rights, representative government, and the rule of law were deeply rooted in the old traditions of English constitutional law: the Magna Carta, the Grand Remonstrance, the Declaration of the Rights of Englishmen, and the political philosophies of 17th-century writers like Thomas Hobbs, John Milton, and John Locke. The Loyalists were supporting the recent changes in government instituted by the king and his ministers that actually changed the traditional status quo. The leaders of the rebellion in America would have considered themselves conservative in their political philosophies, but they were radical in the sense that they were willing to take up arms against the British Empire to reaffirm these philosophies.

John Dickinson was foremost among the moderate leaders in Congress in holding out the hope of reconciliation with Britain. He was convinced that mediation and negotiation might return nominal sovereignty to the Crown while reestablishing the autonomy of the prerevolutionary provincial governments under the benignly negligent oversight of Parliament. In this way, Britain and America could restore the harmony that had once existed between them without losing face. Radicals, like John Adams, were dedicated to independence by any means, but they were busy from the first in preparing for a war not for a negotiation. "This negotiation I dread like death," Adams admitted during the discussion of Dickinson's proposals for opening negotiations with the British in July 1775. "What is the reason, Mr. Adams, that you New England-men oppose our measures of reconciliation?" responded Dickinson. "If you don't concur with us in our pacific system, I and a number of us [in Congress] will break off from you in New England, and we will carry on the opposition by ourselves in our own way."[36] Adams understood that he and the supporters of independency were then in the minority. Those convinced of the need for independence, like Adams, would not admit that the original resistance to British taxation had changed in character, and they allowed the idea of negotiation to be submitted, hoping all along that that idea would be rejected by a stubborn and inflexible Parliament.

Whigs and Tories

The Tory Party in Britain, with which the Loyalists in America were commonly identified, was founded in large measure on "the aristocracy of culture, of dignified professions, of official rank and hereditary wealth."[37] The Whig Party opposed the Tories in Britain. The name Whig was probably derived from Whiggamore, a derogatory term first applied to the Covenanters of 17th-century Scotland, who were supporters of Presbyterianism. The Whigs were backed in Britain by the growing mercantile and industrial interests, the landed but untitled gentry, and the Protestant nonconformists (Presbyterians, Congregationalists, and others outside the Anglican church). Consider for a moment a Whig (in the widest sense of the word) named Thomas Johnson who was a moderate delegate to Congress from Maryland. He hoped to preserve both the British Empire and the traditional constitutional liberties of the American people through a dependence on the same "whiggish principles" that were handed down to him by his ancestors.[38] American revolutionaries rarely referred to themselves as Whigs—U.S. politicians taking up the name only in the 19th century—but historians favor the term in place of unrepresentative and misleading terms for revolutionaries such as *patriots*, *rebels*, or simply *Americans*.

The true Whig moderates in the American Revolution were generally leaders of the revolutionary cause from outside New England—and especially from outside Massachusetts—who regarded war with Britain as a means of forcing acknowledgment of the colonies' legislative autonomy rather than as a path to absolute independence. Many of these men thought that conciliation on colonial terms could better be achieved through warfare than through repeated unproductive negotiations. For some radicals, the outbreak of active warfare made negotiations impossible and reconciliation improbable. For others there was a different paradigm. "Let us beat them into compliance," one man wrote, "they will be glad to receive us on those terms, rather than lose us altogether." Many moderates sought only two goals from the war: the reestablishment of American liberties and a reunion with Britain. Among the important moderate leaders who were dedicated to colonial autonomy rather than outright independence, were the brothers Edward and John Rutledge of South Carolina, Joseph Hewes and William Hooper of North Carolina, Benjamin Harrison and Edmund Pendleton of Virginia, Thomas Johnson and Samuel Chase of Maryland, John Dickinson and James Wilson in Pennsylvania, and John Jay and James Duane of New York.[39]

Although those who resisted the colonial cause in America were often called by the name *Tory*, the Tories in Britain had only briefly controlled Parliament under Prime Minister John Stuart, Earl Bute in 1762–1763. The Whig Party generally opposed them. Nevertheless, party politics in the British Empire was no simple two-party dichotomy. The more politically successful and organized Whig Party in Britain suffered from a severe ideological split between its conservative and liberal branches. The ministers of government with whom the colonies had their greatest disputes over taxation—George Grenville and Charles Townshend, for instance—were not members of the Tory Party, but rather conservatives of the Whig Party in coalition with them. Townshend had been a great favorite of Bute, and Grenville served as the Leader of the House of Commons under the Tory administration. Frederick Lord North, prime minister throughout the war years (1770–1782), had begun his political career under the Newcastle-Pitt coalition. Nonetheless, influential Tories had gravitated around North to form a government and were able thereby to influence the course of colonial policy.

Many American Tories never became overt Loyalists, and others came late to Loyalism. Although most of the late Loyalists came from Pennsylvania, moderates in all the colonies outside New England—where overt Loyalism had been all but extinguished—were having second thoughts concerning the Revolution and were working toward reconciliation. The cynics believed that all their battles ultimately aimed at peace. For the majority of uncommitted Americans, neutrality rather than Loyalism was the characteristic refuge. Many chose to become careful neutrals hopefully waiting for one side or the other to collapse and thereby relieve their dilemma.

The Mob

Before 1764 American colonists generally had accepted the doctrine that Parliament could pass acts regulating trade and imposing duties on imports. They had merely nullified any act that proved too irritating by smuggling, by producing enumerated goods clandestinely, or by simply ignoring the law. After 1764, the voice of a new, more radical group of politically active colonials was raised above the normal background of discontent common to the middle classes. These radicals proposed for the first time the idea that only the colonial legislatures could tax Americans because they were not properly represented in Parliament. Clandestine political grumblings quickly became open confrontations with calls for liberty and the rights of Englishmen permeating the air during the Stamp Act crisis of 1765.

Conservative voices among the loyal population claimed that radicals like John Hancock and Samuel Adams of Boston could instigate a street demonstration in a matter of minutes over any perceived slight to America. Adams was actually accused of having hundreds of protestors in his employ, a charge that was clearly untrue taking Adams's shabby clothing and obvious lack of finances into account. Hancock dressed well, but he was £100,000 in debt to the British revenue service and hardly able to finance a mass demonstration. The people of the colonial waterfront took an increasingly active roll in these public disorders because of their frustration over the enforcement of the Navigation Acts, the Townshend duties, and the Tea tax—many of which affected the way they went about their daily livelihoods.[40] The natural rowdiness of the waterfront denizens ranged from mere mischief such as tavern brawls to sometimes bruising battles between large groups of men known as Liberty Boys, or more generally by their detractors as the mob. Flowing rum, loose women, and pent-up frustrations from being confined aboard ship for long periods made seamen prime candidates for inclusion in any public demonstration.

Repeatedly, resistance to British officials and the enforcement of customs regulations included the type of crowd action that commonly appeared on the waterfront. Sometimes the participants thought in terms of the theoretical concept of political "Liberty;" sometimes they acted in terms of their personal freedom to do as they wished; most times several ideas about liberty were swirling around in their heads simultaneously. "Whatever definitions of liberty appeared on the waterfront, the maritime world's understanding of liberty helped to shape the struggle for American independence."[41] Any effort to restrict trade or limit smuggling threatened the livelihood of a whole segment of the waterfront population, and maritime workers of all types provided the mobs for the earliest calls for liberty in America. It is not surprising, therefore, that the centers of the American revolutionary movement should be found in northern port cities such as Newport, Providence, and Boston.

The Boston Tea Party (December 1773) brought the full weight of British frustration down upon the city of Boston in the form of the Boston Port Act of 1774, which closed the port to commerce. From town meetings and provincial congresses throughout America came words of support for the Bostonians. Among those who exhibited a common cause with them were the people who made their living from the sea. Fishermen, mariners, shippers, shipbuilders, and ship chandlers quickly recognized that their livelihoods could be cut off just as easily in Newburyport, Portsmouth, or Providence as they were in Boston. Those who made their living afloat in Philadelphia, New York, Baltimore, or Charleston could just as quickly be barred from the sea as those in New England. The "Child Independence" may have been born during the Stamp Act Crisis, as John Adams once proposed, but it was drawn forth from the coastal waters of North America in 1775 just as surely as Moses was taken from a floating basket in the Nile in Biblical times.[42]

Supporting the Tory political position in America were many of the most substantial businessmen, the richest landowners, the clergy of the established church, and the legally appointed officers of the British Empire. American Tories were just as indignant as other Americans at what seemed an unjust, arbitrary, and unconstitutional exercise of British authority, but they were repulsed by both the violence of the protest and the overwhelming numbers of lower-class persons, subsistence farmers, laborers, mechanics, tradesmen, religious dissenters, servants, apprentices, adolescents, and blacks that composed the mob. The Tories in America were simply unable to cultivate a positive public opinion for the government from among the moderates in the population. "They [the Tories] were, in fact, afraid of public opinion, afraid of men gathered together, even symbolically, in large numbers."[43] They had beliefs, values, and interests that they were afraid to submit to the rest of the population for approval, choosing instead to be labeled enemies of America.

American Loyalists exhibited the natural conservatism of prosperous and comfortable members of a society trying to maintain the stability and dominance of an imperial system that had proved the foundation of their own power and wealth.[44] In 1767, the British House of Commons reached out to the less prominent Anglo-colonials through the promise of a series of "distinguishing rewards and marks of national favor and approbation" to those who might distinguish themselves by "their zeal and fidelity" to the Crown during the ongoing "tumults and insurrections" against the authority and rights of Parliament.[45] Yet Tory moderates did not generally organize themselves into committees of opposition or try to compete as propagandists with the radicals. In fact, they often failed to consult among themselves except in the most accidental and informal manner as in private letters or through third parties. Important moderates like Joseph Galloway of Philadelphia and Lt. Gov. Thomas Hutchinson of Massachusetts did not even know each other.[46]

Thomas Hutchinson

In the late 1760s and early 1770s, Thomas Hutchinson was one of the most influential of Tory office holders, and he had been respected and admired by many future revolutionary leaders including John Adams. His rationality, sobriety, moderation, and status as lieutenant governor of Massachusetts underlined his natural position as a Tory leader, but these same characteristics left him ill equipped to lead an active opposition to the revolution. Unlike more aggressive Crown officials like William Tryon, governor of New York during the peak of the insurrection, Hutchinson's resistance to radicalism was "passive, instinctive, and narrowly defensive."[47] Faced with radical protests in Boston, he tended to dismiss the upheavals as simply misguided and acted with an unseemly detachment toward the protestors rather than with a forceful purpose in dealing with them. His own house was attacked and burned by the mob, but he continued to hope for the eventual return of tranquility once his countrymen had been convinced that the Crown would exercise its powers prudently in the future. Hutchinson insisted that the destiny of the colonies be left in the hands of those of his own class and moderate sentiment, but he failed to marshal these into a counter-revolutionary movement. In June 1774, he left New England for London with the kind regards of the conservative merchants and moderate gentlemen of Boston, but marked as a traitor by the mob.

Timothy Ruggles

Gen. Timothy Ruggles was a popular military figure from the colonial wars with France, and might have displaced George Washington as commander-in-chief of the American army had he believed that armed warfare against Britain would resolve America's disputes with the mother country. Ruggles, initially a moderate with regard to the disputes with the Crown, was made a delegate from Massachusetts to the first colonial (or Stamp Act) congress of 1765, which met in New York. Being highly respected by the other delegates, he was elected its president, but he refused to sanction the addresses sent by that body to Great Britain. For this the general court of Massachusetts publicly censured him. He claimed at the time to be led by a sense of duty to declare against rebellion and bloodshed. In August 1774, Ruggles was appointed mandamus councilor (the direct representative of the Crown) for Massachusetts. In March 1776, he left Boston for Nova Scotia with the British troops and accompanied Lord Howe to Staten Island where he formed a Loyalist battalion. The Continental Congress confiscated his estates, and in 1779 he received as a reimbursement a grant of 10,000 acres of land from the Crown in Wilmot, Nova Scotia, where he engaged in agriculture until his death.

William Tryon

One historian has called William Tryon "the evil genius of the royal cause in America" because of his many successes in prosecuting the Loyalist raids on Patriot strongholds. Once the governor of North Carolina, Tryon was assigned the task of governing New York just in time to face the beginnings of the insurrection. He stood out as the most principled political architect of Loyalist resistance to the Revolution as well as one of its most aggressive military leaders, especially in New

York and Connecticut. Tryon operated with a force composed of more than 2,000 Loyalist militiamen encamped on Long Island near Flushing, Queens. He organized a stronghold on the north shore near Glen Cove and from there launched amphibious raids across the Long Island Sound into Connecticut.[48]

In April 1777, the Loyalists in brick red or dark green uniforms, commanded by William Tryon, crossed Long Island Sound and landed unopposed at Compo Beach near Westport, Connecticut. They marched inland to raid the towns of Bethel, Ridgefield, and Danbury. The American supply depot at Danbury was burned with a great loss of valuable blankets, preserved meat, and flour. While trying to impede the British return to their ships, Continental general David Wooster was killed, and Col. Benedict Arnold assumed command of the local troops. The British retreat was accomplished only with considerable loss of life, and Arnold rose to national prominence for the first time.

The 1777 raid was followed in July 1779 by a larger affair employing more than eighteen warships and 2,000 Loyalist soldiers. This time Tyron targeted the towns of East Haven, New Haven, West Haven, Fairfield, and Norwalk. The landing at Calf Pasture Beach in Norwalk was the largest amphibious operation mounted by Loyalist forces during the entire Revolutionary War. Described in British records as a nest of privateers, Norwalk, with its protective archipelago of small sandy islands and shallow waters, had served as an American vice-admiralty court for small prizes taken on the Sound. This fact has almost escaped historians because all the court records were burned during the 1779 raid along with eighty-eight homes, dozens of barns, and a church.

Men of Cooler Temper

Possibly due to the natural reticence that sometimes accompanies security and social prominence, many Americans did not come forward to be heard until after the Revolution touched them personally, depriving them of their property or dislocating them from their homes and families. In this way, those who took a moderate stance were often worse off than either the revolutionaries or those dedicated to maintaining the power of the Crown. James Rivington, a pro-British newspaper editor from New York noted that the moderates among the Tory Party in America had been "unfairly censured" for not having exerted themselves in the earliest days of the troubles between the colonies and Parliament. They had quickly been labeled with the pejorative term, Loyalist for not showing an immediate zeal for revolution. The truth of the case according to Rivington was that the average American detested the violence around them but feared to speak out "lest [the storm] should burst on their own heads."[49]

In 1774, the Sons of Liberty (Liberty Boys), led by radicals Isaac Sears and Alexander McDougall, were seemingly turning the struggle over taxation and political rights into a struggle between social classes. More sober conservatives and moderates among the residents in New York, anxious lest the mob in the city turn protest into anarchy, formed a Committee of Fifty-One carefully and judiciously salted with a slim majority of dependable and sensible men of cooler temper—men of property who might push the radicals into the background. The committee rudely ousted Sears from his position of leadership among New York politicians and had McDougall arrested for sedition.

The Committee of Fifty-One then proposed a general congress of colonial delegates (the First Continental Congress) to deal with the grievances of America. The choice of Philadelphia for this congress pleased most conservative and moderate Americans. Under the firm control of Pennsylvania moderates like Joseph Galloway and John Dickinson, and under the legislative domination of Quaker pacifists, Philadelphia (the city of brotherly love) had never developed into a focus of radical activity like Boston or New York. Even the somber Virginians with their carefully worded resolutions and appeals to Parliament were more radical than the residents of Philadelphia. Everyone in Philadelphia seemingly wanted peace and harmony between Britain and America. The moderates badly underestimated the increasing momentum of the radical movement, however, and the Continental Congress quickly fell under the influence and ultimate domination of what were considered overzealous republicans (small "r") from Massachusetts and hot-headed amateur politicians from Virginia.

Dissent proved easiest to undermine where it was least prevalent. Geographic position seems to have been a factor in producing opposition to the rebellion. Although Massachusetts and Virginia were the most uniformly English of the colonies, they supported the greatest proportion of rebels and were the first to effectively suppress Loyalism. Other colonies were more diverse in the national origins of their residents, and in such places large pockets of Loyalism might be found. New York, cosmopolitan by 18th-century standards, was probably the most evenly divided colony in terms of rebellion and Loyalism. There the extremes would come to blows.[50]

Yet the general population of the colonies "seemed to be much inclined to remain peaceable and quiet," to carefully avoid "every ostentatious display" of their sentiments, and mostly to attempt to forestall threats of violence against themselves.[51] Among these Americans were the bulk of religious pacifists and silent anti-revolutionary moderates. They would not be the last *silent majority* in America. With most of the population unwilling to participate in a war or actively support either side in the fighting, the radicals in the Continental Congress could least afford the development of any kind of a neutrality movement that might undermine the momentum of the Revolution.

Some of the radical delegates to the Continental Congress, therefore, moved to force the recognition of its authority among those least likely to resist it—the undecided and moderate portions of the population. Through their local committees of safety, the radicals first attempted to limit the dissent expressed by the moderates by dealing with them in a manner that would not make outright enemies of them. Harsher physical methods, like a jostling in the streets, public carting, or a coat of tar and feathers that could be used against hard-core Loyalists, might prove counterproductive. Many local committees began by resurrecting a compliance with the nonimportation and nonconsumption embargo on trade with Britain that had been established so successfully in 1768 through the Continental Association. All but the most obdurate of Loyalists had followed the embargo. Along with abstention from English items, such as finished cloth and metal goods, no tea was to be used, and Americans who supported the Association made a great show of serving alternative beverages made from herbs, rose hips, and sassafras roots or wearing clothing made from homespun linen and American wool. "We want nothing but self-denial, to triumph," opined a writer to the colonial press.[52]

Those, who took the nonconsumption oath "in name only," found it a mere inconvenience or violated it within the privacy of their own households with a warm cup of tea or a bit of Irish lace. In some localities, harsher means were enacted quickly, and the whole adult population was made to take the Association's oath or declare themselves enemies of American liberty and face public ostracism. The names of those reported to have violated the Association were printed in the newspapers, and merchants who refused to take the nonimportation oath were boycotted[53] or threatened with more severe measures like tar and feathers. No one who organized a boycott at that time could have used the word, because it first appeared in the language only in 1880. In the 18th-century sense, the Continental Association was a collective and organized form of ostracism, a favored tactic of war resistance. In this way, the moderates were forced to acquiesce to the will of the radicals without being forced to march in the streets or take up arms. It was from this point that many of the political lines between radical revolutionaries and hard-core Loyalists were first drawn.

In New England, the social pressure to conform to revolutionary principles was strong, and the radicals were quickly losing patience with their indecisive or moderate neighbors. Many colonials took the stance that open warfare was necessary and that conciliation was impossible. Those moderates who refused to be drawn into the fray were attacked from both extremes. In New England, radicalism was popular, and opposition to the Revolution was usually individual or expressed in quiet tones among reliable friends.

The case of John and Job Westover of Sheffield, Massachusetts, is instructive in this regard. The local committee of safety brought the two brothers before it charged with disaffection to America. John had been overheard to say that the congress was guilty of rebellion against the king, and Job had supported the Parliament's right to tax the colonies. Neither statement was unique to the Westover's, and many moderates held similar beliefs. When asked directly which side they would support in a war between Britain and America, the men vacillated. John found the question too complex to answer directly, and Job opined that America would probably be better off if the British won. Ultimately, one brother, John, voluntarily engaged to obey the congress, while the other, Job refused to make a declaration one way or the other. His punishment was to be labeled an enemy of American liberty. His name was published in the local radical press, and the population was warned to have no dealings with him.[54]

Joseph Galloway

Joseph Galloway was a successful lawyer and merchant who believed that the problems between the colonies and Britain could be resolved by establishing a constitutional federation for Anglo-America with representation in Parliament. He, like his mentor Benjamin Franklin, visualized a better-defined, and thereby more solid, union among the colonies, much like Franklin's Albany Plan of Union of 1754. Although not quite the equivalent of the later British Commonwealth, Galloway's plan would keep America in the family of Great Britain. Just why Franklin and Galloway found themselves on opposite sides in the Revolution is hard to determine. Franklin was also a moderate during the early days of the Revolution and came to be one of its most radical political leaders, whereas Galloway drifted further and further from the cause of America, and toward the support of the king, especially after the outbreak of warfare. Galloway was an open opponent of violence and bloodletting, and the battles of Lexington, Concord, and especially that at Breed's (Bunker) Hill drove him away from the colonial cause.[55]

Galloway was one of the first to see that the overreaching of the radicals in congress was an opportunity for moderates to oppose the Revolution without taking up arms. He viewed congress as something tangible that both moderates and conservatives could attack without attacking the legitimate intellectual and political disputes that America had with Britain. Encouraged by the hostility to the congress among those whom he met in Philadelphia and New York, Galloway determined to oppose the congress publicly. It was unfortunate that he did not sample public opinion farther afield because neither city was typical of American sentiment.

As part of his strategy, he produced a pamphlet printed by the New York Tory publisher James Rivington in 1775 entitled "Candid Examination of the Mutual Claims of Great-Britain and the Colonies." Herein, Galloway attempted to draw a fine line between legitimate and unjustified resistance to the Crown, explaining his actions and condemning both unrestrained resistance and unqualified submission to British authority. The main thrust of his argument was that colonial grievances were genuine but the congress had utterly failed to deal with the problem properly. New Englanders in congress were extremists who had kidnapped a legitimate dispute for their own radical purposes, and southerners were weak for want of moral discipline and inhibited by an undemocratic dedication to black slavery. According to Galloway, they all would soon be overawed and overruled by "the ruthless and cunning Yankees" of New England.[56]

Galloway, a delegate to the First Continental Congress refused to be seated at the Second Continental Congress, and his open disaffection forced him to leave Philadelphia for rural Bucks County where he remained for some time. Yet he found himself in the "utmost danger" from the mobs of radicals that threatened "to hang him at his own door."[57] In 1776, he fled to the British Army in New Jersey for protection. Forced by the persecution of the radicals into being a Loyalist, he became an active adviser to British Gen. William Howe, and in 1777, he was appointed superintendent of police in British-held Philadelphia. When the British abandoned the city in the face of the French alliance, Galloway became dispirited, and he fled to New York and ultimately retired to England where he wrote several pamphlets defending the actions taken by American Loyalists and criticizing the British prosecution of the war on land and sea.

After the Revolution in 1788, Galloway penned "The Claim of the American Loyalists, Reviewed and Maintained upon Incontrovertible Principles of Law and Justice," a call for the Crown to indemnify Loyalists for their losses during the Revolution. "Their claim of justice has not been fulfilled, discussed, or even examined. Hence, it is, that their minds, before too much oppressed by their misfortunes, have remained in the most painful and distressing uncertainty, suspense, and anxiety," he wrote. Of the Loyalist refugees in Nova Scotia, he pointed out, "Many are laboring under the want of means to subsist themselves on their uncultivated farms; many, through the prospect of want, have died of broken hearts; and others have been driven, by their extreme distress, into insanity, and from insanity to suicide, leaving their helpless widows and orphans to prolong their miserable existence on the cold charity of others."[58]

Tory Reaction

Thomas Chandler, a partisan Tory writer from New York, also disapproved of the Congress: "It's first appearance raised our curiosity, but excited no terror," he wrote. "But it was not long, before it turned out to be a perfect monster—a mad, blind monster!"[59] To many, who were otherwise favorable to resisting the ministers of government in London, the delegates to congress had disregarded their original instructions to seek a rapprochement with the Crown, had usurped the powers it had been given, and had assumed the powers of a government unto itself. The Stamp Act Congress a decade earlier had contented itself with successfully protesting the Stamp Act without setting a new government in America as the Continental Congress had gone. Greedy New England shippers and merchants, aided by thoughtless and self-possessed southern gentlemen were accused of using the present misunderstanding with the Crown to establish a republic of their own devising in which they would assume the roll of the ruling class. Chandler maintained that if America could rightfully dissolve its social contract when Britain overstepped its constitutional bounds, than the American people could likewise withdraw their contract with the Continental Congress when it did so. The least congress could do was to consult the people before making a leap in the dark toward independence. The Rev. William Smith of Philadelphia wrote, "Thus we may be [done] out of our liberties, our property, our happiness, and plunged deeper and deeper into . . . war and bloodshed, without ever being consulted."[60]

The Tory writings of Galloway, Chandler, and others like them found acceptance among a growing body of politically moderate colonials in town after town in the Middle Colonies, especially in cities like New York and Philadelphia. Often led by Episcopal (Church of England) clergymen, like Rev. Charles Inglis and Rev. Samuel Seabury, these British-leaning moderates generally refused to select local delegates to the congress, passed resolutions to preserve the established government, or held protest meetings to promote, encourage, and, if called on, enforce obedience to the representatives of the king. Most simply dwelt on the danger of leaving the practical resistance to British oppression in radical hands, and they argued among themselves that the best chance to redress legitimate American griev-ances without violence lay in conservative measures.

It was obvious that the vocal mob would show no mercy to any person who spoke for the king or against the American cause. As a result, the majority of loyal persons "preserved for the most part an arrogant silence toward the arguments of the opposition" and kept their political opinions to themselves.[61] It was difficult to do so. One woman living "between the lines" in Westchester County in New York was awakened in the night by British soldiers demanding entrance to her home with the question, "Are you King's men, or Rebels?" The woman replied calmly that she was "a friend to humanity." The soldiers, ignoring her reply, ransacked the house, stole some items, and went off.[62]

As the siege of Boston progressed through the summer and fall of 1775, many people who wished to remain neutral with regard to the conflict were driven from their homes in the countryside by the more radical elements among the rebels. Timothy Ruggles, chosen as a counselor to Lt. Gen. Thomas Gage because of his neutrality was attacked in the night, and his horse had its tail cropped and was painted over its entire body. Israel Williams, an elderly Tory, was tied in a chair by a mob. With the doors and chimney of his house closed, a fire was set in the fire-place, and the poor old man was smoked for several hours before being released— simply because he refused to take the oath to the united colonies. Daniel Leonard, another Tory advisor, avoided the mobs but had several musket balls shot through his windows. Gen. William Brattle, the elderly keeper of the king's storehouse, had scrupulously delivered to all the colonial selectmen of the region those stocks of gunpowder and ball entrusted to his keeping, but he maintained those of the Crown with equal honesty and care. Brattle later wrote, "Every soldier will say I did but my duty." When he refused to turn over Crown stores to the rebels, Brattle was chased into the British lines as his pursuers fired musket balls over his head.[63]

It seemed impossible to maintain any semblance of neutrality or moderation in a country so charged with hatred. The vast majority of uncommitted persons "rested content in a state of indolence and languid inactivity," failing to enlist in volunteer companies of like-minded persons and take up arms, as had those who had aligned themselves with the rebellion in its earliest days. Some people were loyal because their family or friends chose the side of the king; others, because their personal or political enemies had chosen to be rebels. Family loyalty and kinship bonds were important in determining which side, if any, an individual chose; and political feuds and personal antagonisms often carried more weight than the less substantial issues of taxation, representation, and the rights of Englishmen. When those opposed to the Revolution finally took up arms and formed Loyalist companies and regiments, many of their operations were misdirected, ineffective, or uncoordinated because they failed to develop an effective leadership and a strong organization of their own. They simply relied, as they had in the past, on the bureaucracy of government to maintain the status quo, and on the British regulars to direct their fight.[64]

Not all Loyalists actively resisted the Revolution, and many of the undecided were suspected of harboring Loyalist principles and waiting to see which way the winds of war would ultimately blow. Many were undecided because they feared the legal consequences of joining the rebels who would certainly hang, and others were undecided because they disagreed with the aims of the Revolution. Many feared "how helpless the Colonies would be against the invasion of a foreign power [France or Spain for instance] if there were no protection by the mother country."[65] As the rebellion progressed from isolated clashes between citizens and soldiers in New England to armed resistance across the entire thirteen colonies, many of those who formerly were undecided or against the war were swept onto one side or the other simply because they could not continue to survive in the middle.

Victims of the Few

A Franco-American married to an Anglo-American woman, Hector St. John de Crévecoeur epitomizes the undecided third of the population identified by John Adams as "timid." No adjective could have been more unfairly applied to a person in Crévecoeur's predicament. He had served with distinction as an officer in the Canadien militia in the French and Indian War, and he now had an English wife, a growing family, and a successful farm in Orange County, New York. A British subject by choice rather than by birth he, nonetheless, anguished over the dilemma presented to him by loyalty to the traditions of monarchical rule or the "innovations" of an untried democracy. He wrote:

> How easily do men pass from loving, to hating and cursing one another! I am a lover of peace. If I attach myself to the Mother Country [Britain], which is 3,000 miles from me, I become what is called an enemy in my own region; if I follow the rest of my countrymen, I become opposed to our ancient masters: both extremes appear equally dangerous. . . . I am conscious that I was happy before this unfortunate Revolution. I feel that I am no longer so; therefore I regret the change. What can any insignificant man do in the midst of these jarring contradictory parties, equally hostile to persons situated as I am? . . . The innocent class are always the victim of the few; they are in all countries and at all times the inferior agents, on which the popular phantom is erected; they clamor, and must toil, and bleed, and are always sure of meeting with oppression and rebuke. It is for the sake of the great leaders on both sides, that so much blood must be spilt; that of the people is counted as nothing.[66]

In 1780, the faltering health of his father in France forced Crévecoeur to travel to Europe. Accompanied by his son, he crossed the British-American lines to enter British-occupied New York City, where he was briefly imprisoned as a suspected American spy. Eventually, he was permitted to leave for Britain. In 1782, in London, he published a volume of narrative essays entitled the *Letters from an American Farmer*. The book quickly became the first literary success by an "American" author in Europe and turned Crévecoeur into a celebrated figure. Following the Treaty of Paris in 1783, Crévecoeur returned to New York. He learned that, in his absence, his wife had died, his farm had been destroyed, and his minor children were living with neighbors. Eventually, he was reunited with them. In later years, Crévecoeur served as the French consul for the states of New York, New Jersey, and Connecticut.

Calamity Has Overcome Them

Women—considered largely nonpolitical in the 18th century—often were caught up in the politics of their husbands. Esther de Berdt (Reed), although not a common woman, may be taken as an example nonetheless. Esther was born in England, and her father's house was a place of council for many who sought by moderation and (British) constitutional means to sway the hand of misgovernment over the American colonies without resorting to war. In 1763, the seventeen-year-old Esther met Joseph Reed, a young law student of twenty-three years from America who was in England to finish his studies. The two formed a romance and an engagement to marry, and in 1770, she took ship with her new husband to America to fulfill their dreams. Joseph Reed was deeply involved in the protest movement over colonial discontent, and he held his wife's sympathies. Yet Ester was startled by the outbreak of bloody warfare in Massachusetts and by her husband's appointment as aide and military secretary to George Washington, commander of an American army.

These were life-changing and unnerving events for a young woman who thought of herself as solidly British. Writing in 1848 of Esther's predicament, her biographer, Elizabeth Lummis Ellet, noted the difficulty faced by many wives, mothers, and daughters caught up in the Revolution or in any war:

It is worth a moment's meditation to think of the sharp contrasts in Esther's life. The short interval of less than six years had changed her, not merely into womanhood but to womanhood with extraordinary trials. Her youth had been passed in scenes of peaceful prosperity, with no greater anxiety than for a distant lover and with all the comforts which social position could supply. She had crossed the ocean a bride, content to follow the fortunes of her young husband. . . . She had become a mother, and while watching by the cradles of her infants, had seen her household broken up by a war in its worst form. She too . . . was a native-born Englishwoman, with all the royal sentiments that beat by instinct in an Englishwoman's breast— reverence for the throne, for the monarch, and for all the complex institutions which hedge . . . the British Constitution. Coming to America, all this was changed; loyalty became a badge of crime; the King's friends were her husband's and her new country's enemies. The holiday pageantry of war, which she [had] admired in London, had become the fearful apparatus of savage hostility. Esther, an English woman, was now a fugitive from the brutality of English soldiers.[67]

When her Philadelphia neighborhood fell into British hands in 1777, Esther found her family and herself threatened by the very royal institutions that she had looked to for support and security in England. Personal violence in Philadelphia was rampant, and gentlemen went armed in the streets. "Folly on one hand and fanaticism on the other put in jeopardy the lives of distinguished citizens." With her husband away with the army at Valley Forge, she took her family to the questionable security of Fleming-ton, New Jersey, where one of her little ones succumbed to smallpox. "Calamity has overcome me," she wrote, "and struck the very bottom of my heart. Tell me the work is not yet finished." In May 1780, Esther gave birth to another son, named George Washington Reed, but in September of the same year she fell ill and died at age thirty-four years overtaxed with effort and filled with family cares and anxieties.[68]

Esther and other women like her were often called to "patriotism" or "Loyalism" or "neutrality" through their husbands, brothers, or fathers. They united in a remarka-ble and generous program for the relief of the soldiers and others in their own condi-tion. It was charity in its purest and most genuine form: soliciting contributions, sacrificing their jewelry and trinkets, laboring with needle and thread, and behaving in a businesslike manner at all times. All ranks of women seemed to have joined in the effort with remarkable animation from unnamed black slaves to the Marchioness de Lafayette and the Countess de Luzerne. "During this time . . . humble, homely hero-ism did its good work in helping sustain a spirit that otherwise might have broken."[69]

Young Quakers, members of the Society of Friends, found the antiwar senti-ments of their parents hard to follow in an era of political revolution. This inde-pendent attitude was reflected in a significant increase in the number of mavericks, particularly young women, who defied the authority of the Quaker Meeting to fol-low their own inclinations. One such independent spirit was New York resident Hannah Lawrence who crossed every conceivable religious boundary to marry a non-Quaker Loyalist soldier, Jacob Schieffelin. Worse still, the ceremony was pre-sided over by a Catholic priest. Two days after the Quaker community was informed of the marriage, her Meeting disowned her.

Ironically, Hannah had been a supporter of the congress. Under a writer's pseu-donym, Hannah had found no dearth of topics about which to express her Patriot feelings. She formed a literary society and surrounded herself with a gathering of other young Quakers. Hannah became the standard-bearer of the group communi-cating a message of righteousness and freedom to Quakers in other communities. Although her lover was a British soldier and she an anti-British poet, once the pair had met, a secret courtship had developed. This was followed by an elopement and a dramatic trek to the relative safety of Canada through the Iroquois country of cen-tral New York. During this romantic melodrama, Hannah recorded her feelings for a friend in an unpublished work called "A Journal of a Lady's Courtship." Oddly she seemed not at all to have been distressed at living in a British garrison city in Canada, married to an enemy combatant, and abandoned by her church. Yet she did express some hesitation concerning how her actions would be viewed, "The world, the world will indeed condemn me for imprudence." After the war the couple returned to live in New York.[70]

Refugees

While it is certain that many Loyalists helped the British during the war in the mat-ters of supply, manpower, and information, there is no evidence that active Loyal-ism was as widely practiced in the manner John Adams seemed to suggest. It seems certain, in fact, that the radicals among both Patriots and Loyalists were a minority of positive and determined persons who represented the extremes of their positions. Between them lay the "wavering neutral masses ready to move unresistingly in the direction given by the success of either."[71]

There is no more tragic word concerning the results of warfare than *refugee*. The many refugee families flocking into British-held cities for protection and aid, particularly in the British headquarters in New York City, may have given the Crown a false impression of the overall number of loyal colonials. Nonetheless, the city provided more soldiers to the British forces during the rebellion than any other city in America or Europe. This may explain why the British maintained a constant hope that overwhelming numbers of loyal citizens would turn out elsewhere to support their military operations—a number that never materialized anywhere in America except in New York.

There may have been as many as 100,000 Loyalists (men, women, and children) in New York colony alone, and loyal Delaware was home to more than 20,000. But these were the bastions of Loyalism in America in terms of numbers. The refugees in New York supplied about 25,000 men to the regiments and ships of Britain and all the other colonies about that number again. Half the population of New Jersey may have been loyal, but the pockets of Loyalism there were scattered, geographically isolating most British sympathizers in a sea of uncertainty. The number of Loyalists in the less populous southern colonies, though considerable, was never as great as the Crown's best estimates. In New England, Loyalism was all but exterminated by 1776, and many otherwise loyal citizens had taken ship to Britain or Nova Scotia after the evacuation of Boston in March 1776.

On the afternoon of March 27, 1776, American Commodore John Manly, commanding *Hancock*, noted a parade of 150 British transports and armed vessels sailing from Boston. The fifty-gun men-of-war *Chatham* and *Centurion* took station at the head and tail of the convoy, respectively, and the smaller British warships guarded the flanks, herding in stragglers like sheep dogs. During the few preceding days, Boston had been in great confusion and alarm. The warships and transports were too few and the refugees too many to carry the household effects of all those who wished to escape the besieged city, and what the Loyalists could not take with them was destroyed to keep it out of rebel hands. The British soldiers broke open and pillaged many stores, wantonly defaced furniture, and cast valuable but bulky goods into the waters of the harbor. Crean Brush, a Loyalist originally from New York, was authorized to seize all the clothing and dry goods belonging to Patriot merchants and to place them in the vessels. These outrages produced widespread distress among the population of the city, but the fearful drama ended when the great fleet left Boston, bearing away to Nova Scotia artillery, ammunition, stores, and almost 1,000 loyal Americans.

Manly's squadron of three schooners followed at a safe distance to windward until they came in sight of Nova Scotia hoping to dash in and snap up stragglers, but none of the transports fell behind, even though they sailed through a snow-spitting New England gale for two days. The ability of the officers of the Royal Navy to keep such a large number of sailing vessels on station within the convoy in heavy seas and poor visibility was remarkable and serves as a testament to their seamanship. Reversing course on the first of April, a frustrated Manly brought his three cruisers back south and was rewarded almost immediately with a single straggler. This was the unarmed merchant brig *Elizabeth*, Peter Ramsey (master), that had been detained at Boston by several Loyalists, who had dallied to gather the last of the valuables belonging to the town's citizens. In addition to tons of valuable merchandise that was confiscated, sixty-three loyal civilians were onboard. When examined in Portsmouth, the *Elizabeth* was found to be a valuable prize financially, but it also disgorged twenty-two notorious Loyalist leaders, including Crean Brush.

Brush and others were made prisoners in Boston on charges of having plundered the city and having carried away large quantities of goods, wares, and merchandise, the rightful property of the citizens of Boston. He was handcuffed; denied the use of pen, ink, paper, and candles; and forbidden to converse with any person unless in the presence of the jailer. During his imprisonment, his wife was allowed to visit him, and in 1778, he made his escape in her clothes. Not until the next morning was it discovered that the noted prisoner was gone and that his wife occupied his place in the cell. Mrs. Brush had left a horse tied at a certain spot, and furnished her husband with the means of escape after an imprisonment of more than nineteen months.

Brush immediately set out for the Loyalist stronghold on Manhattan Island in New York. He thereafter directed his efforts at the recovery of his property and tried and failed to obtain from the Crown redress for the injuries he had received and compensation for the losses he had sustained on behalf of the king. Brush had owned about 25,000 acres of land in the State of New York, and nearly the same amount on the so-called New Hampshire grants, almost all confiscated by the Patriots. Being exceedingly despondent, he committed suicide in 1779. In 1783, the British Crown granted 200 acres per person to those Loyalists who settled in Canada.

Test Oaths

Many undecided colonials were required by the rebels to take a *test oath*, and all who equivocated were bound over to Patriot-controlled courts for trial. Most of these proceedings were carried out "under the form of law," but political, legal, and civil disabilities were the "invariable results" of a refusal to take the oath.[72] Isaac Sears, a leader of the Sons of Liberty in New York, was chosen by the local Committee of Safety in 1776 to identify and suppress Loyalist sentiment on nearby Long Island. He noted that many of the residents swallowed the oath of allegiance to America like it was "a four pound shot, that they were trying to get down."[73] Imprisonment, special taxation, and confiscation of property and arms were among the common penalties imposed in various states for failing to take the oath.[74]

Quakers, Moravians, and other Pietist sects generally followed pacifist doctrines of nonresistance and conscientious objection to war. They also rejected the taking of oaths on religious grounds. Despite sacrificing their beliefs and risking expulsion from the Society, many Quakers supported the Revolution while trying to avoid outright belligerence. Famous Quaker patriots like Samuel Wetherell, Jr., Clement

Biddle (who served as quartermaster at Valley Forge), Betsy Ross, and Patriot general Nathaniel Greene believed that they were supporting the creation of a divinely ordained new order of society in America. Nonetheless, during the war there was some concern that the Quakers were not properly loyal to the emerging nation. Quaker dress—the absence of adornments, such as ornamental buttons or lapels on the jacket—made Quakers readily recognizable, and the rebels had arrested some Quakers simply to prevent their acting in favor of the British even though there was little evidence that they supported the Crown in greater numbers than any other discrete group among the undecided moderates.

Nathaniel Greene was a so-called fighting Quaker. Originally from Rhode Island, which had a small Quaker population, Greene began his military career as a brigadier of Rhode Island provincial forces, reorganized the logistics of the Patriot army as its quartermaster general, and commanded the Southern Patriot Army in 1781. It was he who had dissipated the strength of the British forces under General Cornwallis in the Carolinas forcing him into Yorktown where he was defeated by the combined land and naval forces of the Continentals and their French allies. Many contemporaries of Greene, like Henry "Light Horse Harry" Lee, considered him the man who won the Revolution.

During the Revolution, the peace principles of the religious pacifists in America were sorely tried because the vast majority of them refused to serve in the army or take an oath of allegiance to the Patriot government. Their deeply held concepts of passive resistance and patient suffering caused the rebels to remain suspicious of the pacifist commitment to independence. Their stand, while not unexpected, was not accepted by those who felt that the pacifists had as much to gain as other colonists in the fight against the tyranny of the king. The religious opposition to oath taking was generally understood to be an important doctrinal point, but Benjamin Franklin assailed the concepts of nonresistance and conscientious objection in a letter to Richard Price (a Quaker) on October 9, 1780. "I am fully of your opinion respecting religious tests [oaths]. . . . When a religion is good, I conceive it will support itself; and when it does not support itself, and God does not take care to support it so that its professors are obliged to call for help of the civil power, 'tis a sign, I apprehend, of its being a bad one."[75] Thomas Paine, author of *Common Sense* (1776), gave religious objectors his support and noted briefly the relationship he favored between government and religion: "As to religion, I hold it to be the indispensable duty of all government to protect all conscientious professors thereof, and I know of no other business which government hath to do therewith."[76]

Many Quakers supported the ideals of the Revolution, but not its methods. Others supported the Crown in a similar fashion. In many cases, Quakers were simply unable to readjust a lifetime of pacifist belief to the political currents swirling about them, and they suffered because of their failure to fashion a workable response to the situation in which they found themselves.

The story of Christopher Sower, a Mennonite printer from Germantown, Pennsylvania, is instructive in this regard. Sower became a victim of Patriot retaliation for his pacifism after he moved from rural Germantown into British-held Philadelphia. His own account of his difficulties follows:

Having heard how a number of Quakers were banished and carried away to Virginia, and being informed that there were yet some hundreds of substantial inhabitants on the list to be taken up and secured, among which my name was also put down. . . . I considered what I would best do. Knowing that Germantown would always be a disturbed place, for English and Americans would continually march through it, forwards and backwards, and having three of my children already living in Philadelphia, I bethought myself to go there too—to live with them in peace. Accordingly I went . . . and so I lived there quietly and peaceably . . . till May, 1778. . . . [Thereafter] I went back to Germantown again and was in my house . . . when a strong party of Captain McClean's company [Allen McClean's Light Dragoons of Lee's Partisan Corps] surrounded my house and fetched me out of my bed.[77]

Having come out from British-held Philadelphia, Sower's politics and affiliations had become immediately suspect. He was taken through the cornfields to a barn where he was "stripped naked" and frequently prodded in the back with bayonets. Given rags to wear in place of his nightclothes, Sower had his hair and beard cut off, and he was coated with red and black paint. Barefoot and bareheaded, the printer was taken to the American camp near Valley Forge, and put in charge of the provost (military police) charged as "an oppressor of the righteous and a spy." The next day Gen. (John) Peter Muhlenberg visited him, heard him out, and allowed him to petition George Washington for a hearing. Two days later Sower was released, "but it being against my conscience to take an oath to the States, I was not permitted to go home to Germantown."[78]

From 1763 to 1766, Peter Muhlenberg had served in the German dragoons and had become a Lutheran minister before leaving Germany. His brother, Fredrick Augustus Muhlenberg, also a minister, did not approve of the war until the British burned down the latter's church in front of him. Then he joined the military. In January 1776, in a church in Woodstock, Virginia, Rev. Peter Muhlenberg took his sermon text from the third chapter Ecclesiastes, which starts with "To every thing there is a season." After reading the eighth verse, "a time of war, and a time of peace," he declared, "And this is the time of war," removing his clerical gown to reveal an officer's uniform (8th Virginia Regiment of the Continental Army).[79]

Released by Muhlenberg on an order from General Washington, Sower was permitted to live with his daughter Catherine in Methacton near Norristown for several months, and in July, he quietly and secretly moved back into his house in Germantown. Given his previous circumstances, this was an error in judgment. Almost immediately, he was assaulted by Pennsylvania militia for not having taken the loyalty oath, and for having lived in Philadelphia while it was occupied by the British—a charge from which he had already secured his release through Washington and Muhlenberg. "Then they told me," continued Sower's account, "that they were going to take an inventory of my personal estate and sell it . . . and so they passed on with the sale of all my personal estate, and rented out my several houses and lands for one year, and then sold them also [and] published me in almost all the newspapers as a traitor, without any cause and without ever giving me a hearing or a trial." In April 1780, Sower went to live again in Methacton where he died in 1784.[80]

Prosecution for refusal to take the test oath to the revolutionary government was a serious matter. Yet one humorist among the undecided masses penned a parody of Hamlet's soliloquy by Shakespeare that demonstrated the pitiable position into which some who resisted taking the test oath were placed:

> To sign or not to sign, that is the question
> Whether 'twere better for an honest man
> To sign, and be so safe: or to resolve,
> Betide what will, against associations.
> And by retreating shun them. To fly—I reck'
> Not where; and by that flight, t'escape
> Feather and tar and thousand other ills
> That loyalty is heir to; 'Tis a consummation
> Devoutly to be wished.[81]

Many Quakers fled Pennsylvania to Nova Scotia where many Loyalists had taken refuge. Here they suffered from extreme distress. Driven from the United States as enemies of America, the Quakers were held under similar suspicions by the British mainly because they were considered religious dissidents. They quickly found that "the rations allowed by his Majesty's treasury [to refugee Loyalists] had been withdrawn," and that the charitable funds and shipments of flour sent to them by their religious brethren in Pennsylvania had proved inadequate to their maintenance. Rather than finding a refuge, these Quakers—formerly owners of some of Pennsylvania's best agricultural land—found themselves "laboring under the want of means to subsist themselves on their uncultivated farms" in the sparse soils of Nova Scotia.[82]

A generally unsympathetic historian of the late 19th century summarized the reaction of the Loyalist refugees to being hounded from their homes and businesses. "[W]ith nothing to do, [they] needed no temper to find reckless things for their idle tongues to say, one hoped that the rebels would swing for it: another wanted to see the blood streaming from the hearts of the leaders, but would be content to see them become turnspits in the kitchen of some English noble."[83] Madame Higginson, a Loyalist noted for her lack of verbal self-restraint, declared that it would be "a joy to ride through American blood to the hubs of her chariot wheels." Loyalist rhetoric demanded that the Patriot leaders be put to the sword, and those in rebellion have their houses destroyed and their possessions plundered. "It is just that they should be the first victims to the mischief they have brought upon us."[84]

Rooting Out the Pernicious Weeds

When the British evacuated Boston, they took with them to Halifax "102 officials of the crown, 18 clergymen, 105 rural residents, 213 mechanics and tradesmen, as well as some 382 farmers."[85] However, many of those deemed loyal by the radical

Patriots remained behind or fled to the British garrison in New York. By the summer of 1776, neither the British nor the rebel congress considered indecision a legitimate defense to prosecution as an enemy. Those who wished to stand off from the war were "no longer regarded as . . . political opponent[s] to be coerced, but as . . . traitor[s] deserving retributive justice."[86] Samuel Adams—a fractious and unrestrained leader of the rebellion—wrote to another Patriot, Dr. James Warren, in 1777 describing his feelings about those with Tory sympathies remaining in the colonies.

> In my opinion much is to be apprehended from the secret machinations of these rascally people than from the open violence of British and Hessian soldiers, whose success has been in a great measure owing to the aid they have received from them. . . . Indeed, my friend, if measures are not soon taken, and the most vigorous ones, to root out these pernicious weeds, it will be in vain for America to persevere in this glorious struggle for the public liberty.[87]

Maj. William Pierce, a southern Patriot, wrote, "The two opposite principles of Whiggism [revolution] and Toryism [loyalty] have set the people of this country to cutting each other's throats, and scarce a day passes but some poor deluded Tory is put to death at his door."[88] A Patriot soldier who found Loyalists "obnoxious," when asked if he would "murder" loyal refugees if he found them, answered, "It is impossible to commit murder [on] refugees."[89]

The majority of colonials remained loyal or outwardly uncommitted even in the face of rebel occupation of their towns. In the summer of 1776, for instance, the rebel army occupied the city of New York and invested the surrounding areas of Queens and Brooklyn counties on Long Island, Bronx, and parts of Westchester counties on the mainland, Richmond County on Staten Island, and many of the towns on the New Jersey side of the Hudson River. These areas were to witness an ongoing struggle between rebels and Loyalists that focused on food, military supplies and weapons, and recruits for the opposing factions.

The British recruited many fighting men from among the loyal population, and the Loyalists themselves formed many regiments and partisan bands. As many as 8,000 men from New York alone volunteered to serve in Loyal American units or at sea on Loyalist privateers. Most were hard fighting, dependable, and generally effective as soldiers. The refugees possessed a zeal that, coupled with their intimate knowledge of the country, rendered them useful to the Crown. Moreover, Loyalist soldiers—turned on by their neighbors, displaced from their homes by upstart committees, and ill-disposed to the Revolution ideologically—were generally more vigorous than British regulars (redcoats) in the prosecution of their fight against the rebels. It is not surprising, therefore, that Loyalist regiments were associated with many of the atrocities that came to characterize the war. These included the execution of American prisoners and wounded after battles at both Tappan and Paoli.[90]

Loyalist recruits represented fully half of the Crown forces in America, making the combat on the ground more of a civil war between Americans than a war of independence from Britain. More New Yorkers fought for George III than for George

Washington, suggesting that their opposition toward the rebellion was rooted in loyalty to a rightful king and lawful government rather than in antiwar or pacifist sentiments. Nonetheless, the terrors of civil war always create innocent victims and refugees on both sides. In this respect, the American Revolution was little different from other civil conflicts with streams of innocents caught up in an essentially political debate turned to violence.

While the New York provincial congress was trying to secure powder and muskets from Europe and the West Indies for the rebels, Loyalists were receiving arms from Royal Navy ships anchored in New York harbor. A widespread atmosphere of distrust seems to have seized the population, and moderation on any topic even loosely connected with the rebellion quickly disappeared as the politics of the situation became so highly charged that only on the extremes could the average person find support.

Devoted Loyalists controlled almost all of Staten Island and much of Long Island. A Loyalist manifesto written and signed by 788 men from Queens County openly defied the rebels: "Impelled by the most powerful arguments of self-defense, we have at last been driven to procure a supply of those means of protecting ourselves," stated the manifesto in plain language. The list of names freely amended to this document quickly served as warrant for the arrest, prosecution, and confinement of the signers. Squads of rebels led by radical patriots like Isaac Sears scoured the region and attempted to secure the signers for trial.[91]

Richard Hewlitt of Rockaway, along with Jacob Norstrant, Isaac Denton, and John Smith, were reported to have munitions enough for an army hidden in the marshy areas of western Long Island. Joseph Robinson, a Whig informant, warned that these men had organized several dozen Loyalist companies, and had distributed powder and arms to them in preparation for a unified resistance to the rebel army. This report was substantiated by Loyalists arrested and brought in to testify before the Conspiracy Committee of the New York provincial congress, which was formed after a store of 300 small cannons in the Bronx had been sabotaged by having spikes driven into their touch holes and large cobbles jammed into their muzzles.

The Conspiracy Committees met and took evidence concerning questionable activities from witnesses and secret informants. Many of these informants were of questionable integrity. They often took the opportunity to even old scores against their neighbors even when the claims had no validity. Many people were dragged before the tribunals for the most trivial statements, suggesting loyalty to the king or dissatisfaction with the rebellion. Plots and counterplots, most of them false, were uncovered through this means, and just enough of the information proved to be true to maintain the fiasco. This characteristic of making false or highly exaggerated claims remains true to this day, and it requires antiwar and pacifists groups to carefully police their own ranks or have their own motives opened to question.

Many otherwise-moderate Americans joined the Loyalist fold as lukewarm supporters of the Crown in the summer and fall of 1776 because the rebels were seemingly experiencing defeat after defeat at the hands of the redcoats. By December, the Revolution seemed lost, and few could imagine that a single rebel victory over the Hessians at Trenton on Christmas Day would resurrect it.

Nonetheless, the list of committed Loyalists was almost inexhaustible. James Jauncey, a Loyalist member of the New York Assembly, was imprisoned and stripped of property estimated at £100,000. Samuel Tilley of Westchester was imprisoned and had his house plundered for selling provisions to the British, but he escaped and joined a Loyalist regiment. Isaac Low, a member of the First Continental Congress, had a change of mind concerning the wisdom of the Revolution and was forced to flee with his family to the British in New York. Judge Jonathan Fowles and Rev. Samuel Seabury of Eastchester (in Bronx County) were placed under arrest and had their belongings confiscated or destroyed for speaking out against the Revolution. Both men were sent off as prisoners to Connecticut.

As tensions grew, so too did the violence, and rough handling often accompanied an arrest. Many paid for their loyalty with a coat of tar and feathers, a ride out of town on a rail, or a short period of confinement. The tragic treatment suffered during the "carting" of Doctor Kearsley, a leading Loyalist of Philadelphia, was described in the memoirs of Alexander Graydon, who witnessed it:

He [Kearsley] was seized at his own door by a party of militia, and, in the attempt to resist them, received a wound in the hand from a bayonet. Being overpowered, he was placed in a cart . . . [and] paraded amidst a multitude of boys and idlers. . . . The Doctor, foaming with rage and indignation, without his hat, his wig disheveled and bloody from his wounded hand, stood up in the cart. . . . Tar and feather were dispensed with, and excepting the injury he had received in his hand, no sort of violence was offered by the mob to the victim. But to a man of high spirit, as the Doctor was, the indignity in its lightest form was sufficient to madden him. It probably had this effect, since his conduct became [thereafter] so extremely outrageous that it was thought necessary to confine him [in jail]. From the city he was soon after removed to Carlisle, where he died.[92]

Public carting—made famous as a symbol of the Terror during the French Revolution two decades later—was a propaganda device used to great effect to undermine opposition. It attracted large crowds of people and was not so violent that it warranted interruption by the army, the government, or those who might secretly sympathize with the victim. Public spectacles like carting had great deterrent value and were useful in suppressing the undercurrent of opposition. They underpinned the common perception that public safety was being upheld. Carting, tars and feathers, and other punishments were often part of a campaign to divert the attention of the public from some larger issue like a lack of food or a failure on the battlefield. Modern episodes of "public carting" usually involve newspaper headlines, cameraphone videos on MySpace, or appearances before congressional committees on television or in the newsreels (as in the House Un-American Activities Committee hearings that came to focus on figures from Hollywood, the repeated questioning of athletes concerning the use of steroids, or the browbeating of company officials concerning oil prices and executive bonuses).

When detected by the committees of safety, suspected Loyalists were sometimes arrested on charges of disaffection to the cause and confined in jails. The worst of these prisons was undoubtedly the Simsbury Mines in Connecticut, where scores of men were confined underground in dark and damp galleries left behind by the copper miners. Even in August the temperature in the mines rarely rose above 45°F, and water constantly dripped down the rock face, making the environment cold and damp year-round. The inmates were not made to work in the mines, but the floors were tilted and irregular, and few men of average height could find a place to stand upright.

Rebel courts in remote areas were more prone to sentence men to death than to confinement. A Loyalist editor wrote of the revolutionary courts, "They [want] rebel foragers exchanged as prisoners of war, but refugees for the same work [are] treated as traitors."[93] At least 105 Loyalists were sentenced to death by hanging in New Jersey alone. This rather ruthless attitude on the part of the rebels may have been in response to the fact that so many communities in the state were disaffected to the Revolution. Many more Loyalists were victims of lynching without a trial of any sort. Such incidents often reflected the culmination of local hatreds and petty vendettas that predated the war. At least four persons were hanged in a series of associated but separate incidents involving two families in New Jersey, one ardently loyal and the other equally dedicated to the rebellion. Similar atrocities could be found in almost every colony during the war.

No Safety in Neutrality

By 1778, the rebels held virtually all of New England and the region from the Hudson Highlands of New York to the Canadian border. The British commanded Manhattan, much of the Bronx, and all of Staten Island and Long Island. This was their headquarters and base of operations. Much of present-day Westchester County, interposed between the two opponents, was a "neutral ground" throughout the war, and the residents of this region suffered greatly regardless of their allegiance. Both armies attempted to patrol the disputed territory to secure its resources as an open larder for provisions. Once the main focus of war had shifted to the southern colonies after the summer of 1778, the neutral ground surrounding New York evolved into a region constantly upset by the small war, or *petite guerre*, that provided a continual upset for the residents. It was here that many of the worst atrocities taken against civilians took place. The region became the haunt of Loyalist "cowboys" and rebel "skinners"—both really groups of bandits or thugs so named because of their affinity for stealing livestock and robbing people of their goods along the highways and byways of the region. Many of the victims in the neutral ground were from among the uncommitted moderates of the American population.

Evidence suggests that the cowboys and skinners were mere miscreants who sold their stolen goods to either side in the rebellion for cash. Preserved meats, root vegetables, and other provisions were quickly "confiscated" in the name of the Revolution or "appropriated" by the British government. Rebel soldiers often striped bare the larders of "suspected persons," and local committees of safety officially "appropriated loyalist property" by cutting timber, herding livestock, or gathering hay, grain, or fruit found on the land of uncommitted persons under the terms of impressment legislation passed by the congress. As the war progressed, the tendency of the rebels to simply confiscate property became "less restrained," and any person not openly supporting the rebellion was considered suspect and had their stocks of food, fuel, and hay taken. Many of the residents, who simply were trying to ride out the war in peace, were soon destitute of food and fuel for the winter and, therefore, were forced to flee the region. The residents of the Pennsylvania hinterland, much of New Jersey, the Mohawk Valley in New York, and any productive area where military control of the region remained contested were similarly affected.[94]

Those families, whether well-disposed to the Revolution or dedicated to the Crown, that did not take up arms understood the terrible necessity of providing food for the troops who championed their respective causes, but they too often found their larders stripped bare by their own troops. Those who attempted to remain neutral in the maelstrom, or to profit by selling to either or both sides, were often laid waste. Local farmers, who brought produce, flour, meat, or firewood to the military encampments for sale often had their wagons and horses impressed for service. Young men in such circumstances were lucky to find themselves walking home and not drafted into uniform.

Whether an armed Loyalist or antiwar neutral, not being "for" the Revolution often exacted a high price from those who wished to be left out of the war. Joseph Plumb Martin, a private in the Continental Army, described an incident involving a neutral family that arose from a search for Loyalists at Westchester (in Bronx county), a village some miles east of the King's Bridge that connected Manhattan Island to the mainland.

> We found no enemy in this place, but . . . here was a plenty of good bread, milk and butter. We were hungry as Indians, and immediately fell to, and spared not, while the man of the house held the candle and looked at us as we were devouring his eatables. I could not see his heart . . . but I could see his face and that indicated pretty distinctly what passed in his mind. He said nothing, but I believe he had as like his bread and butter had been arsenic as what it was. We cared little for his thoughts or maledictions; they did not do us half so much hurt as his victuals did us good.[95]

Loyalist raiders were no friendlier to neutrals than were the rebels, and they often targeted whole areas, laying waste indiscriminately to neutral farms to keep provisions from rebel troops. Loyalist troops seemed particularly outraged by the fact that their fellow British subjects were not willing to side with the Crown. On a farm in North Carolina, "they immediately entered and plundered the house of everything, carrying away also the corn and wheat."[96] In Philadelphia, Crown forces "plundered at a great rate, such things as wood, potatoes, turnips, etc."[97] The 19th-century historian Elizabeth F. Lumis Ellet recorded, "During the summer, families throughout the country, near the scene of warfare, lived chiefly on roasted corn, without bread, meat, or salt."[98]

The residents of Redding, Connecticut, at first welcomed the proximity of the rebel troops in their winter encampment. Surely they would be protected against Loyalist raiders, but they came to look at the presence of American troops with mixed emotions.

> A few months' acquaintance opened their eyes to some of the ways of the soldiers, and caused them to speed the army [on its way] in the spring as heartily as they welcomed them in autumn. The soldiers . . . plundered the neighboring farmers, whether Whig or Tory, with utmost impartiality. To them a well-stocked poultry-yard or a pen of fat porkers offered irresistible inducements . . . droves of fat cattle . . . were killed and eaten with as little formality as they were taken.[99]

The Camps

Stripped of their belongings and starving, thousands of Loyalists and otherwise displaced persons sat out the war in the urban centers of American because they had no other place to go. If they could, loyal refugees flocked to the British strongholds, especially New York City, Philadelphia, Charleston, and Niagara, where their number "constantly grew in size and in hopeless dependence."[100] As winter approached in 1777, hundreds of women and children arrived at the refugee camps in New York, being "friends of the government" fleeing from the persecution of the rebels. "They were sent off by order of the [Patriot] committees, councils of safety &c. with little more than their wearing apparel, being robbed of their furniture, cattle, &c. and their farms given to strangers."[101]

New York City faced a great shortage of housing made worse by a major conflagration said to have been set by Patriot arsonists when the Rebel Army was driven from the city in autumn 1776. One thousand buildings were completely destroyed even though the townsfolk, redcoats, and naval personnel fought the fire. According to Ambrose Serle, secretary to the British commander Gen. William Howe, a strong wind fanned the flames that extended in a line for almost the length of a mile. The fire was not suppressed before a third of the city was in ashes.

Many women and children were reported to have perished in the fire, and many permanent residents of the city lost all that they owned. The extent of the fire, added to the demand of the refugees for shelter, created a shortage of rooms, bedding, clothing, furniture, and household implements. It destroyed many of the warehouses, shops, and workplaces that might have furnished replacements. Lumber and building materials thereafter were held at a premium, and Patriot control of the hinterland made their importation difficult. In February 1777, 32,000 persons still were residing in two-thirds of a city originally built for 20,000, and these numbers did not include military personnel and Patriot prisoners of war. These people simply could not be housed in the 2,000 buildings left standing.

The extraordinary numbers of inhabitants posed a logistical problem of Herculean proportions for the British administration of the city. The military government allocated little in the way of firewood, food, candles, or clothing to the refugees. The city government undertook a rebuilding program, but the effects of unremitting graft and corruption among the city officials delayed it. The general feeling among the Loyalists was that more money should have been spent on their relief. Dependent refugee families were often left destitute because their men were away on duty with a Tory regiment. Although the families of volunteers received half-rations on the British Army account while they served, no system for forwarding a husband's military pay to his wife or family existed. Many Loyalist husbands and sons were incarcerated in Patriot jails with no provision made for their loved ones.

Charitable subscription for the refugees were taken up among the normal residents of the city, but as the war dragged on, some New Yorkers attempted to maintain the meager remnants of their wealth as a contingency against British defeat. Many other city residents simply wanted the refugees out of the way. Left with little hope of finding decent lodgings in the city proper, the refugees resorted to living in shacks, huts, or other improvised shelters in large Loyalist camps on the forested slopes of the Bronx. The refugee camps were described as wretched and deplorable, but they had a nearby supply of firewood and dependable sources of fresh water.

The former estate of Patriot merchant Robert Morris, known as Morrisania, held one of the largest concentrations of loyal refugees in all the colonies save Halifax, Nova Scotia. Another concentration of refugee families was located in Queens County near the village of Flushing. The camps were on the margins of British control and were open to insult by Patriot forces. They were not without defenses, however. Flushing was the home base of the Loyal American Regiment, and Morrisania served as the base for DeLancey's Refugee Corps. This protection was taken away, however, when these Loyalist units were marshaled for operations away from the city. If a husband was killed in action or died of disease or accident, a wife was under some constraint to find herself a new spouse from among the military personnel or be taken off the ration list by a callous army administrator. Many women and teenage girls resorted to prostitution simply to survive, and contemporary observers reported the dire circumstances these women faced.

Suppressing Dissent

It seems clear that the Patriots were unprepared to found an entirely new form of government when the Revolution ended. The immediate reaction to victory was one of sometimes violent retribution directed at the Loyalist population. Those cool to the Revolution and those Loyalists among the refugees were particularly alarmed by the distinctions made in the fifth article of the capitulation signed by General Cornwallis at Yorktown in 1781 between "British subjects" and "Loyalists who had rendered themselves amenable" to joining them in arms.[102] An estimated 100,000 Loyalists fled to Britain or Canada during the course of the war. Many more waited until late 1782 to take ship with the last of the redcoats to leave New York City, hoping in vain for a positive turn in British fortunes. One historian noted, "The formation of the Tory or Loyalist Party in the American Revolution; its persecution by the Whigs during a long and fratricidal war, and the banishment or death . . . of these most conservative and respectable Americans is a tragedy but rarely paralleled in the history of the world."[103]

Notes

1. Peter Silver, *Our Savage Neighbors: How the Indian War Transformed Early America* (New York; W. W. Norton, 2008), 21.

2. Silver, 34.

3. Ralph Bennett, ed., *Settlements in the Americas: Cross-Cultural Perspectives* (Newark: University of Delaware Press, 1993), 149.

4. Bennett, 149.

5. By 1790, as many as 100,000 German speakers may have immigrated to America. They and their descendants made up an estimated 8.6 percent of the population of the United States; 33 percent of the population in Pennsylvania; and 12 percent in nearby Maryland. The failure of the revolutions of 1848 to establish democracy caused thousands more to leave Germany to settle in America in the 19th century.

6. Silver, 101.

7. Silver, 105–106.

8. David Venditta, "We Are Now the Frontier," *The Morning Call*, http://www.mcall.com/all-fi_mayhemnov26,0,579176.story?page=2 (accessed September 2008).

9. Andrew J. Wahll, ed., *The Braddock Road Chronicles, 1755* (Bowie, MD: Heritage Books, 1999), 377.

10. Armand Frances Lucier, ed., *French and Indian War Notices Abstracted from Colonial Newspapers*, vol. 1 (Bowie, MD: Heritage Books, 1999), 264–265.

11. Silver, 112.

12. Silver, 123.

13. Silver, 31.

14. Silver, 28.

15. H. M. M. Richards, *Report of the Commission to Locate the Site of the Frontier Forts of Pennsylvania*, vol. I (Harrisburg, PA: Clarence M. Busch, 1896), 3.

16. Venditta, 3.

17. Richards, 4–5.

18. Silver, 52–53.

19. Silver, 42–43.

20. Silver, 48.

21. Silver, 133.

22. Silver, 109.

23. Silver, 183.

24. Silver, 97.

25. Colin G. Calloway, *Dawnland Encounters: Indians and Europeans in Northern New England* (Hanover, NH: University Press of New England, 1991), 21.

26. Samuel Eliot Morison, *Sources and Documents Illustrating the American Revolution 1764—1788 and the Formation of the Federal Constitution* (New York: Oxford University Press, 1965), 11.

27. Silver, 188.

28. Silver, 197–198.

29. Morison, 7.

30. Quote taken from a peace medal in the author's collection.

31. Bernard A. Weisberger, *America Afire: Jefferson, Adams, and the Revolutionary Election of 1800* (New York: HarperCollins, 2000), 175.

32. Ralph Ketchum, ed., *The Anti-Federalist Papers and the Constitutional Convention Debates* (New York: New American Library, 1986), 1–2.

33. William H. Nelson, *The American Tory* (Boston: Beacon Press, 1961), 172–173.

34. Richard D. Brown, *Major Problems in the Era of the American Revolution, 1760–1791* (New York: Houghton Mifflin, 2000), 230.

35. Nelson, 106–107.

36. Nelson, 118.

37. Nelson, 119.

38. Nelson, 119.

39. Nelson, 117.

40. See James M. Volo, *Blue Water Patriots: The American Revolution Afloat* (Westport, CT: Greenwood Press, 2007).

41. Paul A. Gilje, *Liberty on the Waterfront: American Maritime Culture in the Age of Revolution* (Philadelphia: University of Pennsylvania Press, 2004), 99.

42. The "Child Independence" quotation is from Richard B. Morris, *The American Revolution Reconsidered* (New York: Greenwood Publishing Group, 1979), 17.

43. Nelson, 19.

44. Claude Halstead Van Tyne, *Loyalists in the American Revolution* (Ganesvoort, NY: Corner House Historical Publications, 1999), 5.

45. Joseph Galloway, *The Claim of the American Loyalists, Reviewed and Maintained Upon Incontrovertible Principles of Law and Justice* (London: G. and T. Wilkes, 1788), 4.

46. Nelson, 19.

47. Nelson, 23–24.

48. North Callahan, *Royal Raiders: The Tories of the American Revolution* (New York: Bobbs-Merrill, 1963), 77.

49. Van Tyne, 2.

50. Nelson, 87.

51. Nelson, 102.

52. John C. Miller, *Origins of the American Revolution* (Boston: Little, Brown, 1943), 51.

53. The boycott was named for the hated Captain Charles Cunningham Boycott, an agent for an English landlord during the 19th-century campaign of the Irish Land League for

reform of the system of landholdings. It's an excellent example of an eponym, a word based on a proper name, like Wellington boots, Macadam roads, Ponzi scheme, or the Mackintosh coat. The word boycott was first used in the *Times* of London in November 1880. It was soon adopted by newspapers throughout the United States and Europe, with versions of the name Boycott appearing in French, German, Dutch, and Russian.

54. Nelson, 95.

55. Callahan, 97–98.

56. Joseph Galloway, *Candid Examination of the Mutual Claims of Great-Britain and the Colonies* (New York: James Rivington, 1775), 59.

57. Callahan, 100.

58. Galloway, *Candid Examination of the Mutual Claims*, vii.

59. Nelson, 79–80.

60. Nelson, 127.

61. Van Tyne, 7.

62. Elizabeth Lummis Ellet, *Revolutionary Women in the War for American Independence: A One-Volume Revised Edition of Elizabeth Ellet's 1848 Landmark Series*, edited and annotated by Lincoln Diamant (Westport, CT: Praeger Publishers, 1998), 84.

63. Dorothy Denneen Volo and James M. Volo, *Daily Life during the American Revolution* (Westport, CT: Greenwood Press, 2003), 71.

64. Van Tyne, 169.

65. Charles E. Green, *The Story of Delaware in the Revolution* (Wilmington, DE: Press of William N. Cann, 1975), 185.

66. J. Hector St. Jean de Crevecoeur, *Letters from an American Farmer*, reprinted from the original 1782 edition with an introduction by Ludwig Lewisohn (New York: Fox, Duffield, Publishers, 1904), 287–288.

67. Ellet, 97–98.

68. Ellet, 98–99.

69. Ellet, 99.

70. Judith L. Van Buskirk, *Generous Enemies: Patriots and Loyalists in Revolutionary New York* (Philadelphia: University of Pennsylvania Press, 2002), 69–70.

71. Van Tyne, 158.

72. Otto Hufeland, *Westchester County During the American Revolution, 1775–1783* (Harrison, NY: Harbor Hill Books, 1982), 94.

73. Miller, 485.

74. Van Tyne, 136.

75. Benjamin Franklin, "Benjamin Franklin on Religion," http://bvml.org/GCIAH/franklin.html (accessed May 22, 2008).

76. Thomas Paine, "Quotes on Separation of Church and State," http://www.humanismbyjoe.com/church_&_state.htm (accessed May 22, 2008).

77. S. F. Sanger and D. Hays, *The Olive Branch of Peace and Good Will to Men: The Antiwar History of the Brethren and Mennonites, the People of the South during the Civil War, 1861–1865* (Elgin, IL: Brethren Publishing House, 1907), 40–41.

78. Sanger and Hays, 42.

79. Sanger and Hays, 42.

80. Sanger and Hays, 44–46.

81. Callahan, 68.

82. Galloway, *Candid Examination of the Mutual Claims*, vii.

83. Van Tyne, 43–44.

84. Van Tyne, 43–44.

85. Callahan, 76.

86. Van Tyne, 100.

87. Richard B Morris and James Woodress, eds., *Voices from America's Past: The Times That Tried Men's Souls, 1770–1783* (New York: McGraw-Hill, 1961), 31–32.

88. Ray Raphael, *A People's History of the American Revolution* (New York: New Press, 1991), 82.

89. George E. Sheer, ed., *Private Yankee Doodle* (New York: Eastern Acorn Press, 1962), 141.

90. Van Tyne, 178.

91. James M. Volo, "The Acquisition and Use of Warlike Stores During the American Revolution," *Living History Journal* (Fall 1986): 12–14.

92. Morris and Woodress, 30–31.

93. Van Tyne, 176.

94. Van Tyne, 275.

95. Sheer, 140.

96. Ellet, 69.

97. Elaine Forman Crane, ed., *The Diary of Elizabeth Drinker: The Life Cycle of the Eighteenth Century Woman* (Boston: Northeastern University Press, 1994), 66.

98. Ellet, 215.

99. D. Hamilton Hurd, *History of Fairfield County, Connecticut* (Philadelphia: J. W. Lewis, 1881), 595.

100. Van Tyne, 146.

101. Holly A. Mayer, *Belongs to the Army* (Columbia: University of South Carolina Press, 1996), 11.

102. Galloway, *Candid Examination of the Mutual Claims*, 12.

103. Van Tyne, 182.

Chapter 5

The New Republic

Why quit our own country to stand upon foreign ground?

—George Washington

To Provide a Common Defense

January 1783 usually marks the end of the American Revolution, but the British continued to hold New York City until the spring. Consequently, the Continental Army that had won America's independence did not immediately stand down. A great fear shared by Americans at the end of the Revolution was that the army, its officers, or even George Washington might fail to cede control of the young nation to civil authorities once they had crafted a government. Would it be possible for the delegates in Congress in Philadelphia to invest sufficient military power in a national government to defend against enemies (foreign and domestic) and ensure civil stability without transforming the United States into an oppressive regime?

The initial encounter with the British (1775–1783) had affected the independence of the colonies, but this independence would not be fully realized, in fact, until Americans faced Britain again as a nation instead of a group of states in the War of 1812. More important, the revolution cemented several false impressions in the minds of Americans that would influence the principles and structure of governance in the United States thereafter. The first was that the militia, an army of self-trained volunteers sprung from the very soil of the continent, could rise at a moment's notice to stand off trained regular troops without considerable reinforcement. The second was that trade and commerce on the seas could be secured by a reliance on privateers (privately owned oceangoing commerce raiders), gunboats, and shore batteries.

From their experience of redcoats in the colonial wars with the French and their Indian allies, Americans had no doubt that they could defeat the British on land, and in 1775, the Continental Congress provided immediately for an army based on the existing provincial militia structure. The colonial representatives doubted the practical value of forming a colonial navy to face the might of the British at sea, relying instead on privateers. Nonetheless, the Revolution had been successful and independence had been won. Yet many in the Congress and in the nation had forgotten that without the military aid of France, Spain, and Holland, and the deployment of several Allied fleets of European warships, the War for Independence might have ended quite differently. These martial myths, upon which the young republic would choose to found its defense in 1783, largely ignored the reality of just how American independence had been accomplished.

The issue of the military—one of the first decisive questions faced by U.S. lawmakers—was fundamental to the question of state versus federal sovereignty, and it had a direct impact on every citizen and their civil liberties. The crux of the problem, as envisioned by the delegates to Congress, was to properly apportion the power of the central government with that of the states and the people. As yet there was no formal division of delegates into political parties, which were thought to be deleterious to the welfare of the republic, but these too were to come.

The nationalists (also known as Federalists) in Congress believed that the strength of the nation lay in a strong central government and a regular military composed of an oceangoing navy and a powerful standing army. The anti-nationalists (also known as Anti-Federalists) wanted to continue the loose confederation of independent states from the revolution and wished to rely for the nation's defense on a gunboat/privateer navy and a traditional militia—a virtual navy and army of armed fishermen and farmers. It was the latter system—with the help of the French—that had defeated the British, but many nationalists thought it could not be depended on to secure the nation without foreign aid.

Mutiny

Some of the worst fears of many Americans with regard to the military were seemingly fulfilled in 1783. The Army of the Main Department (as opposed to that of the Middle or Southern Departments) was encamped at Newburgh, New York, overlooking the Hudson River just ten miles north of West Point waiting for word that the Treaty of Paris had been signed formally ending the War for Independence with Britain. Early in the Revolution, the officers serving in the regular Continental forces were offered a half-pay pension at the close of the war as a recruiting inducement, but by the winter of 1782–1783, with the fighting all but over, nothing had been done to implement the promises of Congress. Moreover, Congress was badly in arrears in terms of their pay. At Newburgh, the officers drew up a petition to the Congress offering to give up a lifetime pension and back pay for an immediate lump-sum payment. The petition was carried to Philadelphia by a delegation of officers, who were greeted positively by the nationalists in Congress. The delegation of officers made it clear that if their *requests* were not met, they would become *demands* backed by the threat of the army rejecting congressional control.

There were historical precedents for this problem. Notably, at the end of the English Civil War (1641–1649), the republican army of Oliver Cromwell had effectively taken over the governance of Britain from Parliament with indisputably bad results, including the ultimate return of the monarchy. Closer to home if not greatly nearer in time, the refusal of the colonial Virginia militia under Nathaniel Bacon to stand down after suppressing an Indian uprising in 1675 ultimately turned white against white as Bacon and the royal governor, William Berkeley, came to logger-heads over how to deal with the Indians. Bacon and his followers refused to disband the army of almost 1,000 volunteers calling for sweeping changes in the colonial government. Even the colony's women played a roll, and they were among the rebellion's most active zealots. Bacon's was a blatant case of disloyal opposition to the government. Bacon's death, unrelated to the crisis, caused the rebellion to collapse, but Governor Berkeley brought in troops to chastise the rebels nonetheless.

The Continental Army, itself, had mutinied twice during the war in January 1781. The Pennsylvania Line (1,300 men) had marched on the Congress for their pay at the end of their enlistments, and the New Jersey Line (only 200 men) had done the same some weeks later. The first mutiny was resolved with payments being made and about half the men going home. The second resulted in the execution of the ringleaders to ensure that the army stayed together to fight the war.

With the war finished by everyone's account in 1783, the seething situation at the Newburgh encampment soon fomented the first civilian-military crisis in the history of the young nation. Executions were out of the question and would have been unjustified in any case. With backing from the nationalists in Congress, two documents were circulated among the military officers at Newburgh. One called for a meeting to discuss redress of the pension issue, but the other denounced the government and threatened the civilian control of the new republic. The letters "drawn with great art, and . . . designed to answer the most insidious purposes" shocked Washington who, initially unaware of these sentiments among his officers, found their behavior "unmilitary" and "subversive of all order and discipline." In March 1783, Washington personally took steps to diffuse what would amount to a possible military coup d'état.[1]

Appearing at the officers' meeting—called by Col. Walter Stewart, who with Gen. Alexander McDougall, was an organizer of the officers' pension movement—Washington quietly took out his eyeglasses to read the offending documents and deliver a prepared speech in which he emphasized that he had grown old and nearly blind in the service of his country. He argued that a coup would tarnish the good reputation of the army and lead to civil discord. "My God!" exclaimed Washington. "What can this writer have in view, by recommending such measures . . . by sowing the seeds of discord and separation between the Civil and Military powers of the Continent?" Finally, Washington implored his officers to continue their unparalleled patriotism and patient virtue.[2]

The speech, and the dramatic use of his reading glasses that his aides de camp later suggested was an affectation, worked an almost miraculous reversal among the officers. Without dissent, all in attendance expressed their confidence in the Congress, and repudiated the "infamous propositions" contained in the letters later found to have been written by Maj. John Armstrong, Jr., aide to Washington's arch rival and perennial nemesis Gen. Horatio Gates. Ultimately, Congress gave in to the officers' demands, agreeing to give the men their back pay and an award of full pay for five years in lieu of a lifetime pension. The first crisis of military power faced by the United States was thereby averted, yet many anti-nationalists in Congress and among the legislators in the individual states remained fearful of the potential power of the army to overturn the civil liberties of the people.

Their anxiety was strengthened in April 1783 when Pennsylvania troops of the Continental line became riotous and fomented a new mutiny, marching on the Pennsylvania State House, where both the state legislature and the national Congress were presently meeting, and demanding to be paid and allowed to go home because Congress had declared the war at an end. Somewhat sympathizing with their case, president of the Pennsylvania legislature, John Dickinson—the only delegate to the Second Continental Congress to refuse to sign the Declaration of Independence—refused Congress's request to bring full military action against the rioters. To their credit, the state legislature of Pennsylvania stared down the mutineers and refused to comply with their demands, while the national Congress voted to remove themselves by the back door to reconvene in Princeton, New Jersey.

Although many delegates, like Elbridge Gerry of Massachusetts, insisted that it had no authority whatsoever to maintain a standing army, Congress turned the issue of the future of the military in the United States over to a committee headed by Alexander Hamilton to make recommendations. Meanwhile, the final demobilization of the remainder of the Continental Army proceeded peacefully.

In May 1783, with the mutiny of the Pennsylvania troops quelled and the Newburgh uprising of discontented officers smoothed over, Gen. Henry Knox, self-trained head of Washington's artillery during the war, chose to form the Society of Cincinnatus. It was an inauspicious time to do so. Knox viewed the society as a fraternal and charitable association of officers, who had fought in the Revolution, and honorary members from among the political elite, who had supported the war without taking up arms. Membership, however, was to be hereditary. Those who distrusted the army saw membership in Cincinnatus as an attempt to initiate a military aristocracy in America and underpin it through the inclusion of important nationalists in its ranks. Of course, in hindsight, this was nonsense promulgated largely by the anti-nationalists in Congress, but it did not seem so at the time. When Washington accepted the presidency of the society, much of the debate over its purpose was alleviated. The mediating figure of George Washington at this time of crisis can not be overemphasized. Nonetheless, the public furor over the creation of the Society of Cincinnatus was intense.[3]

The Loyal Opponent

Although a political moderate, John Dickinson has become one of the symbols of loyal opposition in America during the early federal period. During the Revolution, the old Pennsylvania General Assembly had been dominated by people with Loyalist sympathies, religious pacifists, and political moderates like Dickinson, who did little to support the War for Independence except protest the expenditure of money and second guess the military strategies. The radicals in this assembly ultimately took matters into their own hands, using irregular means to write the Pennsylvania

Constitution of 1776, which excluded from the electoral franchise anyone who would not swear loyalty to the state and the Christian Holy Trinity. In this way, virtually all the Loyalists, many resolute moderates, and Quakers, Mennonites, Moravians, and other conscientious persons who had a religious objection to oath taking were kept out of the government. This peremptory action seemed appropriate at the time, especially as the pacifist-dominated colonial government of Pennsylvania had a history of refusing to support even defensive warfare against the depredations of the French and their Indian allies. Nonetheless, as the Revolution seemingly ground on without end, the moderates gradually regained the majority of seats in the Pennsylvania State House, and Dickinson's election to the Supreme Executive Council of Pennsylvania in November 1782 was seen as the beginning of a reactionary movement against the nationalist influence in American government.

Benjamin Franklin replaced Dickinson as president of the council in 1785 when the moderates lost their majority to the Pennsylvania nationalists, who favored the framing of a new constitution. Not until the revolution had tiny Delaware shaken itself loose of domination by Pennsylvania. Dickinson was an embodiment of the smaller state's lack of an individual identity. He was signer of the Articles of Confederation for Delaware, for a short time simultaneously the president of both the Pennsylvania and Delaware assemblies (1782–1783), and the wealthiest landowner in the state of Delaware. Although a major figure in Pennsylvania politics during the war, he was chosen by Delaware to represent its interests at the Constitutional Convention of 1787.

At the convention gathering in Philadelphia, Dickinson voiced strong reservations regarding the proposed apportionment of representation by population in the national government, setting forth a defense of the small states that led to the Great Compromise in congressional representation. This compromise recognized slaves as three-fifths persons for the purpose of determining state populations for apportioning representation in the House and gave each state an equal vote in the Senate. The politics surrounding the Great Compromise "nicely reflects the prevailing image of the convention as a cumulative process of bargaining and compromise in which a rigid adherence to principle was subordinated to the pragmatic tests of reaching agreement and building consensus."[4]

Dickinson, chief among the small-state leaders, was the voice of moderation and prudence throughout the convention. Rather than seek complete agreement on all the broad principles over which there was disagreement, Dickinson argued that the delegates should proceed to the definition of such powers and repair of such weaknesses that were thought adequate to produce a document to replace the Articles of Confederation. He wrote nine essays at this time under the pseudonym Fabius in support of moderate positions. The choice of the pseudonym Fabius was meaningful. Quintus Fabius Maximus was the Roman general who in the Second Punic War (218–202 B.C.E.) had saved the republic through caution, prudence, patience, and persistence—qualities easily ascribed to Dickinson himself. What Dickinson seemed to leave out of the equation, however, was that the Roman general had used the time gained by his patience to build a larger navy and recruit additional legions to ultimately destroy the Carthaginians.

In answer to those who feared that a strong federal government under the Constitution of the United States would eventually lead to despotism, Dickinson suggested in *Fabius Letter II* and *Fabius Letter IV* that two features of the proposed system of federal-state governance made any despotic eventuality highly unlikely. First, he highlighted "the power of the people" that pervaded the proposed system, together with "the strong confederation of the states." He also emphasized the "common defense" purposes to which the federal government was to be dedicated. At one point in the deliberations, an angry Dickinson reportedly took James Madison aside and warned that the small states—while friendly to the idea of a national government—might sooner submit to a foreign power than be deprived of an equal suffrage in the legislature.[5] Yet, had it not been for the moderating presence of Dickinson, and a handful of other moderate delegates, the extreme nationalists would have prevailed in the convention, and the Constitution might not have been ratified when sent to the states.[6]

In later years, Dickinson's involvement in state and federal matters never slackened. He continued to act and write as a moderate, becoming chairman of Delaware's constitutional convention in 1791. As an enthusiastic Democratic Republican (Jeffersonian Republican) and Francophile, he lent his support and advice to Thomas Jefferson a decade later. It should be noted that Dickinson's intentions in writing the *Fabius Letters* were different from those of the authors of the *Federalist Papers*.[7] Dickinson observed that other writers had commented at length on particular aspects of the proposed constitution. What Dickinson wished to do, he said, was to simplify the subject, to facilitate the inquiries of his fellow citizens.

Historians have labeled John Dickinson overly cautious and too conservative. It is true that he often seemed blind to the flow of the events in which he was embroiled, perhaps as a result of a temperamental revulsion to mass violence. His devotion to the rule of law and to the principles of liberty linked him to the radicals in the early days of the Revolution, but he could not take the step of severing the ties that bound the colonies with Britain. Yet Dickinson never wavered from his core moderate principles, serving briefly under arms in the Continental Army for the rights of Americans, but refusing to bow to popular clamor and support independence. It is perhaps only because of his steadfast opposition to American independence that he is not celebrated with the likes of Washington, Jefferson, and Franklin, appearing instead as a dark character in the musical *1776*, among the main antagonists of John Adams in his quest for independency. Nonetheless, it was Dickinson who helped to set the principles and means of loyal opposition. "It is [the people's] duty to watch, and their right to take care, that the constitution be preserved."[8]

The Military Peace Establishment

The disturbing events involving the military and civilian aspects of government under the Articles of Confederation generally overshadowed congressional deliberations regarding Alexander Hamilton's proposed plan for a postwar military in May 1783. This proposal for a military organization composed of "a few troops" predated the adoption of the Constitution. Hamilton's so-called military peace establishment seems an oxymoron, but it was highly favored by Washington as being "under certain circumstances, not only safe, but indispensably necessary." It was to have four parts:

- First, an officer-heavy regular army of 2,630 officers and men to garrison the Great Lakes West, overawe the Indians, and guard against British or Spanish incursions onto U.S. territory.

- Second, a uniform militia system under federal control in every state as an immediate response force and as a reserve for a quickly expandable standing army.

- Third, federally controlled arsenals and weapons manufactories among the states to support these troops.

- Fourth, one or more military academies for the training of a professional officer corps for the army with special emphasis on engineering and artillery training.[9]

The Continental Army of the Revolution had been formed around a war establishment of eighty-eight understrength battalions that never numbered a total of more than 25,000 (July 1776) men and most often represented less than 7,000 regulars and militiamen. By comparison, the proposed army composed of just 2,630 officers and men arranged in five regiments hardly could be considered an irresistibly despotic force. Although the number of regular troops proposed by Hamilton's plan was one-tenth the number that fought for independence, the fear of standing forces was great nonetheless. In defense of the plan, Washington noted of the proposed national army:

If this number should be thought large, I would only observe; that the British Force in Canada is now powerful, and, by report, will be increased; that the frontier is very extensive; that the Tribes of Indians within our Territory are numerous, soured and jealous; that Communications must be established with the exterior Posts; And, that it may be policy and economy, to appear respectable in the Eyes of the Indians, at the Commencement of our National Intercourse and Traffic with them. In a word, that it is better to reduce our force hereafter, by degrees, than to have it to increase after some unfortunate disasters may have happened to the Garrisons; discouraging to us, and an inducement to the Enemy to attempt a repetition of them. . . . Besides the 4 Regiments of Infantry, [and] one of Artillery will be indispensably necessary.[10]

With the majority in the Congress being anti-nationalists, who favored retaining only the generally disjointed militia system of the old colonial establishment, Hamilton's plan for a regular army—even with Washington's imprimatur—was dead on arrival. Although there was a grudging acceptance that both the extent of U.S. territory and the effective combat style of the Native Americans required a more highly trained force for its defense, Congress had no patience for standing armies of any size. Also of great weight were recurring sectional rivalries among the delegates, and, above all, the persistent economic objections to the cost of maintaining a large army so frequently voiced in the past by a parsimonious Congress. Moreover, in forming his plan, Hamilton had relied on the recommendations of two foreign military officers and the all-but-disgraced American officer who had surrendered an army of 5,500 men at Charleston: respectively Gen. Friedrich Von Steuben, drillmaster of the army; Maj. Gen. Louis Du Portail, its chief of engineers; and Gen. Benjamin Lincoln, the present secretary of war. The opinions of these men did not inspire confidence in Hamilton's suggestions, and they tended, although they were not meant to do so, to offset Washington's favorable opinion of the plan.

A Disabling Weakness

Having rejected Hamilton's plan for a centralized military force for these and other reasons, the delegates disbanded all but eighty-three officers and men from the Continental Army before the ink on the Treaty of Paris of 1783 had dried. Provision for a national army numbering less than 100 men emphasizes the depth of anxiety among the delegates that troops would be employed to police the citizenry. Subsequently, Congress was almost immediately embarrassed by its inability to respond to the British who refused to abandon their posts along the Canadian-American border and in the Great Lakes region in 1784, as they had pledged to do in the peace treaty. These included Pointe au Fer and Oswegatchie in northernmost New York, Forts Oswego and Niagara on Lake Ontario, Fort Erie on the westernmost end of Lake Erie, and Forts Detroit and Michilimackinac at the strategic connections among the larger bodies of water in the lakes region. The long sessions of mediation and compromise in Paris had failed to ensure the good faith of the British diplomats, and the redcoats would not be removed from all these posts until 1796.

Moreover, with independence, the United States had gained sovereignty over and responsibility for tens of thousands of Native Americans within the former boundaries of the British colonies as well as in the Trans-Appalachian West, and some force with constabulary powers (like those of the later North-West Mounted Police or Canadian Mounties, established in 1873) had to protect the scattered settlers and lone envoys to the tribes, evict squatters on Native lands, and counteract British and Spanish influence with the tribes on the frontier. An army of less than 100 men could not suppress the uprising of a single tribe much less overawe the combined force of the Native American nations.[11]

It was no small matter to pacify the western borderlands, and most of those calling for a larger regular army had in mind its deployment to this region. The backwoods settlements were composed largely of Scotch-Irish immigrants from the borders of northern Britain and Northern Ireland. An armed force was thought necessary not only for the protection of these settlers but also to protect the Indians from the whites. Unlike the Virginia and Pennsylvania Quakers, Moravians, and

Mennonites who scrupulously paid for Native land, the Scotch-Irish unabashedly believed that they were foreordained by scripture to take their land from the Native Americans, by force if necessary. "On the frontier, the Scotch-Irish were hewing their way through the woods, killing Indians when it suited them, and developing a righteous indignation against the restraining orders which came from the government."[12] In similar fashion, the German American residents of central New York and the Carolina backcountry were wreaking vengeance on both their former Loyalist neighbors and the Indians who had sided with the British.

These understandings of their wider obligations to the nation finally overpowered the anxieties of many in Congress concerning the establishment of a larger military. In June 1784, Congress established the 1st American Regiment that was to be composed of 700 men recruited for one year from the four states willing to provide troops to a national force: Connecticut (165 men), New York (165), New Jersey (110), and Pennsylvania (260). During its earliest deployment under the Articles of Confederation, this single regiment—the only national U.S. force then in existence—garrisoned the posts west of the Appalachian Mountains on the Pennsylvania and Ohio frontiers. In 1785, the unit was reauthorized for a further period of three years and a Department of War was established under Secretary of War Henry Knox, who was given administrative authority over the troops. A congressional committee (rather than the president as commander-in-chief) retained overall control of the regiment and its discipline. Josiah Harmar was appointed the first regimental commander.

Command by congressional committee proved as much a disaster at the time as it would in future American wars, but the initial failures of the regiment were largely due to the fact that only half the regimental strength (men from New Jersey and Pennsylvania) was marshaled during the first year of deployment. Understrength for the task even at its conception, the 1st American Regiment simply could not patrol the hundreds of miles of frontier effectively. The unit was not brought up to strength until 1785 when men from New York and Connecticut were added for a three-year enlistment. Unfortunately, the antimilitarist majority in Congress failed to learn from the lessons that these developments offered.

Ironically, it was in the northeast rather than on the western frontier that the next military crisis—a rebellion among the citizenry—was to erupt. In 1786, Daniel Shays led a rebellion of heavily indebted farmers against increased government taxation in Massachusetts. This was the very interface between the expression of civil liberties and deployment of military force that many Americans had feared. Mercy Otis Warren (a contemporary of these events) noted in her history of the period that Shays's Rebellion was provoked by a number of the questions circulating in Congress regarding the structure of the national government:

These discontents artificially wrought up, by men who wished for a more strong and splendid government, broke out into commotion in many parts of the country, and finally terminated in open insurrection in some of the states. This general uneasy and refractory spirit had for some time shown itself in the states of New Hampshire, Rhode Island, Connecticut, and some other portions of the union; but Massachusetts seemed to be the seat of sedition. . . . The people met in country conventions, drew up addresses to the General Assembly to which were annexed long lists of grievances, some of them real, others imaginary. They drew up many resolves, some of which were rational, others unjust, and most of them absurd in the extreme. They censured the conduct of the officers of government, called for a revision of the constitution [Articles of Confederation], voted the Senate and judicial courts to be grievances, and proceeded in a most daring and insolent manner to prevent the sitting of the courts of justice in several counties.[13]

To deal with the increasing turmoil engendered by Shays and his followers, the Congress authorized an expansion of the U.S. army to 2,040 men, but was unable to recruit more than two artillery companies before the crisis receded. A local militia of 600 men under the command of Massachusetts general William Shepherd responded quickly to the uprising firing on and scattering the rebels. The arrival of an additional force of 2,000 Massachusetts militia under Benjamin Lincoln put an effective end to the rebellion. The nationalists used Shays's Rebellion to scare the country into supporting a more vigorous government and a larger federal military force. To them, the ineffectiveness of Congress in protecting the nation from internal turmoil was a symptom of the weakness of the Articles of Confederation. The nation under the Articles seemed to be stumbling toward anarchy. The anti-nationalists countered that state and local forces had been sufficient to quell the uprising, and they saw no reason to increase the military power of the central government.[14]

Foundation for Opposition

The debate over state or executive control of the military goes back to the earliest days of intercolonial wrangling over marshalling the militia and provisioning the regulars during operations against the French in British America, as well as the basic argument against unlimited executive power and promiscuous war-making. These served as the basis for much of the antiwar-militarist dichotomy that has plagued the United States throughout its history.

Even in the early days of the American Republic, there were grave doubts about the ability of the central government to discipline itself with regard to the exercise of its powers. In an era when distance created a real separation in time and isolated the consensus of opinion, the bond between Americans and their government always had been strongest on the local level. Voters could expect regular contact and interaction with their elected officials (much greater and more direct than today) and an interchange of ideas and opinions among themselves at town meetings and church services, and in the markets and taverns. Although Washington had helped to cement the concept of civilian control of the military, Americans retained a fear of a strong central government with its standing armies and navies as tools of a possible tyranny. Many immigrants had come to America to escape the widespread warfare and constant threat of conscription characteristic of the states of central Europe, and the Scotch and Scotch-Irish in America were not likely to quickly forget the brutal way the British regulars had put down the Highland uprisings in their homeland in 1719 and 1746.

In working closely with British authorities during the colonial wars that preceded the Revolution, many of the American colonies had sustained significant expense as well as human loss. Just as often, the majority of the colonies resisted preparations for joint expeditions with British regulars. Pacifist Pennsylvania and nearby Delaware (a virtual county of Pennsylvania until the Revolution) regularly refused to support any warlike operations, while New York, Connecticut, New Hampshire, Massachusetts, and Virginia were generally the most supportive. Nonetheless, many of the operations planned and led by regular British forces (redcoats, if you will) were military disasters for the colonials with fleets partially destroyed, hundreds of American men lost to incompetence, poor planning, and disease, and hundreds more impressed into involuntary service beyond their legal term.

The citizens of Massachusetts were particularly affected by these repeated failures because they had answered every call for men and money during the 18th century with a laudable immediacy. Public war debt in the Bay Colony had skyrocketed, and local taxes had almost doubled. One-third of all the military-age Americans in Massachusetts had served with distinction alongside the redcoats, yet nearly one in four had died in service. Of all the colonies that had supported the British army in the colonial wars, only Massachusetts had been able to retire its war debt before 1775. Yet in the end, the Crown had turned against the Bay Colony levying new taxes, closing its ports, impressing its seamen, placing Boston under martial law, and leaving it and other colonies in like circumstances with a poor regard for regular armies and government ministers.

The contrast between the state-over-federal system of sovereignty envisioned after the close of the Revolution and the actual working relationship between the federal and state governments, and those entities and the individual, became obvious to any observant American at the Constitutional Convention of 1787. Called to repair the obvious deficiencies of the Articles, it did not take long for the anti-nationalist (Anti-Federalist) representatives of the states to come into conflict with those nationalists (Federalists) who wanted to extend the powers of the national administration. In fact, among the few points of agreement reached among the parties at the Constitutional Convention was the need to scrap the Articles of Confederation and construct an entirely new document.

Not Short of Despotism

Unfortunately, to provide for free and open discussion during the Constitutional Convention, no official minutes of the deliberations were taken. Were it not for the private notes kept by the delegates, particularly James Madison, little concerning the constitutional debates would be known today. The lack of explicit and indisputable records led to a flurry of analyses by third parties concerning exactly what the delegates meant in fashioning certain clauses of the final document. The customary premise of those who believed in *strict construction* of the Constitution was that the exact wording of the document should be relied on in determining the wishes of the founders, while those who believed in a *broad construction* felt that reliance on literal interpretation made the Constitution a sterile and confining document. A literal analysis provided a conceptual simplicity to government but denied powers to Congress and to the president, which were not explicitly enumerated in the underlying clauses but might be needed in an ever-changing world situation.

Federalists held ideals best expressed by Alexander Hamilton, James Madison, and John Jay, authors of the *Federalist Papers*. These letters and essays were popular with a smaller and more elite portion of the population, generally moneyed interests like bankers, shippers, and the upper classes. The ideas found in the *Federalist Papers* were inspiring enough to support an entire political party for two decades. *Federalist No. 10*, in particular, favored a republican form of governance, discussed the means of preventing political factions, and warned of the dangers to society of a pure popular democracy. It is generally regarded as the most important of the eighty-five papers written from the Federalist philosophical perspective.[15]

The Anti-Federalists—a larger group of writers with more diverse opinions— saw in a strong executive backed by the military threats to the rights and liberties of the people so recently won from Britain. Anti-Federalist authors included John Dewitt (possibly a pseudonym), Melancton Smith, a Federal Farmer (possibly Richard Henry Lee), a Maryland Farmer (possibly John Francis Mercer), and a pantheon of Roman-styled pseudonyms whose identity can only be surmised (Agrippa/ James Winthrop, Brutus/Robert Yates, Cato/George Clinton, Centinel/Samuel Bryan, and Fabius/John Dickinson). They generally shared a positive idealism and a democratic vision far closer to the goals of the Revolution than the political and commercial ambitions of the Federalists would admit. According to the Anti-Federalists, a new age would follow the Revolution during which only the mildest and simplest forms of self-governance would be necessary. The "new order" to be fashioned in the United States would be a model for the world: "novus ordo seclorum" as the great seal of the United States would read.

However, an intense suspicion of corruption, greed, neglect of the people, and lust for power—generally directed at the highest authorities in the central government—colored almost all Anti-Federalist thought. Antiwar conservatives would trot out Anti-Federalist arguments during almost every American war up to the present time. In *John Dewitt I*, for instance, the author makes note of a particularly moving and often-repeated antiwar theme, the endlessness of bloody warfare:

> It must ever prove a source of pleasure to the Philosopher, who ranges the explored parts of this inhabitable globe . . . to close his prospect with this Western world. In proportion as he loves his fellow creatures, he must here admire and approve; for while they have severally laid their foundations in the blood and slaughter of three, four, and sometimes, ten successive generations, from their passions have experience, every misery to which human nature is subject, and at this day present striking features of usurped power, unequal justice, and despotic tyranny. America stands completely systemized without any of these misfortunes.[16]

In *Brutus X*, Robert Yates warned of the dangers of standing armies and the possible usurpation of power by an unscrupulous executive or commanding general subverting the constitutional safeguards of the republic by force of arms:

> [A]n army will subvert the forms of the government, under whose authority, they are raised, and establish one, according to the pleasure of their leader. . . . [T]he liberties of the commonwealth [of Rome] was destroyed, and the constitution overturned, by an army, lead by Julius Caesar, who was appointed to the command, by the constitutional authority of that commonwealth. He changed it from a free republic, whose fame had sounded, and is still celebrated by all the world, into that of the most absolute despotism. A standing army effected this change, and a standing army supported it through a succession of ages, which are marked in the annals of history, with the most horrid cruelties, bloodshed, and carnage; the most devilish, beastly, and unnatural vices, that ever punished or disgraced human nature. . . . I firmly believe, no country in the world had ever a more patriotic army, than the one which so ably served this country [America] in the late war. But had the General who commanded them, been possessed of the spirit of a Julius Caesar or an [Oliver] Cromwell, the liberties of this country, had in all probability, terminated with the war; or had they been maintained, might have cost more blood and treasure, than was expended in the conflict with Great Britain.[17]

During the Constitutional Convention virtually every conceivable principle, device, or structural form of government in effect at the time or conceived in the pen of political theorists up to that time was discussed. Locke, Swift, Hobbs, Voltaire, Montesquieu, and others were quoted, dissected, debated, applied, discarded, and reapplied.[18] Districting schemes, election laws, rotation in office, popular representation, executive prerogatives, voter manipulation, checks on the popular will, the rights of states and individuals, and other facets of governance were all considered. Much of the debate between the parties focused on whether the Constitution should be strictly or loosely interpreted, and many of the positions taken by the delegates on any one issue smelled of political expediency. If strictly interpreted as the Anti-Federalists wanted, the federal government would have only the powers specifically given to it in the final document. The Tenth Amendment of the Bill of Rights, added later, would specifically reserve all other powers to the states or the people. Loose interpretation would allow for the expansion of federal powers into areas not specified in the founding document.

The Federalists would use the so-called elastic clause (Article 1, Section 8, Clause 18) to decide what powers were necessary and proper for the protection of the nation. Moreover, a large federal bureaucracy might require more extensive powers simply to hold its separate parts in check. Hamilton thought that the only way to protect the sovereignty of the individual states was to have a national government that would have a strong central authority and a military force equal to the task of protecting the union from embarrassment or partition by outside forces like France, Spain, or Britain—all of whom had territorial possessions on the boundaries of the nation. Additionally, in the absence of a strong central force, the states might war on each other with the small being gobbled up by the large in a war of attrition over boundaries, arable lands, or other resources.

Anti-Federalist Patrick Henry was somewhat the antithesis to the Federalists. During the deliberations surrounding the ratification of the Constitution, Henry made a speech against a strong federal government in which he said, "I smell a rat!"[19] An isolationist and antiexpansionist, Henry wrote,

> There is no danger of a dismemberment of our country, unless a constitution be adopted which will enable the government to plant enemies on our backs. . . . Then [it is said] the savage Indians are to destroy us. . . . But, sir, it is well known that we have nothing to fear from them. Our back settlers are considerably stronger than they. Their superiority increases daily. Suppose the states to be confederated all around us; what we want in numbers, we shall make up otherwise. Our compact situation and natural strength will secure us.[20]

A necessary premise underlying the Anti-Federalist attack on the proposed constitution was that it was meant to place exclusive jurisdiction over the militia in the hands of the general government. Anti-Federalists believed that the true motive for the assertion of national control over the armed forces, and especially the state militias, was not to use them, but to neutralize them through their amalgamation into the federal forces, and thus eliminate any state-sponsored opposition to an overbearing standing army and an overburdening military budget proposed by the central government. Though the Federalists denied this premise, even Luther Martin and Elbridge Gerry, who had been members of the Federalist group at the convention, affirmed it and opposed any constitution without amendment to secure the individual right to keep and bear arms. It was to prevent such a circumstance that the Second Amendment of the Bill of Rights was adopted. In "The President as Military King," the author (probably Benjamin Workman) opined, "The thoughts of a military officer possessing such powers, as the proposed constitution vests in the president . . . are sufficient to excite in the mind of a freeman the most alarming apprehensions; and ought to rouse him to oppose it at all events."[21]

Ironically, many of the strongest reservations concerning "powers" came from the New England politicians who threatened to pull out of the constitutional deliberations if their demands were not met. The delegates from Virginia also demanded that the powers of the central government be severely limited. Thomas Jefferson warned that if the federal government were allowed to define the limits of its own powers, the result would be not short of despotism. To get approval of the Constitution, a separate bill of rights defining the limits of power alluded to in the principal document was needed to overcome the fear of either an imperial executive or a tyrannical Congress. The Bill of Rights was to be the final security for the civil liberties of the individual.

While Federalists generally favored the concept of executive appointments to positions in government (whether by the president, a governor, or a state legislature), James Wilson, one of America's first great political theorists and later an

Associate Justice of the Supreme Court, believed that the popular election of senators, judges, and others including the head of the executive branch effectively extended the influence of the people over government. Wilson did not fear the executive branch. "They who execute and they who administer the laws, are as much the servants, and therefore as much the friends of the people, as those who make them."[22]

The appointment without election of delegates to the Constitutional Convention unfortunately had established a precedent for the concept of state selection of representatives to high office—particularly that of senators. Many of the framers believed that through the selection of persons to the U.S. Senate, state legislatures would cement their ties with the national government. This would increase the chances for a more republican form of governance and protect the nation from the dangers of uncontrolled democracy. They also expected that senators appointed by state legislatures rather than by the people would be able to concentrate on the business at hand without pressure from the electorate. Unfortunately, this decision by the Constitutional Convention marked the beginning of many contentious battles in the state legislatures as the struggle to appoint "right-thinking" senators reflected the increasing tensions over slavery and state rights. The addition of the Seventeenth Amendment in 1913 modified the Constitution (Article I, section 3) and provided for the direct election of senators by replacing the phrase "chosen by the Legislature" with "elected by the people."[23]

James Wilson noted further his faith in the power of the presidency,

The executive power is better to be trusted when it has no screen. Sir, we have a responsibility in the person of our President; he cannot act improperly, and hide either his negligence or inattention; he cannot roll upon any other person the weight of his criminality; no appointment can take place without his nomination; and he is responsible for every nomination he makes . . . far from being above the laws, he is amenable to them in his private character as a citizen, and in his public character by impeachment.[24]

The Elastic Clauses

Most of the anxieties that populated the nightmares of Anti-Federalists would become reality under the new constitution as the executive branch seized upon the common defense clause to make war, and the Congress used the general welfare clause to proceed with federal programs thought "necessary and proper" for the prosecution of their carefully enumerated powers. These were called the elastic clauses of the Constitution as both branches of the government used them to stretch the powers of the federal government. The courts ultimately brought a third party into the overall scheme of governance assuming the concept of *judicial review* in the *Marbury v. Madison* decision in 1803 to balance the competing powers of the other two branches. Proponents of strict construction pointed for relief to the Tenth Amendment of the Bill of Rights, which specified that those powers not specifically granted to the federal government in the Constitution were reserved to the states or to the people. This, they argued, was further proof that those who had ratified the Constitution had subscribed to the Anti-Federalist interpretation. Although the Supreme Court agreed with the broader view of the Constitution by developing the *doctrine of implied powers* in 1819, constitutional conservatives continued to derive arguments from Anti-Federalist principles.

Partisan Policies

New York was the first seat of the national government under the Constitution. Although it had the potential to be a republican city, the presence of the central government ensured that it was a Federalist town. Important Federalists like Alexander Hamilton, John Jay, and Rufus King had homes there—Hamilton's on Harlem Heights overlooked Morningside Park where a major battle of the Revolution had been fought. Although a long-term Anti-Federalist governor, George Clinton, ran the state of New York, the Federalists in the state had the support of most of the influential newspapers. Moreover, because the city was becoming a financial center, they had access to money. Hamilton and other Federalists had founded the Bank of New York in the 1780s well in advance of any pressing economic need, and their foresight was paying both monetary and political dividends.

The leading families of the city lived closely together, and the political and financial notables were always in close touch. The wealthy merchant traders and shipowners, who lived on State Street overlooking the harbor, annually shipped more than $2 million worth of wheat, flour, beef, pork, furs, raw hides, lumber, and livestock. Hundreds of cargo vessels tied up the New York wharfs in one of the world's finest natural harbors. The social elite mingled at the theater, at sporting events, at the eating-places, and at the coffeehouses.

Fine appointments and details had always graced the homes of the "first families" of the republic, but never before had they been located so close to the gritty machinery that produced their owners' wealth. As a moderate form of separation from the other classes, homeowners erected fences of wrought iron and ornamental brick that enclosed gardens filled with exotic plantings, Far Eastern urns, and classical statuary. Inside the so-called Federalist-style homes, spacious rooms were filled with Chinese porcelains, carved soapstone, embroidered silks, and handsome teakwood furniture. Cantonware graced the dining tables of all but the meanest residences.

Other port cities exhibited similar environmental, economic, and demographic characteristics—if not on the same grandiose scale as New York; and their residents also supported banks, business districts, literary societies, theater groups, cultural activities, and a commonly held theory of government.[25]

Somehow, in fine mansions and reeking grog shops, amid a jungle of crooked streets, shop fronts, hitching posts, refuse piles, dingy stoops, amid sledges and derricks and carts and barrows of construction sites, amid the smell of hogs and goat manure and outhouses, and out of the pushing and hauling of legislators, aroused interest groups, rival factions, elitist manipulations—the government of the young republic emerged.[26]

Americans were living well under their newfound independence, but the buying spree they were on was leading to an unfavorable balance of trade with America's overseas customers, particularly France and Britain. Inflation increased, recession threatened, and the commercial and moneyed interests that had supported the government when the Revolution seemingly had promised limitless opportunity began losing confidence. The rich seemed to be getting richer at the expense of everyone else. In 1794, the bubble seemed ready to burst and destroy the young nation's economy. At that time economic panic was notable—the first of many that affected Americans' ability to work or find a job. It was evident to some that only a strong central authority with the power to levy taxes, collect duties, and regulate the economy could restore the optimism of the nation.

The Great Divide

From 1788 to 1796, President George Washington presided over a national administration that was outwardly unified but actually rife with internal conflicts and problems. The framers of the Constitution had left a large number of questions unresolved even with the addition of the Bill of Rights. The men serving in Washington's administration were trying without the benefit of previous experience to establish departments, procedures, and protocols that buttressed the structure of the republic without offending the freedoms of speech, religion, press, and assembly or the rights to life, liberty, property, and equal protection under the law. This was difficult under any circumstance, but it was more challenging without a clear concept of just how these high-sounding principles related to the realities of governance, the role of political opposition and self-interest, and the effect of an ever-shifting majority opinion.

As the virtually unanimous choice for first president of the republic, Washington is usually classified a federalist (small "f"), not in the political party sense—he detested parties and factions—but in the sense that he wanted to establish a central government that could act quickly, decisively, and authoritatively for the whole nation. That had been the purpose behind the abandonment of the Articles of Confederation and the adoption of the Constitution. "The men around Washington were building a national governmental structure in a cooperative, soldierly, and workmanlike way, yet they differed violently over banks, tariffs, slavery, fiscal policy, foreign policy, presidential power, congressional prerogative, the permanent location of the national capital, and . . . a multitude of philosophical issues."[27] Among the important unresolved political questions, the ambiguous relationship among the federal government, the individual states, and the sovereignty of the people stands out.

It was not that Washington and his administration were not in full command of the government, they were. Yet once the euphoria of self-government had worn off, questions of who should rule—merchants or farmers, shippers or manufacturers, workers or employers—plagued the nation. A foreign observer noted that "American [political] theory is . . . in advance of American practice."[28] The tandem questions of just how much civil liberty could be allowed to the public and how much authority could be granted to the central government were to plague the republic during much of its history. Charles Pinckney had warned during the Constitutional Convention that the nation could depend for guidance neither on the opinion of the people as a whole nor on the wisdom of the elites because each was too prone to selfishness and too hostile to the interests of others. An American-born observer of the process noted that "liberty was not the fashion for the moment, so the American government came in for condemnation because it had not power enough, especially in the executive branch. . . . As a consequence the representatives were too dependent on their constituents and too local in their policy."[29] It was no accident that the first disagreements concerning the establishment of a stronger army and navy came during this period of national stress.

Washington's advisors and secretaries held a wide spectrum of political opinions, but most of his subordinates suppressed their partisanship because the president believed that it was threatening to the success of the republic. Yet two of them stand out from the group. Alexander Hamilton (secretary of the treasury) and Thomas Jefferson (secretary of state) refused to yield on the most divergent of their strongly held and mutually exclusive beliefs. These included the proper military and naval posture to be assumed by the nation.

National politics revolved around Hamilton and Jefferson like a whirlwind, but factionalism rather than political parties was the order of the day within the Washington administration. Even with the formal adoption of party labels, the so-called two-party system of later American history was not as entrenched or well organized as the phrase suggests. Factional leaders attempted, nonetheless, to recruit blocs of voters and popular regional leaders to the ongoing set of policy disputes. The Jeffersonian Republicans (now formed into a political party, the Democratic Republicans) understood the anxiety that many Americans held toward a powerful central government, and they seized on frontiersmen, settlers, farmers, and the lower classes as the foundation of their political power. Jefferson and his followers were the first Americans to form a formal political party since the Revolution. The organization of this party and that of its opponents, the strong-government Federalists, is sometimes called the first-party system. The two-party system, or something closely resembling it, moved along fitfully from the time of the ratification of the Constitution in 1787 to the end of the War of 1812.[30]

Hamilton was the most audacious and provocative of Washington's ministers. He and other likeminded Federalists believed that a weak agrarian republic could not survive in a world of empires. They saw a need to vastly broaden the American economy, underpin its currency, consolidate the foundations of its financial system, and strengthen the republic by giving the wealthy, the well-born, and the educated increased access to and interest in government. Not only were Hamilton's Federalist principles audacious in their details, they were drawn largely from moderate European writers and economists and relied on many British legal precedents. They reinforced the age-old fundamental political inequality of men and women, the inviolability of property, the sanctity of contracts, and the continued reliance on the concept of social deference among the classes. Hamilton was a self-proclaimed militarist and Anglophile who believed that the future success of the republic lay in resolving through strength the old economic questions and impasses that stood between America and Britain. As secretary of the treasury, he submitted his proposals to the president, and Washington adopted them for submission to the Congress.

By way of contrast, Jefferson's ideas of a purely democratic form of governance ruled by the majority of the common people were radically liberal and innovative for their day. He feared that the Federalist principles of Hamilton were a direct threat to individual liberty, personal rights, majority rule, and the political devices that would facilitate true democracy. The men who rallied around Jefferson's position became known as Jeffersonian Republicans (or Democratic Republicans, but they were in no way associated with the 1850s Republican Party of Abraham Lincoln). They were a combination of just plain folk led by the liberal elite, who in the 21st century might be called the intelligentsia. Jeffersonian Republicans feared that a strong central government, supported by a national army and navy and dedicated to international commerce and the accumulation of wealth, would inevitably slip into tyranny. Those who believed as Jefferson did "portrayed themselves as the rightful heirs of the Revolutionary victory, determined to keep taxes and public debt low, to limit government, to avoid entanglements abroad, but to support the rights of man generally and the revolutionaries in France particularly."[31]

In fact, developments in France in the 1790s would demonstrate that the tyranny that Jefferson feared could take many forms beyond the simple tyranny of monarchy. The tyrannies possible under the rule of an exclusive upper class possessed of unfettered wealth were obvious, but the tyrannies of shifting public opinion or of an uninformed and badly led majority of the lower classes were potentially dangerous to individual liberty, personal rights, and life itself. The Jeffersonian Republicans recognized the danger but believed that if the people were truly virtuous in a civic sense they would put aside self-interest and sacrifice comfort, riches, and power for the greatest public good.

The Jeffersonian Republicans were at first elated by the French Revolution (1792), thinking that they had helped to plant the seeds of popular democracy in aristocratic Europe. The red and blue of the citizens of the city of Paris and the white of the Bourbon Dynasty sharing the French Tricolor was thought to signify a generally smooth transition from absolute monarchy to a more republican form of government like that in America with its own red, white, and blue flags and bunting. Before their confinement and execution, even the royal couple, Louis XVI and Marie Antoinette, sported red, white, and blue ribbons in public. Jeffersonian Republicans in America first began wearing red, white, and blue ribbons on their clothing and as cockades in their hats as a symbol of their party affiliation at this time. Federalist gentlemen disconnected themselves from such attitudes by wearing wholly black cockades on their hats, as had the first American militias in the Revolution before the French alliance (after which alliance they wore black with a white center). It is from this point that political partisanship in American's handling of foreign affairs truly takes root.[32]

An egalitarian France, with 25 million new consumers free to purchase American grain, raw materials, and manufactures, initially promised to be a boon to Americans of all parties. The Marquis de Lafayette, himself an icon of both the American and French revolutions, sent the key of the Bastille to President Washington in 1789 as a symbol of understanding and symbiosis between republican France and republican America. In *Rights of Man* (1791–1792) Thomas Paine wrote, "Never did so great an opportunity offer itself to England, and to all Europe, as is produced by the two Revolutions of America and France. By the former, freedom has a national champion in the western world; and by the latter, in Europe. . . . When all the Governments of Europe shall be established on the representative system, Nations will become acquainted, and the animosities and the prejudices fomented by the intrigue and artifice of Court will cease." However, political freedom and international peace did not come with the simple turn of a key, nor did they automatically translate into social and economic equality, as the bloody Sans-Culottes of the Paris mob would show.[33]

The Jeffersonian Republicans were damaged politically in the eyes of many Americans when the French mobs slaughtered more than 1,600 middle- and upper-class persons in a single month—including women and children—and declared war almost simultaneously on Austria, Britain, and Prussia. They executed their king, queen, and many other aristocrats in a barbarous and bloody manner. Finally, the Terror (1793–1794) suspended the rights guaranteed under the French constitution, established a secret police, renewed censorship of the press, repressed religion, and eliminated many of the oldest families in France—seemingly discarding many of the fundamental principles of liberty and justice all within a few months.

To the personal distress of Jefferson, Maximillien Robespierre, leader of the French Committee of Public Safety, openly equated *civic virtue* with the bloody machinations of the Terror, thereby degrading a major foundational tenet of Jeffersonian-style democracy in American eyes. Yet the American Revolution was fundamentally different from that of the French. America had separated itself from British rule, not only politically but geographically. The French were forced by their geography to live among their former rulers, rubbing raw the differences between them. Unfortunately those Frenchmen calling for liberty, equality, and fraternity seemed to have forgotten the concomitant need for humanity, stability, and restraint. The grotesque levels of personal violence, the spiraling instability, and the rivers of blood in France repelled many Americans who noted that they had not resorted to similar excesses in 1776 or in 1787. Many of those formerly open to Jefferson's egalitarianism turned away from the democratic republicanism of Jefferson and left the Federalists firmly in control of the American nation just as President Washington left office.

Alien and Sedition Acts

Washington ended his administration in 1796 with his foreign policy in tatters and his government divided along the very party and sectional lines that he hated, especially with regard to their sympathies for either Britain or France. Noting the momentary embarrassment of the Jeffersonians, the Federalists overreached. The Alien and Sedition Acts refer to the four bills passed in 1798 by the Federalists in Congress and signed into law by the second president John Adams (1796–1800). The acts were ostensibly designed to protect the nation from alien citizens of enemy powers and to stop seditious attacks among its own citizens from weakening the government during wartime. At the time of their passage, the United States stood on the brink of war (the so-called Quasi War 1798–1803) with revolutionary France. The Federalists believed that Jeffersonian Republican criticism of U.S. government policies was disloyal—bordering on treason—and they feared that alien immigrants living in America would sympathize with the French during a war.

While time and anecdote have gilded the reputations of Adams and Jefferson as founders of the nation, the two men were implacable political opponents (enemies, really) during the early period of the republic. Adams was a Federalist ideologue and never a likeable man personally. Moreover, he considered Jefferson and his liberal followers dangerous to the government. The two men refused to speak with one another for more than two decades, and only on their deathbeds was there any hesitant accommodation made between them. The fact that they died on the very same day (July 4, 1826), exactly fifty years after the signing of the Declaration of Independence that they both helped to create, has tended to overshadow the depth of the hatred between them during much of their public lives.

The Alien and Sedition Acts were carefully aimed at suppressing popular dissent. Among a population increasingly composed of foreign-born immigrants, the laws raised the residency requirements for citizenship to fourteen years, authorized the president to deport aliens, and permitted their arrest, imprisonment, and deportation during wartime. The Alien Acts played into the ever-flowing stream of American nativism, but the Sedition Act was a blatant attempt to muzzle the Jeffersonian Republicans and other wholly American Francophiles. It made it a crime for U.S. citizens to print, utter, or publish any negative statements about the U.S. government or its policies.

The Jeffersonian Republicans attacked the acts as being unconstitutional, dangerous to civil liberties, and designed to suppress criticism of the Adams's administration. The redress of unconstitutional legislation under the doctrine of judicial review would not be established for several years. Moreover the Supreme Court of the 1790s was composed entirely of pro-Federalist justices, many of whom were openly hostile to the anti-Federalist point of view. Lacking a precedent-setting decision, in his own presidency Thomas Jefferson (1800–1808) would pardon and order the release of all who had been convicted of violating the laws during the administration of his predecessor.

The Sedition Act, as separate from the Alien Acts, was set to expire in 1801, coinciding with the end of the Adams administration. While its constitutionality had not been directly decided by the Supreme Court, subsequent mentions of the Sedition Act in Supreme Court opinions have assumed that it would have been ruled unconstitutional as a violation of free speech if ever tested in the courts. One of the remaining three acts—the Alien Enemies Act (50 U.S.C. sec. 21–24)—is still in force and frequently has been cited in wartime to justify the actions of the executive branch. The remaining acts expired or were repealed by 1802.

Virginia and Kentucky Resolutions

Meanwhile, Jefferson and Madison had combined their talents in 1798 to define the limits of legitimate federal power through the Virginia and Kentucky Resolutions. In these resolutions, Jefferson and Madison—disciples of principles on different ends of the constitutional interpretation debate—attempted to address the injustices of the Alien and Sedition Acts. They tried to demonstrate that the states were not united on the principle of unlimited submission to the central government, but they were the exclusive and final judges of the extent of the powers delegated to the federal level. Madison and Jefferson had proposed no more than cooperation among the several states in securing the repeal of unfair federal laws or in amending the Constitution. In later years Madison, one of the authors of the *Federalist Papers*, clearly considered the application of the principles that he had delineated in the resolutions by Anti-Federalists a gross misrepresentation of his political opinions with respect to the powers of the federal government.

The Kentucky and Virginia Resolutions brought to the forefront an important matter of concern—that is, a state's right to nullify a federal action (in this case, the widely despised and legally flawed Alien and Sedition Acts). The Federalists said that if a state could nullify a federal action, even a misguided one, then the authority of the central government had no meaning. Supreme authority in America, the Anti-Federalists argued, was not held by the federal government but rather by the people and the states. Congress and the executive branch had only those powers clearly delegated to them in the Constitution. This issue would be settled to some extent in the Civil War through the virtual extinction of the Tenth Amendment by the force of federal arms, but its arguments with respect to the limits of federal power would continue to be made throughout American history and are common into the 21st century.

It is important in this discussion to emphasize the contrast between "rights" and "powers." Ironically, many strong reservations about "powers" came from the Northern states during the constitutional ratification debates. The Massachusetts legislature expressed a fear that the Constitution might be interpreted to extend the powers of Congress, which they feared might abridge states rights, or increase the possibility of extending the war powers of the president whenever he took a position with which the states did not agree. Indeed the New Englanders seemed to trust neither the legislative nor the executive branches of the federal government. Ironically, the northeastern states would assume a radically different position with respect to the federal government in the Civil War.

Massachusetts was not alone in the plasticity of its political principles. Rhode Island proposed a remarkable statement of states' rights similar in sentiment to that used by southern secessionists two generations later. Even Connecticut politicians resorted to their rights and threatened secession if their demands were not met. Among the southern states, the people of Virginia required that the powers granted the national government under the Constitution "be resumed by the states, whensoever the same shall be perverted to their injury or oppression."[34] Both Jefferson and Madison believed that the states were "not united on the principle of unlimited submission to their general government" but reserved "each State to itself, the . . . right to their own self-government."[35]

Both Jefferson and Madison were antimilitarists in their own way. Jefferson's aversion to standing forces was reflective of a pervading distrust of standing forces not only in America, but also throughout the 18th-century world in which conscripted armies and continuous wars among princely states had made life almost intolerable for the common man. Madison was more circumspect in his antimilitarism declaring "armies *in times of peace* [italics added] are allowed by all to be an evil."[36] Yet no such uniformity of principle existed with regard to the expansion of the nation for either man.

It was here that the conservative case against American empire-building could be found. Some suggested that expansion had been among the primary goals of those seeking American independence. "We are on the verge of empire," said the antiwar conservatives of the late 18th century, noting that "we should not cross over into empire's snare."[37] In terms of size, the infant United States was already an unwieldy empire, with 500,000 square miles of area marked on all but one point of the compass (the South) with water access through the Great Lakes, the Mississippi River, and the Atlantic Ocean. Antiexpansionist critics would reiterate these sentiments during the War of 1812, the Mexican War, the Civil War, and the Spanish-American War as the expansionists sought to fill out the "natural boundaries" of the nation.[38]

The Louisiana Purchase

It is ironic that the expanding American empire should have been made possible in its infancy by Thomas Jefferson's clearly extraconstitutional purchase of a territory belonging to a foreign country. Nowhere in the Constitution was the power to add territory to the nation even addressed. The Louisiana Purchase from Napoleonic France in 1803 was considered by some conservative voices in the Northeast "a great waste" of national treasure and a liability that would require the establishment of a massive armed force for its protection and security. Conservatives pointed out that the new frontier states carved from this "unpeopled wilderness" that the expansionists envisioned would give the Jeffersonian Republicans a secure and possibly insurmountable majority in the U.S. Senate, two by two, ultimately condemning the Federalist Party to oblivion.[39]

America's quest for its *Manifest Destiny*—not referred to as such for six decades[40]—had begun as early as 1784 when Thomas Hutchins, geographer of the United States, noted of the great expanse of the North American continent, "If we want it, I warrant it will be ours." He viewed the inhabitants of the young republic as potential possessors of a vast transcontinental empire who had it "in their power to engross the whole commerce of it, and to reign, not only as lords of America, but to possess, in the utmost security, the dominion of the sea throughout the world."[41]

In fact, the exploration and domination of the North American continent was no haphazard series of fortuitous ramblings and random discoveries, but a careful process initiated by Jefferson and programmed thereafter from the urban centers of the Northeast and Midwest, particularly Washington, D.C., and St. Louis, Missouri. Politicians, land speculators, and businessmen formulated specific instructions and sent explorers, traders, artists, and soldiers into the unfenced expanses of grass, the towering mountains, and the formidable deserts to gather information that would further the development of the continent under U.S. rule.

Jefferson had accumulated information regarding the Trans-Mississippi West during his five years (1784–1789) of diplomatic service in France. Jefferson had instituted an expedition into the region in 1794, well in advance of any offer to sell Louisiana made by Napoleon Bonaparte, but had canceled it when the French-born leader he had chosen came under suspicion as a spy. Secretary of the Treasury Albert Gallatin and others had persuaded Jefferson that the power to acquire territory was "implied" by the executive power in the Constitution to "make treaties." Even though Jefferson conceded that it was probably beyond the powers granted to the president in the Constitution, he simply ignored the potential of constitutional difficulties and made the purchase.

In 1805, Meriwether Lewis and William Clark returned from a two-year exploration of the Louisiana Purchase. Their maps, drawings, and descriptions of the territory fired the imagination of the nation concerning the West, and the constitutionality of the deal was quickly forgotten by all but the most vigilant of strict constructionists. Among these was John Randolph of Virginia who considered the Louisiana Purchase the "worst curse" that ever befell the country, and historian Henry Adams (great grandson of the second president) who thought the purchase a "fatal wound" to strict construction.[42]

The practical difficulties of overruling the North American continent from the eastern to the western oceans and from the Mexican Gulf in the South to the frozen lakes of the Canadian North were of minor consequence. Time and space could be overcome. It was America's Manifest Destiny to do so. Mexico, Britain, and even Russia stood in the way no less than the vast prairies, towering mountains, and indigenous native population. The power of Manifest Destiny lay in the national imagination. It was a drama enacted on a corporate level by all but the entire American people.

Individual families normally are not considered powerful agents of nation-building. Surely it is armies, speculators, industrialists, railway magnets, and other economic and political factors that are the impetus of national expansion. Yet this was not always the case in America, and many of these forces tended to follow families rather than to lead them into the new territories. The simplest maps of the unknown interior spurred thousands of Americans to relocate to towns that existed nowhere except on land office surveys. With them, in many cases, came their slaves, forced to emigrate sometimes in ways that forever broke black family ties. Before them stood the Native Americans with their own families, aboriginal inheritors of the land, poised to be swept aside and ultimately to be dispossessed of their heritage.

Warfare on the Frontier

At the end of the Revolutionary War, many of America's Native allies formed treaty relations with the United States, while the Loyalist tribes generally passed to the west of the Appalachians or removed to Canada to take advantage of British protection. Other nations, which had attempted uneasy neutrality during the Revolution, viewed the new republic with cautious curiosity. American diplomats sent to the tribes attempted to resurrect the old ceremonial vocabulary of the "Great Father" and his "Indian Children" formerly utilized by the British in forming treaties with the president taking the place of the king. In the first decades of the 19th century, however, the British retained control of Canada and much of the Great Lakes Region, and they willingly incited the Indians to cause trouble on the American frontier.

In the Proclamation of 1763, Britain had attempted to enforce a western boundary to white settlement along the Appalachian chain that generally had favored the tribes. By comparison after the Revolution, the independent-minded American states seemed weak and disorganized as white settlers and land speculators poured over the mountains and onto Native land. The Mohawk war leader and British supporter, Joseph Brant, worked with Native tribes throughout the Ohio country and the lakes region of Canada to create a Western Confederacy and coordinate a resistance to the United States. Brant set the Ohio River as the border between Native lands and those of the new republic. Americans claimed the entire Midwest and Great Lakes region, and formed a political entity from it called the Northwest Territory, because it was on the northwest margin of those lands recognized by treaty with Britain in 1783.

Brant's confederacy thoroughly defeated two American armies sent to occupy the newly created Northwest Territory in 1790 and 1791, respectively. The force of 1,400 men led by Gen. Arthur St. Clair lost more than 600 killed and 300 wounded, making the defeat one of the worst proportionately ever visited on American troops in any war even into modern times. In response, a punitive force under Gen. "Mad" Anthony Wayne won a battle with the tribes at Fallen Timbers, after which the British virtually abandoned the Native American survivors. This changed a minor victory by American arms into a huge diplomatic success with the Indians, who yielded most of the Ohio country to white settlement. Wayne relied on the threat posed by a thinly spread series of forts from Cincinnati to Fort Wayne (Indiana) rather than on diplomacy to bring the Native leaders to the peace table.[43]

Throughout the crisis, the British had feigned neutrality, but their agents had assured the Indians of their support in terms of arms and ammunition. In 1794, the Jay Treaty required that the British abandon their western posts, but British pretensions to the Old Northwest were not truly erased until 1815, leaving the Native leaders to make the best deal with the United States that they could. During this crisis, the tribes had gained the undying enmity of the western settlers, and most of the tribes abandoned the woodlands within the United States and sought refuge with the British in Canada. This course probably saved a great number of Native American lives. The tribes thereafter utilized the recognized border (the medicine line) with the United States as an invisible, but effective, barrier to pursuit. The Oregon treaty line with Canada—not permanently settled at the 49th parallel until 1846—was used in a similar manner during the Plains Indian Wars of the second half of the century.

Among the major objectives of the Lewis and Clark Expedition (1803–1805) were efforts to make a show of American sovereignty over the Louisiana Territory after its purchase from France, and to establish relations and treaties with the western tribes then resident in the region. These had formerly owed allegiance to or recognized the British, French, or Spanish. Yet from the inception of the United States, treaties and alliances between the federal government and the Native American nations were conveniently broken whenever coveting white settlers became numerous or aggressive enough to work their collective wills upon the politicians. The efforts of the Native population to thwart white incursions into their lands often brought the government to intervene—usually on the side of the settlers and with devastating military force. Nonetheless, in 1809, federal troops forcibly removed 1,700 white squatters from Native lands; however, they were so quickly replaced by other intruders that, without a constant military presence, the policy seemed doomed to failure.

George Washington's Secretary of War Henry Knox initially crafted "Indian" policy at the federal level, and it was carried out by most of the administrations that followed. Knox envisioned a policy of "civilization" and "Christianization" for the tribes. He sought to teach the Indians to abandon their traditional gender-based communal economy of male hunting and warfare, and female agriculture and child-rearing for a Euro-American lifestyle of male-oriented farming and female domesticity that would allow the tribes to prosper on a much smaller land base. This, it was hoped, would open former Native lands to white settlement without eradicating the tribes. Federal agents relentlessly pushed this civilization program, or a near facsimile, throughout the 19th century.[44]

The Quaker Presence

The American Revolutionary War proved to be an extremely difficult period for the Quakers. On the one hand, many of them rejoiced in the possibility of freedom from an intolerant Church of England; but, on the other hand, they abhorred the violence that was bringing about the change. Some Quakers, like Nathaniel Greene, joined the Revolutionary Army forming their own society and calling themselves Free Quakers.

The Religious Society of Friends realized that the American South, generally hostile to the antislavery Quakers, was not the most advantageous place in which to live, and they began to look for new lands on which to settle where they would not be persecuted for their beliefs and practices. To the north, beyond the mountains and beyond the Ohio River, was a new territory called the Ohio Country, acquired from Britain in the peace that ended the Revolution. This region had an abundance of natural resources. The Ohio Country had been organized for survey and sale after

Congress enacted the Land Ordinance of 1785. When the Northwest Ordinance of 1787 guaranteed that neither slavery nor involuntary servitude, except as punishment for crime, was ever to be permitted in any of the territory north of the Ohio River and east of the Mississippi River, the Free Quakers began to think seriously of making a mass migration northward.

Once opened, the Ohio Country attracted immense settlement. Free Quakers in the South began to join the great migration to the new West, which offered economic opportunity and personal and political freedom to its residents. Friends from New Jersey, eastern Pennsylvania, and northern Virginia also began to migrate to the Northwest Territory, not necessarily to escape from the evils of a slave society, but rather to seek a change and to start what many thought would be a better life.[45]

Pacifist Quakers were crucial in supporting Native American rights during this period, yet the Religious Society of Friends never had a unified approach in their dealings with the Indians. The Quakers played varying roles with the tribes: sometimes as partners and advocates, and sometimes as well-intentioned but misguided caretakers. Nonetheless, Quakers distinguished themselves as never having taken up arms against Native Americans, who in turn had never been purposely violent to Friends. Distinctive Quaker clothing and speech often served as a shield against violence. Sometimes Quaker involvement was inappropriate to the needs of Native Americans, but overall, Quakers and Indians enjoyed a relationship marked largely by peace, cooperation, and mutual respect.[46]

Quaker policy varied over time and location. Native Americans, from distinct nations and cultures, also varied in their response to Quaker efforts. Quaker Meetings throughout the states had active committees on Indian concerns, worked as intermediaries between tribes and whites, and initiated projects to assist them. For example, New York Friends provided smallpox vaccinations to the Oneida and Stockbridge Indians and assisted the Montauk and Shinnecock tribes of Long Island with farm equipment and agriculture techniques. In 1794, the Philadelphia Yearly Meeting sent representatives, at the request of the Native Americans, to observe the negotiations between the United States and the Six Iroquois Nations, which resulted in the lasting Treaty of Canandaigua. Established in 1794, Quaker Indian Committees were the longest standing committees of the Philadelphia and Baltimore Yearly Meetings.[47] As Quakers moved into the Ohio Country late in the 18th century, they demonstrated this concern for the welfare of the Indians in various ways, such as through visits to them with the message of Christ and through the establishment of service centers at Sandusky, Upper Sandusky, and Wapakoneta. Of particular interest and importance was the activity at Wapakoneta west of the Mississippi River where a remnant of the warlike and troublesome Shawnee tribe had moved.

Treason and Aaron Burr

Aaron Burr was a founding member of the Democratic Republican Party and senator from New York State (1791–1797). As candidate for president in 1800, Burr had tied Jefferson in electoral votes, sending the election into the House of Representatives. After dozens of ballots, Jefferson was selected president and Burr appointed vice president. Burr served only one term as vice president and was replaced in 1805 by George Clinton, the first governor of New York, and vice president under both Thomas Jefferson and James Madison.

During an unsuccessful campaign for governor of New York in 1804, Burr became insulted by published articles written by Alexander Hamilton. Taking umbrage at remarks made by Hamilton at a dinner party, Burr challenged Hamilton to a duel with pistols in July 1804 at the Heights of Weehawken in New Jersey. In the duel, he mortally wounded Hamilton, whose untimely death fatally weakened the remnants of the Federalist Party. Easily the most famous duel in American history, it had immense political ramifications. Burr was indicted for murder in New Jersey and, though the charges resulted in acquittal, the harsh criticism and animosity directed toward him in political and social circles brought about an end to any hope of furthering his political career in the Northeast. He remained a popular figure in the West and South, however.

In 1805, Burr journeyed into the Ohio River Valley and the lands recently acquired in the Louisiana Purchase to gauge for himself public opinion concerning aggressive rumblings with Spanish America and to have discussions with persons sympathetic to creating a Mexican insurrection against Spanish rule—among them former Ohio Sen. Jonathan Dayton, who was later indicted with Burr for treason. In New Orleans, Burr allegedly began to prepare a private military expedition into New Spain. There were persistent rumors that he planned to carve out a region for himself from among the Spanish possessions, form his own monarchy in the western half of North America, and ultimately secede from the United States.

The so-called Burr Conspiracy had its origins in a series of discussions over the winter of 1804–1805 between Burr and his long-standing friend Gen. James Wilkinson, the newly appointed governor of the Louisiana Territory. The two men had served together in the Revolution, and over the years they often corresponded in a written cipher invented by Wilkinson that smacked of conspiracy on its surface. Wilkinson was a noted intriguer who formerly had established a minor political party in the Trans-Appalachian West that favored a separation of the western states from the Atlantic coastal states. It was Wilkinson who had decided to abandon the plan with Burr, and he determined to undermine Burr by rushing troops to the Mississippi Valley and ordering the militia in New Orleans to be on alert for an attack. A decoded ciphered letter along with one from co-conspirator Senator Dayton, were sent to the president by Wilkinson as evidence of the conspiracy. Jefferson, who seemingly took it as a personal mission to secure Burr's conviction for treason, quickly issued a proclamation of conspiracy.

Burr was in Nashville when he learned that federal authorities were out to crush his plans, and he beat a hurried retreat down the Cumberland River. All of Burr's forces (dwindled to between 60 and 100 armed men) met up at the Falls of the Ohio. Addressing his recruits, Burr told them what he had intended, but circumstances had caused him to defer his plans. Instead, the expedition would head down the Mississippi, where Burr, still ignorant of Wilkinson's betrayal, expected the military backing of his friend. Only upon reaching Bayou Pierre, thirty miles above Natchez, did Burr learn that Wilkinson had turned from co-conspirator into an informant. A militia detachment of thirty men under Capt. Edmund P. Gaines caught up with Burr when he and his followers were camped across from Natchez, on the west bank of the Mississippi. Burr was handed an official letter demanding his surrender. Burr responded to the letter by denouncing Wilkinson whose perfidious conduct had completely frustrated his project. The next day, Burr was convinced to surrender.

On the basis of having conspired to wage a private war on a peaceful power, Burr was arrested and brought to trial on charges of treason in February 1807. John Wickham and Edmund Randolph represented Burr, who also argued on his own behalf. After several weeks, Burr petitioned the court that the prosecution testimony had utterly failed to prove that he had taken any overt act of war. Although members of the expedition had taken aggressive actions, Chief Justice John Marshall, who presided over the case, agreed that Burr had not taken an act of war and sent the case to the jury without further testimony. Burr was acquitted. After failing to convict Burr of treason, the government halfheartedly tried him on a misdemeanor charge of waging war on Spain. This trial, too, ended in acquittal, on grounds similar to the earlier case. Jefferson fumed over Marshall's ruling, which had effectively ended the prosecution, claiming that the United States had no law but the individual will of the judges. The president contemplated responses ranging from proposing a constitutional amendment limiting the power of the judiciary to asking Congress to impeach the chief justice.

The treason trial of Aaron Burr came at a time of great instability, both in Europe and America. The American and French revolutions worried traditional European powers, which were determined to keep the radical new doctrine from undermining the power of their monarchies. After several years in self-imposed exile in Europe, Burr returned to practicing law in New York City and lived a largely reclusive existence until his death.

Several important questions were raised by the treason trial of Burr. Some points were definitively decided during the case, while others were left open to further discussion and revision. Among the questions raised were the following:

- What is the meaning of treason? This was left largely undecided.

- Could the executive branch ignore a court order? No, but the doctrines of *executive privilege* and the overriding importance of national security were left largely unchallenged.

- Did a person accused of a crime have a right to demand the appearance of a witness and the presentation of documents as evidence? Yes, both before and after his indictment.

- What were the characteristics of a competent and unbiased juror? An impartial jury was found to be composed of persons who would fairly hear the evidence and decide according to that evidence. Those who had already formed an opinion of the guilt of the accused were disqualified, as were those who had formed an opinion not on the whole case but on a point so essential that it would have an unfair influence upon the verdict.

- Could a person who organized or instigated the gathering of an armed force be considered as *legally and constructively present* at the commission of the treasonable act, if that person did not directly participate in the armed assembly? No, the Constitution did not extend the concept of treason to the limitation of speech in the absence of overt actions.[48]

From the standpoint of constitutional law, the Burr trial was notable for Chief Justice Marshall's landmark decision narrowly construing the Constitution's definition of treason and thereby making conviction for this crime exceedingly difficult. The Constitution (Article III, section 3) provides that "Treason against the United States, shall consist only in levying War against them, or in adhering to their Enemies, giving them Aid and Comfort. No Person shall be convicted of Treason unless on the Testimony of two Witnesses to the same overt Act, or on Confession in open Court."[49]

The government charged Burr with the first of these two crimes of treason, levying war against the United States. In limiting treason only to levying war and giving aid and comfort to enemies, the framers of the Constitution established a more restrictive definition than had prevailed in Great Britain during the colonial period. The framers' omission of a more discrete definition of treason was intended purposefully to restrict the government from utilizing the concept of *constructive treason*—in other words, speaking or acting to encourage treason—that in England had been exploited to suppress dissent and political opposition.

Before the Burr trial, the few cases of treason heard in the United States were limited to the federal government's prosecution of persons involved in resisting a tax on distilled spirits during the Whiskey Rebellion (1794). This insurrection marked the first time under the new Constitution that the federal government had used military force to exert its authority over the nation's citizens. These cases were not important precedents in the Burr trial, although they provided examples of what some federal judges regarded as the conditions and circumstances necessary to constitute "levying war." Moreover, Burr's case had become deeply embroiled in politics, with Democratic Republicans supporting Jefferson's measures to bring the accused traitor to justice, and Federalists rallying to defend their former nemesis, Burr against the charges.[50]

Luther Martin, who had joined Burr's defense in time for the jury proceedings, had assumed the role of principal attack dog against the executive branch. In one notably vitriolic rant, he denounced Jefferson as a president who had "let slip the dogs of war, the hell-hounds of persecution, to hunt down my friend." Earlier, Jefferson had unwittingly and unwisely made himself vulnerable to such censure by publicly declaring that Burr's guilt was "beyond question."[51] It was possible that the president had thereby tainted the jury pool.

Martin's outburst had come in the midst of an important argument in the proceedings, prompted by Burr's motion for a *subpoena duces tecum* to the president. A *subpoena duces tecum* orders a person to appear in court and "bring with you" certain specified documents. Burr wanted the president to turn over the letter and papers received from Wilkinson, together with copies of the president's reply and certain directives issued by the departments of war and navy. The motion raised the fundamental question of whether the federal judiciary could issue such a subpoena to the president without violating the constitutional principle of *separation of powers*. The subpoena in the Burr trial followed an earlier contest between the Jefferson administration and the Supreme Court concerning the delivery of a commission to a justice of the peace. In that earlier case, *Marbury v. Madison* (1803), the Supreme Court declined for lack of jurisdiction to order the delivery of the commission but rebuked the executive branch for not doing its legal duty. In Burr's case, too, the threatened confrontation did not occur.[52]

Chief Justice Marshall had granted the motion for a subpoena, maintaining that the president was not exempt from court orders designed to protect the constitutional rights of criminal defendants. By the terms of the subpoena, the president was to provide the documents but did not have to appear personally. Jefferson did not acknowledge the court's order but informed the U.S. attorney that he had substantially complied with the subpoena's terms by previously delivering the requested documents to the prosecutor. In so doing, Jefferson claimed to have acted voluntarily and did not acknowledge the judiciary's right to compel him to release executive papers. He also maintained that in the interests of national security the president must be the sole judge of which papers could be safely disclosed. Jefferson here asserted the doctrine known as *executive privilege*.[53]

The Yankee Trader Expands the Nation

Before the end of the Revolution, Americans had shown that they were among the best wind-ship builders in the world, and American mariners had proven themselves among the most courageous of blue water sailors. Soon after the granting of independence, Americans began to revitalize those maritime activities that the British Royal Navy had threatened during the war. Technically allied with France and at peace with most of Europe for the first time in decades, American vessels, whalers, and slavers soon inundated the trading ports of the world, especially those among the rich islands of the West Indies, which the so-called Yankee traders began to view as their own.

By the beginning of the 19th century, the economics of maritime trade had become truly global. Englishmen drank French wine and brandy when they could get it; Frenchmen used spice imported from the Dutch East Indies; Hollanders cooked with Spanish olive oil; and Spaniards ate salted cod from New England. Sugar moved from the New World to the Old, Asian silks and tea were sold in markets from Italy to Philadelphia, and Africans were torn from their homes and forced to labor in the wilderness of America. For the maritime nations of the world, sea power was the fundamental principle that could determine whether an empire would rise or fall. Overwhelming sea power, and the quest to gain or retain it, proved a decisive factor in the history of the period.

Before the Revolution, Americans had been absolutely prohibited from trading in places like China, India, and many of the islands of the East Indies. Even before the ink had dried on the Peace of Paris (1783), however, American vessels were taking on cargoes in these formerly forbidden places. The consortium of British government officials and the directors of the Honorable East India Company in London noted the increase in this activity with some apprehension. Until challenged by the Americans, the British trading empire was a closed and highly profitable economic system that reached halfway round the globe, and if not highly efficient in modern terms at least its lawful side seemed so at the time. The foundation of the British economy and the Empire itself was based on a form of regulated trade known as *mercantilism*.

In 1775, American patriots had been warned that if the colonies left the orbit of the trading empire, London merchants might press the passage of domestic legislation closing British ports to American tobacco, grain, fish, slaves, and naval stores. As an unwanted consequence of winning independence, in 1783 a British Order in Council had indeed barred any American vessel from entering British ports in the Caribbean. The measure cut off the republic's access to its most important markets just as some had predicted. This, it was thought, would ruin the republic's economy, plunge most Americans into poverty, and bring the Yankee traders back into the fold of the British Empire. It almost did.

Cut off from some of its most significant markets, American exports fell precipitously for several years, and unemployed seamen and shipwrights loitered about the wharves and slept in the streets. However, Yankee traders were not to be broken by mere adversity or British pretentiousness. American merchants continued to trade with the French islands of the Caribbean, and they quickly sought out new trading partners in the Baltic and the Mediterranean. Moreover, American merchant vessels were tying up to wharves in India, the East Indies, and the Far East. The Bengali government in India, still independent of British control, offered America the equivalent of most favored nation-trading status severely jeopardizing the monopoly of the Honorable East India Company. However, Yankee expansion into new markets, particularly in the Mediterranean, was not accomplished without adversity— especially with regard to the so-called Barbary States of North Africa.

It was during the early period of maritime expansion that the U.S. Navy reached its utmost popularity as an American icon. However, the French Revolution and the wars for empire that followed changed the political and economic landscape of Europe and the world as America's new trading partners were thrown into two decades of almost unceasing warfare with either Britain or France. Nor did the European allies avoid war with each other. Under these circumstances America tried to profit from its neutrality as a carrier of merchandise to the contending parties, but the cloak of neutrality proved but a mean defense for U.S. flag vessels. If no other lesson can be learned from American history, it is this one, that maintaining absolute neutrality in wartime does not work, that should be remembered.

In 1785, the American merchant sloop *Experiment,* made a direct run from New York to Canton, China, in just four months and twelve days inaugurating a whole series of record-breaking passages by swift sailing wind-ships. Not only had the little American-built trading vessel shown the world its heels, it had also opened a profitable business in trading homegrown Appalachian ginseng for Asian tea, nankeens, china plate, and silk. In the following year, in the company of a French ship trading on the China coast, the American vessel *Empress of China*, under the command of John Greene, turned an amazing profit in excess of 30 percent on a single run to the Far East. Shippers in large cities like Boston, Philadelphia, and Baltimore, and small towns like Providence, Gloucester, and Salem immediately took notice. In 1788, Capt. Jonathan Carnes, in the Salem brig *Cadet*, discovered the long-sought source of white pepper in Sumatra and opened American trade in spices with the natives of the region and with China.

Throughout the Americans' stay, the French continued to be particularly helpful ensuring that the Chinese understood that the Americans "were a free, independent and sovereign nation, not connected with Great Britain, not owing allegiance to her, or any other power on earth, but to the authority of the United States." The Honorable East India Company (sometimes called John Company by its detractors) could do little to enforce its monopoly in the islands other than to refuse to trade directly with the Americans. In 1796, Carnes returned, without foreign assistance, a cargo of pepper that brought a profit of nearly 700 percent.[54]

The China trade quickly became a significant part of America's growing consumer economy. The initial objective of U.S. foreign policy was simply to maintain its new markets and increase its promising trade with France, especially among the islands of the West Indies where American vessels had a long history of doing business. Several smaller European powers also signed trade agreements with America, notably Holland, Sweden, Prussia, and Russia. Soon carved ivory, sharks teeth, boomerangs, mummies, grass skirts, Asian gongs, ostrich feathers, and walrus tusk filled American ports. By the second decade of the 19th century, the duties on imported pepper collected at Salem produced 5 percent of all the tax revenue of the United States.[55]

The young republic's enormous commercial growth overseas created a national dilemma. Trade monopolies, European conflicts, and piracy threatened the sea-lanes of the world, and the continued growth of American shipping required that U.S. flag vessels be protected away from domestic shores. For other nations, the traditional remedies for an exposed commerce had been to post a strong naval force along the major sea-lanes of the world, as had the British, or to pay to have some other friendly nation do so, as had the Venetians, Dutch, Austrians, and Scandinavians. Yet Americans most formidable trading partners were embroiled in their own wars, and a growing sectional cleavage in Congress had separated the delegates of the coastal states from those of the rural interior with respect to the establishment and application of American sea power. As a result, the young republic had neither the warships nor the naval programs sufficient to prevent an "insult" to its shipping.

The dynamic growth of its overseas commerce required that an equally energetic navy protect America's vessels. Spurred on by John Adams—foster father of the Continental Navy in 1775 and chief proponent of a Navy Department in 1794—America's Navy stood poised, on paper at least, to oppose any foreign designs on its merchant shipping as the 19th century opened. Yet the U.S. Navy was to be founded on blatant economic necessity rather than on well-considered military principle.

Notes

1. George Washington, "The Newburgh Address," *The War for American Independence*, http://users.adelphia.net/~revwar/index.html (accessed June 17, 2008).

2. Washington, "The Newburgh Address."

3. Allan R. Millett and Peter Maslowski, *For the Common Defense: A Military History of the United States of America* (New York: Free Press, 1984), 84–85.

4. Jack N. Rakove, "Ideas and Interests Drove Constitution-Making," in *Major Problems in the Era of the American Revolution, 1760–1791*, ed. Richard D. Brown (New York: Houghton Mifflin, 2000), 428–429.

5. Rakove, 434.

6. John Dickinson, "The Letters of Fabius," in *Pamphlets on the Constitution of the United States,* ed. Paul L. Ford (New York: DaCapo Press, 1968), 163.

7. See Clinton Rossiter, ed., *The Federalist Papers* (New York: New American Library, 1961).

8. Dickinson, 216.

9. Millett and Maslowski, 86–87.

10. George Washington, "Sentiments on the Peace Establishment," http://www.history.army.mil/books/RevWar/ss/peacedoc.htm (accessed June 19, 2008).

11. The present Royal Canadian Mounted Police was founded on an establishment of only 22 officers and 287 men who were considered constables rather than soldiers.

12. Louis B. Wright, *The Atlantic Frontier: Colonial American Civilization, 1607–1763* (New York: Alfred A. Knopf, 1951), 224.

13. Mercy Otis Warren, *The Rise, Progress, and Termination of the American Revolution Interspersed with Biographical, Political, and Moral Observations*, Vol. 3, chapter 31, http://www.samizdat.com/warren/rev31.html (accessed June 17, 2008).

14. Millett and Maskowski, 87.

15. See Rossiter.

16. John Dewitt (possible pseudonym), "John Dewitt I, the Anti-federalist Papers," http://www.constitution.org/afp/dewitt01.htm (accessed June 18, 2008).

17. Robert Yates, "Brutus X, the Anti-federalist Papers," http://www.constitution.org/afp/brutus10.txt (accessed June 18, 2008).

18. See Ralph Ketcham, ed., *The Anti-Federalist Papers and the Constitutional Convention Debates* (New York: New American Library, 1986).

19. James R. Kennedy and Walter D. Kennedy, *The South Was Right* (Gretna, LA: Pelican, 1995), 164.

20. Patrick Henry, "Foreign Wars, Civil Wars, and Indian Wars—Three Bugbears," *Anti-Federalist No. 4*, http://patriotpost.us/antifedpapers/antifed4.htm (accessed June 17, 2008).

21. Benjamin Workman (Philadelphiensis), "The President as Military King," *Anti-Federalist No. 74*, http://patriotpost.us/antifedpapers/antifed74.htm (accessed June 17, 2008).

22. Ketcham, 4.

23. Ketcham, 4.

24. Ketcham, 4.

25. James MacGregor Burns, *The Vineyard of Liberty* (New York: Alfred A. Knopf, 1982), 115–116.

26. MacGregor Burns, 82.

27. MacGregor Burns, 91.

28. MacGregor Burns, 61–62.

29. Gaillard Hunt, *As We Were: Life in America, 1814* (1914; rpt., Stockbridge, MA: Berkshire House Publishing, 1993), 33.

30. Michael F. Holt, *The Rise and Fall of the American Whig Party: Jacksonian Politics and the Onset of the Civil War* (New York: Oxford University Press, 1999), 4.

31. Frederick C. Leiner, *The End of Barbary Terror* (New York: Oxford University Press, 2006), 8.

32. There is no evidence that American revolutionaries ever sported red, white, and blue cockades. They began the Revolution with solid black and added a circle or ribbon of white to the black after the French Alliance of 1778. The all white cockade, worn by some frontiersmen, was the archaic symbol of the Scottish revolts against Hanoverian rule of 1715, 1719, and 1746.

33. Quoted in James Dugan, *The Great Mutiny* (New York: G. P. Putnam's Sons, 1965), 14.

34. Kennedy and Kennedy, 162.

35. Kennedy and Kennedy, 164–165.

36. Bill Kaufman, *Ain't My America: The Long, Noble History of Antiwar Conservatism and Middle-American Anti-Imperialism* (New York: Henry Holt, 2008), 15.

37. Kaufman, 15.

38. Bernard A. Weisberger, *America Aflame: Jefferson, Adams, and the Revolutionary Election of 1800* (New York: HarperCollins, 2000), 30.

39. Kaufman, 15.

40. In July 1845, New York newspaperman John L. O'Sullivan wrote in the *United States Magazine and Democratic Review* that it was the nation's "manifest destiny to overspread and to possess the whole continent." This was the origin of the phrase.

41. Henry Nash Smith. *Virgin Land: The American West as Symbol and Myth* (Cambridge, MA: Harvard University Press, 1973,) 9.

42. Kaufman, 19.

43. Daniel K. Richter, *Facing East from Indian Country: A Native History of Early America* (Cambridge, MA: Harvard University Press, 2001), 225.

44. Richter, 227.

45. Duncan Rea Williams, "Quaker settlement in Ohio," http://www.drwilliams.org/iDoc/index.htm?url=http://www.drwilliams.org/iDoc/Web-213.htm (accessed June 18, 2008).

46. Amanda Keil, "The Peaceful People and the First Nations: A Brief History of Friends and Native Americans," American Friends Service Committee, http://www.afsc.org/nymetro/specialprojects/resources/SPpeacefulPeopleAndFirstNations.pdf (accessed June 18, 2008).

47. See Kiel.

48. Charles F. Hobson, "The Aaron Burr Treason Trial," http://www.fjc.gov/history/burr. nsf/page/burr_pdf/$file/BurrTrial(final).pdf (accessed March 2009).

49. Hobson.

50. Hobson.

51. Hobson.

52. Hobson.

53. Hobson.

54. Oscar V. Armstrong, "Opening China," *American Heritage Magazine* 33, no. 2 (February/March 1982).

55. Walter Buehr, *Salt, Sugar, and Spice* (New York: Walter Murrow and Company, 1969), 50.

Chapter 6

Fair Winds and Following Seas

The English Nation may hate me, but I will force them to esteem me too.
—John Paul Jones, 1780

The Natural Defense of the Nation

Immediately after the Peace of Paris in 1783, the United States began to systematically retire its tiny revolutionary navy. The only line-of-battle ship built in America (the seventy-four-gun vessel christened *America*) was given to the French, and the last surviving frigate to serve in the Continental Navy, the thirty-two-gun *Alliance*, had been sold. Not a single capital ship or frigate remained after 1785. It has been noted that an empire requires a navy, and the wholesale dismantling of the tiny American fleet attests to the anxiety that its mere existence engendered among the Anti-Federalists who feared U.S. expansion.

This course of events was followed for a variety of reasons, including a fear of standing armies and navies shared by many of the leaders of the American Revolution. They had undergone a series of disagreeable experiences with standing forces from the Boston Massacre of 1770 and the attacks at Lexington and Concord in 1775 to the naval bombardment of the majority of America's port cites throughout the conflict. In response to the early American success against their ground forces, British ministers in Parliament had urged their naval commanders on the North American Station to keep "the coasts of the enemy constantly alarmed" through bombardments and amphibious raids. This would at least "prevent their sending out a swarm of privateers, the success of which has enabled and encouraged the rebels to persist in their revolt."[1]

In fact, during the course of the Revolution, British vessels had bombarded, burned, or attacked every colonial seaport of appreciable size with the exception of Baltimore and Salem. Besides creating a good deal of local terror, these tactics had little positive effect on the British war effort. The policy served better for the patriots as antigovernment propaganda than for the British as a means of cowing the American public. By generally steeling the determination of the rebels to resist, the

171

attacks utterly failed to meet the expectations of the strategic planners in London. Yet there was no indication in the 1790s that the British had abandoned this strategy of war with regard to America.

Some Americans, and particularly the Jeffersonian Republicans, saw no need for a federal navy except as a possible tool of popular oppression in the hands of a central government run amuck. Surely a flotilla of shore-based gunboats and floating batteries supported by a series of strong coastal fortifications would keep the British, or any other foreign naval power, away from American shores. The War of 1812 would test this supposition and find it wanting.

In *Federalist No. 12*, Alexander Hamilton noted the need for an oceangoing navy,

> The world may . . . be divided into four parts [the Americas, Europe, Asia, Africa], each having a distinct set of interests. Unhappily for the other three, Europe, by her arms and by her negotiations, by force and by fraud, has in different degrees extended her domination over them all. Africa, Asia, and America have successively felt her domination. . . . Let the thirteen [American] states . . . concur in erecting one great American system superior to the control of all transatlantic force or influence and be able to dictate the terms of the connection between the old and the new world!"[2]

Hamilton's ultimate object was to create a navy—supported by all the states, not just the maritime ones—through which the republic might influence the conduct of European nations. The navy he envisioned would "not vie with those of the great maritime powers," but would at least be of respectable enough force that "if thrown into the scale of either of two contending parties" it would shift the balance of maritime power. "This would be more particularly the case in relation to operations in the West Indies . . . [where] a few ships of the line, sent opportunely to the reinforcement of either side, would be sufficient to decide the fate of a campaign."[3] Hamilton hoped by such a course to place a value on American friendship as an ally or, in the reverse case, make American neutrality a diplomatic objective for the warring nations of Europe. Hamilton's ideas would be incorporated into the *fleet in being* concepts proposed by U.S. Adm. Alfred Thayer Mahan more than a century later in *The Influence of Sea Power upon History, 1660–1783* (1890). This book's arguments influenced naval policies of governments for decades. In particular, it encouraged President Teddy Roosevelt to support a larger navy and motivated the government to project American power abroad through its navy, thus contributing to American imperialism as many of the delegates to the Constitutional Convention had feared a century earlier.[4]

Although Hamilton mentioned "ships of the line" in his plan for a limited navy, his initial proposal was a modest one asking only for frigates and sloops of war similar to those built in the Revolution. He hoped in this manner to win over those in Congress who were opposed to a standing navy. Written during the crisis of ideas that surrounded the Constitutional Convention, Hamilton's proposals "worked only a small influence upon the course of events during the struggle over ratification," and many of his most controversial ideas regarding the establishment of a federal navy had to be set aside for the moment to ensure the success of the vote. He would have to wait many years to see the beginnings of the naval force he envisioned.[5]

The Revenue Marine

Unable to force the establishment of a formal navy, in 1790, Hamilton used his position as secretary of the treasury to deploy a small force of armed cutters to enforce the maritime and revenue laws of the nation. This force was called the Revenue Marine (later the Revenue Cutter Service), and it was operated under the authority of the Department of Treasury. As such, it was an arm of the executive branch generally outside the control of Congress. In the years immediately following the Revolution, the United States was struggling with its finances. The national income was based largely on the collection of import tariffs, and the government was desperately distressed by the rampant increase in smuggling. There was, therefore, a need to strongly enforce the tariff laws.

The most lucrative profits to be realized through illegal overseas trade proved to come from the genial addictions—a nice cup of coffee or hot chocolate, a hot buttered rum or beaker of flip, a pinch of seasoning in the broth, a cake or confection to sooth a sweet tooth—all "exotic rarities converted into cravings."[6] Dutch coffee and chocolate were high on the list of smuggled items. The consumption of alcohol, in particular, had not yet taken on the negative associations commonly voiced by temperance advocates in 19th-century America. Besides domestically produced rum and beer, wines, brandies, and liqueurs of many types were imported. Whiskeys, gins, and other distilled beverages were not particularly popular except as home brews intended for the privilege of enjoying a temporary intoxication. The crisis over the taxation of these home brews would work itself out in 1794 on the Pennsylvania frontier as the Whiskey Rebellion. For most Americans, imported coffee, cocoa, and seasonings, especially from the East Indies, were more highly valued than distilled liquor.

Better homes stocked a fairly generous supply of caffeinated and alcoholic beverages, and business establishments such as taverns and coffeehouses that catered to the "addicted" were common sights in most towns. Americans willingly spent a fair penny for their favorite extravagances, but they greatly resented paying import duties on them. They therefore depended in large part on smugglers to provide low-cost, high-quality products.[7]

In 1789, James Madison had made his first order of business in Congress the establishment of import duties, or tariffs. These duties, along with fines and a small income from licenses, were designed to pay for the entire cost of the central government. Faced with the effectiveness of smuggling, Madison stood up in the Congress and declared the economy of the country to be in danger. He demanded that Congress insure the stability and integrity of the economy by establishing an elaborate system of duties eerily similar to those under which Americans had suffered during their time as British subjects. Rum, beer, molasses, cocoa, coffee, and sugar were all targeted. His proposals aroused a furious debate among the legislators.

On August 4, 1790, Congress passed Hamilton's Revenue Cutter Bill. A revenue cutter was assigned to each of ten ports on the East Coast. The *Massachusetts*, first of the original ten lightly armed vessels, was sixty-feet long, with a crew of ten seamen. The term "revenue cutter" dated back to the early 1700s in England, where their Revenue Service patrol vessels were all cutter-rigged, that is, with a single mast and two or more jibs.

Cutter captains were answerable to and received their sailing orders directly from the Customs Collector of the port to which they were assigned. All crew pay, requests for supplies, arrangements for repairs to the cutter, and mission-specific tasking came directly from the port's Customs House. The Collector of the port was given wide latitude in how he could task "his" cutter, and situations requiring the Secretary of the Treasury to intervene directly in the affairs of the Collector were rare.

Twin Crises

Within ten years of the signing of the Constitution, the republic found itself involved in its first foreign war. The major seafaring industries of the Barbary states of North Africa were slave trading and piracy carried out against the vessels of any seafaring nations passing through the Mediterranean who were viewed as too weak to retaliate. Under normal circumstances, the major maritime powers of Europe kept the Barbary pirates in check—Portugal being particularly dedicated to patrolling the western Mediterranean. However, the French Revolution had turned Europe's attention landward, and in the 1790s it was absorbed with containing France's revolutionary spirit.

The French Revolution had several consequences for American commerce. Chronologically, the first serious consequence of European introspection was a series of unwarranted attacks on American shipping by Algerian pirates.[8] The British government unknowingly aggravated the situation for U.S. shipping by arranging a peace treaty between the Algerian corsairs and the Portuguese government, whose navy had previously policed Algerian activities and isolated attacks to the Barbary Coast of North Africa. Consequently, the pirates had expanded their operations into the Atlantic. In 1791, the Algerians required that the United States pay a bribe of $60,000 for the return of eleven captured vessels and the ransom of more than 100 seamen. They made a further demand for a $100,000 annual bribe (equivalent to $2.5 million in 2009) to secure the future safe passage of American flag vessels through the region. The initial diplomatic response to these demands has been described as one of "powerless outrage." Congress had to choose to pay up (as other nations did) or fit out a naval force of its own to oppose the pirates.[9]

The French Revolution produced a second diplomatic crisis in America. Technically allied to the French since 1778 and beholden to the Bourbon monarchy for arms, supplies, and naval support during its own republican revolution, Americans were faced with a diplomatic dilemma when the French people sought to overthrow their king. Conceptually, Americans had been the first successful revolutionaries in generations, and they initially favored the French insurgents. This led to a debate between those in Congress who favored the spread of republicanism and those who believed that they had to honor America's decade-long commitment to the French king. Chief among the former group was Thomas Jefferson, an open Francophile who initially favored the revolutionaries.

In 1793, Jefferson gleefully received a young Frenchman named Edmond Charles Genêt in Philadelphia as a representative of the French revolutionary government. Genêt came to ask for a prepayment of America's war debt from the War of Independence to the revolutionary government, and Congress managed to interpret its obligations to the French Crown as narrowly as possible. Unfortunately, Genêt used his diplomatic position to secretly outfit and arm a former British vessel moored in the port as a French privateer (*La Petite Democrate*) and to recruit Americans to attack French Louisiana—clear violations of American neutrality. The proposed military expedition, to be led by American war hero George Rodgers Clark, never materialized, but Genêt could not be stopped before the warship had slipped down the Delaware River and out to sea where it could prey on British shipping. These diplomatic outrages coupled with the bloody image of the Terror (1794) as well as the attraction of increased trade with Britain swung the balance of public opinion toward those Anglophile forces in Congress backed by American merchants, shippers, and bankers. Alexander Hamilton suggested that President Washington dispatch a highly regarded representative to the Court of St. James to repair the damaged diplomatic relations with the British.

John Jay, practiced diplomat and chief justice of the Supreme Court, was chosen to make the trip to London, but it was Hamilton who drafted his instructions. Jay, like Hamilton, was a New York Federalist anxious to retain British trade. Although he secured the admission of American vessels to British ports in both the East and West Indies, only vessels of limited capacity and carrying specific cargoes would be allowed. The Jay Treaty of 1794 was hardly a generous agreement, and it seemed less than respectful of America as a maritime trading nation. The outstanding questions that remained between the two nations were not addressed. These questions included the impressment of American seamen (up to 5,000 of them), the search of American shipping, and the seizure of American cargoes deemed to be contraband of war. Upon publication of its terms, protest meetings were held in many seaports, and both Hamilton and Jay were pilloried in the popular press for succumbing to British pressure. Nonetheless, the Senate ratified the document at the behest of Washington after striking some of the more restrictive language.

The Navy under Adams

John Adams was the first vice president of the United States serving under Washington during his two terms. In this office, he often came into contention with Washington's first secretary of state, Thomas Jefferson, concerning U.S. relations with Britain and France. Jefferson's opposition to pro-British federal policies generated so much friction in the administration that Edmund Randolph, a staunch Federalist, replaced him as secretary of state during Washington's second term. Jefferson at the end of 1793 retired from government to his Virginia home at Monticello where he continued to orchestrate opposition to Hamilton and Washington. Jefferson wanted to strangle Britain without actually going to war, and it became an article of faith among Democratic Republicans that "commercial weapons" and "diplomatic strategies" would suffice to bring Great Britain to any terms the United States chose to dictate.[10]

Adams favored more open trade relations with Britain and a strong navy and Navy Department to protect the American merchant marine. When Adams became the second president in 1796, he was forced by the conventions of the electoral college to accept Jefferson as his vice president during his single term. The tension between Adams and Jefferson led to an estrangement that lasted until the end of their lives, but Adams as chief executive had the support of two strongly Federalist secretaries of state, Timothy Pickering followed by John Marshall.

The ongoing difficulties with France prompted Adams to push vigorously for construction of the navy that had been neglected since the ratification of the Constitution. Congress, torn by divided counsels, had been unable to commit to the financing of a permanent naval force under the Articles of Confederation, even though the framers of that document had endorsed the creation of a naval force in principle. With the heavy fighting ships of the European navies cautiously eying one another in foreign waters, it was thought that a miscellaneous collection of privateers, armed merchantmen, and revenue cutters would suffice to attain America's defensive needs as a neutral country. Such views dismissed the more sobering consequences of a greatly expanding and far-reaching transoceanic American commerce. Only by being a major naval power itself could the United States afford the luxury of maintaining its neutral rights at sea.

John Jay posed the essential question surrounding naval appropriations squarely, "Whether it would be more wise in the United States to withdraw our attention from the sea, and permit foreigners to fetch and carry [merchandise] for [us]; or to persevere in concerting and pursuing measures as may . . . render [ourselves] a maritime power."[11] Edmund Randolph of Virginia declared, "He who commands the sea will command the land." David Humphreys, American ambassador to Spain, noted, "If we mean to have commerce, we must have a naval force to defend it."[12] Even Jefferson—who would as president resist the establishment of a navy—admitted that the American people seemed determined to share in the occupation of the seas with the great powers of Europe.

A British official observing the progress of the political debate in the United States noted, "It is not probable that the American States will have a very free trade. . . . They cannot protect themselves . . . [and] cannot pretend to a navy."[13] Under these circumstances, it seemed that the United States would be forced to undergo the insults of the petty emirs and corsairs of the Barbary States, of the bloody-handed Sans-Culottes of Revolutionary France, or of an increasingly arrogant and confrontational John Bull, Limited of Britain.

The pro-navy sentiments had survived the antimilitary anxieties of the Constitutional Convention, and the founding document had given Congress the specific power "to provide and maintain a navy." James Madison noted at the time that few other areas of contention regarding the formation of the federal government had been so specifically and forcefully addressed in the Constitution. In *Federalist No. 41*, Madison wrote, "The palpable necessity of . . . a navy has protected that part of the Constitution against a spirit of censure which has spared few other parts. It must, indeed, be numbered among the greatest blessings of America that as her Union will be the only source of her maritime strength, so this will be a principal source of her security against danger from abroad."[14]

Unfortunately, even some of those in favor of the naval-building program failed to grasp its full implications. A fear of government tempered even Madison's support of a navy. "The [naval] batteries most capable of repelling foreign enterprises on our safety are happily such as can never be turned by a perfidious government against our liberties."[15] Even Adams had initially supported the idea that America's navy be "separated and scattered as much as possible from New Orleans [in the Gulf of Mexico] to Passamaquoddy [Maine]."[16] This would require a deployment of vessels along a coastline of more than 2,000 miles in extent, the establishment of numerous naval installations and shipyards, and the development of logistical and repair facilities.

The congressmen also had only a vague idea concerning the task of building capital ships like the huge seventy-four-gun ships-of-the-line that presently represented the common warships composing foreign fleets. In the Revolution, American shipyards had produced only one such vessel, the 2,000-ton *America*. Moreover, in 1792 with the death of John Paul Jones (who had served as admiral of the Russian Imperial Fleet for a time), no serving American sea officer had commanded such a capital ship and no American admiral had ordered such a fleet. Jefferson—almost alone among the luminaries who had prosecuted the Revolution—had concluded that "to aim at such a navy as the greater nations of Europe possessed would be a foolish and wicked waste."[17]

Adams was possibly the most eloquent and steadfast of the pro-navy politicians during the constitutional debates. He wrote:

Neither nature nor art has partitioned the sea into empires, kingdoms, republics or states. . . . Let Mahomet, or the Pope, or Great Britain say what they will, mankind will act the part of slaves and cowards if they suffer any nation to usurp domination over the ocean or any part of it. Neither the Mediterranean, the Baltic, the four seas, or the North Sea are the peculiar property of any nation. A naval power is the natural defense of the United States. Our seacoasts, from their great extent, are more readily annoyed and more easily defended by a naval force than any other. With all the materials our country abounds; in skill our naval architects are equal to any; and commanders and seamen will not be found wanting.[18]

The anti-navy forces, which had lost the naval establishment argument at the Convention, did not altogether abandon their fight, however. In Congress, they almost defeated the proposed naval building program, trailing in the final vote in 1794 by only six votes (47–41). Opposition leaders like Albert Gallatin and William Maclay, relying on a general misunderstanding of the function of large warships and exploiting the past success of the thirty-two-, twenty-eight-, and twenty-four-gun American frigates of the Revolution, attempted to retrieve a partial victory from their Constitutional defeat by limiting the size as well as the number of U.S. warships to be built. In this regard, the pro-navy forces in Congress allowed consensus politics to dictate policy and kept the navy within the most modest limits compatible with the protection of the republic's immediate seacoasts and ports. Congress decided that a small, well-organized naval force of six large cruisers (frigates of forty-four guns) would be sufficient to command respect for American shipping during periods when Europe's maritime powers were at war with each other and their attention was thereby directed elsewhere. This was essentially an isolationist position that largely ignored the practical need to protect America's far-flung foreign trade.[19]

It would be no simple task to build a navy of the dimensions needed to render the nation respectable in the eyes of foreign powers. Gouverneur Morris, a Federalist diplomat serving in revolutionary France, proposed a more significant naval force than the antimilitarists. "We could now maintain twelve ships of the line, perhaps twenty, with a due proportion of frigates and smaller vessels." With such a

THE "CONSTITUTION."

The U.S. frigate Constitution, *better known as "Old Ironsides," was the best known of the early U.S. naval warships. (Library of Congress Prints and Photographs Division, LC-USZ62-46545)*

navy "no nation on earth [would] dare to insult the United States."[20] It has been noted, however, that such a building program entailed a major commitment of funds and of national will that did not seem to be in the offing. "Not only had timber to be cut and seasoned, but other materials collected, the vessels designed, shipyards built or rented, skilled workmen employed, the work of construction rigidly supervised, ordnance secured, stores and supplies purchased, competent officers found and commissioned, crews recruited and assembled—all these and many other details, before the ships would be ready for sea."[21]

Meanwhile, an extensive set of shore installations needed to be made ready to support a fleet. These included well-equipped naval shipyards, large storehouses, ordnance depots, ropewalks, timber storage facilities, ship's cradles, slipways, drydocks, and foundries. The establishment of hundreds of shore batteries needed to protect these installations was less a matter of contention and more one of their extent because both nationalists and anti-nationalists agreed that they were a necessary first line of defense for America.

While shipbuilding was a major industry in America, the majority of its shipyards were generally appropriate only for the production of small commercial craft used in the coasting and fishing trades. The government had not a single naval shipyard of its own, and the Congress leased commercial facilities in six major port cities to spread the advantage of a major government-sponsored building project. Nonetheless, naval shipbuilding was a specialized trade, and a commercial dockyard apprentice was unlikely to gain sufficient experience in designing and building vessels of war without working in a government shipyard for some time. Fortunately, some men, like Josiah Fox, had worked in Admiralty yards in Britain and had received formal training in the design and construction of frigates and smaller warships before coming to America; and others had shown some talent in designing and building frigates and sloops of war during the Revolution.

The technical problems raised by the need to "fight a ship" efficiently were much harder for shipwrights to resolve than the trade needs of most merchant vessels. The weight of the armament and the inherent requirements created by the dynamic stress of firing large guns from a seagoing platform made of wood proved to be the most troublesome aspect of warship development. The weight of the sails and rigging added to the mass of projectiles in the shot lockers, the weight of hundreds of seamen, and the weight of the provisions needed to keep them alive (especially the drinking water) made the production of a seaworthy fighting platform exceedingly difficult for shipbuilders. To resolve these problems "compromises were made in dimensions and proportions, which soon became national characteristics of their men-of-war."[22]

Benjamin Stoddert,[23] the first secretary of the navy under the Constitution, was tasked with the creation of a navy in the midst of two crises: one posed by the continued insults of the Barbary pirates and the other a product of the French Revolution. Stoddert was an energetic and competent man, who quickly set the machinery of the navy into motion. By May 1798, with one cruiser ready for sea (*Constellation*) and a number of small makeshift vessels of war converted from merchantmen, the Congress authorized hostilities against French armed vessels off the coast of

America. Stoddert, however, eventually resigned his office because he was disgusted with Congress's vacillation toward the navy.

Meanwhile, ambassador David Humphreys had negotiated a reasonable treaty with Morocco, the least belligerent of the Barbary pirate states, but the Dey of Algiers refused to receive any American delegation. Also coming into power in the 1790s was the Bashaw of Tripoli, Yusuf Qaramanli, who would reign for forty years amid a series of internal dynastic squabbles with his brothers trying throughout to raise that country to the level of a maritime power at the expense of American shipping. The Bashaw, a perennial thorn in America's diplomatic side, chopped down the flag pole at the American consulate in 1801, an act deemed a declaration of war. An anonymous American despaired, "Our flag is about as much respected among the different nations as an old rag that's hung up in a cornfield to scare crows."[24]

The Quasi-War with France (1798–1803)

Adams entered the presidency in 1796 with a foreign crisis on his hands. Charles Pinckney had been sent to France as a special envoy by the previous administration in an attempt to repair the diplomatic breech with the French republic caused by the ratification of the Jay Treaty. He had been rebuffed, his credentials had been questioned in a officious manner, and he had fled to Amsterdam when threatened with imminent arrest. The French ambassador, Pierre Adet, had been recalled from the United States without replacement as soon as Adams's election had become known. Adams wrote to his son John Quincy of "a misunderstanding with France, which I shall endeavor to reconcile, provided that no violation of faith, no stain upon honor is exacted. . . . Nor do I think we ought to wait a moment to know whether the French mean to give us any proofs of their desire to conciliate with us. I am for pursuing all the measures of defense which the laws authorize us to adopt, especially at sea."[25]

After the diplomatic break, the French Directory had issued a series of orders to its sea captains to seize all American shipping bound for Britain or carrying British goods. Within a year, more than 300 American flag vessels were seized under these directives. Moreover, in 1797, the French Directory declared that all seamen found serving on enemy vessels—who were nominally citizens of neutral governments—were to be considered pirates. This put a large number of American seamen, involuntarily impressed into the British Royal Navy, in jeopardy of their lives at the hands of a French government already knee deep in blood because of the Terror. In January 1798, Adams proposed, as one of his first acts from the new executive residence, the creation of a navy department, and he asked Congress for funds to put the military on a war footing. By December 1798, the United States had a total of twenty-one warships (limited to frigates, sloops, and cutters). By way of comparison, Britain had 800 naval vessels—more than 300 of them ships-of-the-line.

Unlike his contemporaries, Hamilton and Washington, John Adams did not recommend providing for a regular army. Indeed, Hamilton wanted to raise a temporary emergency force, with Washington called out of retirement to command it, to make war on the French. Instead Adams suggested to Stoddert that some of the new ships being built be sent to cruise the coast of France and show the American flag in an aggressive manner.

Adams essentially had sought to avoid war by building up the American Navy to protect U.S. ships at sea. During his presidency the USS *Constitution* ("Old Ironsides") and several similar warships were launched. At home, Federalist Anglophiles from New England were cheering, while the Jeffersonian Republicans were appalled that the president was taking the country into a needless war with France. In March 1799, *Constellation* captured the French frigate *L'Insurgente*, after an extended single-ship encounter near the Caribbean island of Nevis, and in October 1800, *Boston* fought and took *LeBerceau*.

The undeclared Quasi-War (1798–1803) with the French revolutionaries, and the Tripolitan War (1801–1805) with the Barbary pirates that were waged simultaneously at times, tested the mettle of America's Navy for the first time and produced officers like John Barry, Samuel Nicholson, William Bainbridge, Stephen Decatur, Richard Dale, John Rodgers, David Porter, and Edward Preble. The French war produced only moderate results for the U.S. Navy because it simply failed to encounter a large number of French warships at sea. This failure was mainly due to the effective blockade of the French coast by Britain. The Barbary problem would not be resolved to the satisfaction of the United States until 1816.

The Navy under Jefferson

Adam's maritime defense at sea was successful only in that it deterred further French aggression during his administration, a circumstance obviated under the isolationist policies of his successor in the presidency, Thomas Jefferson. The more meaningful result of the Quasi War was the establishment of a functioning Navy Department and an ongoing naval shipbuilding program.

Meanwhile, the Barbary pirates of Algiers, Tripoli, and Tunis continued to insult American shipping. The U.S. frigate *Philadelphia* was accidentally run aground in Tripoli Harbor, its crew (including Captain Bainbridge) captured, and the ship appropriated by the Tripolitan government for its own use. Isolationists pointed to the incident as a prima fascia example of how a navy served as a gateway to foreign entanglements, leading Jefferson to say in despair, "Our navigation [in] the Mediterranean has not resumed at all."[26] Four months later Lt. Stephen Decatur led a mission to burn the *Philadelphia* at its anchor in what was called by British Adm. Horatio Nelson "the most bold and daring act of this age."[27]

The American merchant marine did not want war made in its name. It jealously guarded its neutrality as a way to make money by carrying war materials and contraband between warring parties. Blockading squadrons of British warships maintained a constant presence along the approaches to the European continent from the Scheldt Estuary to Toulon Harbor to close off the French from their sources of supply. This effectively prevented American carriers from making profitable voyages to France without incurring unreasonable risks.

One of the cardinal rules of naval warfare regarding *blockade* was that it had to be effective to be lawful. This concept banned so called paper blockades, those that were declared but not actively enforced. This required the active deployment of vessels along the margins of the blockaded nation. Whether or not a blockade was seen as lawful depended on the laws of the nations whose trade was influenced by the blockade. A lawful blockade allowed the blockading party to seize the cargo of neutral states trading with blockaded harbors. Lawful blockades were not formally defined in international law until the Congress of Paris in 1856. The same congress outlawed privateering among all the signatories to the agreement. The United States refused to sign the document.

By 1807, the British had virtually destroyed the national fleet of Denmark at Copenhagen (1801), had routed—but not totally eliminated—the French and Spanish presence in the Mediterranean at the battles of the Nile (1798) and Trafalgar (1805), and would so frighten the Russians with their preemptive attack on the Dano-Norwegian fleet in 1807 that the Russian ships rarely would leave the Baltic during the next decade. Nonetheless, British warships were kept constantly at sea minding the French ports at Brest and Toulon.

Unknown at the time, no nation would again challenge the dominance of British seapower in a fleet battle for more than 100 years. That battle, the World War I engagement at Jutland in 1916 between the British and German imperial fleets, would also be the last major fleet action between steel battleships in any war. The engagement was a standoff, as the Germans, outmaneuvered by the larger British fleet, managed to escape and inflicted more damage to the British fleet than they received. Thereafter, major sea battles would be fought between aircraft carrier task forces sometimes hundreds of miles apart.

For a decade (1805–1815), both the French and the British navies—while embroiled in their own life and death struggle in Europe—continued to take advantage of a weak U.S. naval presence on the high seas through the harassment and seizure of its neutral merchantmen. In *Federalist Paper No. 11*, Hamilton recognized the reality of this situation, "A nation, despicable by its weakness, forfeits even the privilege of being neutral."[28] French and British warships stopped American vessels at sea and demanded to examine their papers and seized their cargos. The British went further in illegally impressing American seamen into the service of the Royal Navy if there was the least question concerning the origin of their U.S. citizenship. Britain's reading of the legal protections to impressment afforded by foreign (that is, American) citizenship required that a mariner be born after the conclusion of the Revolution and never have been a citizen of Britain at any previous time. This outlook was a large noose around all those Americans born in British North America before January 1783. It included—according the British way of thinking—most able-bodied seamen between twenty and forty years of age ostensibly still Englishmen though born in New York, Philadelphia, or Boston. Over 1,200 clearly American-born sailors were seized. Overzealous British officers flogged one American seaman to death before they admitted their error in seizing him and added insult to injury by sending a curt apology to U.S. diplomats. Americans foresaw their merchant marine "reduced to ruin, just like those of Holland, Hamburg, Prussia, and every other community squeezed by the British."[29]

In an effort to stem the crisis, Congress initially passed the Non-Importation Act of 1806, which made it illegal for Americans to trade with either Britain or France, and Jefferson, as president, unwisely closed all American ports to foreign trade in the Embargo Act of 1807 in an attempt to keep American vessels from harm's way by declaring absolute neutrality and restricting maritime trade to coasting, fishing, and whaling. This was a huge expansion of the limits of presidential power. Yet as leader of a rising agrarian party, Jefferson simply closed the ports and disavowed his earlier advocacy of a navy. Jefferson wrote, "It is of utmost importance to diminish our expenses [which] may be done in the Navy Department."[30] Whether this statement was from a change in conviction on Jefferson's part or from an attempt to conform to the prevailing antiwar sentiment in the backcountry of America is not certain. Closing one's own ports in the name of neutrality was an unprecedented move. The immediate result of Jefferson's botched attempt at the *diplomacy of neutrality* was to put a large segment of the nation's maritime service out of business.

Throughout 1807 and 1808, American ships sat rotting at their moorings; deepwater sailors wandered the waterfront looking for a berth on coasters and fishing smacks; and commercial shippers tried to weather the financial storm of rising port and dockage fees. New England—the epicenter of American oceanic shipping—was particularly hard pressed. It soon became apparent that the Embargo Act with its nonintercourse clause to limit American trade was having no effect on the European powers while it was decimating the U.S. economy. Anti-administration protests were developing on the waterfronts, and the path to peace through commercial neutrality that Jefferson had chosen was becoming increasingly more difficult to follow. In late 1808, the act was repealed and trade resumed with both France and Britain.

Jefferson considered the embargo an alternative to war; however, his political opponents among the Federalist thought it a prelude, which secreted a hidden Jeffersonian Republican agenda of exploiting British misbehavior to bring New England shipping interests to the support of France by choking off their commerce. "The embargo was followed by war, as embargoes are wont to be," but with Britain in 1812 rather than with France.[31]

In 1808, a young and intemperate William Cullen Bryant wrote of the embargo as the "curse" of the nation and the "dark womb" of its miseries and woes.

While our sage Ruler's diplomatic skill,
Subjects our councils to his sovereign will;
His grand "restrictive energies" employs,
And wisely regulating trade—destroys . . .

How foul a blot Columbia's glory stains!
How dark the scene! Infatuation reigns!
For French intrigue which wheedles to devour,
Threatens to fix us in Napoleon's power;

Anon within th' insatiate vortex whirl'd,
Whose wide periphery involves the world.
Oh, heaven defend, as future seasons roll,
These western climes from Bonaparte's control.[32]

After giving up the drudgery of a law practice, Bryant became editor of the New York *Evening Post*, a Federalist-leaning paper originally established with the help of Alexander Hamilton. Eventually, the *Evening Post* became not only the foundation of Bryant's fortune but also the means by which he exercised considerable political power in his city, state, and nation. Bryant was a proponent of a "laissez-faire," that is, hands-off economic policy. In his elder years, he opposed tariffs of any kind, as he had in his satire of the embargo written as a youth. He was against slavery, endorsing the Free-Soil Party and the Republican Party of Abraham Lincoln. His influence from the editorial desk of the New York *Evening Post* was great. Bryant's views were always progressive, though not quite as populist as the followers of Jefferson. Yet upon Bryant's death in 1878, he was eulogized as a foremost champion of the same antiwar philosophy that Jefferson had espoused.

Jefferson should not be seen as a Machiavellian villain with regard to the imposition of the embargo. Nevertheless, no politician from the period has left so many sincere statements of the anti-imperial, antimilitarist, and isolationist nature of the America he imagined. His philosophy was one of peace, noninvolvement, and nonintervention in the absence of foreign aggression, and it contains many of the fundamentals of American antiwar pacifism. In 1799 Jefferson had written:

> I am for relying, for internal defense, on our militia solely until actual invasion, and for such a naval force only as may protect our coasts and harbors from such depredations as we have experienced [in the Revolution]; and not for a standing army in time of peace which may overawe the public sentiment; nor for a navy which by its own expenses and the eternal wars in which it may implicate us, will grind us with public burdens [taxes], and sink us under them. I am for free commerce with all nations, political connection with none, and little or no diplomatic establishment, and I am not for linking ourselves, by new treaties with the quarrels of Europe.[33]

To Render Ourselves Respectable

The wooden warships that had fought in the American Revolution were all but indistinguishable from those used in the first half of the 19th century, and the Royal Navy set the standards by which all other navies were judged. Yet British shipwrights were of a conservative turn of mind and were content to provide ships that were soundly built.[34] Whereas the French were constantly effecting minor improvements in their ships-of-the-line and frigates, the mantle of leadership in marine design had actually passed to the Americans, particularly those on the New England coast. By the end of the 18th century, Americans had become the master commercial wind-ship builders of the world, and this same excellence would be lent to the design of their warships.

American shipwright Joshua Humphreys, noted for his work during the Revolution, may have designed many of the best wooden vessels of war ever produced during the early 19th century.[35] The credit given Humphreys as designer of the Revolutionary Era frigates has long been a matter of controversy. The lack of physical evidence for his designs, such as plans and diagrams from the 1770s, has led some historians to believe that unwarranted credit has been given to his role in the Revolution because of his groundbreaking and carefully documented work in designing the Constitution class of flush-decked frigates for the Federalist-era Navy. It is known with certainty, however, that Humphreys appeared before Congress on December 13, 1775, with "the plans of several men-of-war," but none had flush weather decks.[36] Only three flush deck warships are known to have been built during the Revolution, and none have been definitely attributed to the Wharton and Humphreys shipbuilding firm. Based on the totality of his work, however, it remains highly likely that Humphreys personally designed the vessels that are commonly associated with his shipyard.[37]

The flush deck was a technological advance in frigate design. It added rigidity to the hull, which if too blunt at its bow and stern might sag in the water, or if too sharp-ended might hog (like the arched back of a pig). Both of these conditions put strain on the keel especially in a wooden warship that was carrying cannons along most of its length. The privateer *Mohawk* built in Salem, Massachusetts in 1779, was flush-decked. Lost under the command of Capt. John Carnes to a slightly larger British vessel, *Mohawk* was taken into the Royal Navy, and its lines and measurements were taken at Deptford Dockyard, England, in 1783. The vessel had an original copper bottom and was considered a good, fast sailer. The main battery was composed of eighteen cannon on the gun deck, and the flush spar deck was fitted for eighteen smaller guns, which seems to look forward somewhat in terms of design to Humphreys's later plans for flush two-deck frigates carrying between thirty-six and forty-four guns of the Constitution class made famous during the War of 1812. His designs remained in common use in U.S. naval warships throughout the age of sail.

Naval author and historian C. S. Forester noted the fine quality of the American two-deckers that fought in 1812. Although they were vastly superior to other vessels of their class, Forester pointed out that they were not "extra powerful frigates" but rather "not-too-small two-decked ships of the line." The U.S. Navy deployed its first three-decked ship of the line in 1815.[38]

The waterfront of a seaport town, even a small one, was a virtual forest of masts, yards, ropes, and pulleys. The wooden sailing ship was the largest and most complex mechanical system in the world before the introduction of steam. At mid-century John Ruskin wrote the following concerning the wooden battleships of his day:

A Ship of the Line is the most honorable thing that man . . . has ever produced. . . . Into it he has put as much of his human patience, common sense, forethought, experimental philosophy, self-control, habits of order and obedience, thoroughly wrought handiwork, defiance of brute elements, careless courage, careful patriotism and calm expectation of the judgment of God as can be put into a space 300 feet long by 80 broad. And I am glad to have lived in an age when I could see the thing so done.[39]

Naval vessels were largely referred to by the number of gundecks or the available armament on board as in the forty-four-gun frigate Constitution—that is, thirty cannon firing balls weighing twenty-four pounds and fourteen firing twelve-pound balls. There is virtually no universally accepted system for recording this information, but the meaning of each notation is usually clear from the context of the discussion.[40]

The Americans entered the naval war in 1812 with six frigates, five sloops of war, two brigs, and sixty-two gunboats ready for sea. Nine new vessels were building in various harbors, including two new line-of-battle warships of seventy-four guns each, but these would not be ready for sea trials until late 1814. Only one American vessel was patrolling Lake Ontario, although several other warships were being built or refitted for service on the Great Lakes. It seems obvious, therefore, that the American plan for its naval defense was somewhat optimistic. A navy twenty times the number would have been needed to stand eyeball to eyeball with any of the fleets of Europe. The British Royal Navy had more than 100 warships larger than seventy-four guns, while the frigates deployed by the Americans had no hope of standing up to a lone fifty-gun warship.

The naval strategies of the congressional War Hawks included the idea that Britain would be too busy blockading the French coast to deploy many ships to North America. This idea was quickly shown to be faulty as the British immediately set almost 100 warships on station solely directed against the American coastline. To counter the British presence, the Americans had six large frigates designed to carry forty-four guns and several smaller two-masted vessels of the Essex class. Nonetheless, the double-banked American frigates proved vastly superior to any other warships in their class. Like many American merchant vessels of the day, these frigates were particularly fast and could run from any vessel they could not match in size. Their superiority over other warships in their class was largely due to the attention to detail of their designer Joshua Humphreys and to the talent of their officers and crew.

Of the six vessels—*Constitution, President, United States, Chesapeake, Constellation,* and *Congress*—the best known was *Constitution* with its many single-ship actions, including the defeat of the British frigates *Guerriere* and *Java.* The strength of *Constitution*'s sides in these battles was so great that many of the enemy's shot bounced off into the sea. This observation led to the frigate's nickname, "Old Ironsides." The *United States* brought Capt. Stephen Decatur to renewed prominence when he trounced the thirty-eight-gun *Macedonian* and brought it into the American Navy. Yet not all went well for the U.S. Navy. The thirty-eight-gun *Chesapeake* was lost in an ill-considered ship-to-ship duel with the thirty-six-gun *Shannon* within sight of Boston. Late in the war, *President,* the fastest of the six

Humphreys's frigates, was pounded into submission by a small squadron of British ships, including the forty-four-gun *Endymion,* a British large frigate. The remaining U.S. frigates captured a few merchant vessels in the Atlantic but generally failed to distinguish themselves otherwise.

Notes

1. Quoted in Stanley Weintraub, *Iron Tears: America's Battle for Freedom, Britain's Quagmire, 1775–1783* (New York: Free Press, 2005), 164.

2. Alexander Hamilton, "Federalist No. 12," in *The Federalist Papers,* ed. Clinton Rossiter (New York: New American Library, 1961), 90–91.

3. Alfred Thayer Mahan, *The Influence of Sea Power upon History, 1660–1783* (New York: Dover Publications, 1987).

4. Mahan.

5. Hamilton, 87–88.

6. Simon Schama, *A History of Britain: The Wars of the British, 1603–1776,* Vol. II (New York: Hyperion, 2001), 409.

7. Schama, 409.

8. As of January 2009 pirates were attacking ships off the cost of Somalia.

9. Frederick C. Leiner, *The End of Barbary Terror* (New York: Oxford University Press, 2006), 4.

10. Nathan Miller, *Sea of Glory: A Naval History of the American Revolution* (Annapolis, MD: Naval Institute Press, 1974), 143–144, 148–149.

11. Harold Sprout and Margaret Sprout, *The Rise of American Naval Power, 1776–1918* (Annapolis, MD: Naval Institute Press, 1990), 18.

12. Sprout and Sprout, 15.

13. Frances Diane Robotti and James Vescovi, *The USS Essex and the Birth of the American Navy* (Holbrook, MA: Adams Media Corporation, 1999), 9.

14. James Madison, "Federalist No. 41," in *The Federalist Papers,* ed. Clinton Rossiter (New York: New American Library, 1961), 260.

15. Madison, 260–261.

16. Robotti and Vescovi, xvii.

17. Sprout and Sprout, 14.

18. Theodore Roscoe and Fred Freeman, *Picture History of the U.S. Navy* (New York: Charles Scribner's Sons. 1956), 252.

19. Sprout and Sprout, 47.

20. Sprout and Sprout, 34–35.

21. Sprout and Sprout, 34–35.

22. Howard I. Chapelle, *The History of the American Sailing Navy: The Ships and Their Development* (New York: W. W. Norton, 1949), 16.

23. Spelled Stoddart by Paullin and others. There seems to be no consensus as to the correct spelling.

24. Stephen Howarth, *To Shining Sea: A History of the Unites States Navy, 1775–1991* (New York: Random House, 1991), 51.

25. Frederick C. Leiner, *Millions for Defense: The Subscription Warships of 1798* (Annapolis, MD: Naval Institute Press, 2000), 12.

26. Howarth, 51.

27. Dorothy Denneen Volo and James M. Volo, *Daily Life in the Age of Sail* (Westport, CT: Greenwood Press, 2002), 284–285.

28. Ian W. Toll, *Six Frigates: The Epic History of the Founding of the U.S. Navy* (New York: W. W. Norton, 2006), 40.

29. Arthur Herman, *To Rule the Waves: How the British Navy Shaped the Modern World* (New York: HarperCollins, 2004), 410.

30. Jefferson to Albert Gallatin quoted in Howarth, 67.

31. Bill Kauffman, *Ain't My America: The Long, Noble History of Antiwar Conservatism and Middle-American Anti-Imperialism* (New York: Henry Holt, 2008), 21.

32. William Cullen Bryant, "The Embargo," *The Works of William Cullen Bryant*, http://www.4literature.net/William_Cullen_Bryant/Embargo/ (accessed June 17, 2008).

33. Kauffman, 14.

34. John Creswell, *British Admirals of the Eighteenth Century* (London: Anchor Books, 1972), 15–16.

35. See David Wells, *Our Merchant Marine: How It Rose, Increased, Became Great, Declined and Decayed* (New York: G. P. Putnam's Sons, 1890), 15–16. Shipbuilding in the colonial American South is often ignored; however, some of the best designs for 18th-century vessels developed in the Chesapeake Bay area of Maryland and Virginia.

36. Chapelle, 57–58.

37. John Fitzhugh Millar, *Early American Ships* (Williamsburg, VA: Thirteen Colonies Press, 1986), 146.

38. C. S. Forester, *The Age of Fighting Sail: The Story of the Naval War of 1812* (Sandwich, MA: Chapman Billies, 1956), 44–45.

39. Leiner, 2.

40. The author has attempted to be consistent in the forms that he uses. However, prime sources such as journals, diaries, and traditional reference works—worthy of citation—may use slightly different methods to convey this information. The author has decided to leave such material in the form found in the original works.

Chapter 7

War of 1812

I am for free commerce with all nations, political connection with none, and little or no diplomatic establishment, and I am not for linking ourselves, by new treaties with the quarrels of Europe.

—Thomas Jefferson

Mister Madison's War

Because of the continued aggressive acts of Britain, America ultimately was drawn into war in 1812. James Madison, secretary of state under Jefferson, was himself elected president in 1808 making Virginians three of the first four executives-in-chief in the short history of the nation. Only Adams had come from New England, and he had not been reelected. The domination of Virginia under the first two decades of rule under the Constitution (soon to be twenty-four of twenty-eight years by the time Madison left office) was not lost on the New England states, and they were not reticent about making their disapproval known.

During the first year of Madison's eight-year administration, the United States prohibited trade with both Britain and France; then in May 1810, Congress authorized trade with both, directing the president, if either nation would accept America's view of neutral rights, to forbid trade with the other. Napoleon announced that he was ready to comply late in 1810, and Madison—taken in by the phantom diplomacy of Bonaparte—proclaimed nonintercourse with Great Britain. In Congress, meanwhile, a group of young legislators including Henry Clay and John C. Calhoun, the War Hawks, pressed the president for a more militant policy toward Britain.

There was a lot of talk in 1812 of freedom of the seas and the evils associated with the impressment of American seamen. Yet it was the expansion of American maritime trade by leaps and bounds—and the fact that both America and Britain were in a fighting temper—that made the clash inevitable. Ultimately, these concerns brought the United States to enter a second Anglo-American conflict—the War of 1812, sometimes called Mister Madison's War. The opposition Federalist

Party opened a vociferous antiwar propaganda campaign with the public that was the first significant antiwar tirade based on policy in U.S. history. The horrors and bloodshed of warfare, the religious and moral imperatives against it, played no significant part in the antiwar rancor of the Federalists. Theirs was an opposition based mainly in political obstruction and for political purposes supported by the idea that war with Britain was bad for business.

Madison's devotion to his republican ideals had stopped him from building a formidable army and navy during peacetime. Therefore, it was difficult for him to organize an effective war machine amid opposition from New England Federalists, whose shipping had greatly suffered from nonintercourse. The regular army was weak—almost nonexistent in its scattered deployment—and Madison feared that he would need to fill the ranks of his ground forces by compulsion. Daniel Webster, a Federalist, claimed that the Madison administration failed to adhere to a strict construction of the Constitution when it began to gather state levees to fight in a major land war. Webster expressed a fear that if Congress acquiesced to the use of state troops to fight in wars engaged in by the central government, it could create the equivalent of a military dictator in the Executive Mansion (the White House).

The president resisted declaring war for four years, but the political influence of about two dozen outspoken proponents of war with Britain in the Congress convinced him to declare war in June 1812 just months before opening his reelection campaign. These War Hawks expected the war to be short, and they were convinced that the United States could gain part or all of Canada while Britain was expending most of its energy fighting the French. However, the British retained control of the seas, had bases in nearby Canada and the Caribbean, and enjoyed the allegiance of many tribes of Native Americans residing in the Great Lakes region and on the sparsely settled border regions of the great southeast particularly in parts of Alabama, Georgia, and Florida. These tribes had a great and proven potential to do harm. To enter a war against Britain was to invite attack from almost every quarter.

Nonetheless, the ordinary residents of America's developing midsection held a widespread and less cynical conviction that Britain had insulted their national dignity and their republican ideals during the period since the end of the American Revolution. Calling for volunteers in 1812, Andrew Jackson, major general of the Tennessee state militia and eager proponent of the war asked, "Are we the titled slaves of George the third? The military conscripts of Napoleon the great? or the frozen peasants of the Russian Czar? No," he concluded. "We are the free born sons of America; the citizens of the only republic now existing in the world; and the only people on earth who possess rights, liberties, and property which they dare call their own." The arguments and expansionist hopes of the War Hawks were less important to Jackson than making war on the Indians. Many whites like Jackson considered attempts to live peacefully with Native Americans futile, and Henry Clay once confided to a fellow congress member that the Indians were destined for extinction and not worth preserving as a race in any case.[1]

Nonetheless, Jackson also reflected the more commonly held belief that Britain had threatened America's place in history as the torchbearer of popular liberty for the world through its policy of instigating war between the tribes and American set-tlers. Jackson described the purpose of the war as an attempt by a free people "to reclaim by the power of their arms the rights which God has bestowed upon them, and which an infatuated King has said they shall not enjoy."[2]

In the war that followed, the U.S. Army regulars did not win a single major battle without the aid of the militia, and the grandiose plans to invade and seize Canada collapsed under an immense weight of government stupidity and military ineptitude. The efforts of the regulars had been dismal. With the help of Choctaw and Cherokee allies, however, Jackson and his volunteers were able to carry the war to the Gulf Coast region. He had dragged himself wounded (in a knife fight) from a sickbed in 1813 to lead his Tennessee and Kentucky volunteers to victory over the British-allied Creek Nation in the so-called Red Stick War, seizing in the process large chunks of Alabama and Mississippi from the Indians. On his own ini-tiative, he invaded Florida, because the Spanish governor had supplied the tribes with arms and munitions, and he drove a small British force out of Pensacola. Jack-son emerged as a hero and man of the people from the Battle of New Orleans in 1815. His victories were heralded as both a vindication of republican principles and of the militia system. His successes had helped to further entrench the myth that militias alone could be relied on to secure the nation.

A modified version of a Jeffersonian-style Embargo Act was enforced on American shipping for only a few months in 1813 with little success. In fact, only the U.S. Navy stood up to Britain with any effect. Although the little squadron of U.S. warships could not hope to decisively defeat the fleets of two-deckers that the British could bring to bear, it did hit the enemy hard enough in the Atlantic, the Caribbean, and the Great Lakes to save America's prestige. Historian Henry Adams, grandson and great-grandson of presidents, noted that the classic single-ship encounter between the heavy U.S. frigate *Constitution* and the heavy British frigate *Guerriere* in 1812 raised the United States to a first-class naval power "in one half hour of hot and heavy work." *Constitution* would experience its most effective period as a warship during the course of the war, capturing numerous merchant vessels and defeating four British warships: *Guerriere, Java, Cyane,* and *Levant.*[3]

Even with these circumstances taken into account, American entry into the war in 1812 is still somewhat of an enigma, and the study of Madison's decision to go to war has filled numerous volumes. Although no American troops were detailed to serve in the European theater, the free-trade Federalists of New England were vociferously opposed to involvement in what they considered a foreign conflict between Britain and France.

At the time of America's entry into the war, British land forces seemed preoccu-pied in Spain and Portugal, and American privateers, who had once before faced down the supposed might of the Royal Navy, sincerely believed that they could do so again. American privateers (517 vessels armed with 2,893 guns) would fight alongside the tiny regular U.S. Navy from 1812 to 1815. A tavern song from the revolutionary period had been revived for the new war at sea, "They talk of Sixty Ships, Lads, to scourge our free-born Land. If they send out Six Hundred we'll bravely them withstand."[4] With only sixteen seaworthy vessels of war (six frigates,

Table 7.1 The U.S. Naval Establishment, 1812

U.S. vessel type/name	Gun rating
Heavy frigates	
President	44
Constitution	44
United States	44
Chesapeake	36
Congress	36
Constellation	36
Corvettes/light frigates	
Adams	28
John Adams	28
Sloops of war	
Wasp	18
Hornet	18
Siren	16
Argus	16
Schooners	
Enterprise	12
Nautilus	12
Vixen	12
Viper	10

two corvettes, two sloops of war, two brigs, four schooners, and no ships of the line) in America's regular blue water navy versus Britain's estimated 800-plus warships of all sorts, the United States would need to fight a hit-and-run oceanic war with no hope of rivaling its large opponent. In no other war did the U.S. Navy's survival depend more on seamanship, marksmanship, and leadership. Of course, the British Navy had many other critical assignments, including maintaining a blockade of all of Europe, that would limit the number of warships that could be brought to bear on American shores.

Moreover, in 1812, Napoleon was the master of the European continent. Jeffersonian Republicans had greeted the French Revolution with joy and anticipation, yet Bonaparte had come to personify the culmination of all their antimilitarist fears. He had used the army to topple the French republic and crown himself emperor. He had installed his family members as kings and queens in more than a half-dozen European states and had made his infant son, Napoleon François, King of Rome thereby founding a dynastic line. He had recently invaded Russia—getting back out was going to be the trick. His brother Joseph was the king of Spain and the Peninsula War, having dragged on for years, had not yet become an abject failure.

Madison and the War Hawks had no way of knowing when they went to war *against* Britain (rather than *for* France) that the French initiatives on the continent would blow up in Napoleon's face. By mid-April 1814, Napoleon would abdicate, thereby freeing the redcoats to fight in America. Under the Treaty of Fontainebleau, he would be assigned to the island prison of Elba. With almost 1 million dead

Frenchmen littering the fields of Europe, no one considered that Napoleon would return to power during the Hundred Days, rebuild his armies, and fight the world again at Waterloo in 1815. Thereafter, Napoleon would run out his life imprisoned on St. Helena, and hundreds of headstrong French Bonapartists would seek asylum in the United States, especially along the Gulf Coast.

Meanwhile, the British policy of inciting Native American raids on the American frontiers in 1812 made a major war against the tribes likely for the understrength U.S. Army. The British warship *Orpheus* commanded by Capt. Hugh Pigot actually ascended the Apalachicola River to arm with muskets 3,000 warriors recruited from ten local bands of Creek and Seminole warriors to act against the American settlements. Constant trouble with the Indians on the frontiers and the threat of a British attack at almost any point on the Atlantic seacoast or on the border with British Canada would keep the American volunteers constantly in the field throughout two years of fighting.

The Men

With the declaration of war in June 1812, Madison called up all the state militias to serve the purposes of the federal government with each state satisfying a particular quota. This was late in the season to be marshaling forces, and the likelihood was great that the men would have to serve into the winter months. Except for a few hundred regulars scattered about the nation, the United States had no standing army at the time, and it relied on the citizen soldiers of the local militias and state-sponsored regiments for defense. In America, independent riflemen and rangers had patrolled the backwoods areas since colonial times, but a well-regulated and trained militia was thought to provide the most practical solution to the defense needs of most frontier settlements in times of crisis. There remained, as a relic of Revolutionary tradition, the cherished and romantic concept of the militia as a mythical army of self-trained and self-armed warriors, springing from the native soil in times of trouble. This picture hardly aligns with the known facts from the War for Independence during which a regular Continental Army had been established as the foundation of the Revolution with the militias serving as auxiliary forces.

As discussed earlier, for most Americans, the most noxious tool of impending tyranny was a standing army, whereas a militia system designed for the common defense was considered a sign of a healthy and vigorous democratic society in which citizens took on the responsibilities of actively safeguarding property, liberty, and life itself as had the ancient Greeks. The local militia companies—composed largely of fathers, sons, grandfathers, nephews, cousins, neighbors, and friends—were merely a local stop-gap, a quick response force for dealing with Indian raids and minor emergencies, not the foundation of a national defensive posture. While less than adequate to substitute for a regular military, the militia was, nonetheless, able to defend the settlements, drive back the Native American raiders, and hold open the newly abandoned Native lands for white acquisition. The reality of continuing to rely on the militia for national defense or for the prosecution of a war against a foreign power quickly proved a disastrous illusion.

It would be unfair, incorrect, and naïve to assume that the entire army of 1812 suddenly sprang from the soil of America composed of farmers, shopkeepers, or mechanics and commanded by a cadre of inexperienced lawyers, plantation owners, and merchants. Although almost all Americans were military amateurs, most previously had served under arms in some capacity. Because the last major war had ended almost three decades earlier, few young men had tasted battle. However, unlike European civilians who were denied the civilian use of firearms under the law, Americans were familiar with the processes of loading, aiming, and shooting, and most owned weapons of some type. Unfortunately, Americans also lacked military training, fire discipline, and respect for their officers. They were willful, disobedient, and unruly, but they would fight if they believed in the cause.

Those men between the ages of sixteen and sixty commonly were formed into local units for training, but formal state militias were more pragmatically composed of well-armed adult males in the prime of life rather than of old men armed with fowling pieces and young boys carrying squirrel guns. Almost all the men who served in the war from 1812 to 1815 were true volunteers, unlike the soldiers of European armies who may have been impressed or conscripted. The United States lacked a European-style professional officer corps, but many of the older Americans now serving as officers or noncommissioned officers had seen service in the Revolution or with their state militias on the frontiers.

Although no formal institution for the development of naval officers existed at the time, Congress had formally authorized the establishment and funding of the U.S. Military Academy (USMA) at West Point in 1802. Classes numbering as many as thirty-two "cadets" between the ages of ten and thirty-seven years had been undergoing training in artillery and engineering studies at the site since 1794. The U.S. Naval Academy (USNA) at Annapolis, Maryland, would not be established until 1845.

Firm congressional sanction for the USMA, signed by President Jefferson, separated the engineers from artillerymen and authorized a corps of cadets with a total of seven officers and ten students. Interpretations of Jefferson's intent in establishing the USMA vary, and because of his open antimilitarism, the evidence is inconclusive. Given the violent partisanship of the 1790s, there is evidence that Jefferson as president may not have been confident of the loyalty of those officers commissioned by his predecessors. He may indeed have hoped to foster a "national university" for scientific research, or he may have wanted to use the academy as a way to commission officers from among the "common people" who might be more loyal to a democratic form of government at a time when most army officers had come from more elitist and upper-class backgrounds. In any case, it was commonly agreed that artillery and engineering were precise and complicated areas of military training, mastery of which required specific instruction.[5]

Nonetheless, "wracked by cadet resistance to attending class, personal disputes and threats of violence among cadets, officers, soldiers, and civilians . . . the Military Academy was barely functioning at all by 1812." Indeed, only a single cadet and a single instructor were present at that time, and only eighty-nine cadets had graduated from West Point since its founding ten years earlier. The impending war with Britain caused Congress to authorize a more formal system of education at the military academy, and increased the size of the Corps of Cadets to 250 men. The Academy did not gain its reputation for discipline and academics until taken in hand by Col. Sylvanus Thayer, who served as superintendent from 1817 to 1833. Since 1812, all the superintendents at the Academy have themselves been West Point graduates.[6]

Despite the proclamations of the governors of the various states describing distinctive uniforms and standardized weapons, many Americans went to war in 1812 in the everyday clothing in which they had enlisted. Others attempted some degree of regimentation by adopting distinct emblems, hats, or pieces of clothing. Capt. Henry Brush of Virginia left a precise description of the newly enlisted men who turned out to fight in 1812. The soldiers were outfitted for service with unbleached, coarse linen hunting shirts and trousers almost identical to those used in the Revolution four decades earlier. In many cases, their clothing was fashioned in the pragmatic style of the backwoodsman, failing entirely to approach anything military in appearance. Yet it was well fitted to the vicissitudes of the weather and the physical exertion that would be expected of soldiers on campaign. Ironically, this lack of uniformity engendered a feeling of camaraderie and common cause among the volunteers and helped to dispel to a great extent any antigovernment feeling among the population.

Almost all military firearms used in the War of 1812 were based on the same standard smooth-bore, flintlock technology that had served in the American Revolution and continued to characterize the weapons of the Napoleonic Wars in Europe. Most firearms, including pistols, fired a generally large lead ball between 0.63 and 0.75 caliber weighing almost an ounce, but other calibers were used. The effective range of muskets remained less than 100 yards, while the visually intimidating pistols were actually useful only at very close quarters. The slow-moving and massive musket ball produced gruesome wounds—smashing bones and redirecting itself within the body. So-called clean wounds were rare, and postinjury infections were common, making amputation of limbs a common prophylactic procedure. Rifle fire, provided by the technology that gave America the Kentucky and Pennsylvania long rifles, was particularly accurate even at long ranges of 300 to 400 yards. Although the rifle was slow to load and fired a smaller ball (generally 0.36 to 0.58 caliber), the spin imparted to the projectile by the spiral grooves in the barrel (rifling) made it a deadly and precise weapon. Muskets were used for comparatively rapid, unaimed volley fire, and the average conscripted soldier could be easily trained to use them. The (muzzle-loaded) rifle was originally a sharpshooter's weapon used for targets of opportunity and deliberate aimed fire.

The effectiveness of the rifle had been proven in the American Revolution, and most European armies had adopted at least some rifle companies in the interim—notably the Prussian Jägers, French Voltiguers, and British Green Jackets.[7] Whereas the British and French riflemen were "chosen men" trained as light infantry and skirmishers, the Prussian Jägers were patriotic volunteers, bearing the cost of their weapons and uniforms at their own expense or with the help of contributions from friends and neighbors, and often organizing into clubs and leagues. Because of a slower loading time than a musket, rifles generally were issued only to specialized troops and not adopted for whole armies. The development of cartridge ammunition and breech-loading in the American Civil War was concurrent with the general adoption of rifles as standard-issue infantry weapons thereafter. The extreme range of the rifle should not be overemphasized, however, as most practical infantry targets proved to be well within 300 yards.

Campaigns

The War of 1812 was fought in three major theatres: (1) on the oceans, in the Gulf of Mexico, and the Caribbean where the warships and privateers of both sides preyed on each other's merchant shipping; (2) along the extended Great Lakes frontier between the United States and Canada; and (3) in the southeast of the American continent drained by the Alabama, Apalachicola, and Tombigbee Rivers and largely populated by the woodlands Native American nations. As the war progressed, the American coastline was blockaded with increasing regularity by the British who mounted numerous large-scale raids in the later stages of the war particularly those that had targeted the national capital at Washington, D.C., and the city of New Orleans, Louisiana.

By 1814, both sides had become weary of the costly and indecisive war, and they began peace conferences in 1814 at the city of Ghent (currently in Belgium). The war added some £25 million to the national debt of Britain, and about $105 million to that of the United States. Since the British pound (£) was worth about five times more than the U.S. dollar ($), the cost of the war to the United States was only slightly greater than that for the British. Nonetheless, the cost to U.S. trade because of the British blockade was significant, and maritime insurance rates of 75 percent were some of the highest ever charged during wartime.

British losses in America were about 1,600 killed and 3,700 wounded. In addition 3,300 British died from disease. U.S. losses were 2,300 killed and 4,500 wounded. While the number of Americans who died from disease is not known with certainty, the estimates vary wildly from 4,000 to 17,000. These figures do not include deaths or losses among Native American tribes. In addition, tens of thousands of American slaves escaped to the British lines because of the offer of freedom issued by the Crown. Other slaves just fled the plantations and farmsteads of their owners during the chaos of war hoping to find refuge among the tribes or in Canada. The Seminole of Florida were heavily infiltrated with former black slaves at this time, and the British settled the few thousand blacks who fled to Canada in Nova Scotia after the armistice.

The northern border of the United States was the first to feel Britain's wrath. Although U.S. troops would stand face-to-face trading volleys with British regulars at Chippewa and Lundy's Lane, the lack of a professional army was clearly evident throughout the American operations in the north country. Here Americans would learn the hard lesson of relying on a largely untrained militia led by an equally untrained group of officers making three attempts to invade their neighbor to the North. The tiny village of Sackett's Harbor, New York, on Lake Ontario was the scene of two important battles. In the first battle in 1812, the U.S. sloop of war *Oneida* and the American shore batteries established on the lakeside repulsed an attacking force of five British vessels operating from Canada. In the second battle in May 1813, a British land force was transported across Lake Ontario and attempted to capture the town and the principal dockyard for the American naval squadron on the lake. They were repulsed by a combination of American regulars and militia. The village of Sackett's Harbor became a major base of operations, both for the Navy (including the U.S. Marine Corps) and Army, for the duration of the war. Thereafter, it housed a training school for naval officers before the establishment of the U.S. Naval Academy.

The main American forces on the border between the United States and British Canada were stationed at Sackett's Harbor under Maj. Gen. Henry Dearborn and Commodore Isaac Chauncey. The U.S. lake squadron under Chauncey was superior in number to the opposing British vessels at Kingston, and the volunteer troops concentrated under Dearborn could outnumber the British at any point on their extended front. In April 1813, the Americans had missed a chance to storm Kingston, which would have eliminated the British squadron and perhaps allowed the Americans to secure almost all of Upper Canada, but Dearborn and Chauncey exaggerated the number of British regulars stationed there and chose to defend their base.

In late May 1813, the Americans attempted a final invasion of Canada and lost the final opportunity to seize much of Upper Canada. An amphibious force of 4,000 men under Col. Winfield Scott was ferried across Lake Ontario by Commodore Oliver Hazard Perry and proceeded to attack York (Toronto), the provincial capital at the other side. The Americans won the ensuing battle, occupying and looting the town and setting fire to the parliament building; but they then blundered into an ambush at Stony Creek and withdrew to the mouth of the Niagara River in disorder. The British reoccupied Fort Niagara in December. Having gained a martial reputation in the Mexican War in the late 1840s, Scott would continue in the U.S. Army until the opening of the Civil War when he was the highest-ranking Union general. Scott would formulate the so-called Anaconda Plan, which would strangle the Confederacy during the Civil War by closing the Mississippi River and the Atlantic and Gulf coasts to shipping.

On September 10, 1813, nine vessels of the U.S. Navy (sloops, schooners, and brigs) defeated and captured six vessels of the Royal Navy on Lake Erie. The losses on each side were about 100 men. After defeating the British fleet in the Battle of Lake Erie, Perry, commander of the American fleet, dispatched one of the most famous messages in military history to Maj. Gen. William Henry Harrison. It read: "We have met the enemy, and they are ours, two ships, two brigs, one schooner and one sloop."[8] This victory ensured American control of Lake Erie for the remainder of the war, which in turn allowed the Americans to recover Fort Detroit and win the Battle of the Thames River that broke the Native American confederation led by Tecumseh.

Further east, a redcoat army of 14,000 veteran troops supported by an inland British squadron attacked south from Canada through Plattsburg, New York, planning to drive the Americans before them. A remarkable American naval victory on Lake Champlain turned back the invasion. The British army under Lt. Gen. Sir George Prévost and the naval squadron under Capt. George Downie had converged on the lakeside town, which was defended by American troops under Brig. Gen. Alexander Macomb and ships commanded by Commodore Thomas MacDonough. Downie's squadron attacked shortly after dawn on September 11, 1814, but was defeated after a hard fight in which Downie was killed. Prévost then abandoned the land attack and retreated to Canada. The battle at Plattsburg (Second Battle of Lake Champlain) took place before the conclusion of peace negotiations in Europe, thereby giving American diplomats at Ghent, who had knowledge of it as well as of the previous series of lake victories, leverage to demand exclusive control over the Great Lakes and to negate any British claims against occupied territory in the New England states.

Notwithstanding these victories, the general U.S. war strategy along the Canadian border was mismanaged in that a number of opportunities were missed elsewhere: the gunboat navy on the Atlantic Coast proved useless; Chesapeake Bay was blockaded, Norfolk attacked, and Hampton Roads sacked. Fort McHenry in Baltimore harbor withstood a determined British attack in 1814, and its defense provided inspiration for Francis Scott Key's "Star-Spangled Banner." Yet the capital at Washington, D.C., was briefly captured and the Executive Mansion burned, possibly in retaliation for the burning of the Canadian Parliament building at York. Finally, Madison's enemies in his own party thwarted any attempt to seize parts of Spanish Florida for the United States.

With the armistice in December 1814, Madison found that not a single American war aim had been attained. After two years of war, there was even little enthusiasm left among abolitionists for creating new antislavery states from Canadian territory and thereby undermining southern control of the Senate. Notwithstanding these setbacks, history has dismissed the dismal failure of American arms in Mister Madison's War for the less-bitter illusions of success offered by the victories of the U.S. frigate *Constitution;* the successful defense of Fort McHenry; the chastisement of the southeastern tribes; and the minimal naval successes on Lakes Ontario, Champlain, and Erie.

The only truly decisive engagement of the war was the defeat of the British regulars at the Battle of New Orleans—significant in that it was to catapult Andrew Jackson to national prominence. The American riflemen at the Battle of New Orleans were particularly effective because they were stationed behind giant cotton bales arranged as temporary fortifications with supporting artillery, whereas the British, armed with smooth-bore muskets, marched in a line formation restricted to the width of the open levees that held back the swamps as they were mowed down. Many of these British regulars were veterans who had fought Napoleon in Spain. Upon hearing of the extent of the victory Rep. Henry Clay exulted, "Now, I can go to England without mortification."[9] Unknown to the participants, the most decisive battle of the war had had no effect on the terms of the peace because it had been fought after the treaty had been arranged in Europe. Had the battle been fought earlier, or had the peace been concluded later, the United States might have forced

Britain to cede sole control of the Great Lakes or a northern boundary at the 54th parallel.

Opposition to the War

Strong support for the war came from southerners and from those in frontier communities, but the Federalists, especially those in New England, opposed Mister Madison's War with Britain from beginning to end. As the Federalists had feared and predicted in 1812 the war had not gone well. Over time, the New Englanders became increasingly frustrated over how the war was affecting their states. For example, Castine, overlooking Penobscot Bay in Maine (then part of Massachusetts and a center for shipbuilding and coastal trading) was occupied by British troops. American troops were garrisoned in Castine, but they were unable to defend the town against a superior British force supported by the Royal Navy. American ropewalks, sail lofts, and ship chandlers providing necessary goods and services for the New England maritime trade with the West Indies and England were captured or put out of service. The use of a major salt depository supplying the Grand Banks fishing fleets was also lost. In times of peace, hundreds of fishing ships were anchored in Penobscot Bay at Castine harbor. The town, once taken, would be held by British forces until 1815.

Many New Englanders considered the deployment of militias outside their states under federally appointed officers unconstitutional. Massachusetts troops should have been used to protect New England interests, not the frozen border of New York with Canada. The increased wartime taxes, shortages of goods brought on by the British blockade, and the occupation of other parts of New England by enemy forces also agitated public opinion. Their's was a two edged sword of protest. Although they were against the war, the New Englanders also were complaining that the federal government was not investing enough militarily to defend their states and their commercial vessels. The state governments should have the right to recall their own militias from deployments outside their home states. Under such circumstances, the prowar party could do little to satisfy them.

As a result, at the Hartford Convention (December 1814–January 1815) held in Connecticut, twenty-six representatives from the northeast asked the federal government to fully restore the states' powers it had seemingly undermined. Unfortunately for the delegates, many of their meetings were held in secret, and no written records of the proceedings were kept. After openly choosing George Cabot (a merchant, seaman, and politician from Boston) as president, and Theodore Dwight (a distinguished lawyer, member of Congress, and journalist from Hartford) as secretary, the convention shut itself up and remained in secret session for three continuous weeks. A great deal of anti-Southern (and antislavery) sentiment filled the discussions. Surviving letters of contemporaries suggest that the Federalist representatives labored intensely among the delegates to procure the immediate secession of New England from the United States.

Assembling each day amid rumors of conspiracy and treason, the members were watched by an army officer who was conspicuously stationed near the entrance to the hall taking down the names of the attendees and pestering those coming in and out of the deliberations for information. This was an open attempt at intimidation. The majority of the Hartford delegates intended, however, only to embarrass Madison and their prowar opponents in Congress by publicly issuing a series of antiwar, anti-administration resolutions. They threatened the president with the secession of the entire region east of the Hudson River only in the final months of the conflict when peace was clearly on the horizon and the threat of secession was hollow.

The Federalists had voted against the declaration of what proved a generally popular war, and they had continued to harass the war efforts of the administration in all the states controlled by the party. The Federalists tried to use their opposition to the war as the basis for power negotiations between New England and the other sections of the country. The attempt had not been well carried out. Few believed that the New England states would actually secede. Nonetheless, both the Hartford Convention and the Federalist Party became synonymous with disunion, secession, and treason, especially in the South and on the frontier.

While the war was less than decisive, it was cathartic for the majority of Americans who continued to harbor anti-British sentiments left over from the Revolution. Many felt that they had been made to win their independence twice to take unqualified possession of it. Also important was the fact that the British had finally agreed to abandon their claims to the Great Lakes region and had set the boundaries of several U.S. states with Canada. Significantly, the boundary between Canada and the United States in Maine was set at the St. Croix River rather than along the line of the Penobscot River adding one-third to the area of the region to U.S. sovereignty. Moreover, the pro-British Indians, who had threatened the frontiers for most of the three decades since independence, had been clearly chastised. While the war was hardly a triumph, the Democratic Republicans were able to present it as such, and the antiwar Federalists would not survive the confrontation as a viable political party.

Although the Federalists would maintain more than a minimal presence in states like Massachusetts and Delaware until the national elections of 1816, the party was clearly in decline. The large, but unstable Democratic Republican Party essentially took over American political life. The nation had shifted from the dominance of Federalist thought to the dominance of Democratic Republican thought in less than a decade, and many hoped that the resurgence of a unified concept of governance would usher in a era of active bipartisanship and national consensus. At the same time, the newly elected president (in 1816), James Monroe remained suspicious of lurking Federalist principles but spoke of the opposition in the blandest platitudes possible lest he create a reactionary resurgence of the party. The editor of a New England newspaper declared the Monroe presidency an "Era of Good Feelings," and the name stuck.

The failure of the Federalist Party initiated a brief period of virtual one-party rule in America. Four of the first five presidents of the United States had come from Virginia, coloring the office with a pro-Southern, pro-agrarian, and pro-slavery outlook. The only New Englander among these chief executives was John Adams, a Federalist who had served a single term. Yet the differences between the moderates and the more radical members of the Democratic Republican Party soon became evident. The twin evils of factionalism and sectionalism once again raised their heads fueled by slavery, tariffs, banking, and other internal questions. Former War Hawks like Henry Clay of Kentucky and John C. Calhoun of South Carolina continued to support a militant nationalism with respect to Britain, but the Democratic Republicans found that a total reliance on an agrarian economy had been a serious disadvantage to America's military efforts during the war. Domestic industries had sprung up during the war years, foreign imports had decreased, and many of those formally repulsed by the industries of the northeast (the South excepted) found themselves supporting protective tariffs. A majority of those who had railed against Hamilton's National Bank in 1811, when it was allowed to pass out of existence, suspended their constitutional objections to the establishment of a Second National Bank in 1816. This resurrected the question of the bank as a political issue (especially in the Midwest) and strengthened the perceived evil of growing sectionalism. Many former anti-nationalists began to seek federal subsidies for internal improvements within their states, especially with respect to roads and canals that would connect the settlements on the frontiers to the markets in the East.

In 1825, Monroe approved a federal purchase of stock in the Ohio Canal Company, a move considered by some "old republicans" as clearly unconstitutional. Among these "old republicans" were strict constructionists like John Randolph and John Taylor of Virginia and Nathaniel Macon of North Carolina who believed that the accumulation of wealth, the growth of industry, and the expansion of urban areas were signs of a fatal corruption in the fabric of the nation. "The tariff, bank, and internal improvements would stimulate commercial interests unduly, undermine agriculture, centralize power in the federal government, and violate the Constitution."[10]

Sectionalism had grown but increased intraparty political tension was often most obvious at the state level where "old party republicans" and "new party republicans" fought for control of their caucuses in the state legislatures and disputed the power to choose gubernatorial candidates, U.S. senators, and other state officials. Ironically these were precisely the evils of an unchecked popular democracy that had been predicted by the Federalists during the Constitutional Convention.

Continued internal wrangling led to the presidency of John Quincy Adams (1825–1829), candidate of the short-lived National Republican Party, and ultimately to a new two-party system. This so-called Second-Party System was dominated by Democrats (the modern party formed from the Democratic Republicans in 1828 under Andrew Jackson) and by Whigs (formed in 1833 in opposition to Jacksonian policies) during the next eight presidential election cycles. During a long political career (1803–1848) as ambassador, state senator, secretary of state, congress member, and president, John Quincy Adams was a member of five distinct national parties—the Federalist, Democratic-Republican, National Republican, Anti-Masonic, and Whig parties—attesting to the volatility of the American political structure in the first half of the 19th century.

Meanwhile on the global front, the removal of Napoleon Bonaparte from the stage of European politics in 1815 caused many nations to face inward for the first time in a generation. The world entered an era of extended peace among nations. For most of the next fifty years, European countries struggled with the internal social upheavals that culminated in widespread national revolutions from 1848 to 1860. The Sicilians and Neapolitans revolted in Italy under Garibaldi; the Piedmontese struggled with Austria; and the Sepoys mutinied against the British in India. In 1854, the world briefly focused on the Crimea, as the once-unthinkable alliance of France and Britain moved against Turkey and Russia in what some historians consider the first modern war. Meanwhile, the United States passed through a long period of internecine political brawling over Native American removal, nullification, states' rights, and slavery, which ultimately led to the Civil War.

Notes

1. Harry L. Watson. *Liberty and Power: The Politics of Jacksonian America* (New York: Hill and Wang, 2006), 53.

2. Watson, 48–49.

3. Watson, 78.

4. William Bell Clark, *George Washington's Navy* (Baton Rouge: Louisiana State University Press, 1960), 228.

5. West Point Bicentennial, "The Early Years, 1776–1817," Official USMA Bicentennial Web site, http://www.usma.edu/bicentennial/history/1776.asp (accessed April 2009).

6. West Point Bicentennial.

7. The 95th Rifle Brigade (Prince Consort's Own, made famous in the fictional Richard Sharpe series by Bernard Cornwall) was the first to use military camouflage regiment-wide. The purpose of the regiment, was to be the sharpshooters, skirmishers, and scouts of the British Army. The unit played an important role in the Peninsular War. The first four regular battalions had been raised as regular line battalions, but a fifth battalion was raised and equipped entirely with the Baker rifles and wore dark green jackets.

8. Theodore Roosevelt, *The Naval War of 1812; or The History of the United States Navy during the Last War with Great Britain* (New York: G. P. Putnam's Sons, 1882), 326.

9. Watson, 78.

10. Watson, 60–61.

Chapter 8

The War with Mexico (1846)

Future years will never know the seething hell and the black infernal background, the countless minor scenes and interiors of war; and it is best they should not. The real war will never get in the books. In the mushy influences of current times, too, the fervid atmosphere and typical events of those years are in danger of being totally forgotten. . . . Think how much, and of importance, will be—how much, civic and military, has already been—buried in the grave, in eternal darkness.

—Walt Whitman[1]

Expansion

President John Tyler spent much of his presidency maneuvering to get Texas annexed to the United States. He considered this goal a great benefit to the United States, but he left the war with Mexico that followed his decision to be fought by his successor, James K. Polk. The Mexican War was wildly popular with the electorate, but it generated the first truly *intellectual justification* of antiwar principles in America through the pen of Henry David Thoreau. Although a simple and somewhat quixotic man, Thoreau has become an icon to many antiwar intellectuals and progressive academics.

In 1845, Massachusetts senator Charles Sumner—ironically, a leading proponent of abolishing slavery by military means in 1861—provided pacifists with an early springboard for opposition to the war with Mexico when he gave a Fourth of July oration regarding the approaching Texas crisis. "Can there be in our age any peace that is not honorable, any war that is not dishonorable?"[2] More than 400 New York businessmen, fearful that the war would ruin their business, signed a petition in protest of the conflict, and in 1846 the New England Anti-slavery Convention—fearing a further expansion of slavery into any territory that the United States might acquire in the Southwest—declared that it thought the prosecution of a war with Mexico unconstitutional. The inclusion among the antiwar voices of the literary and political elite of New England—chief among them Henry David Thoreau, Ralph Waldo Emerson, Theodore Parker, Margaret Fuller, John Quincy Adams, Daniel Webster, and other like-minded persons among their acquaintances—legitimized antiwar sentiment and passive war resistance from 1846 through 1849.

To Rebel and Revolutionize

The Mexican War brought forth for the first time many of the intellectual foundations of the later American antiwar movement. The classic antigovernment essay of Henry David Thoreau, "On Civil Disobedience" (1849), was written to protest the use of tax money to prosecute the Mexican war, a conflict he considered unjust and blatantly aggressive. Thoreau believed the purpose of the war was to extend American slavery into new territories at the expense of its weaker neighbor. "When a sixth of the population of a nation [the United States] which has taken to be a refuge of liberty are slaves, and a whole country [Mexico] is unjustly overrun and conquered by [our] army and subjected to military law, I think it is not too soon for honest men to rebel and revolutionize."[3]

Although the money paid to his local magistrate was not actually being spent on the war, by refusing to pay his poll taxes, Thoreau had protested the concept of war funding and was hauled off to jail. His aunt quietly paid his poll taxes, and Thoreau was released after spending a single night in the local lock-up, sharing a cell with a man accused of setting fire to a barn. "It was like traveling into a far country, such as I had never expected to behold, to lie there for one night," wrote the sometimes overly melodramatic author.[4] No one took notice of the incident save Ralph Waldo Emerson, James Russell Lowell, Margaret Fuller, and a small circle of relatives and friends, among them the group of writers and intellectuals known as the Transcendentalists. Emerson observed of the incident, "My friend Mr. Thoreau has gone to jail rather than pay his taxes. On him they could not calculate."[5]

The episode of Thoreau's imprisonment, brief as it was, produced a literary work of political philosophy so profound that it reached out to the pacifist minds of Mahatma Gandhi and Martin Luther King, Jr., more than a century later, and it helped to build the bona fides of antiwar sentiment on America's college campuses and among its university faculties. Gandhi adopted some of these ideas and recommended the study of Thoreau's "Civil Disobedience" to all his followers. Martin Luther King, Jr. wrote of Thoreau, "Here, in this courageous New Englander's refusal to pay his taxes and his choice of jail rather than support a war that would spread slavery's territory into Mexico, I made my first contact with the theory of nonviolent resistance."[6]

Thoreau—a Harvard alumnus, ex-schoolteacher, poet, essayists, and sometime recluse—had begun his solitary stay at Walden Pond just as Polk was entering the White House. The property around the pond, which was only a short walk from his aunt's home, belonged to Emerson who had given his friend free use of it, and Thoreau built a shack near the water's edge in which to live. During his stay, Thoreau was no hermit in sackcloth and ashes. His aunt and female cousin often visited him there, brought him meals and baked goods, and took away his dirty laundry to be cleaned. Although the facts surrounding Thoreau seem incongruous to the themes of individual freedom, resistance to government, and civil rights that he set in motion, a few of his contemporaries recognized in him an important nexus in the conflict between expansionism and antislavery. Thoreau helped set in motion a new antiwar movement, the first since the Federalists in New England had protested the War of 1812, but one that had an intellectual as well as a political conscience.[7]

Transcendentalism

The Transcendentalists, who practiced a form of Christian humanitarianism at Brook Farm in Massachusetts, were both antislavery and antibusiness. They had an effect on the intellectual development of New England out of all proportion to their number, which totaled no more than a few dozen persons. Ralph Waldo Emerson, Theodore Parker, Margaret Fuller, and Bronson Alcott spent time there, and Emerson supplied funds to the failing commune in the last year of its existence. The group had coalesced around the rising social religion known as Unitarianism. In 1831, a devotee described Unitarianism as being nothing more than the spirit of freedom and individuality with no established creed or symbol, its members aiming for the social harmony of earth with mankind.[8] The purposes of the Mexican War, as the Transcendentalists perceived them, were the antithesis of the spirit of the Utopian community that they had formed.

A 19th-century feminist (women's rights) leader, Fuller served for a time, as did Alcott, as editor of the Brook Farm literary publication, *The Dial*. Among their essays and poems, the Transcendentalists published a full range of antiwar sentiments. Fuller wrote that in opening a war with Mexico, the United States had become "a scourge" on humankind that hid behind the flag.[9] Yet no amount of literary effort or intellectual argument could stop the forces driving a popular war. Emerson did most of his writing in journals with a small circulation, and much of what was written had little effect on the general public. The rather insular circle of Emerson's friends often felt that to speak against the war publicly was either "mistaken or futile." Nor could they convince a majority of U.S. citizens that war with Mexico was immoral or unjust.[10]

Other notables among New England's intellectual community expounded on the war-slavery connection. The venerable senator Daniel Webster agreed that some limit must be put to the territorial expansion of the United States if its institutions were to remain viable: "The government is very likely to be endangered," he wrote, "by a further enlargement of its already vast territorial surface."[11] As the number of Mexican and American war casualties increased, John Greenleaf Whittier moralized on an antiwar theme in *Yorktown*; Herman Melville castigated the government in *Typee*; and William Lloyd Garrison proclaimed Polk's presidency "a curse to the country" and wrote that if blood was to flow in Mexico, it should be American blood.[12]

Not Just Abolition

Garrison was never restrained in his criticism of any topic he considered iniquitous or unjust. In his crusade against slavery, he more than once called for the

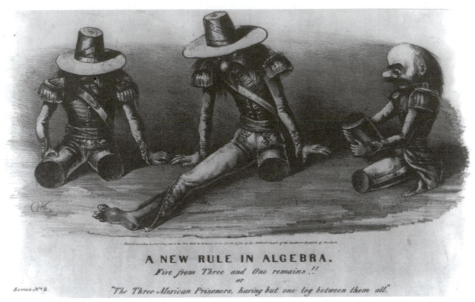

A NEW RULE IN ALGEBRA.
Five from Three and One remains .!!
or
"The Three Mexican Prisoners, having but one leg between them all."

A biting and somewhat morbid satire about the fate of wounded Mexican prisoners of war in the hands of American doctors. During the Mexican War, amputation was considered the surest way to prevent the infection of an injured limb, and American doctors were accused of performing unwarranted medical procedures. The cartoon shows three Mexican soldiers seated, in obvious alarm, on the ground. Of the three men, only the soldier in the center has a leg remaining. (Library of Congress Prints and Photographs Division, LC-USZ62-9915)

abandonment of the Constitution and was not beyond disrupting the services of churches not dedicated to abolition. Yet he was thoroughly committed to nonviolence. In 1831, in the very first issue of his antislavery newspaper, the *Liberator*, Garrison stated, "I do not wish to think, or speak, or write, with moderation. . . . I am in earnest—I will not equivocate—I will not excuse—I will not retreat a single inch—and I will be heard!"[13]

Although best known as an abolitionist, Garrison, like many other 19th-century social reformers, was also a committed war resister who rarely ceased finding fault with the government. As early as 1838, Garrison had prepared a declaration for the peace convention that had met in Boston to establish the Non-Resistance Society. In the "Declaration of Sentiments Adopted by the Peace Convention," he wrote, "Our country is the world. . . . The interests, rights, liberties of American citizens are no more dear to us than are those of the whole human race. Hence, we can allow no appeal to patriotism, to revenge any national insult or injury."[14]

Frustrated in its attempt to convert southern moderates to abolition and unable to sustain itself without violence in any slave state, the abolitionist movement of the late 1840s became closely focused on being heard by a northern audience. The abolition leadership, however, disagreed among itself over how best to proceed, and a serious rift developed among dedicated abolitionists over the question of tactics. Consequently, two large factions formed in the antislavery movement—one dedicated to Garrison and the other coalescing around New York financier Louis Tappan.

Those who followed Garrison included many free black men and women who had previously been "non-actors in American politics." These black abolitionists often supported pacifism, nonresistance, social utopianism, anarchism, and full women's rights—causes thought by some in the antislavery movement to be highly impractical objectives. When an international antislavery convention in London in that same year refused to recognize female delegates, Garrison dramatically took a seat among the women in the gallery in protest. In 1840, Garrison's following peaked at about 2 percent of the white male voting public of the Northeast.[15]

The Garrisonians tended to embrace religious views outside the evangelical mainstream. They tended to be Unitarians, Transcendentalists, or fallen-away Quakers (those who had seceded from the mainstream meeting house discipline). They were thought by some to be more closely aligned with the pacifism as expressed by members of regional utopian communities such as at Hopedale or Northampton in Massachusetts than with the goals of the wider evangelical reform community. Former Episcopalians Angelina and Sarah Grimké, for instance, joined the Quaker Meeting Discipline in Philadelphia in 1835, but they found the absolute pacifism and nonresistance of the Friends frustrating. The sisters from South Carolina began to speak out against slavery and for women's rights in public. They were among the first women in the United States to break out of the designated domestic sphere society had established for women of their class making them somewhat of a curiosity. Whittier approved of the sisters, but he also suggested that they restrain themselves by limiting their activities to emancipation of slaves rather than that of women.

Meanwhile, Garrison's negative attitudes toward government in general aligned him more closely with the antiwar principles and personal civil disobedience of men like Thoreau. Consequently, about half the membership of Garrison's American Anti-Slavery Society split from the organization and, under the leadership of Tappan, formed the American and Foreign Anti-Slavery Society. Unlike Garrison, who generally eschewed political involvement, the Tappanites had no objection to political activism—supporting the antislavery candidates of the Liberty Party and other parties. Garrisonians tended rather to focus on moral and religious agitation, shunning the political arena and calling for the preeminence of moral principles over constitutional law.[16]

The Wilmot Proviso

In August 1846, David Wilmot, a Democrat from Pennsylvania, introduced an amendment to a war appropriations bill requested by President Polk that stipulated that slavery would be barred from all lands acquired from Mexico as a result of the war. Although Wilmot had sought to quiet antiwar resentment concerning the underlying objectives of the war by this action, the Wilmot Proviso polarized northerners and southerners in Congress and failed to pass. The proviso tended to equate opposition to slavery with opposition to the war, and the war with Mexico was a popular conflict. The issues raised by the proviso did, in fact, drive the debate over the war, thereby bringing hundreds of antislavery activists into an otherwise-unpopular antiwar movement. Among these were a large number of young women active in the religious enlightenment and camp meeting phenomenon raging in the Northeast and Midwest. Already acting outside the cultural establishment of traditional churches, these women provided the antiwar movement with a "great silent army of volunteers and fund-raisers."[17]

Antiwar protests concerning the so-called Mexican Cession—a term used with respect to lands newly acquired from Mexico—were by no means confined to the antislavery issue. The effort to prosecute the war had negative implications for a range of social reformers. Many activists preferred that the government dedicate its human resources and limited treasure to economic development, public education, public works, or social improvements rather than on soldiers, bullets, cannon, and ships. In a letter (July 7, 1847) to Richard D. Webb, founder of the Hibernian Anti-Slavery Society, Garrison wrote of the Mexican campaign:

It was begun and is carried on against the deep moral convictions of the sober portion of the people; its real object, the extension and preservation of slavery, no intelligent man honestly doubts; still, the diabolical motto, "Our country, right or wrong," gratifies national pride, appears in a patriotic garb, and obtains a sanction practically that is almost universal. Besides, American arms have been crowned with extraordinary success; and there is little doubt that Generals [Winfield] Scott and [Zachary] Taylor will be reveling in the halls of the Montezumas, in the city of Mexico, on the 4th of July, our glorious day of freedom and national independence. . . . Now, boldly and continually to denounce the war, under such circumstances, as bloody and iniquitous—to impeach the government and the administration—to deplore instead of rejoicing over the victories won by our troops—to wish success to the Mexicans, as the injured party, who are contending for their firesides and their country against enslaving and remorseless invaders—as you can easily imagine, subjects us to great odium, and brings down upon our heads the heavy charge of "treason" and "traitors to the country." But our testimony is not in vain. It burns like fire upon the national conscience.[18]

No Appeal to Patriotism

Chief among the voices raised in protest of the war with Mexico was that of former president John Quincy Adams (1825–1829), who as a member of the House of Representatives (elected in 1830), was one of only fourteen members of Congress to vote against the war. Adams was an outspoken opponent of slavery, and it was he who had spoken before the U.S. Supreme Court in 1839 in support of the Africans on the captured slave ship *Amistad* and helped to obtain their release and freedom. Adams believed that the government's secret and immoral purpose in making war was to seize new territory into which slavery might be expanded. On February 21,

1848, the House of Representatives were discussing the matter of honoring U.S. Army officers who had served in Mexico. Adams firmly opposed this idea, so when the rest of the house erupted into "Ayes," he cried out, "No!"—his voice, usually small with age, stunning the chamber. At that precise moment, Adams collapsed, having suffered a massive cerebral hemorrhage that led to his death.

Adams's son, Charles Francis Adams, had supported the former president in his antislavery and antiwar beliefs. The younger Adams was a lawyer, editor, and politician, and he printed scathing antiwar editorials in the *Boston Daily Whig*, the unofficial voice of the so-called Conscience Whigs. Because of his antislavery position and articles he had written in the *Boston Courier* in 1840 critical of President Martin Van Buren, the Whig Party asked him to run for a seat in the Massachusetts legislature. He served as a state representative (1840–1843), and then as a state senator (1843–1845). Beginning with the 1843 session, Charles Francis Adams led the antislavery struggle in the Bay State legislature. That year, he successfully brought about passage of a resolution opposing the annexation of Texas as a slave state. After the national Whig party endorsed the admission of Texas to the Union, he separated himself from the majority of so-called Cotton Whigs, and associated only with the antislavery Conscience Whigs. After the death of his father in 1848, he joined the Free Soil Party, composed of former Conscience Whigs and other dedicated abolitionists. He chaired their national convention that year and the Free Soilers nominated him for vice president. After his unsuccessful candidacy, Adams temporarily withdrew from active politics, devoting himself to writing and business. He was particularly effective as the ambassador to Great Britain during the Civil War.

The father-son Adams team was able to produce a significant public uproar concerning both abolition and war resistance throughout the late 1840s that ended in a stream of pacifist memoranda and antiwar petitions coming out of the abolition societies of Massachusetts. The two issues had become virtually inseparable. The commonwealth's legislature rejected a bill to outfit a state volunteer regiment raised to fight in the war, and its governor, James Briggs, refused to commission officers for service in Mexico. The legislature ultimately passed a "sense of the assembly" condemning the military operations set in motion by Polk as "a war of conquest, so hateful in its objects, so wanton, unjust and unconstitutional in its origins and character, that it must be regarded as a war against humanity, against justice, against union . . . and against the free states."[19]

The Extension of Slavery

The bulk of the antiwar unrest was related to the abolition movement, which feared the expansion of slavery within the Union. One of the strategic errors made by pro-slavery apologists was to allow the abolitionists to turn the antiwar argument into a debate over whether the practice of slavery would extend into the vast expanse of unorganized territories that the nation was assembling in meeting its Manifest Destiny. Although the South vociferously demanded a fair share in the nation's territorial opportunities, by mid-century, the question of slavery in the territories had, in fact, become nothing more than symbolic. Few regions remained into which slavery could be introduced economically. Cotton, rice, and sugar—the labor-intensive crops that seemingly demanded a slave workforce for their cultivation on a commercial scale—could not be grown in most of the bone-dry desert Southwest or in the cold and damp Northwest of Oregon. Crops like rice and sugar demanded moisture, and cotton needed at least 200 frostless days of growth. These facts limited their practical production to those areas of the South in which it already existed. All of New England had given up slavery by 1848 and began to rely on white immigrant wage labor from Europe in its stead. It seemed equally unlikely that slaves could have been employed economically among the apple orchards of Oregon or the vineyards of California when there seemingly existed a swarm of Asian laborers (mostly Chinese) willing to work long hours for little pay. Nonetheless, southerners rarely made these arguments, and the question of the extension of slavery persisted as a flash point for both abolition and war resistance. The debate remained a focus of sectionalism and a catalyst for discord throughout the 1850s and was not resolved until the Civil War.

Antiwar tactics at this time proved ineffective. The American Peace Society urged Mexico and the United States to mediate their differences as if some magical logic expounded at the negotiating table would alter their geopolitical differences or deter the United States in its quest for its manifest destiny. The war in Mexico also affected Elihu Burritt, who was the American founder of the first International Peace Congress held in Brussels in 1848. Playwright Victor Hugo presided over the second International Peace Congress in Paris in 1849. Successive meetings from 1850 through 1853 were all held in Europe and attended mostly by Europeans. In 1854, the Crimean War jolted Burritt into a realization that both his fellow countrymen and the leaders of other nations were unimpressed by pacifist calls for world brotherhood and international arbitration, and he turned his attention to abolition, temperance, and justice for Irish immigrants in America. He was consul to Great Britain during the Lincoln administration.

The focus of antiwar disaffection with the Mexican War in the United States was generally to be found among the academic communities of New England. It was the war with Mexico that brought the "university" into the antiwar fold. Significant constitutional questions concerning the deployment of American troops in a foreign land remained unresolved, but the usual antiwar proponents among constitutionalists and isolationists were conspicuous in their relative silence.

Historians have fallen into the habit of underestimating the Mexican forces partly because they lost most of the battles and partly due to a residual ethnic prejudice. The Mexican military in 1846 was quite substantial and experienced, but the American military was well led and competent enough to use its resources to good effect. Due to the foundational importance of this period to the history of war resistance, this chapter has been deliberately foreshortened with regard to the U.S. Army, its structure, and the battles that it fought in Mexico. Yet a few words must be added because the army that fought a foreign enemy in 1846 was very like the ones that fought each other in 1861.

At the end of the War of 1812, an American officer—tongue firmly in cheek—expressed his opinion of the army's lackluster performance: "We certainly have every reason to be proud of many parts of our war however unadvisedly and without proper preparation it may have been begun." [20] Yet within three decades the United States brought to bear upon Mexico two fully functional armies, and, without regard to any justification of the war, each behaved gallantly and was led decisively. Most importantly, the U.S. artillery was brilliant, providing tremendous firepower at opportune moments and completely overawing its Mexican counterpart, while the American navy provided dependable transportation and both strategic and logistical support to the ground forces.

The army that fought in 1846 was stronger on logistics than previously, but it remained weak in organizational structure. The individual infantry, cavalry, artillery, and engineering branches of the U.S. Army at midcentury each had its own characteristic weaknesses, yet they worked well as a whole when properly led. Copious supplies and advanced weapons made battles possible, but leadership kept the army from degenerating into unorganized mobs. It must be remembered that there is nothing natural or easy about long lines of men tramping about on a battlefield shoulder-to-shoulder shooting, stabbing, and hacking at another group similarly composed and with identical intent. The inherent tendency of such operations is to fall into chaos, and a successful battle requires a great deal of pre-engagement regimentation and training. That training was largely a product of education—particularly the education afforded young officers at schools like West Point. The Mexican War vindicated the institutional forms, military doctrines, and organizational structures taught at the U.S. Military Academy and ensured that they would be followed dutifully by both sides in the Civil War. No major changes were made in these military paradigms until Elihu Root reformed the system at the turn of the twentieth century.[21]

Notes

1. Walt Whitman, *Specimen Days* (Philadelphia: David McKay, 1883).

2. Walter Millis, *Arms and Men: A Study of American Military History* (New York: A Mentor Book, 1956), 91.

3. Bernard DeVoto, *The Year of Decision, 1846* (Boston: Little, Brown, 1943), 208–209.

4. Joseph Wheelan, *Invading Mexico: America's Continental Dream and the Mexican War, 1846–1848* (New York: Carroll & Graf Publishers, 2007), 258–259.

5. Wheelan, 258–259.

6. Martin Luther King, Jr., *Autobiography of Martin Luther King, Jr.*, http://www.stanford.edu/group/King//publications/autobiography/chp_2.htm (accessed October 2008).

7. Wheelan, 259.

8. Wheelan, 261.

9. Wheelan, 261.

10. Richard V. Frangaviglia and Douglas W. Richmond, eds., *Dueling Eagles: Reinterpreting the U.S.-Mexican War, 1846–1848* (Fort Worth: Texas Christian University Press, 2000), vii.

11. Bill Kauffman, *Ain't My America: The Long, Noble History of Antiwar Conservatism and Middle-American Anti-Imperialism* (New York: Henry Holt, 2008), 4.

12. Wheelan, 261.

13. William Lloyd Garrison, "The First Editorial by William Lloyd Garrison," *The Liberator,* January 1, 1831, URL: http://www.wfu.edu/~zulick/340/garrisonliberator1.html (accessed October 2008).

14. William Lloyd Garrison, "Declaration of Sentiments Adopted by the Peace Convention," September 28, 1838, http://teachingamericanhistory.org/library/index.asp?document=564 (accessed October 2008).

15. William E. Freehling, *The South vs. the South: How Anti-Confederate Southerners Shaped the Course of the Civil War* (New York: Oxford University Press, 2001), 34.

16. Daniel Walker Howe, *What God Hath Wrought: The Transformation of America, 1815–1848* (New York: Oxford University Press, 2007), 648–649.

17. Howe, 650, 767.

18. William Lloyd Garrison, "Letter on the Mexican-American War," July 1, 1847, http://teachingamericanhistory.org/library/index.asp?document=498 (accessed October 2008).

19. Wheelan, 260.

20. Wayne Wei-Siang Hsieh, *West Pointers and the Civil War: The Old Army in War and Peace* (Chapel Hill: University of North Carolina Press, 2009), 23.

21. See Hsieh.

Chapter 9

The Civil War (1861–1865)

To you [Mr. Lincoln] we look for a restoration of friendly relations between the States, only to be accomplished by peaceful and conciliatory means, aided by the wisdom of Almighty God.

—Fernando Wood, Peace Democrat and mayor of New York, 1861[1]

Let us confess our sins, and beseech Him to give us a higher courage, a purer patriotism, and more determined will; that will convert the hearts of our enemies; that will hasten the time when war, with its sorrows and sufferings, shall cease, and that He will give us a name and a place among the nations of the earth.

—Robert E. Lee, prayer after Gettysburg, 1863[2]

I do not expect to live to the end of this contest, nor do I wish to, if we do not have victory.

—Thomas "Stonewall" Jackson, 1862

The soldier's courage and sacrifice is full of glory, expressing devotion to country, to cause, to comrades in arms. But war itself is never glorious, and we must never trumpet it as such.

—Barack Obama, 2009

Brother versus Brother

Statesmen of the 19th century seemed willing to accept what Margaret Fuller described as the "scourge of war" to reshape not only the map of the United States but also American society. Militarism rather than diplomacy was to prove the most efficient tool for achieving the nation's Manifest Destiny of stretching from coast to coast during the 19th century. Internecine warfare would also be the mechanism by which the issue of slavery would finally be resolved. Moreover, the American public from New York to New Orleans and from Charleston to Chicago generally supported these military efforts, followed their development, and attended to the war news in particular with rapt attention. The shifting tides of Civil War battle often were viewed like a sporting event.[3]

In 1790, the entire U.S. Army numbered just eighty men and there was not one ship in the U.S. Navy. By the time of the Civil War, there would be more than 2 million men under arms and more than 100 warships and scores of gunboats and ironclad monitors—an American force unimaginable just a generation earlier. The Confederacy had established its own formidable land force but no navy beyond a few dozen gunboats and a handful of commerce raiders. The American military system of the mid-19th century had become so specialized that it needed to be described on a series of schematic diagrams, yet the old tradition of cavalier gallantry—drinking, carousing, and fighting—remained alive, permeating the ranks of both the army and the navy. Pretensions to gentility among the officers, however, caused friction in a republican America, and officers sent to Europe to acquire military knowledge were often resented at home. Still, European military paradigms—developed during the fight with Napoleon—remained the standard for military training.[4] The military was seen, nonetheless, as an acceptable professional career for many men and formal education in the concepts of warfare generally were not looked down upon as they are in some 21st-century circles. A contemporary observer expressed the absolute faith that 19th-century Americans had in their military, "It is our army that unites the chasm between the culture of civilization in the aspect of science, art, and social refinement, and the powerful simplicity of nature."[5]

Warfare was studied as a profession not only at institutions dedicated to warfare like Annapolis, West Point, the Citadel, and VMI, but also as a course of study at hundreds of academic schools and colleges across the nation. In 1857 Justin Smith Morrill introduced a land-grant bill that gave 30,000 acres of federal land for each sitting senator and representative to support or establish a college in his district.[6] The bill was not unique. Michigan State University and Pennsylvania State University had both been formed under less generous land-grants in 1855. The original intent of the Morrill Act was to make available to members of the working classes courses in scientific agriculture and mechanical engineering. Added to the enabling legislation, however, was a requirement that recipient institutions offer courses in military science and tactics. Artillery and engineering were considered so intricate and specialized as to warrant formal military instruction. The government also needed a well-articulated system of military training and an educated officer corps to develop and control its geographic conquests. The military training requirement behind the land-grant concept had been resisted for several years, but in July 1862 the wartime need for trained military officers helped to push the Morrill Act through Congress. The first school created under the act was Kansas State University (1863).

It was the American Civil War, rather than any foreign conflict, that served as a watershed with regard to the development of a more comprehensive war resistance in the 19th century. Before the Civil War, there was no draft in America to be resisted, and although Thoreau had withheld his local poll tax in 1848 and was jailed in protest of war until it was paid, government loans and bonds rather than any form of direct taxation had financed warfare before Lincoln imposed an involuntary income tax for that purpose for the first time in U.S. history. Strong public sentiments existed in the antebellum period, but street riots, noisy protests, and brutal violence were thought to be the weapons of proslavery, antitemperance, and anti-immigrant agitators, not of pacifists, conscientious objectors (COs), and other war resisters. Moreover, previous administrations—like that of James K. Polk and unlike the Civil War administration of Abraham Lincoln—were often careful in questioning the loyalty of the critics of earlier wars choosing instead to ignore the protestors. For instance, few Americans of the Mexican War period, outside a small circle of transcendentalists and academics, knew that Thoreau existed, much less that he had penned a significant contribution to antiwar literature and pacifist doctrine. This would not be the case with Lincoln's administration, which excoriated its antiwar opponents and used the full weight of government against them.

The antiwar protests of the Civil War period were somehow different than those that went before, and they shared a rhetoric that transcends time and remains alive in the modern antiwar movement. Antiwar hostility, verging on an actual loathing of the Lincoln administration among war resisters, was profound. The president was called a warmonger, a criminal, and a liar who had goaded the South into secession, prosecuted an illegal and unconstitutional war, and denied his fellow citizens their legal rights. Similar epithets would be hurled at almost all the future presidents who would lead the nation in wartime, and much of the extreme rhetoric of the 1860s would be familiar to the 21st-century ear. Moreover, this unrestrained and formerly atypical use of language was not isolated only to those who supported the Confederacy, or to those who sought to gain favor with the South, but could also be found among many loyal unionists.

Many peace proponents believed in strict construction of the Constitution, and they saw no interpretation of the document or of the powers with which the executive branch was endowed that allowed Lincoln to wage offensive war on the South or on any member state of the Union. It was illogical at least that maintaining domestic tranquility and providing for the common defense would include warring on ones neighbors just because they no longer wanted to associate with you. Besides a desire for peace, many antiwar conservatives were fundamentally concerned about the apparent loss of personal and civil liberties under the Lincoln presidency. They castigated the president for a laundry list of violations, including suspending habeas corpus, suppressing the press, imprisoning editors, instituting the income tax and the draft, holding military tribunals for civilian prisoners, and declaring martial law in some areas. Opponents pointed out the president's apparent lack of constitutional authority in ordering a naval blockade of American ports, calling it an act of war and a regulation of commerce that was solely the province of Congress. Herein they were only technically correct because Lincoln, like Jefferson before him, had the power to *close the ports* as well as to blockade them. By declaring a blockade Lincoln had erred, however. He had treated the Confederacy as an independent power and was forced thereafter to maintain the blockade against foreign shipping for it to be considered legitimate by foreign powers. "Their [the dissidents] fears about the threats of government power, combined with their understanding of the Constitution, made them extremely wary of, and often alarmed by, the way Lincoln wielded power during the war—indeed, in some cases, by the very fact of the war itself."[7]

In 1862 John Stuart Mill, a British economist and philosopher, sided with Lincoln regarding the steps he had taken to underpin the federal government, writing:

> The doctrine [of suspending civil liberties in wartime] in itself is no other than that professed and acted on by all governments—that self-preservation, in a State, as in an individual, is a warrant for many things which at all other times ought to be rigidly abstained from. At all events, no nation which has ever passed "laws of exception," which ever suspended the Habeas Corpus Act or passed an Alien Bill in dread of a[n] . . . insurrection, has a right to throw the first stone at Mr. Lincoln's Government.[8]

William H. Rehnquist, chief justice of a more recent Supreme Court (1986–2005), commenting on the wartime actions of the Lincoln administration, pointed out that the federal government's legal officers—many fewer than today—were seriously disorganized at the beginning of the Civil War—barely three months into a new administration. Moreover, although there was an attorney general (Edward Bates) who sat in the president's cabinet, he did not oversee a justice department as such, nor did he have practical control over the actions taken by the individual U.S. attorneys in their various judicial regions. In such a position, the attorney general was unable to play a significant role in the decisions taken by the administration. Bates, a minor rival with Lincoln for the Republican nomination for president in 1860, was far to the president's ideological right and had been supported by a combination of conservative Republicans, diehard Whigs, and members of the nativist Know-Nothing Party. Furthermore, Bates "had neither the desire nor the ability to compete with them [other members of the cabinet] in attempting to influence the policy of the administration."[9]

Secretary of State William H. Seward was more than willing to fill the vacuum, and he undertook to develop the internal-security policies of the administration even though he was officially tasked only with foreign policy considerations and may have been at variance with the views of the president. Seward believed that he was the true beacon of the Republican Party, while Lincoln—who had little experience in the federal government and none as an administrator—served as a mere figurehead. He similarly overrode the responsibilities of Secretary of the Treasury Salmon P. Chase and Secretary of War Simon Cameron. A "duplicitous side" to Seward would resurface when he served in the cabinet of Andrew Johnson. In February 1862, many of these internal-security tasks ultimately were transferred from Seward to the new Secretary of War Edwin M. Stanton, thereby somewhat defanging Seward.[10] Stanton, a prowar Democrat, was better suited to the war department than his predecessor, Cameron, but Stanton was arguably even more arbitrary than Seward with respect to the wartime violation of individual civil liberties.[11]

Rehnquist noted in his analysis of the early months of the Civil War the lack of a past history upon which Lincoln's administration might base its treatment of those deemed disruptive of the purposes of the federal government. A single significant case stood out as a precedent. President Andrew Jackson had faced down the threat of secession in South Carolina during the Nullification Crisis of 1832 by assembling a federal force to enter the state if it persisted in its refusal to allow the collection of the tariff. Yet Jackson had done so under the authorization and legal cover of the Force Bill passed by the Congress. At that time South Carolina had marshaled its state militia to defend itself much as the Confederate states were doing in 1860, and in both instances, a shooting war was clearly possible. Nonetheless, the 1832 crisis had been adverted through a face-saving compromise proposed by Henry Clay in which a less draconian tariff was passed, and South Carolina retained the legal fiction that it could nullify any federal law with which it did not agree. Nonetheless, the compromise had only postponed the confrontation. In nullification, the South had found a weapon to use against the power of the central government just short of secession—an intriguing political device based on the Tenth Amendment that soon got out of hand. The radicals in the South had raised nullification to the level of a principle of governance known as states' rights, for which they ostensibly had gone to war in 1860. Meanwhile, Lincoln had found in the Force Bill of 1832 a precedent for entering a recalcitrant state to demand its acquiescence to federal dictates by force.[12]

The specter of war in spring 1861 had vastly expanded the responsibilities of all the facets of government to levels never before experienced. "The reaction of the Lincoln administration to conspiracy, disloyalty, and dissent was, therefore, without precedent." Moreover, there was virtually no extended public criticism outside the South for Lincoln's apparent disregard for the civil liberties of the secessionists. This fact alone may have produced some of the pressure to abridge civil liberties during the critical first year of the war.[13] Thereafter, the process of apprehending suspect civilians and suppressing internal opposition to the war became more regular and orderly; but it would also become a system largely based on unfettered martial law that was considerably dangerous to civil liberties. Since "few of those so treated resorted to the courts to challenge these measures . . . they [the abridgements civil liberties] would remain as benchmarks for future wartime presidents."[14]

Separate Causes

The Civil War is thought to have been the formative event in the history of the American nation. It shaped the future of antiwar protest from one of largely uncoordinated individual pacifism to that of mass movements for peace. Meanwhile North and South fought for four desperate years (1861–1865) to reset the course of a nation that was seemingly caught among a number of powerful crosscurrents with mutually exclusive outcomes. Among these were aristocracy or republicanism, federal or state supremacy, industrialization or agriculture, tariffs or free trade, modernism or tradition, freedom or slavery, union or secession, social order or individual liberty, and war or peace. Although all of these factors played their role

The states illustrated here—South Carolina, Florida, Alabama, Mississippi, Georgia, and Louisiana—were the first to secede from the Union in 1861. With the quick addition of Texas, it was thought that the entire rebellion might be limited to just seven states. For this reason, early Confederate national flags had only seven stars. Virginia, Arkansas, Tennessee, and North Carolina joined the rebellion a few months later making the total eleven. Missouri and Kentucky were occupied by federal forces before they could secede, and the Confederate flag of thirteen stars reflected their determination to join the South. (Library of Congress Rare Book and Special Collections Division, LC-USZ62-92048)

in bringing about the Civil War, ultimately, it was secession that pushed the nation over the brink from rhetoric to armed confrontation.

During the secession crisis, many Democrats in the North were more conciliatory toward the South than were their Republican rivals, preferring political compromise to military action as the surest remedy for national discord. The majority of Northern Democrats supported the effort to save the Union, but a strong and active minority asserted that the antislavery Republicans (so-called Black Republicans) had provoked the South into secession and were waging an illegitimate war to establish their own domination, suppress civil and states rights, and impose racial equality on society. These Peace Democrats believed that military means would never restore the Union. Their Republican opponents nicknamed them "Copperheads," describing the antiwar Democrats as silent (as opposed to rattlesnakes) and poisonous vipers waiting in the weeds to strike a blow in favor of the South.

The first reference to these peace proponents as Copperheads appeared in an Ohio newspaper in 1861. Accepting the Copperhead name as a badge of honor, many opponents of the war began to use the portrait side (Goddess of Liberty) of copper pennies as badges and tokens for identification and promotion of their cause. This gave a double meaning to the term Copperhead, one that Peace Democrats

This image ran in the February 28, 1863, issue of Harper's Weekly *above the caption: "The Copperhead Party—In Favor of a Vigorous Prosecution of Peace!" (Library of Congress Prints and Photographs Division, LC-USZ62-132749)*

accepted and even cherished. Copperheads should not be confused with the Quakers, Mennonites, or other COs from the period who continued to follow absolute pacifism based on their religious beliefs. Nor were they traitors and spies. On the contrary, they seem to have been sincere in their belief that the Lincoln administration and the majority Republic Congress were overstepping their constitutional bounds in waging war on the South.

History has been skeptical of the underlying motives of the Peace Democrats because they seemingly sided with the detested proslavery elements in the South. Yet the Copperheads never openly acknowledged Confederate independence or the right of states to secede. The extent of their plan for peace was a return to the status quo antebellum. They failed to identify, however, just how this unrealistic plan for peace was going to resolve the problems of slavery and states rights that continually had plagued the nation for seven decades.

We Have Flags: Red, White, and Blue

Disunion was very popular in the South, not only among the social and political elite, but also with the average white southerner. Many southerners who would have shrunk to defend slavery or to malign the protective tariff, nonetheless, defended secession from the federal union. "The unanimity of the people was simply marvelous," wrote a Southern observer. "So long as the question of secession was under discussion opinions were both various and violent. The moment secession was finally determined upon, a revolution was wrought. There was no longer anything to discuss, and so discussion ceased." In expectation of rising commodity prices, southern planters warehoused bales of cotton and sheaves of tobacco to trade in Europe, and yeomen farmers cleared a slightly larger garden area for their kitchens. "Men got ready for war, and delicate women with equal spirit sent them off with smiling faces."[15]

Northerners responded to the act of disunion in a variety of ways. A young woman wrote, "The storm has broken over us. . . . How strange and awful it seems."[16] Yet initially the majority of the people in the North celebrated the coming of the storm with fervor and enthusiasm. In expectation of increased wartime demand, midwestern farmers put in bumper crops of wheat and corn. Women and girls gathered to sew uniforms, make flags, and roll bandages in the churches and the local courthouses, and young men lined up at the recruiting stations.

Remarkably, both *Unionists* and *Secessionists* chose to use the red, white, and blue—popular as national colors since the American Revolution—to signify their separate causes. A young woman wrote in her diary, "We have flags on our papers and envelopes, and have all our stationery bordered with red, white and blue. We wear little flag pins for badges and tie our hair with red, white and blue ribbons and have pins and earrings made of the buttons the soldiers gave us."[17] The writer's allegiance was to the Union, but her comments mirrored equally well the dedication of southern ladies to similar symbols—flags, pins, bunting, and secession aprons all done in red, white, and blue—that they also considered distinctly American. Both the Confederate national flag and its battle flag (the so-called Stars and Bars) sported colors identical to the Federal national emblem (the Stars and Stripes).

The Civil War was initially popular, and thousands of men volunteered before the imposition of conscription. (Library of Congress, LC-USZ62-93555)

These symbols were so alike that they were often misconstrued on the battlefield leaving observers confused as to the identity of friend or foe at a distance.

Patriotic aprons were worn by both sides, but the secession apron was best known for its appearance on Southern streets worn over women's everyday dresses. They were made in cotton, silk, or wool (similar to wool flag bunting). The designs varied greatly, from simple to elaborate. The stars (usually seven or thirteen in the South) were almost always on the upper pinner portion, but sometimes on a stomacher, both of which would serve as a blue background. The stripes in the apron portion varied depending on the allegiance of the wearer, North or South. In the South, there were always three, usually red/white/red like the Confederate National Flag. In the North, the aprons had more stripes, making it look more like a standard U.S. flag.

Of course, both sides in the secession crisis shared a common political origin, a common frontier experience, a common set of heroes and heroines from the colonial and revolutionary wars, and a common list of former foes. They had fought side by side to defeat the British and the Indians in 1812 and the Mexicans in 1846, and they had cooperated in adding a considerable part of the North American continent to the boundaries of the United States. Nonetheless, northerners and southerners were initially more alike than different, but they had somehow drifted apart culturally and had become polarized politically. When contrasting societal values result from such a comprehensive set of shared experiences, "history becomes a contested ground where alternative versions of the past vie for supremacy."[18] The Mexican War in particular had been a watershed event that raised the political rhetoric of earlier generations into a death struggle, pitting slaveholders and abolitionists against one other over the expansion of slavery into the new territories.

The idea of secession had first been floated by the New England states as part of their resistance to the War of 1812, but the secession crisis that led to the Civil War began at least a decade before the first bullet was fired at Fort Sumter, and it endured for more than a decade after another bullet—itself among the last used in anger—was fired at Ford's Theater in Washington, D.C. Southern secession had been proposed by South Carolina in the late 1820s and again in the 1830s as a response to the tariff question, state nullification, and the possible prohibition of slavery in the territories. These issues finally brought the subject of disunion to a head during the national elections in 1860. The election of Lincoln, an open abolitionist, was a signal for action, yet it was the actual act of secession that caused Americans to take up arms and go to war. One prominent abolitionist, Charles Russell Lowell, wrote, "Who cares now about slavery? Secession, and the Oligarchy built upon it, have crowded it out."[19]

In the earliest days after secession, few antiwar voices were raised. Nonetheless, in the North the stock markets fell and banks began to call in their loans. Many northern businessmen, forgetful of their recent enthusiasm for abolition, panicked at the specter of a near bankruptcy brought on by defaulted loans below the Mason-Dixon Line. Yet regiments of regulars paraded along the avenues of large cities lined with cheering anonymous masses, and companies of volunteers proudly marched through small town streets filled with family and friends. A clerk in the

Confederate War Office in Richmond wrote of the volunteers in April 1861: "A great many separate companies are accepted . . . provided they have arms. . . . What a deal of annoyance and labor it will be to organize these into battalions, regiments, brigades, and divisions."[20]

The Federal War Department could not provide for all the volunteers arriving in Washington, and clerks placed them in warehouses and markets to sleep until proper camps could be arranged on the ring of hills around the city. "It seemed," wrote Theodore Winthrop, "as if all the able-bodied men in the country were moving, on the first of May, with all their property on their backs, to agreeable, but dusty lodgings on the Potomac."[21] Soldiers in gray and blue, and in the garish red, forest green, or butternut uniforms of Zouaves, Chasseurs, and Dragoons, carried their regimental flags past the White House. Six regiments of volunteers from three different states arrived in Washington in such close succession that their separate parades formed "a continuous procession." Like irresponsible children, some soldiers joined the gaily dressed and carefree crowds that roamed the city, even to the grounds of the Executive Mansion, waving flags to the strains of patriotic songs such as "Yankee Doodle," "The Girl I Left Behind Me," and "Columbia, the Gem of the Ocean."[22] Lincoln's call for 75,000 volunteers to force reunion on the South had been answered with a vengeance.[23]

It was expected that the main federal army would march on the main Confederate Army, win the ensuing battle, take the Confederate capitol at Richmond, and end the rebellion. "On to Richmond!" was the call. Only gradually did the dire reality of the situation take hold. The American Civil War was the first major conflict in which both sides were completely armed with more accurate rifled muskets—at least during the last two years of combat—and these may have introduced a new lethality and ironic indecisiveness into warfare. At no time since humans first learned to control fire had warfare been so profoundly affected by technology.[24]

Tent life of the 31st Pennsylvania Infantry (later, the 82nd Pennsylvania Infantry) at Queen's farm, vicinity of Fort Slocum, Washington, D.C. This young wife and her children are visiting. (Library of Congress)

The lists of dead and wounded (2,952 Union and 1,752 Confederate) from the battlefield of Manassas, Virginia (First Bull Run)—the largest number of casualties in American history—shocked the public and stunned the general staff. No such number of Americans had been killed before in a single day of war, and both armies stood back somewhat during the remainder of 1861 to gain a breath and reconsider their strategies. Two years later, the casualties at Gettysburg (23,186 Union and 31,621 Confederate, killed, wounded, and missing), the worst totals of the war, would dwarf the Bull Run figures. At Cold Harbor, Virginia, almost 7,000 men would die in just twenty minutes of fighting.

Foreign governments generally stood in favor of the secessionists because they wanted to see a weakened United States, but they were sensitive to the issue of continued slavery. At the same time that many Europeans were decrying the barbarity of the war in America, other more hypocritical Europeans (especially in Austria, Belgium, Britain, and France) were providing firearms to both sides. Although Confederate records are incomplete, it seems certain that the South imported a remarkable store of military supplies from Europe through the federal naval blockade. More than 400,000 rifles, 3 million pounds of lead, and 2 million pounds of saltpeter for gunpowder production, as well as uniforms, shoes, accouterments, and medicines were brought through the blockade. To pay for these supplies, more than 500,000 bales of cotton were shipped out of the South during the war, and cotton bonds for tens of thousands of additional bales worth millions of Confederate dollars (CSD) were issued to creditors and bankers mostly located in England and France. The Federals, while waiting to get their armament production onto a wartime footing, also purchased 1.2 million long arms from Europe, including almost 500,000 brand new Enfield rifles directly from British government sources.

The introduction of the long-range rifled musket—considered an improvement in infantry weapons over the old smoothbore—has been identified as the cause of the mass casualties characteristic of Civil War battles in which linear tactics were used. All armies acting on the defense have always had some advantage over the attacker, and period tactical theory suggested that the offense needed a three-to-one ratio with regard to numbers to overcome these advantages. Nonetheless, linear tactics were generally effective during the war even if they limited individual initiative and hampered the tactical decision-making accorded subordinate officers.

It was the lethal efficiency of the rifled artillery and the highly efficient versions of the exploding shells designed by a British officer, Henry Shrapnel, in the previous century, however, that were responsible for 40 percent of all Civil War battlefield casualties. Filled with small iron or lead balls and fitted with a time fuse, the Shrapnel container burst open during its passage over the enemy position giving the effect of an oversized shotgun fired from overhead. Exploding projectiles were not new to warfare, but the novel arrangement envisioned by Shrapnel made the weapon grotesquely efficient. At ranges of up to 300 yards these rounds (spherical case shot) were highly lethal even against men lying prone to the ground or behind entrenchments. This type of killing from great range—of destroying the lives of otherwise-brave men hunkering down on the ground and taking refuge behind tree stumps, rocks, or the dead bodies of their comrades—introduced an impersonal and gruesome quality into American warfare that dissembled the ages-old chivalric concepts of personal struggle and individual honor on the battlefield.

To What Extent Sacrifice

The psychological effect of this new type of warfare affected even those who rained death down upon their opponents. Col. Wm. B. Hazen, Army of the Cumberland, noted, "The battle . . . the dreadful splendor . . . all my description must fall vastly short."[25] Capt. John T. James, 11th Virginia Infantry, wrote, "At every step some poor fellow would fall, and as his pitiful cry would come to my ear I almost imagined it the wail of some loved one he had left at home."[26] A professional writer in civilian life, Capt. John W. De Forest, Twelfth Connecticut Volunteers, reported,

> The terror of battle is not an abiding impression, but comes and goes like throbs of pain; and this is especially the case with veterans. . . . [A] man lay near me, dying from a terrible wound through the abdomen, his fair face growing whiter with every laboring breath and his light blue eyes fixed vacantly on the glaring sky. . . . I glanced at him pitifully from time to time as he patiently and silently drew towards his end. Such individual cases of suffering are far more moving than a broad spectacle of slaughter.[27]

Failed mass assaults and steadfast defenses that resulted in thousands of dead and wounded like those of the Federals at Fredericksburg (12,000 Union casualties) and Cold Harbor (15,000 Union casualties), or of the Confederates at Gettysburg (32,000 Southern casualties) and at Chickamauga (18,000 Southern casualties) were not seen as the fault of tactical formations or more lethal weapons but rather as a lack of humanity and ethics on the part of the commanders who ordered them.

From the first great push at Fort Donelson, Tennessee, in February 1862 to Lee's surrender at Appomattox, Virginia, in April 1865, giant armies trudged across the Southern hinterland in efforts to defend the Confederacy or dismantle the "slavocracy" of the Old South with its characteristic lifestyle. While only 5 percent of all federal soldiers who served were killed or mortally wounded in combat, almost 12 percent of the Confederates suffered a similar fate. The death rate from all causes, including accidents and sickness, was much higher. Six hundred thirty thousand (630,000) Americans died in the conflict. As many as 25 percent of all southerners who took the field may have died. (Confederate documents are frustratingly incomplete and often lack disarticulation into killed, wounded, and missing). The North actually suffered more war deaths, almost three men for every two lost by the South. The number wounded or maimed for life was much greater. The Battle at Gettysburg had the highest number of casualties in the war, and it was also the largest battle in terms of the number of men engaged in the Western Hemisphere—up to 170,000 combatants depending on which ancillary units are included in the tally. One-third of all those involved were inflicted with serious or lethal wounds of some kind. In terms of the number of wounded and killed as a portion of the forces engaged, the bloodiest battle of the war was Shiloh; the bloodiest single day took place at Antietam; and the greatest losses suffered in the shortest time were at Cold Harbor. The willingness of Civil War soldiers to face death in a conflict that offered no chance of personal gain remains one of the most remarkable characteristics of the war. The single worst one-month period for casualties was May 1864. Almost 100,000 Americans (Federal and Confederate combined) lost their lives or were wounded in battle in this period, and Ulysses Grant was called a butcher for continuing his campaign in the face of so many casualties. Yet it was Grant's willingness to fight a war of attrition with the manpower-strapped South, regardless of negative public opinion, that turned the fortunes of war toward the Union.

Ultimately, one in four men engaged in battle during the entire Civil War were dead, wounded, or missing. Parts of the South were said to actually stink with the odor of death. Oliver Wendell Holmes wrote after seeing the photographs of battle-field corpses at Antietam, "What a repulsive, brutal, sickening, hideous thing it is, this dashing together of two frantic mobs to which we give the name of armies. The end to be attained justifies the means, we are willing to believe; but the sight of these pictures is a commentary on civilization such as a savage might well triumph to show its missionaries."[28]

The southern landscape at war's end was littered with debris—skeletons of horses and mules left unburied, human remains washed from their shallow graves, broken muskets and wagon wheels decorating the sides of rutted ditches that once had been pleasant lanes through the countryside. Many homes had been burned, shelled, or dismantled to build fortifications or for fear that they might be used as a refuge for snipers. Bridges had been dismantled in the face of an advancing enemy, and fences had been burned as firewood. Trenches, artillery shells, and the movement of thousands of horses, mules, wagons, and cannon had scarred the land in many places almost beyond recognition. Meadows, pastures, and family farms had been churned into fields of mud. Meanwhile, the spectacle of the North fighting a great war with many of its young farmers in military service, while still producing a surplus of foodstuffs, contradicted all common logic.

An incalculable number of civilian lives were permanently disrupted by the Civil War even in the absence of death or mutilation. While many men wrote regularly to their families and expressed pitiable longing and loneliness for them, a federal officer testified about receiving a letter from a destitute young wife, anxious for news of her husband. She had received no word of the scoundrel in months and only nine dollars since he had enlisted. She and her children had therefore been evicted from their home. "Here are four pages of pathos that make me want . . . to kick him for not deserving them," wrote the officer.[29] Certainly similar scenes were played out many times, and many others had tragic endings.

In just 1,500 days of armed conflict more than 630,000 soldiers died from wounds and disease. This meant that an average of more than *400 men per day* died, dwarfing the war death rates of all other U.S. wars.[30] Moreover, the grief visited both the South Carolina plantation house and the New York tenement. When a nation is at war with itself, it is not just the soldiers whose lives are changed. The lives of the civilians who remain behind, whether they are joined to the battle by the ties of love or not, are altered just as irrevocably. Tens of thousands of children were left fatherless or orphaned by the vagaries of campaigning, and as many more among the young women were made widows. No meaningful measure can be made of their suffering.

Nor was the death in battle of a loved one the fullest extent of the sacrifice made by their families. Wounded, maimed, and mutilated men required care, nursing, and compassion that was expected to be found in the home. Once off the battlefield, the plight of the wounded was complicated by limited medical knowledge, malnutrition, and disease. While American military hospitals were better than those in Europe, they were nonetheless inadequate. The military hospitals of the South were overwhelmed by the task before them, and wounded men were often shipped home to recuperate under the care of their families. The survivors of battle, who were of no further use to the military because of their physical disabilities, placed a burden on their loved ones and their communities that was perhaps more long lasting and more difficult to discharge than that required for those who had died.

A number of civilian organizations helped fill the need for additional medical care. The Women's American Association for Relief was closely associated with a number of eminent doctors in New York and furnished medical supplies to the army. Beyond this the U.S. Sanitary Commission made provisions for the relief of the sick, provided ambulances, and cared for the wounded and the dead. Commission representatives, operating in the east and in the west, oversaw the diet and personal cleanliness of the soldiers in camp, provided housing for white refugee families, and raised money to expand their work.

College and so-called high school enrollments suffered as idealistic young men and boys rushed to join the forces of their cause, and teachers and administrators suddenly found themselves unemployed for a lack of students. Notably, all those who fought during the first two years of the Civil War were volunteers. Caroline Cowles Richards listed in her diary a number of young men who talked of leaving college and going to war. She described a rally at the Canandaigua Academy, New York, and detailed how the academy boys drilled in military tactics on the campus every day. Southern colleges had the additional complications of the loss of funding, physical destruction from battle, and conversion to hospitals, barracks, and headquarters.

It is commonly thought that at the outset of war the economy of the American South was deficient when compared to that of the North in many critical areas of industry, including manufacturing, transportation, and communications. Such metrics attempt to make the progress of the conflict into a simple mathematical model consisting of force ratios, railway mileage, and logistical comparisons. Yet the physical reality of warfare was filled with chaos, chance, and uncertainty governed largely through an interaction of competing strategies, tactical opportunities, and martial skill. These factors made the overall outcome something more than a quadratic equation expressing the likelihood of success and something less than a completely random lottery independent of generalship, morale, or genuine heroism. Shortly after the war had ended, William Dean Howells addressed the question. "The fighting, in itself horrible, and only sublime in its necessity and purpose, was but a minor part of the struggle."[31]

While bullets, artillery, and bayonets destroyed the opposing forces, the effects of war wrecked havoc on the lives of civilians also. The war policies of both governments so extended into the lives of the local populations that southerners and those living in the so-called border states came to look seriously upon the result as the hard hand of war. Meanwhile, the terrible cost of war, measured in tens of thousands of lives and millions of dollars, afflicted the North with a palpable weariness.

Watching a Free Government Die

Antiwar sentiments were not peripheral issues during the Civil War. They were argued over on the national stage and in the newspapers as well as across the farmyard fence. The rhetoric used against Lincoln, and the hostility that it engendered, was quite similar to that used on the television nightly news against Lyndon B. Johnson and George W. Bush with respect to the wars that they conducted (Vietnam and Iraq II, respectively). Somehow according to their detractors these leaders had brought on the war, made the situation worse by fighting, or engendered a conflict that would not have happened except for some presidential dedication to a sinister hidden agenda. On the day after the firing on Fort Sumter in 1861, the *Dubuque Herald* wrote of Lincoln, the Republicans, and their abolitionist supporters:

> Nothing will satisfy the fanatics of the North but a provocation to civil war, in which they may accomplish their darling object that which they have toiled for many years: the incitement of slaves to insurrection against their masters, and . . . the consequent emancipation of those slaves, the abolition of slavery, and the ruin and subjugation of the South to the political thralldom of Northern fanaticism.[32]

Matthew Bulkley of Connecticut, a Peace Democrat, was astounded that his fellow citizens could not perceive the dangers inherent in Lincoln's apparent disregard for the Constitution. "If we have any desire to maintain, and preserve our government, and free institutions," he wrote, "sacrifice everything, but honor and principle and unite as brothers, and give this corrupt, imbecile and . . . God abhorred administration to understand that they can no longer usurp power and trample upon the sacred rights guaranteed to us by our constitution and laws."[33]

The fact that Copperheads existed also caused a flurry of accusations regarding disloyalty and even treason. The county sheriff of Hartford City, Indiana and twenty-one other men were accused of inciting and participating in a riot to prevent the draft when they argued with the enrolling officers over who should supervise the proceeding. The sheriff refused to have anything to do with conscription, and the mob tore up the enrollment records, destroyed the lottery wheel, and chased the enrolling officers out of the local courthouse. Two men in Union County, Illinois, reported to federal authorities that their region was the most proslavery in the state. Men were making speeches against the government, claiming that

Jefferson Davis was a better president than Lincoln, and holding secret meetings in the woods. Many Democrats readily admitted forming paramilitary units for the personal safety of the residents in their area from runaway slaves, deserters, and foragers. Even former president Franklin Pierce was accused of being a member of a group whose secret objective was to overthrow the federal government, and Secretary of State William H. Seward wrote to Pierce for an acceptable explanation of the rumor. Reports of disaffection were made to state governors scrambling to fill the officer rolls of their volunteer units. Governors, especially in the border regions and the states of the Midwest, were earnestly urged to send troops to disband newly formed Copperhead militias that may or may not have existed, and for which task in either case they had no available troops.[34]

The Dynamics of Tyranny

On May 25, 1861, Lt. John Merryman, an officer in the Maryland state cavalry, took a leading role in demolishing a bridge to block any federal troop movements through his state. Merryman was arrested at his home by Union troops, indicted for treason, and confined in Fort McHenry; his jailers ignored a writ of habeas corpus. As a petitioner to the courts for relief from imprisonment, Merryman became one of the best-known habeas corpus cases of the American Civil War. Under an Executive Order of April 25, 1961, Lincoln also had nineteen prosecession or antiwar members of the Maryland legislature arrested so that they could not vote for their state to secede. Such a move was unprecedented and patently unconstitutional.

Chief Justice Roger Taney ruled against Lincoln in the federal district court with regard to the suspension of habeas corpus and the arrest of civilians by the military, but the full Supreme Court never heard the case (*Ex parte Merryman*, 17 F. Cas. 144 1861). After the war, the Supreme Court held in a similar case that Lincoln had exceeded his powers as commander-in-chief only in declaring martial law in those parts of the country not in rebellion where the ordinary civil courts were open and well-functioning. In this decision, the geographical rather than the constitutional jurisdiction triumphed. The authority of federal courts to review claims of habeas corpus was not clearly established until Congress adopted a statute (28 U.S.C. § 2254) granting federal courts that authority in 1867, as part of the post–Civil War Reconstruction.[35]

Lamdin P. Mulligan had been arrested, tried, and sentenced to death in a military court for joining and aiding, between October 1863 and August 1864, a secret society known as the Order of American Knights, or Sons of Liberty (a Copperhead group) to overthrow the government of the United States. The Court found it significant in the case (*Ex Parte Mulligan*, 71 U.S.C. 2, 1866) that the petitioner was a private citizen not connected with military service who lived in Indiana, was arrested there in 1864, and had not been a resident of any of the states in the rebellion or a prisoner of war. The court found that the guarantee of trial by jury contained in the Constitution was reserved for individuals in both a state of war and a state of peace; and was equally binding upon rulers and people, at all times and under all circumstances. The court also found that Congress had power, under the

Constitution, to provide for the organization of military commissions (tribunals rather than courts), and for trial by those commissions of people engaged in conspiracy against the United States, if the Congress chose to use them.[36]

Lincoln had ignored the early rulings of the court in cases like these maintaining that he had no choice but to bend the law in response to the gravity of the national situation. The Supreme Court had only six active justices in 1861 and four of these had agreed in principle with the pro-Southern Dred Scott Decision while the remaining two were so ill of health or infirmed by age as to make their entry into the decision-making process impracticable. Given the judicial track record of the active justices, it was unlikely that any action taken by Lincoln against the South would have met with the approbation of the majority of the court. "Must a government . . . be too strong for the liberties of its own people, or too weak to maintain its own existence?" Lincoln asked as if caught on the horns of a dilemma. Given these realities, Lincoln chose to ignore the court.[37]

The Constitution clearly stated that habeas corpus could be "suspended" (Article 1, Section 9) in the case of a rebellion or an attack on the nation, but it was equally unclear which branch or branches of government were empowered to enact the suspension. Lincoln acted as if the power of suspension were within the presidential prerogatives, and as an equal branch of government, he refused to be gainsaid by the Congress. Few participants in the government thought that secession was anything other than a form of rebellion, but until the president had issued the suspension, no one had ever considered that the executive might act in such a situation under his own prerogatives without the consent of Congress or the imprimatur of the judiciary. Lincoln, immediately faced with the greatest threat ever to the United States, had no time to finesse a highly articulated response to secession. The crisis had come on too quickly to allow for extensive debate on these questions, and Lincoln had rolled out a series of war powers for the executive branch to ensure the Union's preservation and resist its destruction by force. Asserting his prerogative, Lincoln asked rhetorically, "Are all the laws, but one [habeas corpus], to go unexecuted, and the government itself to go to pieces, lest the one be violated?"[38]

Similar wartime expedients initiated by Jefferson Davis in the Confederacy seem to have left Lincoln with some modicum of political cover for the steps he had taken. In the South, Davis had suspended habeas corpus and imposed martial law, in part to maintain order during the secession crisis and in part to speed the marshalling of southern defense forces. The details surrounding the administration of Davis in the South have attracted a good deal of second-thinking concerning his abilities as a political leader and the nature of the government's ideological roots. The Confederate government lasted somewhat less than the six years its constitution had envisioned making scholarly arguments concerning the lack of a two-party system, a single-term presidency, and the effects of state's rights on a centralized system of governance and supply in wartime somewhat superfluous.

Absent definitive directives to the contrary printed in the Constitution, opponents of the federal administration in the U.S. Congress could do little in 1861–1865 to thwart Lincoln's prosecution of the war in any manner he found acceptable. The Peace Democrats in the 37th Congress (1861 and 1862) were at a severe numerical

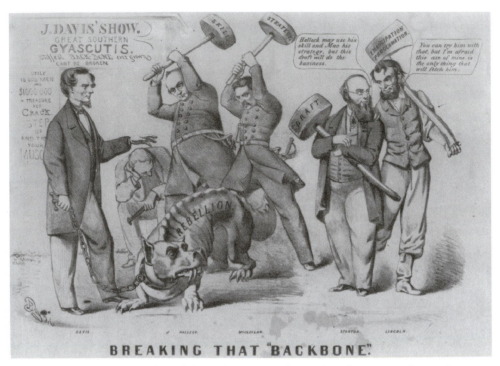

Federal generals Halleck and McClellan take aim at Jefferson Davis's "creature" named rebellion in an attempt to break its back with "skill" and "strategy." Secretary of War Stanton believes that the "draft" will do the job, but Lincoln puts his faith in the Emancipation Proclamation. (Library of Congress Prints and Photographs Division, LC-USZ62-42560)

disadvantage politically. With the secession of eleven states, the number of Democrats in the House and Senate had been significantly diminished. The House alone lost fifty-five members due to secession. Some of the remaining members were Unionists or War Democrats, generally unfriendly to the antiwar position of others in their party, but equally interested in weakening the Republicans in the next two-year election cycle.

Despite the exit of twenty-one Southern senators during the Civil War, the U.S. Senate continued to push forward with its legislative duties. Some senators left the body to aid the military efforts of the war, while others attempted to balance simultaneous careers in the Senate and on the battlefield. When the Senate convened, the seats from all eleven Confederate states were vacant with the single exception of Andrew Johnson of Tennessee. Johnson denied the right of a state to secede and maintained his allegiance to the Union. He left the Senate in March 1862 to become the military governor of his state under the federal occupation and served later (1865) as vice president and president of the United States.

The Republican Party, which had elected Lincoln in 1860, was for the first time in U.S. history the majority party in both houses (In the House: Republican 108, Democrat 44, Unionist 28, Constitutional Unionist 2, Independent 1. In the

Senate: Republican 31, Democrat 15, Unionist 3, vacant 1). In an admittedly unlikely scenario in which the southern states had maintained their representation in the Congress, in the manner that Tennessee had a sitting senator in the person of Andrew Johnson, Lincoln's power in Congress, and in the executive role, might have been curtailed. Yet such a course would have weakened the cause of secession and undermined the clean break that the Confederate states were trying to make with the Union. As it was, the few Copperheads remaining in Congress would have to speak their piece against the war and hope for the best.

Through an innocuous bill to increase the soldiers' pay passed by both Houses without significant further debate, the 37th Congress quickly added a conspiracy provision with a penalty of death to Lincoln's executive order of April 25, 1861. It was argued that the provision was ostensibly meant to thwart "rebellious activities," but it was actually aimed at suppressing antiwar protests particularly of the type found in opposition newspapers—especially those in New York, which were thought to have a disproportionate impact on antiwar sentiment in the rest of the country. Remarkably, the pro-administration newspapers failed to rally around those in the press who were being suppressed, and might even have been accused of gloating concerning their predicament.[39]

No one was put to death under the conspiracy provision of Lincoln's order. California Democrat James McDougall put forward the frightening contention that all civil liberties were automatically superseded under the exigencies of war, and that habeas corpus was only a "peace right." To ratify the president's acts, protested John C. Breckinridge of Kentucky in response, was to effectively amend the Constitution—an action clearly "beyond Congress's authority." It was of course nothing of the sort. Ratification of unauthorized acts after the fact had a long and honorable history in the law. In the end, the 37th Congress found that the president had not transcended his power.[40]

In addition, the Congress made conspiracy a federal capital crime if its object was to overthrow the government, to levy war against the United States, to obstruct the execution of the laws, to seize government property, or to recruit soldiers to fight against the United States. This was spreading a wide and hardly discriminating net for potential dissenters. Congress authorized the president to prohibit commercial intercourse with rebel states; required federal officers to take an oath of allegiance to the nation; and removed a source of ambiguity in the president's authority to enforce the laws by empowering him to call out the armed forces and militia for that purpose whenever it was "impracticable" to enforce them by ordinary judicial means. These measures were all innocent enough in constitutional terms, and none of them met with significant constitutional objection. In contrast, a revolutionary but innocuous bill to establish a Department of Agriculture encountered stiff resistance in the Senate, although it too ultimately was enacted.[41]

However, the main measures taken under consideration by the 37th Congress were financial in nature: a legal tender bill, an internal revenue bill, a confiscation bill, and various loan bills. These bills were all debated at length and their passage was not generally along party lines. Owing to the initial expectation of a short war, the federal government raised its war chest chiefly by taking loans and issuing paper money and bonds. The government generally failed to raise enough funds through these methods, running in deficit throughout the conflict. Expenses ran eight times the revenue from taxes. A novel source of war funding was found in the adoption of a personal income tax, the first tax of its kind ever levied by the U.S. government. As first envisioned, it fixed a 3 percent tax on family incomes over $800, but by June 1864, the exemption threshold fell to $600 and the minimum rate rose to 5 percent on incomes up to $5,000. The first *tax-the-rich scheme* envisioned by the federal government had quickly set the common pattern for all those that would follow.

The 37th Congress was memorable for the measures by which the state of Virginia was divided and the new Commonwealth of West Virginia was formed, as well as for the Militia Act, the Homestead Act, the Morrill Tariff, the Pacific Railroad Act, and the Enrollment Act (military conscription). The nonmilitary legislation of the Civil War years reflected a veritable revolution in the understanding and scope of federal authority. By the end of the war, the central government was "a far ampler sovereignty than it earlier had been, more powerful, more ambitious, and more besought." Indeed, an observer went so far as to call the legislation passed by the first Civil War Congress a "blueprint for a new America."[42]

The biennial elections for 1863 were disappointing for the Lincoln administration. Many Americans had given Lincoln the benefit of the doubt for two years, but after two years of war with no seeming success, a number of them jumped to the antiwar camp. Horatio Seymour the Democratic candidate for governor in Connecticut ran on the slogan "Restore the Union as it was, and Maintain the Constitution as it is."[43] Republicans lost the governorships of New York, New Jersey, and Illinois; but Michigan, California, and Iowa all went Republican. Democrats—many of them Peace Democrats—gained twenty-eight House seats, many in places that the Republican Party had thought safe like Indiana, Ohio, Pennsylvania, and Lincoln's own home state of Illinois. Yet a closer look at the results showed that the Democrats gained seats only where they had been strong before 1860 and in smaller numbers than the minority party in an off-year election might have expected. The Republicans maintained a small majority (eighty-five to seventy-two) over the Democrats in the House and actually gained two seats in the Senate.

The first session of the 38th Congress was characterized by a serious confrontation between the president and Congress over control of the process for reconstructing the governments of the formerly self-styled Confederate States. Otherwise, it was largely a repetition of the previous Congress providing troops, voting supplies, adjusting finances, and establishing the Freedmen's Bureau (Bureau of Refugees, Freedmen, and Abandoned Lands). In June 1864, Congress enacted a brief statute with the astonishing title "An Act to repeal the Fugitive Slave Act of eighteen hundred and fifty, and all Acts and Parts of Acts for the Rendition of Fugitive Slaves." A close look at the statute confirms that it did just what the title said it was intended to do. When the 38th Congress adjourned, the end of the war was not far off. In less than six weeks after the adjournment of the 38th Congress, the Confederacy collapsed.[44]

The Antiwar Press

In calling for secession, the fire-eating radicals of the South were aided by a highly partisan and radical press. Public orations, debates, and harangues were a popular instrument of the fire-eaters and were well attended. Yet these forums addressed only those who could be present, producing a somewhat-transient enthusiasm for the particular topic of discussion. Therefore, the 19th-century citizen favored the newspaper as a more individualized and permanent form of communication. Newspapers gained influence steadily during the first half of the century. An amazingly large number of local publications appeared. Speeches were printed in their entirety within a few days of being given. Printed political arguments, essays, letters to the editor, and discussions among dedicated readers—both genuine and planted for effect—flowed in the wake of every issue.

People read alone or in small groups with the leisure to reread and analyze what was printed. The power of the press to influence a wider audience than could be assembled at any one place and time was not to be underestimated. Some papers tried to remain neutral, but others sought out political alliances either because of the agenda of the editors, or, more commonly, to attract a lucrative trade in political advertising and public printing. Neutrality on any topic of public interest often doomed a newspaper to failure. "We have perfect unanimity in the press," wrote one southern observer early in the war. Local newspapers commonly filled their pages with reprinted articles and speeches reported in other journals from around the country, often with biting editorial preambles.[45] When there was no crisis to rally around, the radical secessionists were fully capable of fabricating one. In 1859, for example, Southern leaders in Congress had proposed the reopening of the transatlantic slave trade without hope of the question being resolved in their favor so that the radicals might use the issue to good effect as propaganda.[46]

The widely heralded claim of unanimous support for secession was not quite correct especially after the summer of 1863. The *North Carolina Standard*, published by William Woods Holden, began to run editorials critical of the Davis administration in the aftermath of the loss of Vicksburg and the Gettysburg defeat. Holden began by suggesting a negotiated settlement between North Carolina and the federal government and ended by encouraging soldiers to desert the army to force the government in Richmond to seek a diplomatic solution to the war. In response, Gov. Zebulon Vance of North Carolina issued a proclamation against individuals who promoted resistance to Confederate laws or who urged a separate peace settlement by the state. While he stopped short of muzzling newspapers like Holden's, he proclaimed them disloyal and allowed the public to take matters in their own hands.

A group of southern sympathizers led by Confederate soldiers tore down the doors of the *Standard* office in Raleigh, scattered the type, overturned the furniture, and dosed the office with a plentiful spattering of printers ink. They then turned to demonstrate at Holden's home, which the publisher had wisely abandoned. The next day, Holden supporters mobbed the pro-government *State Journal* in Raleigh destroying the presses and perpetrating serious damage. The violence and counter-violence spread to every paper in the city with the exception of the *Raleigh*

Progressive, which wrote scathing editorials condemning the escalating intensity of the behavior. Gov. Vance shortly thereafter published a letter warning of anarchy and promising to use troops to restore order. The *Standard* resumed publication within the month.[47]

While many antiwar protestors inside the Confederacy were absolute pacifists who drew no distinction between war waged by North or South, a great deal of violence was perpetrated against them. Even minor confrontations with Southern Unionists were declared a crisis upon whose immediate resolution rested the very survival of the Confederacy. One southern officer noted that "hatred and revenge had filled the hearts" of many secessionists leading to "burnings, hangings, and whippings" of those thought disloyal to the Confederacy.[48]

Copperheads

Antiwar northerners (and those with pro-Southern sentiments in the border states) were known as Copperheads. There were three distinct types of Copperhead: (1) those who believed the war could not be won; (2) those who believed that the war had a hidden agenda and were alarmed by Lincoln's actions with reference to emancipation; and (3) those who supported the Confederate right to secede from the very first but were unwilling to join in the act of secession. The first group was the least dedicated to antiwar pacifism and quickly abandoned their positions and returned to supporting the war with every dramatic Confederate reversal on the battlefield. The second group was composed largely of deeply racist persons who wished to retain the dictates of race-based supremacy. Many of these had supported the war when its sole purpose was maintaining the Union, but they jumped to the Copperhead side when confronted with the looming reality of universal black emancipation. One member of this group wrote, "The object of the administration [is] to kill off the people of the South and liberate the slaves." Another said that the "true object" of the war was to liberate the "n—s, elevate the black race, and degrade the white."[49] Finally, those who supported the concept of secession from the onset grew increasingly distressed as Lincoln took unprecedented steps to force the seceded states back into the Union through military action. This last group made up the stable inner core of the Copperhead movement throughout the war.

Several Peace Democrats participated in a mass meeting of delegates from twenty-one of the thirty-four states held in the Willard Hotel in Washington, D.C., during early 1861. The delegates hoped to convince the recently inaugurated president (Lincoln) to either agree to the Confederacy's demands to get it to rejoin the Union or to simply let the southern states secede. All three of Lincoln's opponents in the 1860 presidential election—Stephen A. Douglas, John Bell, and John C. Breckinridge—visited Lincoln at the Willard Hotel. Only Douglas, himself a Northern Democrat, stood squarely behind the president, and he was one of the first public figures to suggest that those who did not embrace the war effort were traitors. "There are but two parties, the party of patriots and the party of traitors."[50]

Most people who participated in the peace convention at the Willard affiliated themselves with the so-called Peace Democrats. They were unhappy with Lincoln's

Swarms of former black slaves attached themselves to the Federal Army sometimes choking the roads and unwittingly slowing down operations. The officers of the army were sorely pressed as to what to do with this mass of humanity whose care they were ill-prepared to organize. (Library of Congress, LC-USZ62-112169)

preparations to invade the South that included calling up 75,000 nine-month volunteers, but mostly they reflected a long-standing dislike for a number of Republican policies especially their dedication to the universal abolition of slavery. They strongly supported the resurrection of the Crittenden Plan, proposed by Sen. John J. Crittenden of Kentucky in December 1860. Crittenden proposed peace based on diplomacy, the "manly and prudent discussion . . . in accordance with popular government and constitutional guarantees" for maintaining slavery and strengthening the fugitive slave laws.[51] The "popular government" alluded to by Crittenden was a conceptual recognition of states' rights in the form of the old idea of popular sovereignty, and the "constitutional guarantees" were those that supported the continuation of slavery where it already existed and the enforcement of the fugitive slave laws throughout the country. In 1861, the House adopted this resolution by a vote of 117–2, and the Senate followed suit by an almost equally lopsided margin. In argument before the House, Pennsylvania representative and antislavery radical John Hickman noted that there was no constitutional guarantee for slavery regardless of the Crittenden compromise, and in its second session, the 37th Congress took steps to limit slavery in any case.[52]

Peace Democrats were most numerous in the Midwest (especially in the southern tier of Ohio, Indiana, and Illinois), a region that traditionally had distrusted the northeastern business and banking interests and that had economic, cultural, and sometimes kinship ties with the South. Many of the residents here were so-called *butternuts*—southern-born farmers who had relocated to the Midwest much like

Lincoln's own father. Of this population, 10 to 12 percent may have been born in the South. The Lincoln administration's arbitrary treatment of dissenters caused great bitterness in this region. Above all, antiabolitionist midwesterners feared that emancipation would result in a great migration of blacks into their states. Some feared that freedmen would flood the region looking for jobs and forcing whites to compete with them for employment.

Immediately after the firing on Fort Sumter, armed antiabolition organizations reportedly were forming in New England, the very home of abolition. Activities like these were reactionary and short-lived. One antiabolitionist from New Haven, Connecticut, promised that he would raise and equip two companies of 100 men each to fight for the South. Former Connecticut governor Thomas Seymour wrote, "Free the blacks and enslave the whites; that seems to be the policy of the Lincoln dynasty. If freemen are pleased with this, they may get enough of it."[53] Connecticut had allowed race-based slavery until 1848, and it was the last New England state to end the practice. Although the bigotry was unforgivable and the rhetoric inflammatory and unhelpful, the sentiments expressed by white farmers and workers were not surprising.[54] It was widely believed that former slaves would come north to compete with lower-class whites and recent immigrants for scarce jobs in the cities, and the effects of the economic downturns in 1857 and 1858 did not help to relieve this fear. Moreover, the treatment of blacks in northern states was often brutish, and they were despised and treated with contempt almost everywhere.

Many Copperheads were convinced that the war, from its inception, was really about a Republican Party–abolitionist conspiracy to secure universal emancipation and full social equality for blacks while circumventing the will of Congress and the oversight of the courts. Those Peace Democrats, who based at least part of their antiwar protest on racism, fretted that the deteriorating military situation for the federal army prior to 1863 would soon allow the Lincoln administration to turn to African Americans for help by placing arms in their hands. The enlistment of black soldiers was a consistent demand of abolition radicals—one that was realized before the war ended. If white men could not save their own government, these Copperheads thought it was better to allow the nation to collapse than to raise the black race to equality by making them soldiers. These sentiments were particularly common after the Confederacy clearly routed the federal forces sent to end the rebellion at Manassas, Virginia, in 1861. The *Chicago Times* insisted in an editorial that if white men proved unable to save the Union, and only then, should arming blacks even be considered. The idea of arming slaves "is disgraceful to the civilization of the age, and disgraceful to ourselves," wrote the editors. "The slaves are practically barbarians. Their instincts are those of savages."[55]

Even among those who volunteered to fight for the preservation of the Union, there was little sympathy for the abolitionists. One federal soldier wrote at the beginning of the conflict, "I don't blame the South an atom. They have been driven to desperation by such lunatics as [William Lloyd] Garrison and [Wendell] Phillips, and these men ought to be hung for it."[56] Another federal recruit wrote to his family, "I want to see those hot-headed abolitionists put in the front rank and shot first."[57] Feelings against abolitionists had run deep for decades. Elijah P. Lovejoy, was murdered by a mob in the free state of Illinois in 1837, and Garrison was once dragged through the streets of Boston on a rope by a group of men without much of his clothing. He was rescued with great difficulty and consigned to the local jail for safety. George Thompson, a lecturer who was the subject of continued outbursts of rage, actually fled to England so that he might continue his crusade against slavery. Abolitionist speakers were threatened with tar and feathers in New England towns in the 1850s.[58] Phillips was pelted with eggs while trying to deliver a speech as late as 1862, and James Gordon Bennett of the *New York Herald* wrote, "If this is a war of ideas then let the abolitionists fight for their ideas, and let all others stand back."[59]

Antiabolitionist sentiment was evident among women, especially those who felt that the squabble over secession and emancipation was directly affecting their families. Maria Lydig Daly, wife of the a prowar Democrat in New York wrote, "It is a pity that the abolition female saints and the Charleston female patriots could not meet in a fight fair and mutually annihilate each other."[60] Another woman saw the political issues ripping her family apart. For her, politics had become sadly personal. She was the only Unionist left among her prosecession relations, and she wrote once the war had begun, "None of them love me as they once did."[61]

Fernando Wood

Mayor of New York Fernando Wood, an antiwar politician running for reelection in a northern state, was a prominent spokesmen for the Peace Democrats. Formerly a political partisan who had tried to bring together all the diverse groups within the Democratic Party, Wood was by 1861 clearly a Copperhead. During the presidential race of 1860, both Wood and the corrupt Tammany organization that ran the city had agreed that abolitionism rather than slavery was the cause of America's difficulties. In good demagogic fashion, Wood denounced the Republican Party as a "fiend which stalks within the narrow barrier of its Northern cage" and contrasted this with the nationwide support enjoyed by the peace-loving Democratic candidates who believed in compromise and nonpartisanship. In a blistering speech that was anything but bipartisan, Wood said that the Lincoln Republicans "would pursue the war as long as slavery existed [and] Southern blood was still available to be shed [provided that] they themselves are removed from the scene of danger." The mayor made a clear appeal to the antiwar sentiment to be found among the urban immigrant population of the North. "They [the Republican abolitionists] will get Irishmen and Germans to fill up the regiments and go forth to defend the country under the idea that they themselves remain at home to divide the plunder that is to be distributed."[62]

Wood sincerely believed that much of New York's prosperity depended on its southern connections and that an accommodation with the planter aristocracy of the South was in the city's best interest. He was not alone in this assessment. The financial basis of the city was lodged in its trade dominance and the enormous tariffs it collected. On the eve of the war, New York was exporting more cotton to Europe than Charleston, South Carolina, and much of the annual export tally of 5 million bales was transshipped to New York from other southern ports including New Orleans. In January 1861, after Lincoln's election, Wood suggested that Manhattan, in combination with Staten Island and Long Island, secede from the United States and the State of New York and become an independent city-state. Abandoned by the Tammany machine, Wood's proposal marked the end of his career as Manhattan's leading political figure. When the South fired on Fort Sumter, Wood proved himself a political chameleon capable of reversing himself whenever the situation required, but he never favored an active prosecution of the war. Nonetheless, he helped organize a federal volunteer regiment and seemed thereafter to be waving the flag of patriotism as fervently as anyone. Duly elected to Congress from New York in 1862, Wood became a leader of the Peace Democrats in the House and served as such for the duration of the war.

The Third Nation

Copperheads in a number of midwestern states also floated the idea of exiting the Union in much the same manner as had the South, but without aligning themselves with the Confederacy. William B. Wedgewood published a tract proposing the division of the country into three or more independent republics and then reuniting them under a totally new Constitution in the form of a so-called Democratic Empire, or more correctly an American commonwealth. A strong midwestern—Pacific Coast identity had existed for years, and midwestern sectionalism was almost as popular as the southern variety. The outbreak of war did not dampen sectional talk in the Midwest. On the contrary, it took on a new urgency. Meanwhile, there was great anxiety that west coast Copperheads might be successful in prying away California and the mining-rich mountain territories from the Union.

Midwestern hostility toward Yankee New England was rooted in both political and economic fundamentals. Farmers from this region were much more closely tied to the Mississippi River for the exportation of their produce than they were to the rail lines that connected them to New York or Baltimore. The loss early in the war to northern troops of New Orleans as a point of transshipment was a blow to many of those farmers friendly to the South who now had no choice but to use the rails to the east. The hard feelings were increased when the war caused the default of many unsound banks in the Midwest. These banks had circulated a great deal of paper currency whose value plummeted leaving the farmers with the loss. Nearly half the banks in Wisconsin failed, and 85 percent of those in Illinois were defunct in the first year of the war. The 1861 Morrill Tariff increased the pain by placing duties on finished goods and making it more difficult to sell produce abroad. Only a European grain shortage saved the farmers of the Midwest from financial ruin, but it also dispelled any concept of forming a third nation.

Conscription

Much of the violent protest during the Civil War was because of the draft. The concept of compulsory service seemed to some to contradict the aims of the war.

Antiwar northerners and anti-Confederate southerners (mostly from the border states) thought the concept of conscription un-American and the application of the draft unfair. Through the draft, Americans North and South were exposed to a new bureaucracy that had greater reach and authority over their lives than they had ever known, and the government was not adverse to using this bureaucracy to pursue its enemies. After First Bull Run, arrests for draft evasion rose dramatically giving the Peace Democrats a substantial issue on which to focus their protests. As many as 38,000 civilians in the North were arrested by the military during the Civil War. Most were suspected of draft evasion, desertion, or sabotage.

Even though the war was popular in the South, the Confederacy—with a smaller white population than the North—was the first forced to resort to conscription to preserve its forces in the field. The Confederate Conscription Act of 1862 was the first general draft of soldiers in America. Neither the Confederate Congress nor Jefferson Davis wanted it, but conscription was seen as an absolute necessity. Its purpose was twofold. The twelve-month enlistments, entered into in the spring of 1861, were about to run out. It was feared that these men, now veterans of war and free from many of the romantic notions they had brought to their first muster, would fail to reenlist. Conscription ensured that the Confederacy would retain the men it had in the army, and, since the war had already lasted longer than anyone had predicted, it provided for the additional men that would be needed. Conscription passed through the Confederate Congress in 1862 by more than a two-to-one vote. The act made all white males from the ages of eighteen to thirty-five eligible for three years of service. The U.S. Congress followed with its own Conscription Act in August of the same year, but Lincoln refused to sign it into law until March 1863 so that it would not coincide with the promulgation of emancipation (January 1863).

The draft, almost identical in its characteristics both North and South, was universally unpopular, but it was accepted with a certain equanimity, rather than reservation, in the South. In the North, the first drawing of names in July 1863 set off a violent four-day long riot with a mob of more than 50,000 working men swarming through the streets of Manhattan. Federal troops, just back from the grim scene at Gettysburg, were called on to quell the riots, leaving more than 1,000 rioters dead. Small disturbances also broke out in Boston, Troy, and other towns in the East and in Ohio.

Men could avoid the drafts in a number of ways. If he was found to have a physical disability, he would be exempt. Disqualifying disabilities included genuine health problems like blindness, missing limbs, lung disease, venereal disease, or an unsound heart. Other genuine problems were less evident. Urine samples were taken; a man's balance and coordination were tested; and even if he could see, his eyesight needed to be normal or at least correctable with the use of glasses. Those who were epileptic or insane were exempt. Chronic conditions such as coughing, shortness of breath, and back pain were more difficult to prove and harder for the authorities to evaluate. Two simple physical characteristics also freed a man from conscription. He could not be less than five feet six inches tall, which suggests that people were not really shorter in the 19th century than they are today. Second, as a purely practical matter, he needed at least two opposed teeth because the bullet cartridge needed to be torn open with the teeth in firing the musket.

A man could have an exemption from the draft based on a war-related occupation considered more critical to the cause than his service at the front. Iron founders, machinists, miners, and railroad workers; ferrymen, pilots, and steamboat workers; government officials, clerks, and telegraphers; ministers, professors, teachers of the handicapped, and private teachers with more than twenty pupils; and other occupations exempted men from the draft. Protests erupted over the exemptions; but the only outcome of a public outcry was an extension of the exemption to physicians, leather workers, blacksmiths, millers, munitions workers, shipyard workers, salt makers, charcoal burners, some stockmen, some printers, and one editor for each newspaper or publishing house. COs, belonging to recognized pacifist sects, did not have to serve if they provided a substitute or paid $500 to the government.

One of the more flagrant exemptions under southern law was that one slaveholder, with more than twenty slaves under his care, would be exempt from each plantation. White overseers were exempt because of the fear of slave uprisings. Many felt that this exemption led to "a rich man's war and a poor man's fight." Although this attitude was strongly held in many circles, many slaveholders and their sons voluntarily served in the war, very often as officers and leaders of local partisan groups.

Finally, in both the North and the South, a man could buy his way out of the draft by finding a substitute. Two future U.S. presidents, Chester Arthur and Grover Cleveland, hired substitutes in order to avoid active service. As much as $400 in gold was offered to willing candidates in the North in 1863 for a draft substitute. A tremendous amount of fraud was perpetrated in the hiring of substitutes, and this may have been the greatest weakness of the draft system. Physically unsound men were found to replace sound substitutes before they reached the training camps; underage boys and overage men were used in the same manner; and many paid substitutes simply deserted, often repeating the process over and over again under different names. Scams like this often caused legitimate recruits to be herded together like criminals to prevent desertion until they reached the training camps.

The Conscription Act and the exemptions were modified as the war progressed, and more and more men became eligible for the draft. The federal act made all men twenty to forty-five eligible. The Confederates accepted boys of seventeen and men between forty-six and fifty as local defense forces or as railroad guards. These men who were too young or too old to fight on the front lines were able to free up thousands of other soldiers to do so. The draft had the positive effect of retaining veteran soldiers in the ranks. Without these soldiers, the southern armies would soon have collapsed. The conscription system was, nonetheless, amazingly inefficient, and filled with abuses. Moreover, it provided a rallying point for antiwar sentiment.

Because service seemed inevitable, the draft induced some men to enlist in local regiments, but as arrests rose because of evasion, more and more men began to speak out against the war and discourage others from joining the army. From the institution of conscription to the end of the war, state and federal files filled with reports from government agents reporting on the activities of individual antidraft activists and secret organizations established to damage conscription. Five young men were arrested in a single day in Burlington, New York, for trying to escape to Canada. Almost forty prominent Copperheads and administration critics were arrested in Illinois and Iowa. Among these were a number of anti-administration newspaper editors. Daniel Voorhees, an important Copperhead congress member from Indiana, had agents assigned to follow him on all his speaking tours. Voorhees had announced on the floor of the House as it passed the Conscription Act that he was a witness to "the melancholy spectacle" of watching "a free government die." Government officials considered arresting him for his "objectionable" speeches, but did not think they could prove the case that he was spreading sedition and draft resistance. The agents feared that an arrest of Voorhees would spawn violence.[63] Outraged anticonscription activists openly intimidated, threatened, and assaulted recruitment officers, rioted in the streets of several major cities, and endangered (but did not derail) the reelection of Abraham Lincoln in 1864.

The Draft Riots

European immigrants in America showed a particularly strong prejudice against blacks, and war resistance advocates used this to enlist them in the antidraft movement. According to some, any man who would enlist as a volunteer or submit to the draft "was a G-d d—d fool, besides being a G-d d—d black abolition son of a b—h."[64] Nonetheless, the poor immigrant Irish who voluntarily joined the Union Army made many brave stands. The 63rd and 69th New York (Fighting Irish), the 9th and 28th Massachusetts, and the 116th Pennsylvania Infantry made up the so-called Irish Brigade. A Second Irish Brigade (the 155th, 164th, 170th, and 180th New York Infantry) was formed by war's end. Of the 140,000 immigrant Irish in the Union Army, one-third came from eastern cities (chiefly Boston, Philadelphia, and Pittsburgh), one-third came from New York City alone, and the remainder served in scattered units raised in the Midwest and western theaters of the war.

The number of Irish killed, especially at the Battle of Fredericksburg in December 1862, was shocking. The Irish Brigade was involved in the assault on the stone wall in the sunken road in front of Marye's Heights. In this action, the brigade suffered its most severe casualties of the war with its fighting force reduced from more than 1,600 to only 256. Irish immigrant members of the Fenian Brotherhood often faced each other in battle. The casualty rolls, featuring the names of friends and relations, strengthened the otherwise-dormant antiwar sentiment of many poor urban residents. War widows with children often tried to cope with the situation faced by their fatherless brood, and the federal government had begun to award pensions to the widows of soldiers and sailors as early as July 1862. Yet the wife of a private soldier received only $8 per month without regard to the number of her children. This was the same pension given to wounded men disabled in the war, but it simply was not enough. Many of the Irish, who made up a large part of the draft resistance in urban areas, took out their frustrations with the draft on blacks largely because they believed that

THE MEETING OF THE FRIENDS,
CITY HALL PARK.

An unflattering cartoon portraying the New York drafts rioters as drunkards and brutes. (Library of Congress Prints and Photographs Division, American cartoon print filing series, LC-USZ62-96391)

"the abolitionist [hated] both Irish and Catholics and want[ed] to kill them off." The abolitionists it was claimed, always "put them in the front of the battle."[65]

The Catholic archbishop of New York, John Hughes, took an unquestionably militant stand in defense of his church. He rallied the largely Irish Catholic population of the city in defense of Catholic institutions and surrounded Catholic churches and schools with armed guards. He was said to be in control of 2,000 to 3,000 men. This response clearly sharpened the dispute and swelled the ranks of the Nativist, or Know-Nothing, political party, which used anti-Catholicism and the evils of popery as foundation stones of their all-American rhetoric.

Disaffection with conscription was most obviously manifest during the mid-July 1863 New York City draft riots. One New Yorker wrote, "The draft began on Saturday, the twelfth, very foolishly ordered by the government, who supposed that these Union victories [Gettysburg and Vicksburg] would make the people willing to submit. By giving them Sunday to think it over, by Monday morning there were large crowds assembled to resist the draft. All day yesterday there were dreadful scenes enacted in the city."[66] Beyond a few recruiters and government officials who happened to be in the wrong place at the time, the targets of the mostly Irish rioters were generally black. *Harper's* reported that "no class of our foreign population is more jealous of its own liberties than the Irish, and there is also none which more strongly resents every liberty accorded to the Negro race." One black was "seized by the mob, and, after his life had been nearly beaten out, his body was suspended from a tree, a fire kindled under him, and, in the midst of excruciating torments, he expired." There may have been upwards of seventy black victims among the servants and workers of the hotels and restaurants in New York. An observer noted, "These things were done deliberately, and not in the heat of passion . . . and were moved by a political prejudice."[67]

Col. Edward S. Sanford telegraphed Washington, D.C., several times on the first night of the disturbances:

Hon. E. M. STANTON,
Secretary of War.
SIR: The situation is not improved since dark. The programme is diversified by small mobs chasing isolated Negroes as hounds would chase a fox. I mention this to indicate to you that the spirit of mob is loose, and all parts of the city pervaded. The *Tribune* office has been attacked by a reconnoitering party, and partially sacked. A strong body of police repulsed the assailants, but another attack in force is threatened. The telegraph is especially sought for destruction. One office has been burned by the rioters, and several others compelled to close. The main office is shut, and the business transferred to Jersey City.

In brief, the city of New York is to-night at the mercy of a mob, whether organized or improvised, I am unable to say. As far as I can learn, the firemen and military companies sympathize too closely with the draft resistance movement to be relied upon for the extinguishments of fires or the restoration of order. It is to be hoped that to-morrow will open upon a brighter prospect than is promised to-night. If troops are to come in any numbers, all the equipments of the roads should be put on the Amboy line, which can be easily guarded, and boats enough sent from here to Amboy. The troops can land from on board boats at any desired point, and under cover of gunboats, if necessary.
Respectfully,
E. S. SANFORD.[68]

One of the buildings destroyed in the riot was the Colored Orphan Asylum that had been founded by a Quaker group in Manhattan in 1836. The three-story brick structure was attacked and burned by the largely Irish immigrant mob. The orphans, mere children who were turned out into the streets by the enraged white rioters, found temporary refuge in a nearby local police station and an asylum for white children. Maria Lydig Daly recorded some of her experiences during the riot in her diary:

At last the riot is quelled, but we had four days of great anxiety. Fighting went on constantly in the streets between the military and police and the mob, which was partially armed. The greatest atrocities have been perpetrated. Colonel O'Brian was murdered by the mob in such a brutal manner that nothing in the French Revolution exceeded it. Three or four Negroes were hung and burned; the women assisted and acted like furies by stimulating the men to greater ferocity. Father came into the city on Friday, being warned about his house, and found fifteen Negroes secreted in it. . . . They came from York Street, which the mob had attacked, with all their goods and chattels. Father had to order them out. We feared our own block on account of the Negro tenements below MacDougal Street, where the Negroes were on the roof, singing psalms and having firearms.[69]

The City of New York was not the only location in which the drafts riots occurred. Similar reports came from other cities, like this one from Boston:

Col. E. S. SANFORD :
SIR: Considerable excitement and gathering of people at North End yesterday; some fighting. Two police injured. Two companies regulars ordered up from Fort Independence; also two companies artillery from Readville. About 8 P.M. crowd made an attack on armory in Cooper street. All window glass demolished by brickbats. Troops fired a round of blank cartridges, and made a bayonet charge on mob, which retreated toward Charlestown street. Troops returned to armory, crowd following. A disturbance more intense. Large breach made in door of armory, which was then thrown open, and 6-pounder brass field pieces, loaded with canister shot, discharged full in the crowd. One man killed and several wounded. The crowd still refusing to leave, infantry marched out by platoons, and fired. One man and one woman killed by this discharge, and several wounded. Cooper street was then cleared.
    Later in evening a battalion of dragoons [mounted infantry] formed line in Cooper street. Part of the crowd assembled at Dock Square, and a hardware store was broken into. Police fired fifteen or twenty shots.
    At 8.40 P.M. alarm bells were rung, and another squad of police sent to Dock Square, which succeeded in keeping it clear until arrival of dragoons and company of infantry.
    At 10 P.M. dragoons returned to Cooper street, the disturbance in Dock Square being quelled.
    At 12.30 armory discovered to be on fire, but was saved from destruction by military. The Forty-fourth Massachusetts Regiment notified to assemble at their armory at 6 this morning.
G. F. MILLIKEN.[70]

The absolute pacifists among the antiwar movement denounced the violence of these acts and were outraged by their inclusion as alleged perpetrators of them; however, they remained unsure whether the protests did not further their own antiwar agenda. Many Peace Democrats supported the draft for political reasons of their own, but they were not a majority. Most disdained not only conscription, but also anyone who submitted to it. Former governor of Connecticut, Thomas Seymour, wrote that he was disgusted by men who submitted to conscription. "The American people are the easiest enslaved of any people in the world," he wrote. "The only class that shows any signs of remaining manhood are the farmers [of the Midwest]."[71]

Equating the pride and honor of serving to preserve the Union with white slavery was probably a tactical error. The rising tide of antiwar sentiment, at a time when the Battle of Gettysburg and the Fall of Vicksburg suggested that victory was at hand, was alienating the federal troops in the field, who thought that the Copperheads were undermining their ability to win the war. "It is a common saying here," wrote one soldier, "that if we are whipped, it will be by Northern votes, not by Southern bullets." Most men thought that at the least the antiwar sentiment was prolonging the war.[72]

Vote for Peace

Rep. Clement Vallandigham of Ohio was the best-known Peace Democrat. He organized a rally for the Democratic Party at Mount Vernon, Ohio, on May 1, 1863, that caused a great stir among Lincoln supporters. Vallandigham, Samuel S. Cox, and George H. Pendleton all delivered speeches denouncing General Order No. 38 that had been issued by Gen. Ambrose Burnside, commander of the Department of Ohio in April 1863. Burnside hoped to intimidate Confederate sympathizers with General Order No. 38, which stated the following:

> The habit of declaring sympathy for the enemy will not be allowed in this department. Persons committing such offenses will be at once arrested with a view of being tried . . . or sent beyond our lines into the lines of their friends. It must be understood that treason, expressed or implied, will not be tolerated in this department.[73]

Burnside also declared that, in certain cases, violations of General Order No. 38 could result in a sentence of death. Vallandigham was so opposed to the order that he allegedly said that he "despised it, spit upon it, [and] trampled it under his feet." He also encouraged his fellow Peace Democrats to openly resist Burnside. Vallandigham went on to chastise Lincoln at a public gathering for allowing Burnside to thwart citizen rights under a free government. Federal agents wearing civilian clothes attended the meeting and took careful notes. Made aware of Vallandigham's protests, Burnside ordered his immediate arrest. On May 5, 1863, a company of soldiers placed Vallandigham in custody at his home in Dayton and brought him to Cincinnati to stand trial before a military tribunal.[74]

Vallandigham offered no serious defense against the charges, contending instead that military courts had no jurisdiction over his case. Judge Humphrey Leavitt of the federal circuit court rejected Vallandigham's argument. He agreed with Burnside that military authority was necessary during a time of war to ensure that opponents to the U.S. Constitution would not succeed in overthrowing it and the rights that it guaranteed its citizens. The military tribunal found Vallandigham guilty of treason and sentenced him to remain in a federal prison for the remainder of the war. Cox, a newspaper editor from Ohio and former U.S. ambassador to Peru, wrote a moving letter to the president asking for Vallandigham's release: "If not

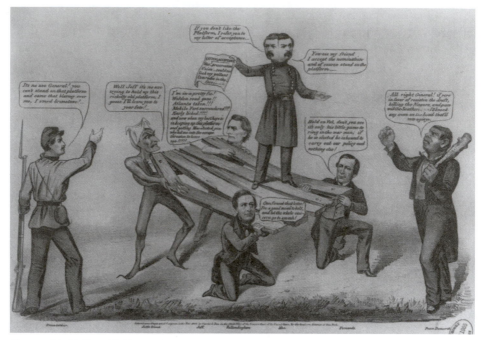

George McClellan, 1864 presidential candidate, on his Peace Platform. The corners of the platform are supported by (clockwise) Jefferson Davis, Fernando Wood, Clement Vallandigham, and the Devil. These are flanked on the right by a brutish anti-black Peace Democrat and on the left by a disapproving Union soldier. (Library of Congress Prints and Photographs Division, LC-USZ62-21706)

accounted magnanimous, by reason of the bitterness of the times, [such a course] may nevertheless prevent that ill will and distrust between the people and its agents, which the wisest of Statesmen ever seek to avert."[75] Cox, considered a moderate among Copperheads, was one of the most vehement and outspoken critics of the Lincoln administration in terms of his verbal attacks against the president and the war. Lincoln knew that confining Vallandigham might make the Ohioan a rallying point for opposition and cause Peace Democrats across the North to rise up to prevent his detention. The president, therefore, commuted Vallandigham's sentence to exile in the Confederacy, and on May 25, Burnside sent Vallandigham into Confederate lines. Vallandigham made his way to Canada and proceeded to run for Governor of Ohio from that distance, but lost the race.

Throughout the war, Lincoln was confronted with widespread disaffection and profound hostility. "Less ideologically minded" antiwar dissidents brought repeated violent protest to many parts of the North, both in the East and West and in rural as well as urban settings.[76] Yet dissent had an unexpected by-product. As disputes over how the war should be waged divided towns and counties across the Union, Republican politicians—especially the state governors—embraced the administration's position to a degree they otherwise might not have. "In dealing with this resistance, they turned repeatedly to the federal government for help, even if it meant surrendering state powers and becoming more dependent on a centralized infra-structure in the process."[77]

The influence of the Peace Democrats varied with the fortunes of war on the bat-tlefield. When things were going badly for the Union on the battlefield, larger num-bers of people were willing to entertain the notion of making peace with the Confederacy. When things were going well, Peace Democrats could more easily be dismissed as mere defeatists. But no matter how the war progressed, Peace Demo-crats constantly had to defend themselves against charges of disloyalty. Revelations that a few had ties with secret organizations such as the Knights of the Golden Circle, or the Sons of Liberty helped smear the rest. The administration exaggerated the Copperhead menace for political advantage, and the stories of secret plots and treasonous associations were mostly false. Government officials estimated that more than 100,000 persons belonged to these organizations, but most historians discount the figure as being dramatically higher than the group's actual numbers.

The Copperheads mobilized behind the 1864 election to throw Lincoln from office and gain their objectives at the ballot box, but they generally opposed the Democratic Party's nomination of Gen. George McClellan. A War Democrat candi-date for president in 1864 McClellan refused to accept Copperhead demands for an immediate peace. They were influential enough in the party, however, to set a peace plank in the party platform and place one of their own, George H. Pendleton of Ohio, as the Democratic vice presidential candidate. Pendleton had begun his politi-cal career during the 1850s. He first served in the Ohio Senate, and in 1856, voters elected him to the U.S. House of Representatives. He held his seat until March 1865. He was a committed Peace Democrat and strongly opposed the Union war effort. He was a close associate of Vallandigham.

The Peace Democrats made a good deal of headway among Democratic voters in the North during 1861 and 1862 with an argument that the war could not be won and was not worth winning, but this line of attack generally infuriated the soldiers serving in the federal armies who wanted to win the war. These men voted in increased numbers for Lincoln in 1864 and helped to persuade their family and friends at home to do so also. Historian James M. MacPherson has noted that the demands made by the Peace Democrats for "peace at any price, even the price of defeat and disunion," exemplified "the naïveté of the Copperheads insistence that an armistice and negotiations would bring the Confederate states back into the Union."[78] Southern leaders had consistently set Confederate independence as a first condition for any formal talks.

In a letter to Lincoln in July 1864, Horace Greeley of the *New York Tribune* begged the president to forego an attempt at reelection while the war persisted. "Our bleeding, bankrupt, almost dying country," Greeley wrote, "longs for peace—shudders at the prospect of fresh conscriptions, of further wholesale devas-tations, and of new rivers of human blood. I entreat you to submit overtures for pacification to the Southern insurgents." A month later, Greeley made his feelings public. In an editorial in the *Tribune* he declared: "Mr. Lincoln is already beaten. He cannot be elected. And we must have another ticket to save us from utter overthrow."[79]

Due largely to major northern victories at Savannah and Atlanta and the backing of Lincoln by federal soldiers, the McClellan-Pendleton ticket lost the election. With the successful conclusion of the war in 1865, the Peace Democrats were thoroughly discredited. Most northerners believed, and not without reason, that the Copperheads had prolonged the war beyond 1864 by encouraging the South to continue fighting in the hope that the North would abandon the struggle after the election.

By the end of the war, the Copperheads were in total disgrace. Many Democrats struggled to distance themselves from any previous political associations with the peace faction of their party. Humiliated, most stopped talking about their antiwar sentiments and anti-Lincoln politics and vanished from public sight. Most of what they had said against the war in their heyday—even among many Copperhead leaders—can be found only in the public record, not among private writings like diaries and journals. According to historian Jennifer L. Weber, the larger Democratic Party was "so tainted by the exploits of the Peace Democrats that only two Democrats occupied the Executive Mansion between 1868 and 1932, by which time most of the Civil War generation had died away."[80]

The Anti-Confederate South

Anti-Confederate southerners from the border regions made important contributions to the northern victory, but their protests against the Confederate government in Richmond were rooted largely in war weariness, food shortages, and antiblack prejudices rather than pacifist sentiment or allegiance to the Union. Although they generally found fault with the Davis administration, they also acknowledged that Lincoln had freed and armed slaves in contravention of the law, had suppressed civil liberties, and had repressed opposition newspapers, jailed antigovernment editors, and limited access to telegraphic dispatches and the mails. Ironically, government officials on both sides of the Mason-Dixon Line claimed that antiwar agitation in the border states encouraged the enemy and protracted the conflict.

The Lincoln administration could not wage a war effectively in the South without neutralizing the pro-Confederate and anti-administration sentiment in these border states. If the border states insisted on proclaiming their states' rights, they could refuse to allow federal forces to pass through their states or across their boundaries to bring the Confederates to battle. Lincoln, hoping to recruit border residents in the fight to suppress the Confederacy, first attempted to attract white support in the region to the cause of *perpetual union* by promising to leave slavery alone. Understanding that many neutral border state residents were against secession, but also deeply racist and Negro-phobic, in his inaugural address of 1861 Lincoln said, "I have no purpose, directly or indirectly, to interfere with the institution of slavery in the States where it exists. I believe I have no lawful right to do so, and I have no inclination to do so."[81]

Although Tennessee had seceded with the rest of the Confederate states, more than 30,000 men from the eastern part of the state ultimately served in the federal forces. Five times this number—mostly from the western and central regions—served the Confederacy, yet no border state donated more men to the Union cause. By downplaying abolition, emancipation, and citizenship for blacks, and by treating escaped slaves as so-called *contrabands*, Lincoln was generally successful in attracting manpower, resources, and positive public opinion in the white-belt border regions. This was especially true in 1861 and 1862 when Lincoln most needed the border states as staging areas for the incursion of federal forces into the Confederacy. He also needed to secure with a minimum of force better access to the Ohio, Tennessee, Mississippi, and other rivers for the operations of the federal gunboat navy.

In September 1862, after the marginal success at Antietam in Sharpsburg, Maryland had ended the Confederate Army of Northern Virginia's first invasion into the borderland, Lincoln tactfully broached the idea of using the war as an opportunity to free slaves. In introducing the Emancipation Proclamation (taking effect January 1863) he carefully "freed" only those slaves residing in areas *not* held by federal forces. He thereby exempted the federally controlled border regions from the proclamation and salved the sometimes-racist propensities of borderland residents.

In March 1861, Captain Nathaniel Lyon arrived in St. Louis, Missouri, in command of a company-sized detachment of the 2nd U.S. Infantry. Before the secession of South Carolina, Lyon had been extensively involved in establishing the St. Louis Wide Awakes, a pro-Union paramilitary organization composed of antisecessionist Missouri residents. He realized that prosecession forces under command of the state governor Clairborne "Fox" Jackson, intended to arm themselves from the federal arsenal in the city and muster into the ranks of the Confederate Army. Upon obtaining command of the arsenal, Lyon armed the Wide Awake units and had most of the excess weapons in the arsenal secretly moved to Illinois. Lyon was aware that secessionists had shipped captured artillery from the U.S. arsenal in Baton Rouge to the Missouri State Militia camp near the city. On May 10, he led the Missouri volunteers and the 2nd U.S. Infantry to the camp, forcing its surrender. Riots broke out in St. Louis as Lyon marched his secessionist prisoners through the city, and he ordered his men to fire on the demonstrators, killing twenty-eight and wounding approximately fifty. Lyon was promoted to brigadier general and oversaw the instillation of a pro-Union state government. He was killed on August 10 at the Battle of Wilson's Creek while dramatically rallying his badly outnumbered men, the first Union general to be killed in the Civil War.

In July 1861, John C. Fremont had taken command of the Western Department of the federal army headquartered in St. Louis, Missouri. Lyon had secured the federal arsenal in the city, but Fremont found disorder everywhere. The terms of enlistment of the three-month militia who were holding the state for the Union were expiring, and they were unwilling to reenlist because they had not been paid. Fremont had little money or arms at his disposal to battle the active Confederate minority in the southwestern portion of the State. He applied to the U.S. Treasurer at St. Louis for $100,000 of the cash on hand and with the money Fremont secured the reenlistment of many of the home guards. He strongly fortified St. Louis and proceeded to garrison the nearby river city of Cairo, Illinois, by moving nearly 4,000 troops to the city on river steamers. The Confederate troops in Kentucky and

Missouri that were gathered for the purpose of seizing Cairo were dissuaded from the attempt.

Fremont immediately proclaimed martial law in Missouri, and he appointed a provost-marshal in St. Louis. Some of the most active secessionists were arrested, and the publication of newspapers charged with disloyalty was suspended. Because of Fremont's avowed determination to confiscate the property and free the slaves of those disloyal to the Union, a storm of indignation suddenly arose among the residents of the border states. This alarmed the national government, and the president, wishing to placate the rebellious spirit of those states, requested Fremont to modify his position on these points. Fremont declined to do so, and his military career was suddenly placed in check. False accusers, public and private, ultimately cost Fremont his command. Meanwhile, the Missouri state convention defrocked the prosecessionist governor (Jackson), rejected any lingering idea of disunion, and declared itself the permanent wartime government of the state. The quick actions of Lyon and Fremont had secured Missouri to the Union.

In sharp contrast to the situation in Missouri, the state of Kentucky was so divided politically that initially only neutrality seemed possible. The state legislature voted 2–1 "to take no part in the civil war now being waged except as mediators and friends to the belligerent parties."[82] Gov. Beriah Magoffin issued a strong Neutrality Proclamation warning that only death awaited any who defied Kentucky's decision. Hundreds of Kentuckians immediately enrolled in the state guard ready to enforce its neutrality. Lincoln carefully stayed away, but Confederate Gen. Leonidas Polk violated Kentucky's neutrality by seizing first Columbus and then Bowling Green. Two days later, Gen. Ulysses Grant entered Kentucky with federal forces claiming that he came to save the state. The state legislature, in a lopsided vote, insisted that Polk retire across the border, but invited Grant to stay. The state was safe for the Union, and in the next election, Unionists carried three of every four seats in the Kentucky house. More than 70 percent of the state's young men (approximately 190,000) remained out of the fighting, one of the highest proportions of eligible men to remain undrafted among any of the states that saw fighting on its soil. Nonetheless, Kentuckians served in both armies. Federal recruiters did better in bringing men (50,000) into the army, but Confederates found the southwest section of the state a prime recruiting ground for men (25,000), mostly guerillas.[83]

Bitter guerilla raids were conducted in many of the border states. With its history of Missouri-Kansas border conflicts from the 1850s, Missouri was possibly the most terrorized region in the Yankee-occupied South. No other border state had "such entrenched antislavery and proslavery regions or such experience with the nighttime raid and the daytime ambush. . . . It's embittered black belt offered guerillas their launching pad against the Federal dominion."[84] Western Virginia and eastern Tennessee had no convenient marshalling areas for guerilla activity, but their mountainous topography and numerous fords were ideal for cross-border irregular operations. Delaware with less than 1,800 slaves and fewer than 600 slaveholders in a population of 90,000 hardly needed any force to quell secessionist sentiment, and almost all the antigovernment activity in Maryland centered in Baltimore, raising its head on a single day (April 19, 1861) when Massachusetts troops were attacked by a mob. Thereafter, secessionists in Maryland caused little unrest besides street grumbling. They called Gen. Ben Butler a beast and President Lincoln a despot; a few hundred Marylanders crossed to Virginia to enlist in the Southern cause, but they raised no local forces to oppose the federal occupation of the state. White Marylanders in convention had chosen the Union by a 2–1 margin.

The white-belt areas of the border states overwhelmingly supported the Union in the Civil War, thereby allowing the federal forces to secure important avenues into the Confederate breadbasket in the Shenandoah Valley and the strategic heartland of the Mississippi Valley. Confederate raiders would move in and out, but a wall of border states generally loyal to the Union now faced the South. Only a combination of minimal federal forces with an anti-Confederate local sentiment could have so swiftly secured these regions. Lincoln's army had imposed little or no coercive force on the majority population of the white-belt regions, and a minimum of federal repression had been applied to borderites, who on their own had chosen to remain in the Union. Only with the support of loyal border residents could Lincoln expect to guard these borderland winnings against Confederate insult.[85]

Conscientious Objection

By 1787, no member in good standing of the Society of Friends was a slaveholder. Quakers did not, however, advocate the abolition of slavery by violent measures. In the Civil War, *peace church* leaders sought blanket exemptions for their draft-age young men based on religious teachings, but most cases of conscientious objection throughout the war were resolved individually. Although Quakers and Mennonites (up to 200,000) made up the majority of religious pacifists in 1860, members of several smaller pacifist religious groups defied Union and Confederate officials in the defense of their conscientious scruples against bearing arms. They tended to suffer most severely in the South, where manpower shortages, a martial spirit, and invading armies left little sympathy for men unwilling to fight. But under each of the opposing governments, they sometimes endured violent persecution by their civilian neighbors, brutal punishment by military authorities, or in rare cases, death by firing squad.

The federal Militia Act of 1862 made no provision for COs, though the Draft Act of 1863 did. In December 1863 Secretary of War Edwin M. Stanton eased the situation by paroling all COs held in custody and ordering that no more to be called up. This resulted in a flood of individual petitions from potential draftees claiming personal religious scruples against serving in the army. Finally, in February 1864, Congress dealt with the question by ruling pacifists subject to the draft but assuring noncombatant assignments to members of those religious groups whose articles of faith clearly expressed opposition to bearing arms. They were also given the option of paying $300 for the relief of sick and wounded soldiers. The draft, however, failed to closely define any CO outside the discipline of a recognized pacifist sect. During the Civil War, 143 Quakers reportedly enlisted as Union soldiers, but the majority of their pacifist brethren supported the Union through service in hospitals, caring for sick and wounded soldiers in their homes, or working among the so-called contrabands.

COs in the South were sometimes offered a government exemption for the payment of $500. Pacifists in combat-torn regions such as the Shenandoah Valley, however, were subject to rough treatment. Considered disloyal to the cause, they hid or fled with their families to escape being hunted by home guards. Some southern pacifists enlisted voluntarily for combat positions. Among them were approximately two dozen Quakers who decided to fight for abolition with the federal forces, and two companies of Brethren men from Forsyth City, North Carolina, who were mustered into the Southern Army in June 1861. Most of these were expelled from their sects during the war but were readmitted afterward.

The draft laws of both the Union and the Confederacy recognized the existence of religion-based war resistance, but could not deal with the dilemma posed by forced conscription. Neither government definitively resolved the problem posed by conscientious objection during the war. Thereafter, U.S. officials debated the issue at the national level, ultimately offering the option of noncombatant service, which remained in effect through World War 1.

Notes

1. William H. Rehnquist, *All the Laws But One: Civil Liberties in Wartime* (New York: Vintage Books, 1998), 6.

2. Alexander Mendoza, *Confederate Struggle for Command* (College Station: Texas A&M University Press, 2008), 28.

3. Walter Millis, *Arms and Men: A Study of American Military History* (New York: A Mentor Book, 1956), 13.

4. Wayne Wei-Siang Hsieh, *West Pointers and the Civil War: The Old Army in War and Peace* (Chapel Hill: University of North Carolina Press, 2009), 19.

5. Randolph B. Marcy, *The Prairie Traveler: A Hand-book for Overland Expeditions* (1859; rpt., Bedford, MA: Applewood Books, 1993), xi.

6. First proposed and passed in 1857, but vetoed by President James Buchanan.

7. Jennifer L. Weber, *Copperheads: The Rise and Fall of Lincoln's Opponents in the North* (Oxford: Oxford University Press, 2006), 2.

8. See footnote 1 in John Stuart Mill, "The Contest in America," *Fraser's Magazine* (1862), http://en.wikisource.org/wiki/The_Contest_in_America (accessed September 2008).

9. Rehnquist, 44.

10. Rehnquist, 57.

11. Rehnquist, 51.

12. Dorothy Denneen Volo and James M. Volo, *Daily Life in Civil War America* (Westport, CT: Greenwood Press, 1998), 22.

13. Rehnquist, 58.

14. Rehnquist, 179–180.

15. George C. Eggleston, A *Rebel's Recollections* (1874; rpt., Bloomington: Indiana University Press, 1959), 12.

16. Caroline C. Richards, *Village Life in America, 1852–1872* (Gansevoort, NY: Corner House, 1997), 131.

17. Richards, 130–131.

18. Colin G. Calloway, *The Shawnees and the War for America* (New York: Viking, 2007), 174.

19. Thomas A. Lewis, *The Guns of Cedar Creek* (New York: Bantam, 1991), 163.

20. Earl Schenck Miers, ed., *A Rebel War Clerk's Diary, by John B. Jones, 1861–1865* (New York: Sagamore Press, 1958), 22.

21. Volo and Volo, 26–28.

22. Margaret Leech, *Reveille in Washington* (New York: Harper & Brothers, 1941), 66–67.

23. Volo and Volo, 26–28.

24. Earl J. Hess, *The Rifle Musket on Civil War Combat: Reality and Myth* (Lawrence: University Press of Kansas, 2008), 30.

25. Peter Cozzens, *No Better Place to Die: The Battle of Stones River* (Urbana: University of Illinois Press, 1990), 165.

26. Editors of Time-Life, *Voices of the Civil War* (New York: Time-Life, 1995), 121.

27. James H. Croushore, ed., *A Volunteer's Adventure, by Captain John W. De Forest* (New Haven, CT: Yale University Press, 1949), 138.

28. Oliver Wendell Holmes, "Doings of the Sunbeam," *Atlantic Monthly,* July 1863, 12.

29. Croushore, 46.

30. In Vietnam *monthly* rates ran as high as the hundreds, and the total deaths in seven *years* of war in Iraq had not exceeded 4,000 as of December 2009.

31. William Dean Howells, "Question of Monuments," *Atlantic Monthly,* May 1866, 647.

32. Weber, 22.

33. Weber, 66.

34. Weber, 23–24.

35. Rehnquist, 26.

36. Rehnquist, 167.

37. Weber, 32.

38. Weber, 33.

39. Rehnquist, 46.

40. Weber, 36; David P. Currie, "The Civil War Congress," *University of Chicago Law Review* 73: 1131–1226, 1139, http://lawreview.uchicago.edu/issues/archive/v73/fall/Currie.pdf (accessed June 14, 2008).

41. Currie, 1141.

42. Currie, 1132.

43. Weber, 66.

44. Currie, 1174.

45. Miers, 14.

46. Mendoza, 34.

47. Mendoza, 32–33.

48. Mendoza, 34.

49. Weber, 54.

50. Weber, 14.

51. Weber, 14.

52. Currie, 1147.

53. Weber, 23.

54. Weber, 23.

55. Weber, 39.

56. John D. Billings, *Hardtack and Coffee* (Boston: G. M. Smith, 1887), 20.

57. Billings, 20.

58. Dumas Malone, ed., *Dictionary of American Biography* (New York: Scribner's Sons, 1943). The information on prominent abolitionists that follows is taken largely from this source.

59. Weber, 29.

60. Maria Lydig Daly, "New Yorkers and the War," July 14, 1863, http://ny1863.wordpress.com/author/mld1863 (accessed June 12, 2008).

61. Weber, 47–48.

62. Weber, 39.

63. Weber, 129.

64. Weber, 50.

65. Weber, 50.

66. Daly.

67. Alfred H. Guernsey and Henry M. Alden, ed., *Harper's History of the Great Rebellion* (New York: Gramercy Books, 1866), 652.

68. Reports of Mr. Edward S. Sanford, U.S. Military Telegraph Service, July 13–16, 1863, "Draft Riots in New York City, Troy, and Boston O.R." Series I, Volume XXVII, no. 2 [S# 44] http://www.civilwarhome.com/essanfordor.htm (accessed March 2009).

69. See Daly.

70. See Sanford.

71. Weber, 51.

72. Weber, 70.

73. Weber, 94–95.

74. Weber, 96.

75. Samuel Cox to Abraham Lincoln, June 14, 1863, http://memory.loc.gov/mss/mal/maltext/rtf_orig/mal054f.rtf (accessed May 27, 2008).

76. Weber, 2.

77. Weber, 2.

78. Weber, x.

79. Horace Greeley, "Letter to Abraham Lincoln," July 7, 1864, http://teachingamerican-history.org/library/index.asp?document=1473 (accessed February 2009).

80. Weber, 1.

81. William W. Freehling, *The South vs. the South: How Anti-Confederate Southerners Shaped the Course of the Civil War* (New York: Oxford University Press, 2001), 39.

82. Freehling, 52–53.

83. Freehling, 52–53.

84. Freehling, 55.

85. Freehling, 57.

Chapter 10

International Diplomacy in the Civil War Period

In peace, in war, united they move;
Friendship and Glory form their joint reward. . . .
"What god," exclaimed the first, "instills this fire?"
Or, in itself a god, what great desire?

—Lord Byron

Suppression of the Atlantic Slave Trade

The role of the U.S. Navy during our nation's first tottering steps toward the international abolition of race-based slavery is often overlooked. Slavery within the United States was not completely abolished when Abraham Lincoln signed the Emancipation Proclamation of 1863. That would have to wait for a constitutional amendment. Nonetheless, President Thomas Jefferson had made the international trade and transportation of slaves illegal a half-century earlier in 1808 by signing the Slave Trade Act. This provided the first occasion for the United States to act as an international partner with the other nations of the world (principally Britain) in enforcing global maritime law.

From the start, the act proved unenforceable largely because of Jefferson's opposition to an advanced program of naval shipbuilding. The lack of ships denied the central government any power to halt the slave trade where it was weakest—in the Middle Passage at sea. At the same time, rising cotton production in the South was expanding the demand for slave labor, and slave ships continued to take blacks from West Africa and the Caribbean and secretly bring them into American ports for black-market sale and trade. Profits from cotton in the Carolinas and from sugar in Louisiana provided a financial bulwark for slavery in the Deep South. The archaic plantation system would have faded into obscurity were it not for the ability of slavery to provide the labor needed to produce these crops. Nonetheless, estimates show that by 1860 more than 3.6 million blacks were enslaved in the states that were to form the Confederacy thought by most observers to be a self-sustaining population separate from the overseas slave trade.

Meanwhile, during the previous five decades, the efforts of the U.S. Navy to suppress the international slave trade through cooperation with the British Royal Navy were hindered due to antagonisms between the countries left over from the Revolution, and all efforts were suspended during the War of 1812. Under several treaties between 1817 and 1830, the Spanish and Portuguese also made the oceanic slave trade illegal. The plantation South despised these agreements, but the U.S. Navy, nonetheless, was required to enforce them. It was common for abolitionist forces in America and Britain to complain that the Americans were not taking the law seriously. They pointed out that while the British Royal Navy went out of its way to actively patrol the West coast of Africa and the Caribbean for slavers, the Americans seemed to enforce the restrictions only when it was convenient. Of course, the British had more far-reaching maritime assets, including a navy eight to ten times larger than that of the United States. Nonetheless, Sir George Collier, commander of the British antislavery squadron, reported that the American Navy on all occasions acted with the greatest zeal and the most perfect unanimity with British forces with respect to stopping the slavers.

In May 1820, Congress passed a new bill that called for severe punishment for violation of the Slave Trade Act. Slaving at sea was thereafter considered an act of piracy and any American caught could be punished with death. The navy was empowered to seize slave ships wherever they were found. President James Monroe allocated $100,000 to enforce the act immediately, sending a flotilla of warships to the African coast. Here the U.S. Navy acted in loose consort with antislaving patrols of the Royal Navy.

Among those sent to patrol the waters of West Africa was Lt. Matthew C. Perry, whose family had been associated with the establishment of the American Colonization Society in 1816. He escorted the first group of former black slaves as settlers to African Liberia in 1820. The American navy captured ten slavers in its first season of patrolling. At least six of these were registered in Baltimore, Charleston, or New York. In 1821 the ten-gun schooner *Shark* was launched from the Washington Navy Yard with the specific objective of eliminating piracy and slave trading in the reef-filled waters of the West Indies. Perry was chosen as the schooner's commander.

In the 1830s an illegal commercial liaison formed between slavers in Cuba and the builders of quick-sailing Baltimore Clippers in the United States. It was almost impossible to prove that the Americans were in a conspiracy to trade slaves. However, Nicholas Trist, the American consul in Havana from Virginia, was found to be deeply involved in fraudulently authenticating these sales to hide the paperwork trail from builder to slaver. An embarrassment to the diplomatic corps, Trist was removed from his post in 1841, but the trade flourished in the interim.

In June 1839, the *Amistad*, a slave ship belonging to Spanish owners, sailed from Havana for another Cuban port. On the journey the African slaves aboard, under the leadership of a warrior named Cinque, overcame the crew and took control of the ship. In the process, they killed the captain and the ship's cook. With the coerced help of the surviving crew, they proceeded to sail north along the Atlantic coast of the United States. Some months later, the Navy found the vessel at anchor off the shore of Long Island, New York, and the Anti-Slavery Society brought suit in the Supreme Court. In 1841, Justice Joseph Story claimed the freedom of the "Africans" under existing U.S. Law even though Cuba had no law against the slave trade. The court ruled that they were at liberty to return to Africa, if they wished, on the grounds that they had always been free men under Spanish law.[1] On November 27, 1841, with money raised for the purpose among interested abolitionists, thirty-five of the surviving Africans were returned to their homeland along with five white missionaries and teachers. A Christian mission to Africa was established there and remained prosperous for many decades.

In 1843, a permanent African squadron under Matthew C. Perry was sent to patrol all known slave harbors on the west coast of Africa, but he was called away to serve with the Gulf Squadron during the Mexican War in 1846. Perry had entered the navy as a midshipman in 1809 and did his first service under his brother Oliver Hazard Perry. In the War of 1812, he had been promoted lieutenant, but he had waited to receive a captaincy until 1847. From 1838 to 1840 as commander of the steam frigate *Fulton*, Perry had made a number of important experiments with power naval operations. In 1853, he was sent with a squadron to show the American flag in the Pacific, where in 1854, he helped to open Japanese ports to American shipping for the first time.

The Trent Affair

In March 1861, the Confederate secretary of state dispatched several diplomats to Europe. Among these were William L. Yancey, Pierre Rost, and A. Dudley Mann. Each carried letters from the Confederate government promising advantageous treatment with regard to southern cotton. The price was recognition of the Confederate States of America. These men were received cordially but coolly in Britain and France. In May, Queen Victoria extended so-called belligerent rights to Confederate vessels and neutral shipping carrying military supplies and raw materials to the South. The United States government was furious at this development, but nothing else seemed likely to happen on the diplomatic front.

In November 1861, James M. Mason and John Slidell sailed from Havana, Cuba, on the British ship *Trent*. The next day, while in international waters, the U.S. warship *San Jacinto* overtook the *Trent*, and a boarding party removed Mason and Slidell. Charles Wilkes, the federal captain, brought the two men under arrest to Boston. The British were incensed and threatened war. U.S. Ambassador Charles Francis Adams did all he could to calm the situation, suggesting strongly that Wilkes had acted without orders, and promising that Mason and Slidell would be released. By the time the two southern diplomats reached London and Paris, respectively, the furor had died. Neither man was greatly effective in their diplomatic role.

The Southern Quest for Recognition

The southern war effort in Virginia and Tennessee was supplemented at the time by the efforts of Confederate agents in Europe, such as Mason and Slidell. Although foreign recognition escaped them, several Confederate agents were successful in other ways. James D. Bullock was responsible for building and arming a number of Confederate vessels in Britain. Bullock has been characterized as "worth far more to the Confederacy than most of its best-known generals."[2] Edwin De Leon, former U.S. consul to Egypt, resigned his federal post and sailed to Europe to oversee southern propaganda efforts in Britain and France. He was quite critical of the efforts of his colleagues, however. His candid visit with the British Prime Minister Palmerston in July 1862 convinced De Leon that recognition by Britain was a virtual impossibility as long as the South supported slavery. He left his interview with Napoleon III of France, however, with greater expectations, suggesting that the Confederates would promise to initiate gradual emancipation of slaves and to give France a monopoly on southern cotton production in return for diplomatic recognition. These efforts failed largely because of the attitudes of the Confederate Congress. By the end of 1863, De Leon had been dismissed as a Confederate diplomat, his plans never having approached fruition and his frustration apparent.[3]

There was also an effort made by Confederate diplomats to wrest the states of Nuevo Leon, Baja California, Sonora, and Chihuahua from northern Mexico. All four states were virtually independent of the central government in Mexico City and the rebel government of Benito Juarez in Vera Cruz. The gold and silver mines of Sonora and Chihuahua would have been a great resource for the Confederacy, and their coastlines—especially the 1,500 miles on the Pacific side—were virtually immune from an effective blockade.[4] The annexation of these Mexican states was not a new idea, and southerners had howled with rage when the United States failed to demand them at the end of the Mexican War in 1849. In 1861, many southerners thought their inclusion in the Confederacy would strengthen the South, but they failed to realize the need to defend the added territory with men and munitions and the added coastline with ships and fortifications. Nonetheless, also in 1861, Confederate Secretary of State Robert A. Toombs dispatched John T. Picket as a confidential agent to Mexico to attempt the arrangement. It soon became apparent that Picket was no peaceful diplomat, but rather an agent provocateur trying to stir up an independence movement in Mexico. This created a severe diplomatic crisis between the Confederate states and the Mexican government. Napoleon III sent French soldiers (as part of a British, Spanish-French contingent) to collect debts owed in Mexico. The French troops stayed capturing Mexico City in June 1863 and eventually installing the Austrian Duke Maximilian as Emperor of Mexico. Picket's successor was Hamilton Bee of Texas who forged a positive relationship with Maximilian in 1864, but Bee was not able to advance the southern strategy.

Other less notable Southern agents were George N. Sanders, who would later play an important role in the secret service activities of the Confederacy in Canada (particularly the raid on the banks in St. Albans, Vermont), and several regular Confederate naval officers, including J. Thomas Scharf and Raphael Semmes, skipper of the CSS *Alabama*. These men were successful in building and arming several state-of-the-art commerce raiders in British shipyards, producing (but not deploying) the so-called Eads Ironclads in France, and recruiting a swarm of blockade runners. They also proved sufficiently effective in portraying the success of the raiders' activities to warrant a report in the *New York Times* (August 4, 1863) that British opinion was of the mind that U.S. shipping had become almost valueless in consequence of the seizures made by the Confederate cruisers.[5] Little effort was made to determine the reliability of these assertions at the time, but they failed to bring the diplomatic recognition that the South desired. The dual defeats suffered by the Confederates at Gettysburg and Vicksburg in early July 1863 all but made such recognition impossible. When word of the defeats reached Europe, both Britain and France withdrew their support for the Confederate vessels building in their harbors. Britain placed an embargo on any further Confederate sailings, and France confiscated the ironclads that were being built. The United States felt secure enough thereafter to invoke the terms of the Monroe Doctrine announcing its displeasure at foreign intervention in its internal affairs.

The Alabama Claims

Many of the most effective vessels of the Confederate Navy were built and armed in Britain. These included *Alabama, Tallahassee, Shenandoah*, and a half dozen other raiders. Since the Confederate raider *Alabama* made the largest share of the Civil War–era seizures of U.S. shipping, the resulting litigation between the United States and Great Britain over damages and punitive payments came to be known as the "Alabama Claims." The United States, in an arbitrated settlement in 1872, received more than $15 million in reparations from the British for that nation's complicity in building, supplying, manning, and otherwise aiding the raiders. The two governments also agreed to arbitration of the northwest boundary with Canada, which was decided in favor of the United States along with a partial settlement of a Grand Banks fishing dispute (completed in 1877).

In laying the foundation of its case against the British in the Alabama Claims, Charles Francis Adams, representing the U.S. government, also demanded payments for the virtual destruction of American maritime commerce during the war years. This demand amounted to an assertion that the raiders and, by extension, Great Britain were entirely responsible for the decline of the U.S. merchant marine during the Civil War period. These *indirect damages* ultimately were disallowed by the Geneva Arbitration Tribunal that oversaw the settlement of the case.

The rationale of the government's argument for indirect damages, which serves as a foundation for the "Flight from the Flag" theory, was rooted in the concept that the existence and reported success of the Confederate raiders had undermined American preeminence in the foreign carrying trade to the extent that British carriers were unfairly able to displace the Americans.[6] By driving war risk insurance premiums higher than was warranted by the accomplishments of the raiders, Adams argued that U.S. commerce was forced to suffer. American shippers were forced to seek neutral carriers, often British ones. Moreover, he charged that Lloyd's of London, which set the underwriter's standards for vessels and held the position as the largest marine insurer of the world's fleet, had given British vessels favorable treatment. Northern shippers, already working on small profit margins, had been forced to "sell foreign" (that is, legally sell to foreign owners) in the face of the financial ruin brought on as port charges mounted on their unused vessels.

The terminology of *selling foreign* and that of *flying a flag of convenience* are often confused, yet they continue to be used by the maritime industry to avoid unfriendly domestic legislation or attack in time of war. Vessels that were sold foreign were considered to actually have been sold so that their former owners no longer held a financial stake in their operations. Flying a flag of convenience was a different matter. It amounted to a paper transaction, wherein the former owners still retained financial and practical control of the vessels, but legally had transferred their ownership to another national registry.

In the face of scrutiny by the tribunal, however, the activities of the Confederate commerce raiders faded as a cause for the severe distress documented to have taken hold of the U.S. merchant marine trades. The importance of the raider's depredations in the patchwork of causes for the decline of the American foreign carrying trade seemed to be based more on anecdotal evidence provided by former Confederates and the owners of economically distressed shipyards rather than on documented statistics. Although the wartime figures evidence a decline, they do not seem to support a general abandonment of the U.S. flag or an extinction of its commerce.

Rather than a general abandonment of U.S. registry, the facts seem to indicate that only a minority of owners, generally of large sailing vessels, deserted the flag. Moreover, the reliance on the psychological apprehension of loss and on the fear of high war risk rates as compelling mechanisms for owners to change registry fails to answer one salient question convincingly. Given that the owners of vessels captured or destroyed by the Confederates were paid for their vessels and cargoes by insurance or by the foreign purchasers, in the case of sale, why were these vessels not replaced after the Civil War as the hundreds of captured and destroyed merchant vessels had been after the Colonial and Revolutionary wars of the 18th century? Furthermore, the insurance rates returned to their prewar levels with the end of hostilities, but foreign carrying continued to decline even in the absence of the raiders. Here is a central weakness in the argument of the "continuing effect" of the raiders, especially as it fails to suggest a mechanism by which the immediate effects of the raiders could prove so enduring.[7]

Diplomatic Trouble with Mexico

The Mexican Civil War that brought Benito Juarez to prominence ran from 1857 to 1861. It was a war of reform launched by the liberal forces in Mexico dissatisfied with the reigning conservative government with its strong ties to the Catholic Church. The so-called War of Reform ended in 1861 with the installation of Juarez as president in Mexico City and the development of a new constitution that reflected the principles of the Great Charter of 1857. This document called for general elections, the expansion of the franchise, and the establishment of federated states under a republican system of central governance. The United States had supported Juarez and his republican forces, but Lincoln (who viewed the conflict in

Mexico as disturbing) found that he was too busy with his own Civil War to intervene on the part of the Juarez government.

The Juarez government abrogated many private contracts and nullified the debts owed to British, French, and Spanish business interests. In response, the three European countries sent troops to Mexico to intervene over the objections of the Lincoln administration. The Spanish and British quickly withdrew their forces, however, when it became apparent that the French planned to conquer Mexico. Although the French army suffered an initial defeat at Puebla on May 5, 1862 (the origin of the Cinco de Mayo holiday still celebrated by Mexicans), they eventually defeated the Mexican republican forces. The members of the Juarez government were forced to retreat to Vera Cruz, taking the government treasury with them. French troops entered the capital at Mexico City in June 1863, and a conservative junta of thirty-five persons was established to govern the country under French oversight.

Meanwhile, Napoleon III of France offered the so-called Mexican throne to Duke Maximilian of Austria. It is difficult to believe that the French would have so brazenly challenged the precepts of the Monroe Doctrine had the United States not been involved in a civil war of its own. A rightful member of the Habsburg line that had ruled in Europe, Maximilian was enthroned as emperor of Mexico, and he and his wife Carlotta arrived in Mexico City in May 1864. Maximilian was no dictator, and he believed in a limited form of monarchy tempered by an elected legislature. He also took steps to abolish child labor, limit working hours, and reform the system of land tenancy. In so doing, he was abandoned by the conservative elements in society and quickly was left with no support whatsoever. The conservatives who initially had cheered his acceptance of the throne were put off by his liberal ideas, and the republican Juarista's considered Maximilian an enemy simply because he existed. This circumstance also cooled Napoleon III's ardor somewhat and left Maximilian with few friends and numerous enemies.

The U.S. Congress passed a unanimous resolution opposing the establishment of any monarchy in Mexico. American diplomats demanded that the French withdraw their forces and that Austria recall Duke Maximilian, but nothing happened. Immediately after the end of the American Civil War, however, President Andrew Johnson took steps to visibly threaten the French by supplying arms to the Juarez government. General Phillip Sheridan was ordered to place 50,000 federal troops on the U.S.-Mexican border along the Rio Grande, and the U.S. Navy set up a blockade of the Mexican coastline to prevent French reinforcements.

Napoleon III withdrew his support of Maximilian in 1867, and the Mexican emperor was forced to capitulate. The capture and execution of Maximilian (June 19, 1867) ended the crisis. Juarez restored order to the country and was reelected president. He died in 1872, and left Sabastián Tejada as president. It was during this period that the United States was attempting to suppress the Apache, who had used the diplomatic uncertainties along the U.S.-Mexican border to their advantage.

Meanwhile under Tejada, certain beneficial constitutional reforms were enacted in Mexico, but a cabal supported by the Catholic Church and Mexican business interests overthrew Tejada making Porfiro Diaz president in 1876. Diaz ruled Mexico fairly well from 1876 to 1911, but his policies allowed for a great deal of foreign influence in Mexico, especially from U.S. railroad and industrial interests. By 1911, political and social stresses had developed to the extent that Diaz was overthrown by Francisco Madero. The next five years were extremely factious with competing forces in open revolt with the Mexican federal government. Numerous leaders (Huerta, Carranza, Obregón, Villa, Zapata, and others) controlled various regions of the country and installed separate governments. The United States formally recognized only the government of President Venustiano Carranza.

In 1916, General Francisco Villa led a raid into the United States (Columbus, New Mexico) that caused an American punitive expedition to be dispatched over the border under Gen. John J. "Black Jack" Pershing. The American troops fought several sharp actions with Villa's forces, but were withdrawn in 1917 because of growing concern over World War I in Europe. The Mexicans were greatly disturbed by the U.S. invasion of their country and were largely sympathetic to Germany during World War I. There was even talk between Germany and Mexico of opening a second front against the United States on the southwest border to prevent American troops from deploying in France. U.S.-Mexican diplomatic relations across the border remained problematic throughout the first half of the twentieth century.

Notes

1. Fred J. Cook, "The Slave Ship Rebellion," *American Heritage,* February 1957, 60–64, 64. See also Howard Jones, *Mutiny on the Amistad* (New York: Oxford University Press, 1987).

2. Philip Van Doren Stern, *The Confederate Navy: A Pictorial History* (Garden City, NY: Doubleday, 1962), 34.

3. See William C. Davis, ed., *Secret History of Confederate Diplomacy: Edwin De Leon, Late Confidential Agent of the Confederate Department of State in Europe* (Lawrence: University Press of Kansas, 2005); Francis R. Stark, *The Abolition of Privateering and the Declaration of Paris* (New York: Columbia University Press, 1897); and James D. Bullock, *The Secret Service of the Confederate States in Europe*, 2 vols. (New York: Putnam's, 1884).

4. See Robert Perkins, "Diplomacy and Intrigue, Confederate Relations with the Republic of Mexico, 1861–1862," http://members.tripod.com/~azrebel/page11.html (accessed August 2007).

5. See *New York Times*, August 4, 1863, 1:1.

6. See G. W. Dalzell, *The Flight from the Flag: The Continuing Effect of the Civil War upon the American Carrying Trade* (Chapel Hill: University of North Carolina Press, 1940).

7. Dorothy Denneen Volo and James M. Volo, *Daily Life in the Age of Sail* (Westport, CT: Greenwood Press, 2002), 288–291.

Chapter 11

Churchmen and Pacifists during the Indian Wars

Then I heard the voice of the Lord saying, "Whom shall I send? And who will go for us?" And I said, "Here am I. Send me!" . . . Then I said, "For how long, O Lord?" And he answered: "Until the cities lie ruined and without inhabitant, until the houses are left deserted and the fields ruined and ravaged, until the Lord has sent everyone far away and the land is utterly forsaken."

—Isaiah 6:8, 11–12

War in the New Promised Land

Farmers were the chosen people of the United States, and after the Civil War the vast farmlands of the Great Plains were the new Promised Land. While city dwellers and manufacturers changed the face of the nation with their factories and belching steam engines, farm families maintained their commitment to the traditional *Protestant work ethic* through the cultivation of the soil and the propagation of livestock. Farmers—fathers, mothers, and children—were thought to work in harmony with nature as a cooperative and contented team. The industrious person was considered to be a good person, a moral person. Good work brought both religious and economic rewards. Moreover, with thousands of migrants and immigrants moving west, the universality of the farming culture among them was thought to uphold the family and guarantee the stability, continuity, and order of the frontier community. Many churchmen and politicians believed that the Native American population of the plains should discard their traditional ways and assume white values like these.

Indian policy at the federal level was initially crafted by Secretary of War Henry Knox during Washington's first term of office, and it was carried out by most of the administrations that followed. Knox envisioned a policy of "civilization" and "Christianization" for the tribes that remained government policy into the 20th century. This policy sought to teach the Indians to abandon their traditional gender-based communal economy of male hunting and warfare and female agriculture and childrearing for a Euro-American lifestyle of male-oriented farming and female domesticity that would allow the tribes to prosper on a much smaller land base. This, it was hoped, would open former Indian lands to white settlement without eradicating the tribes. Federal agents and well-meaning churchmen relentlessly pushed this civilization program, or a near facsimile, throughout the 19th century.[1]

Meanwhile, the Native American population was being displaced by a numerically and technologically superior group of immigrants who transplanted their way of life, culture, religion, and language, while dispossessing the Indian population of its own. "The displacement of the native population in North America was accelerated by certain biological, technical, and cultural advantages enjoyed by European immigrants at the time of contact." Among these was a surplus white population in the cities that was prepared to emigrate; an acquired immunity to specific biological infections; the availability of sophisticated military weapons and tools; and an absolutist religious belief that the white race was meant by God to rule America.[2]

The Oregon Territory had been the destination for many white migrant families and Christian missionaries in the 1840s and 1850s. The influx of intruders into what was considered Indian land was not without turmoil. In 1847, Marcus and Narcissa Whitman, a married couple serving as missionaries to the Native Americans in Oregon for the American Missionary Board, were killed along with fourteen other whites by Cayuse warriors who were upset by the death of nearly all their sick children during a measles epidemic brought on by exposure to infected whites. Although the Whitman's administered to all the sick, only half of the infected white children had died, an outcome unacceptable to some among the distraught Cayuse. The death of the Whitman's served as a benchmark in the troubled relations between the federal government and the Native American tribes for the remainder of the 19th century. Subsequent to the murders, the local militias counterattacked, indiscriminately killing Native men, women, and children and escalating a regrettable but isolated incident into a full-fledged genocidal war.

From 1851 to 1856, whites undertook a number of punitive raids against the Cayuse, but they also attacked the nearby Yakima and Walla Walla nations that had had nothing to do with the murders. In 1855, Yakima retaliatory attacks on parties of prospectors brought in the U.S. regular army, which forced the tribes onto reservations. Not until the interposition of Gen. William S. Harney did the raiding and counterraiding end. Harney, promoted to general and transferred from the Plains to the command of the Oregon Territory in 1858, used his understanding of Indians to initiate a relatively peaceful settlement out of the ongoing troubles in the Northwest.

Pre–Civil War Indian Fighters

For a time, voters in the antebellum period (1815–1860) became fond of Indian fighters and military men in general, as political candidates. A good Indian fight on one's résumé could catapult an otherwise unspectacular local politician to national status. This fascination, which replaced an earlier but similarly inspired

The interior of an Indian Agency store. The purpose of the Indian Agency or Reservation was to alter the traditional lifestyle of Native Americans, making them more like whites. The actual effect was to impoverish the tribes and make them dependent on the largess of the government. (Library of Congress Prints and Photographs Division, LC-USZC2-768)

enchantment with the long-gone military heroes of the Revolution, began in earnest with the election of Andrew Jackson, seventh president of the United States (1829–1837), who fought the Creek nation at Horseshoe Bend in 1813, virtually wiping out the Upper Creek, which was forced to relinquish 23 million acres of tribal homeland to white settlement. The remnants of the tribe moved west to Arkansas and ultimately to Oklahoma. Jackson thereby set a militaristic protocol for dealing with recalcitrant Indian bands.

The fascination with Indian fighters continued with William Henry Harrison, ninth president (1841), who fought the Shawnee under Tecumseh at Tippecanoe in 1812, and with Zachary Taylor, twelfth president (1849–1850), Seminole Indian fighter in 1837 and hero of the Mexican War of 1846. So persuasive was this pro-military sentiment among the electorate that Abraham Lincoln, sixteenth president (1861–1865), relied on his service in the militia during the Black Hawk War, a minor Indian uprising in 1832, to qualify himself as executive timber.

Lincoln, who had been elected captain of his local militia unit, helped to chase Black Hawk and his followers back into the Wisconsin wilderness, but he was no military man. The Black Hawk War was Lincoln's only military experience, yet as president during the Civil War, he consistently interfered with his generals in the field, second-guessing their strategies, and sending preemptory orders by way of the U.S. Military Telegraph. Ulysses S. Grant, eighteenth president (1869–1876), also rose to office based solely on his Civil War performance.[3]

The Rise of Native American Power

The withdrawal of Federal troops to the East to fight the Civil War changed the nature of the Indian Wars during 1861–1865. On the Great Plains in the 1850s the army had been active in mounting offenses against the tribes. In 1854, Harney, then a colonel, had mounted a series of bloody raids on the villages of the Lakota Sioux in Nebraska; in 1857, Col. Edwin V. Sumner attacked a large body of Cheyenne warriors on the Solomon River in Kansas; and finally, Col. Earl Van Dorn fought the Comanche at Rush Spring in Oklahoma and at Crooked Creek in Kansas in 1859 and 1860, respectively.

In 1861, the federal government was concentrating on winning battles in Virginia and Tennessee, and it more or less ignored the growing "Indian problem" in the Great Plains, leaving the policing of the tribes to volunteer forces and irregular partisans. What resulted was a series of mistakes, blunders, and massacres throughout the Civil Wars years made by part-time soldiers and amateur officers. As one observer noted, "Every once in a while the soldiers themselves got cleaned out, [and] the Indians . . . massacred everyone in the whole place."[4] Unfortunately, many of these same errors would be repeated by regular troops in the second half of the century.

In 1861, an irregular force of white militiamen attacked a previously peaceful encampment of Chiricahua Apache under the leadership of Cochise. The Apache Wars that followed this incident lasted for the next quarter-century. In 1862, a column of California volunteers under Col. James Carleton fought several skirmishes with the Apache in Arizona. Also in 1862, the Santee Sioux of Minnesota opened a series of raids against settlers, traders, missionaries, and lumberjacks, killing nearly 1,000 whites and losing hundreds of their own people. Gen. Henry Sibley, a former fur trader and governor of the territory, met the Santee in battle at Wood Lake and defeated them. Sibley sentenced 303 captured Santee warriors to death by hanging, but President Lincoln commuted the sentences of all but thirty-eight of the Native American leaders. These men were hanged en masse in December 1862 as a lesson to other Plains tribes.

The relatively peaceful Navajo of the Southwest were engaged by militia and frontier forces in 1861. Kit Carson, the frontier scout, made his reputation fighting the Navajo. With the outbreak of Civil War, Carson resigned his post as Indian agent in New Mexico, and organized a volunteer militia for the territory. With the rank of colonel of volunteers, he commanded 60 percent of the Union forces in the territory, and he fought the Texas Confederates under Sibley at the Battle of Valverde in 1862. Thereafter, all regular Union forces were called East, and Carson instituted a scorched-earth policy against the Navajo. He was aided by Ute warriors who were long-standing enemies of the Navajo. In 1864, he added to his reputation at the battle at Canyon de Chelly, where dozens of warriors were killed and hundreds captured. In the spring of that year, 8,000 Navajo men, women, and children were forced to march 300 miles to reservations near Fort Sumner.

Finally in 1864, Col. John M. Chivington and the Third Colorado Volunteer Cavalry attacked a peaceful Cheyenne/Arapaho village at Sand Creek. The Indians under Black Kettle—men, women, and children—were horribly massacred and many of their bodies desecrated. The horrors of the Sand Creek Massacre set off renewed warfare with many of the Plains tribes. In 1865, the Arapaho and Lakota tribes sacked Julesburg, Colorado, cut the telegraph, destroyed the supply trains, and drove the cavalry into their forts on the South Platte River and in the Powder River country.

Notwithstanding all the military activity taken against them in the prewar decades of the 19th century, the eight years of the Grant administration (1868–1876) stand out as a time of remarkable turmoil and despair for Native Americans. The peoples of the Plains were confronted with the decline of the buffalo, the outbreak of epidemic diseases, devastating plagues of grasshoppers and interminable droughts, warfare with their neighbors—Native and white—and the intrusion of railroads, telegraphs, farmsteads, and towns. Moreover, the War Department continued to emphasize that the Indian bands would find peace only by staying on their reservations and adopting white ways. "Peace within, war without," was one of the many quips uttered by Gen. William T. Sherman with regard to the so-called Indian problem. During the Grant administration, the army would undertake more than 200 military operations against the Native tribes.[5]

The New Indian Fighters

The military heroes of the antebellum period were often professional career army officers who had used their prominence to secure a political career at the state or territorial level. Their service in the field usually could secure a place for them in the local legislature, or they could use their service to embarrass a political opponent who had not served. After the Civil War, with almost every adult male capable of claiming war service, no political party was forced to emphasize the military career of a candidate to win high office. The failure of George B. McClellan, the federal commanding general from 1861 to 1862 to beat a disliked, handicapped, and weakened incumbent (Lincoln) in 1864 presaged this development, and the inglorious presidency of Ulysses Grant left future military candidates in disfavor. Presidential candidate Rutherford B. Hayes had been wounded five times in the Civil War, yet he failed to carry the popular vote in 1876 and received the electoral victory only after an election committee, voting along strictly partisan lines, decided three disputed states in his favor. Not until the era of Teddy Roosevelt would martial prowess again be held in high esteem.

The Indian fighters of the last half of the 19th century were the "boy generals" of the Civil War. Chief among these were George Armstrong Custer, Nelson A. Miles, and George A. Crook. Army officers serving in the West in the 1860s and 1870s were usually Civil War veterans. Many, like Custer who was a brevet (temporary) major general during the war emergency, reverted after 1865 to their formal rank. This was not a demotion, but a return to the officer's actual rank. Custer was a lieutenant colonel, but many of his admirers, including his wife, continued to call him "General," the highest rank he had ever held. Under army regulations at the time, this was perfectly correct. Many high-ranking officers from the Civil War served against the Native tribes in grades from colonel down to lieutenant. This could cause severe strains among former officers serving together whose relative superiority was now somehow upended.

Officers, like those serving in the 21st century, usually brought their families to live with them at the forts and larger posts where there was only a minimal danger from attack. A limited number of noncommissioned officers (NCOs)—usually long-term sergeants—were permitted to bring their families on the posts. The wives of officers and those of enlisted men formed two mutually exclusive societies on the post. This was reinforced by a strict military caste system that applied to all persons related to those in the military. However, the presence of civilian women and their offspring created a number of more practical difficulties for army families, especially in terms of their homes, which often were limited to a set of rooms in simple frame buildings similar to the barracks in which the soldiers lived. Some women attempted to set up schools for the young children taught by the educated wives and mothers, but anything other than a rudimentary schooling had to be sought elsewhere, usually in the East.

The cavalry and infantry companies that fought the Plains tribes numbered about seventy-five men. An infantry regiment had ten companies and a mounted unit had twelve troops of cavalry. Volunteer recruits after the Civil War were hard to find, and there was no draft at any time during the so-called Indian Wars. Many recruiters depended on enlisting unemployed immigrants from the crowded cities of the East to fulfill their quotas. Many ex-Confederate soldiers and officers served in the ranks, sometimes under assumed names. When posted to their regiment, recruits rarely changed establishments. Once assigned, their squads and companies quickly became their home and family. The men ate, slept, and fought together, and they were forced by circumstances to trust each other implicitly.

Prominent among the men who fought in the Indian Wars were the *buffalo soldiers* of the 9th and 10th Cavalry, and the 24th and 25th Infantry. These were black soldiers, many of whom had volunteered to remain in the service after the Civil War. Although they were commanded by white officers and had strict segregation practiced against them, they did have their own NCOs and were treated with respect as Indian fighters. Custer had been offered the command of the 9th Cavalry, but demurred because he considered blacks poor soldiers. Instead he accepted the 7th Cavalry, a unit noted for the number of alcoholic Irishmen in its ranks.

The Plains tribes had first been encountered by the Lewis and Clark Expedition as it crossed the Northern Plains during their exploration of the Louisiana Purchase (1803–1805). These nations included many interrelated tribes and discrete bands, some of which were bitter enemies. These included Arapaho, Ute, Pawnee, Crow, Nez Percé, Cheyenne, and Sioux. Many recognized bands were actually subdivisions of others. For instance, the Blackfoot generally were considered to be part of the Siouan language family, while others like the Cheyenne and Sioux formed political or defensive alliances. Other nations like the Cheyenne and Crow were traditional enemies. The Pawnee fought a forty-year war of attrition with the Teton Sioux that left the former tribe in abject poverty by 1870, and internal dissension split the once powerful Oto into two factions in the third quarter of the 19th century.

This photograph purports to show the departure of a war party of Plains Indians. (Library of Congress Prints and Photographs Division, Edward S. Curtis Collection, LC-USZ62-46959)

The most historically colorful of the Plains tribes were the Sioux (Lakota or Dakota), who gave their name to two U.S. states. Their several bands generally followed the migrating herds of buffalo, camping freely in Colorado, Wyoming, Nebraska, western Kansas, southern Montana, the Dakotas, and parts of Canada. The holy ground and cultural anchor of the Sioux was an area of Wyoming known as the Black Hills. When first contacted by Lewis and Clark, the Sioux were found to be so unfriendly as to be labeled hostile, yet they freely traded with French Europeans, the agents of the British Hudson's Bay Company, and the mixed-race Métis in the 18th century and early 19th centuries.

In 1849, the federal government purchased a trading establishment at the confluence of the North Platte and Laramie Rivers and made it into a military post. Rechristened Fort Laramie, the substantial structure was meant to protect and aid travelers along the newly developed Oregon Trail and to establish a central position from which to trade with the Indians. In 1851, a commission headed by David Mitchell, superintendent of Indian Affairs, extracted a commitment from the local tribes for the safe passage of wagons to Oregon. This was one of the earliest of many negotiations into which the tribes would enter only to find in less than a generation that the government had no intention of keeping its word. John Young Nelson, a white who lived on and off among the Sioux from 1845 to 1888, wrote:

The Indians saw their doom by the increased traffic through their country, and protested. A commission was sent out by the Government to negotiate, with a view to guaranteeing the safety of the caravans upon receiving an annual subsidy. This was fixed at some thousands of dollars, and it was agreed that it should be paid in goods, such as blankets, cloth, cotton stuff, powder, muskets, beads, kettles, and in fact whatever articles were required. These were sent to Fort Laramie, the general rendezvous, where the various tribes would come for their share of the tribute. Government agents were appointed, and everything was fixed to the satisfaction of both the contracting parties.[6]

The Civil War stemmed the flow of settlers moving through Indian country on the Oregon Trail. The only recognized and significant attempt to move through the Powder River country north of Laramie by another route during the war years was made by a group of men led by a trailblazer named John M. Bozeman. Attracted by gold strikes on the Salmon River in Montana, twenty-five-year-old Bozeman left a wife and three small daughters in Georgia in 1862 and went west with fifteen companions. His father, William, had left a wife and five children to chase gold in California in 1849. Neither father nor son ever returned home. Because the new trail through the Bighorn and Yellowstone country was outside the treaty area, the tribes drove the Bozeman party back.

At the end of the Civil War, in 1866, the federal government established three outposts on the Bozeman Trail to secure passage through the region. Beginning in June 1866, the Ogallala Sioux, under the leadership of Red Cloud and Crazy Horse, began to raid wagons and forts along the trail. Although the tribal leaders had initially allowed the trail to be cleared and used under treaty, the agreement had been broken by the whites. Consequently, war parties under the direction of Red Cloud began attacking isolated groups of woodcutters that left the protective confines of the fort to bring in lumber and firewood. Ultimately, these outrages produced their own brand of conflicts and victories.

On December 21, 1866, William J. Fetterman, "an impetuous officer who had contempt for the fighting qualities of the Indians," went out with eighty men to relieve a party of woodcutters ostensibly under attack by a small party of Sioux believed to be led by Crazy Horse. Fetterman decided to carry the fight to the Indians and rode out of sight of the fort in pursuit. The small party proved to be a decoy, and Fetterman and all his men were killed in an ambush.[7]

On August 2, 1867, Red Cloud attacked a party of fourteen woodcutters' wagons under the command of Capt. James W. Powell. Once alerted, Powell formed an enclosure of wagon boxes and prepared to repulse the attack of more than 100 mounted warriors. Native warriors had learned to attack whites in successive waves, the first to draw their fire and the second to close before the standard muzzleloader could be reloaded, yet on this day they attacked again and again, each time receiving undiminished fire from the wagon-box enclosure. The attackers were repulsed with great loss of life. It seems that Powell's men were armed with breech-loading Springfield rifles, which had been developed at the end of the Civil War. These could be loaded almost as quickly as they were fired, using a new 0.50 caliber self-contained brass cartridge.

Notwithstanding the new weapons, the attacks along the Bozeman Trail became so vehement that the government agreed to abandon the forts and remove from the region. The victorious warriors burned both Fort C. F. Smith and Fort Phil Kearny after they were abandoned. This was a great victory for Red Cloud, yet the government used the quiet after the crisis to call for a treaty negotiation at Fort Laramie in 1868. The Fort Laramie Treaty brought temporary peace to the Plains by closing the Bozeman Trail and promising that no new forts would be built. "We [the government] will protect you against all future inconvenience," promised the diplomats at the meeting. "We wish to set aside a part of your territory for your nation, where you may live forever, you and your children. . . . [And] so that your children may become as intelligent as the whites, we wish to send to you teachers who will instruct them." Among those who signed the treaty was Red Cloud. Congressional leaders ratified the document but insisted that the government was not perpetually bound by it. This attitude laid the groundwork for conflict in the 1870s.[8]

Gen. William T. Sherman—the man who burned Georgia on his march to the sea—was put in charge of the Indian problem in the American West after the Civil War. His strategy included a continued attack on the small number of villages not on reservations, the destruction of their "pony herds," and the unremitting pursuit of those bands deemed hostile by the government even during the winter months. Sherman envisioned the coordinated advance of several columns of troops (usually three) to converge on the Native encampments and prevent their escape. Yet Sherman did not take the field against the tribes, leaving the tactical command to younger, or more active, men, notably George Armstrong Custer of the Seventh Cavalry and Nelson Miles of the 6th Infantry. Considered a rash and impetuous glory hunter, the figure of Custer would dominate the late Indian Wars even though men like Miles would be more effective from a military standpoint. Other commanders took the field, but these two were among the very few who were not seemingly handicapped by senility or a sickbed.[9]

A Civil War hero—some say he saved the day for the Union during the cavalry battle at Gettysburg—Custer began fighting Indians at age twenty-six. He was a flashy and courageous fighter, who had been given the brevet rank of major general of volunteers during the war, but in the postwar years had reverted to his permanent rank of lieutenant colonel of the 7th Cavalry Regiment. In November 1868, Custer and the 7th were called on to retaliate for Indian raids throughout Kansas and Colorado by a group of warriors from the Fort Larned Reservation. At dawn Custer swept down through the snow-filled morning onto the village of Black Kettle on the Washita River. "Half-naked braves popped out of their tepees, sounding the war whoop. Grabbing their rifles, bows and arrows, they sprang behind frosted trees or bounded over the frozen banks and into the snow-filled gullies. Armstrong and Tom Custer picked them off with their revolvers as they weaved in and out of the trees and pounded around the lodges . . . shouting like buffalo hunters riding down game."[10] At battle's end, 103 warriors had been killed, and twenty soldiers, cut off in the fight, had been killed. Seventy-five lodges had been burned and fifty-three women and children captured. Black Kettle, who died early in the fight, had had little to do with the original depredations. The frontier newspapers acclaimed Custer and the Seventh Cavalry, and declared the result proper treatment for all Indians.[11]

In 1873, Custer began a rush to the Black Hills by confirming the discovery of gold there. The Sioux, under the religious leadership of Sitting Bull of the Teton band and the military leadership of Crazy Horse of the Ogallala band, resented the intrusion of white miners on their sacred ground and refused to sell the region to the government. On June 17, 1876, the well-mounted warriors under the overall command of Crazy Horse fought Gen. George A. Crook's command composed mostly of infantry to a standstill on the Rosebud River. Then at the Little Bighorn River on June 25, Custer's ten troops of cavalry, accompanied by a contingent of Crow Indian scouts, several civilians including newspaper reporters, and several male members of Custer's family (his brothers Tom and Boston, brother-in-law James Calhoun, and nephew Armstrong Reed) were met by unexpectedly over-whelming numbers of warriors. The attack stirred up a hornets' nest of Sioux, Cheyenne, and Arapaho who poured forth in defense of their own families. No white man knows what happened to Custer and his 215 men. The last trooper to see him alive was an Italian-American dispatch rider, Giovanni Martini. The rest of the Seventh Cavalry dug in on a ridge and fought off repeated attacks until evening, but they suffered heavy losses. The Custer "massacre" became one of the greatest defeats visited upon regular American troops by Native American forces in history. Gen. Phil Sheridan attributed the disaster to "a misapprehension of the situation and a superabundance of courage."[12]

Nonetheless, Lt. James H. Bradley felt that Custer wanted to "get there first and win all the laurels for himself and his regiment."[13] In fact, Custer had attacked within just hours of his planned rendezvous with columns under Crook and Alfred Terry, who were the first to reach the site of the battle from the north. Custer, who had just passed the minimum age to be president of the United States in 1876, may have been positioning himself for a run at the Executive Mansion in 1880. Certainly in the months before the Little Bighorn campaign, Custer had purposely embroiled himself in a public debate with President Grant concerning corruption in the Indian Department. He made headlines everywhere.

The year 1876 saw the end of a full century of American independence. Colorado, the Centennial State, was admitted to the Union. America had grown into a modern industrial giant, and many Americans believed that there was no reason to continue to coddle so-called savages in their midst. With the death of George Custer, the minds of the general public became completely closed to the plight of Native Americans. The alliances between the tribes dissolved as the individual bands tried to evade detection or made for the Medicine Line in Canada.

Nelson A. Miles now took the reins in the Indian Wars. In 1876, the Modocs of northern California and southern Oregon were forced to flee and fight for their lives at Tule Lake, and in 1877, the Nez Percé were removed from Oregon to reserva-tions in Idaho. The Nez Percé refugees made an attempt to flee to Canada but were stopped by the U.S. Cavalry just a few miles short of the Medicine Line. Crazy Horse and Sitting Bull escaped to Canada during the spring of 1877. By September, Crazy Horse was dead, killed by the bayonet of a guard at Fort Robinson, who was himself a Native American of a different tribe. Word of the warrior's death caused 2,000 additional Indians to flee to Canada.

Part of Miles's strategy was to keep the recalcitrant tribes from their traditional food source—the buffalo. The migrating herds flowed north in summer into the

Canadian plains and south in winter into the United States. For generations the Plains Indians depended on the annual buffalo hunt. Government policy encouraged the slaughter of the herds by white buffalo hunters so that the remnant bands, faced with starvation, would be forced onto the reservations where they were promised beef, corn, flour, and blankets. Miles also might have turned his Indian fighting glory into a political career, but he was more interested at the time in commanding the army and had not sufficiently paved his way with a campaign of public relations.[14]

In 1881, the great shaman Sitting Bull and 176 of his most loyal followers reentered the United States and surrendered at Fort Bufford on the Missouri River. The chief, who would appear as part of Buffalo Bill Cody's Wild West Show before his murder at the Standing Rock Agency in 1890, said at the surrender, "I wish it to be remembered that I was the last man of my people to surrender my rifle."[15] Yet the surrender of Sitting Bull did not close the last chapter of America's disgraceful fight to dispossess Native Americans of their birthright.

The Apache Wars

Since 1821, the Mexican government had followed an official policy of genocide regarding the Native bands of the great Southwest, and the Treaty of Guadalupe Hidalgo that ended the Mexican-American War and the Gadsden Purchase had thrown much of the Southwest and much of the Indian problem into American hands. Initial contacts with the Native tribes of the region were peaceful, but these soon became strained as Americans refused to recognize tribal rights, and miners and settlers arrived in the territories. In a series of despicable incidents, Americans pretending friendship to the Indians killed or poisoned them, setting off a series of wars with the tribes of the Southwest that lasted from 1850 until 1886.

The desert tribes, particularly the Comanche, Kiowa-Apache, and Apache, had defied the authority of both the Spanish and American governments and had managed to delay white settlement of much of Texas, Arizona, and New Mexico for more than 100 years. The Comanche were originally residents of the Yellowstone region of Wyoming and Colorado, where they split away from their Shoshone relatives after acquiring horses. The Kiowa were refugees from Teton Sioux aggression in the Black Hills.

Local leadership among the Apache was supplied through the family hierarchy, but tribal or band leaders rose to prominence through the force of their personality. Ably led in the second half of the 19th century by Mangas Coloradas, Cochise, Vitorio, Geronimo, and others, small marauding bands of Apaches attracted few friends, Native American or white. They were tireless and implacable enemies when pursuing a vendetta, however. When on the prod, they exhibited an uncanny slyness, a bottomless well of physical reserve, and a macabre and sometimes gruesome cruelty.

Up to the time of the Mexican-American War of 1846, the Apaches reveled in attacking Spanish settlements and less aggressive tribes such as the pueblo tribes or the Navajo. The pueblo tribes and Navajo Indians were no complacent people— "digger Indians," as some whites called them. The pueblo tribes had staged a concerted rebellion against the Spanish in 1680, destroying virtually every mission in

New Mexico and parts of Arizona and treating the padres to some particularly grue-some deaths, but their time had passed. Few remained recalcitrant into the 19th century and most had found life on federal reservations adequate if poor. From their long exposure to the Catholic missionaries of Spain, it is not surprising to find that many southwestern bands were exclusively Christian, while others followed their traditional religion in part or in whole. Many spoke fluent Spanish, which facilitated communication and relieved misunderstandings somewhat. Yet, the bands railed under poor government treatment from both Mexico and the United States, and small groups of warriors regularly left the agencies and raised terror throughout the region.

The Chiricahua Apache gained in reputation and status in a series of strikes and counterstrikes against the whites during eleven years of war with the Americans (1861–1872). The entire Southwest was considered to be under threat from the Mescalero Apaches from 1866 to 1886. The Mescalero raided on both the Mexican and Texan sides of the Rio Grande. In 1874, the war chief named Geronimo (Goyath-lay) was able to recruit a small band of Chiricahua Apache to raid across New Mexico and Arizona. He had a deep belief in the traditional Apache spirits and seemingly was entrusted by the other bands with avenging the many Apache deaths that had taken place over time. Geronimo acquired a recognition among his people as an intrepid and cunning fighter. He seemingly moved in and out of Mexico at will even though the American Army and the Mexican Army were constantly trying to intercept him. When Geronimo finally surrendered to General Nelson A. Miles in 1886, he was one of the best-known Native warriors in the country. He and his people were sent to Florida with almost 500 other Apache and their families. In 1892, the Apache were removed to Oklahoma, where Geronimo sustained his family by ranching, farming, and selling autographed photographs. He appeared at the St. Louis World's Fair and marched in Teddy Roosevelt's inauguration parade. The Apaches were released from confinement in Oklahoma by an act of Congress in 1913.

The Indian Peace Policy

On February 25, 1869, the *Boston Daily Advertiser* published a front-page article suggesting that the newly elected president Ulysses S. Grant was planning a radically different policy with regard to the Native American population. The article maintained that Grant wanted to place the Native tribes on reservations and root out the bands of speculators and thieves that inhabited the Indian Bureau. Grant was a fighting man, and there was no doubt that he would bring military force to bear on any Native band considered "hostile." To this effect the paper stated, "All Indians who are disposed to peace will find that the policy of the new Administration is a peace policy."[16] Grant's plan to confine, reform, and educate Native Americans to white ways seems a monstrosity when viewed in hindsight, but it was filled with good intentions meant to displace the genocidal war practices prosecuted against the tribes in the past. The term *Indian peace policy* was used both by the president in his speeches and by his backers in Congress. The plan is generally considered to have misfired.

Grant thought from the inception of his policy to appoint agents from among the pacifist religious denominations to administer it, and he chose a number of Quakers for the job. In command of these agents, Grant chose as the first Commissioner of Indian Affairs Ely S. Parker—an experienced Native American (Seneca) military officer and friend of the president who had studied at Rensselaer Polytechnic Institute and worked as an engineer until the Civil War. Grant also established a Board of Indian Commissioners composed largely of noted philanthropists and churchmen, including Henry Whipple, the Episcopal bishop of Minnesota; Thomas Wistar, a Quaker leader from Philadelphia, and George Stuart, a personal friend of the president's and also a Quaker from Philadelphia.

The Quakers brought good intentions to the Indian reservations volunteering to serve as agents and representatives of the government. Honest Quakers strove to assimilate the Native Americans under their care into white society while maintaining the identity of the individual, but they often were blind to the real problems that affected their charges. The record of their labors at the agencies was largely one of frustration and failure. "Well-meaning white friends" simply could not solve the complex issues that confronted the tribes, and the Indians found that they had lost control of their own fate as well.[17]

The selection of so many Quakers to serve as agents on the reservations caught the attention of the public and ultimately brought down a good deal of criticism on Grant. Yet by harkening back to colonial times, Grant's initial choices were applauded as an attempt to "Quakerize" the hostile tribes. Herein the word was used to mean a general pacification of the tribes rather than an attempt to convert Native Americans to the Quaker religious sect. The *New York Times* (May 1, 1869) expressed the hope that the Quakers would find a cheap and effective means of dealing with the so-called Indian problem. Benjamin Hallowell, secretary of the Baltimore area Society of Friends noted:

President Grant, in looking to the Friends for some assistance in the improvement of the Indians . . . was not led thereto by any belief in the superiority of theirs over other religious organizations . . . but that it was because of the entire record of the Society of Friends towards Indians, from the time of William Penn to the present day, was an unbroken one of kindness, justice, and brotherly friendship, which is traditionally known to the different tribes of Indians at the time. . . . [T]hese traditional facts will give the Society of Friends a prestige with the Indians, which, if properly used, might tend to restore that confidence in the National Government, which has been so sorrowfully impaired by the maladministration of Indian affairs.[18]

Quaker work in the antislavery movement and in race relations after the Civil War, as well as their traditional peaceful relationships with the tribes, provided a legacy for their work on the reservations. In assigning duties to the men and women at each agency, the Quakers followed their own religious concepts and set the tone for the daily regime. Quakers always had recognized the spiritual equality of the sexes, but they generally did not extend their ideas of gender equality beyond the religious

Two children of the Havasupai Apache sit outside a crude house made of stones and logs, at Supai village in Havasu Canyon, Arizona, in 1942. Some 200 Havasupai live in this remote area west of the South Rim of the Grand Canyon, the smallest Indian reservation in the country. (AP Photo)

realm. Instead, they adhered to the same social norms that recognized the rights of women to deal with female matters. This included the partition of tasks for the agents themselves into male and female occupational roles. The men worked as blacksmiths, farmers, and traders, while the women served as teachers, matrons, and housewives. At the agencies, Quaker women taught Native American girls the female skills of sewing, food preparation, and housekeeping. The Quaker men undertook to teach the Native American men and boys simple woodworking and metal forming trades as well as modern farming and husbandry techniques. It was understood by both male and female Quakers at the agencies that the traditional dominance of Native women in the organization of village agriculture had to be overturned. Native American men had to be convinced to give up their wide-ranging hunting forays for work in the shops and fields, while the females left the fields to work in the home.

No other facet of Quaker work illustrates so well that good intentions were not enough to solve the problems faced by whites and Native Americans on the reservations. Even honest agents, who did not abuse or cheat the Indians, failed to understand them fully or to appreciate their cultural traditions. They hoped to turn Indians into whites by assuming that the establishment of single-family farms among Christianized Natives would bring on full assimilation into the white world.

Even sincere Quakers believed in "too simple a solution" to the Indian problem, and failed to learn from their own failures and frustrations.[19]

Critics of the administration found fault in the obvious Quaker dominance of the Office of Indian Affairs and the Board of Indian Commissioners, but by the mid-1870s, the religious solution to the operation of the agencies had expanded to include a number of non-Quaker Protestant groups and the Roman Catholic Church. Ultimately, Quakers and other pacifist sects became associated with the annual religious conferences held at Lake Mohonk near New Paltz, New York. These were called in part to deal with the problems confronting the Protestant religious missions to the Native tribes in the American West. Initiated by Albert Smiley, a Quaker member of the Board of Indian Commissioners, the Mohonk meetings effectively superseded nearly all the functions of the Office of Indian Affairs into the early 20th century.

Notes

1. Daniel K. Richter, *Facing East from Indian Country: A Native History of Early America* (Cambridge, MA: Harvard University Press, 2001), 227.

2. Bernd C. Peyer, *The Tutor'd Mind: Indian Missionary-Writers in Antebellum America* (Amherst: University of Massachusetts Press, 1997).

3. Thomas Mitchell, *Indian Fighters Turned American Politicians: From Military Service to Public Office* (Westport, CT: Greenwood Press, 2003), 2.

4. Francis Marion Watkins as told to Ralph Leroy Milliken, "The Story of the Crow Emigrant Train of 1865," in a 1935 pamphlet reprinted by *The Livingston Chronicle,* January 1937, 12.

5. Charles A. Milner II, *With Good Intentions: Quaker Work Among the Pawnees, Otos, and Omahas in the 1870s* (Lincoln: University of Nebraska Press, 1982), 4.

6. John Young Nelson as told to Harington O'Reilly, *Fifty Years on the Trail: The Adventures of John Young Nelson* (Norman: University of Oklahoma Press, 1963), 104.

7. Alvin M. Josephy, Jr., *The Patriot Chiefs* (New York: Viking Press, 1962), 283.

8. Dorothy Denneen Volo and James M. Volo, *Family Life in Native America* (Westport, CT: Greenwood Press, 2007), 166–167.

9. D. A. Kinsley, *Favor the Bold: Custer, the Indian Fighter* (New York: Holt, Rinehart, & Winston, 1968), 205.

10. Kinsley, 88.

11. Kinsley, 88.

12. Kinsley, 232.

13. Kinsley, 203.

14. Mitchell, 207.

15. Alvin M. Josephy, "The Custer Myth," *Life* 71, no. 1 (July 2, 1971): 48.

16. Milner, 1–2.

17. Milner, xii.

18. Milner, 5.

19. Milner, 25.

Chapter 12

The Era of Small Wars

Patriotism means to stand by the country. It does not mean to stand by the president.
— Theodore Roosevelt

The half dozen rash spirits that ventured to disapprove of the war and cast doubt upon its righteousness . . . quickly shrank out of sight and offended no more in that way.
— Mark Twain, 1904

Resurgent Militarism

The rapid industrialization of the United States at the end of the 19th century catapulted the nation to international prominence, and the country responded by building a modern navy to protect its maritime commerce. In 1889, the U.S. Navy was the twelfth largest in the world; a decade later it was the third largest. The expansion of the U.S. Army during the same period was somewhat more problematic. With the repression of a few Native American tribes, seemingly their only domestic assignment, and with no external enemy on the horizon, calls from militarists to expand the ranks of the regular army fell on generally deaf ears in Washington.

The precipitating event of the Spanish-American War was the destruction of the U.S. battleship *Maine* in Havana Harbor. This event changed the military status quo, and the American public evidenced an almost wild and uncharacteristic enthusiasm for combat overseas. Congress seemingly understood the popularity of opening a war against Spain at this time and raised the army authorization from a mere 29,000 in 1897 to more than 260,000 enlisted men in just two years.

As the traditional opponents of large-standing armies and navies had feared for more than 100 years, the developing military and naval power of the United States led it to the use of force in pursuit of its foreign policy and in support of its economic and domestic goals. Unlike the Civil War or World War I with their massed battles and gruesome causalities, the wars with Spain and in China featured relatively small-scale operations against vastly inferior military forces. These were swift, decisive, and inexpensive battles that generated relatively few American casualties. Nonetheless, through the use of its newly acquired naval power, the United States effectively projected its foreign policy to the other side of the world for the first time.

Unlike earlier conflicts that had many vocal critics, among them the isolationists and intellectuals of the northeast like Henry David Thoreau, hardly a negative comment could be found regarding the deployment of American troops to foreign places at the end of the century. American global economic expansion, the formal closing of the western frontier in 1890, Social Darwinism, scientific racism, the Gospel of Wealth, the rise of the nation to great power status, as well as a new, more belligerent vision for American manhood seemingly pushed the entire people of the United States to undertake several imperialist ventures abroad.

A careful reading of the historic record suggests that warfare is acceptable to the majority of Americans when it is quick, decisive, cheap, and relatively bloodless. America's wars at the end of the 19th century seem to fill these requirements, and it is difficult to discuss the antiwar sentiment at the end of the 19th century because it was simply so rare. In this chapter, the debates surrounding the Spanish-American War and the Boxer Rebellion in China are considered.

Eloquent but Few

Among the rash spirits who spoke out against the growing public demand for war with Spain in 1897 were Speaker of the House Thomas Brackett Reed of Maine, a few senators (notably Sen. George F. Hoar of Massachusetts and Sen. A. O. Bacon of Georgia), and some members of the business community. None of these were able to engender enough support in the legislative branch to prevent the war with Spain.

Thomas "Czar" Reed, as he was known, was Speaker of the House three times from 1889–1891 and again from 1895–1899. He had arbitrarily used the Speaker's powers in the House to facilitate the orthodox Republican agenda in the face of strong opposition. A typical isolationist of the period, Reed was an advocate of high tariffs. He strongly opposed the war with Spain, the annexation of Hawaii, and the ongoing program of colonial expansion that had been in effect since the end of the Civil War. Reelected in 1898, he retired from Congress in 1899 and practiced law in New York City until his death in 1902.

Sen. George F. Hoar of Massachusetts was one of the most eloquent antiwar and anti-imperial speakers in the Senate. In a speech given in 1898 he noted,

> It will be a sad thing for the country, it will be a sad thing for mankind, if the people of the United States come to abandon their fundamental doctrine. We are giving it a hard strain in our dealing with the Negro at the South. We are giving it a hard strain in our dealing with the great problem of immigration. But it cannot stand if this country undertakes also to exercise dominion over conquered islands, over vassal States, over subject races; if in addition to the differences of race and

the differences of education we attempt to govern great masses of people, aliens in birth, of strange language, of different religions. If we do it, our spirit will not, I am afraid—God grant that I may be wrong—the American spirit will not enter into and possess them, but their spirit will enter into and possess us."[1]

Sen. A. O. Bacon of Georgia, a former Confederate soldier considered an proponent of racist views while in the Senate, was the current champion of constitutional separation of powers between the legislative and executive branches. As Foreign Relations Committee chair, Bacon could be a formidable foe especially when backed by a small clique of Democratic senators. During a secret legislative meeting held in the Capitol in May 1898 to discuss the occupation of the Philippines and the annexation of Hawaii, Bacon asked, "I desire to know under what constitutional power [can] . . . the President of the United States . . . seize the territory of a neutral nation if it becomes a military necessity—a neutral nation, not a nation with which we are at war." He was reelected three times and remained an antiwar constitutionalist in the Senate until his sudden death 1914.[2]

William Graham Sumner, ordained in the Episcopal Church and noted as a tutor and lecturer at Yale University, added an academic voice to the anti-imperialist protest. In 1899, he became the vice president of the National Anti-Imperialist League. The original Anti-Imperialist League had been founded in New England as a regional association. Many of the League's leaders were classical liberals and so-called Grover Cleveland Democrats who believed in free trade, a gold standard, and limited government. Prominent statesman and congress members joined the organization, and Sen. George S. Boutwell of Massachusetts served as the organization's national president from its inception in 1898 to his death in 1905. Lawyer and civil rights activist Moorfield Storey then assumed the presidency until the League dissolved in 1921. Storey is noted for the following comments regarding American colonialism. "When the white man governs himself that is self-government," he declared, "but when he governs himself, and also governs another man, that is more than self-government—that is despotism." Storey also noted, "Imperialists assume that with the destruction of self-government in the Philippines by American hands, all opposition here will cease. This is a grievous error. . . . we regret that the blood of the Filipinos is on American hands, we more deeply resent the betrayal of American institutions at home."[3]

In the war's aftermath, there was raised among American anti-imperialists considerable opposition to its consequences, just as Senator Hoar had predicted, specifically to the idea of retaining former Spanish territories as overseas American colonies. During the post–Civil War period, the United States had established a number of overseas bases, and the American public largely supported the continued possession of these and the former Spanish colonies. Nonetheless, a few prominent critics spoke out against growing American imperialism.

Those who were prominent as well as eloquent in this regard included William Jennings Bryan, who served during the war with Spain as colonel of the 3rd Nebraska Volunteer Regiment but saw no combat. Bryan, a perennial presidential candidate, ardent supporter of bimetallic currency reform and evangelical reformer, protested the retention of overseas colonies and felt certain that the American people would repudiate any administration that declared for annexation of the former Spanish possessions. Bryan was often considered the cornerstone of the Democratic Party, and his famous "Cross of Gold" speech had rocked the Democratic National Convention in 1896. At age thirty-six he was the youngest candidate ever to run for the presidency simultaneously receiving the nominations of the Democrat, Populist, and the Silver Republican Parties. Nevertheless, he lost two consecutive elections (1896 and 1900) to McKinley.

In the 1890s, Bryan became involved in the issues surrounding the Spanish-American War, but he was often criticized for the inconsistency of his actions during this time, which seemed choreographed to win him high office. With the advent of the controversy in Cuba, Bryan remained unusually uninvolved and continued to remain focused on agrarian and currency issues. As the political currents shifted in favor of a conflict with Spain, he began to ardently campaign for Cuban independence, arguing that America had an obligation to spread the virtues of democracy to such a nearby neighbor. Waving a small Cuban flag in one hand and a small American one in the other, he excited large crowds in favor of intervention.

After the war, Bryan became a staunch supporter of the Anti-Imperialist League and protested the annexation of the Philippines, declaring that his support of the war had been purely in the name of freedom. Colonialism contradicted the very values for which the war had been fought. Running for president again in 1900, he continued in the role of anti-imperialist, ironically finding himself (a long-time populist) in alliance with Andrew Carnegie and other anti-imperialist millionaires. Republicans mocked Bryan as indecisive and hypocritical, and he became increasingly irrelevant as a party leader. In 1913 he was appointed secretary of state under Woodrow Wilson, but he resigned in 1915 because he was rarely consulted by the president who seemingly made all the major foreign policy decisions for the administration alone.

Mark Twain (Samuel Clemens) was almost alone among American celebrities in expressing his antiwar sentiments. As with much of his work, Twain painted pictures with words for his readers, and in "The War Prayer" (ca. 1904), an extremely short narrative, he did not disappoint. Twain's work was then and remains now one of the most eloquent and thoughtful antiwar statements ever written. Yet his family believed the work would be regarded as an anti-American sacrilege, and they urged him not to publish it.

Written some time between 1904 and 1905, a manuscript copy was found among Clemens's papers after his death in 1910, but it was not published until 1923 when the battlefield realities of World War I had changed the warlike mood of the American people. In the selection reproduced below, Twain noted the euphoria with which the Spanish war was greeted, the lack of antiwar opposition to it, and the unspoken message of the militarist:

It was a time of great exulting and excitement. The country was up in arms, the war was on, in every breast burned the holy fire of patriotism; the drums were beating, the bands playing, the toy pistols popping, the bunched firecrackers hissing and sputtering; on every hand and far down the receding and fading spread of roofs and balconies a fluttering wilderness of flags flashed in the sun; daily the young volunteers marched down the wide avenue gay and fine in their new uniforms, the proud fathers and mothers and sisters and sweethearts cheering them with voices choked with happy emotion as they swung by; nightly the packed mass meetings listened, panting, to patriot oratory which stirred the deepest depths of their hearts, and which they interrupted at briefest intervals with cyclones of applause, the tears running down their cheeks the while; in the churches the pastors preached devotion to flag and country, and invoked the God of Battles. . . . It was indeed a glad and gracious time, and the half dozen rash spirits that ventured to disapprove of the war and cast doubt upon its righteousness straight away got such a stern and angry warning that for their personal safety's sake they quickly shrank out of sight and offended no more in that way. . . . Upon the listening spirit of God . . . fell also the unspoken part of the prayer. . . . [W]e also go forth from the sweet peace of our beloved firesides to smite the foe. O Lord our God, help us to tear their soldiers to bloody shreds with our shells; help us to cover their smiling fields with the pale forms of their patriot dead; help us to drown the thunder of the guns with shrieks of their wounded, writhing in pain; help us to lay waste their humble homes with hurricanes of fire; help us to wring the hearts of their unoffending widows with unavailing grief; help us to turn them out roofless with their little children to wander unfriended the wastes of their desolated land in rags and hunger and thirst.[4]

To relieve the doubts of the anti-imperialists concerning the war, Congress had passed the Teller Amendment in the months before the conflict with Spain commenced in 1898. Proposed by Sen. Henry Teller of Colorado and passed 42–35, the debate in the Senate featured some of imperialism's most articulate intellectual offerings. Senators Hoar and Bacon were among the nation's most outspoken anti-imperialists, while Sens. Albert Beveridge and Henry Cabot Lodge countered that annexation would allow the United States to enter the ranks of the world's great powers. Beveridge exclaimed:

The Philippines are ours forever . . . [a]nd just beyond the Philippines are China's [unlimited] markets. We will not retreat from either. We will not repudiate our duty in the archipelago. We will not abandon our opportunity in the Orient. We will not renounce our part in the mission of our race, trustee under God, of the civilization of the world. The Pacific is our ocean. . . . China is our natural customer. . . . The power that rules the Pacific . . . is the power that rules the world. And, with the Philippines, that power is and will forever be the American Republic. . . . Let men beware how they employ the term "self-government." It is a sacred term.[5]

Believing that military strength was a prerequisite to diplomatic power and commercial success, Senator Lodge also firmly believed that America deserved a prominent global role, and he argued for increased army and navy appropriations as well as a more engaged role in the arena of international diplomacy. Despite his always dapper appearance, Lodge was ill-tempered, sharp-tongued, and the equal of President Wilson or any of his supporters in terms of stubbornness in an argument. "We should never suffer Cuba to pass from the hands of Spain to any other European power," noted Lodge (September 1, 1900). He continued:

> We make no hypocritical pretense of being interested in the Philippines solely on account of others. While we regard the welfare of these people as a sacred trust, we regard the welfare of the American people first. We see our duty to ourselves as well as to others. We believe in trade expansion. By every legitimate means within the province of government and constitution we mean to stimulate the expansion of our trade and open new markets.[6]

The Teller legislation stated that Cuba would not be annexed and should be free and independent. Yet the ultimate approval of the Teller Amendment had less to do with senatorial rhetoric than with McKinley's grant to Louisiana's Democratic senators of control over the state's federal patronage in exchange for their votes. Nonetheless, in 1901, Secretary of War Elihu Root drafted a set of articles to serve as guidelines for future Cuban-American relations. The so-called Platt Amendment (named for Sen. Orville Platt who proposed the legislation on Root's behalf) became part of the Cuban Constitution and provided that the Unites States retain the right to stabilize Cuba by military force if needed to ensure that American companies would not be damaged by any unforeseen changes on the ground. It also provided for the establishment of a permanent naval base at Guantanamo Bay ostensibly as a coaling and fueling station for the U.S. Navy.

The Platt Amendment virtually gutted the underlying principles of the Teller Amendment. The desires of the Cubans were ignored, and Cuban delegates to the peace conference were given the status of observers. The U.S. government allowed the Cubans to write an independent constitution, but this generally recognized and ensured U.S. economic interests and political control over the population. Often considered a wholly self-serving document, the Platt Amendment also addressed a number of important issues left unresolved in the Cuban constitution, including the establishment of standards for disease prevention, urban sanitation, and public financing. The Platt Amendment remained in force until 1934.

The political history of Cuba, and U.S. involvement therein after the close of the war, is important. In 1902, Tomás Estrada Palma became Cuba's first president. In contrast to the corruption of many Cuban leaders, Palma was noted for his honesty. However, in 1906, both Palma and his vice president resigned after an uprising led by Jose Miguel Gomez. U.S. troops, acting under the Platt Amendment, were sent to help control the island and remained for five years. Palma won reelection in 1905 while the country experienced an economic boom. U.S. troops again returned in 1917 to strengthen Mario García Menocal's presidency after his reelection in 1916. Several other presidents reigned until 1924 when Gen. Gerardo Machado y Morales was elected and turned the presidency into an open dictatorship. The United States again intervened in 1933, forcing Machado to resign and hoping to find a peaceful solution to the troubles in Cuba before protests could turn into civil war. In 1934, the administration of Franklin D. Roosevelt recognized Sergeant Fulgencio Batista y Zalvidar as the Cuban leader, but Batista named Carlos Mendieta as president. In 1940, the popular Batista was elected president in his own right. After leaving office in the mid-1940s, Batista returned to Cuba in 1951 and announced that he would once again run for the presidency. He feared that he would lose the election, however, and thus overthrew the government in 1952. Fidel Castro led a failed revolt against him in 1953. Castro was pardoned by Batista and went to Mexico. In Mexico, Castro met "Che" Ernest Guevara and began leading a new socialist-oriented group. His return to Cuba was followed shortly afterward by the 1958 elections, which were rigged. On January 1, 1959, Batista fled, taking a good portion of Cuba's treasury with him. Although tens of thousands of Cubanos fled the island to live in the United States, the Communist government set up by Castro continues to rule Cuba today.

Another of the unforeseen consequences of the Spanish-American War was that the United States became a colonial power—a small power when viewed against the influence of Britain, France, or Germany, but with enough far-flung possessions to force the government to look overseas to the establishment of coaling and watering stations and military outposts. The idea of naval bases located in the Caribbean, the Pacific, and the Far East predated the war and became even more attractive when the French engineer De Lesseps began construction of an interocean canal in Panama. Possession of the Philippines, Guam, Hawaii, Puerto Rico, and a base at Guantanamo Bay in Cuba provided these outposts.

In addition in 1899, John Hay, American secretary of state, had received assurances from the European powers of a so-called *open door* to equal commercial opportunities in China. The final years of the 19th century were also the final years of Manchu rule (Qing Dynasty) in China. The instability of the Chinese government provided a small, but significant test of the role of the United States as a world power. American participation in an alliance with the great powers of Europe in the Boxer Rebellion in China ultimately would put the United States at loggerheads with the raising sun of imperial Japan.

Overseas Ventures

By the mid-1880s, virtually all the erstwhile hostile Native American tribes of the West had been confined to specific reservations, and troops had been assigned to overawe those who remained restless and to prevent outbreaks. The commercial extermination of the buffalo left the Plains Indians totally dependent on government beef, and local Indian agents attempted to introduce new ways among those who had but recently been unfettered hunters, raiders, and warriors. The early reservation period of the 1880s was a time of sore trial for these western Indians. Soldiers would police the Indian country for decades to come, chasing isolated outlaws and breakaway bands, but never again would they meet the Native Americans in a major action.

The census of 1890 reported that the frontier was closed. The "unsettled" areas of the country had been so broken up by isolated bodies of settlement that a line for the frontier could no longer be traced on a map. The nation, initially isolated on a thin strip of land along the Atlantic coast, had attained its Manifest Destiny by stretching from sea to sea in little more than a single century. Many expansionists felt that the country should now become a transpacific power, a multiocean player among the other colonial empires in the world.

As early as 1851 this notion of an American role in the Pacific had been formalized and approved by Secretary of State Daniel Webster. The mid-19th-century period was noted for the series of treaties between the European powers and East Asian governments, particularly China and Japan. These treaties generally were forced on the Asians through simple demonstrations of naval power known as *gunboat diplomacy.*

Commodore Matthew Perry of the U.S. Navy had forced a commercial treaty on Japan in 1854 through the use of gunboat diplomacy. The previous year Perry had steamed unannounced to Edo Bay (later called Tokyo Bay) with four black-hulled ships mounting sixty-one guns and carrying more than 1,000 sailors. He did all that he could to impress the Japanese with American power and prominence warning them that if they did not treat with him on his return they might suffer the same fate as had Mexico in the recently concluded war. He returned in 1854 with an even larger fleet.

The so-called Convention of Kanagawa entered into by Japan and America in 1854 effectively ended Japan's 200-year-long policy of seclusion from western influence. The treaty opened the ports of Shimoda and Hadodate to American trading vessels, provided for a permanent American consulate in Japan, and ensured the safety of American mariners shipwrecked on Japanese shores. The treaty ports were relatively isolated and inaccessible, but their existence would ensure a refuge for shipwrecked sailors. The agreement was made between Perry, as representative of the United States, and Tokugawa Ieyoshi, the leading Shogun (de-facto ruler) of Japan. Representatives of other foreign powers soon followed Perry to Japan and secured treaties similar to that of the United States.

Shortly after the Perry treaty was concluded, the American government sent its first consul general, Townshend Harris, to reside at Shimoda. Harris was from New York, a capable diplomat and merchant familiar with East Asia. During his stay in Japan, Harris came to admire the Japanese people and appreciate their culture. Harris's experiences may have been the inspiration for Giocomo Puccini's opera *Madame Butterfly* (1904), which itself was based on the short story "Madame Butterfly" (1898) by John Luther Long.

The principal objective of the Harris mission was to secure a full commercial treaty with Japan. Harris sought to convince the Shogun that the limited intercourse established by the treaty of 1854 was no longer adequate or practical. The prospects of success were small. The appearance of the Americans had precipitated one of the great crises of Japanese history by threatening their highly valued tradition of cultural purity and isolation. From the moment Harris landed, the Japanese used every device of obstruction and deceit to discourage and defeat him, including the murder of one of his servants. The threat to Harris was very real. Seven diplomats of other foreign governments were killed in a single eighteen-month period at this time—some of them hacked to pieces by street gangs.

Nonetheless, in January 1858, the Shogun agreed to the principal terms of a new agreement. Despite bitter division of opinion among the ruling clans, the treaty was signed in July 1858. It provided for formal representation at the capitals of both powers, the opening of new treaty ports, civil and criminal extraterritoriality, freedom of foreigners to practice their own religions, and the prohibition of the opium trade. The Harris treaty became the fundamental document in Japan's foreign relations until 1894, and the European powers accepted it as a model. Ironically, as other foreign governments established treaty relations with Japan, American influence waned, and by 1861, when Harris left Japan, Britain had assumed the greatest influence over the Shogunate.

At the close of the Civil War, America's Far East naval squadron was the only foreign naval force in the Pacific without a local base of its own, and the navy was repeatedly beset with logistical problems. Due to the need to maintain coaling and watering stations for its whalers, traders, and steamships in the Pacific, in 1867, the United States took possession of Midway Island—America's first foreign outpost. It then acquired coaling rights at the island of Tutuila (with its excellent harbor at Pago Pago) and a protectorate over the remaining Samoan Islands in consort with Britain and Germany.

Also in 1867 Alaska was added to America's far-flung possessions by purchase from Russia for $7.2 million. Secretary of State William H. Seward was the major proponent of the purchase, and Alaska was referred to as "Seward's Icebox" for many years. Eight decades earlier, Boston skippers had opened a trade in seal furs, and later in gold, with the northwest coast of North America and the Aleutian Islands. Both were highly desirable items in China, and for a time gold bullion was the major U.S. item of export to China. Seward, if no one else in government, understood the value of Alaska as the first cog in the wheel of the fabulously lucrative China trade.

In Asia, continued problems concerning American sailors shipwrecked on the Pacific coasts of the Asian continent caused Rear Adm. John Rodgers to make a visit to Korea with a squadron of five ships in 1871 in an attempt to overawe a Korean government that continued to treat distressed American mariners as criminal interlopers. Nonetheless, it was not until 1882 that a treaty of commerce was signed with that nation. Meanwhile, the Samoan Islands had become a hotbed of international intrigue among Britain, Germany, and the United States, with each government keeping vessels on station to protect their national interests in the Pacific. Ultimately, the island group was divided by treaty among these naval powers into a series of colonial possessions. American Samoa was one of the southernmost of these island groups.

Throughout the 19th century, Hawaii had remained an independent island kingdom and a meeting place for Americans mariners working the Pacific whaling grounds. Along with the China traders who stopped there for water, fresh provisions, and cargoes of fragrant sandalwood, the whalers made Hawaii practically a suburb of any American mainland city. Some locations on the islands were virtual facsimiles of neighborhoods around Boston. For many years, the largest building in Honolulu was the large stone church built of coral block by American missionaries in the image of a New England–style meetinghouse.

In 1840, King Kauikeaouli began a twelve-year program, known as the Great Mahele (division), to dismantle the traditional system of tribal land tenure. He gave up his monarchial interests in all island lands, retaining ownership only in selected estates, and promulgated a constitution with provisions for a Hawaiian legislature. This was followed, later in the decade, by laws establishing an American-style cabinet, civil service, and judiciary. Under the 1852 constitution, all male citizens received the right to vote in elections for a legislative lower house. Missionaries and other foreigners regularly served in Hawaiian cabinets through the end of the monarchy in 1893.

American, British, and Japanese interests in the Pacific were generally uncomfortable with a growing German influence in the Hawaiian islands. German settlers had married into native families, and German sugar growers had been among the first to set up European settlements and plantations among the indigenous population. The discipline, leadership, and technical skills of the German immigrants played an important role in the growth of the Hawaiian sugar industry.

As far back as 1867, U.S. Adm. David Porter, Sr. had said, "Honolulu is bound to be the principal stopping place between China and California and a point of great importance to American commerce."[7] In 1872, an American treaty with the government of the islands set up safeguards that would prevent Hawaii from falling under foreign (that is, German) domination. In 1887, a clause was added to the treaty that allowed the United States to set up a fortified base at Pearl Harbor ostensibly as a defensive outpost for the west coast of California and the approaches to a possible canal planned at the Central American isthmus. Finally, in 1893, American businessmen aided by the U.S. Consul John L. Stevens and 150 marines from USS *Boston* overthrew the government of Queen Liliuokalani in a bloodless coupe. Sanford B. Dole, a major pineapple farmer and business leader in the American community, formed a short-lived independent republican government.[8]

Meanwhile, Britain, France, and Germany had divided the large island of New Guinea among themselves in the 1880s, and Germany had seized control of New Britain (Neu Pommern), New Ireland (Neu Mechlenberg), and several other small islands before the end of the century. The inhabitants of these islands lived in great isolation and saw little of their European nationals other than missionaries, who tried to "promote to the utmost the material and moral well-being and social progress of the inhabitants."[9] In July 1898, Congress annexed Hawaii partially due to its increased importance as a staging area for war with the Spanish Pacific fleet, partially to secure the rich fields of sugar cane and pineapple that had been developed, and partially to counter the growing German presence in the Pacific. American possession of Wake Island was effected in 1899, rounding out the U.S. expansion before the war with Spain.

The expansion of U.S. interests in the Pacific brought the nation into potential conflict with other European nations, particularly Germany, which had seized the port of Tsingtao in 1897 as a home port for its navy in the Pacific. In the 1914 edition of his book, *How Germany Makes War*, German Gen. Friedrich von Bernhardi noted that his nation could not continue to support a population of 65 million persons within its own national borders, and he found the situation intolerable. The following remarkable statement was written only a few months before the outbreak of World War I:

> There is no question, agriculture and industry of the home country cannot give permanently sufficient employment to such a steadily increasing mass of human beings. We therefore need to enlarge our colonial possessions so as to afford a home and work to our surplus population, unless we wish to run the risk of seeing again the strength and productive power of our rivals increased by German emigration as in former days. Partitioned as the surface of the globe is among nations at the present time, such territorial acquisitions we can only realize at the cost of other States or in conjunction with them; and such results are possible only if we succeed in securing our power in the center of Europe better than hitherto. With every move of our foreign policy today we have to face a European war against superior enemies. . . . On this depends not only the possibility of carrying into execution the political aims befitting the greatness and the wants of our country, but also the very existence of our people as a civilized nation.[10]

Naval Development

For the United States, the last twenty years of the 19th century were a time of transition from an inward-looking agrarian nation to an outward-looking industrial one. For the U.S. Navy, these decades were largely ones of reconstituting its former maritime greatness. During the first century of its existence (1775–1875), the U.S. Navy had been built of wood and largely powered by the wind. Americans were then the best wind-ship builders in the world. U.S. naval strategy had been one of coastal defense, commerce raiding, and single-ship encounters. Then came the dividing years of American maritime decline and British ascendancy in the mid-19th century. The wooden wind-ship designs that Americans were so expert in building had reached their practical engineering limits with the development of the clipper ships of the 1850s, and the failure of the U.S. Navy to adopt modern steam-driven, metal-hulled vessels had left the America fleet "as antiquated as Roman galleys" before the century had ended.[11] Although economical sailing coasters and fishing vessels continued in service, large American commercial sailing ships were condemned to hauling ice from the Arctic circle or fertilizer (guano) from the west coast of South America to eek out a living. The final decades of the century—the American Industrial Revolution—ultimately witnessed the birth of the so-called New Navy built of American iron and steel, powered by triple-expansion steam engines, and governed by a strategic deployment of oceanic fleets.

Of the world's major fleets, the British Royal Navy had made the transition to modern naval technologies with the least difficulty moving early and steadily from wind-ships to coal-fired steamers throughout the 19th century. The marine environment was thought to be one of the most corrosive for metal hulls, but the British had overcome many of the most restrictive disadvantages through the innovative use of copper and nickel alloys in combination with iron and steel. Although the Civil War era USN *Monitor* and CSN *Virginia* were the first steam-powered ironclads to fight (1862), HMS *Warrior* (launched 1860 and in commission in the Royal Navy from 1861–1883) is often considered the first modern steam-powered, metal-hulled warship. The other fleets of the world (French, German, Japanese, and Spanish) started making strides toward maritime modernity while America's attention was focused on post–Civil War reconstruction and transcontinental expansion.

The change from old to new was not easy for Americans. Commercial shipyards in the United States were heavily invested in woodworking technology, and the transition to metal shipbuilding required a heavy investment in new tools and machinery at a time when most spare capital was flowing into railroads, mills, and factories. On the government side, financing a modern fleet was less a problem than overcoming the prejudices of the navy itself. The wind-ship-oriented Old Navy officers greeted even competent naval engineering officers of the new American steam navy with bias, injustice, and indignity.

Nonetheless, from 1862 to 1885, Benjamin F. Isherwood, chief engineer of the Navy's Bureau of Steam Engineering, oversaw the change from just 27 to almost 600 steam warships and the adoption of a screw propeller design that would be used into the 20th century. After serving in the Mexican War as a young naval lieutenant, Isherwood had been assigned to the Washington Navy Yard, where he assisted in designing engines and carrying out experiments with steam as the sole source of power for propelling ships. Throughout the 1850s and into the Civil War, Isherwood compiled operational and performance data from steam engines in U.S. and foreign commercial vessels and warships. He used these empirical data to analyze the efficiency of engine types then in use. He designed and built engines rugged enough to withstand the shock of combat, as well as the poor treatment to be expected from ill-trained operators. Isherwood was the nation's most prolific antebellum technical writer. He published the results of his own original thermodynamic experiments in numerous pamphlets and wrote the two-volume *Engineering Precedents for Steam Machinery* (first published in 1859). In 1862, Isherwood displaced Chief Engineer Alban C. Stimers as the oversight officer for the building of the new generations of ironclad monitors.

Stimers was an Old Navy officer, but he willingly worked with John Ericsson, the Swedish-American inventor, to produce the first three generations of ironclad monitors for service in the Civil War. His career was marred by the scandal that enveloped the Casco-class monitors (generation 3.5, if you will) after they were found to be unseaworthy in operation. Placed in charge of an overly ambitious project to construct twenty light-draft monitors for use in shallow inland waters, Stimers unfortunately miscalculated the buoyancy needed for these vessels in fresh (actually brackish) rather than saltwater. Consequently all twenty of the ironclad vessels produced on Stimers's design found their decks awash in calm water and were recalled to be fitted with wooden ballast tanks. The error, unacceptable in the work of even a first-year marine engineering student, demonstrated the inherent difficulty of successfully shepherding complex technological endeavors through a navy department dedicated to a wooden-hull technology. To be fair to Stimers, none of the Casco-class monitors sank, but the foundering of an earlier monitor, *Weehawken,* in December 1863 with great loss of life (thirty-one officers and seamen) added drama to a situation that historians otherwise would have found laughable. After the Casco-class debacle, Stimers returned to the seagoing Navy serving until the end of the Civil War. He retired in 1865 to pursue a second career as a civil engineer.

Isherwood, as the first commanding officer of the Bureau of Steam Engineering (established 1862), introduced a core of naval engineering concepts that would be the basis of steam experimentation and naval shipbuilding around the world until the adoption of the World War I–era dreadnaught. Secretary of the Navy William H. Hunt (1881–1882) supported the efforts that Isherwood had placed in motion and set up the first Naval Advisory Board to consider changes in the navy in an unbiased and analytical way. The assassination of James A. Garfield in 1881 brought Chester A. Arthur to the presidency. Arthur made the development of the New Navy his personal goal—almost a hobby—and he had regular naval gun drills staged for him at the naval bases at Newport and Norfolk.

There is good evidence that the establishment of the U.S. Naval War College in 1885 at Newport, Rhode Island, served as the chief support for New Navy ideas in America. Rear Adm. Stephen B. Luce conceived the Naval War College project and carried it through to completion with the support of President Arthur. He did so in the face of internal departmental indifference and the hostility of many serving naval officers. Some antiwar civilians who feared the potential elitism of the officers who taught and studied at the school raised protests. These objections were similar to those raised against the establishment of the U.S. Military Academy at West Point and the U.S. Naval Academy at Annapolis at the beginning of the century.

The appointment of Capt. Alfred Thayer Mahan in 1885 as the first instructor in naval tactics and strategy at the Naval War College had an unprecedented affect on the future of naval history and operational doctrine. The work of the college, and of Mahan in particular, has been described as vitally important to a true understanding of America's naval needs in the 20th century. In 1887, Mahan met and befriended a young visiting lecturer at the college named Theodore Roosevelt, who would become president in the new century. The extent of Mahan's influence on Roosevelt's naval thinking is unknown, but Mahan's strategic objective for the New Navy was clearly the development of a fleet capable of destroying the enemy's main force in a single, decisive battle. Thereafter, a blockade against enemy merchant ships and the destruction of their remaining lighter ships would be made more feasible. The establishment of the War College is generally credited for improving officer personnel in the art of naval warfare, and for establishing a sound body of naval doctrine based on historical analysis and practical experimentation rather than the anecdotal impressions of sea officers.[12]

From 1885 to 1889, Secretary of the Navy William C. Whitney carried forward the progress of the New Navy, and his able hand produced the first group of modern American war vessels made of steel. These were the *Atlanta, Boston, Chicago,* and *Dolphin,* sometimes called the *A, B, C, Ds* because of their initials. Completed in 1887–1888, these vessels with their uniformly white-painted hulls were more commonly called the White Squadron. The "unarmored" cruisers of the White Squadron composed the core of the New Navy. The later "armored" cruisers (like the *Maine* and *Texas*) had a thick steel belt at the waterline, and the "protected" cruisers that fought at Manila Bay had an additional steel deck up to three inches thick. "Fast armored" cruisers (up to twenty-one knots) of the New York class, and protected battleships of the Iowa class mounting twelve- and thirteen-inch guns were authorized in 1892. Ships like these, serving not singly but in well-organized squadrons, were the backbone of the U.S. fleet during the war with Spain in 1898, and they presaged the development of the massive battleships of the 20th century known as *dreadnaughts*.

Spain had nothing to match battleships like the *Iowa, Indiana, Massachusetts*, or *Oregon*. The only advantage that Spain had in the Pacific was its dozen or so fast torpedo boats of which the Americans had none in theater. These were a larger steam-powered type than the diesel-powered patrol torpedo (PT) boats common to World War II operations. An innovation of the Italian/Illyrian naval designer Giovanni Luppis in 1860, steam-powered torpedo boats ranged from 380 to 750 tons each, and could take down a battleship with a well-placed shot. The United States had launched an all-steel torpedo boat prototype, the *Cushing*, in 1890 and deployed it to the Florida Keys in 1898 in preparation for the invasion of Cuba, but it saw no action.

Torpedo boats had seen rapid development among several naval powers after 1875 with the development of the Whitehead self-propelled torpedo first demonstrated in 1866. By 1890, Britain, Germany, France, and Japan had acquired comparable flotillas of torpedo boats numbered in the dozens of vessels projected for tactical use as coastal and seagoing defenses. In reaction to the deployment of torpedo boats, Britain had introduced in 1893 the torpedo boat destroyer, the direct antecedent of the more seaworthy destroyers of the 20th century that focused on suppressing the submarine activity that brought the United States into World War I.

With victories over Spain in the Pacific and the Caribbean, America's New Navy had firmly established itself. In 1907, President Theodore Roosevelt was able to review the sixteen great battleships of the U.S. Atlantic Fleet sailing in a long column of four squadrons out of Hampton Roads, Virginia. Every one of these giants had been commissioned since the end of the Spanish-American War. This was Roosevelt's Great White Fleet manned by 14,000 sailors and marines and commanded by Rear Adm. Robley "Fighting Bob" Evans. These vessels would circumnavigate the globe showing the American flag in far-flung foreign ports, steaming 43,000 miles in just fourteen months in one of the greatest naval achievements of the period before World War I.

The Holy Fire of Patriotism

The Spanish-American War started as a popular outpouring of sympathy among Americans for the Cuban people (Cubanos) who were struggling under the harsh governance of Spain just ninety miles from the shores of the United States. The poor Cuban revolutionaries had been fighting for their independence from Spanish colonial rule for decades. This support was fanned by the publication in the American popular press of astonishing tales of atrocities carried out by Spain. Men, women, and children fell prey to Spanish intransigence. Captives were mistreated and prisoners were often executed without trial. Spain had killed more than 200,000 Cuban insurrectionists by the beginning of 1898.

The emergence of "yellow journalism" at the end of the 19th century has come to characterize the news publications of the period. This characterization has been imprinted on the American historical psyche for more than a century, but to the extent that the actions of the Spanish government in Cuba were truly inhumane, "yellow journalism" is a somewhat pejorative phrase. Subjective reporting and a lack of restraint, with their potential to incite readers to outrage, were characteristic of the entire arena of news reporting, and the newspaper correspondents at the time made no pretense that their reporting was objective. Correspondents made little overt effort to misrepresent the facts to the reader, but the articles did not shrink from giving detailed accounts of controversial actions. Opinions, reactions, and conclusions were openly included in most so-called news stories to an extent unacceptable to modern concepts of unbiased journalism.

When informed that conditions in Cuba were not bad enough to warrant a war, newspaper mogul William Randolph Hearst was supposed to have told the artist Frederick Remington, "You furnish the pictures, and I'll furnish the war." In later years, Hearst strongly denied that he ever said such a thing, but the quote is still attributed to him and was paraphrased to great affect in Orson Well's movie *Citizen Kane* (1941) for which title character Hearst was supposedly the inspiration. Hearst was so angered by the film that he refused to have it mentioned in his papers, and he attempted to buy up and destroy all the prints and negatives of the work. Because of the interruption of World War II, *Citizen Kane* was little seen and virtually forgotten until its rerelease in postwar Europe, where it gained considerable acclaim, particularly from French film critics. A perennial late-night television favorite in the 1950s, the film has been rated in the 21st century by several agencies as the best ever created.

The flagship paper of the Hearst organization was the *San Francisco Examiner*, but at his peak, Hearst owned controlling interest in twenty-eight major newspapers and eighteen magazines, along with several radio stations and movie companies. His New York papers were particularly flamboyant. Inspired by the journalism of his competitor Joseph Pulitzer, Hearst turned the newspaper business into a venue for many social reforms, but it was lurid sensationalism that created a following among his readers. Hearst was twice elected to the U.S. House of Representatives, but he was defeated in 1906 in the race for governor of New York. Nonetheless, through his newspapers and magazines, he exercised enormous political influence through the 1940s.

Although the opening of a war with Spain is often attributed to the machinations of the press, American popular support for the Cubans in the 1890s was clearly sincere as illustrated by the fact that western, midwestern, and southern farmers—suffering from terrible economic misfortunes of their own and traditionally focused on internal domestic affairs—demanded U.S. interference abroad. The Populist Party was so moved as to call for the government to actively support the Cuban independence movement as early as 1890. Although religious pacifists declined their endorsement for the war, support for popular independence movements like that in Cuba was not inconsistent with the antiwar principles of many nonsectarian war resisters.

Altruism aside, American economic interests in Cuba required the protection that a successful U.S. military operation would afford them. U.S. companies had roughly $50 million invested in Cuban sugar, mining, and utilities. These were endangered by the continued Spanish operations against the Cuban rebels. Furthermore, U.S. trade with Cuba had averaged more than $100 million per year, and this had fallen by two-thirds because of the fighting. American foreign and immigration policies remain intimately concerned with Cuba and its people more than 100 years later.[13]

Operations in Cuba

As President Cleveland left office in 1896, his administration had attempted to negotiate with Spain, urging the empire to seek peace in Cuba on the basis of home rule. The Spanish politely refused. The incoming president, William McKinley (1896–1901) was originally against the war with Spain, but once decided on his course, he carefully guided the nation toward intervention in Cuba while trying to avoid having tensions in the Caribbean and Central America explode around him. Many foreign powers controlled islands in the region, including Britain, Denmark, France, and Holland. Intrusion by any one of them into the conflict on the side of Spain could have impaired U.S. war plans.

McKinley's diplomatic juggling act was even more impressive given the incredible popular pressure for war among the American electorate that was fanned by the intense anti-Spanish jingoism of Pulitzer's *New York World*, Hearst's *New York Journal*, and other newspapers. In February 1898, the *New York Journal* published a letter written by a Spanish government official that excoriated McKinley in the most unflattering terms and enraged many Americans. Six days later the battleship USS *Maine* exploded in Havana harbor, killing 274 U.S. sailors aboard including thirty-three black stokers in the boiler rooms. This disaster was widely blamed on Spanish agents, although at least four postwar investigations suggested that the disaster was actually due to an accidental explosion inside the coalbunkers of the vessel.

On March 17, 1898, Vermont Sen. Redfield Proctor delivered one of the most significant speeches of the Spanish-American War era. After an observation visit to Cuba, Proctor returned to the United States and told Congress about Cuba's bleak situation. "To me the strongest appeal is not the barbarity practiced by [the Spanish], nor the loss of the *Maine* . . . but the spectacle of a million and a half people . . . struggling for freedom and deliverance from the worst misgovernment of which I ever had knowledge."[14] Senator Proctor's words, unlike those of the

A highly overdramatized illustration of the destruction of the USS Maine. *(Library of Congress Prints and Photographs Division, LC-USZC4-1572)*

sensationalist press, were taken seriously by Congressional Republicans and by the U.S. business community with interests in Spanish America. On April 19, a joint resolution of the two houses of Congress gave the president the authority to intervene. On April 22, the North Atlantic Squadron of the U.S. Navy was ordered to blockade Cuba. Spain declared war two days later, and by April 25 the United States had declared war on Spain. "Remember the *Maine*, and to Hell with Spain," filled the newssheets.[15] Congress opened the war by authorizing the president to employ the entire army and navy of the United States against Spain, and more than $35 million was appropriated for the war.

On the day of the *Maine* disaster, the regular army of the United States numbered just under 29,000 officers and enlisted men spread across the North American continent. Many of these were posted to police the Native American reservations of the American West. Spain, on the other hand, had 80,000 soldiers in Cuba alone, and these had been seasoned to the climate and hardened to war by decades of suppressing and fighting Cuban insurrectionists. The professional soldiers in the U.S. War Department had been urging an expansion of the regular army for some time, and in April 1898, they settled on a figure of 104,000 men. These numbers were to be recruited to fill existing companies and to allow a return to the basic regimental structure of the 1860s. Congress, envisioning a return to the volunteer regiments of the Civil War, at first authorized an increase in the regulars to just 65,000 and relied on state troops and Nation Guard units to supply the desired balance.

National Guard proponents had been badgering their respective state governors for inclusion in the war since word of the destruction of the *Maine* had appeared in the press, and their political power was such that they could not be ignored. However, the regular army organization favored the incorporation of the entire National Guard contingent under regular army control rather than the piecemeal brigading of detachments from different states. Even entirely new units raised for the war at the state level would be accepted into the federal volunteer organization with their own state-appointed officers, but only if the unit volunteered as a body for federal incorporation. Under these rules, the 71st New York National Guard entered service as the 71st New York Volunteers, and the 1st Minnesota National Guard entered as the 4th Minnesota Volunteers. The enabling legislation also granted that volunteer units with special qualifications could be recruited from scratch from the nation at large in the same manner that the U.S. Colored Troops or the Veteran Volunteers of the Civil War had been organized. Such volunteer units were to have federally appointed officers, but they were not to exceed 3,000 men.

The majority of the troops recruited from the nation at large were formed into the 1st, 2nd, and 3rd Volunteer Cavalry regiments and brigaded under the command of former Confederate Civil War veteran Gen. "Fighting" Joe Wheeler. The activities of the latter two regiments were almost completely ignored by newspaper observers during the conflict, however, as they were lost in the publicity glare surrounding the activities of the 1st Volunteer Cavalry (known as the Rough Riders). The highlighting of this regiment was no accident. Col. Leonard Wood, who commanded this unit with Theodore Roosevelt as lieutenant colonel, had been the White House physician to President Grover Cleveland in 1895. Roosevelt, once police commissioner of New York City and presently assistant secretary of the Navy, was an enthusiastic proponent of the war with Spain who planned to run for the office of governor of New York after the war. The press could not ignore such high-profile officers.

Besides the volunteer cavalry, a brigade of 3,500 army engineers was also formed, and ten volunteer infantry regiments were established. Six of the infantry regiments were composed entirely of white troops, and the remaining four were of black soldiers. The black volunteers were generally, and incorrectly, considered the "immunes" because it was thought they were racially resistant to the extremes of the tropical climate and to attacks of yellow fever and malaria.[16] Booker T. Washington, eminent scientist and influential leader of the black community, wrote, "At least ten thousand loyal, brave, strong black men in the south . . . crave the opportunity to show their loyalty to the land and would gladly take this method of showing their gratitude for the lives laid down [during the Civil War] and the sacrifices made that the Negro might have his freedom and rights."[17]

All the volunteers—white, black, cavalry, engineers, and infantry—were intended for overseas service. This clearly violated a long-standing constitutional principle of keeping militia and volunteer forces inside the United States. To avoid this problem, each person in a volunteer unit was sworn into service as an individual. Yet when the 3rd Volunteer Infantry (recruited mostly in Georgia) was chosen to go to the yellow fever region of Cuba, Senator Bacon of Georgia, an outspoken anti-imperial constitutionalist, raised a cry of protest against exposing them to the disease. Bacon's protests, however, were not reflective of the mood of the Georgian troops who were anxious to go to war. These men were the children of the post–Civil War generation and to them war was largely a complete novelty, a heroic dream based on stories, novels, and newspaper reports of the wars their fathers and grandfathers had fought.[18]

It was at this time (1895) that author Stephen Crane published *The Red Badge of Courage*. This story set in the Civil War is considered one of the most influential works in American literature spanning the intergenerational gap between combat veterans and young men who are asked to go to war for the first time. As a boy living in Port Jervis, New York, Crane became fascinated with the stories told by the elderly Civil War veterans around the cannon and memorial in the local park, and he constantly read and reread issues of the *Century Magazine*, which were devoted to famous battles and military leaders from the Civil War. Because it can be viewed either way, authorities are divided over the idea that Crane's work might be one of antiwar sentiment, but they do agree that the novel is a prime example of literary realism applied to the war story genre.

It is clear that the U.S. government had no trouble securing enough manpower for the war effort in Cuba. McKinley had called for 100,000 volunteers, and 1 million men had responded. Both antiwar isolationism and constitutionalism seem to have been forgotten in the wave of sympathetic sentiment for the Cubans. Volunteers came from all walks of life and were so plentiful that the regular establishment of almost 59,000 enlisted men was quickly filled, although three-quarters of those applying were rejected for medical reasons or failure to meet the minimum physical standards. Commodore Dewey's quick naval victory at Manila Bay increased the manpower requirements somewhat unexpectedly, however, because troops would thereafter be needed to garrison the Philippines and deal with the Filipino insurrection. McKinley issued a second call for volunteers to address these needs, which was met with equal enthusiasm by the public. When the war ended, there were 11,108 officers, and 263,609 regular and volunteer enlisted men on the army rolls.

The relief and reinforcement of the insurgents in Cuba served as the primary grounds for war with Spain, and the capital city of Santiago de Cuba was the focus of the land combat. Nonetheless, there were other theaters and earlier operations during the brief conflict. The war in the Pacific was largely a naval affair beginning with the deployment of the U.S. Navy from Hong Kong in April 1898 and moving to the Philippines, where the first major operation of the war took place at Manila Bay in May 1898. There was also a landing on June 20 at the Pacific island of Guam in the Northern Marianna's 1,600 miles east of Manila and 3,800 miles west of Hawaii. Also in May, reconnaissance-in-force was made on Puerto Rico 400 miles northeast from Havana.

The initial preparations for the invasion of Cuba suffered from a lack of logistical organization and preparedness brought on by more than three decades of shrinking military appropriations since the end of the Civil War. No agency in the Department of War was responsible for mobilization planning, and the bureaus that *were* created lacked imagination and vigor of execution. Expenditures were limited to existing congressional appropriations, and no contracts could be finalized that exceeded these limits.

U.S. strategic planning was woefully inadequate. The War Department concentrated its land forces for the invasion of Cuba in the relatively few military camps in the department of the Gulf while they awaited transportation to the island. Some fifteen camps eventually were used to assemble and train troops, but the most important of these were at Chickamauga Park, Georgia, and Port Tampa, Florida. The War Department was properly faulted for failing to make sufficient preparations for so many troops in these locations, especially in the early weeks of the mobilization.

There was also a shortage of combat clothing and equipment because the Quartermaster's Department had stockpiled only a three-month supply for the original regular army of 29,000 men and an excess for 10,000 more troops. This was less than half of what was needed to fit out 100,000-plus soldiers just once. Finally, a severe shortage of modern Krag-Jorgensen rifles and smokeless ammunition forced most volunteers to be armed with single-shot Springfield rifles that left a cloud of white smoke that enabled the enemy to locate the shooter. The American artillery suffered from similar problems, and the artillery units that got into action were badly outmatched in terms of counterbattery fire from hidden Spanish guns that fired smokeless powder.

The newspapers that reported the war—including the *World, Journal, Sun*, and *Herald* of New York, the *Tribune* and *Times-Herald* of Chicago, the *Tribune* of Boston, and the *Chronicle* and *Examiner* of San Francisco—all had correspondents on the scene. The Associated Press (a wire service) sent reports by telegraph to those papers that had no correspondent present. In large part due to the extensive popular interest in the war, correspondents sought to make sensational headlines by grasping at each logistical problem that arose during these operations. While remaining uniformly hopeful of an American success, these reporters tended to put the worst face on every minor failure or logistical oversight.

Though the press had conveyed an impression of thorough ineptitude in the supply department, the procurement of equipment and clothing actually had gone fairly well when the massive nature of the mobilization was taken into account. The depot quartermaster at New York was able to have 100,000 blouses and trousers made in just two weeks, and the Krag-Jorgensens had been issued to all volunteers by August. Still the soldiers were expected to serve in the tropics in woolen flannel uniforms or in canvas duck that was not much cooler. These soldiers were issued a lighter weight and more appropriate uniform before the end of the war.

Transporting the troops to the camps proved a much greater problem because the camps were located in the Gulf Coast South where the railway transportation network was less well developed than elsewhere. The Quartermaster's Department failed to devise an efficient method of loading and unloading the railcars as they made their way to the departure point in Florida, and the camp in Tampa had only two single-track railway lines serving it for the movement of men, supplies, and equipment. Nonetheless, the greatest single problem remained moving the troops by water from Tampa Bay to Santiago Bay. This required an unprecedented coordination between the Army and Navy.

The grumbling began when the soldiers were visited with a nauseatingly continuous diet of canned boiled beef as they waited aboard transport ships for two weeks to be taken from Florida to Cuba. The delay was occasioned by the fear that Spanish naval cruisers or torpedo boats might be lurking in the Straits of Florida to pounce on the slow-moving steamers. Once in Cuba, the troops found that the rations set aside for consumption in the field had been placed in the deepest parts of the ships requiring that they be offloaded last. They often spoiled in the steamy temperatures in the holds. At other times, the canned meat ration, while safe to eat, was stringy, tasteless, and disagreeable in appearance.[19]

The secondary theater of the Spanish-American War, the one that would give the United States the most long-lasting difficulties, was in the Philippines. The initial operation of the American fleet against the Spanish in Manila Bay was quick and decisive, but the casualty figures for the postsurrender period between 1898 and 1902 (at which date Theodore Roosevelt simply declared hostilities in the Pacific at an end) were sobering. Two major cholera epidemics killed more than 100,000 civilians and soldiers, and dysentery killed U.S. troops at a rate 50 times that of the most disease-infected theater of World War II.

Moreover, the transfer of power from Spain to the United States led directly to a second round of combat with Filipino insurgents under Emilio Aquinaldo, who was bent on freeing the islands from any foreign control, including that of the United States. Heroic, but poorly armed and led, this rebellion (the so-called Filipino-American War) ultimately collapsed only to be replaced by a more virulent conflict with the Moro inhabitants of the southern islands based in Mindanao. From 1902 to 1916, these intensely Islamic people fought the American forces in a long and savage confrontation based largely on their continuance of their traditional tribal way of life that included polygamy, slaveholding, and piracy. This was the second major confrontation between America and Islam, the first being that with the Barbary States of North Africa almost a century earlier. The fourteen-year war against the Moro was one of the longest ever fought by U.S. forces against an indigenous people. Gen. John J. Pershing, then a captain serving in the Philippines (1913), noted that the Moro were a unique and ferociously independent people.

Combat during the Spanish-American War lasted a mere 113 days and consisted of little more than two naval battles (one at Santiago de Cuba and the other at Manila Bay in the Philippines), which proved disastrous for Spain, and a few small land encounters in Cuba prominent among them El Caney, San Juan Hill, and the siege of Santiago. Operations also took place on Guam in the Pacific and on Puerto Rico in the Caribbean.

The 71st New York Volunteers suffered under some of the harshest criticism from the press because they broke under fire and refused to continue forward at San Juan Hill under a withering fire to which they could not reply. This conduct was contrasted to the heroics of the Rough Riders on an adjacent hill (Kettle Hill, part of San Juan Ridge) and to the operations of the citizen soldiers of the VIII Army

Americans wounded in Cuba receiving first aid in the field. (Library of Congress Prints and Photographs Division, Farm Security Administration—Office of War Information Photograph Collection, LC-USW33-042486)

Corps on the far side of the world, who were sent to the Philippines to put down the Filipino insurrection.

After the successful attacks at San Juan Hill and El Caney, the American advance ground to a halt before the island capital. Spanish troops successfully defended Fort Canosa, allowing them to stabilize their lines and bar American entry to Santiago. The Americans and the Cuban insurrectionists began a bloody strangling siege of the city. During the nights, rebel Cuban troops—relegated to the inglorious role of drudges by the American commanders—dug successive series of trenches (actually raised parapets) in parallels toward the Spanish positions. Once completed, U.S. soldiers occupied these parapets and a new set of excavations went forward the next night. Both the American soldiers and the Cuban allied troops of Gen. Calixto Garcia, while suffering losses from Spanish fire and snipers, sustained far more casualties from heat exhaustion and mosquito-borne disease than from gunfire. The men were faced with inadequate hospital services for the wounded and the sick.

The position of the Spanish was hopeless, however. Hostilities were halted on August 12, 1898, with the signing in Washington of a Protocol of Peace between the United States and Spain. The Cubans participated only as observers. The U.S. Senate ratified the formal peace treaty that ended the war with Spain on February 6, 1899.

The war had been a two-ocean encounter, the first such attempted by the United States. Every supply problem faced during the Spanish-American conflict pointed out the need for an overhaul of the logistical organization of a nation just entering the international arena of military affairs. Yet naval operations in the Pacific had provided a relatively easy series of victories. The Spanish fleet under Adm. Patricio

Montojo y Parasón, while superior in firepower on paper (five cruisers and a dispatch vessel), was actually in poor condition. With the support vessels left a safe distance offshore, the American squadron advanced "in perfect and majestic order" as the Spaniards opened fire, but the battle ended in Spanish surrender after just seven hours. The catalog of destruction was extensive: more than 200 Spanish dead, and 500–700 wounded, while the Americans had only seven wounded and one dead from heat prostration in the boiler room of an uncommitted cutter. Four other firemen collapsed from the heat and were taken to sickbay during the engagement.[20]

A month later, and 1,600 miles away, Capt. Henry Glass opened the sealed orders that had reached him aboard USS *Charleston*. He was ordered to steam to the Northern Marianna's Islands and capture the Spanish base at Guam. Arriving on June 20, Glass fired his cannon at the island and was greeted by a clueless Spanish officer who came out to the cruiser in a launch to ask to borrow some gunpowder so that the ill-equipped garrison might return the American salute. Glass informed the Spaniard of the state of war between their countries and sent him under parole to inform his comrades that they were at war and should consider discussing the terms of surrender. The following day, the entire Spanish complement of fifty-four men surrendered, and the island was placed in U.S. hands. Guam would play a pivotal role in World War II.

The war with Spain served to cement the northern and southern American states against a common enemy for the first time since the Mexican War of 1846. An active press had swayed American public opinion against Spain by appealing to the territoriality and ethnocentrism of its readers. Total American fatalities (3,289

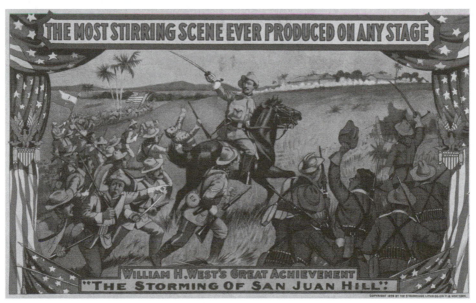

The attack on San Juan Hill as portrayed in a poster advertising one of the many theatrical recreations of the event. (Library of Congress Prints and Photographs Division, Minstrel Poster Collection, LC-USZC4-12429)

soldiers and sailors) during the war were generally from disease and far outnumbered those caused by Spanish attacks (432). These figures do not include losses to America's Cuban or Filipino allies. Spanish deaths have not been precisely calculated but 5,000 to 6,000 is a common estimate.

As wars go, the Spanish-American War had two virtues: It was short, about sixteen weeks, and it was decisive. Once war was declared, there was little waiting around and once commenced there was little doubt about who had won. American combat casualties were small when compared with those losses expected in a tropical setting. These factors kept domestic war-weariness at bay and provided a popular memory of the war that was clean and sharp. More important, the press showed northerners and southerners, blacks and whites fighting together against a common foe rather than against each other.

Among the 274 American dead on the *Maine* were 33 black sailors. Partly for this reason and partly because of their dedication to freedom for all men, the members of the black community in America strongly supported the Cuban rebels. Booker T. Washington argued that his race was uniquely suited to render service to the country in the peculiar and dangerous tropical climate of Cuba. The community of black soldiers gained a great deal of prestige through their performances in the Spanish-American War.[21]

The war also brought Theodore Roosevelt to national acclaim and ensured his inclusion as a vice presidential prospect to replace Garret A. Hobart who had died in 1899. As assistant secretary of the Navy in 1897, Roosevelt had arranged for the appointment of Commodore George Dewey to command of the Asiatic Squadron. It was Roosevelt who had recognized that, if war came, Spain would be vulnerable in places other than Cuba that might be of interest to the United States. Upon hearing of the *Maine* disaster, he used his authority as assistant secretary to dispatch orders to the U.S. Navy in every part of the world. Guns were shipped from the navy yard in Washington, D.C., to be fitted to American merchantmen bound for the war zones. Squadron commanders were put on high alert and told to fill their coal bunkers and gather their vessels. Roosevelt's war hero status with the Rough Riders in Cuba would launch his bid for high political office, first as governor of New York and then as vice president and president.

Significantly, the war marked America's entry into world affairs as a virtual equal among imperial powers. As noted earlier, the successful prosecution of U.S. naval operations in the Pacific against a major European power (Spain) in the far away Philippines removed the protective barrier of physical isolation from the American nation. With the victory, the Unites States gained a far-flung, if small, empire from Spain that now added Guam, Puerto Rico, the Philippines, and Cuba to its previous acquisitions like Hawaii, Alaska, Samoa, Wake, and Midway. The notion that America would continue on after the war as a nation with colonies of its own was hotly contested during the election of 1900, but so was the idea that it would not. The election of 1900 was a replay of the 1896 contest and a referendum on the war. The McKinley-Roosevelt ticket and the imperialists defeated a vocal Democratic slate once again headed by William Jennings Bryan who had supported the war but opposed the continued possession of colonies.

Foreign Repercussions

In 1900 a war broke out in South Africa between the pastoral farmers of the Orange Free State and the Transvaal (known collectively as Boers) and gold-mining interests supported by the military might of Great Britain. The conflict was brutal, and the British were widely condemned for conceiving of the idea of the concentration camp for confining Boer civilians. Although the common analogy to this circumstance was that of the global response to the concentration camps established by the Germans and Italians in World War II, another might be found in the virulent response of the antiwar opposition to the more recent detention of terrorist detainees by the United States at Guantanamo Bay, Cuba.

There was a good deal of pro-Boer sentiment in Congress in 1900 even though the South Africans openly supported racial segregation, white supremacy, and white domination of the African people. Nonetheless, the Boers were seen as fighting in a struggle for liberty, and their hit-and-run tactics were thought to be very much like those used by Americans in the Revolution. Senator Bacon and several other senators submitted a resolution of sympathy for the South African Republic (that is, the Boers) to Congress. Roosevelt, who was governor of New York when the Boer War began and president when it ended in May 1902, continued his interest in the conflict from beginning to end.

A Boer delegation arriving in America in 1900 toured the country from coast to coast like celebrities. The city council of New York and the common council of Boston both passed unanimous votes of sympathy for the Boers, and the governor of Illinois made a personal appeal for money on behalf of the Boer Relief Fund. Everywhere the South African delegates were given a warm and sympathetic reception, another indication of the predominant American mood with respect to wars of national liberation as the Victorian Age neared its end. Americans seemed especially supportive of conflicts that were waged by an apparent underdog against some major imperial power other than the United States.

It was somewhat hypocritical for Americans to side with the Boers who were fighting for their independence from Great Britain, while at the same time American soldiers in the Philippines continued to hunt down and kill insurgent Filipinos who were fighting for their independence from the United States. The situations in South Africa and the Philippines were embarrassingly similar, a circumstance pointed out by a young British newspaper correspondent (son of a prominent British politician) named Winston Churchill who was writing in confinement from the Boer-controlled prison in Pretoria. It was Churchill's reporting concerning the Boer War and his book detailing his dramatic escape from this prison that catapulted him at a young age into politics in Britain.

The Boxer Rebellion

In late 1899, a movement arose in Shandong and Shanxi provinces of China among the lower-class peasants that was anti-foreign, anti-Christian, and anti-imperial in nature. The Chinese name for the secret society (*I Ho Ch'uan*) behind the uprising translated in English as The Righteous and Harmonious Fists. From a literal translation, the peasant followers of this movement were widely known as boxers, and the crisis that they initiated is generally known as the Boxer Rebellion (1899–1901). It was a reactionary movement caused by growing foreign influence in trade, politics, religion, and technology in China. The Boxers called for the ousting of the foreign devils and the cleansing of all Christians from the Chinese population.

Americans had forged strong commercial relations with China throughout the 19th century. In the first half of the 19th century, American Clipper ships opened trade with China, the South Seas, and Japan; and in the second half-century the U.S. Merchant Marine entered its heyday under canvas only to be supplanted late in the century by British steam. Rare spices and unusual fragrances from the Far East could be found in most upscale U.S. markets, and many wealthy Americans had collections of Chinese porcelain, silks, lacquered ware, and various other Oriental items like rugs, draperies, and wallpaper sometimes arranged in special rooms "a' la Chinoise." It should be noted that the so-called China Trade was actually a misnomer involving an American commercial presence in a half dozen or more major trading centers other than China in the Far East. These included—besides mainland China and the island of Formosa—India, the East Indies (Spice Islands), the Siamese and Malay peninsulas, Java, Japan, Korea, and the Philippines.

The desire for spices, coffee, tea, authentic Chinese items, or other Asian products drove the American China Trade, and New England skippers lined up to get command of trading vessels destined for the western and southern Pacific, the Indian Ocean, or the South China Sea. The Chinese government was largely unconcerned about regulating the trade of its own people, but had become concerned when the first European vessels arrived in mainland ports in the 16th century. Before the Opium Wars with Britain in 1842 that opened four ports to outside trade, all foreign vessels whatsoever were prohibited from traveling further up the Zhujiang River toward the trading center at Canton than the Whampoa Island anchorage, and white traders were allowed inland only under harsh restrictions. The Treaty of Nanking that ended the Opium War effectively overthrew the original Chinese mercantilist system by forcing open the ports of Canton, Amoy, Foochow, Ningpo, and Shanghai to British trading.

When American merchants had first arrived in China in 1785, they were considered interlopers by the established European powers resident there. For almost six decades, the Americans interacted with China merely through their business transactions, without government-to-government communication—piggybacking off the agreements between China and other foreign traders. The American decision to acquiesce in this way was based on the twin assumptions of the futility of a direct and forceful confrontation with the Chinese government, and the profitability of letting the British flex their imperial muscles, while the Americans posed as friends and allies. Seeing that Britain easily could eliminate foreign competition in China after the 1842 agreement, the Americans—who had wisely stayed on the sidelines during the Opium War—needed to establish formal diplomatic relations and a commercial equality in China.

In 1844, President John Tyler sent Caleb Cushing to negotiate a commercial treaty with China that would give Americans the same privileges as Britain. The Sino-American Treaty of Wanghia (1844) achieved this goal and was a monumental agreement in that it laid the foundation for more extensive and better regulated American trade with China. The U.S. government had achieved through negotiations all the same privileges and immunities realized by the British through the use of force without poisoning the Sino-American diplomatic relationship.

In the last decade of the 19th century, European influence in China had been mounting. Giant trading establishments housing hundreds of white traders and known as *factories* had sprung up in Chinese port cities. Significantly, China and Russia had a railroad construction agreement in 1896, and China and Germany had a commercial treaty in 1898, which was followed closely by a similar pact with Japan. These agreements created a scramble for trade concessions from China among the foreign powers, and it was clear that what was best for the Chinese people was largely being ignored. The Americans were equally rapacious in this regard, but they did support reinvestment of some of the wealth that they accumulated from the China Trade, not only in stateside philanthropic ventures, but also in such Chinese enterprises as the Shanghai Steam Navigation Company and charitable projects like the Canton Hospital, which was comparable in scale to stateside public endowments.

The Boxer Rebellion was a bloody and brutal affair. Although the rebellion was finally suppressed, it spelled the end of Manchu rule and further entrenched foreign influence over the Chinese government. The uprising oversaw the murder of 20,000 Chinese Christians—mostly Roman Catholics—and more than 200 Christian missionaries. The diplomats of several nations, including Europeans, Americans, and the Japanese, were besieged in the capital city of Beijing (Peking) by thousands of armed rebels. The Boxers killed 230 non-Chinese residents of the city in June 1900. The Dowager Empress Tzu Hsi (who had precipitated the crisis by illegally seizing the throne) stood by in seeming helplessness as foreign diplomats and civilians, embassy guards and employees, and some Christian Chinese retreated to the foreign legation compound in the city, set up temporary fortifications, and withstood the assault of thousands of Boxers. The siege lasted for fifty-five days.

The Boxer Rebellion and the Chinese government's inability to deal with it effectively offered an opportunity for unfettered exploitation of China by the foreign powers. The foreign navies in the region, which included U.S. warships stationed in the Pacific, began building a presence in Chinese waters as early as April 1900, and before the legations were closed to relief that summer, 435 sailors from eight countries—among them sixty U.S. Marines—were dispatched to reinforce the embassies at their request. These men represented the Eight-Nation Alliance that included Austria, Britain, France, Germany, Italy, Japan, Russia, and the United States. Eventually more than 54,000 foreign troops would be committed to putting down the Boxers and relieving the legations. The largest contingents were from Japan (20,000), Russia (13,000), and Britain (12,000). The American force—the China Relief Expedition hesitantly dispatched by President McKinley from the Philippines—was composed of only 6,300 men. The international force won a major battle over the Boxer forces at Tianjin during July and soon thereafter relieved the foreigners in the compound.

American inclusion among the forces of the other world powers was significant as a symbol of U.S. maturity in the eyes of the diplomatic elite. Once scorned by Europeans as culturally backward, by the turn of the century, the United States had assumed an important role as an international cultural, political, and industrial power. The transformation was not instantaneous, and it was by no means clear that the 20th century would come to be called "the American Century." The United States had become a great power but was not yet part of the *great power system* that seemingly ruled international affairs. Significantly, a Japanese officer had commanded the international force—another symbolic event with similar qualifiers with respect to Japan. Both the United States and Japan thereafter became major players in the volatile politics of East Asia.[22]

Among the results of the Boxer Rebellion was the weakening of the dynasty and of the Chinese national defense. Imperial Chinese troops had shown that they were unable, or unwilling, to stand against the Boxers. Although the Boxers were virtually exterminated, the obvious weakness of the Qing government led to a new nationalist revolt led by a Christian Chinese man named Sun Yatsen who formed the Tung Meng Hui (a society dedicated to displacing the rule of the Manchu) thereby laying the foundations for a modern Chinese republic. In 1905, a boycott of American goods in China was used as a protest against the exclusion of all Chinese immigrants to the United States. This protest marked a growing national consciousness among the Chinese.

In the United States, anti-Chinese bigotry was at its height. The effects of repeated depressions, especially the Panic of 1873, had lingered, and the Chinese were the particular targets of prejudice because of their race, exotic clothing, and unfamiliar customs. Many unemployed American laborers were anti-immigrant nativists who considered the seemingly endless supply of foreign workers as a drag on wages. They were especially vicious in their attacks on the Chinese who they considered treacherous, slovenly, and ignorant. Tales were spread of their carrying terrible diseases, including a number of illnesses that existed only in the popular imagination.

In 1882, Chinese laborers had been specifically banned by the federal government from entering the country under the Chinese Exclusion Act. In 1885, a further act of Congress made the entrance of all Chinese laborers, even those under temporary contract to white employers, illegal. In 1902, the exclusion was made perpetual and extended the immigration prohibition to Chinese living in Hawaii and the Philippines. Subsequent to the Exclusion Act, many Chinese returned to their homeland, a greater proportion than any other major immigrant group. The official Chinese population in America, which had stood at 5 million in 1880, was only 37,000 in 1940.

The American combat units that took part in the defense and relief of the legations during the Boxer Rebellion gained a martial reputation from their participation in the brutal fighting. Many added a golden dragoon to their regimental coats of arms. Meanwhile, the expansion of Japanese influence in East Asia, coupled with

American annexation of the Philippines, Hawaii, and other Pacific islands at the end of the Spanish-American War, set the stage for Japanese-American confrontations in the 20th century.

Among the foreign powers participating in the suppression of the Boxers, Japan had gained the most in terms of regional prestige. Because of the leading role its military had played in suppressing the rebellion, it was seen for the first time as a major world power. Japanese attitudes toward other Asians supported concepts of racial and ethic inferiority for all non-Japanese. These prejudices, like the Aryan supremacy of the Nazi's, would play out in the 1930s and 1940s to the detriment of world peace.

Russia—second only to Japan in its active participation in quelling the rebellion—viewed the development of Japanese influence in the region with some discomfiture. Recognizing that conflict between them was inevitable, the Japanese offered the Russians a compromise: Japan would accept the Russian occupation of Manchuria in return for Russian acceptance of the Japanese claims to Korea. The Russians rejected the proposal confident that no Asian country could successfully challenge a major European military power. Just three years after the close of the Boxer Rebellion, Russia and Japan went to war over their common pretensions to Manchuria and Korea (Russo-Japanese War of 1904–1905). It was to end this war that Roosevelt had called together the Portsmouth Peace Conference in 1905. Roosevelt's diplomacy in ending this conflict brought the United States onto the world stage in 1905 as an international diplomatic player with the moral authority of proven success as the peacemaker.

The Russo-Japanese War

The Russo-Japanese War of 1904–1905, fought in Korea, Manchuria, and the Sea of Japan, may have been history's first modern war. With the largest land and sea battles ever fought between two industrial nations, the war is now sometimes known as World War Zero for the modern weapons employed, the huge armies and navies engaged, the tactics of entrenched positions defended with machine guns and long range artillery, and its effect on European colonialism and the international balance of power.

For several years, Czarist Russia had been penetrating southward into Manchuria with the Trans-Siberian Railroad—putting itself on a collision course with the newly expanding empire of Japan. The ultimate Russian objective was the occupation of Korea. Japan also sought to extend its hegemony over Korea and to get revenge for Russia's interference during the 1894–1895 Sino-Japanese War, which had resulted in Russian troops seizing Port Arthur and limiting the Japanese occupation of the Liaotung Peninsula. Between 1900 and 1903, Russian soldiers secretly infiltrated across the Yalu River into northern Korea fully prepared to fight the Japanese for control of the country's rich mineral wealth. Japan countered those moves with a movement of 25,000 troops to the independent Hermit Kingdom.

The threat of war between a European power and an Asian nation sent journalists from around the world rushing to the Far East during the first weeks of 1904 to report on the Russo-Japanese conflict. Among the contingent of war correspondents on the Korean Peninsula was Jack London of the Hearst newspapers. London had no experience as a reporter, but he had already received acclaim for his novel *The Call of the Wild* and other stories about the 1897 Klondike gold rush. His photographs of Korea—many considered unflattering to the Japanese way of making war—were the first pictures of the conflict to arrive in the United States. During his travels London became acquainted with socialism, which became his personal "holy grail." He cast his socialist beliefs into *The Iron Heel* (1908), imagining a world in which a ruling party rises to complete domination of the proletariat. In later years he ran unsuccessfully for mayor of Oakland, California, as the Socialist Party candidate, and he became known as the "Boy Socialist of Oakland" because of his passionate pacifist oratory.[23]

The war did not go well for the Russians. The Russian fleet experienced major defeats at the siege of Port Arthur, and the retreating Russian infantry formations disintegrated as fighting units. Nonetheless, the Japanese failed to destroy either completely. The Japanese themselves had suffered large casualties and were in no condition to pursue. Although defeated in battle, the Russians had not been decisively whipped, and the final victory would depend on a naval battle in the Tsushima Straits between Japan and Korea.

The Russian Baltic Squadron had sailed 18,000 miles—via the Cape of Good Hope because Britain refused it access through the Suez Canal—to reinforce its Far East Fleet near Vladivostok. The Japanese engaged the Russian vessels with torpedoes and heavy guns where they could not maneuver in the narrow Tsushima Straits on May 27–28, 1905. The Russian fleet was virtually annihilated, losing eight battleships, numerous smaller vessels, and more than 5,000 men, while the Japanese lost only three torpedo boats and 117 men. The victory left the Japanese Imperial Fleet with a much-enhanced reputation. After the Battle of Tsushima Straits, the Japanese Army occupied the entire Sakhalin Islands chain.

Despite winning most of the battles and sinking the Russian fleet in the Tsushima Strait, Japan could not decisively defeat the Russian Army in Manchuria. Continuation of the struggle threatened both Russia and Japan with financial ruin, destabilized the established balance of power in Asia and Europe, and risked drawing the other European powers into the conflict through a complicated network of alliances as later happened in World War I. As leader of a neutral power not aligned with either warring party, President Roosevelt seized the opportunity to become a peacemaker.

Careful to make certain that both parties understood that the United States was not imposing its own view on the situation, Roosevelt offered Portsmouth, New Hampshire, as a neutral host city for peace negotiations, respecting the Japanese and Russian insistence on direct, face-to-face diplomacy without third-party interference. With the naval base at Kittery, Maine, across the anchorage serving as a reminder of U.S. naval power, Roosevelt encouraged an open atmosphere for both formal and informal meetings between the parties. Roosevelt's brilliance was as a realistic diplomat who could suggest compromises through back-channel contacts, but he also ensured that the belligerents could communicate without the interference of any other government. Ultimately, the Russians and Japanese established a framework that balanced power between Russia and Japan in Asia until World War II. American pacifists greeted the Treaty of Portsmouth as "the glorious triumph of arbitration."[24]

Notes

1. George F. Hoar. "Speech before the Massachusetts Club, July 29, 1898," http://virtual.yosemite.cc.ca.us/smithaj/against_imperialism.htm (accessed February 2009).

2. Secret U.S. Senate Debate, "U.S. Seizure of Hawaii during the Spanish-American War," May 31, 1898, http://74.6.239.67/search/cache?ei=UTF-8&p=senator+augustus+bacon&y=Search&fr=yfp-t-120&u=www.hawaiiankingdom.info/C1769281028/E20061216080505/Media/Secret_Debate.ppt&w=senator+senators+augustus+bacon&d=Kisnfw-YSJLW&icp=1&.intl=us (accessed February 2009).

3. Moorfield Storey, "Platform of the Anti-Imperialist League, October, 1899," http://www.wwnorton.com/college/history/ralph/workbook/ralprs30a.htm (accessed February 2009).

4. Samuel Clemens (Mark Twain), "The War Prayer," http://www.lexrex.com/informed/otherdocuments/warprayer.htm (accessed February 2009).

5. Albert J. Beveridge, "In Support of an American Empire," *Congressional Record*, 56 Cong., I Sess., pp. 704–712: 704, http://teachingamericanhistory.org/library/index.asp?document=639 (accessed February 2009).

6. See James H. Blount, *American Occupation of the Philippines, 1898–1912* (New York: 4 Knickerbocker Press, 1913), 27. See also "Henry Cabot Lodge Quotes," http://www.brainyquote.com/quotes/quotes/h/henrycabot295166.html (accessed February 2009).

7. Stephen Howarth, *To Shining Sea: A History of the United States Navy, 1775–1991* (New York: Random House, 1991), 241.

8. Howarth, 241.

9. John Vader, *New Guinea: The Tide Is Stemmed* (New York: Ballantine Books, 1971), 34.

10. Friedrich von Bernhardi, *How Germany Makes War* (New York: George H. Doran Company, 1914), x.

11. Henry George, *Protection or Free Trade: An Examination of the Tariff Question with Especial Regard to the Interests of Labor* (New York: Henry George and Co., 1886), 200.

12. Carroll S. Alden and Allan Westcott, *The United States Navy* (New York: J. B. Lippincott Company, 1945), 286–287.

13. Joel Shrock, *The Gilded Age* (Westport, CT: Greenwood Press, 2004), 21–22.

14. Joseph E. Wisan, *The Cuban Crisis as Reflected in the New York Press, 1895–1898* (1934; rpt., New York: Octagon Books, 1965), 24.

15. Wisan, 24.

16. Russell F. Weigley, *History of the Unites States Army* (New York: Macmillan, 1967), 296–297.

17. Willard B. Gatewood, Jr., *Black Americans and the White Man's Burden, 1898–1903* (Urbana: University of Illinois Press, 1975), 29.

18. Weigley, 299.

19. Weigley, 300–301.

20. Howarth, 255–256.

21. Gatewood, 29.

22. George C. Herring, *From Colony to Superpower: U.S. Foreign Relations Since 1776* (New York: Oxford University Press, 2008), 336.

23. "Jack London: Russo-Japanese War Correspondent," *Military History*, June 12, 2006, http://www.historynet.com/jack-london-russo-japanese-war-correspondent.htm (accessed May 2009).

24. S. F. Sanger and D. Hays, *The Olive Branch of Peace and Good Will to Men: The Antiwar History of the Brethren and Mennonites, the People of the South during the Civil War, 1861–1865* (Elgin, IL: Brethren Publishing House, 1907), 190.

Chapter 13

The Great War: World War I

It is a fearful thing to lead this great peaceful people into war, but right is more precious than peace.

—Woodrow Wilson, 1917

I understand why war is not popular, but I also know this: the belief that peace is desirable is rarely enough to achieve it.

—Barack Obama, 2009

Culture of Death

The initial reaction in the United States to the outbreak of World War I was to let the European nations fight their own battles. Originating from the diplomatic maneuvers of the European states during the previous decade and the assassination of Archduke Franz Ferdinand of Austria and his wife Sophie in 1914, the war seemed to put into question an entire decade of diplomatically crafted success toward world peace. Nearly a century of noninvolvement in Europe's quarrels had disinclined most Americans to change their minds with respect to remote and bloody confrontations on the continent. The first months of fighting dispelled any illusion about a quick decisive war, or about America's ability to significantly change the tide of battle without committing troops. American entry into World War I in 1917 generated a great deal of war resistance in the United States.

With its honor affronted by the act of a Serbian nationalist assassin, Austria-Hungary gained German support for war and set out to punish tiny Serbia. Russia mobilized behind the Serbs to prevent an invasion, and the Germans responded with a declaration of war. A month of threats, counterthreats, and entangled alliances quickly pitted Britain, France, and Russia (the Allied Powers) against Germany and Austria-Hungary (the Central Powers) in the Great War, or the so-called War to End All Wars. Ultimately, dozens of countries were drawn into the conflict. Numerous other states joined the Allies, most notably Japan in August 1914, Italy in April 1915, and finally the United States in April 1917. The Ottoman Empire joined the

Officially neutral until April 1917, the United States supplied the fresh troops that were decisive in smashing the German's last big offensive on the Western Front in 1918. Here American infantrymen fire at a German position in France. (AP-Photo)

Central Powers in October 1914, followed a year later by Bulgaria. Warfare spread even to the colonial possessions of the belligerents in Africa and Asia. By the conclusion of the war, only Monaco, the Netherlands, the Scandinavian nations, Spain, and Switzerland remained officially neutral among the European countries.

A number of influential persons in the United States were initially anxious to enter the war on the side of Britain, an Allied Power. All European trade was vitally important to the U.S. economy, but the extent of trade with Germany when compared to that of Britain was insignificant. Britain purchased more than $900 million in U.S. goods annually leaving the nation's financial system more closely tied to the Allies than to the Central Powers. Eastern (U.S.) banking interests immediately extended more than $80 million in credit to the Allies. Ultimately, they would receive close to $10 million a day in U.S. financing. Oddly, tiny Finland would prove to be the only nation that would pay back its war debt to America.[1]

A long line of failed offensives early in the fighting made U.S. intervention on the side of the Allies highly unlikely, however. New technologies in artillery, machine guns, aircraft, and gas warfare had created a culture of death on the battlefield unknown since the religious wars of the 17th century. In the five months of fighting in 1914 alone, the combatants in Europe had incurred staggering losses. France counted 300,000 deaths among a total list of casualties (killed, wounded, and missing) of more than 900,000. Losses like these frightened and sobered many would-be interventionists. Massive casualties should have brought the belligerents to the peace table, but the vast alliance system had encouraged the leaders facing defeat to continue on in the expectation of support from the outside. The total French and German dead during the Verdun campaign (February to December 1916) was greater in less than one year than the combined losses of both the Federal and Confederate armies during four full years of civil war. The carnage was so horrible that the U.S. ambassador to Great Britain, Walter Hines Page, thanked God for placing America on the far side of the Atlantic Ocean away from the fighting.[2]

The majority of U.S. citizens favored ties with the British and thought that the Allies held the high moral ground, but public opinion was solidly against entering the war. A large minority of Americans was of German origin, and it was thought that they would support the Central Powers simply for this reason. Many Irish-Americans despised Britain, and British suppression of Irish Republicanism would not help to win their support. Moreover, there were large contingents of Russian Jews and Scandinavian immigrants in America that hated Czarist Russia for a large variety of reasons. Unlike World War II when they fought in tandem, Italy and Germany were on opposite sides in World War I, and in 1914, U.S. cities were filled with recent Italian immigrants aggressively staring down their neighbors from Germany.

Believing that most foreign-born and first-generation Americans remained more loyal to their countries of origin than to the United States, President Wilson urged all Americans to restrict their rhetoric concerning the war. "We have to be neutral since otherwise our mixed population would wage war on each other."[3] In fact, Wilson was mistaken. Most Americans regardless of their national origin—even those with family remaining in Europe—saw no direct stake in the struggle that was taking place there in 1914.

Maintaining the nation's neutrality proved difficult. Americans in favor of intervention insisted that the nation's defenses were inadequate and proposed that military training would toughen American youth and help Americanize foreign immigrants. They promoted their cause with parades, pamphlets, and cartoons filled with caricatures of Huns (Germans) in their characteristic spiked helmets. They used the new popular medium of film to produce anti-German propaganda movies. On the other hand, war resisters and pacifists denounced preparedness as "a scheme to fatten the pockets of big business" and to enrich armament manufacturers, financiers, and international bankers. They warned that increased military expenditures were unnecessary and simply a large step closer to entering the war. Many war resisters spoke out, questioning the stories of German war atrocities, passed out antiwar handbills professing that Christ was an absolute pacifist, or simply refused to purchase War Bonds. Others including teachers, minor public officials, and merchants, who had spoken against the War before 1917, were forced into a profound silence once the United States joined the Allies. The national will seemed split.[4]

The German industrial base had, by 1914, overtaken that of Britain. In the years running up to the war, a race to possess the strongest navy arose between Britain and Germany, each country building large numbers of battleships. This was intensified by the 1906 launch of HMS *Dreadnought*, a revolutionary vessel and first of its type whose size and power rendered all previous battleships obsolete. The warship was so remarkable that it lent its name to a whole category of powerful battleships—*dreadnoughts*—that would become the future focus of serious arms limitation talks. Between 1908 and 1913, the total arms spending by the Great Powers (Britain, Germany, France, Russia, Austria-Hungary, and Italy) increased by 50 percent. Political opponents of President Wilson, like Sen. Henry Cabot Lodge, insisted that the nation improve its defensive posture, but Wilson was loathed to increase American military preparedness at the outset of the war because of the likelihood that it would increase the pressure for intervention in Europe.

Following American victory in the Spanish-American War, Lodge had come to represent the imperialist faction in the Senate maintaining that the United States needed to have a stronger navy and be more actively involved in foreign affairs. He and another powerful senator, Albert J. Beveridge, pushed for the construction of a new American navy. Lodge was a staunch advocate of entering World War I on the side of the Allied Powers, attacking Wilson's perceived lack of military preparedness and accusing pacifists of undermining American patriotism.

Wilson was a internationalist who saw the war as an opportunity to establish not only U.S. leadership in world affairs through negotiated diplomacy, but also as a chance to found a new world order based on a system of collective security in which the United States would take a leading role. The latter task would require additional U.S. military resources. The National Defense Act of 1916 responded to the needs of both parties increasing the size of the regular armed forces and the National Guard and providing the funds for four additional dreadnaughts and eight more cruisers for the U.S. Navy.

Nonetheless, Wilson resisted entering the war. Even the sinking of the passenger liner *Lusitania* by German submarines in May 1915 with 138 Americans on board failed to bring about U.S. intervention. Some months later with mounting death tolls on the battlefields of Europe and the fighting stagnated into an extended period of indecisive trench warfare, this seemed a visionary policy. Consequently, Wilson was able to run for reelection in 1916 on the slogan, "He kept us out of war." His victory was a narrow one, however, suggesting perhaps that American sentiment regarding the war was shifting somewhat.

The Kaiser's declaration of unlimited submarine warfare in February 1917 seemed to confirm Germany's reputation for brutality and ruthlessness in wartime, and it caused the United States to break off diplomatic relations—usually considered the last stage before an open declaration of war. Meanwhile, Ambassador Page sent a dire message to Wilson from the embassy in London reporting that without American help the Allied front in the west of Europe was doomed to break under Central Power pressure. As ambassador to Britain, Page—a man accused in some quarters of questionable and self-interested connections to financier J. P. Morgan—may have been overzealous in defending British policies to Wilson, thereby helping to shape a pro-Allied slant in the administration. Page's warning in March and the concurrent sinking of three American flag vessels without warning and with considerable loss of life brought the United States into the war one month later.

A Second War in Mexico

Among the minor events that drove the decision to enter the war in Europe was the revelation of the so-called Zimmermann Telegram, a diplomatic communiqué between Germany and Mexico (leaked to the United States through British sources) that offered the return of Arizona, New Mexico, and Texas for a military alliance that would increase the already high tensions in the American Southwest and pin down American troops on the U.S.-Mexico border. U.S. troops had been operating along this border and up to 350 miles inside of Mexico since 1916 in an effort to capture Gen. Francisco "Pancho" Villa. On March 9, 1916, Villa had crossed the border in defiance of Mexican president Venustiano Carranza and attacked the American town of Columbus, New Mexico. Villa was driven back by U.S. troops with an untold number of Mexican casualties (possibly near 100) and seventeen Americans killed. In response to the raid, a punitive force of more than 6,000 U.S. regulars led by Gen. John J. "Black Jack" Pershing invaded Mexico to capture Villa with strict orders to otherwise respect the sovereignty of the Carranza government. Wilson's firm but measured response to Villa's attack helped get a military preparedness bill through Congress, but Pershing's failure to bring Villa to heel left U.S.-Mexico relations strained and American military prowess in question.

A Peaceful People Moved to War

Wilson moved slowly as the events in Mexico unfolded and tensions with the Carranza government calmed somewhat. Yet he was cognoscente of the need to respond to Germany's open and inhumane violation of America's rights as a neutral on the seas. The president finally decided in April that the time had come to intervene in the war in Europe. "It is a fearful thing to lead this great peaceful people into war," he stated in his address to Congress, "but right is more precious than peace."[5] As a result, between early autumn 1917 and late autumn 1918 (approximately sixteen months), the United States became actively involved in World War I calling up 4 million men for military service of whom nearly 1.5 million served on the battlefields of Europe.

In 1917, Americans were generally unprepared for war, and in 1918, they were equally unprepared for Wilson's concept of peace. For the president, the decision to go to war was taken more to gain a seat for the United States at the negotiating table, where he could help to direct the postwar peace, than to gain an immediate and unlikely victory on the battlefield. In this manner, Wilson hoped to bring about a lasting world peace founded on a form of global governance to be known as the League of Nations.[6] Americans understood that a good and lasting peace would require some kind of international cooperation and good will, but they did not realize that they would have to permanently abandon their protective blanket of isolation and take some responsibility for policing the new world order.[7]

The decision to enter the war under these circumstances split the American public over its legitimacy. Britain had brutally suppressed the Irish Easter Rebellion in

The world community joined together to topple the Hun. (Library of Congress Prints and Photographs Division, Caroline and Erwin Swann Collection of Caricature and Cartoon, LC-USZ62-84857)

the spring of 1916, and the execution of Irish Republican leaders inflamed many Americans who normally would have been sympathetic to the Allies. In 1917 there were potentially "millions of Americans—Socialists, Progressives, German-Americans and Irish-Americans—opposed [to] American participation in the war."[8] Moreover, there had been no attack or invasion of American territory around which to solidify public opinion, and in fact, the American deaths on *Lusitania* two years earlier had presented a more pressing case for entering a war 3,000 miles across the Atlantic than the fewer than the two dozen more recent deaths at sea. Finally, in June 1917, internal revolution was sweeping Russia from the war, making Allied success seem even less likely. Would America enter an unpopular war in Europe only to be numbered among the losers?

In response to these arguments for not intervening in Europe, Wilson established the Committee on Public Information, led by journalist George Creel, to craft and communicate America's message. Beyond shifting public opinion, the nation's first propaganda agency did its job too well. With its shrill anti-German message, it stirred up hatred of Germans and German culture in the United States. A number of state and local councils of defense—both those formally founded as government agencies and those that arose spontaneously among the hyperpatriotic—adopted similar methods and added their weight to the cultural inquisition by burning German language books including Bibles, forbidding the teaching of German in schools, and creating many long-lasting and negative ethnic stereotypes.[9]

The Bolshevik Revolution, rather than American intervention, may have been the transforming event of the Great War. The success of the Russian revolution had been unexpected. Many Americans initially cheered the overthrow of the repressive Czarist regime, viewing the new and more moderate Provisional Government of the Revolution as a fit partner in the new world order envisioned by President Wilson. Elihu Root, serving as Wilson's representative among the revolutionaries, promised almost a half billion dollars in aid to the provisional government and arranged for relief teams from the Young Men's Christian Association and the American Red Cross to encourage the Russian people to support the moderate anti-Czarists while continuing the war effort against the Central Powers. However, the United States did not have sufficient capabilities to influence Russian politics, and the Bolshevik Leninists overthrew the more moderate provisional government sparking a prolonged civil war among Leninists, Czarists, and Russian moderates. The followers of Vladimir Lenin then stunned the Allies by forming a separate peace with the Central Powers at Brest-Litovsk.

These developments essentially resolved the war on the Eastern Front in favor of the Germans leaving the Central Powers with a brief advantage over the Allies in the West. The United States never could quite make up its mind as to what to do with Bolshevik Russia. Wilson was just enough angered by the Bolsheviks to hope for their early collapse, but not nearly dedicated enough to actively attempt to achieve the aim of the non-Communists and anti-Communists—the active overthrow of Bolshevism.

With Russia removed from the Allied team, Germany gambled that it could win the war before increasing U.S. intervention would become a decisive factor. Buoyed by the promise of U.S. help (initially consisting of only a token force of U.S. doughboys under Black Jack Pershing) France and Britain had unfortunately launched offensives in the summer of 1917 that proved disastrous to the Allies, thereby giving the Central Powers an additional advantage. The Germans responded by mounting a concerted drive toward Paris in the hope of quickly knocking France from the war or forcing an advantageous mediation. This offensive failed miserably. At Château-Thierry and in other operations, the Americans had been filtered into the front lines and had shown that they could fight, and the Germans had suffered irreplaceable losses in men and materiel. The addition of 850,000 fresh U.S. troops made possible an effective counteroffensive in the summer of 1918 that drove the Germans back to the so-called Hindenburg Line, which was successfully breached a number of times during the Allied Hundred Days Offensive that September. With 3 million more American men in training, it was unlikely that any future end-the-war offensive would succeed for the Central Powers. It was, therefore, agreed by all parties that the guns should fall silent and that peace should return to Europe at the eleventh hour, of the eleventh day, of the eleventh month of the year (November 11, 1918).

Resistance during the Great War

World War I generated a great deal of war resistance. The twenty years since the war with Spain had changed the mood of America once again. Although it operated from a converted mansion overlooking the Hudson River in Nyack, New York, the

Fellowship of Reconciliation (FOR) had begun its opposition to the war in Europe in early 1915, well before U.S. intervention was contemplated. At the outbreak of the hostilities, Henry Hodgkin (an English Quaker) and Friedrich Siegmund-Schultze (a German Lutheran) began the organization after participating in a Christian pacifist conference held in southern Germany. FOR was rooted in an essentially Christian vision and was associated, in principal, with a wide range of smaller groups of absolute religious pacifists. Once America entered the war in 1917, FOR served as the principal community of support for conscientious objectors avoiding the draft, while it continued its program of promoting social justice and internationalism as stopgaps to future world conflicts. The organization had up to 12,000 members who "explicitly pledged neither to take part in war nor to sanction military preparations for it." FOR expressed a belief in a *militant nonviolence* similar to those precepts later found in the writings of Mahatma Gandhi or Martin Luther King, Jr.[10]

The Women's Peace Party (WPP) was also founded in 1915, and it was the first autonomous national women's political organization in the United States. The organization's European counterpart was the nonsectarian International Committee of Women for Permanent Peace. Conceived in late 1914 by settlement house advocates Jane Addams (chairperson) and Lillian Wald, suffrage leader Carrie Chapman Catt, labor advocate Crystal Eastman, peace advocates Fannie Fern Andrews and Fanny Garrison Villard, and other female social reformers, the WPP was the most radical women's political organization of its time, encouraging women to be active in their protests for peace. On January 10, 1915, more than 3,000 likeminded women attended the initial mass meeting of the WPP in the ballroom of the New Willard Hotel in Washington, D.C. The WPP demanded that women connect their responsibilities within the home to the free exercise of their political rights, as seen from its founding statement of purpose.

We women of the United States, assembled in behalf of World Peace, grateful for the security of our own country, but sorrowing for the misery of all involved in the present struggle among warring nations, do hereby band ourselves together to demand that war be abolished. As women, we are particularly charged with the future of childhood and with the care of the helpless and the unfortunate. We will no longer endure without protest that added burden of maimed and invalided men and poverty-stricken widows and orphans which was placed upon us. We demand that women be given a share in deciding between war and peace in all the courts of high debate—within the home, the school, the church, the industrial order and the state. So protesting and so demanding, we hereby form ourselves into a national organization to be called the Woman's Peace Party.[11]

Invited members of the WPP attended an international congress of women in The Hague in April 1915. Out of this meeting the Women's International League for Peace and Freedom (WILPF) was born with Addams as international president. Many of the organizers of The Hague Congress were prominent women in the International Suffrage Alliance, who saw the connection between their struggle for equal rights and the struggle for peace. The WILPF foremothers rejected the theory that war was inevitable, and they defied all obstacles to their plan to meet together in wartime. Attendance at a protest during wartime—even one demanding peace—was condemned in many circles in America as treasonable. Nonetheless, the WILPF assembled more than 1,000 women from warring and neutral nations to work out a plan to end World War I and lay the basis for a permanent peace.

Before the United States entered the war, American representatives of the WPP traveled to many of the critical capitals in Europe, including London, Berlin, Vienna, Budapest, Rome, Berne, and Paris to speak with members of the various governments. During these visits, they placed a great deal of significance on their own country's neutrality, which for them carried with it a moral obligation for America to mediate a peace. The fact that these women did not hold political or governmental offices, and had refused financing for their travels, even from other pacifist organizations, added to the effectiveness of their efforts as peace advocates. Their insistence on being unofficial envoys may have resulted in more forthright discussions with a wider range of officials than otherwise would have been expected.

Among the organizers of this effort was American suffragist Alice Paul, a Quaker who would stage the first political protest to picket the White House for any reason (January 1917). The picketers, known as "Silent Sentinels," held banners demanding the right for women to vote for many weeks, but were arrested and imprisoned on a trumped up charge of obstructing traffic (but actually for publicly embarrassing the president while America was fighting a war overseas). The incident emphasizes the interconnection of persons active in social reform and those dedicated to war resistance during this period. Paul and her associates were cruelly treated while confined and were forced to resort to an extended hunger strike to realize their freedom. Ironically, in January 1918, President Wilson announced that he favored women's suffrage as an urgently needed war measure. This announcement resulted in 1920 in the passage of the Nineteenth Amendment to the Bill of Rights (women's suffrage).

Former president Theodore Roosevelt, who favored entering the war on the side of the Allies, attacked the WPP in the press and spoke against the women as "hysterical pacifists" and called their proposals "both silly and base." As a recent Nobel Peace Prize Laureate (1907) and a popular political figure, Roosevelt's remarks were stinging, and they tended to brand the women's peace movement as being radical in the extreme. Addams was selected for particular criticism and described as easily duped and largely uninformed. The WPP was widely denounced as pro-German or anti-American. Nevertheless, by 1917 the WPP had grown to 40,000 members. After the United States entered the war, however, the WPP fragmented somewhat over the concept of protesting a war while Americans were actively fighting in the field. Some of its members dropped out to actively support the war or to take a more passive antiwar stance by rolling bandages, working in hospitals, or doing social work among the widows and orphans the war had created.[12]

Significant among the leaders of the WPP was Crystal Eastman, who attempted to turn the energies of this women's society into a dramatic and vigorous instrument of social protest. She shared the position of editor of *The Nation* and, with other pacifists, founded the American Union against Militarism. In 1917, Eastman joined her brother Max on the staff of the antiwar publication *The Liberator*. For two years, they fought against war and on behalf of world socialism. The Bolshevik Revolution in Russia was potentially the embodiment of the utopian dreams of many socialists, and they watched Central Europe with the high hope of the spread of worldwide socialism fueled by the famine and devastation wrought by the war. They hoped the events in Russia would make the working classes in the rest of Europe more conscious of their plight and cause them to join the socialist movement. Eastman later helped to found the American Civil Liberties Union (ACLU), possibly her most long-lasting and influential accomplishment.[13]

Emma Goldman viewed the Selective Service Act of 1917 as an exercise in militarist aggression, driven by capitalism. She declared in her newsletter *Mother Earth* her intent to resist conscription, and to oppose U.S. involvement in the war. With her long-time lover and partner Alexander Berkman, she organized the No Conscription League of New York. The group became a vanguard for antidraft activism, and chapters began to appear in other cities. When police began raiding the group's public events to find young men who had not registered for the draft, Goldman and the others turned their focus to spreading antiwar pamphlets and other written work. She played a pivotal role in the development of anarchist political philosophy in North America and Europe. In June 1917, Goldman and Berkman were arrested during a raid of their offices, which yielded what was termed anarchist propaganda by the authorities.[14]

Goldman, a self-proclaimed anarchist and free-thinking woman, had a long history of friction with the authorities. She and Berkman had planned to assassinate Henry Clay Frick in 1892 in revenge for the death of seven striking steelworkers who were killed by the Pinkerton detectives Frick hired as strikebreakers. Though Frick survived the attempt on his life, Berkman—who had carried out the attack alone—was sentenced to twenty-two years in prison. Goldman was imprisoned several times in the years that followed, for inciting riots and illegally distributing information about birth control.[15]

In 1901, Leon Czolgosz, an unemployed factory worker with a history of mental illness, shot President William McKinley twice during a public speaking event in Buffalo, New York. Czolgosz identified a speech by Goldman as the inspiration for his actions. Although she was arrested and detained, no evidence was found linking Goldman to the attack. Nonetheless, many newspapers held the anarchist movement responsible for the murder. The assassination proved a watershed event, and many American radicals abandoned anarchism for the less violent doctrine of socialism. During her life, Goldman was both lionized by her admirers and derided by her critics as an advocate of politically motivated murder and violent revolution. However, her writing and lectures spanned a wide variety of issues, including prison reform, atheism, freedom of speech, open marriage, free love, family planning, and homosexuality. Goldman died in 1940 almost forgotten. The radical feminist movement of the 1970s rediscovered her, and her writings informed a resurgent anarchist movement. Actress Maureen Stapleton won an Academy Award for her portrayal of Goldman in the 1981 film *Reds*.[16]

The American Friends Service Committee (AFSC) also began in response to the World War I draft. The group was founded in 1917 by American members of the Religious Society of Friends to assist civilians caught up in the draft. It was largely a Quaker oriented organization that hoped to provide alternative service for conscientious objectors (COs). One of the first tasks was to identify potential COs, find the army camps where they were located, and then visit them to provide spiritual guidance and moral support for their pacifist position.

The offices of the AFSC were located in Philadelphia, and the organization was closely associated through its Quaker connections with the Friends Committee on National Legislation (FCNL), a political lobbying organization with offices in Washington, D.C. After the end of the war in 1918, AFSC began working in Poland, Russia, and Serbia with orphans and with the victims of famine and disease, and in Austria and Germany, where they set up soup kitchens to feed hungry children.

In the early 21st century, AFSC continues to support programs related to peace, immigrant rights, restorative justice, civil rights, and other causes. Its affiliates protect and support American draft evaders and military war resisters (considered deserters in the United States) in both Australia and Canada. Many socially conservative groups have alleged without specific evidence that AFSC supports Communist activities, and they disagree with its assistance to illegal aliens wishing to stay in the United States.

Since the 1970s, criticism has also come from liberals within the Society of Friends, who charge that AFSC has drifted from its Quaker roots and has become indistinguishable from other political pressure groups. Quakers expressed concern with AFSC's abolition of their youth work camps during the 1960s and with what some saw as a decline of Quaker participation in and theological underpinning of the organization. The criticisms became most prominent after rank-and-file Quakers at the Friends General Conference in Richmond, Indiana, in the summer of 1979 called for a firmer religion-based orientation toward public issues. AFSC has been charged with an anti-Israel bias because of its long history of support for Palestinians.

Suppressing Dissent

In June 1917, Congress passed the Espionage Act directed against traditional forms of spying, interference with manufacturing, sabotage, and other items of concern common to wartime. However, included in the legislation were policies directly affecting the civil liberties of war-resisting Americans, including penalties for the willful attempt to cause insubordination, disloyalty, or mutiny among the U.S. armed forces, as well as willfully interfering with the draft or the recruitment or training of soldiers. Included in the legislation was a widely structured section that banned seditious utterances and antiwar printed matter. Acknowledging that many foreign-born Americans opposed the war, President Wilson noted that censorship of this sort was absolutely necessary for public safety, "The gravest threats against our national peace and safety have been uttered within our own borders. There are citizens of the United States, I blush to admit, born under other flags . . . who have poured the poison of disloyalty into the very arteries of our national life."[17]

The Espionage Act made it a crime to help enemies of the United States, but the Sedition Act that was amended to it in 1918 made it a crime to utter, print, write, or publish any disloyal, profane, scurrilous, or abusive language about the U.S. form of government. Most U.S. newspapers showed no antipathy toward the act and even seemed to welcome its speedy enactment. Antiwar protesters were arrested by the hundreds for having spoken out against the draft and the war under this law. Other U.S. citizens, including members of the Industrial Workers of the World (IWW), were also imprisoned for their antiwar dissent under the provisions of the Sedition Act. The IWW, an international union that promoted worker solidarity in the revolutionary struggle to overthrow the employing class, attracted hundreds of socialists, anarchists, and radical trade unionists from across the United States. IWW membership reached 100,000 in the 1920s. The act was repealed in 1920 largely because of the many apparent abuses of civil liberties that it fostered.

A number of people were charged with violation of the speech and press sections of the Espionage Act. Charles T. Schenck, for example, was convicted of violating the act by distributing leaflets that urged resistance to the draft. His case was ultimately brought before the Supreme Court of Chief Justice Oliver Wendell Holmes, which unanimously upheld the conviction on the grounds that his words were not protected by the free speech clause of the First Amendment. The court found that his words presented a "clear and present danger" of bringing about a conduct (in this case draft evasion) that Congress had a right to prevent. Meanwhile, Postmaster General Albert Burleson achieved a virtual censorship of antiwar material by declaring many items nonmailable under the Espionage Act. Ultimately, the Supreme Court upheld virtually all of Burleson's decisions declaring that certain newspapers and magazines were "intended to interfere with the success of United States military operations and tended to obstruct the recruitment and enlistment services of the United States military."[18] A series of arrests, interrogations, and deportations of supposed anarchists also took place under the legislation toward the end of the war. These events generally are lumped together by historians as the Palmer Raids because they were carried out under the auspices of Attorney General A. Mitchell Palmer.

When not decided unanimously, Justices Holmes and Louis D. Brandeis were the only dissenting voices in many of the war resistance cases that came before the Supreme Court during this period. Two of the cases in which they dissented stand out as examples of the application of the Espionage Act to war resisters. In *Pierce v. United States*, the defendants were convicted of having circulated a seditious pamphlet arguing that U.S. entry into the war was an attempt to protect the loans made by J. P. Morgan and other financiers to the allies. In *Abrams v. United States*, five Russian immigrant defendants living in New York City were convicted of printing and distributing pamphlets essentially urging support of the Bolshevik regime that had come to power in Russia. The pamphlets and leaflets, some written in Yiddish, were intended to "incite, provoke, and encourage resistance to the United States in said war," and designed to curtail the production of necessary war materiel. In both cases, the majority of the justices (7–2) upheld the convictions.[19]

In their written minority dissent in *Pierce*, Brandeis pointed out that these were largely cases of individuals expressing their opinion, and that it was incorrect for the government to criminalize such expression simply because it was "unfair in its portrayal of existing evils, mistaken in its assumptions, unsound in reasoning, or intemperate in language." Holmes, writing for the minority concerning *Abrams*, added that he felt that conviction under the Espionage Act required that the defendants actually intended to impede the war effort through their expressions.[20]

The best-known person prosecuted under the Espionage Act in this period was Eugene V. Debs, labor organizer and perennial candidate for president representing the Social Democratic Party. (Debs last ran for president in 1920 from prison.) Debs never polled more than 6 percent of the vote (in 1912), which remains the all-time high for a Socialist Party candidate in America. Immediately following the declaration of war in 1917, Debs had issued a party manifesto denouncing America's involvement in a European conflict, but this was ignored. In the following year, however, he was prosecuted for publicly praising draft resisters and those who supported them. The unanimous decision of the court upheld Debs's conviction. The court found that the "purpose of the speech . . . was to oppose not only war in general but this war; and that opposition was so expressed that its natural and intended effect would be to obstruct recruiting." Debs was sentenced to ten years in prison, but was pardoned in 1921 by President Warren G. Harding.[21]

Through prosecutions like these, the Wilson administration came to resemble that of Lincoln a half century earlier in that it sought to suppress harsh criticism of its war efforts in any way possible. Although there were no suspensions of habeas corpus or trials before military courts during Wilson's tenure in office, this was largely because Wilson rejected the enabling legislation proposed by a willing Congress. The Supreme Court gave little relief to antiwar defendants who were exercising their civil liberties in the areas of free speech and press. In one majority opinion, Justice John Clarke called the defendants "anarchists" and found their publications "an attempt to defeat the war plans of the government of the United States, by bringing upon the country the paralysis of a general strike, thereby arresting the production of all munitions and other things essential to the conduct of the war."[22]

Many governments have tolerated pacifist views and even accommodated pacifists' refusal to fight in wars, whereas others have outlawed pacifism and antiwar activity. During the period between World War I and World War II, pacifist literature or public antiwar advocacy was banned in many nations, including Italy under Mussolini, and Germany after the rise of Hitler. In these nations, pacifism was denounced as cowardice. Ironically, the U.S. Congress had passed the Sedition Act in 1918 largely because Woodrow Wilson—like Mussolini, Hitler, and other leaders and presidents before him—opposed dissent in time of war, a stance that he would have abhorred in times of peace.

Notes

1. George C. Herring, *From Colony to Superpower: U.S. Foreign Relations Since 1776* (New York: Oxford University Press, 2008), 404.

2. Herring, 398–399.

3. Herring, 399.

4. Herring, 405.

5. Herring, 410.

6. Herring, 410.

7. Henry Seidel Canby, *Prefaces to Peace: A Symposium* (New York: Columbia University Press, 1943), ix.

8. William H. Rehnquist, *All the Laws But One: Civil Liberties in Wartime* (New York: Vintage Books, 1998), 172.

9. Rehnquist, 172.

10. Charles DeBenedetti, *An American Ordeal: The Antiwar Movement of the Vietnam Era* (Syracuse, NY: Syracuse University Press, 1990), 21–22.

11. Statement issued by the Women's Peace Party, January 10, 1915, "The Women's Peace Party," http://www.spartacus.schoolnet.co.uk/USApeaceW.htm (accessed December 2008).

12. "How Did Women Activists Promote Peace in Their 1915 Tour of Warring European Capitals?" http://womhist.alexanderstreet.com/hague/intro.htm (accessed December 2008).

13. "Crystal Eastman," Spartacus International. http://www.spartacus.schoolnet.co.uk/USAWeastman.htm (accessed November 2009).

14. "Emma Goldman," American Experience (transcript). http://www.pbs.org/wgbh/amex/goldman/filmmore/pt.html (accessed November 2009).

15. "Emma Goldman."

16. "Emma Goldman."

17. Rehnquist, 173.

18. Rehnquist, 178.

19. Rehnquist, 180.

20. Rehnquist, 180.

21. Rehnquist, 180–181.

22. Rehnquist, 181–182.

Chapter 14

The Interwar Period (1918–1941)

Then another horse came out, a fiery red one. Its rider was given power to take peace from the earth and to make men slay each other. To him was given a huge sword.

—Revelation 6:4

No man can sit down and withhold his hands from the warfare against wrong and get peace from his acquiescence. The world must be made safe for democracy. Its peace must be planted upon the tested foundations of political liberty.

—Woodrow Wilson, 1917

Toward Global Peace

Peace activism peaked in the wake of World War I, and in its heyday, the "movement" had an estimated 12 million adherents and a combined income from donations of more than $1 million, a vast sum at the time. War resistance attracted leaders from among ministers, veterans, and women's rights and student groups. Student participation was significant for the first time during this period. During the interwar period, President Wilson's passion for the establishment of global peace through the League of Nations came to dominate American politics at the same time that Bolshevism, Fascism, and Nazism threatened Europe.

Among the most significant and long-lived of antiwar organizations formed in the postwar period was the War Resisters League (WRL) founded in 1923 as the American branch of War Resisters International. The purpose of the group was to move pacifist principles based on conscientious objection onto a wider and more comprehensive conceptual foundation of collective and public resistance to war rather than to continue to rely on the slender religious grounds formerly required of conscientious objectors (COs). A few democratic socialists and European believers in anarchism initially dominated the organization, as well as Americans who rejected the violent and manipulative strategies used by many politicians in the

United States. The WRL, the oldest purely secular antiwar organization in America, claimed no special dispensations from military service based on religion and held no meetings or mass conclaves. It worked through small groups of like-minded persons who organized local antiwar and anticonscription protests to publicize their views. Until World War II, the organization had a small staff housed in a single office in Manhattan and fewer than 1,200 members.[1]

In the early 21st century, the group has six offices in New England and local chapters in two dozen states. Central to its core philosophies are the nonresistance teachings of the Indian leader Mohandas Gandhi, civil rights leader Martin Luther King Jr., pacifist-feminist activist and theorist Barbara Deming, labor organizer Cesar Chavez, and peace agitators A. J. Muste and Dave Dellinger. The organization recognized that interwoven systems of domination and exploitation were at the roots of social inequality and global injustice, and that to remove all the causes of war, pacifists had to collaborate and stand in solidarity with oppressed people around the globe. By this means socialists and anticapitalists increasingly came to control the activities of the WRL.[2]

Another important antiwar group founded in the interwar period was the Catholic Worker Movement (CWM). The CWM had an effect on the antiwar movement much larger than its small membership should have warranted. Founded in 1933 at the height of the Great Depression by a French religious mystic, Peter Maurin, and an American journalist, Dorothy Day, the organization reached out to COs from its social service center on Manhattan's East Side. The foundations of the CWM were rooted in a belief in social justice, and it reached out to the public through the *Catholic Worker*, a penny press newssheet targeting the English-speaking Catholic population of major cities. The circulation of the paper quickly reached 150,000, but it plummeted drastically during the Spanish Civil War (1936) and World War II, when in the face of Fascist aggression, the editorial position of the paper remained consistently pacifist. Many CWM volunteers and staff members went to prison or public service camps for refusing to submit to the World War II draft.

Co-founder of the CWM, Peter Maurin entered the United States from Quebec looking for work during the Great Depression, and he prospered as a private teacher of the French language. Initially he founded houses of hospitality in the cities for those members of the community at large who had been wounded in war and responded to their needs through the direct practice of the "corporal and spiritual works of mercy." CWM farming communes were established in rural areas in the hope of obviating unemployment and forming "cells of good living" as a practical alternative to a moribund society. In city houses and farming communes regular meetings "for the clarification of thought" would be held.[3]

The fourteen so-called Works of Mercy, or Acts of Mercy, under which the CWM operated are actions and practices that the Roman Catholic Church considers expectations to be fulfilled by all its believers, and which are recognized as spiritual aids among members of other Christian denominations. They find their origin—as does much of the so-called Social Gospel—in the Sermon on the Mount as recorded in the Gospel of Matthew (5:1–12). The term Social Gospel came to be applied to a way of thinking that linked religious obligation to social progress. The Salvation Army was one of the first organizations to take up the work of the Social Gospel.

The traditional Catholic presentation of the Acts of Mercy is to divide them into two sets of seven. The *corporal works* of mercy are as follows:

- To feed the hungry
- To give drink to the thirsty
- To clothe the naked
- To give shelter to the homeless
- To visit the sick
- To ransom the captive
- To bury the dead

The *spiritual works* of mercy are:

- To instruct the ignorant
- To counsel the doubtful
- To admonish sinners
- To bear wrongs patiently
- To forgive offenses willingly
- To comfort the afflicted
- To pray for the living and the dead

It is notable that conscientious objection and war resistance are not specifically enumerated among these principles, but they can be inferred under the overall concept of "Love Thy Neighbor." Consequently, the Roman Catholic Church is not considered a traditional Peace Church. Nonetheless, the CWM pursued the idea of laypersons (not ordained or members of a religious order) applying basic Christianity to social problems, and it had thirty-one houses of hospitality operating by 1941. Both Day and Maurin traveled widely, visiting Catholic Worker communities and speaking at colleges and churches wherever they could find audiences. Day's uncompromising pacifism was hard listening for a nation angered by the excesses of pre–World War II totalitarianism, and the burgeoning war economy diminished much of the need for hospitality to the unemployed, and many Catholic Worker houses closed in the postwar boom.[4]

Dorothy Day was a city woman, a so-called bohemian (a term used to describe the untraditional lifestyles of marginalized and impoverished artists, writers, musicians, and actors in dense urban enclaves like New York) as well as a pioneer of the so-called engaged journalism of the Left. She was born in New York City, and she grew up there as well as in Oakland, California, and Chicago, Illinois, before returning as a young adult to Manhattan and a staff assignment at the *Daily Socialist Call*. She worked on the staff of *Liberation* and was acting editor with Crystal Eastman of *The Masses* when it was closed by order of Attorney General Mitchell Palmer during the First Red Scare after World War I. Palmer was a zealous opponent of anarchists (those who advocated the abolition of the state and capitalism in favor of a network of voluntary associations, workers' councils, and communes) and other radicals who advocated the violent overthrow of the U.S. government. Day was jailed for picketing the White House (along with American suffragist Alice Paul) during President Wilson's administration for the women's vote and was placed in solitary confinement for participating in a hunger strike at Occoquan Prison.[5]

Day's close friends and fellow workers were self-identified socialists, anarchists, and Communists. She was an intimate as well among the literary circles in New York that centered around playwright Eugene O'Neil, dramatist Kenneth Burke, and literary critic and social historian Malcolm Cowley. Day never ended her quest for peace and social justice. At age fifty-three, she was jailed for not taking shelter during the mandatory air raid drills during the "duck-and-cover" A-Bomb scares of the 1950s, and she was arrested for protesting in support of Cesar Chavez and the United Farm Workers in 1972 when she was seventy-five years old. Day thereby gave cohesiveness and longevity to the CWM that she co-founded and ensured her place in the annals of peace-making.[6]

The distinguishing marks of the CWM have remained rooted in the efficiencies of remaining small, decentralized, and personally responsible. The hallmark of the CWM was the "gentle personalism of traditional Christianity" (the personal response to those in need by direct encounter). In the 21st century, more than 185 Catholic Worker communities are active, mostly in the United State. They remain committed to nonviolence, prayer, and hospitality for the immigrant, homeless, exiled, hungry, and forsaken. Catholic Workers continue to protest injustice, war, racism, and violence of all forms, but they also are known for activity in support of labor unions, rural communes, and farmers cooperatives.[7]

The advent of the post–World War II nuclear age sharpened the awareness of many war resisters to the need for global disarmament and alternatives to war. Yet the widening gap between rich and poor in the United States and between the industrial and developing nations of the world spurred on these activists to call for the simultaneous establishment of a more just social order with a greater urgency. The two objectives of their opposition to the status quo—the eradication of both social injustice and the end of global warfare—have become so intertwined that, in many cases, they are indistinguishable.

The Battle for the League

Although isolation from European events had long been part of America's antiwar tradition, World War I (the Great War) was the conflict that firmly implanted the idea of *benign interventionism* into the national vocabulary. The emergence of a dual-natured interventionism—*conservative* and *progressive*—precipitated a more formal form of American isolationism in response. Those mainly Republican or upper-class men who came to be called *conservative interventionists* such a President William Howard Taft and Elihu Root promoted the ideas of international law and arbitration. They vaguely embraced notions of collective security and benign intervention that would be enforced by a world parliament of which the United

States would be a member. They also supported a buildup of U.S. military strength, a *community of power* rather than a *balance of power* arrangement among nations, and the use of collective military force to protect vital international interests. Former president Theodore Roosevelt—a major critic of the isolationists of the past and a leader among the conservative interventionists—favored vastly increased military readiness for the nation.

Progressive interventionists fervently insisted that world peace was possible only through the advancement of social reforms—both foreign and domestic—in the areas of labor, social justice, women's rights, and education. Progressive interventionists like Woodrow Wilson hoped to end war through the establishment of *peace without victory*. The mechanisms of this peace would be compulsory arbitration, economic sanctions, and multilateral disarmament. Progressive intervention espoused ideas of a social world order that most Americans, rightly or wrongly, considered antithetical to their traditional constitutional principles, a brake on national sovereignty, and an abridgment of their personal liberties.[8]

Henry Cabot Lodge, Massachusetts Republican senator, chairman of the Senate Committee on Foreign Relations, and senate majority leader (after 1918), proved a long-term adversary of President Wilson and ultimately his nemesis with respect to the approval of American involvement in the League of Nations. Conservative and conventional, Lodge was no isolationist. A friend and supporter of Theodore Roosevelt, Lodge believed that President Wilson represented a danger to traditional American values with his set of progressive notions that were anathema to conservatives. Wilson and Lodge shared a mutual and ill-concealed hatred of one another. Lodge used his powerful position as senate majority leader to oppose U.S. participation in the League of Nations, and Wilson used the bully pulpit of his presidency to try to accomplish U.S. involvement in the organization. Lodge noted, "The United States is the world's best hope, but if you fetter her in the interests and quarrels of other nations, if you tangle her in the intrigues of Europe, you will destroy her powerful good, and endanger her very existence."[9] Lodge lacked a following outside New England, but his power within the Senate was unquestioned. By proposing a series of amendments to Wilson's bill ratifying the peace treaty at the end of World War I, Lodge succeeded in preventing U.S. involvement in the League, while simultaneously encouraging popular opposition to Wilson and the Democrats.

Wilson was a true believer in the concept of collective security, and his articulation of the interventionist position—regardless of being conservative or progressive—was revolutionary at the time. It was mainly through his efforts that the League of Nations was established as part of the Treaty of Versailles and recognized by each of the lesser bilateral peace treaties of 1919. Wilson firmly believed that any compromise on the League would render the peace all but useless. Wilson, however, did recognize that his thinking was "a hundred years hence." Yet it was his own self-centered leadership style and a poorly chosen advisory group devoid of members from the opposition political party that most hampered his success at bringing the United States into the organization. Republican Party victories in the 1918 elections weakened him politically, and his health failed before the treaty with its League membership for the United States could be ratified.[10]

It is doubtful that a more robust Wilson—he could not have been more forceful—would have succeeded in having the treaty ratified by the U.S. Senate with League membership in place. The president simply had misread the temper of the American public with regard to the price it was willing to pay for the promise of perpetual peace. Ethnic groups in America in particular poured out their resentment. German Americans found the entire treaty punitive; Italian Americans thought the League system unfavorable to the just territorial claims of their homeland (especially Italian territorial interests in Ethiopia, Somaliland, and Egypt); and Irish Americans castigated it for failing to even consider the question of Irish independence from Britain. Many others pointed out that some of the treaty's articles could be used to suppress anticolonial or nationalist movements or to bind the United States to reactionary European powers. Finally, a great deal of conservative (all-American or America first) opposition was expressed over the concept that the United States would surrender some of its freedom of action and part of its sovereignty to an untested world governing body. Membership in the League, it was argued, might lead the United States into involvement in disputes that were not in its vital interest or even of its concern. It might also threaten control of domestic issues such as immigration policy, or take from Congress its constitutional prerogative to declare war. These were very real possibilities in a world in which collective security and global governance had never been tried outside the demonstrated tyranny of an imperial system like that of ancient Rome or Napoleonic France. In 1922, the ubiquitous Elihu Root noted that the war-making and peace-making processes discussed during the dispute over the League had taught Americans more about international relations in their eight years than during the preceding eighty.[11]

In 1943, amid the pressures of a second great war, Wendell Willkie, Republican candidate for president in 1940, looked back two decades and noted the following concerning Wilson's plans for peace at the end of the First World War:

It has become almost a historical truism that *that* was a war without victory. . . . Woodrow Wilson, our Commander in Chief, [had in 1917] stated our purpose in eloquent terms. We were fighting to make the world safe for democracy . . . by setting up a full-fledged international structure to be known as the League of Nations. That was a high purpose, surely. But when the time came to execute it in a peace treaty, a fatal flaw was discovered. We found that we and our allies had entangled themselves in secret treaties; and they were more intent upon carrying out those treaties, and upon pursuing traditional power diplomacy, than upon opening up the new vista that Mr. Wilson had sought to define. The net result was the abandonment of most of the purposes for which the war had supposedly been fought. Because those purposes were abandoned, *that* war was denounced by our generation as an enormous and futile slaughter. Millions had lost their lives. But no new idea, no new goal, rose from the ashes of their sacrifice. . . . Nothing of importance can be won in peace which has not already been won in war [but] the details must be worked out at the peace table and at the conferences succeeding the peace table—details which cannot be judiciously worked out under the pressure of war. . . . What we must win now [1943], during the war [World War II], are the principles [and] innovations [that] lay in the future, nourished only by the brains of a few great political thinkers.[12]

Idaho Sen. William E. Borah also opposed the entrance of the United States into the League, and he believed that America had risen to a position of respect and admiration in the world "by minding her own business." Entrance into the League would only drag America into foreign wars. "If the political independence of some nation in Europe is assailed . . . What will . . . the United States do . . . send troops without the consent of Congress? . . . but [under the] vast protection [of] unanimous consent."[13] In one of the oratorical masterpieces of the 20th century, Borah continued:

> I do not wish to speak disparagingly; but has not every division and dismemberment of every nation which has suffered dismemberment taken place by unanimous consent for the last three hundred years? Did not Prussia and Austria and Russia by unanimous consent divide Poland [three times: 1772, 1793, 1795]? Did not the United States and Great Britain and Japan and Italy and France divide China and give Shantung to Japan [1915]? Was that not a unanimous decision? Close the doors upon the diplomats of Europe, let them sit in secret, give them the material to trade on. And there will always be unanimous consent.[14]

Borah, known thereafter as the Great Opposer, had moved Lodge to tears in sympathy with his views. Vice President Thomas R. Marshall and members of the press in the Senate gallery passed notes to Borah on the Senate floor complimenting him on his triumph, and Indiana Sen. Albert J. Beveridge conceded that he could not recall "a speech that more perfectly satisfies my conception of the standard of taste and genuine eloquence. Nobody can answer it—nobody will try to answer it."[15]

While Borah helped to keep America out of the League of Nations, he was no stay-at-home conservative isolationist, but rather an active interventionist on the side of reestablishing the former world order. As early as 1931, Borah had declared that he was in favor of undoing many parts of the Versailles Treaty (1919). He was also in favor of revising the Treaty of Trianon (1920) that divided many of the lands from the old Austro-Hungarian Empire between Austria, Czechoslovakia, Romania, and Yugoslavia. This established the borders of a smaller post–World War I Hungary and deprived it of about two-thirds of its ethnic inhabitants. Officially, the treaty was intended to confirm the right of self-determination of nations with new nation-states replacing old multinational empires. Borah also believed that the question of the so-called Polish Corridor should be revisited. Ironically the last of these issues proved to be the tipping point into a second world war.

The Polish Corridor—a strip of land between the German territories of Pomerania and East Prussia awarded to Poland at the end of World War I—afforded that country access to the Baltic Sea. The Germans resented the transfer even though the region had once been Polish before the partition and was inhabited by an ethnic Polish majority. Poland refused to accede to Adolf Hitler's demands for extraterritorial highways across the corridor and for cession of the free port city of Danzig

(Gdansk) to Germany. Poland's rejection of these demands was supported by French and British guarantees against German aggression. Continued friction over control of the area was the immediate cause of the German invasion of Poland (September 1, 1939) that marked the beginning of World War II.

Upon hearing of Hitler's attack on Poland, Borah sighed: "Lord, if only I could have talked with Hitler, all this might have been avoided."[16] The senator's obvious diplomatic naiveté was the subject of partisan attacks in the press, and he was accused of favoring appeasement in much the same manner as British Prime Minister Neville Chamberlain's diplomatic sojourns had with respect to the Munich Accords in 1938. Borah's last major speech on October 2, 1939, was in support of the Neutrality Act embargo that required that all U.S. trade with belligerents be conducted on a cash-and-carry basis. The Neutrality program, which pre-dated the Lend-Lease policy of Franklin Roosevelt, was aimed at preventing U.S. intervention in the war. It required foreign buyers to send their own ships to U.S. ports to pick up war material, thereby lessening the threat of U.S. vessels being torpedoed. Borah died in 1940 before the Pearl Harbor attack drove the United States into World War II. One of Borah's many nicknames was "The Lion of Idaho" given to him because of the stands he had taken against the governor of his state and his own party. Another was that of "The Great Opposer" for his stance against the League. Unfortunately, yet another was that of "The Spearless Leader," which was given to him because of his antiwar and isolationist sentiments.

The German American Bund

The German American Bund, or *Amerikadeutscher Volksbund* (AV) was America's largest and best-known ethnic organization in the 1930s, and its members quite predictably resisted U.S. entry into World War II. The Bund wore military-style uniforms and touted swastikas, but actually had few ties to Nazi Germany. Their support among the larger German American community was minimal. Originally known as the Friends of New Germany (established in 1924) the organization remained small with a membership of between 5,000–10,000. Its ranks were mostly composed of German citizens living in America and German emigrants only recently arrived in the country. It busied itself with verbal attacks against Jews, Communists, and the Versailles Treaty and strove through its political wing to bring Nazi-style fascism (National Socialism) to the United States.

After Hitler's rise to power in 1933, additional German Americans joined to support the Nazi Party in Germany and attempt to influence American attitudes toward the war in Europe. Until 1935, the Friends of New Germany was openly supported by the Third Reich, although Nazi officials soon realized the organization was doing more harm than good in America. In December 1935, Rudolph Hess (second in command of the German National Socialist Party) ordered that all German citizens leave the Friends of New Germany and that all the group's leaders return to Germany.

The most notorious of the German ethnic groups that formed to replace the Friends of New Germany was the German American Bund, which attempted to

incorporate the strength of America into Nazism and capitalize on American tolerance of political pluralism to establish the adoption of those portions of National
Socialism (Nazism) that might aid in the economic recovery of the United States
from the Great Depression. Bund membership nationwide was about 20,000 regular
members with about 80,000 auxiliary members known as "patrons." The membership was organized into 100 local units located in forty-seven U.S. states. The Bund
also established a security force—the OD (*Ordnungsdienst,* Order Division)—consisting of about 3,000 men at the height of the Bund's strength. The OD was considered a group of strong-arm thugs by their detractors and it was not adverse to
strengthen this opinion through outward posturing and vitriolic rhetoric. It is estimated that around 25 percent of Bund members were German nationals—the rest
being mostly first- or second-generation German Americans.[17]

The Bund included—apart from the general membership and the OD—a wives
organization, a youth group for boys (*Jugenschaft*) and for girls the (*Madenschaft*).
The Bund ran approximately two dozen youth summer camps across the country
for family and youth activities. A camp known as Nordland in New Jersey was the
largest of these with 204 acres. The Bund leadership was fond of drawing a loose
analogy with the Boy Scouts and Girl Scouts of America to legitimatize the continued existence of their Bund Youth Groups. It owned various companies through
which it published propaganda material and maintained its economic solvency.[18]

The organization brashly promoted the same anti-Semitism as that practiced in
Germany by the Third Reich. It handed out Aryan (white supremacist) pamphlets
outside Jewish-owned establishments and campaigned in the 1936 presidential
election against Franklin Delano Roosevelt—who they charged was part of the
Jewish-Bolshevik conspiracy. The Bund was vehemently anti-Communist as well
as anti-Semitic. The Bund actually held slight influence over the millions of
German immigrants living in the United States, and its activities often made average Americans less sympathetic to Germany. The organization's extreme Aryan
and pro-Nazi views did not sit well with the American public. Even Nazi Germany
realized this and attempted to distance itself from the Bund.

Fritz Kuhn was the American leader of the Nazi Party. In 1936, Kuhn and a few
of his followers traveled to Berlin to attend the Summer Olympics. During his visit,
Kuhn was welcomed at the Reich chancellery and had his picture taken with Adolf
Hitler. The Bund began attracting the attention of the federal government in the
summer of 1937 as unsubstantiated rumors spread that Kuhn had 200,000 men
ready to take up arms. During that summer, a Federal Bureau of Investigation (FBI)
probe of the organization was conducted but no evidence of wrongdoing was found.
Later in 1938 Martin Dies, member of the House Un-American Activities Committee (HUAC), estimated that Kuhn had almost 480,000 followers. Yet most records
show that in 1938 Kuhn had 8,500 Bund members and barely another 5,000 dedicated sympathizers.[19]

The active membership of the Bund may have been small, but its anti-Communist
stance and white supremacist rhetoric drew many hangers-on and considerable
attention from onlookers. In February 1939, Kuhn and the Bund held their largest
rally in Madison Square Garden. In front of a crowd of 22,000, flanked by a massive

Nearly 1,000 uniformed men wearing swastika armbands and carrying Nazi banners parade past a reviewing stand in New Jersey. On July 18, 1937, the German American Bund opened its 100-acre camp at Sussex Hills. (AP Photo)

portrait of George Washington, swastikas, and Americans flags, Kuhn attacked Roosevelt for being part of a Bolshevik-Jewish conspiracy, calling him names, and criticizing the New Deal. The OD, the militant arm of the Bund, were on hand and fistfights broke out in the crowd among those who had come to heckle Kuhn, including a group of Jewish War Veterans from World War I. After the rally, New York District Attorney Thomas Dewey arrested Kuhn on charges of larceny and forgery. He was convicted of these charges in May 1939, and he also confessed to pocketing $15,000 from the Madison Square Garden rally. New York's Mayor Fiorello La Guardia described the Bund simply as "a racket." The Bund leadership voted to cease all activities with the advent of World War II.[20]

Unfortunately, many loyal Americans were held in contempt for their antiwar opinions during the pre–World War II period. The California Joint Fact-Finding Committee on Un-American Activities was begun by Sam Yorty, mayor of Los Angeles, in 1940 to investigate the *People's Daily World*, the West Coast media organ of the Communist Party. The committee's first report published information on a wide range of organizations with antiwar views, lumping together the Communist Party, the German American Bund, pro-Italian and pro-Japanese fascists organizations, the Ku Klux Klan, and pro-Nazi groups based in Mexico. The attention of the committee led to the Alien Registration Act of 1940 requiring all foreign residents to register with the Department of State. Within four months of its passage, almost 5 million aliens had registered under the Act's provisions.

Many hyphenated Americans, who posed no real security risks to the United States, were interned during the Second World War, including German, Italian, and Japanese Americans. Many of those arrested were interned as family groups in Crystal City, Texas, at a camp run by the U.S. Army. Conditions were relatively good, but the nation groups were kept apart. Most of the active Bund members were placed in these internment camps for the duration of the war and later deported. Kuhn was among them. Deported to East Germany, he died there in 1951.

Prosecutions under the Alien Registration Act—aimed at pro-Nazi, pro-Communist, and pro-Socialist groups—continued in the post–World War II years. In 1951, for instance, twenty-three leaders of the Communist Party in America were indicted for failing to register, including Elizabeth Gurley Flynn, a founding member of the American Civil Liberties Union. A series of Supreme Court decisions in 1957 threw out most of the convictions as unconstitutional. The principal decision, *Yates v. United States* (354 U.S. 298), ruled unconstitutional the conviction of fourteen Communist Party leaders distinguishing between advocacy of an idea for incitement and the teaching of an idea as a concept.[21]

Notes

1. Singeli Agnew, "Thoreau's Army," http://alibi.com/index.php?story=7442&scn=feature (accessed November 2009).

2. Agnew.

3. Tom Cornell, "A Brief Introduction to the Catholic Worker Movement," http://www.catholicworker.org/historytext.cfm?Number=4 (accessed February 2009).

4. Rosalie G. Riegle, "Mystery and Myth: Dorothy Day, the Catholic Worker, and the Peace Movement," http://web.archive.org/web/20011215154532/www.forusa.org/fellowship/fel1197-11.htm (accessed February 2009).

5. Riegle.

6. See Cornell.

7. See Cornell.

8. George C. Herring, *From Colony to Superpower: U.S. Foreign Relations Since 1776* (New York: Oxford University Press, 2008), 408.

9. William E. Borah, "The League of Nations," November 19, 1919: 3, http://www.senate.gov/artandhistory/history/resources/pdf/BorahLeague.pdf. (accessed November 2009).

10. Herring, 416.

11. Herring, 430.

12. Henry Seidel Canby, *Prefaces to Peace: A Symposium* (New York: Columbia University Press, 1943), 121.

13. Borah.

14. Borah.

15. See Borah.

16. See Borah.

17. Jim Bredemus, "American Bund: The Failure of American Nazism: The German American Bund's Attempt to Create an American Fifth Column." Traces, http://www.traces.org/americanbund.html (accessed November 2009).

18. Bredemus.

19. Bredemus.

20. Bredemus.

21. See Francis MacDonnell, *Insidious Foes: The Axis Fifth Column and the American Home Front* (New York: Oxford University Press, 1995).

Chapter 15

World War II

Does anyone believe that victory is possible without facing danger?
—Franklin D. Roosevelt, 1941

Military experts, as well as our leaders, must be constantly exposed to democracy's greatest driving power—the whiplash of public opinion, developed from honest, free discussion.

—Wendell Willkie, 1943

Inter arma, silent leges [In time of war, the laws are silent].
—William Rehnquist, quoting a Latin maxim

The Rise of Militarism

World War II was the greatest military conflict in history, and its outcomes affect the world today in ways inconceivable to the generation that fought it. Among the significant outcomes of World War II for the United States was that common everyday Americans came to believe that *war worked*, that it was worthwhile to undertake armed conflict to alleviate the ills of the world. This idea overturned not only the American experience in World War I, but also generations of political thought that said that involvement in the affairs of others was a danger to American democracy at home. The idea that war was an effective tool of diplomacy was not new, but it was new to America. More civilians died in World War II than soldiers, but because of the former war there has been no World War III. Ideas like this, expressed by President Barack Obama during his acceptance of the Nobel Peace Prize in Oslo (2009), have driven U.S. policy into the 21st century.[1]

The treaties that had ended World War I did not stop the growth of militarism, or the inevitable opening of a Second World War. In fact, they led to the virtual extinction of the disarmament movement in many of the nations that would become the Allied countries of World War II. In the post–World War I world, Britain, France, Italy, and Japan were numbered as the only heavily armed nations remaining among the great powers. Recovering from the chaos of the Bolshevik Revolution, Communist Russia soon joined them, leading the rearmament race after World

War I. Benito Mussolini continued the military buildup of the former regime as part of the Fascist takeover of Italy, and Adolf Hitler repudiated the disarmament of Germany contained in the Versailles Treaty as soon as he was in power.

Under the terms of the peace, the Germans were forbidden to possess offensive weapons like bombers and tanks. Yet Germany trained its young men using gliders and dummy tanks, and tested its equipment in other countries like Spain and the Soviet Union "in order to circumvent the treaty."[2] Moreover, Hitler's well-documented prewar greed for territory was based on a combination of economic necessity, diplomatic opportunism, and strategic forethought. Regardless of the pretext, even Hitler's earliest diplomatic ploys were always directed at gathering strategic resources for the rearmament of Germany.

In 1935 and under the scrutiny of the world's diplomats, Hitler quietly absorbed the Saarland and its coalfields, and the following year he reoccupied the demilitarized manufacturing region of the Rhineland. His "liberation" of the Germans living in the Sudetenland provided him with the Skoda armament works and the Czech technicians and workers that he "desperately needed to supplement his meager tank force."[3] He needed not only the raw materials, but also the existing factories in these areas to produce his weapons before the world caught on to what he was doing. These included the ball bearing works in Austria and the oil refineries at Poleste in Rumania. He started small and ultimately embroiled the whole of Europe in a massive arms race.

The Air Arm

Italy, Japan, and Germany had begun their arms race by producing a new generation of warplanes. Through these means, the Axis began World War II with a highly competent air force designed around some of the best airplanes in the world. Meanwhile, Britain and the United States were making technological strides in commercial aviation. One of the American commercial designs, the DC-3, would be converted into the workhorse of World War II military aviation (the C-47). The armed forces of many countries used the DC-3 and its military variants for the tactical movement of airborne and ground troops, as tugs for gliders, and as transports for cargo, supplies, and the wounded.

In the theory of aerial warfare and in the organization of their air forces, the Italians were initially much further advanced than the Japanese or the Germans. Mussolini had hoped that the Italian Air Force (*Regia Aeronautica*), with its approximately 2,600 first-line aircraft, would prove a dominating factor in control of the airspace over the Mediterranean. The hope was not fulfilled because Italy's aircraft industry proved particularly unequal to the demands of large-scale wartime production.

The German Air Force, or Luftwaffe, reached its full potency under Hitler's air chief Hermann Göring, a World War I combat pilot and squadron leader. Both men recognized that air power would play a huge role in the next war, and once the Nazis took control of Germany, the development of German air superiority became a high priority. Determined to rebuild their military aviation, the Germans found ways to circumvent and then openly violate the terms of the Treaty of Versailles.

The treaty restrictions had little effect in any case because German aircraft manufacturers promptly established subsidiary companies in neutral countries, where the production of aircraft could proceed without regard to the agreement. The Luftwaffe was, therefore, well ahead of its potential enemies when Hitler came to power. Moreover, many German pilots and crews gained valuable experience in the Spanish Civil War, where the Ju-87 (Stuka) and Me-109 began their notorious reputations.

The German vision for air power was a tactical one—quick and powerful support for the infantry and armor on the battlefield, which fit perfectly with the *blitzkrieg* style of warfare. Blitzkrieg replaced the swarms of vulnerable men used as an aggressive force in World War I with fast-moving machines, including motorcycles, tanks, and dive-bombers. The German tactical coordination of its combat arms was so fluid that its dive-bombers were able to serve as flying artillery taking out enemy strong points and artillery in advance of the infantry and armor.

Though the London Naval Treaty of 1930 restricted Japan's naval construction to replacement vessels, the Japanese continued to expand their naval air force, and four replenishment plans were approved by the Japanese high command during the 1930s. Night aircraft carrier training began in 1933, and both the carrier and shore-based strength of the naval air force continued to grow. Japanese aircraft were some of the best in the world. The Mitsubishi Zero (A6M2) and Aichi D3A (Val) dive-bomber were among some of the most recognizable and effective aircraft of the war. The Nakajima B5N (Kate) was an excellent torpedo plane that made early Allied models seem primitive by comparison. Moreover, as the war commenced, the fighter aircraft of the Japanese Navy had a much greater range of operation than anything the Allies could put in the air. This would be important in the Pacific Ocean, the largest *battlespace* in the history of warfare.

The Japanese theory of air attack was thoroughly professional and well executed, and their pilots were methodical in performing their duties. Yet Japanese air power was separated into army and navy units, and the naval squadrons were much superior. The average first-line Japanese pilots in 1941 had more than 800 hours of training. Some 600 of the best pilots were assigned to aircraft carrier units each year. The remainder were assigned to the army.

The functions of the two Japanese air forces also were clearly divided. The army air force was designed solely to support the army ground forces, while the naval air force, in addition to supporting the fleet, was responsible for coastal defense, convoy protection, and sea and antisubmarine patrols. Apparently little cooperation existed between the two forces. Japanese aircraft designers provided no armor for the engine or the pilot, emphasizing both the tactical and the cultural philosophy of Japanese society. The poor record of Japanese army pilots in China led foreign observers to conclude that their army air force was inferior in both training and efficiency to their naval air force.

In China in 1937, Japanese army bombers without fighter protection made daylight attacks on Nanking and other cities, but they were exposed to disastrous encounters with Chinese pursuit planes, including a squadron flown by American volunteers known as the Flying Tigers (American Volunteer Group until July

1942). Furthermore, in the Russo-Manchurian fighting of May 1939, the Japanese Army Air Force received a severe and devastating test of its strength. The Soviet Air Force, designed primarily as an immediate support to the Red Army, administered a resounding defeat to the Japanese pilots with simple but formidable aircraft that presaged the development of Soviet Yakovlev (Yak) 9 fighter.

Soviet aircraft production increased significantly in the early years of the 1930s and toward the end of the decade the Soviet Air Force was able to introduce several formidable fighters and bombers. One of the first major tests for the Soviets came in 1936 during the Spanish Civil War, in which the latest aircraft designs, both Soviet and German, were employed against each other in fierce air-to-air combat. The Soviets, however, failed to supply planes in adequate numbers, and their aerial victories were soon squandered. The defeats in Spain coincided with the arrival of Stalin's "Great Purge" of the ranks of the Russian military leadership, which severely affected the combat capabilities of the rapidly expanding Soviet Air Forces.

Shortly before the start of the Spanish Civil War, a Soviet Volunteer Group was sent to China to train Chinese pilots for the air war with the Japanese. These experiences proved of little use to the Russians in their own war against Finland in 1939, in which scores of inexperienced Soviet bomber and fighter pilots were shot down by a relatively small number of equally inexperienced Finnish pilots. Believing their airframe designs had reached their engineering potential, the Soviets turned to Ilyushin ground assault bombers and Yak fighters, both of which became the most produced aircraft of all time in their respective classes. These planes brought the Soviets into air parody with the Luftwaffe by 1941. On the Eastern Front, the bombers were capable of defeating the thick armor of the German Panther and Tiger I tanks, and the Yak fighters were numerous enough to occasionally take down a Me-109 fighter.

As was the case with military aviation in America, the survival and growth of the Royal Air Force (RAF) after World War I was accomplished only with difficulty in the face of isolationist opposition to military appropriations. From 1935 forward, however, the British Air Ministry proceeded with the development of long-range, heavy bombers that fit their night-bombing strategy. For the urgent needs of defense, the Hurricane and the Spitfire, two superlative fighter planes, were put into production after 1936. Production in quantity came slowly because adequate manufacturing facilities were not immediately available. The RAF also produced one of the most famous light bombers to serve on the frontlines in Europe, the all-wood framed de Haviland Mosquito. By autumn 1939, the RAF possessed a modest but well-trained force of airmen. Its bombers, fighters, reconnaissance planes, and flying boats were few in number but efficient in operation.

Although America remained in the throws of isolationism and nonintervention, the military alliances agreed to among Germany, Italy, and Japan in the 1930s provoked a resurgent rearmament among the other great powers of the world, including the United States. In March 1939, American aviation engineers finally began designing technologically advanced bombers and fighter escorts. Under the impact of repeated Axis successes in Europe, the United States evolved a dynamic, if rather cynical, concept of strategic defense. The new concept was influenced by the military tactics of the Nazis as well as by their unbroken string of diplomatic victories. The pattern of political infiltrations, violent air attacks, and machine-like blitzkrieg encouraged the conviction that defense of the Western Hemisphere was closely linked with the independent survival of each of the Allies, especially of Britain. An Allied victory would forestall an Axis invasion of the Americas, should it come, and by merely prolonging Allied resistance, the United States could gain the time needed for building its own defenses.

The weight of America's vast industrial complex would prove the difference in the outcome of the war. Hundreds of American P-40 Tomahawk fighters and B-24 Liberator bombers were shipped to Britain. American engineers would design a number of excellent airframes, and American pilots would fly some of the most significant aircraft developed during the war, including the F-4F Wildcat, the Dauntless SB Dive-Bomber, the long range P-51 Mustang fighter escort, and two state-of-the-art strategic bombers: the B-17 and the B-29. On America's entry into the war in Europe, the U.S. Army Air Force (USAAF), with its own emphasis on strategic bombardment, would find in the RAF a stout and understanding ally.

Naval Rearmament

The terms of the Washington Naval Treaty (Five Power Naval Treaty) of 1921 were modified by the London Naval Treaty of 1930 and the Second London Naval Treaty of 1936. Naval arms limitations had been the objective of many of the treaties in 1920s and 1930s, but the great powers quickly ignored them. The only signatories of the second London treaty were the governments of Britain, France, and the United States. The government of Japan, which had been a signatory of the Washington treaty and the first London treaty, had withdrawn from the conference because of the diplomatic crisis brought on by its actions in Manchuria. Italy declined to participate under similar circumstances, largely as a result of public hostility over its invasion of Ethiopia (Abyssinia). Heavy battleships had been the naval weapons of choice since their development late in the 19th century. Ironically, battleships would play only a secondary role in naval warfare in the next major war. World War II would be the carrier war.

Although capable of launching catapult aircraft from their battleships, the *Aquila* was considered Italy's first true aircraft carrier. The vessel was an ambitious conversion that, completed sooner (still incomplete in 1943), might well have proven a formidable adversary for its British counterparts in the Mediterranean during World War II. Because the Italian Navy was expected to operate primarily in the relatively narrow confines of the Mediterranean and not on the world's oceans, its lack of carriers seemed a small omission, especially given that aircraft carriers were an expensive and unproven battle platform in 1940. The Italian mainland and its islands such as Sicily were viewed as natural unsinkable aircraft carriers, whose many airbases, operated by the Italian Air Force, could provide adequate fleet air coverage in the Mediterranean when requested by the navy. Since France was considered Italy's most likely foe, keeping parity with its battleship navy was a far greater concern.

Despite its lack of aircraft carriers, the Italian Navy succeeded in fulfilling its two wartime objectives: preventing the Allies from severing Italy's maritime supply routes to Axis forces in North Africa and maintaining itself as a viable "fleet in being." Although Britain's Royal Navy operated up to eight of its twelve aircraft carriers (1939) in the Mediterranean at varying times during the war, they failed to achieve any decisive or long-lasting results in terms of halting the flow of supplies to North Africa.

Already armed with thirty battleships and heavy cruisers, Britain began preparing for another naval Armageddon with Germany like the Battle of Jutland in World War I by laying down nine new battleships in 1939,[4] but Germany failed to produce a massive war fleet during World War II. Hitler instead deployed his handful of so-called pocket battleships, cruisers, and auxiliary cruisers as ocean commerce raiders. Outside of these, Germany relied almost exclusively on submarines (1,141 of them) as their aggressive arm at sea. Unlike Japan, Germany also neglected to produce any aircraft carriers. Nonetheless, a great deal of concern was generated when war vessels such as *Deutschland, Graff Spee, Admiral Speer*, or *Bismarck* were on the loose in the Atlantic, or when *Scharnhorst, Gneisenau*, or *Prinz Eugen* were running the gauntlet of the English Channel. Each breakout of German cruisers was followed by headlines in London, New York, Paris, and elsewhere around the world.

While channeling funds to the production of aircraft and tanks, Germany built these armored ships (*panzerschiffe*) to add strength and prestige to a fleet that was badly depleted after World War I. Conceived in 1928, the new warships were designed according to weight restrictions (10,000 tons) imposed by the 1919 Treaty of Versailles. Carrying massive eleven-inch guns, they resembled small battleships. Reputed to be faster than a battleship and more powerful than a cruiser, they caused some alarm in international naval circles. The brilliantly engineered warships, with prototype diesel engines and electrically welded hulls, remained an enigma to potential enemies who wondered how such powerful vessels could comply with the treaty restrictions.

As early as 1921, Japan was secretly restructuring it naval expansion specifically to fight the U.S. Navy. Japan's strategic doctrine of the "decisive battle" planned to allow the U.S. Navy to cross the Pacific, and then using submarines to weaken it, engage the Americans in a predetermined battle area near the home islands. The plan was similar to the one used against the Russians at the Tsushima Straits in 1905. With this strategy in mind since the end of World War I, the Japanese had continually expanded their naval and air bases a Truk Atoll in the Caroline Islands (the Gibraltar of the Pacific) specifically to counter American strategic planning in region.

Japan's numerical and industrial inferiority to the powers of the Western Hemisphere led it to seek technical superiority in fewer but faster and more powerful ships. It was thought that maneuverability and aggressive tactics could overcome the size and number of the enemy. An island nation like Britain, Japan's naval expenditures quickly reached nearly 32 percent of its national budget. In December 1941, the Imperial Japanese Navy possessed forty-eight battleships and cruisers, and ten aircraft carriers (Italy and Germany had none). *Yamato*, the largest

Table 15.1 Total Surface Battle Fleets Deployed in
December 1941 (United States/Japan)

Battleships	16/10
Aircraft carriers	6/10
Cruisers	37/38
Destroyers	171/112

Source: Compiled by author based on data by Walter J. Boyne.

and most heavily armed battleship in history, was launched in 1941. By comparison, the United States had fifty-three battleships and cruisers, and six aircraft carriers spread across two oceans and the Caribbean.

The vast global military machine, which well-meaning diplomats had put so thoughtfully into its box after World War I, had turned once again toward war and away from peace. Moreover, by 1940 those weapons and systems thought most formidable at the end of World War I had been made largely antiquated or obsolete through continued military research and development. Certainly Japanese planners had never envisioned American long-range bombers attacking the home islands as they did in 1942 (the Doolittle Raid).

From 1932 to 1938, the annual arms expenditure of the world increased fourfold from $4 billion to almost $18 billion (in 1939 U.S. dollars). Such a sum seems small today in a world where a single fighter jet costs $50 million (in 2009 U.S. dollars), but in the 1930s, this sum of money could have relieved most of the acute poverty in the Western Hemisphere left over from the Great Depression. The $18 billion was also twelve times greater than all the appropriations spent by all the belligerents in 1914 preparing for World War I.[5]

One of the most significant lessons of the World War II rearmament experience was that the American economy, when operating at a level approaching full capacity, could provide enormous resources for military purposes while simultaneously providing a high standard of living for its citizens. Wars, even immoral ones, make for good business especially for those nations that can sell arms and remain neutral. After allowing for price changes and inflation, personal consumption expenditures in the United States rose by almost 20 percent between 1939 and 1944, even as the amount of resources going to government use rose by $60 billion (38 percent gross national product [GNP] in 1939 dollars). It is safe to say that U.S. militarism was motivated first and foremost by a global geopolitical struggle, but it showed at the same time that the war was essentially costless (even beneficial) to the U.S. economy. In a parody of economic choices, Americans found that they could have both more guns and more butter. The buildup to war was thus viewed as a win-win solution for a U.S. economy recovering from the Great Depression. On December 7, 1941 (Pearl Harbor), the United States still had a 14 percent unemployment rate, yet just six months later, women were being brought into the previously all-male work environment for the first time to fill the need for industrial workers.

Nationalism

At the same time that the great powers were rearming, nationalism increased. The British found a renewed resentment of their colonial rule in India and parts of Africa, and the French and Dutch were dealing with nationalist ferment in Southeast Asia and Indonesia. German nationalism was rampant. Although Hitler and his grotesque concepts of racism and Aryan supremacy contributed to the persecution of Jews and other racial minorities, the peace treaty that ended World War I had set somewhat irrational political boundaries to include dominion over many areas of mixed ethnicity. It placed many Russians, Lithuanians, and Germans inside Poland; many Hungarians, Bulgarians, and Russians within Czechoslovakia, Yugoslavia, and Rumania; many Germans in parts of Czechoslovakia and France; and many Arabs under British colonial rule in the Mideast. In addition, imperialism once again reared its head. Hitler looked with avaricious eyes toward Austria and the Sudetenland; Italy desired Ethiopia and Somaliland; Soviet Russia wished to extend its Communist form of government to Finland, the Baltic States, Georgia, Azerbaijan, and Outer Mongolia; and Japan wished to expand its rule to China, Korea, Indochina, and much of the western Pacific.

The Nazis and Italians also supported the Nationalists of Francisco Franco in the Spanish Civil War (1936–1939). Although long portrayed as a dress rehearsal for World War II with the Germans using the conflict as a proving ground for World War II tactics, the civil war is best understood as a uniquely Spanish phenomenon. Nonetheless, the German Condor Legion did use the war in Spain to experiment with close air support of infantry operations by their fighter aircraft and bombers—a core tactic of the Blitzkrieg. There was a sharp contrast between the intermittent clandestine aid of France and Russia to the Spanish Republican government and the committed support of Fascist Italy and Nazi Germany for the successful Nationalists. The Nationalists also were assisted by some 60,000 Italian, 20,000 Portuguese, and 15,000 German "volunteers" sent to fight by their governments in Spain. Officially, Britain, France, the Soviet Union, and the United States adopted a strict policy of nonintervention in Spain, but the independent units composed of men from these nations fought there nonetheless.

The Italians alone deployed a total of 758 aircraft in Spain (Fiat fighters and Savoia-Marchetti bombers), and the Germans deployed 100 aircraft (Junkers and Dornier bombers). The bombing of the Basque town of Guernica on market day (April 26, 1937) caused widespread destruction and civilian deaths. As many as 1,600 civilians may have been made casualties (250–350 killed). The raid was made by planes of the German Luftwaffe Condor Legion and the Italian Fascist Aviazione Legionaria. The Republican government commissioned artist Pablo Picasso to create a large mural of the atrocity for the Spanish display at the Paris International Exposition in the 1937 World's Fair in Paris. *Guernica* showed the tragedies of war and the suffering war inflicts upon individuals, and in particular, innocent civilians.

The German Stuka JU-87 dive-bomber—the virtual symbol of German aggression—made its combat debut in the Spanish Civil War, and operated with further success in North Africa and the Balkans. In the Battle of Britain, it proved vulnerable to RAF fighters, however. Its potency as a precision ground attack aircraft made it valuable to the Axis war effort nonetheless. In March 1939, the hard-pressed Republican forces in Spain finally surrendered, and Madrid, beset by civil strife between Communists and anti-Communists, fell to the Nationalists. About 500,000 people died in the civil war, some 100,000 of these being executed prisoners. The war's end brought a period of dictatorship under Franco that lasted until the mid-1970s. The Spaniards were deeply scarred by the trauma of this civil strife, and while friendly to Italy and Germany, the Franco government generally stayed out of World War II.

Imperialism

Meanwhile, Italian imperial aggression in Ethiopia (Abyssinia) in 1934 had exposed the inherent weaknesses of the League of Nations. The independence of Ethiopia was interrupted by the Second Italo-Abyssinian War and the Italian occupation (1936–1941). During this period, Ethiopian Emperor Haile Selassie appealed to the League of Nations (1935), delivering an address that made him a world-renowned figure and the 1935 *Time* magazine Man of the Year. Like the Mukden Incident (the Japanese annexation of three Chinese provinces including Manchuria) in 1931, the so-called Abyssinia Crisis was a clear example to the world of the ineffectiveness of the League. Both Italy and Ethiopia were member nations, yet the League was unable to control Italy or to protect poorly armed Ethiopia when Mussolini clearly had violated the League's own rules. The Italians also deployed between 300 and 500 tons of mustard gas in Ethiopia both as bombs and artillery shells, despite having signed the 1925 Geneva Protocols that prohibited its use. The deployment of gas was not restricted to the battlefield, however, as Italian forces targeted civilians as part of their attempt to terrorize the local population. The Italians carried out gas attacks that effected Red Cross camps and ambulances.

As the 1930s opened, Japan was in turmoil. Between 1930 and 1932, the nation had been in the clutches of a right-wing revolution. Four major political figures had been assassinated, and two coups had been attempted. The empire had broken most of the disarmament agreements into which it had previously entered. Each incident had strengthened the military leadership and their expansionist policies. In 1931, the extremists put forward the ancient concept of *Hakko Ichiui*, the incorporation of the eight corners of the Pacific world under the one roof of Japan. This was updated and presented to the world as the concept of a Greater East Asia Co-Prosperity Sphere by Foreign Minister Shigenori Togo.

The Japanese economic presence and political interest in Manchuria had been growing ever since the end of the Russo-Japanese War of 1904–1905. The weak state of the Republic of China, its tenuous control over Manchuria, and the highly militaristic outlook of the Japanese Army were all factors driving Japan to detach Manchuria from China. The Five Power Naval Treaty had guaranteed a certain degree of Japanese hegemony in the Far East, and any intervention on the part of its signatories would have been a breach of the agreement.

On the morning of September 19, 1931, two Japanese artillery pieces installed at the Mukden officers' club opened fire on the Chinese garrison near a Japanese-owned railway. Within five months of the Mukden Incident, the Japanese Army had overrun all the major towns and cities in the provinces of Liaoning, Kirin, and Heilongjiang. The League of Nations ordered Japan to remove its troops from China, but the Empire rejected the League's mandate, literally stormed out of the assembly, and resigned its membership (March 1933).

The Will for Peace Thwarted

During the twenty years following the end of World War I, the global will for a lasting peace had never been stronger. All the military activity of the 1930s added up to popular unrest, political uncertainty, and diplomatic chaos. Many of the problems thought to stand in the way of peace in 1918 supposedly had been addressed by two decades of diplomacy, conciliation, and multilateral agreement. They had seemingly become only worse during what has been termed "the greatest definite effort of mankind to organize peace and international cooperation in history."[6]

The effort for peace had been impressive. The global community had established the League of Nations and the World Court, and sixty-three nations had signed the Kellogg-Briand Pact, which provided for the renunciation of war as an instrument of national policy. The great powers had signed the Five Power Naval Treaty (1921), which limited rearmament, and the Treaty of Locarno (1925), which attempted to normalize post–World War I relations with Germany. Yet these were only the highlights among the numerous armaments reduction and weapons limitation conferences that were held before 1938 in an attempt to secure Europe from another world war.

Victory in World War II may not have been so hard-earned had the Allies been better prepared for war. The diplomacy and agreements had failed. "There is no little irony in the fact that a major cause for World War I was the naval armament race between Germany and England, while a major cause for World War II was the almost mindless quest for naval disarmament."[7]

This attitude was a revival of the old pacifist argument that preparations for war led only to war, as well as that of the militarist argument that weakness invited attack. Neither seemed correct on their face, but neither could be proved wrong by the unraveling of events. It seems enough to assert that diplomatic agreements are creatures of the moment and only worthwhile if the parties do not lie to one another.

Chief among those clamoring for arms limitation in 1921 was Britain who, with an economy ravaged by the costs of World War I, could no longer afford to fund a navy of the size needed to rule the waves. British diplomats attempted to hold the Royal Navy's traditional place as the leading naval power by downsizing everyone else. In the Five Power Naval Treaty (1921) the United States, Britain, Japan, France, and Italy had agreed to maintain a respective proportion of capital ships of 5:5:3:1.75:1.75, respectively. In addition, a ten-year moratorium from building

The League of Nations meeting in Geneva, Switzerland. By the opening of World War II it was a largely dysfunctional and meaningless institution. (AP Photo)

capital ships was enacted. Japan accepted the agreement with the proviso that the United States could not strengthen its island bases west of Hawaii, and that Britain would not strengthen their base at Singapore. These would be among the first targets of Japanese raiders in 1941. While the 5:3 ratio was thought to be a safeguard against Japanese aggression, the agreement was actually a brilliant diplomatic victory for Japan, because the United States had two oceans to defend, while Britain had three oceans plus a presence in the Mediterranean to maintain. Japan with only the Pacific Ocean as an area of immediate concern was effectively left stronger than either nation, and at least at parity with them should they act in concert. The French, with aspirations in Indochina, were even more greatly disadvantaged, needing a three-ocean navy with a half-size (almost) fleet. The Italians, with no oceans to secure, would be more than happy with a fleet the same size as France to patrol their traditional *Mare Nostrum* (the Mediterranean). The Italian Navy would almost single-handedly supply the Axis forces in North Africa from 1939 to 1943.

Yet the pressure on the Allies to disarm in the 1920s and 1930s was based neither in diplomatic gamesmanship nor in pacifist ideology. It was primarily economic. It was the "butter or guns" argument that stressed the rededication of limited resources from military security to social security. This was especially true in light of the grim social consequences of the worldwide economic downturn of the 1930s. It thus became first politic, and then fashionable, to preach disarmament; and the aspect of reduced expenditures for arms was wildly popular with social progressives who sought finances for their domestic projects and programs. Yet in the ensuing euphoria for peace, none of the democratic nations had foreseen that a former Allied power (Italy), a defeated Germany, and a newly ascendant Japan would take advantage of their altruism and fiscal restraint to precipitate a new war.

Appeasement

No set of events in modern times has so damaged the reputation of the antiwar movement than those that led up to the Nazi invasion of Poland in 1939. Although Americans were merely interested onlookers at the time, the consequences to the future of U.S. foreign policy were significant. Among these, the concept of appeasement has become negatively linked as a cause of World War II with the Munich Agreement of 1938 signed by Adolf Hitler and British Prime Minister Neville Chamberlain.

Antiwar and peace advocates are constantly accused of being in favor of Chamberlain-like appeasement when they oppose the use of force as a tool of foreign policy. This charge may be unfair. At times, the best intentioned diplomatic ploys and compromises result in war, and a review of the circumstances surrounding the beginning of World War II is necessary to judge the worth of such accusations.

Appeasement is defined as a multifaceted diplomatic process dealing with the pursuit of conciliatory policies toward another political entity through mediation, bargaining, and compromise. However, the term *conciliation* is considered by many to be an operative word suggestive of the idea of paying blackmail or buying off an aggressor by giving him what he wants. Nonetheless, in the 1930s appeasement had wide popular support among a British public fearful of being swept into another great war. World War I had all but slaughtered an entire generation of young British men as well as tens of thousands of Austrians, Frenchmen, Germans, Italians, and others. Many Britons argued that German rearmament, the remilitarization of the Rhineland, and the reacquisition of the Saarland (administered by the French under a League of Nations mandate since 1920 and readmitted into Germany by a 90 percent plebiscite in 1935) were merely examples of the Germans taking back what was rightfully theirs two decades after an arguably unfair peace had ended World War I. The Conservative Party in Britain gradually adopted this view as a political expedient. Others believed that since the Treaty of Versailles had created the boundaries of the states of Poland and Czechoslovakia on the basis of the concept of self-determination, it was unjust to deny the same opportunity to Austrians and Sudetenlanders of German decent who might want to join themselves to the German polity. These issues came to a head during the several political crises that rocked 1938.

The first of these took place in March 1938. Hitler gave an ultimatum to Chancellor Kurt Schuschnigg of Austria demanding that he resign and allow a new candidate for chancellor to stand for election. Schuschnigg had succeeded the assassinated Engelbert Dollfuss as chancellor in 1934, and ever since the Austrian

Fascist Party had been in turmoil. Hitler had pledged Germany's support to the opposition Austrian Nazi Party (Austrian National Socialist Party) threatening that German troops would march into Austria, if the demands for an election were not met. With Schuschnigg's resignation, a new Chancellor, Dr. Arthur Seyss-Inquart, a Nazi puppet within the Austrian cabinet, took control. Through the use of intimidation rather than invasion, Hitler had attained without firing a shot the *Anschluss*, an effective unification of Germany and Austria under Nazi control.

Shortly thereafter, Schuschnigg attempted to regain control of Austria through a plebiscite, protesting that the country had reached the limit of its concessions to Germany, but he was arrested by Nazi storm troopers and confined at the concentration camp at Dachau. He was liberated by American soldiers on May 5, 1945, and taught in the United States until his death in 1977.

Hitler next turned to the reacquisition of the Sudetenland, a former part of Germany then under Czech governance but inhabited by a majority of ethnic Germans. Applying the concept of self-determination to the situation, Chamberlain decided to acquiesce to Hitler's demands for the return of the Sudetenland to Germany. French Prime Minister Edouard Daladier agreed with Chamberlain, and Italian Prime Minister Benito Mussolini suggested a conference of the major powers in Munich to work out the terms of the agreement. No Czechoslovak representative was invited to these discussions.

In a letter to his sister Hilda (October 2, 1938), Chamberlain described his late-night meeting with the German leader at the Munich conference:

> I asked Hitler about one in the morning . . . whether he would care to see me for another talk. . . . I had a very friendly and pleasant talk, on Spain, (where he too said he had never had any territorial ambitions) economic relations with S.E. Europe, and disarmament. I did not mention colonies, nor did he. At the end I pulled out the declaration [ceding the Sudetenland to Germany], which I had prepared beforehand and asked if he would sign it. As the interpreter translated the words into German Hitler said, "Yes I will certainly sign it. When shall we do it?" I said "now," and we went at once to the writing table and put our signatures to the two copies which I had brought with me.[8]

When Chamberlain returned home, he was mobbed by overjoyed crowds of Britons expressing their relief that a new war with Germany had been averted. He proclaimed:

> My good friends . . . a British Prime Minister has returned from Germany bringing peace with honour. I believe it is *peace for our time* [italics added]. . . . We, the German Führer and Chancellor, and the British Prime Minister, have had a further meeting today and are agreed in recognizing that the question of Anglo-German relations is of the first importance for our two countries and for Europe. We regard the agreement signed last night [September 29–30, 1938] . . . as symbolic of the desire of our two peoples never to go to war with one another again. We are resolved that the method of consultation shall be the method adopted to

deal with any other questions that may concern our two countries, and we are determined to continue our efforts to remove possible sources of difference, and thus to contribute to assure the peace of Europe.[9]

Peace in Our Time

The Nazi invasion of Poland one year later, coupled with Chamberlain's braggado-cio in front of the newsreel cameras claiming the dawning of "peace in our time," set the stage for his political downfall and crippled the British peace movement for a decade. Chamberlain was vilified as being unrealistic in following the policy of appeasement when it had little chance of permanent success. His political rival, Winston Churchill, used the ultimate failure of the appeasement policy to highlight the corruption of Chamberlain's Conservative Party government and to heighten his own political prestige. Churchill's "blood, toil, tears, and sweat" speech appealed to British patriotism and steadfastness in the face of war, and it established him as a strong and able war leader.

The Road to War

Although war-making and peace-making are intimately related, it is not the purpose of this volume to follow all the details of the military campaigns of World War II. Only the significant military operations are noted. However, the formation of alliances and the use of diplomatic ploys predating U.S. involvement in the war are instructive of the theme of comparing the characteristics of war and peace even when compressed into a timeline of events.

The fiasco at Munich had the unexpected consequence of increasing the likelihood of a more widespread war. The Munich agreement of 1938 had severely shaken the Soviet Union's faith in its temporary alliances with both Britain and France, and it confirmed Joseph Stalin's suspicion that Britain hoped to provoke a Soviet-German death struggle by encouraging Hitler to turn his aggression to the East.

Shortly after his invasion of Czechoslovakia in 1939, Hitler began to form a series of alliances similar to those that had entangled the world during World War I. In May 1939, shortly after Italy had invaded Albania, Mussolini formed the Pact of Steel (that is, The Pact of Friendship and Alliance) with Germany, thereby becoming the first voluntary ally of Hitler. The pact consisted of two parts: the first section was an open declaration of continuing trust and cooperation between Germany and Italy, while the second section contained a so-called Secret Supplementary Protocol encouraging a joint military and economic policy and the promotion of an improved image for fascism.

In August 1939, the Soviet leader, Joseph Stalin signed a totally unexpected Non-Aggression Pact with Germany that seemed shockingly out of character for an antifascist Communist regime. Through this pact, the Soviets received half of Poland in return for ignoring Hitler's aggression, but more important, they received an opportunity to grow stronger and retool their own military machinery. Thus, in

1939, Stalin decided to "sacrifice Marxism-Leninism on the altar of Machiavelli."[10] Shortly thereafter Britain and Poland signed a Mutual Assistance Treaty.

The road to another world war thereafter was a fast one. On September 1, 1939, Germany invaded Poland, and two days later Australia, Britain, France, and New Zealand declared war on Germany. Canada joined the Allies on September 3. The United States shamefully proclaimed neutrality on the same day that the German troops crossed the Vistula River in Poland (September 5). This act by the United States sent the wrong message to Hitler—one of indolent patience. The Soviets invaded Poland from the east on the September 17 and by the end of the month had divided that nation with Germany. While Stalin seemingly had held the British policy of appeasement in contempt, he later justified his policy toward Hitler as no more than what Chamberlain had done in Munich the previous year. By the end of the year, the Soviets had also invaded their traditional enemy Finland (November 30). The Russians were quickly expelled from the League of Nations (December 14) for these actions—a meaningless gesture of frustration on the part of an already failed institution.

Had Hitler known that he would have to face an alliance of Britain, France, and the Soviet Union (and eventually the United States), there might not have been a war in 1939. Even Hitler's generals—rarely timid about aggression—had warned him against such formidable coalitions. Meanwhile, the Soviets had strengthened the Nazi war machine by closing their embassies in countries conquered by the *Wehrmacht* (German Army), and they recognized the pro-Nazi governments through the sale of supplies of grain, petroleum, metallic ores, and rubber that ultimately went to Germany. This compliant attitude astounded even Hitler, who had already decided to launch a preemptive attack (Operation Barbarossa) against the Russians the following year to end the German-Soviet Nonaggression Pact.[11]

Month by month the war spread. During the first half of 1940, Germany invaded Denmark, Norway, France, Belgium, Luxembourg, and the Netherlands. Each surrendered to the Nazi war machine in its time. From May 26 to June 3, there was a massive evacuation under fire of Allied troops from Dunkirk, and on June 10, Italy declared war on the badly beaten British and French. Mussolini was reported to have entered the war at this point so that he would have a seat at the peace conference that he expected to take place before the end of the year. The Italian leader claimed that 10,000 Italian casualties would guarantee him a front-row seat.

Meanwhile, the Soviets began their occupation of the Baltic States, and by July, Lithuania, Latvia, and Estonia were occupied. In August, the Italians occupied British Somaliland in East Africa and attacked Egypt a month later. In September, Japan signed on to the Tripartite (Axis) Pact with Germany and Italy thereby spreading an already active war in China to much of French Indochina and threatening British India. Meanwhile, in October, Germany attacked Romania, and Italy invaded Greece. Hungary and Romania joined the Axis in November.

As can be seen from this highly compressed timeline, 1940 was a wondrous year for the dictators and a bad one for the world. One nation after the other quickly fell before the Axis war machine. French Marshal Philippe Pétain proclaimed the formation of the Vichy government on July 10, 1940. The legitimacy of Vichy and

Hitler and Mussolini, masters of Europe in September 1941. Within four years both leaders would be dead, one murdered by his own people, one by his own hand. (AP Photo)

Pétain's leadership was challenged by General Charles de Gaulle, who claimed to represent the legitimacy and continuity of the French government in the form of a *resistance*. There were some Axis setbacks in 1940, but the Greek defeat of the Italian 9th Army, the British advances against Italy in North Africa, and a British torpedo bomber raid that crippled the Italian fleet at Tarentum stood as the only positive events for the Allies.

Meanwhile from September 1940 to May 1941, the Germans prosecuted a pitiless bombing campaign (the Blitz) against Britain and especially the city of London. While the British had some success against the Italians in Africa, Germany came to Mussolini's aid in Greece and in North Africa in the form of the Afrika Corps commanded by Erwin Rommel, one of Hitler's best generals. Yugoslavia—in the midst of its own anti-Communist civil war—officially became an Axis ally, Greece surrendered to Nazi forces, and the war spread to Lebanon, Syria, and Iraq, the last signing on as an Axis power.

American supineness during this period was remarkable, but the lack of U.S. commitment suggests the strength of American *noninterventionism*. Not until March 1941 did President Roosevelt sign the Lend-Lease Act, and it took until June for the United States to finally freeze German and Italian assets in America. In May 1941, German airborne troops invaded the Greek island of Crete in the first major aerial operation of its kind. It was also the first time that invading German troops encountered mass resistance from a civilian population. In light of the heavy casualties suffered by his parachutists and glider troops, Hitler forbade further large-scale airborne operations even though he captured the island. Nazi paratroopers proved, nonetheless, to be among Hitler's best troops. The German capture of Crete, particularly as a result of the failure of the intervening British land forces to recognize the strategic importance of airborne operations, served as a wake-up call for military strategists. The Allies were impressed by the potential of the new *vertical warfare* and started to build their own airborne divisions.

In June 1941, Hitler finally turned on the Soviets launching a massive attack (Operation Barbarossa) designed to crush the Russians even before he had concluded his war with Britain. Joseph Stalin, the Soviet leader, in 1941 had made a fundamental, but understandable, diplomatic miscalculation concerning his agreement with Hitler. He had not expected an attack without a provocation on his part or at least an ultimatum from Germany. Moreover, it had taken Hitler only months instead of the years that Stalin had contemplated to conquer most of Western Europe, and Stalin was now faced with a colossal Nazi war machine filled with the pride of success and the confidence of its seeming invincibility. In his first radio message to the Soviet people after the German attack, Stalin tried to save face noting that he had secured the motherland from attack by dealing with Hitler in the same manner that Czar Alexander had Napoleon at Tilsit in 1807 or Lenin had the Kaiser at Brest-Litovsk in 1917.

In July 1941, Stalin formed a strategy to regain the support of the Soviet people for the war with the Axis. This was something new. Formerly, popular resistance to the policies of the Soviet government had been suppressed through fear of arrest, imprisonments, and nationwide purges. Yet Stalin understood that the Soviet people were not going to willingly give their lives for Communism, and he appealed rather to their love of the motherland. He conjured up images of the Russian people's past resistance to invasion and of an entire population fighting against the Nazi hordes to protect Mother Russia. Like Churchill in Britain, Stalin appealed to national loyalties, rather than party loyalties, to drum up support for the war. As with Napoleon before him, Russia quickly became Hitler's worst nightmare.[12]

German Submarines Again

In anticipation of war in September 1940, the U.S. Congress passed the Selective Training and Service Act that provided for the annual induction of 900,000 unmarried men between the ages of twenty-one and thirty-six into the U.S. Army. In October, 16.5 million men registered. One month later the first group of conscripts, called selectees, was called into service. Many men looking for alternatives to Army life—including escape from marching, muddy foxholes, cold rations, and sleeping in tents—opted to enlist in the Navy or the Coast Guard, where a dry bunk, warm food, and constant transportation seemed a better way to fight a war.

In March 1941, American, British, and Canadian military staffs met in Washington to discuss the role of each nation in defeating Germany. They drew up the ABC-1 Staff Agreement that established a strategic role for the United States, *if America entered the war*. Meanwhile, Roosevelt ordered the Coast Guard to take into protective custody two German ships, twenty-six Italian vessels, and thirty-five Danish vessels then in America's neutral ports. The interned vessels were turned over to the U.S. Maritime Commission, and after the United States entered the war, they were renamed, reconfigured, and used to defeat their former owners.

In April 1941, the President signed Transfer Directive D-27-T, which made ten U.S. Coast Guard (USCG) Lake-class cutters available to the Anglo-Canadian convoy system. In May, as Greece and Yugoslavia fell to the Axis, Roosevelt increased the U.S. presence in the North Atlantic by agreeing to protect the neutrality of Iceland with a 4,000-man force of Marines. The Navy established a base at Reykjavik. This base, along with those in Newfoundland, Greenland, and Northern Ireland, would enable the United States to convoy supply ships through the mid-Atlantic if necessary. Long-range aircraft would be used to locate Axis submarines and vector in destroyers and sub chasers. It has been pointed out that "although the North Atlantic looks large, it is really a small place when there are hundreds of ships to ferry across safely and tens of U-boats trying to stop them."[13]

Maintaining U.S. neutrality at sea was also difficult. In May 1941, the USCG cutters *Madoc* and *Northland* found themselves accidentally sandwiched between the German raider *Bismarck* and three British naval vessels preparing to do battle. The cutters were in the line of fire. Moreover, British *Swordfish* torpedo planes from the British aircraft carrier HMS *Victorious* were warned off mistakenly attacking the Americans only by the giant U.S. flags draped over the sides and on the decks by the USCG crews. Deciding that they were in the wrong part of the ocean to hang around and watch the fireworks, the two cutters made flank speed and left the scene.[14]

In August 1941, amid great secrecy, British Prime Minister Winston Churchill and President Roosevelt met aboard USS *Augusta* in Canadian waters to work out an Allied statement of principles that came to be called the Atlantic Charter. This document set out the following ideas, including the right of all people—

- to choose their own leaders
- to trade freely with one another
- to access raw materials on equal terms
- to improve their economic lot
- to disarm aggressors
- to be free from want
- to be free from fear
- to be free to traverse the high seas and oceans without hindrance

The last phrase was directed at Hitler's U-boats and provided justification for the United States to take part in escorting convoys across the Atlantic.

In the autumn 1941 (September 4), the neutral American destroyer USS *Greer*, traveling in consort with the USS *Carney*, was fired on by an unidentified submarine (later identified as *U-625*). *Greer* and *Carney* dropped nineteen depth charges on the aggressor but lost contact with it. Thereafter, the last vestiges of U.S. neutrality were gone. Roosevelt ordered all U.S. warships to show no lights at night and to be ready for combat at any time. On September 11, 1941, Roosevelt publicly accused the Axis of piracy and declared that he had ordered the American Navy and Army Air Force to shoot on sight at any German or Italian war vessel in waters protected by U.S. warships. The first land encounter between U.S. and Nazi forces took place on the next day when U.S. Marines seized and destroyed a Nazi radio station and its operators in Greenland. On October 17, a torpedo from an unidentified submarine struck the USS *Kearny* killing eleven American sailors and wounding twenty-two of the crew. Roosevelt once more expressly affirmed to the American public in his radio address that his shoot-on-sight order was in force. On October 30, the U.S. oil tanker *Salinas* was torpedoed south of Iceland by *U-106*, and escorting destroyers ran the aggressor off. Finally on October 31, while escorting a convoy out of Halifax, Nova Scotia, the USS *Reuben James,* a post–World War I destroyer was torpedoed by the German submarine U-552 and sank along with a crew of 115. The *Reuben James* was the first U.S. vessel destroyed by the Axis Powers. Yet the German attacks on neutral American warships did not bring about a declaration of war. American naval forces were again being attacked in a war in which they remained mere onlookers as they had in 1802, 1812, and 1914.

Recognizing the danger to America if Germany occupied all of Europe, Roosevelt had pledged to give Britain all the aid it needed short of war. Sentiment in the United States was greatly divided with regard to siding with Britain, but the attacks on American naval vessels shifted the center of agreement somewhat toward intervention. Consequently, Congress repealed the Neutrality Act, sending fifty antiquated destroyers to the Royal Navy and passing a draft law in the United States. Nonetheless, many Americans, especially in the Midwest, continued to believe that the best way to secure America was to stay out of Europe.[15]

It is certain that Roosevelt's personality imprinted American foreign policy at this time, and Roosevelt's "cavalier and feckless diplomatic style" would become something of a trademark of his administration. For instance, Roosevelt had recognized the legitimacy of the Soviet Union in 1933 because he saw no useful purpose in withholding it any longer. Hard-core anti-Communists in the United States passionately opposed this move. Although Roosevelt had worked vigorously for U.S. participation in the League of Nations as a vice presidential candidate in 1920, domestic problems brought on by the Great Depression had clearly affected his legislative and foreign agendas since his election as president in 1932. The first 100 days of his administration saw a deluge of domestic legislative initiatives flood Congress. None of them had relieved the worst symptoms of the long economic downturn that began in 1929, and several of his programs had been found unconstitutional by the courts.[16]

Influential Republican Rep. Hamilton Fish III warned that Roosevelt's policies toward the Soviets in particular were making the world vulnerable to international Communism, and that America was in danger of becoming a willing accomplice in prosecuting a war against Germany to save an outdated British colonial empire. Fish denied being an isolationist, saying he was merely a noninterventionist who wanted negotiated settlements of disputes rather than American involvement in another foreign war. Nevertheless, as the fighting continued between British

Hurricanes and Spitfires and German Stuka and Henkel bombers, sympathy in America for the embattled British mounted. Britain's battle for survival had focused American attention on Europe, and Japan's attack on Pearl Harbor caught the United States looking at the wrong ocean.

Pearl Harbor

It took the Japanese attack on Pearl Harbor on December 7, 1941, to bring the United States into the war. Roosevelt asked for and immediately received a declaration of war against Japan, but even as he did so, it was Germany that declared war on America rather than the other way round. Justice William Rehnquist, writing in regard to this circumstance, noted,

> Germany, in one of Hitler's major blunders, declared war on the United States. Had he not done so, it seems questionable whether Congress at that point would have declared war against Germany, since there would have been a substantial segment of public opinion that would have favored concentrating United States resources in the war against Japan in the Pacific.[17]

The Japanese had attacked the U.S. Naval Base at Pearl Harbor, and almost simultaneously struck Hong Kong, Malaysia, and the Philippines. A subsequent series of stunning Japanese attacks and victories in the Pacific continued almost without interruption in Thailand, Guam, Wake Island, and Manila. Allied forces seemed overwhelmed and incapable of withstanding the Japanese Imperial Army. On December 10 off the coast of Malaya, two British warships (*Repulse* and *Prince of Wales*) were destroyed within minutes by eighty-six Japanese torpedo planes and dive-bombers from the 22nd Air Flotilla based in Saigon. Wake Island withstood the initial December 11 attack, but was overwhelmed on December 23. On December 8, Japanese bombers had destroyed the U.S. Navy Yard at Cavite in the Philippines, and two days after Christmas, Gen. Douglas MacArthur evacuated the capital at Manila.

In January 1942, Japan invaded Burma, the Dutch East Indies, New Guinea, and the Solomon Islands, and they captured Manila, Kuala Lumpur, and Rabaul. After being driven from the Malay Peninsula, Allied forces in Singapore attempted to resist, but then surrendered to the Japanese in February 1942. Almost 90,000 British troops in Singapore surrendered to a determined Japanese army one-third its size supported by superior aircraft. Approximately 130,000 Australian, British, Dutch, and Indian personnel became prisoners of war during these operations. Also in February, the Japanese bombed the port of Darwin on Australia's northwest coast. By March 1942, Japan gained control of Bataan and Corregidor in the Philippines, and by May, Java had surrendered, Rangoon (capital of Burma) had been occupied, and the Philippines had completely fallen—considered a great military disaster for the United States. "India and Australia were tremblingly aware that their turn might come next." In June, the Japanese attacked Dutch Harbor, Alaska, and gained a foothold on Attu and Kiska Islands in the American Aleutians.[18]

Allied Strategy

With the ANZAC (troops from Australian and New Zealand), British, Dutch, and Indian forces already drained by years of war with Germany and Italy in Europe and heavily committed in the Middle East, North Africa, Greece, and elsewhere, they were unable to provide much more than token resistance to the battle-hardened Japanese. In consultation with Great Britain and the Allies, the United States decided to follow a *coalition strategy* of first defeating the Germans on the ground in Europe while pursuing a *holding action* in the Pacific using those forces commonly assigned to the navy, including torpedo boats, submarines, aircraft carriers, and the Marines.

Initially, the United States had established a (secret) distribution of its military resources in a global ratio of 85 percent to 15 percent with the lion's share being deployed in Europe. The United States sent an entire infantry division, the 41st, and 40,000 support troops to Australia by May to hold back the Japanese. While some of the ANZACs returned home, the Allies established an ANZAC defense area in the southwestern Pacific under an American Supreme Commander Pacific, Douglas MacArthur. In January 1943, at the Casablanca Conference between Roosevelt and Churchill, however, a more appropriate 70 percent to 30 percent division was put into effect under the concept that it would be more productive of overall success. To achieve this new distribution, the Allies had to agree to a delay in the invasion of Europe until 1944.

It should not be concluded from this circumstance that America fought both Germany and Japan with anything other than equal tenacity. The United States was the only country among the major Allies that had spoken in the prewar years of Germany *and* Japan in the same strategic breadth. Although at odds with its aggression in China, neither France nor Britain had any anxiety over the Japanese potential to attack their interests. Germany had been a much closer and older rival of both nations. Russia had had closer interactions with Japan including a major war with the Rising Sun Empire at the beginning of the century, and China had been fighting with Japan for much of the 1930s.

As has been discussed, American geography had forced the United States to look both East and West in its foreign policy. The United States had vulnerable colonial possessions and an extended coastline in the Pacific, and an important transoceanic commerce involving both Europe and Asia. Both Germany and Japan had been among America's deepest concerns for decades—first as fierce competitors, but also as promising markets. Now it seemed an American responsibility to undertake a war in both oceans. This was emphasized in 1942 when a Japanese submarine shelled oil installations in Santa Barbara, California, while German submarines torpedoed U.S. shipping within sight of the beaches of New York and New Jersey.[19] In January 1941, German U-boats torpedoed twenty-five commercial vessels off the coast of Long Island, some of them silhouetted by lights from New York and other cities.[20]

Nonetheless, these aggressor nations (and their Axis partners) represented more than the military challenge of a so-called *two-ocean war*. In the view of America, they operated according to principles and standards that were threateningly different. These were rival societies to America "bursting onto the world stage with enormous force and speed."[21]They were more highly ordered and restrictive in their social and industrial orders than the United States. Their governments ruled with an iron fist, and their populations were subordinated to the aims of their leaders in a way that Americans generally found offensive. Here were two nations, Germany and Japan, "whose disastrous miscalculations caused them to attempt to change the existing world order by force, resulting in the deaths of some fifty million people."[22]

These nation-states were something else for those who blamed the United States for the diplomatic failures of the 1930s that ended in a surprise attack—a mirror of America itself, rich, greedy, and overconfident in a world that was generally poor, hungry, and pessimistic. This train of thought—it hardly qualified as a form of logic given the facts—contained a common thread of antiwar sentiment that blamed the victim for its refusal to negotiate and compromise away its advantages at the conference table. War had been forced on an America that previously had been largely disinterested in problems outside of its own advantage or even isolationist in its comportment.

Soldiers in the Field

As the United States filled its manpower needs in 1942, it found that it could be selective in choosing recruits from among the thousands of young volunteers lining up to join the various services. The Marines seemed to have the stiffest entry requirements, while the Army accepted men "irrespective of fine physical gradations . . . whether a man would engage in hand to hand fighting, march long distances on foot, carry a heavy pack, or go without sleep and food counted very little in his original assignment."[23]

Although it was not known at the time, the armies of World War II would have a much smaller proportion of draftees and conscripts in their ranks than those of World War I. However, the infantrymen of 1939–1945—when compared with pilots, artillery, armor, and naval personnel—suffered the bulk of the injuries in battle. This was particularly true of the Americans who entered the war against veteran enemy troops as relative novices in 1944. "The U.S. infantry divisions that fought in North-West Europe between D-Day on 6 June 1944 and VE-Day on 8 May 1945 had an average manpower turnover of approximately 100 per cent."[24] In an extreme case, the U.S. 4th Infantry Division turned over 35,000 men—almost two and a half times its organizational strength of 14,000. Quite a few men were willing to be wounded (the so-called million dollar wound) to escape the virtual meat grinder of battle. The particularly dangerous nature of infantry work was not recognized by the U.S. Army until late 1943 with a Combat Infantry Badge, which carried with it an additional hazard pay ($10 per month) like that offered to paratroops and submariners. Other Allied and Axis infantry units suffered similar infantry losses, but those governments tended to rotate or even disband units that suffered mass casualties rather than continuously fill the ranks with successive waves of conscripts as did the Americans.[25]

The appalling casualties of World War I led U.S. military leaders to believe that public opinion would not tolerate a similar squandering of life in a second war, and the universal teaching of sophisticated combat skills to American soldiers had developed in the interwar years. By 1942, certain concepts came to be accepted as defining features of the U.S. foot soldier. Infantry was required to move efficiently over difficult terrain both in massed formations of march and in small inconspicuous tactical groups. They were expected to take advantage of cover and utilize terrain to advantage. Their main purpose in battle was to attain maximum fire effect, to conserve personnel, and to facilitate the maneuver and employment of reserves of ground forces, airpower, artillery, and armor.[26]

The deployment of infantry as a base for all further military action was thought to be absolutely necessary. Infantry protects all the points of strategic importance for an army, and it compels the withdrawal or surrender of the enemy. It is the most adaptable and the most generally useful of all military arms and is more capable than the others of defending itself under most circumstances. With the exceptions of independently walking on water or flying through the air, infantry is capable of operating over wide differences in terrain, during both day and night, and in almost any type of weather. An airborne or coastal naval operation attempted without the deployment of infantry—as was the U.S.-led NATO air intervention in Bosnia in 1995 (Operation Deliberate Force)—simply cannot produce a permanent result. In Bosnia, coalition ground forces filled the role of infantry.

The U.S. infantryman's personal equipment (uniform, helmet, web belting, pack, poncho, grenades, and so on) was scientifically designed and fairly good, but the designated quantity of ammunition to be carried by each man in the field fell far below what he needed. Strategic planners feared that the men would waste their ammunition in promiscuous fire. Improvements in supply lines and advances in technology almost always lagged behind the fast-moving realities of actual combat. In Europe, camouflage clothing was all but neglected, and rubberized snowshoes were not widely distributed until late 1944. The excellence of the M1 Garand rifle developed in 1934–1935 and widely distributed in the European theater was surprising. According to Gen. George Patton, the semiautomatic (eight-shot) M1 was "the greatest battle implement ever devised,"[27] and it made each squad of riflemen capable of independent attack and defense when supported by the Browning automatic rifle (BAR) or the Thompson submachine gun—the favorite "Tommy Gun" of rum-running gangsters in the interwar period.

The Germans, Italians, and Japanese by comparison had a much wider distribution of automatic weapons and heavy machine guns, but their riflemen used standard bolt action weapons that were accurate but slow to fire. The standard Italian Carcano infantry rifle was made famous as the weapon that was used to assassinate John F. Kennedy. The British lay somewhere between the two extremes in terms of their firepower distribution balancing their Enfield bolt actions, with automatic Bren guns.[28]

Soldiers were not stupid, and they realized that there were severe gaps between what they needed to know in the field and what they had been trained to expect. They soon learned to recognize the comparative risks that they ran from particular operations or tactics. Bayonets, although widely carried by all sides, produced few injuries while artillery fire, dive-bombers, mortar fire, machine guns, and rifle fire caused the greatest number of casualties. Of 20,000 casualties recorded for a particular American infantry division in 1944 only thirteen wounds were due to bayonets. By comparison bombs, mortars, and artillery shells accounted for 75 percent of the casualties. Prolonged shelling was a stern test of men's morale. Bullets, mines, booby-traps, and so-called friendly fire were identified in 10 percent of the cases, and accidents and other injuries common to men working around dangerous materials and heavy equipment filled out the remainder.[29]

Hundreds of men are lost to noncombat accidents even when they are not deployed in active combat. People fall sick and die, trucks overturn, aircraft crash, and weapons discharge unintentionally. So-called *battle inoculation* using live ammunition and realistic environments during training to inure green recruits to combat conditions are an effective but dangerous expedient.[30] Up to 20 percent of the casualties (including deaths) among troops are nonhostile in nature and expected to occur during training and transportation.[31]

The War in the Pacific

At Pearl Harbor, America had lost the use of almost its entire Pacific Battle Fleet. Fortunately as it turned out, the U.S. aircraft carriers and their escorts had been at sea, and they ultimately would provide a new dimension to naval tactics in the Pacific through the development of the Carrier Task Force. These would win most of the major naval battles against Japan (Coral Sea, Midway, Guadalcanal, Philippine Sea, Leyte Gulf, Okinawa) in what would be the ultimate ocean war in the largest battlespace ever envisioned in the era of conventional weapons. Meanwhile, the U.S. Navy deployed its fleet of patrol torpedo (PT) boats to harass the Japanese and attack enemy logistics while the Navy recovered.

When the Pearl Harbor attack occurred only eighteen PT boats were deployed in the Pacific. For the next three months, the boats almost single-handedly defended the Pacific. They were credited with shooting down the first enemy plane at Pearl Harbor, and of being the last American presence to leave the Philippines.

Before the Pearl Harbor attack, American PTs were completely untried, and their combat tactics and strategic deployment were still being formulated. With a top speed of about forty knots, heavily armed, and costing only $0.5 million apiece, it proved the perfect weapon to use in a crisis of military unpreparedness. In December 1941, the U.S. Navy had just twenty-nine PTs. Two years later, there were twenty-nine squadrons of them deployed around much of the world. Ultimately, a total of forty-five squadrons composed of twelve to sixteen boats each were commissioned. These 500-plus vessels served in the Pacific, the Aleutians, the Mediterranean, the Panama Canal Zone, and in Northern Europe fighting a variety of enemy E-Boats, S-Boats, R-Boats, armed barges, destroyers, minesweepers, submarines, and aircraft. Even the Italian MAS-Boats proved a challenge, "the most aggressive and warlike [craft] in all the Italian Navy."[32]

The PTs could be formidable adversaries anywhere they were deployed. In March 1942, with only three boats left operable in the Philippines, the PTs under John D. Bulkeley, a Medal of Honor recipient, were ordered to evacuate General MacArthur, his family, and his aides from Corregidor in one of the most dramatic small flotilla operations of the war. *They Were Expendable* (1945), a film based on the book of the same name by William L. White, related the real-life story of these exploits. The characters played by Robert Montgomery and John Wayne were highly fictionalized, but the film depicted typical actions undertaken by PT boats, including the evacuation of MacArthur. The crews that manned the PTs were all volunteers from assorted backgrounds, and one historian has produced a study suggesting that the officers were heavily recruited from the upper-class sporting set because "PT officers should be tough and athletic." One of these, a young man from Massachusetts named John F. Kennedy, would become president of the United States.[33]

While on patrol one moonless night, a Japanese destroyer appeared suddenly out of the darkness and cut Kennedy's torpedo boat (PT 109) in half, instantly killing two crewmen. Kennedy led the survivors in swimming from the floating wreckage to a distant deserted island. Hiding from Japanese coastal patrols, after a few days, Kennedy encountered two natives and gave them a message carved on a coconut, which they took to an Australian coastwatcher, who arranged for a rescue. The coconut was kept on Kennedy's presidential desk in the Oval Office. With the election of Kennedy as president in 1960, interest in his exploits during the war in the Pacific increased.[34] The film *PT 109* (1963) was the accurate story of Kennedy's service in the war. Before his death in November 1963, the president had selected Cliff Robertson to play him in the movie after viewing a number of screen tests and meeting with the actor.

The Makin Island raid (August 1942) led by Lt. Col. Evans Carlson's 2nd Marine Raider Battalion was conspicuous as the first American land offensive of the Pacific War. The Raiders, who were delivered to the island by submarines, swiftly defeated the Japanese garrison and retired. Nine Marines were inadvertently left behind. They were subsequently captured and executed by Japanese forces—one of the first war crimes of the conflict.

The U.S. Marine Corps did not fight the ground war in the Pacific alone, but they did make the most difficult and bloody amphibious landings, and many of the rugged attacks on enemy strong points. Army infantry and U.S. air units then came in to "mop up" and garrison the islands. Meanwhile, the United States undertook major offensives against the enemy beginning with the hard-fought battle for Guadalcanal in the Solomon Islands in 1942 and continuing with an island-hopping strategy (including Tarawa, Bougainville, New Guinea, Iwo Jima, Saipan, Tinian, and Okinawa) that bypassed Japanese strongholds and brought U.S. strategic bombers closer and closer to the Japanese mainland islands. Bombers carrying atomic weapons would fly out of Tinian in August 1945.

American submarines were active in the Pacific throughout the war. Not a single U.S. submarine was lost in Central Pacific waters until the loss of *Pickerel* in April 1943, sixteen months after the start of the war. The submarines paid heavily for their successes, however. Fifty-two American subs were lost thereafter, representing a loss of 18 percent of those deployed. While high in comparison to the losses sustained by other types of ships of the Allied Forces, this is considered remarkably low when taken in relation to the results achieved, or when compared with the losses sustained by enemy submarine forces. With but meager results to show for their submarine effort, the Japanese in World War II lost 128 submarines and had fifty-eight remaining at the end of hostilities.

Task Force Warfare

From 1942–1945 most of the naval battles in the Pacific between capital ships were fought by aircraft—the vessels of the Carrier Task Forces never being in sight of the enemy. In the beginning of 1942, Japan had ten aircraft carriers in the Pacific to America's three operational vessels. Five other U.S. carriers, including the obsolete *Langley* and *Ranger*, were deployed elsewhere or undergoing repairs.[35] By August 1942, Japan had four carriers to oppose only one American carrier (*Enterprise*), and U.S. strategists were asking for help from the British Royal Navy.[36]

At the Battle of Coral Sea on May 7, the carrier forces from the two sides exchanged airstrikes over two consecutive days. The American fleet carriers *Lexington* and *Yorktown* joined the Australian light carriers *Australia* and *Hobart* in the first carrier-to-carrier sea battle in history. On May 7, the U.S. sank the Japanese light carrier *Shōhō*, while the Japanese sank a U.S. destroyer and a fleet oiler. The next day, the Japanese fleet carrier *Shōkaku* was heavily damaged, the U.S. fleet carrier *Lexington* was sunk by planes from the fleet carrier *Zuikaku*, and the U.S. fleet carrier *Yorktown* was damaged. The Japanese light carriers *Mogami* and *Mikuma* later collided. The first was damaged and the latter was sunk by U.S. aircraft. Before Coral Sea, the Japanese had not lost a warship larger than a destroyer—only barges and transports. Now they had lost two capital ships. With both sides having suffered heavy losses in aircraft and carriers damaged or sunk, the two fleets disengaged and retired from the battle area. The loss of *Lexington* was significant given American disadvantage in numbers of such vessels. Yet the battle was essentially a tactical draw, and the Japanese had been frustrated in their invasion approach to New Guinea.

In June 1942 the Japanese Imperial Fleet of 200 vessels steamed east across the Pacific possibly destined for an invasion of the U.S. base at Midway Island. The U.S. naval (naval air) victory over the Japanese invasion fleet at the Battle of Midway was decisive because it ended any realistic Japanese threat to the west coast of the United States or even to Hawaii. The Japanese planned to bomb the island garrison of Midway into submission destroying its aircraft and runways, but the Americans, having broken the Japanese code, wanted to draw the Japanese fleet into a battle of attrition while they attacked the unsinkable island garrison.

As the enemy made a diversionary attack on the Aleutian Islands, Japanese aircraft from the main body attacked the island base at Midway. Meanwhile, American carrier aircraft quickly sought out the enemy carriers. Not expecting the presence of U.S. carrier aircraft, Japanese Admiral Nagumo had arranged his own carriers within a protective screen of sixteen nearby ships. The formation was woe-fully vulnerable to surprise attack because the Japanese did not possess radio detection and ranging (RADAR) and lacked good damage control procedures. It depended largely on an overhead Combat Air Patrol (CAP) of fighter planes.[37]

At Midway, the two American carrier task forces involved (*Enterprise*/*Hornet* and *Yorktown*) were kept just far enough apart to make it unlikely that they would be detected by a single enemy scout plane or submarine, but close enough so that each group's fighter screen could support the other should the need arise. *Hornet*'s SBD Dauntless dive-bombers initially failed to find a target, but its fifteen TBF torpedo bombers gamely attacked the carrier *Hiryū* (Flying Dragon). Only one man survived, Ensign George H. Gay, and not one torpedo found its mark. While the torpedo attack failed it pulled the fighter cover away leaving the Japanese carriers vulnerable to U.S. dive-bombers. The Dauntless SBDs scored fatal hits on three separate first-line Japanese aircraft carriers within a six minute time span. Photo air reconnaissance of the battlespace showed numerous columns of black smoke rising from the burning Japanese fleet.[38]

By the end of the battle, the Japanese had lost four fleet aircraft carriers, 272 air-craft, and hundreds of pilots and mechanics to the Dauntless dive-bombers. Enemy counterstrikes had left *Yorktown* a derelict, but as it turned out, it floated throughout the night. It was attacked the next day by Japanese submarines, and ultimately was sunk by the U.S. Navy. Of the forty-one TBF torpedo planes launched by the three American carriers, only six returned. These negative aspects of naval air warfare would have to be addressed. One of the flyers shot down and rescued was nineteen-year-old George H. W. Bush, then the youngest pilot in the navy and later 41st president of the United States.[39]

After Midway, naval warfare in the Pacific changed. Japan could (and did) build more carriers, but its greatest loss was the death of approximately 4,800 trained naval and air personnel and technicians. Japanese pilots had been engaged in real combat since 1935, and the massive loss of life among these veterans left Japan with generally inexperienced rookies at the same time that U.S. pilots were gaining in experience and confidence. At Midway, the Japanese found that even their best pilots could not sink an island or protect their vessels from concerted American air attacks. Most of the car-riers and the Japanese heroes that had attacked Pearl Harbor were gone in a single day.

In 1942, there was a very real fear that Japanese aircraft carriers would sit off the U.S. Pacific Coast and serve as floating airfields for attacks on the U.S. mainland. Before the war, the United States had started production of twenty-four new large Essex-class carriers as a defense for this eventuality. In 1943, as the new American carriers began to enter service, this fear had been dispelled. None of the new Essex-class carriers would be lost, not even to the kamikaze attacks late in the war.

Kamikaze ("divine wind") attacks were new to naval warfare, equivalent to today's suicide bombers and improvised explosive devices (IED) in their lethal nov-elty. They began in October 1944, following several critical military defeats for Ja-pan, and initially the Americans were hard-pressed to defend against them. The word *kamikaze* harkened back to the destruction of a great Mogol fleet in a typhoon in the 13th century. The first divine wind had saved the island homeland. With the fall of Saipan, Vice Adm. Takijiro Onishi, who was in charge of the Japanese Air Force in Manila, understood that it was impossible to win a naval battle with so few aircraft and trained pilots. For this reason, he decided to form a suicide attack force, the Special Attack Unit. An initial group of twenty-four student pilots volunteered for the mission. Over the next few months, more than 2,000 pilots made suicide attacks. The number of vessels sunk by kamikaze is a matter of debate (70 of the 380 reportedly hit seems a safe estimate), but it appears certain that suicide attacks accounted for up to 80 percent of the U.S. naval losses in the final phase of the war in the Pacific. The high point of kamikaze attacks came from April 6 to May 25, 1945, during the Battle of Okinawa.

On April 18, 1943, Adm. Isoroku Yamamoto, the architect of the Japanese attack on Pearl Harbor, was shot down and killed by U.S. aircraft acting on certain intelligence over South Bougainville. The Japanese secret code, decrypted by the U.S. Navy, had given Yamamoto's itinerary, and he was met by eighteen P-38 Lightning fighters that shot down both bombers carrying his party. The Japanese admiral had taken off from the main Japanese base in the South pacific at Rabaul. About 110,000 troops were based in Rabaul. Yamamoto's death was a propaganda triumph for the United States.

At Coral Sea the Japanese advance in the Pacific had been stopped, at Midway the odds had been made more even, and thereafter the enemy began its retreat. In February 1944, an American carrier-based attack eliminated Japan's ground-based air force and antiaircraft defenses at Truk Atoll over just two days. The same carrier task force attacked targets in the Mariana Islands. Japanese aerial resistance was all but completely suppressed. These operations proved that carriers could take on land-based aircraft and win.

With the U.S. fleet largely invulnerable to Japanese air power by 1944—decreasing Japanese aircraft production, the decimation of its veteran pilots, and overwhelming U.S. numbers—the Japanese fleet did not stand a chance of surviving through 1944. With the death of its admiral-in-chief and the destruction of Japanese naval aviation went any hope that Japan had of victory. Nonetheless, the Japanese still possessed a powerful surface navy in the absolute sense with excellent surface ships and dedicated sailors, but the main elements of their strength were no longer relevant to the developing exigencies of modern warfare at sea. The 400-year-long naval dominance of the surface battleship had been transferred almost overnight to the aircraft carrier, thus proving the adage that future wars are often fought with the knowledge and weapons of the past.

Jungle Warfare

Although Americans had fought in the jungles of the Philippines in the Spanish American War at the opening of the century, they had to relearn how to fight in jungle environments during their island-hopping campaigns of World War II. The pioneers who methodically developed *jungle warfare* as a specialized branch of combat—the unconventional, low-intensity, guerrilla-style type of fighting—were the British. Examples of early jungle warfare forces were the Chindits and other

Table 15.2 Naval Air Assets in the Pacific (Japan/United States)

	1942	1943	1944	1945
Fleet aircraft carriers	6/3	4/2	4/7	2/14
Light aircraft carriers	4/0	3/4	4/22	2/65
January totals	10/3	7/6	8/29	4/79

Source: Compiled by author based on data by Walter J. Boyne.

small bodies of soldiers, equipped with no more than small arms and explosives, who were rigorously trained in guerrilla tactics (particularly in close-quarter combat). Formed in the later stages of the Pacific War in support of conventional forces, the Chindits (Long-Range Jungle Penetration Groups) were the true jungle warfare experts whose unconventional combat skills and tactics were specially developed for use in the jungle environment to harass Japanese logistics and communications.

The jungle operations in Burma of America's Merrill's Marauders (officially named the U.S. 5307th Composite Unit) commanded by Gen. Frank Merrill introduced U.S. fighting men to the hardships of fighting a war in mainland Southeast Asia. The Marauders were a new volunteer special forces unit patterned after the Chindits. U.S. Gen. Joseph Stilwell was determined throughout the war that U.S. combat troops in the Southeast Asia theater would not serve under British command. This left a good deal of bad blood between the British and American headquarters.

The Hollywood movie *Objective Burma* (1945), starring Errol Flynn, pictured U.S. paratroopers attacking behind enemy lines in the jungles of Southeast Asia. The story line was loosely based on the actual operations of Merrill's Marauders. The recapture of Burma had taken place during late 1944 and the first half of 1945. The British were initially upset with *Operation Burma* because it seemingly underrepresented the contribution to the war of British Commonwealth soldiers in Burma stemming from the unwarranted Americanization in the film of what had been a mainly British, Indian, and Commonwealth conflict. In fact, Winston Churchill was so infuriated by the movie that it was not exhibited in Britain until 1952 when it was accompanied by an apology for the oversight.

The War in Europe

The Battle of the Atlantic pitted U-boats and other war vessels (E-boats, S-boats, and so on) of the German Navy against Allied convoys. Besides submarines, the *Kriegsmarine* (German Navy) had a well-articulated fleet of surface raiders, sub chasers, and armed minesweepers. The British people required that virtually everything needed to sustain life in the island kingdom be imported by convoy through a cordon of enemy vessels. The convoys, coming mainly from North America and going mainly to Britain or the Soviet Union, were protected for the most part by British and Canadian warships and aircraft. The campaign began on the first day of the European War in 1939 and lasted for six years, involving thousands of ships and stretching over hundreds of miles of ocean. During this period, there were more than 100 convoy battles and perhaps 1,000 single-ship midocean encounters. The Allied forces were aided by ships and aircraft of the United States beginning in September 1941, but the major American contribution to the Battle of the Atlantic was the Liberty Ship—specially designed cargo transports crewed by U.S. merchant seamen. Germany also deployed tens of thousands of floating mines in the bays, inlets, and channels of the North Atlantic and the Baltic. More than 1.8 million tons of Allied shipping was sunk by these silent denizens of the deep. German mines were still being removed as late as 1957.

The bloody skirmishes, numerous sinkings, and mounting death tolls in the Atlantic has come to be known as the Battle of the Atlantic. For almost 2,100 days, the Allies tried to control an area of ocean stretching from above the Arctic Circle south to the Cape of Good Hope in Africa and west from the Coast of England to the Caribbean and the bulge of South America. The center of the Atlantic was outside the range of protective aircraft. Every convoy passed through some part of this U-boat hunting ground bringing war material to the Soviets at the ports of Archangel and Murmansk or to the British at Liverpool. The Allied forces in the Mediterranean were supplied by way of Gibraltar or the Suez Canal. In the Mediterranean, they faced Italian submarines and surface raiders, including the very efficient MAS torpedo boats. The submarines and surface raiders of the Axis navies came within a hair's breath of winning this battle and thereby the war in Europe.[40] Nonetheless, the Germans (who had lost 178 submarines in World War I) lost between 700 and 800 submarines in World War II. The Italians by comparison lost 102 submarines in the Mediterranean, (a half dozen or so scuttled at the moorings when Italy left the war in 1943), and Japan lost 128 submarines in the Pacific and Indian oceans and surrendered fifty-eight at war's end.

In late 1941, discussions had been held in Washington concerning the idea that the U.S. Navy would take over those portions of the U.S. Coast Guard (USCG) that might be used to escort these convoys or fight in the war. Two scenarios were discussed. In the first, the Navy would assume and retain for the duration of the emergency control of the entire Coast Guard down to its lifeboats and aircraft, and in the second, it would return those parts that it did not want to control to the Treasury Department. The second plan was deemed impractical due to the administrative chaos it would cause, so the Navy subsumed for the duration of the war the entire USCG on November 1, 1941, by presidential order.

The transfer of authority did not sit well with many men who had enlisted in the Coast Guard, especially in terms of its effect on the morale of the men and the friction it created between USN (U.S. Navy) and USCG officers. Some predictable operational difficulties emerged during the initial USN-USCG attempts at convoy escort. Among these was a lack of short-range voice radio known as TBS (talk between ships) that provided fast and secure communications between vessels without using frequencies that would attract the attention of enemy submarines and surface raiders. The design differences between USN vessels and USCG ships in terms of fuel were profound. The Navy destroyers were continually leaving the convoy to refuel because their designers had sacrificed fuel capacity for firepower. Consequently, the USN vessels did not have enough fuel for extended operations at sea as did the USCG ships.

After 1942, much of the convoy escort duty fell to the USCG vessels—a fact not clearly enunciated in period propaganda films or later histories of the war.[41] Although structured as a military service, the Coast Guard was normally a part of the Treasury Department, yet for this aspect of the war, it possessed two unique skills. Coastguardsmen had a long working experience in Arctic or near-Arctic conditions that made their expertise invaluable on the runs to Russia, and they had a proficiency in safely maneuvering small boats on and off beaches in heavy surf—a skill set not practiced by Navy personnel at the time. Consequently it was the Coast Guard that manned most landing craft and provided most convoy escorts.

Bombing Campaigns

Strategic bombing during World War II was greater in scale than any wartime attack the world had witnessed, and it attracted the attention of antiwar protestors due to the human carnage that it wrought. Britain had a policy of using aerial bombing only against military targets such as ports and railways that were of direct military importance. Accidental bombing of civilians and nonmilitary targets (so-called collateral damage), however, was a common consequence of the British strategy of nighttime bombing. The dark of night protected the bomber crews somewhat, but thousands of civilians were killed. On August 24, 1940, German aircraft (Luftwaffe) over London dropped bombs in the east and northeast of the city causing widespread devastation and severe civilian casualties. A period of reciprocal retaliation began, mainly focused on industrial areas.

The United States entered the war intending to use strategic daylight precision bombing in Europe, which was used with mixed success and never officially abandoned as a policy. Daylight bombing proved deadly to U.S. bomber aircrews, who had an average life expectancy of less than fourteen missions. They would be rotated home after twenty-five missions, but with an optimistic attrition rate of 4 percent (25 × 4 percent =100 percent) survival was unlikely. In May 1944, the United States began attacking German petroleum resources particularly in the so-called 1,000 plane raids on the heavily defended oil fields at Ploesti in Rumania. With nothing but synthetic fuels (painstakingly produced from coal) for their tanks, by the end of 1944, many units of the German army were forced to travel on foot or revert to horse-drawn transportation. Because of the lack of oil, the army that had conquered Europe with a novel mechanized form of warfare (*blitzkrieg*) straggled back over the Rhine River looking more like a beaten medieval host than a modern army.

Beginning in February 1945, British and American raids saw 1,300 heavy bombers in four divisions drop more than 3,900 tons of high-explosive bombs and incendiary devices on Dresden, destroying thirteen square miles of the city and causing a firestorm that consumed the city center. It was the worst bombing raid of the war in Europe in terms of its inhumanity. Estimates of civilian casualties vary greatly, but recent researchers place the figure at nearly 40,000 persons.

At about the same time in the Pacific theater, Air Corps Gen. Curtis LeMay switched to low-altitude, nighttime incendiary attacks on Japanese targets, a tactic senior commanders had been advocating for some time. The first raid using low-flying B-29s carried incendiaries to drop on Tokyo in a night raid in late February 1945. The 174 bombers destroyed approximately one square mile of the city and the largely wooden Japanese structures could be seen burning for many miles. LeMay declared that if the fire-bombing shortened the war by a single day, the attack would have served its purpose.

The bombing casualties during the war were suffered disproportionately by the various participants. This is especially true regarding civilian casualties. The United States, which suffered no general bombing campaign on its population, amassed 417,000 military deaths, but only 1,700 civilian deaths. Strategic aerial bombardment claimed the lives of more than 160,000 Allied airmen in the European theater, 60,595 British civilians, and between 300,000 and 600,000 German and Axis allied civilians. American precision bombing, fire-bombing, and atomic bombing in Japan killed between 300,000 and 500,000 Japanese civilians. Japanese strategic bombing was independently conducted by the Japanese Navy and Army air service. Bombing efforts mostly targeted large Chinese cities such as Shanghai, Wuhan, and Chonging, with around 5,000 raids. Although hard numbers are unavailable, estimates of Chinese civilian deaths approached a total of 4 million, with the deaths due to bombing certainly approaching 1 million. The Pacific War ended with the deployment of atomic bombs at Hiroshima and Nagasaki in 1945 killing between 40,000 and 100,000, but the fire bombings of German and Japanese cities killed many more people.

Presidents Roosevelt and Truman justified these inhumane tactics by referring to estimates based on losses during attacks on Okinawa and other islands that 100,000 American troops would be killed if Japan had to be invaded. According to Dr. Gregory H. Stanton, international lawyer and president of Genocide Watch, "The Nazi Holocaust was among the most evil genocides in history. But the Allies' fire-bombing of Dresden and nuclear destruction of Hiroshima and Nagasaki were also war crimes. . . . We are all capable of evil and must be restrained by law from committing it."[42] In his anti-American diatribe, Stanton carefully avoids speaking to the Allied deaths in Europe caused by Axis bombing.

Antiwar observers looking back to 1943 from the threshold of the atomic age also declared that the United States could have undertaken a (questionably) more humane strategy against Japan—that of starving the island nation into submission:

Instead of conducting an island-hopping campaign, during which the lives of thousands of Americans and hundreds of thousands of Japanese were lost, some contend that the United States should simply have intensified the unremitting economic warfare already underway. Rather than invading the Philippines, taking the Marianas and undertaking the B-29 bombing campaign with its atomic denouement, the argument is made that Japan could have been blockaded so effectively by surface ships, submarines and carrier-based air power that her war-making capacity would have evaporated, and she would have had to surrender, thus sparing the lives of hundreds of thousands of fighting men and Japanese civilians.[43]

This idea ignores several important factors, including the mood of the American people to finish the war quickly, and the announced dedication of the Japanese to defend their home islands and endure starvation, disease, and suffering for as long as their beloved Emperor told them to do so. The pattern of their stubborn resistance, as seen on their isolated island outposts cut off from food, medicine, ammunition, and other supplies, suggests that the home islands could have held out for five to seven years with more Japanese civilians succumbing to slow starvation and disease than ultimately died in the American bombing campaign. This could hardly be considered a better fate.[44]

Moreover, when the bombing strategy was adopted in 1943, Japan was far from beaten and still occupied Indochina, Malaya, the Dutch East Indies, the Philippines, and enormous areas of China. Previous experience with Japanese occupation suggests that these captive populations would have been exploited to the greatest extent under this scenario. "Five more years of the ruthless occupation of those countries would certainly have resulted in additional tens of millions of civilian deaths, as well as the deaths of thousands of Allied prisoners of war."[45] Rather than blaming American leaders for not having a more compassionate vision of the means of ending the war, it might be more sensible to ask the Japanese why they persisted in the fight when all reasonable hope of victory was gone.

The Invasion of Europe

The major U.S. amphibious landings in the European theater of war were in North Africa, in Italy (Sicily, Anzio, and Salerno), in the south of France (between Toulon and Cannes), and at Normandy, the so-called D-Day. Upon breaking out of Normandy in August, the Americans worked their way east across France in a sometimes-difficult coordination with their British and Free French allies. Allied forces also drove north from southern France and along the boot of Italy. Soviet forces moved west at the same time forcing the Germans to retreat to their homeland. Everyone was focused on Berlin.

Halfway through the war Italy was seen to be failing on every front. By January 1943, half of the Italian forces serving on the Eastern Front in Greece had been destroyed, the African campaign had collapsed, and the Balkans remained unstable. Once the darling of the Italians, Mussolini had lost the support of the people for having led a disastrous war effort. The Italians wanted an end to the war, and they celebrated the fall of Mussolini who was ultimately murdered by Italian Communist partisans (April 1945). The Italian government had officially surrendered in September 1943. However, German forces replaced them in the trenches and retreated slowly up the boot of Italy as the Allies advanced, taking strong defensive positions and giving great resistance. The Allies had a great and plausible fear that the war effort would bog down in Southern Europe if a second invasion (Normandy) was not quickly completed. As more Italian territory was ultimately occupied by the Allies, they were welcomed as liberators by the population, who opposed the continued German occupation. The German Army in Italy did not surrender until May 1945.

German armor (especially the Panzers and Tigers) outclassed Allied tanks until the very end of the war, and Panzer and Panzergrenadier units were greatly feared by the Allied infantry. Hitler had been preparing a massive counter-attack in the West since the Allied breakout from Normandy. The plan was actuated in the Ardennes in December 1944 resulting in the Battle of the Bulge—the last major German offensive of the war and its biggest battle. Hitler believed he could split the Allied forces by attempting a drive toward Antwerp led by his tanks. He planned thereafter to persuade the Americans and British to sue for a separate peace, independent of the Soviet Union. During the German operations, some captured Americans (approximately 150 unarmed men) were sent to stand in a field near the crossroads at Malmedy where most were shot down in cold blood. The Massacre at Malmedy was a serious blow to German prestige. After initial successes in bad weather, which gave them cover from the Allied air forces, the Germans eventually were pushed back to their starting points. In the wake of the defeat, many experienced German units were left severely depleted of men and equipment.

The Allied crossing of the Rhine into Germany was achieved at four points— one of them by U.S. mechanized forces across the Ludendorff bridge at Remagen, which the Germans had failed to blow up. Pressed by the Allies in the west and the Soviets in the east, Germany was quickly overrun. Hitler and many of his close associates committed suicide in Berlin rather than fall prisoner to the Soviet Army. On May 7, 1945, at his headquarters in Rheims, Supreme Allied Commander Gen. Dwight Eisenhower took the unconditional surrender of all German forces to the western Allies and the Soviet Union from the German chief of staff, Gen. Alfred Jodl. Many Axis leaders, officers, and soldiers were tried by a military tribunal at Nuremberg after the war, charged with a variety of war crimes including the deaths of 12 million concentration camp prisoners.

Prisoners of War

The International Red Cross (IRC) made periodic inspection visits of all the military prison camps covered by the Geneva Conventions. (Japan was not a signatory to the conventions and ran its prisoner-of-war [POW] camps as it pleased). Had it not been for food parcels sent in via the IRC, nutrition would have been a serious problem in all POW camps regardless of what nation ran them. The recommended intake for a normally healthy active man is 3,000 calories, but the Germans and Italians allowed only between 1,500 and 1,900. Although acceptable for a short period, the issued official rations provided only prolonged and unpleasant starvation over longer periods, and the IRC food parcels often made up the difference between health and sickness or even life and death. On average, the IRC provided one parcel per week per man. Those sent and paid for by relatives and containing a mixture of goods, and "bulk" parcels (for general distribution, sent and paid for by the IRC, and containing a supply of a single item) were pooled. Thus, replacement clothing, shaving and washing kits, coffee, tea, tinned meat, jam, sugar, and other items were distributed equally.

The phrase *death march* is most often associated with a single word: Bataan. When Japanese troops overran the Philippines in 1942, they forced thousands of GIs and Filipinos to march across sixty miles of the Bataan Peninsula in tropical heat with little or no food and water. Hundreds of Americans and thousands of Filipinos died in the week-long trek that came to be called the Bataan Death March, one of the greatest war atrocities ever perpetrated against American fighting men.

The film *Back to Bataan* (1945) starring John Wayne and Anthony Quinn was meant as a tribute to the U.S. Army personnel and the Filipino resistance during the pacific war. Two-thirds of the way through filming, the real invasion of the Philippines occurred, causing several script changes and rewrites to keep up with current events. This included the release of hundreds of "Bataan Death March" survivors held captive since the fall of the islands in 1942. Many of the actual survivors of the Japanese prison camp at Cabanatuan appeared at the end of the film.

The Great Raid (2005), starring Benjamin Bratt, Joseph Fiennes, and Filipino actor Cesar Montano, was a more focused and historically correct telling of the 1945 raid on Cabanatuan by the 6th Ranger Battalion and Filipino guerillas to rescue almost 300 Americans held at the Japanese POW camp. Regardless of which film better depicts the rescue—the 2005 film has better production qualities and more extensive real-life footage of the rescued men—the operation itself remains noteworthy as an example of a well-planned and expertly conducted small-unit mission behind enemy lines.

Japanese Interment

The attack on Pearl Harbor stunned the American people, and the shelling of an oil installation and a minor bombing on the Pacific coast by elements of the Japanese Navy (including two fold-away seaplane bombers delivered by submarine) in February 1942 left residents of California, Oregon, and Washington fearful of the ethnic Japanese among them. Although the fear was largely unwarranted, it was nonetheless palpable.

Those ethnic Japanese (*Issei*) who emigrated to the United States in the prewar decades had not been allowed to become citizens, and they were prohibited by law from owning land and were segregated from the rest of society in many ways. Their children born in the United States (*Nissei*) were citizens from birth. More than 100,000 of these resided on the U.S. Pacific Coast. Nonetheless, public officials responding to the anxiety of the majority population began to call for the wholesale relocation of persons of Japanese ancestry to interior regions of the country. These persons were not POWs, but relocated civilians. Nor were the Japanese interned simply because of their race. Although not in equal numbers, many alien Germans and Italians—white foreign nationals and not citizens—were treated similarly in 1942 under the provisions of the Alien Act of 1798, which (with some amendment) was still in force.

Former Chief Justice William Rehnquist, acting as a historian of the Supreme Court decisions in this regard, noted, "These distinctions seem insufficient to justify such a sharp difference of treatment between Japanese and German and Italian aliens in peacetime. But they do seem legally to support the difference in treatment between the two classes of enemy aliens in time of war."[46] Part of the chief justice's finding was based on the concept that the law, as it was understood at the time of his writing in 1998, was "be no means so clear in 1943 and 1944." Moreover, the Fifth Amendment to the Bill of Rights provided for due process and the Fourteenth Amendment for equal protection, both seemingly violated by the apparent unfairness. Yet at the time, the former amendment was incumbent on all levels of government, while the latter did not place any limits on the actions of the federal government. The doctrine of equal protection would not be extended to federal action for a decade.[47]

Military commanders in the Western Defense Command of the United States initially resisted the idea of internment, but state and local officials—especially in California—were insistent and were supported by their congressional representatives. If a forced evacuation was to be in effect, however, it would need the president's explicit approval as commander-in-chief. Secretary of War Henry L. Stimson informed Roosevelt of the situation and received his "vigorous" agreement. Stimson wrote further in 1947:

> [M]indful of its duty to be prepared for any emergency, the War Department ordered the evacuation of more than 100,000 persons of Japanese origin from strategic areas of the west coast. This decision was widely criticized as an unconstitutional invasion of the rights of individuals many of whom were American citizens [*Nissei*], but it was eventually approved by the Supreme Court as a legitimate exercise of the war powers of the President.[48]

Attorney General Francis Biddle speculated on Roosevelt's feelings concerning the wholesale evacuation of Japanese instituted by Executive Order No. 9066, which authorized the internment:

> I do not think he was much concerned with the gravity or implications of this step. He was never theoretical about things. What must be done to defend the country must be done. . . . The military might be wrong, but they were fighting a war. Public opinion was on their side, so that there was no question of any substantial opposition, which might tend toward the disunity that at all costs must be avoided.[49]

Congress followed the presidential order with enforcement legislation and issued regulations under which it would be implemented. They imposed a curfew on ethic Japanese, ordered them to report to evacuation centers, and finally moved them to camps in interior California and the mountain states. Although it is impossible to measure the emotional stress this placed on the *Issei* and *Nissei*, there was no blatant brutality such as prodding with bayonets or the use of shackles. Yet the internment camps were generally meager in their appointments (similar to standard U.S. military barracks, but partitioned for family groups), and there was a great deal of personal dislocation in terms of employment, schooling, and social connections. As the war progressed, some restrictions were relaxed, and internees were issued work permits that allowed them to leave the camps. Most of those interned were released before January 1945. By 1999, reparations had been awarded to more than 80,000 Japanese Americans or their heirs at a cost of $1.6 billion.

The Japanese American (*Nissei*) volunteers of the 442nd Regimental Combat Team were largely recruited from among these camps, and fought in the European theater especially against the Germans in Italy. There was a certain irony in ethnic Japanese Americans fighting bravely for the United States while that same country interned their families. Yet this unit became the most heavily decorated military command in the history of the U.S. Army, as well as one of the regiments with the highest casualty rates.

Internment of *Nissei* citizens was challenged in the courts during the war, and the Supreme Court had to respond to the charge that distinctions based on race alone were unconstitutional. Such distinctions by their very nature should be odious to a free people who are governed under the doctrine of equality. The court found that race and ethnicity *alone* afforded no grounds for such confinement, but that the attack threatened by Japan rather than some other nation had effectively set the Japanese Americans apart from others, thereby legitimizing the measure. The court criticized the military for lumping together a few truly disloyal Japanese aliens (found to be involved in the raids on Hawaii and the Philippines) with all those loyal noncitizen *Issei* and citizen *Nissei* against whom no similar showings had been made. In the case of Mitsuye Endo, for instance, the court found that the Japanese American woman—who had followed all the regulations of the internment— was entitled to be released because she had proven her loyalty to the United States.

The Supreme Court also recognized that it was the duty of the military to secure the nation under uncertain circumstances, not to make legal assessments regarding civil liberties. This was an important distinction that embraced a legal logic similar to that followed during the American Civil War and in the years after the September 11, 2001, terrorist attacks. The traditional unwillingness of courts to decide constitutional questions in wartime illustrates the Latin maxim *Inter arma, silent leges* (In time of war, the laws are silent). It should be noted that the American Civil Liberties Union (ACLU) and other civil liberties watchdogs were also silent during the initial stages of the internment.[50]

The most common postwar criticism of the Court in this regard was that it recognized the overriding necessity of military considerations. The Court had found:

Whatever views we may entertain regarding the loyalty to this country of the citizens of Japanese ancestry, we cannot reject as unfounded the judgment of the military authorities and of Congress that there were disloyal members of that population, whose number and strength could not be presently and quickly ascertained. We can not say that the war-making branches of the Government did not have grounds for believing that in a critical hour such persons could not readily be isolated and separately dealt with, and constituted a menace to the national defense and safety, which demanded that prompt and adequate measures be taken to guard against it.[51]

Certainly, Gen. Walter Scott and Adm. Husband E. Kimmel, charged with the security of Pearl Harbor, had been pilloried for their failures to anticipate the Japanese attack, and it seems unfair to military leaders to denounce their decisions with regard to the possibility of additional enemy agents when they were erring on the side of caution. In considering these actions, Rehnquist noted that it was not incumbent on the Court to invalidate decisions simply because they were based on military concerns. He wrote, "Judical inquiry, with its restrictive rules of evidence, orientation towards the resolution of factual disputes in individual cases, and long delays, is ill-suited to determine an issue such as military necessity."[52]

Pacifism and Criticism

During World War II, there was very little opposition to government policy regarding the prosecution of the war. The Church of the Brethren worked with the government to create a system of alternative service, which would allow religious conscientious objectors to serve their nation and humanity through nonviolent service. Alternative service evolved into the Brethren Volunteer Service, a church agency that placed many young people and some older persons in volunteer human service jobs, usually for a one-year term. Despite the church's official peace stance, many members of the Church of the Brethren did not agree with its pacifist stance during World War II, and many of its men entered active duty in the military. Others served as noncombatants in the military with only 10 percent taking conscientious objector status.

In 1933, the American Friends Service Committee (AFSC) was chartered by the government to help provide the U.S.-sponsored relief efforts in Europe. During the rise of Nazism, Quakers from the AFSC provided relief for children on both sides of the Spanish Civil War, helped refugees escape from Germany, and provided relief to refugees in Vichy France. After World War II ended, AFSC did relief and reconstruction work in China, Europe, India, and Japan. The extraordinary relief work of AFSC during World War II earned the organization the Nobel Peace Prize in 1947. In 1948, they worked to resettle refugees from the partition of India, Palestinians from the Gaza Strip, and other displaced persons. In 1955, the Committee published *Speak Truth to Power,* a seventy-one-page pamphlet focusing on the Cold War and the need to reduce or eliminate nuclear weapons. The phrase "Speak Truth to Power" would come to be a common weapon in the arsenal of war resistance.

Partisan Political Criticism

One World, a plea for international peacekeeping at the conclusion of World War II authored by Wendell L. Willkie, Republican candidate for president in 1940, was highly popular in its time and sold millions of copies. It spent four months atop the *New York Times* bestseller list beginning in May 1943. The book, written while the outcome of the war was still in question, was no mere humanitarian essay. It was based on the things that the former presidential candidate learned first hand on a wartime trip around the world, and it was based on the views of world leaders, men and women of many nationalities and races, with whom he met.[53]

Willkie, a former Democrat, was a well-known progressive figure in American politics. He had spoken often of the need to end racism in America, and he had addressed the convention of the National Association for the Advancement of Colored People (NAACP) in 1942, one of the most prominent whites ever to do so up to that time. When a violent race riot broke out in Detroit in the summer of 1943, Willkie went on national radio to criticize both Republicans and Democrats for ignoring the "Negro question." In his remarks, he emphasized the similarity between American racism toward blacks and Nazi anti-Semitism. During this time, Willkie also worked with Walter White, executive secretary of the NAACP, to convince Hollywood to change its portrayal of blacks in the movies.

Willkie as a politician embodied a nonpartisan spirit of cooperation during wartime and supported Roosevelt's creation of a military draft. An unlikely ally with the president against the isolationists of his own party, Willkie's support turned into criticism of Roosevelt's seeming lack of preparedness in military matters. During the election campaign of 1940, however, Roosevelt expanded military contracts to blunt the attacks of the opposition. Although Willkie initially had supported the draft, he reversed his stance when opinion polls showed that opposition to entering another world war was an issue inflaming the electorate. Although the United States was still neutral in 1940, the nation was deeply divided between isolationist and interventionist sentiment. Three of the leading candidates in competition with Willkie (a former Democrat) for the 1940 Republican nomination, Robert Taft, Arthur Vandenberg, and Thomas E. Dewey, were all isolationists to varying degrees. To court the powerful isolationist wing of the Republican Party, Willkie began to claim that Roosevelt was secretly planning to take the United States into the European War against Germany. The isolationists only thinly supported his candidacy, while his greatest support came from the benign interventionist wing of the party, which felt that America needed to provide all aid to the Allies short of war.

As a wartime measure, Willkie noted that Americans were being asked to give up temporarily some of their individual freedoms and civil liberties to crush the Axis powers, but he also noted that these rights must be recovered and restored after the war. In 1943, he sided with the critics of the administration regarding the "misdirected censorship" imposed by the Roosevelt administration:

It is the utmost folly—just short of suicide—to take the position that citizens of any country should hold their tongues for fear of causing distress to the immediate and sometimes tortuous policies of their leaders. We have been told, for example, that private citizens, particularly those not expert in military affairs or those unconnected with government, should refrain from making suggestions about the conduct of the war—military, industrial, economic, or political. It is said we must remain silent and allow our leaders and the experts to solve these problems unmolested. This position threatens, I believe, to become a tight wall which will keep truth out and lock misrepresentation and false security within.[54]

Some of the ideas proclaimed by Roosevelt (and Churchill) in the Atlantic Charter greatly distressed Willkie and other members of the opposition. They forecast the recreation of Western Europe at the end of the war with Germany in its same-old divisions of small nations "each with its own individual political, economic, and military sovereignty."[55] This they considered an outmoded system that restricted trade, manipulated the power of politics, and "made impoverishment and war inevitable."[56] Willkie supported the reincorporation of the former governments of Europe as political units, but not as economic or military ones. Roosevelt and Churchill were not the only leaders whose words and activities invited criticism. Stalin's failure to formulate and announce specific aspirations for Europe after his entry into the war also made them anxious. Willkie wrote:

While we fight, we must develop a mechanism of working together that will survive after the fighting is over. Successful instruments of either national or international government are the result of growth. . . . They must be made workable and smooth-running, under the emery of day-to-day effort in the solution of common problems.[57]

Willkie as a spokesperson for the opposition thought it all but useless to talk about creating mechanisms of peace-keeping between nations after the war "unless the parts of the machinery have been assembled under the unifying effort and common purpose of seeking to defeat the enemy."[58]

Willkie (who died in 1944) assumed that the United States would be faced with three alternatives at the conclusion of the war:

- a narrowly defined nationalism that might serve as a means to the ultimate loss of American civil liberties
- an international imperialism that would require the sacrifice of the civil liberties of others
- the creation of a form of world government devoted to the equality of opportunity of every race and nationality

He was sure that Americans would choose the last alternative. "To win this peace three things seem to me necessary," he wrote, "[F]irst, we must plan now for peace on a world basis; second, the world must be free, politically, economically, for nations and for men, that peace may exist in it; third, Americans must play an active, constructive part in freeing it and keeping its peace."[59]

Former president Herbert Hoover also wrote an analysis of problems confronting the world at the end of the war. In *The Problems of Lasting Peace* (1943) he wrote, "The men who gather at the peace table . . . have but a fleeting opportunity to make secure the foundations of lasting peace." He noted in particular,

The difference between aims and peace treaties is the same difference as that between the Declaration of Independence and the Constitution of the United

States. It takes little imagination to picture the results, if, instead of elaborating a Constitution, the Founding Fathers and their descendants had endeavored to govern this country under the terms of the Declaration. . . . The vital question in the peace is how our aims and ideals are to be made to work. That is, by what means, what powers, what machinery, is peace to be made to prevail.

Among Hoover's first principles were that peace had to be *founded on victory*, and overseen by some organization, some machinery for international cooperation that would think about the problems of peace in a larger framework than ever before.[60]

Henry A. Wallace, wartime vice president of the United States until 1944, was a long time voice for peace. In *The Price of Free World Victory* (1943), he noted that even in the midst of a world war, the interventionists were plotting a new, subtle, and therefore dangerous form of militarism that he felt would lead the nation straight to a third world war. He wrote:

The people are being told that a world war every generation is inevitable and that we can have national security only by maintaining the biggest army, the biggest navy, and the biggest air force in the world. Even if we could indefinitely stand the expense and the privation of such a program, it would not necessarily protect us.[61]

Wallace rejected these militarist concepts as propaganda. If the democracies of the world wished to survive in the postwar era and retain their human rights, he felt that they must convince their citizens to be as willing to give wholeheartedly and unselfishly the same type of service to their democratic nations that citizens of totalitarian powers gave to theirs.

In 1942, Wallace delivered his most famous speech, which became known by the phrase "Century of the Common Man," to the International Free World Association in New York. Wallace's speech, grounded in Christian references, laid out a positive vision for the world beyond the simple defeat of the Nazis. The speech, and the book of the same name that appeared the following year, proved quite popular, but his obvious acceptance of Socialist principles earned him enemies among the Democratic Party leadership, important Allied leaders like Churchill, and business leaders and conservatives.

In 1941, the International Free World Association had begun publishing a magazine called *Free World*, which openly envisioned a world government superseding the sovereignty of nations in the postwar world. The statement of purpose of the organization included the following frank statement:

World peace can be created and maintained only under world law, universal and strong enough to prevent armed conflict between nations. . . . Therefore, while endorsing the efforts of the United Nations to bring about a world community favorable to peace, we will work primarily to strengthen the United Nations into a world government of limited powers adequate to prevent a war and having direct jurisdiction over the individual.[62]

The frankness with which the proponents of one-world government discussed their plans alarmed many Americans who objected to surrendering their sovereignty and even their basic right to self-determination. Explicit in the proposal was the power of taxation over the individuals of all nations by a world legislature. Many feared that such an organization would be dominated by have-not nations envious of the great wealth and industry of the United States, where only 6 percent of the world population resided, but which controlled half the world wealth and production capacity. These suspicions were magnified when the secretary of the group, Louis Dolivert was later identified as a member of the World Communist Party. Another person active in the group was Carlo Emmanuel a Prato, who was a member of the International Editorial Board of *Free World*. Prato, an Italian Communist, had been expelled from Switzerland as a Soviet agent and had entered the United States under a false name on a Czech passport.

On April 26, 1945, representatives of most of the recognized nations of the world met in San Francisco to create an organization of nations that would ensure lasting peace to a world long weary of war. The conference was completed on June 26, 1945, with the adoption of the United Nations Charter. The Subcommittee on International Organization at the conference was headed by Sumner Welles, of the U.S. State Department and a close advisor to Roosevelt. Welles provided a direct link between the old League of Nations and the new United Nations and called for a return to the principles of disarmament and the establishment of world economic justice as instruments to bring about a peaceful and equitable postwar world. In *Blueprint for Peace* (1943) Welles outlined two unalterable premises for world peace:

> First . . . the abolition of offensive armaments and the limitation and reduction of defensive armaments and of the tools which make construction of such armaments possible can only be undertaken through some rigid form of international supervision and control. . . .
>
> Second . . . no peace which may be made in the future would be valid or long lasting unless it established fully and adequately the natural rights of all people to equal economic enjoyment. So long as any one people or any one government possesses a monopoly over natural resources or raw materials which are needed by all peoples, there can be no basis for a world order based on justice and peace.[63]

With regard to the unbroken record of failure in attaining peace set by the previous generations of antiwar progressives, Welles noted that their idealism was not the problem to be overcome in establishing world peace. Rather it was the "defeatist philosophy of the cynic who, because of the failures of the past, cannot envision the successes of the future."[64]

Many statesmen had theorized that increased interaction and interdependency among nations would bring world peace. Thus, the United Nations was created and the internationalist movement among pacifists acquired a momentum rooted in free commerce and an appreciation of diversity, as well as the desire for mankind to be free from war. In 1947 the United World Federalists was founded by merging several other organizations interested in world government, including Americans United for World Government, the World Federalists, the Massachusetts Committee for World Federation, the Student Federalists, the World Citizens of Georgia, and the World Republic. Yet along with increased worldwide commerce, communication, and travel in the postwar world, the poison of the destructive power and widespread distribution of the weapons of war had increased exponentially.

The United Nations had been created to help form this peace, and well-intentioned diplomats from all parts of the globe had assembled to establish what they viewed as mankind's last hope for achieving it. Many in the wealthy nations of the world viewed the United Nations as little more than a forum for poor nations to advocate for the transfer of wealth to their regions and work against the interests of the most powerful ones. The United Nations would not become a world government, as many well-intentioned idealists had purposed. Rather, it became a composite, or conglomerate, of assembled nations (or blocs) each pursuing their own interests, goals, and objectives. To condemn the United Nations as a cause of continued world conflict is irresponsible, but to claim that it has brought about peace is utterly foolish.[65]

Although the simultaneous evils of Nazism, fascism, and imperialism had been turned back and soundly defeated, one of the unfortunate outcomes of World War II for U.S. foreign policy was that Americans came to believe that war worked—that it could be used to resolve seemingly insoluble problems, work out thorny issues, and bring lasting peace. In the 1960s, U.S. diplomats attempted to resolve the problem of spreading world Communism by defeating it in detail (nation by nation) on the battlefield. Whenever the United States had stood up to its enemies in the past, America had won, and Americans had flourished. The next attempt would prove disastrous.

Notes

1. Jeffrey E. Garten, *A Cold Peace: America, Japan, Germany, and the Struggle for Supremacy* (New York: Random House, 1993), 47.

2. Anthony Tucker-Jones, *Hitler's Great Panzer Heist: Germany's Foreign Armor in Action, 1939–1945* (Mechanicsburg, PA: Stackpole Books, 2007), 2.

3. Tucker-Jones, 2.

4. See the appendix, "Major Peace Organizations, 1960s and 1970s."

5. Herbert Hoover and Hugh Gibson, "The Problems of Lasting Peace," in *Prefaces to Peace: A Symposium* (New York: Columbia University Press, 1943), 248.

6. Hoover and Gibson, 249.

7. Walter J. Boyne, *Clash of Titans: World War II at Sea* (New York: Simon & Schuster, 1995), 17.

8. See Neville Chamberlain, "Chamberlain's radio broadcast before 10 Downing Street (transcription)," September 30, 1938, http://eudocs.lib.byu.edu/index.php/Neville_Chamberlain%27s_%22Peace_For_Our_Time%22_speech (accessed October 2008).

9. Chamberlain.

10. John G. Stoessinger, *Why Nations Go to War* (New York: St. Martin's Press, 1993), 41–42.

11. Stoessinger, 49.

12. Stoessinger, 50.

13. Michael G. Walling, *Bloodstained Sea: The U.S. Coast Guard in the Battle of the Atlantic, 1941–1945* (New York: McGraw Hill, 2004), 25.

14. Walling, 18.

15. William H. Rehnquist, *All the Laws But One: Civil Liberties in Wartime* (New York: Vintage Books, 1998), 185.

16. George C. Herring, *From Colony to Superpower: U.S. Foreign Relations Since 1776* (New York: Oxford University Press, 2008), 495.

17. Rehnquist, 186.

18. Rehnquist, 187.

19. Garten, 46.

20. Walling, 41.

21. Garten, 47.

22. Garten, 47.

23. Stephen Bull and Gordon L. Rottman, *Infantry Tactics of the Second World War* (Westminster, MD: Osprey Publishing, Ltd., 2008), 7–8.

24. Bull and Rottman, 18.

25. Bull and Rottman, 18.

26. Bull and Rottman, 21.

27. Bull and Rottman, 42.

28. Bull and Rottman, 42.

29. Bull and Rottman, 11–12.

30. Bull and Rottman, 11–12.

31. Robert Burns, "Deaths outside Combat Increase Recently," http://www.signonsandiego.com/uniontrib/20050220/news_1n20casualty.html (accessed June 2009).

32. Bern Keating, *The Mosquito Fleet* (New York: G. P. Putnam's Sons, 1963), 125–126.

33. Keating, 93–94.

34. Five U.S. presidents saw combat in World War II: Eisenhower (supreme Allied commander), Kennedy (PT commander, Navy/Marine Corps Medal), Johnson (Navy, Silver Star), Reagan (1st Motion Picture Unit, AAF), and G. H. W. Bush (Navy Torpedo Plane Pilot, DFC, three Air medals). Nixon was a Navy commander dealing with logistics in rear areas. He saw no combat.

35. Clark G. Reynolds, *The Carrier War* (Alexandria, VA: Time-Life Books, 1982), 63.

36. Reynolds, 121.

37. John B. Lundstrom, *The First Team* (Annapolis, MD: Naval Institute Press, 1984), 323.

38. Boyne, 193.

39. Boyne, 188.

40. Walling, xii.

41. Walling, xii.

42. Gregory H. Stanton, "How We Can Prevent Genocide, Building An International Campaign to End Genocide," http://www.genocidewatch.org/HOWWECANPREVENTGE NOCIDE.htm (accessed February 2009).

43. Boyne, 281.

44. Boyne, 281.

45. Boyne, 281.

46. Rehnquist, 211.

47. Rehnquist, 211.

48. Rehnquist, 190.

49. Rehnquist, 191.

50. Rehnquist, 101.

51. Rehnquist, 107.

52. Rehnquist, 205.

53. Wendell Willkie, "One World," in *Prefaces to Peace: A Symposium* (New York: Columbia University Press, 1943).

54. Henry Seidel Canby, *Prefaces to Peace: A Symposium* (New York: Columbia University Press, 1943), 123.

55. Canby, 126.

56. Canby, 126.

57. Canby, 126.

58. Canby, 126.

59. Canby, 146.

60. Hoover and Gibson, 155.

61. Henry A. Wallace, "The Price of Free World Victory," in *Prefaces to Peace: A Symposium* (New York: Columbia University Press, 1943), 364.

62. Wallace, 350.

63. Sumner Welles, "Blueprint for Peace," in *Prefaces to Peace: A Symposium* (New York: Columbia University Press, 1943), 420.

64. Welles, 427.

65. David C. Pack, "Can the UN Bring Peace to the World?" *The Real Truth Magazine*, http://www.realtruth.org/articles/070119-001-un.html (accessed February 2009).

Chapter 16

The 1950s: Korea, the Cold War, and Banning the Bomb

We have all witnessed the stifling choking effect of McCarthyism, the paralysis of initiative, the discouragement and intimidation that follow in its wake and inhibit the bold, imaginative thought and discussion that is the anvil of policy.

—Adlai Stevenson, 1951

Moving into a Postwar World

The post–World War II decades were a time of great economic prosperity for the United States. However, critics of this period have remarked on the widespread conformity that permeated many U.S. communities. Pockets of rebellion and alternative lifestyles existed, but they were largely under the surface and either ignored or persecuted by mainstream America. As Roosevelt's New Deal paternalism and Hot War–thinking of the 1940s gave way to Truman's Fair Deal capitalism and Cold War–thinking in the 1950s, Americans entered a period of remarkable *sameness*, where media, corporations, and communities reinforced the norms, and government policed and disciplined those who deviated from them.

The period saw the ownership of row upon row of affordable (but eerily identical) houses in the suburbs as a goal to be pursued. Public schools took on a regional sameness, and Main Street became a cardboard cutout virtually interchangeable in any number of American towns. There was also a widespread acceptance of seemingly controversial government activities like those of the House Un-American Activities Committee (HUAC), involvement in a United Nations–sponsored war in the Korean Peninsula, and the establishment of a vast nuclear weapons program as part of America's strategic policy.[1]

Several factors explain the postwar conformity that characterized much of America in the 1950s and early 1960s. Foremost among these were the residual sense of national unity from fighting the recent war and the perceived threat of a Cold War with the Soviets. These factors helped ease political distinctions over foreign policy and contributed to a sense of American togetherness—at least among those considered anti-Communists. The recent victory over Fascism suggested that war worked as a means of spreading democracy, and the Korean Conflict (1950–1953) convinced most in the United States that the nation needed to challenge Communist China and the Soviet Republic in a contest for the sociopolitical soul of the world. This would require both a military and an economic response from the American public.

In addition, the increased adaptation of mass production techniques in a rising postwar economy led to the mass consumption of domestic goods and an improved lifestyle that seemed to dispel much of the attraction that Socialism had had for a large segment (possibly as high as 35 percent) of the Great Depression generation. Along with home ownership, automobile ownership soared helped by the establishment of a new federally sponsored Interstate Highway System. Maintaining middle-class conformity, a middle-class lifestyle, and a middle-class dedication to capitalism was deemed essential for the continuation of this American utopia. Herbert Hoover's pre-Depression election slogan, "A chicken in every pot, and a car in every garage" (1928) had virtually become "a house on every lot, and all your kids in college."

Finally, the troubling continuation of racial, ethnic, and economic segregation (in housing, education, employment, and other areas) prevented a wide range of alternative perspectives from reaching the public eye, while the explosion of traditional white family values on the new medium of television (*Father Knows Best, Leave It to Beaver, Ozzie and Harriet*, and so on) contributed to the Baby Boom era's sense of what constituted the new modern Americanism. By the mid-1950s, television had displaced the Depression-era silver screen (*Andy Hardy, Nancy Drew, Ma and Pa Kettle*, and so on) as the conveyor and guardian of the wholesome American family image. Whereas in former times the extended family (grandparents, aunts, and uncles living together under the same roof) was commonly portrayed, almost everywhere in the 1950s the nuclear family unit (mom, dad, and children) was held forth as an ideal. Not until the late 1960s and early 1970s would alternative family structures return to the world of TV (*The Andy Griffith Show, My Three Sons, The Brady Bunch*, and so on).

The most dramatic change in America's new life of conformity was the establishment of a peacetime universal draft in the United States. The Selective Service Law (1950)—the first of its kind in American history and unthinkable in the past—required eighteen-year-old males to register for conscription in the absence of a war or the threat of war and established a two-year active service obligation in the military followed by an additional term in the reserves. The social impact of the peacetime draft saw hundreds of thousands of young Americans undergoing educational, economic, and personal dislocation in their lives (usually at the end of high school or before entering the workforce from college) to receive basic military training and active deployment to bases in the United States and also throughout Europe, Asia, and elsewhere to counter Communism. This program overturned two centuries of American protocol with respect to peacetime foreign service in the military.

Postwar Foreign Policy

Postwar Soviet-American relations had degenerated from an atmosphere of cooperation at the Yalta Conference in early 1945 to one of deep distrust in less than twelve months. Harry Truman seemingly lacked the self-confidence of Franklin Roosevelt in the role thrust upon him by the president's death, and it showed in Stalin's attitude toward him. Roosevelt had been a larger-than-life president for thirteen years, and Truman, while familiar to the American people and the diplomatic world, projected an unassuming and folksy whimsy. He ultimately overcame the low expectations of many political observers who compared him unfavorably with his highly regarded predecessor, yet at different points in his presidency, he earned some of both the highest and the lowest public approval ratings that had been recorded. In the early 21st century, Truman is generally considered to have been a good president.

Truman's administration was initially torn by the forces of a growing popular conservatism and a preoccupation with anti-Communism. He used executive orders to launch a system of *loyalty checks* to remove thousands of Communist sympathizers from government office, but he strongly opposed mandatory loyalty oaths for government employees, a stance that led to largely unjustified charges from the right that his administration was soft on Communism. Overlapping jurisdictions within the different departments in the administration often produced conflicting foreign policy initiatives. This was especially true when the militarists at the Central Intelligence Agency (CIA) came to loggerheads with the diplomats at the Department of State.[2] Truman's second term (beginning in 1949) was grueling, in large measure because of foreign policy challenges connected directly or indirectly to his attitudes regarding the need to thwart the spread of world Communism.

Rather than forcing the Soviets into an accommodation through a balance of economic sanctions and trade initiatives, for instance, Truman's hard-line policies reinforced Russian apprehensions about Soviet security and Western Hemisphere hostility. Soviet foreign policy has always been dominated by the desire to have a buffer of friendly satellite states along the geopolitical borders of Russia with Europe and Asia. It is not unfair to say that the Union of Soviet Socialist Republics (USSR) existed to protect Russia. Much of Soviet foreign policy can best be understood with this basic premise in mind. This was a novel paradigm to those in the United States, where the idea of forty-nine states existing to protect just one, Ohio for instance, would be thought ridiculous.

Western Hemisphere objections to Soviet policies in Eastern Europe indicated to Stalin their intention to crush Communism and isolate the Soviet regime. Partially for this reason, Stalin closed off East Germany to his former allies. The Soviets saw the Berlin Airlift—a massive campaign that delivered food, fuel, and other supplies to the isolated capital using military airplanes—and the attempt to revitalize the West German industrial economy as provocations. Stalin wanted a weak and divided Germany on his borders, so he denuded the eastern half of its factories, its military materials, its technological documents, and its scientists. He then moved them (even the factories) inside Russia for safekeeping and dropped what Churchill called an *iron curtain* across Europe, plunging the world into a long period of bipolar political maneuvering and military gamesmanship.

The developing diplomatic tensions between the United States and the USSR would come to dominate American foreign policy for almost forty years, and at the end of the so-called Cold War, only one would survive as a great power. America's core policy, enunciated by the Truman administration and followed for years to come, was called *containment* (see discussion of NSC 68 in the section, "A National Security State"). The United States would continue to use economic and military aid to advance its influence in the world community and would attempt to disrupt any Communist revolutions or anticolonial insurgencies that might threaten international stability and give root to Communist influences. "Once the champion of social justice and the right of revolution, the United States increasingly pitted its might against any change that it did not control."[3]

In 1947 the National Security Act created the National Security Council (NSC), which combined the departments of defense and of state with the CIA as a tripartite advisory body to the executive branch. The 1950s oversaw a federal budget that devoted more than 50 percent of its revenues to defense in peacetime as the nation began an accumulation of a vast arsenal of nuclear weapons. While this was only one-third (14 percent of GNP) of what was spent during World War II (38 percent of GNP), this level of military spending in peacetime had never been experienced during any previous period of U.S. history. Although Truman was no friend of the military (he particularly despised the Marine Corps), the demand on the economy to develop military technologies and defense systems increased during his administration. The nation saw the peacetime development of corporations and industries devoted to the business of producing conventional weapons, strategic aircraft, and vessels of war to make a profit (known as the military-industrial complex). Nevertheless, reductions to traditional areas of military spending continued, adversely affecting America's conventional (that is, not nuclear) defense readiness. Meanwhile, John Foster Dulles (secretary of state under Eisenhower) defended the stockpiling of nuclear weapons as cheaper and more effective than drafting even more young Americans to serve in what he called the "global police force."[4]

At any other time in U.S. history such programs would have raised the voice of protest among the vast majority of the electorate. Yet in a decade of conformity, Americans passively submitted to a European-style conscription similar to that established by Napoleon 147 years earlier and a centralization of military power in the hands of the executive similar to that practiced by Hitler. Instead of protest, an entire generation of American families supinely became accustomed to the required military service of their sons and brothers throughout the 1950s and 1960s with barely a whimper.[5] Membership in antiwar groups plummeted, and some pacifists like journalist I. F. Stone questioned whether any semblance of a peace movement remained in America.[6]

A National Security State

In early 1949, Under-Secretary of State Dean Acheson drew up a formal outline for Truman's foreign policy based on a number of assumptions and observations that would become the basis of U.S. Cold War–thinking for decades. Although developed by a Democrat administration, these premises would come to characterize the foreign policy assumptions of both Democrat and Republican administrations for much of the 20th century. The NSC white paper presented by Acheson, called NSC 68, laid out the premises of this program for the approval of President Truman. Among these were the following:

- There can be no distinction between U.S. national security and world security.
- The Soviets intend to stamp out freedom and dominate the world through the imposition of world Communism.
- World freedom depends on the spread of democratic capitalism and freedom from Communist-style Socialism.
- Negotiations with the Soviets are futile because they do not bargain in good faith.
- The administration will take a hard anti-Communist stance everywhere that Communism appears.[7]

Adoption of the principles contained in NSC 68 effectively made the United States a "national security state: a leviathan with overwhelming military power, a wide variety of economic weapons, and an extensive capacity for covert operations." Those who advocated negotiations with the Communists or social initiatives outside the norms associated with capitalism were to be considered "fomenters of disunity and disrupters of conformity" because they weakened the cultural and social fabric of America.[8]

Yet even in an ocean of conformity, not all the voices in government were in agreement, and opposition to many of Truman's policies came from both extremes. Democrat Henry A. Wallace, for example, as a spokesman for "a world community favorable to peace" advocated a more cooperative attitude toward the Soviets, warning that the United States had everything to lose by "beating the tom-toms against Russia." He warned that the United States should have "no more business in the political affairs of Eastern Europe than Russia has in the political affairs of Latin America."[9] A former vice president, Wallace—who was fired as Truman's secretary of commerce shortly thereafter—argued that a secure and prosperous USSR would be more accommodating than a frightened and hungry one.[10]

At the same time, a constant stream of crises—the closing of Berlin, the failure of Nationalist China, the development of a Soviet atomic bomb—unsettled the opposition party with regard to Communism. When a former State Department official, Alger Hiss, was accused of passing documents to Soviet agents, the search for Communists in America was taken up with a will. Sen. William E. Jenner, Republican of Indiana, charged that the Truman administration consisted of a "crazy assortment of collectivist cutthroat crackpots and Communist fellow-traveling appeasers." Jenner declared on the floor of Congress, "This country today is in the hands of a secret inner coterie which is directed by agents of the Soviet Union. We must cut this cancerous conspiracy out of our government at once . . . [and]

impeach President Truman."[11] The powerful *China lobby*, composed of conservative business leaders and supporters of Sen. Joseph McCarthy, blamed the administration for the loss of China to Communism. In the end, Truman maintained the
loyalty of his midwestern progressive base, but he was unable to shake the image
of being unable to purge his administration of subversive influences. When an
unexpected Communist coup took control of Czechoslovakia in 1949, it set off an
anti-Communist crusade in the United States the likes of which the nation had
never before seen. The traditional American right of dissent would be one of the
first serious casualties.[12]

A Second Red Scare

The administration's Office of War Information that had controlled (shaped) Hollywood's propaganda response to the Nazis under the direction of Joseph Goebbels
throughout World War II was staffed by some of America's most famous intellectuals, including veteran CBS newscaster Elmer Davis, Pulitzer Prize–winner Robert
Sherwood, and the Librarian of Congress Archibald MacLeish. These men had
worked to shape the films that were released during the war years. The United
States also established so-called Motion Picture Units within the Army, Navy
(Marines), and Army Air Force for the purpose of producing wartime propaganda.
Ironically, it was the film industry's self-censorship system, the Hays Office, and
the Production Code Administration that opened the door for government censors
to rewrite screenplays and edit movies in the postwar era so that they portrayed an
idealized image of a harmonious American society united in the fight against
Communism.

The HUAC, initially formed to investigate Communist infiltration in American
government, expanded its jurisdiction in the 1950s under Sen. Joseph McCarthy to
include Hollywood. World War II–era screenwriters Dalton Trumbo (*Thirty Sec-
onds over Tokyo*) and John H. Lawson (*Action in the North Atlantic*, *Sahara*) were
among the early victims of the Second Red Scare of the postwar years. These
two men also were part of the Hollywood Ten, a select group of American movie
professionals—primarily screenwriters, directors, and producers—who were either
actual members or alleged to have been members of the American Communist
Party (also know as Communist Party USA). All ten were ultimately blacklisted by
the Hollywood studios. Although both Lawson and Trumbo had produced wartime
films helpful to the Allied cause, many of their screenplays were politically incorrect and seemingly embraced Socialist concepts, such as Lawson's tribute to the
U.S.-Soviet alliance formed during World War II, *Counter Attack* (1945), or Trumbo's *Tender Comrade* (1943) that showed American women on the home front
living in communal bliss while their husbands were away at war. He also wrote *We
Who Are Young* (1940) about a young couple struggling to make ends meet in an
unfriendly and unsympathetic capitalist world. In addition Trumbo's antiwar novel
set in World War I, *Johnny Got His Gun*, had won the American Book Sellers
Award in 1939, and plans were on file to make it into a movie. Also among the
Hollywood Ten was Edward Dmytryk, director of *Tender Comrade* and *Crossfire*

(1947). The latter film examined anti-Semitism in the United States. It caused great controversy at its release and may have been the major reason for Dmytryk's summons from HUAC. Dmytryk admitted a brief membership in the Communist Party and named twenty-six other Communists or Socialists in the film industry. Dmytryk's testimony opened a floodgate of accusations, denials, and pleas to the Fifth Amendment guarantee against self-incrimination.

Although Trumbo had aligned himself with the American Communist Party before World War II, he did not officially join the party until 1943. There is little doubt that Trumbo was political in his screenwriting—he even bragged of the level of Communist influence in Hollywood in *The Daily Worker*—a newspaper published in New York City by the American Communist Party. After the outbreak of war in September 1939, he and other American Communists publicly argued against U.S. involvement because (before June 1941) the Soviet Union was at peace with Germany.

After Trumbo was blacklisted, some Hollywood actors and directors agreed to testify and to provide names of fellow Communist Party members to Congress. Many of those who testified were immediately ostracized and shunned by their former friends and associates. After completing his eleven-month jail sentence, Trumbo and his family moved to Mexico where he wrote up to thirty scripts under pseudonyms. He even won an Academy Award for *The Brave One* (1956) under the name Robert Rich. In 1960, the unrepentant Trumbo was publicly acknowledged as the screenwriter of both of that year's super-films *Spartacus* and *Exodus*. This event is usually considered the breaking of the blacklist and the end of the Hollywood Red Scare.

Meanwhile, screenwriter John H. Lawson, the president and organizing force of the Screen Writers' Guild, made many members of the Guild suspect because he also was the acknowledged and self-identified leader of the American Communist Party in Hollywood. In October 1947, he became the first "unfriendly" witness subpoenaed to testify before HUAC. After his testimony, a week-long session followed during which numerous studio heads, screen stars, and others spoke at length about purported Communist activity in the film industry. During that first week, film critic and screenwriter John Charles Moffitt detailed Lawson's supposed instructions to other writers on how to incorporate pro-Communist propaganda into film scripts. This testimony paralleled the public statements of Trumbo in the Communist press.

With the nine other "unfriendly" witnesses, Lawson gambled that the Committee would issue contempt citations for their refusal to answer questions about their political associations and beliefs, and that after a court case and appeal, the Supreme Court would rule that such questioning violated their First Amendment rights. Further HUAC interrogations would thus be stopped. In 1949, however, before the appeal reached the high court, two liberal justices died, and in 1950, the newly constituted Supreme Court refused to hear the appeal. The Hollywood Ten were sent to prison as a result, and in 1951, HUAC continued its Hollywood probe.[13]

Also testifying in 1947, Hollywood studio executives—including three major "friendly" witnesses, studio heads Jack L. Warner of Warner Bros. and Louis B.

Mayer of Metro Goldwyn Meyer (MGM), and Russian-born novelist and screen-writer Ayn Rand—agreed with HUAC that some wartime films—particularly *Mission to Moscow*, *The North Star*, and *Song of Russia*—could be considered pro-Communist propaganda. Nonetheless, they also claimed that the films had been valuable in the context of advancing the Allied war effort.

In any case, the films under question by HUAC had been made under the general authority of the propaganda office or at the request of the White House. This was especially true in the case of *Mission to Moscow* (released 1943), which Roosevelt had specifically requested. It was argued that if making *Mission to Moscow* was a subversive activity, then the American Liberty ships it portrayed, which carried food and guns to Soviet allies, and the American escort vessels, which protected them, were likewise engaged in subversive activities. The films had been made only to help a desperate war effort and not for the conversion of posterity to Communism.

HUAC did not simply target all pro-Soviet films in a scattergun fashion, only those that in its unchallenged opinion promoted Communism. *Days of Glory* (1944), for instance, was a blatantly over-the-top tribute to the courage and resourcefulness of a small band of Soviet guerilla fighters during the war. It was possibly more pro-Soviet than other films, but the characters (actors Gregory Peck and Tamara Toumanova) spoke in long, somewhat stilted monologues filled with inoffensive platitudes concerning broad areas such as freedom, sacrifice, and the indomitable human spirit. They never praised the Communist system or defamed capitalism. Although listed among suspect films, none of those associated with its production seem to have come under HUAC's scrutiny.[14]

Several leading Hollywood figures, including director John Huston (whose father Walter starred in both *Mission to Moscow* and *The North Star*) and actors Humphrey Bogart and Lauren Bacall organized the Committee for the First Amendment and flew to Washington to protest the government targeting of their industry. Other notable protestors included screenwriter Philip Dunne; film director William Wyler; actresses Myrna Loy, Katharine Hepburn, Jane Wyatt, and Marsha Hunt; actors Henry Fonda, Gene Kelly, John Garfield, and Edward G. Robinson; and entertainers Danny Kaye and Frank Sinatra. In later years, Bogart, Garfield, and Robinson wrote articles suggesting that they were "duped" into supporting the Hollywood Ten, some of whom were indeed associated with Communism. Wyatt's film acting career—best remembered for her roles in Frank Capra's film *Lost Horizon* (1937) and television's *Father Knows Best*—was temporarily damaged for her outspoken pacifism and for having hosted a performance by the Russian Bolshoi Ballet during World War II, even though it was at President Roosevelt's request. Her reappearance on television as the typical American middle-class mother figure in the 1950s was considered a small victory by the acting community.[15]

Several Hollywood professionals, including Ronald Reagan, then head of the Screen Actors Guild, actor Robert Taylor, and animator Walt Disney, testified to HUAC that the threat of Communists in the film industry was a serious one. In his testimony before the committee, Taylor protested that he had made *Song of Russia* (1944) under duress from the studio, a claim echoed by actress Ginger Rogers for her appearance in *Tender Comrades*. Many actors used this rationale to explain to the community of film artists why they were friendly witnesses during the HUAC hearings. Under the pressure of the Red Scare, many film artists seemed willing to throw the screenwriters, producers, and directors "under the bus." Trumbo maintained that those who testified under pressure from HUAC or the studios were equally victims of the Red Scare, an opinion for which he was severely criticized in liberal circles. On November 17, 1947, the Screen Actors Guild voted to make all its officers swear a non-Communist pledge, and during the following week the House of Representatives voted 346–17 to approve citations against the Hollywood Ten for contempt of Congress for refusing to testify. Thereafter, HUAC agreed to stop investigating the studios or the content of their films, and to limit their inquiries to individual persons.

Eventually, more than 300 artists—including directors, radio commentators, actors, composers, and screenwriters—were boycotted by the studios for supposed leftist connections. Besides actual membership in the Communist Party, things like social activism, homosexuality, and pregnancy outside of marriage seem to have been gateway offenses to the "blacklist." Among those blacklisted were major figures in their respective fields like playwright Lillian Hellman, singer Pete Seeger, and composer Elmer Bernstein. Some, like comic Charlie Chaplin and screenwriter John H. Lawson, left the United States to find work abroad—one to Europe, the other to Mexico. Others, like Trumbo, wrote under pseudonyms or the names of colleagues.

In 1946, Paul Robeson, black singer, actor, and social activist, had been questioned by the California Fact-Finding Committee on Un-American Activities. He was one of the first to come under the microscope of the Red Scare. Nine years later, after numerous court fights to suppress the subpoena, HUAC asked him whether he was a member of the Communist Party. Robeson replied that he might as well have been asked whether he was a registered Democrat or Republican—in the United States the Communist Party was equally legal. This claim was not quite true. In 1950, Congress had passed the Internal Security Act (also known as the McCarran Act) that required the registration of all Communists residing in the United States. It also strengthened the espionage and immigration laws, and provided for the establishment of detention camps for spies and saboteurs. In his somewhat rambling but poignant statement before HUAC, Robeson noted:

> Could I say that the reason that I am here today, you know, from the mouth of the State Department itself, is: I should not be allowed to travel because I have struggled for years for the independence of the colonial peoples of Africa. For many years I have so labored and I can say modestly that my name is very much honored all over Africa, in my struggles for their independence. That is the kind of independence like Sukarno got in Indonesia. Unless we are double-talking, then these efforts in the interest of Africa would be in the same context. The other reason that I am here today, again from the State Department and from the court record of the court of appeals, is that when I am abroad I speak out against the injustices against the Negro people of this land. I sent a message to the

Bandung Conference [a meeting of 29 non-aligned African and Asian countries] and so forth. That is why I am here. This is the basis, and I am not being tried for whether I am a Communist, I am being tried for fighting for the rights of my people, who are still second-class citizens in this United States of America. My mother . . . was a Quaker, and my ancestors in the time of Washington baked bread for George Washington's troops when they crossed the Delaware, and my own father was a slave. I stand here struggling for the rights of my people to be full citizens in this country. And they are not. They are not in Mississippi. And they are not in Montgomery, Alabama. And they are not in Washington. They are nowhere, and that is why I am here today. You want to shut up every Negro who has the courage to stand up and fight for the rights of his people, for the rights of workers, and I have been on many a picket line for the steelworkers too. And that is why I am here today . . . I say that . . . you gentlemen [of the HUAC] belong with the Alien and Sedition Acts [1798], and you are the non-patriots, and you are the un-Americans, and you ought to be ashamed of yourselves.[16]

Robeson invoked the Fifth Amendment several times during his testimony, but he added as an afterthought that he was not a Communist. After this appearance, Robeson's passport was revoked, but he worked tirelessly for civil rights within the confines of the United States despite being barred by the HUAC from traveling internationally.

The disturbing nature of the HUAC hearings is best summarized by a few examples of how individuals were targeted. Lillian Hellman appeared before HUAC because of her work as screenwriter for *North Star* and because of her longtime love interest, writer Dashiell Hammett, who had been a Communist Party member. Hellman offered to testify as to her own activities if she would not be forced to inform on others. When the Committee refused her request, she took the Fifth Amendment and was blacklisted. In refusing to name names, she said that she found it impossible to "cut her conscience to fit the year's fashions."[17]

Elmer Bernstein faced censure during the 1950s, but he was "gray-listed" (not banned, but kept off major projects) simply due to his open sympathy for liberal causes. While composing the score for *To Kill a Mockingbird* (1962), Bernstein said he had difficulty writing a musical score about racism as seen through the eyes of children. Singer and actor Burl Ives (also gray-listed for several years) named fellow folksinger Pete Seeger as a suspected Communist before HUAC.

Seeger had been a fervent supporter of the republican (anti-Fascist) side in the Spanish Civil War in 1936. At the age of seventeen, he had joined the Young Communist League (YCL), then at the height of its popularity and influence in the United States, and in 1942 he became a member of the American Communist Party. In his testimony before HUAC, Seeger noted:

I resent very much and very deeply the implication of being called before this Committee that in some way because my opinions may be different from yours . . . that I am any less of an American than anybody else. I love my country very deeply . . . I have sung for Americans of every political persuasion, and I am proud that I never refuse to sing to an audience, no matter what religion or color of their skin, or situation in life. I have sung in hobo jungles, and I have sung for the Rockefellers. . . . I have never refused to sing for anybody because I disagreed with their political opinion.[18]

Seeger was blacklisted along with all the other members of the singing group known as *The Weavers*. In the 1960s, Seeger reemerged on the public scene as a pioneer of protest music in support of international disarmament and civil rights (he supported the Black Panthers), and he was a tireless activist for environmental causes.

Spreading McCarthyism

Sen. Joseph McCarthy was the driving force behind the Second Red Scare, but he was never able to substantiate his most sensational charges. Nonetheless, the term *McCarthyism* has been added to the American idiom as a descriptor of unwarranted prosecution for disloyalty or subversion due to one's political views. Considered a "witch hunt," the HUAC hearings that he chaired have become the focus of what most persons view as McCarthyism. Yet having legitimatized its crusade by uncovering a number of actual Communists in government and film, HUAC next extended its reach beyond these.

In 1953, HUAC ordered USIS (the U.S. Information Service established overseas to facilitate cultural and education exchange in promotion of U.S. national interest) to remove certain books from its libraries that praised Communism or were written by so-called dangerous thinkers. Included were works by Henry Thoreau, African American intellectual W. E. B. Du Bois, and Foster Rhea Dulles, an anti-Communist history professor who was the cousin of Secretary of State John Foster Dulles. Thousands of books were removed from USIS libraries in several Western European countries, including the fiction of Dashiell Hammett, Herman Melville, and John Steinbeck. With the Nazi book burnings of World War II still fresh in the collective American memory, the irony of the situation did not escape commentators of the time. Dwight Eisenhower openly criticized this action. "We have got to fight Communism with something better," he declared.[19]

HUAC defenders noted that the removal of the books was in retaliation for similar actions by the Communist government of Czechoslovakia, which had succeeded in closing a U.S. embassy library in Prague in late 1949 and had also succeeded in driving information from the public library system that challenged Communism. Censorship that limited access to reading materials that contradicted Communist doctrine was common in the USSR and other Eastern bloc states, but should have been anathema to the civil liberties of America.

Libraries in Czechoslovakia in the 1950s were, like many other totalitarian government agencies, influenced by Soviet policy and doctrine. Closed stacks and notions depicting librarians as guardians and arbiters of knowledge exemplified the Soviet style of librarianship. In response, the USIS staffs had established a

Disney-themed retaliation on the part of the United States throughout Eastern Europe. The Disney characters—Donald Duck and Mickey Mouse—were seemingly innocuous images, but at the same time, they represented Western capitalism and culture. Under President Eisenhower in 1953, the USIS created a new selection policy for books and other materials in the overseas libraries, which stated that the collections should represent a balanced collection of American thought, including works by Socialist and Communist-leaning writers.

Although they threatened to circumscribe American liberty, McCarthy's censorship attempts had nothing to do with libraries or books held *within U.S. borders*, but they had an unexpected effect on professional librarianship in the United States nonetheless. The overseas library controversy greatly influenced American librarians and their policies regarding intellectual freedom and resistance to censorship, defining attitudes and values that still permeate the profession in the 21st century. The Cold War and McCarthy's Red Scare actually worked to strengthen and define a more progressive and possibly more liberal librarianship than had previously existed, giving the American Library Association (ALA) and the profession's leaders an opportunity to formulate a strong stance on intellectual freedom based on the First Amendment right to free speech.[20]

In succeeding years, McCarthy seemed unable to control himself. In his hunt to expose additional Communist sympathizers in the U.S. government—his so-called enemies from within—he made accusations of Communist infiltration into the State Department, the administration of former President Truman, the offices of Voice of America, and the officer corps of the U.S. Army.[21] The last charge proved his downfall. The Army hearings were an obvious disgrace, and the Senate voted by a large margin to censure McCarthy in 1954. In the wake of McCarthy's downfall, the prestige of HUAC began a gradual decline. By 1959, the committee was being denounced by former President Truman as the most un-American thing about the country.

Conspicuous among the members of the HUAC was Richard M. Nixon. Although he was eligible for an exemption from military service, both as a Quaker with Quaker parents and through his job working for the Office of Price Administration (OPA), Nixon did not seek one and was commissioned into the United States Navy as a lieutenant commander in August 1942. Nixon first gained national attention in 1948 when his investigations for HUAC broke the impasse over the Alger Hiss spy case. Nixon believed that Hiss, a high State Department official, was a Soviet spy. He discovered that microfilm reproductions of incriminating documents showed that they were typed on Hiss's personal typewriter. Hiss was convicted of perjury in 1950 for statements he made to HUAC.

The discovery that Hiss, who had been a close adviser to Roosevelt, could have been a Soviet spy thrust Nixon into the public eye and made him a hero to many of Roosevelt's enemies on the anti-Communist right, and a perennial enemy to many in the Democrat Party. In reality, his support for internationalism and nonconfrontational diplomacy put him closer to the center of the political spectrum. Nixon, a Republican, was elected senator in 1950, was chosen as vice president under President Dwight D. Eisenhower in 1952, and was twice elected president in his own right from 1968 until his resignation (under fire for the Watergate Affair) in 1974.

HUAC and the Courts

In 1940, Congress passed the Smith Act (2 U.S.C. § 192) as a preemptive measure, making it illegal to advocate the overthrow of state or national governments. Although the act was not used against members of the Communist Party during World War II, eleven Communist Party leaders were convicted under the Act in 1949. In the group's defense, Eugene Dennis (one of the defendants) declared,

> Our Communist Party Constitution acknowledges not only that we learn from Marx and Lenin but that we owe much to and learn from the teachings of men like Thomas Jefferson, Abraham Lincoln, Frederick Douglass, William Sylvis, and Eugene V. Debs. . . . We Communists are second to none in our devotion to our people and to our country, and . . . we teach and advocate and practice a program of peace, of democracy, equality, economic security, and social progress.[22]

The Supreme Court upheld the guilty verdicts in 1951, ruling that government action against the defendants was required under the "clear and present danger" test enunciated by Chief Justice Oliver Wendell Holmes after World War I. The ruling further found that the American Communist Party, which was "in the very least ideologically attuned" with Communist foreign powers, had formed "a highly organized conspiracy" that created the present danger to the government. In subsequent years, Congress passed additional anti-Communist laws, and prosecutors obtained ninety-three convictions of Communist Party members.[23]

Under the Communist Control Act of 1954 (50 U.S.C. § 842), HUAC had been armed with the power to compel testimony under subpoena and to punish offenders with citations for contempt of Congress. After the liberal-leaning Warren Court's 1956 ruling that mere advocacy of revolution was insufficient grounds to convict under the Control Act, the U.S. government ended their prosecution of persons solely for Communist Party membership.

The activities of the HUAC under the Smith Act, which seem obvious draconian violations of civil liberties to many today, were challenged in the courts as unconstitutional by a minor government official from California named Frank Wilkinson. *Wilkinson v. United States* was initially heard by the lower courts during the height of the McCarthy Era in 1952 and by the Supreme Court (365 U.S. 399, 400) in 1961 almost a decade later when the crusading glow of HUAC had largely faded.

The fervor to subpoena Frank Wilkinson, a Housing Authority official, arose out of political criticism concerning recommended sites for instituting the Public Housing Act of 1949. During questions related to eminent domain in California, Wilkinson, testifying as an expert on the conditions in the barrios and ghettos, was asked about his political associations, if any, with Socialists and Communists. He refused to answer and was cited for contempt.

Wilkinson challenged his conviction under the Smith Act, which made it a misdemeanor for any person summoned as a witness to refuse to answer any question pertinent to the issue under inquiry. Wilkinson, supported by the American Civil Liberties Union (ACLU), had refused to appear under a subpoena before HUAC or to say whether he was a member of the Communist Party. His conviction was sustained in a 5–4 ruling of the Supreme Court in 1961. Dissenting opinions were filed by Chief Justice Warren and Associate Justices Douglas, Brennan, and Black. Nonetheless, the majority of the activities under HUAC had been found constitutional.

Before beginning his one-year jail sentence, Wilkinson—now a liberal martyr and outspoken civil libertarian—was honored by Dr. Martin Luther King, Jr., at a reception of African American ministers held at Morehouse College. Wilkinson ultimately became executive director emeritus of the National Committee Against Repressive Legislation and also executive director of the First Amendment Foundation.[24]

The American Civil Liberties Union

Founded in 1920 by Crystal Eastman, Roger Baldwin, and Walter Nelles, the ACLU was the successor organization to the earlier National Civil Liberties Bureau (NCLB) founded during World War I. Baldwin was a disciple of Emma Goldman, who had played a pivotal role in the development of anarchist political philosophy in North America and Europe in the first half of the 20th century. Eastman had co-founded the Women's Peace Party (WPP) in 1914, and Nelles was an activist war resister, a professor of law at Yale, and a frequent attorney in conscientious objector and civil rights violation cases.

An independent outgrowth of the American Union against Militarism, the NCLB had opposed American intervention in World War I and provided legal advice and aid for conscientious objectors and those being prosecuted under the Espionage Act of 1917 or the Sedition Act of 1918. In 1920, the NCLB changed its name to the American Civil Liberties Union. In 1925, the ACLU persuaded school teacher John T. Scopes to defy Tennessee's anti-evolution law in a court. Scopes lost, and the Tennessee Supreme Court later upheld the law but overturned the conviction on a technicality. The ACLU was also involved in the 1920s in the murder trial of Italian anarchists Sacco and Vanzetti, and in the challenge to the ban on James Joyce's *Ulysses*.

The ACLU became prominent in the McCarthy era. In 1940, the organization formally barred Communists from leadership or staff positions and advised against Communists or any person who supported totalitarianism in any country from becoming members. In 1954, the ACLU filed an amicus brief (friend of the court) in the case of *Brown v. Board of Education*, which led to the ban on racial segregation in U.S. public schools. In 1973, the ACLU was the first major national organization to call for the impeachment of President Richard Nixon, giving as reasons the Nixon administration's violations of civil liberties.

The organization frequently has come under criticism for backing unpopular causes on both sides of the political spectrum, including the separation of church and state, the right of Neo-Nazis to demonstrate, the legality of interracial marriage, the abolition of capital punishment, and cases involving government funding of organizations that discriminate against homosexuals and atheists—prominently that involving the Boy Scouts of America. The ACLU has remained a controversial organization with most of its support coming from the progressive left and with opposition from the conservative right. While willing to pursue cases defending all the civil liberties of Americans contained in the Bill of Rights, the ACLU refuses to defend the Second Amendment right to firearms (a thorn in the civil rights theology of most liberals), arguing that the National Rifle Association (NRA) provides sufficient support in those cases. Nonetheless, the ACLU has otherwise remained generally consistent in its outlook toward the defense of civil liberties.

Spies among Us

Britain, Germany, and the United States all tried to develop an atomic bomb during World War II. Upon U.S. entry into the war, the British and U.S. efforts were combined into the Manhattan Project. During the war, German advances in atomic theory led America to believe that the Nazis were ahead of them in the race to make the bomb, but in reality, the major effect of the German atomic program was that it kept pressure on the Manhattan Project to be the first to succeed. The secrecy surrounding the Manhattan Project made Allied intelligence agencies jittery.

With the end of the war, the United States believed that it had a ten-year jump on the Soviet Union in terms of producing atomic weapons. The theory behind producing an atomic bomb was completed in 1939 and clearly understood by Russian scientists, but the practical engineering aspects of producing an atomic weapon (weaponizing the theory) was still a closely guarded secret. However, it became clear through the interception of secret Russian communications that the Soviets had infiltrated the U.S. wartime program as early as 1943. In 1949, Soviets suddenly tested a functioning atomic bomb. The test frightened literally all of America.

The final significant trial of Communists in the McCarthy era was that of Julius and Ethel Rosenberg, who were arrested for passing atomic bomb secrets to the Soviets. Convicted of espionage in 1951 mainly on the testimony of Harry Gold and David Greenglass (Ethel's brother), the Rosenbergs were found to have transmitted information concerning the inner workings of the atomic bomb to the Soviets. The couple was reviled in the press at the time as having given the bomb to Russia. Their executions as "atomic spies" in 1953 fixed the attention of the whole world, and raised an argument over the imposition of capital punishment based on the testimony of other more deeply involved defendants and little in the way of physical evidence.

It seems certain that Julius Rosenberg and his wife were "unrealistically committed to communism as a means to making a better world," and Julius had in fact given away some military secrets during more than fifty meetings with Soviet agents between 1943 and 1946. It is also true that Greenglass had worked on the bomb and was capable of divulging important technical data to the Rosenbergs. Moreover, Alexander Feklisov, an admitted Soviet agent, had frequent direct contacts with the couple. Yet their roles as messengers for the allegedly stolen information hardly seemed to warrant the death penalty. This was particularly true for

Ethel, a mother of two small boys, who seems to have been caught up in the case due to her devotion to her husband and her dedication to Communism as a political philosophy. She clearly knew of her husband's activities, but she may never have considered that they might be executed for playing such a minor role in the espionage.

In this regard, British physicist Klaus Fuchs acknowledged in 1950 that he had stolen atomic plans from Los Alamos (where the bomb had been developed). Fuchs's testimony confirmed that he had contacted a former friend in the Communist Party of Germany, who put him in touch with Feklisov. Fuchs's statements to British and U.S. intelligence agencies were used to implicate Harry Gold, a key witness in the trials of Greenglass and the Rosenbergs in the United States. Gold also admitted his role as a Soviet agent (going back to 1933), and it was he who had interfaced with Greenglass.

Found guilty of conspiracy to commit espionage, Fuchs, Gold, and Greenglass had been sentenced only to prison terms. Morton Sobell, an American engineer working for General Electric on military and government contracts, was also found guilty of spying for the Soviets along with the Rosenbergs, and was sentenced to thirty years in prison. In 2008, Sobell admitted his role as a Soviet spy, but only with respect to nonatomic espionage.[25] It seems true that the hand-drawn diagrams and other atomic bomb details that were acquired by Greenglass and passed to Julius were of little direct value to Soviets in building a bomb, but they were used to corroborate what the Russians had learned from the other espionage sources.

The Rosenbergs, seemingly minor characters in the case, were executed at sundown in the electric chair at Sing Sing Correctional Facility in Ossining, New York, on June 19, 1953. Two factors mitigated against clemency for the Rosenbergs. One of these was certainly the anti-Communist fervor that had gripped the United States in the postwar period, but this would have been equally directed at the other perpetrators in the case. The second—and possibly the more influential factor—was the couple's refusal to cooperate with the justice system once they had been caught. On the witness stand, Julius asserted his right under the Fifth Amendment to not incriminate himself whenever asked about his involvement in the Communist Party or with its members, and Ethel followed his lead. Neither defendant was viewed sympathetically by the jury. The Rosenbergs were the only two American civilians to be executed for espionage-related activity during the Cold War. The Rosenberg's two sons spent years trying to prove the innocence of their parents until 2008, when they admitted that their father (at least) likely had been involved in espionage.

The imposition of the death penalty by Judge Irving R. Kaufman, and the denial of clemency by President Eisenhower in the face of pleas from Pope Pius XII and other intellectuals around the world, supported the widely held consensus among postwar liberals and progressives that there would be "little humanity" found for those who rigidly pursued the Communist ideology. "Their execution seized the literary, mythic imagination and continues to haunt the definition of American justice. Even many who believed in capital punishment were appalled at the lack of moderation in the justice system."[26] Their case has been at the center of the controversy over Communism in the United States ever since, with supporters steadfastly maintaining that their execution was an egregious example of persecution typical of the "hysteria" of the McCarthy era and likening it to the witch hunts that had marred Salem and medieval Europe. In the hierarchy of liberal intellectualism and social activism, the Rosenbergs were placed among abolitionist John Brown, slave rebel Nat Turner, and anarchists Sacco and Vanzetti as American martyrs. "Recent evidence does indicate that the Rosenberg's were involved in minimal espionage, but whether the punishment fit the crime remains an ongoing matter of debate."[27]

Korea: A Police Action

The outbreak of the Korean War would serve as the first true test of the world's commitment to a collective response to aggression. If the United Nations failed to respond convincingly, or if it let the war on the Korean peninsula expand into a wider conflict, it would become another link in the chain of aggressive acts by European and Asian adventurers that might lead to a third war world. The peaceful principles of the U.N. Charter that the nations of the world had ratified with such high hopes in 1945 were to be sorely tested in 1950. Several delegates to the general assembly suggested publicly that the United Nations was fighting for its life as a viable organization during the crisis.

Trygve Lie, a Norwegian labor party politician, was selected as the first secretary general of the United Nations, and he was in office when the Korean conflict broke out. Lie was known as a man of strong convictions and had gained the displeasure of the U.S. State Department by publicly supporting the application of the People's Republic of China (Communist China) for recognition as a member of the U.N. General Assembly and a permanent member of the Security Council. Although the Nationalist opposition Republic of China had governed only Taiwan and outlying islands (Pescadores, Kinmen, and Matsu) since 1949, the Nationalists were recognized by most Western Hemisphere nations and the United Nations as the sole legitimate government of China. Taiwan had been placed under the administrative control of the Chinese Nationalist Party of General Chiang Kai-shek by the United Nations Relief and Rehabilitation Administration (UNRRA) in 1947, and the Nationalists had placed Taiwan and the outlying islands under military occupation. This was at a time when HUAC and Senator McCarthy were searching for disloyal Americans among the domestic members of the Communist Party.

Korea provided a first test of the United Nations with regard to the activities of its member nations (essentially the United States and Red China) within another member nation (North and South) Korea. Similar circumstances involving the League of Nations (Italy in Ethiopia, and Japan in China) had caused that organization to fail because it was unable and disinclined to take action. The conflict arose from the attempts of North and South Korea to reunify the peninsula, each aiming to do so under its respective government. Under the aegis of U.N. Resolution 84, nations allied with the United States intervened on behalf of South Korea. Although the United Nations contingent was taken from seventeen member nations, the United States provided 480,000 men of these and British Commonwealth nations provided 100,000 men. South Korea fielded 590,000 men, while North Korea and China brought more than 2 million to the field—more than three-quarters of them Red Chinese.

The war that followed was a unique combination of the techniques utilized in both world wars, beginning with swift, fast-paced infantry advances following well-choreographed air operations by the American military and its U.N. allies. After rapid advances in a South Korean counterattack, Communist-allied Chinese forces intervened on behalf of North Korea, shifting the balance of the war and ultimately leading to an armistice that approximately restored the original boundaries between North and South Korea. Throughout the conflict, the United States limited its response to conventional weapons, although it possessed the technology to field tactical atomic devices.

American policymakers were somewhat torn between two goals in the Korean War. As joint U.S.-U.N. forces penetrated into the North, they encountered Chinese volunteers, and then regular Chinese troops. The fundamental question was whether the restoration of the 38th parallel as a boundary between North and South was *victory enough*. Simple containment would leave the peninsula divided and a satellite of Communist China. A total rollback of the North and its Chinese allies would unite Korea and leave it under American influence.[28]

American troops, members of the Korean military advisory group, march toward Kimpo airfield, west of Seoul in South Korea after evacuating the South Korean capital ahead of advancing North Korean and Chinese Communists. (AP Photo)

The exact reasons behind the outbreak of the Korean War remains a mystery. North Korean Premier Kim Il Sung was an independent leader capable of taking aggressive actions. As a global figure in the quest for world Communism, however, he was a second rater when compared with Russia's Joseph Stalin, China's Mao Tse Tung, or Yugoslavia's Joseph Tito. A successful incorporation of South Korea (South Korea's president was Syngman Rhee) under the Communist North in 1950 would have advanced Kim Il Sung to the first rank of world Communist leaders.

Historians believe that the North Korean leader may have been inspired by Stalin who wanted to open a war in Asia to drive a diplomatic wedge between the United States and Red China. Although it was the Chinese Communists who came to Kim Il Sung's aid in the conflict, North Korea was certainly in the Soviet sphere of influence before the opening attack, and China—busy dealing with the consolidation of its own power—had little influence there at the time. Nonetheless, it was the Communist Chinese rather than the Soviets who came to the aid of the hard-pressed North Korean government.

The North's well-planned attack with about 231,000 troops, tanks, and planes achieved surprise and quick successes. Within days, South Korean forces (68,000), often of dubious loyalty to the southern regime, were in full retreat. North Korea's hope for a quick surrender by the Rhee government and the reunification of the peninsula evaporated when the United States and other foreign powers intervened with U.N. approval. By August, the South Korean forces (Republic of Korea or R.O.K.) and the U.S. 8th Army had been driven back into a small area in the southeast corner of the Korean peninsula around the city of Pusan. The desperate holding action of these troops became known in U.S. military history as the Defense of the Pusan Perimeter.

Meanwhile, in the face of growing U.N. reinforcements and with weak logistical support, the North Korean forces found themselves undermanned and hard-pressed. The idea to land U.N. amphibious forces at Incheon far up the coast from Pusan was suggested by commanding Gen. Douglas McArthur after he visited the Korean battlefield four days after the war began. The successful Incheon landings caught the North Koreans by surprise. The U.S.-U.N. troops then attempted to move on the southern capital at Seoul. In contrast to the quick success at Incheon, the advance on Seoul was slow and bloody. The U.S.-R.O.K. troops broke out of Pusan, but because U.N. forces had concentrated on taking Seoul rather than cutting off the enemy withdrawal, up to 30,000 North Korean soldiers escaped to the north across the Yalu River where Red Chinese forces awaited them. The U.N. troops had driven well past the old 38th parallel dividing line to the North Korean border with Red China. South Korean victory and reunification of the peninsula seemed at hand.

At the Yalu, the Red Chinese regulars made contact with American troops on November 1, 1950. Thousands of Chinese attacked from the north, northwest, and west against scattered U.S. and R.O.K. units moving deep into North Korea. The Chinese seemed to come out of nowhere as they swarmed around the flanks and over the defensive positions of the surprised UN troops. U.S.-U.N.-R.O.K. troops were seen to be in full retreat almost everywhere. The police action seemed a disaster.

By provoking the Red Chinese to enter the war at Korea's Yalu River, the U.S.-U.N. contingent probably prolonged the war by eighteen months. Truman had rejected MacArthur's request to attack Chinese supply bases north of the Yalu, because he was gravely concerned that further escalation of the war might draw the Soviets into the conflict. Nevertheless, MacArthur had promoted his plan to Republican House leader Joseph Martin, who leaked it to the press. On April 11, 1951, Truman fired MacArthur from all his commands in Korea and Japan. Relieving MacArthur was among the least popular decisions in presidential history. Truman's approval ratings plummeted (22 percent), and he faced calls for his impeachment from many sources. Truman was forced to cancel his 1952 reelection campaign. Meanwhile, MacArthur returned to the United States to a hero's welcome, and a parade for the general attracted 7.5 million people almost twice the crowd that had greeted Eisenhower after World War II. There was talk of a MacArthur run for the presidency that did not materialize. When Republican candidate Eisenhower promised to go to Korea and end the war, he received both applause and votes.[29]

Active fighting ended in Korea only because the principal actors became exhausted and despaired of victory. The Incheon landings had been a tactical

A group of U.S. Marines fighting their way out of the Communist encirclement at Chosin, Korea, take a rest in the snow somewhere on the route in December 1950. (AP Photo)

masterpiece, but the following advance to Seoul was so slow that it constituted an operational disaster. Finally, the expansion of the war to include the Red Chinese was an unintended consequence of a strategy that largely had negated any of the other tactical successes. The diplomatic negotiations to end the fighting were tedious and unproductive, and the American public tired of the "no-win policy" that they represented. The 1953 armistice (not a peace, but a cease-fire) agreed to at Panmunjom, never signed by South Korea, split the peninsula along the demilitarized zone near the original demarcation line of the 38th parallel.

The American dead amounted to 37,000 and South Korean forces suffered more than 800,000 casualties. The North Koreans had more than 500,000 casualties, and the Chinese may have lost up to 1 million men. Yet the war ended in an inconclusive truce with the two Koreas remaining armed camps on either side of the 38th parallel, bitterly hostile to one another for more than fifty years. The Red Chinese gained North Korea as a troublesome and sometimes-erratic satellite, yet they also gained major power status through their convincing fight with an atomic-armed America. Nonetheless, the strategic lessons learned in Korea may have kept China out of the war in Vietnam.

The United States clearly could have used atomic weapons on the Korean Peninsula to end the conflict quickly, but the Truman administration—that had ordered their use to end the war with Japan—resisted such a move. This may have seemed weakness at the time. Truman's decision had provoked a dramatic clash between civilian and military authorities concerning the need to contain Communism by any means. The general public seemingly opposed the concept of *limited war* in this regard. Truman had pressed for a full-scale conventional commitment to victory in Korea, and even over China. Yet he had then backed away and fired MacArthur, one of the public icons of warfare from World War II, after needlessly squandering the lives of tens of thousands of young American men when, in the public's opinion, a single atomic bomb would have done the job.

Truman and the Democrats had spent the weight of twenty years (1932–1952) of accumulated political capital on a single foreign misadventure. Sen. Robert Taft charged that the Truman administration had "invited the attack on South Korea" to involve itself further in Asian politics. Taft quickly emerged as the dominant opposition figure in the Senate arguing that the Democrats under Truman had abandoned the necessary measures taken by the New Deal and moved the United States toward a Socialist state. His reputation for honesty and integrity gained him the admiration even among the more conservative Republicans.[30] Joseph P. Kennedy, former U.S. ambassador to Great Britain and father of a future Democrat president (John F. Kennedy), had raised similar issues in 1950: "[G]et out of Korea—indeed . . . out of every point in Asia which we do not plan realistically to hold in our own defense [such as occupied Japan]."[31] Not until the Vietnam War did the antiwar movement gain wider acceptance as a significant force in opposition, nor had any antiwar movement before shown such a significant impact on national politics or policies.

War had failed, but the clearest lesson of the Korean War was that it uncovered the great weaknesses in the concept of collective defense and peacekeeping as then structured under the U.N. Charter. Collective security meant *global policing*. If one side in a crisis could capture the United Nations diplomatically (as did the United States in the Korean conflict), it could make the organization into an instrument of its own foreign policy to the detriment of the other side. In such a situation, the United Nations would be diminished in its peacekeeping role as an unbiased referee of world conflict. On the other hand, the absolute veto power of each of the five permanent members of the Security Council (China, France, the Soviet Union, the United Kingdom, and the United States) could be used as weapons to prevent clearly justifiable interventions in crisis situations. Even Trygve Lie admitted that the presence of both China and the Soviet Union as veto-casting members of the Security Council could derail the United Nations from taking the steps that might be necessary to reestablish peace and maintain security in a nuclear armed world.

The smoldering Korean conflict had served as inspiring content for antiwar films about the madness of continued U.S. involvement overseas like *Fixed Bayonets* (1951) or *The Steel Helmet* (1951). After four years of war in Europe and the Pacific, the American public was showing definite signs of war weariness and was unwilling to involve itself further in Northeast Asia. Years later, Robert Altman's offbeat dark-comedy *M*A*S*H* (1970) stressed the antiauthoritarian and antibureaucratic sentiment of an entire generation of American youth. Although the film (and subsequent television production) was set in the Korean War, its real focus of attention was the frustrating and ongoing Vietnam conflict.

The ubiquitous symbol of war protest and arms limitation was originally created to protest the atomic bomb. (author's illustration)

Ban the Bomb

The first anti-atomic-bomb wave in 1946 was the strongest of all because it was generated by revulsion attendant to the nuclear devastation of Hiroshima and Nagasaki. At that time, the atomic bomb constituted the most powerful threat known to humankind. The prospects of influencing national policy in the post–World War II era rested largely on the question of atmospheric nuclear testing, and many peace organizations formed in the prewar period turned their attention to overseeing American nuclear development in the postwar years. The same liberal-minded activists who had opposed the concept of world war (with which nuclear weapons had become virtually unthinkable) tried to lead the nations of the globe away from an ongoing competition for armed nuclear superiority.

Successive domestic and international crises in 1956, however, put a premium on safe politics in the place of radical protest. The USSR and Red China were at odds with each other, and mass anti-Soviet uprisings in Poland and Hungary, although cruelly suppressed, suggested a weakness in the effort toward establishing world Communism. In October, Egypt closed the Suez Canal and Britain and France sprang to the defense of Israel; but the nuclear-armed United States and USSR aligned on the side of an immediate cease-fire. This unnatural pairing of rival superpowers initially stunned peace activists into comparative silence. Both Washington and Moscow had seemingly shifted the focus of the Cold War from Europe to the developing world. In January 1957, the U.S. president proclaimed the Eisenhower Doctrine, which pledged U.S. intervention in the Middle East to preserve the status quo.

Nonetheless, the lessening of world tensions opened novel opportunities for dedicated pacifists. Robert Pinkus, a member of the American Friends Service Committee (AFSC), organized a program called Acts for Peace, coordinating the activities of more than a dozen antiwar groups in reaching out to chambers of commerce and parent-teacher associations (PTAs) in the United States to explain their nuclear disarmament principles. Dr. Albert Schweitzer, famed humanitarian, issued a Declaration of Conscience calling for a nuclear test ban, and Nobel Laureate in Chemistry Linus Pauling submitted a nuclear test ban petition signed by more than 11,000 scientists from forty-nine countries. In Britain, the Campaign for Nuclear Disarmament (CND) was established by a coalition of pacifists, peace workers, and left-leaning activists, and developed the inverted Y in a circle "peace" symbol that was ubiquitous during Vietnam War protests. It was understood that many of the older antiwar groups like Women's International League for Peace and Freedom (WILFP) and AFSC would support direct action against the nuclear arms race, and take steps, through this route, to achieve a general disarmament.

Two new groups emerged at this time that were dedicated to the same objectives: the Committee for Non-Violent Action (CNVA) and the Committee for a Sane Nuclear Policy (known as SANE). These groups had the support of a new cadre of antiwar notables known as *nuclear pacifists*, who lent their credibility to war resistance but were interested primarily in eliminating the threat of a nuclear Armageddon rather than war in general. Unfortunately for SANE, there was a sharp

A young protestor sports a "peace crawler" sign on her cap as she makes her way around the Lincoln Memorial during a peace rally in Washington, D.C., on October 21, 1967. (AP Photo)

division between its absolute pacifists and its antinuclear members. Moreover, *U.S. News and World Report*, a weekly news magazine, detected what its editors termed a disturbing pattern among antinuclear groups and reported that much of the agitation against nuclear testing was actually Communist inspired.[32] Thereafter, several SANE members or associates were openly accused of having Soviet sympathies. These circumstances hurt both SANE and other antibomb organizations in the eyes of the public. Nonetheless, the pacifist community was well enough organized by 1958 to press its case for a nuclear test ban on an American public already fearful of deadly fallout and thermonuclear war.[33]

When a global nuclear strategy originated among military planners after World War II, among its basic tenets was the reliance on the omnipotence of the United States with its unique atomic bomb. Tested at Alamagordo, New Mexico, and deployed at Hiroshima and Nagasaki, the threat of massive retaliation by the United States was the presumed hammer by which America would realize lasting world peace. The strategic theory of the United States was to impose the proper rules of the game of warfare on the world community that would maximize the one-sided technical advantage of America at any given moment and minimize the capabilities of its potential adversaries by denying them offsetting advanced technologies. The nation hoped to squeeze a maximum diplomatic gain at the United Nations from the technological lead it enjoyed. Although no nuclear weapons have ever again been used on the battlefield, the development of similar weapons in the Soviet Union and Peoples Republic of China burst this strategy to shreds.

With the development of larger and more numerous nuclear weapons, multiple warheads, submarine launched systems, and intercontinental ballistic missiles (ICBMs) in a number of countries, the concept of an imposed peace under the threat of massive nuclear retaliation collapsed in theory, if not in reality. To emphasize the dissolution of America's primacy in the area of nuclear weapons, the Soviets tested a fifty-six megaton weapon in the atmosphere (not underground) that produced a blast radius of thirty miles, the largest manmade explosion ever on the face of the earth. Although more recent analyses suggest that many of the Soviet advances in the arena of nuclear weapons technology were a well-played bluff, uncontrolled nuclear warfare on dimensions like these frightened most Americans at the time.

Massive retaliation was quickly replaced by the theory of a disarming first-strike capability, which required the United States to produce nuclear weapons and delivery systems on a tremendous scale. These would have the theoretical capability of reducing the effect of a potential USSR counterstrike to *acceptable* levels by taking out its nuclear assets before they could be used and thereby "winning the war." From 1960 to 1965, the United States increased its nuclear arsenal on a tremendous scale: ICBMs increased forty-six-fold and submarine-based nuclear weapons increased fifteen-fold. Western Hemisphere proponents of the theory of *nuclear deterrence* developed a weapons strategy that "like any cult . . . had its rites and Holy Apostles, not to mention numerous disciples who recite the atomic catechism day and night."[34]

The Cuban Missile Crisis

During the 1950s, the USSR built and equipped the Puerta Pesquero (Fishing Port) on the site of the Havana city dump ostensibly to expand Cuba's commercial fishing industry. However, the port also served as Russia's largest terminus outside the Soviet Union for its intelligence-gathering fleet of "fishing trawlers" and mother ships that commonly cruised the coasts of the United States. During the 1961–1962 Cuban Missile Crisis, President John F. Kennedy established a naval blockade of Cuba ostensibly to prevent these Russian trawlers from entering the island nation with nuclear warheads on board.[35]

Although it may seem that the seven days collectively known as the Cuban missile crisis had moved forward quickly, the event was the culmination of a longer process. In June 1961, while still in the early months of his presidency, Kennedy attended a summit with Khrushchev in Vienna to discuss Cold War confrontations between the east and west, in particular the situation in Berlin. The failure of the two leaders to resolve any of their differences during the summit led Khrushchev to view Kennedy as a weak president who lacked the power or support to negotiate any meaningful concessions in the arms race.

The climax period of the crisis began on October 8, 1962, when U.S. reconnaissance photographs taken by an American U-2 spy plane revealed Soviet missile bases being built in Cuba. Kennedy insisted that the bases be removed. In meetings with his advisors, Kennedy asserted that an invasion of Cuba would break the impasse, and he ordered the State Department to make plans for the establishment of a civilian government in Cuba after an invasion. Consequently, planning proceeded for massive air strikes against military targets in Cuba. Soviet Premier Nikita Khrushchev authorized his field commanders in Cuba to launch their tactical nuclear weapons if attacked by U.S. forces.

The crisis ended two weeks later on October 28, 1962, when Kennedy and U.N. Secretary General U. Thant reached an agreement with the Soviets to dismantle the missiles in Cuba in exchange for a no-invasion agreement and a secret removal of North Atlantic Treaty Organization (NATO) missiles from Turkey. Although unacknowledged publicly at the time, the most dangerous moment in the crisis was on October 26, 1962, when the destroyer USS *Beale* ineffectively depth-charged an unidentified submarine that was in fact a Soviet vessel armed with nuclear weapons.[36]

Bridging the Gaps

To maintain a position of strength, the U.S. Pentagon became the generator of an arms race by alleging a series of so-called technological gaps with the Soviet Union. In the mid-1950s, there was a "bomber gap" that required an expansion of the United States fleet of B-52s and a new generation of B-1 bombers. This would allow the U.S. Air Force to go behind the lines to deliver its weapons. This was followed by a "missile gap" in the 1960s that overestimated the abilities of the USSR to reach parity in the number of ICBMs. Finally, early in the 1970s, there was the "throw-weight gap" that compared the forty-five-megaton warheads on Soviet missiles to the twenty-five-megaton weapons standard on U.S. missiles as if the detonation of either over Moscow or Washington, D.C., would leave an impressionable difference in its result on the population of those cities.[37]

The Strategic Arms Limitation Talks (SALT) began in 1969. These bilateral talks and corresponding international treaties between the USSR and the United States centered on the issue of nuclear armament control. The two rounds of talks and agreements were known as SALT I and SALT II. The series of meetings began in Helsinki with the U.S. delegation headed by Gerard C. Smith, director of the Arms Control and Disarmament Agency. After a long deadlock, the first results of SALT I were announced in May 1971, and further discussions brought the negotiations to an end one year later. The agreement known as SALT I froze the number of strategic ballistic missile launchers at existing levels and provided for the addition of new submarine-launched ballistic missile (SLBM) launchers only after the same number of older ICBM and SLBM launchers had been dismantled.

SALT II, the second round of negotiations begun by Richard Nixon and Leonid Brezhnev and lasting from 1972 to 1979, sought to curtail the manufacture of strategic nuclear weapons rather than the launching systems. It was a continuation of the progress made during the SALT I talks. SALT II was the first nuclear arms treaty to provide real reductions in the number of strategic forces in all categories of delivery vehicles on both sides. Under the treaty, the United States preserved their most advanced systems like the underwater delivery called Trident and the low-flying unmanned cruise missiles, which President Jimmy Carter wished to use as his main defensive weapons as they were too slow to have first-strike capability.

In the 1970s, another gap appeared as a result of better computer-aided targeting technologies. This was the "ABM [antiballistic missile] gap." A tremendous fuss was raised over the ABM—a weapon ostensibly designed to take down offensive ICBMs in flight. The Pentagon pushed through Congress allocations for the construction of both Project Sentinel and Project Safeguard ABM complexes, which were used as bargaining chips in the U.S.-Soviet arms reduction treaty of 1972. Throughout the 1970s, the U.S. Department of Defense presented Congress with requests for increased funding for a whole series of cutting-edge strategic and tactical systems: cruise missiles, Trident submarines, AWACS radar systems, new attack aircraft, attack submarines, and surface ships. The price tag was in the tens of billions of dollars. "In the post-Vietnam environment, with a slump in the United States economy and a climate of détente [with the USSR and China], it [was] no simple task to substantiate the 'need' for recarving the federal budget in favor of the military sector" without presenting it "as a response to Soviet military measures" or a "growing Soviet threat."[38]

With the buildup of tension between the USSR and the United States, President Ronald Reagan decided to deploy Pershing II and cruise missiles under NATO command in Western Europe. These were intended to strike targets on the battlefield if the Soviets invaded West Germany. These moves reflected a continuing growth of tactical war-fighting arsenals between the two nuclear superpowers with well over 10,000 strategic nuclear warheads being deployed by each side. In 1983, Reagan announced his much-maligned Strategic Defense Initiative (SDI), a space-based defensive shield capable of protecting the country from nuclear attack. This became known as the Star Wars Defense by Reagan detractors. Some critics used the term derisively, implying it was an impractical science fiction fantasy, but supporters adopted its development on the grounds that yesterday's science fiction is tomorrow's cutting-edge engineering.

Reagan argued that it was senseless to rely on the idea of deterring war through Mutually Assured Destruction (MAD). "The defense policy of the United States is based on a simple premise: The United States does not start fights," he noted. "We will never be an aggressor. We maintain our strength in order to deter and defend against aggression—to preserve freedom and peace."[39] To rely on the specter of nuclear retaliation, he noted, was "a sad commentary on the human condition . . . Wouldn't it be better to save lives than to avenge them?"[40] Reagan called upon the scientific community to turn their talents from the production of weapons to the means of rendering them "impotent and obsolete." The president's proposal was not antiwar or pacifist in any way. He wanted to make the nuclear-armed world safer. Yet Reagan did not believe war to be inevitable. "[Q]uite the contrary," proclaimed Reagan. "[W]hat must be recognized is that our security is based on being prepared to meet all threats. There was a time when we depended on coastal forts and artillery batteries because, with the weaponry of that day, any attack would have had to come by sea. Well, this is a different world and our defenses must be based on recognition and awareness of the weaponry possessed by other nations in the nuclear age."[41]

In 1987, Reagan and Soviet President Mikhail Gorbachev signed the Intermediate-Range Nuclear Forces (INF) Treaty. The treaty eliminated *tactical* nuclear and conventional ground-launched ballistic weapons (Pershing Ib and Pershing II) and cruise missiles with intermediate ranges, defined as between 300 and 3,400 miles. Despite dissatisfaction with the deployment of U.S. weapons in Europe, the USSR agreed to open negotiations in 1980. The key to the negotiations was the U.S. proposal of a phased reduction of INF launchers in Europe and Asia to none by 1989. Under the treaty, both nations were allowed to inspect each other's military installations in a practical application of Reagan's maxim of "Trust but Verify." By the treaty's deadline of June 1, 1991, a total of 2,692 of such weapons had been destroyed, 846 by the United States and 1,846 by the Soviets.[42]

The End of Cold War

Meanwhile, Reagan's "duel in space" between offensive nuclear missiles remained undeveloped. The high-tech defensive weapons deployed in space that he envisioned would fight weapons rather than cities and people. In such a situation, the aggressor nation would be deprived of its tools of war, and humanity would be the winner. Reagan detractors considered the proposals unrealistic or even diabolical. Surely the president was simply trying once again to make nuclear warfare an acceptable alternative to diplomacy.

Physicist Hans Bethe, who had worked with Edward Teller (Father of the Hydrogen Bomb) on both the atomic bomb and the hydrogen bomb at Los Alamos, claimed that a laser-based defense shield (that is, SDI) was unfeasible. He said that such a defensive system was costly and difficult to build, yet simple to destroy. The Soviets easily would use thousands of decoys to overwhelm it during a nuclear attack. Bethe had been one of the primary voices in the scientific community behind the signing of the 1963 Partial Test Ban Treaty, which prohibited further atmospheric testing of nuclear weapons. Ashton Carter, from Massachusetts Institute of Technology and a former Carter administration official, assessed SDI for Congress in 1984, saying there were a number of difficulties in creating an adequate missile defense shield, with or without lasers. Finally, SDI was criticized from the political right for potentially disrupting the older strategic doctrine of MAD that had seemingly deterred nuclear war for almost forty years. David Lorge Parnas of the SDI panel argued that the software required by the Star Wars system would never be trustworthy and that such a system inevitably would be unreliable and constitute a menace to humanity in its own right. Dr. Parnas was a strong promoter of technological ethics in the field of software engineering.

Among other nonpolitical critics of SDI was the popular astronomer Carl Sagan, who pointed out that to defeat the Star Wars system, the Soviet Union had only to build more missiles, allowing them to overcome the defense by sheer force of numbers. Proponents of SDI responded that this strategy would hasten the Soviet Union's downfall. Communist leaders would be forced to either shift larger portions of their gross domestic product (GDP) to counter perceived Star Wars weapon systems or watch as their expensive nuclear stockpiles were rendered obsolete. After decades without being used on the battlefield, the military utility of nuclear weapons had never been lower.

The space weapons race that followed helped to bankrupt the USSR. After decades of Soviet military buildup at the expense of domestic development, economic growth was at a standstill. Failed attempts at reform, a stagnant economy, and war in Afghanistan led to a general feeling of discontent, especially in the Baltic republics and Eastern Europe. Greater political and social freedoms, instituted by Gorbachev, created an atmosphere of open criticism of the regime. Among the first indications of this was the fall in 1989 of the Berlin Wall—a physical symbol since 1961 of the ongoing Cold War.

In 1990, the Central Committee of the Communist Party of the Soviet Union agreed to give up its monopoly on political power, and over the next several weeks, the fifteen constituent republics of the USSR held their first competitive elections. Faced with growing republic separatism, Gorbachev first attempted to restructure the Soviet Union into a less centralized state, but he could not forge a compromise among the independence-seeking republics. On December 17, 1991, alongside thirty-two European and non-European countries, twelve of the fifteen Soviet republics signed the European Energy Charter in The Hague as separate sovereign states. Shortly thereafter, the Soviet ambassador to the United Nations delivered to the secretary general a letter by Russia's president, Boris Yeltsin, informing him that Russia alone was the successor state to the USSR for the purposes of U.N. membership. After being circulated among the other U.N. member states with no objections raised, the statement was declared accepted on December 31. As the Cold War ended with the implosion of the Soviet Union, the space weapons race between the two superpowers ended, too. A second application of space militarization to the targeting of land-based weapons has since given the world the Global Positioning System (GPS), which also is useful in nonmilitary applications.

Landmines

During the American Civil War, landmines had been improvised and deployed in tiny numbers by the Confederacy. However, these were much closer in design to the improvised explosive devices (IED) presently encountered in Iraq and Afghanistan than those used in conventional applications. It was not until World War II that landmines became a prevalent weapon on the battlefield. World War I had witnessed the introduction of tanks to break the impasse of trench warfare. Antitank mines were developed to counter this new invention. During World War II, more than 300 million antitank mines, filled with both powerful and lightweight explosives, were deployed by all warring parties.

The military use of antitank mines was compromised, however, because they could be removed easily and redeployed by the enemy. Smaller antipersonnel landmines were developed to address this problem. They initially were deployed around the antitank mines to prevent their removal. Nonetheless, military weapons design-ers soon began to develop and deploy the antipersonnel landmine as a weapon in their own right. One of the most effective antipersonnel landmines of World War II was the German-made "bouncing betty," which was designed to jump from the ground to hip-height when activated and to propel hundreds of steel fragments within a wide range.

Soldiers during World War I and World War II lived in constant fear of land-mines and invested valuable time and energy clearing suspected mined areas. So-called nuisance minefields—two or three mines placed at the entrance of a house, along the gateway in a road, or in a designated priority area—were intended to have a demoralizing psychological effect on enemy troops. After World War II, advances in weapons technology accelerated rapidly. In the 1960s, an antipersonnel landmine was developed that could be delivered by air and automatically activated as it hit the ground. These scatter mines made it possible to rapidly deploy large numbers of devices, rather than the more traditional, time-consuming method of manually planting each mine by hand. Scatter mines were first introduced by the United States during the Vietnam War. They had severe consequences for U.S. troops, who often found themselves retreating through their own, unmarked minefields. Nearly one-third of all U.S. casualties during the war were caused by landmines, often planted by U.S. forces.

With the proliferation of low-intensity conflicts in the developing world in the 1960s and 1970s—many in less developed areas of the world—landmines became the weapon of choice for hard-pressed government troops, paramilitaries, and gue-rilla forces. They were cheap, effective, and durable weapons of war, readily avail-able, and easy to manufacture or procure locally. As landmines became more prevalent, the distinction between their defensive and offensive uses became blurred. The impact of landmines on war-torn societies was devastating because they impeded the ability of mine-affected communities to fully recover from con-flicts after the cessation of hostilities. Children were particularly vulnerable to land-mines because of their natural curiosity and small physical size. Beyond the immediate dangers to the life and limb of civilians (26,000 hurt or killed per year worldwide), landmines imposed a heavy economic burden on these communities because they were costly to safely remove. Additionally, their presence displaced effected areas of woodland, farmland, and pasture from economic production. In some cases, the exigencies of farming and fuel gathering forced residents to take the risk of working in dangerous mined areas.[43]

The International Campaign to Ban Landmines was a coalition of nongovern-mental organizations whose goal was to abolish the production and use of antiper-sonnel mines. Although the problems posed by unremoved mines were more than a half-century old, the coalition was not formed until 1992. The campaign thereafter spread to groups working on other human rights issues, arms control, peace, and economic development in more than ninety countries. A prominent supporter before her death was Princess Diana of Wales. The organization and its chief spokesper-son, Jody Williams, jointly received the 1997 Nobel Peace Prize for their efforts. The Mine Ban Treaty signed in Ottawa, Canada, in 1997 was the principal international agreement that banned antipersonnel land mines, but several major powers including the United States, both Koreas, India, China, and Russia are not signatories.[44]

Notes

1. Andrew Collins, "1943–1954, Years of Conformity," http://www.duke.edu/~ajc6/7up/Conformity.htm (accessed March 2009).

2. The CIA replaced the wartime Office of Strategic Services (OSS) in September 1945.

3. Norman L. Rosenberg and Emily S. Rosenberg, *In Our Times: America Since World War II* (Englewood Cliffs, NJ: Simon & Schuster, 1987), 11–12.

4. Randall M. Miller, ed., *The Greenwood Encyclopedia of Daily Life in America* (Westport, CT: Greenwood Press, 2009), 99.

5. Miller, 99–100.

6. Charles A. DeBenedetti, *An American Ordeal: The Antiwar Movement of the Vietnam Era* (Syracuse, NY: Syracuse University Press, 1990), 27.

7. Rosenberg and Rosenberg, 16.

8. Rosenberg and Rosenberg, 16.

9. Rosenberg and Rosenberg, 13.

10. Rosenberg and Rosenberg, 13.

11. Rosenberg and Rosenberg, 14–15.

12. Rosenberg and Rosenberg, 14–15.

13. John H. Lawson, "They Want to Muzzle Public Opinion," http://historymatters.gmu.edu/d/6441 (accessed March 2009).

14. An acclaimed ballet star in France, Tamara Toumanova, was said to have been born on a train heading for Paris while her parents were fleeing the Bolshevik Revolution. Her husband, Casey Robinson, was the film's screenwriter. This fact and Robinson's resume of equally over-the-top pro-American films (like *This Is the Army*) may have spared the screenwriter scrutiny. The film was also Peck's screen debut, and he was nominated for an Academy Award for his role in *The Keys of the Kingdom* in the same year, which showed the Chinese in a sympathetic light. Peck, who also avoided blacklisting, wrote a letter of protest to HUAC.

15. The Hollywood Ten included screenwriters Alvah Bessie, Lester Cole, Ring Lardner, Jr., Albert Maltz, John H. Lawson, Samuel Ornitz, and Dalton Trumbo; directors Herbert Biberman and Edweard Dmytryk; and producer Adrian Scott.

16. Paul Robeson, "You Are the Un-Americans, and You Ought to Be Ashamed of Yourselves," http://historymatters.gmu.edu/d/6440 (accessed March 2009).

17. Lillian Hellman, "I Cannot and Will Not Cut My Conscience to Fit This Year's Fashions," http://historymatters.gmu.edu/d/6454 (accessed March 2009).

18. Pete Seeger, "I Have Sung in Hobo Jungles, and I Have Sung for the Rockefellers," URL: http://historymatters.gmu.edu/d/6457 (accessed March 2009).

19. Miller, 96.

20. T. Morgan, *Reds: McCarthyism in Twentieth-Century America* (New York: Random House, 2003), 446–447.

21. Joseph R. McCarthy, "Enemies from Within: Senator Joseph R. McCarthy's Accusations of Disloyalty," http://historymatters.gmu.edu/d/6456 (accessed March 2009).

22. John F. X. McGohey and Eugene Dennis. "Prosecution and Defense Statements, 1949 Trial of American Communist Party Leaders," http://historymatters.gmu.edu/d/6446 (accessed March 2009).

23. McGohey and Dennis.

24. Frank Wilkinson, "Revisiting the McCarthy Era," http://llr.lls.edu/volumes/v33-issue2/wilkinson.pdf (accessed February 2009).

25. *New York Times*. September 11, 2008.

26. Miller, 100.

27. Miller, 100.

28. Rosenberg and Rosenberg, 17.

29. Rosenberg and Rosenberg, 18.

30. Dean G. Acheson, "National Press Club Speech," January 12, 1950, http://www.j-bradford-delong.net/TCEH/Acheson_Korea.html (accessed October 2008).

31. Joseph R. Stromberg, "The Old Cause: A Lost Episode of the Old Right: The 'Great Debate,' 1950–1951," http://www.antiwar.com/stromberg/pf/p-s022100.html (accessed October 2008).

32. DeBenedetti, 30.

33. DeBenedetti, 34.

34. Henry Trofimenko, "The Theology of Strategy," in *Arms Control and Security: Current Issues*, edited by Wolfram F. Hanrieder (Boulder, CO: Westview Press, 1979), 99.

35. John D. Harbron, *Trafalgar and the Spanish Navy* (Annapolis, MD: Naval Institute Press, 1988), 51.

36. In October 1996, The John F. Kennedy Library released a set of tape recordings documenting the crisis for the period October 18 to 29, 1963. These recordings were made in the Oval Office. They include Kennedy's personal recollections of discussions, conversations with his advisors, meetings with the Joint Chiefs of Staff, and members of the president's executive committee. See "The Cuban Missile Crisis, October 18–29, 1962," http://www.hpol.org/jfk/cuban/ (accessed June 2009).

37. Trofimenko, 102.

38. Trofimenko, 104.

39. Ronald W. Reagan, "Address to the Nation," Washington, D.C., March 23, 1983, U.S. Department of State, *Current Policy* No. 472.

40. Reagan.

41. Reagan.

42. Reagan.

43. "The Campaign to End the Use of Land Mines," http://www.menstuff.org/issues/byissue/minehistory.html#history (accessed March 2009).

44. "Campaign to End the Use of Land Mines."

Chapter 17

Vietnam: The Cult of Victory Broken

To take no action, is itself an action.

—Zen-Buddhist principle

Whoever has no sword is to sell his coat and buy one.

—Luke 22:36

By the sword we will bring peace to the world.

—Roman Emperor Constantine

We seek no wider war.

—Lyndon B. Johnson

Clouds over Camelot

Americans, or at least middle-class Americans, began to worry about maintaining their happiness in the 1950s, and "worrying about worrying" soon became a disease of affluence. Heretofore, such concerns had been crowded out by more important things like winning a war, having enough to eat, having the "connections" to avoid the rationing of tires and gasoline, paying the mortgage, or putting aside some money for a child's education or one's retirement. Added to these was the very real worry of being incinerated in a thermonuclear attack. It is difficult for those who did not live through this period of the Cold War to understand just how palpable this fear was.

In the mid-1950s, the concept of psychoanalysis replaced the archaic practices formerly associated with mental illnesses (total physical control and close confinement of the inflicted) to deal with the stresses of worry. Many states instituted mental health legislation that dealt with a whole range of social problems, including marital counseling, delinquency services, alcoholism, drug usage, and unwed motherhood. Each of these seemed a danger to America's vision of itself, and there was a marked increase in the number of professionals doing social work. Women entered colleges in large numbers following World War II, and social workers and attendant professions became a powerful interest group in their own right for the first time. Many of these young women and professionals would serve as the spearhead of the antiwar movement of the 1960s.[1]

In the post–World War II era, psychology became an important ingredient in the strategy of warfare. In the lexicon of psychological warfare were found psychodynamic theories, functional theories, labeling theories, and class conflict theories, and "some of the simplest models of reality were developed from the most partial data."[2] Among the new objectives of war were psychological operations to "win the hearts and minds of the people," or to "convince the enemy that they could not win," or "to demonstrate the strength of commitments to allies." Assumptions were made based on complicated rationalist chains of reasoning: If the United States does this, the enemy will do that; or if the allies do x, the enemy will do y. This incrementalist style of strategic thinking came to dominate the councils of defense intellectuals, but it proved to be grounded on a landfill of false premises.[3]

The 1960 presidential election seemed devoid of issues that did not revolve about the relations between the United States and the Soviet Union. The candidates, John F. Kennedy and Richard M. Nixon, were both searching for some question on which they might draw a significant difference. Both favored better education, better health care, and a better environment. With regard to foreign policy Kennedy stressed the "missile gap" with the USSR, while Nixon reminded the voters that as vice president he had stood up to the Soviets for eight long years. Their television debates were described as "bloodless and boring," and Kennedy was the winner largely because he looked better than Nixon on a television screen. One commentator suggested that the lack of a substantive debate in American political life represented the "end of ideology." He foresaw "a malaise of spirit" and a "lack of content in the political dialogue." Nonetheless, in a few short years, the nation would burst forth in a political dialogue that would be "full-throated enough" for any observer, and ideological doctrine would often come to blur rational thought.[4]

Kennedy's election was not based on his experience—certainly Nixon was the more experienced candidate in any number of critical areas. Yet JFK's youth, vigor, charm, and grace totally overshadowed the older and less likeable Nixon. Murray Kempton, a *New York Post* columnist, suggested that Kennedy was "something fresh, something innocent of all the sins and mistakes of the past [and a] hope for the future."[5] Kennedy was offering a new attitude toward government, a confident and outgoing style that was absent from the Eisenhower administration. Kennedy was part of a new generation of Americans who saw the world differently than their fathers. He would bring about a New Frontier, a new Camelot. The charisma of Kennedy, his wife Jackie, and his family of two small children led to the figurative designation of "Camelot" for his administration, credited to his affection for the Broadway musical of the same name. Kennedy and his wife were younger in comparison to the presidents and first ladies that had preceded them, and both were popular in ways more common to pop singers and movie stars than to politicians.

As one of his first presidential acts, Kennedy asked Congress to create the Peace Corps, a program manned by American volunteers deployed to help developing nations in areas such as education, farming, and health care. He was eager for the United States to lead the way in the space race, and set the moon as the goal. He wanted to dismantle the selection of immigrants into the United States based on countries of origin, and he saw this as an extension of his other civil rights policies. "Kennedy had such wonderful star quality that he might have assumed the leadership of any movement he chose, had he survived."[6] The death of Kennedy and the confusion surrounding his assassination marked a decline in the faith of the American people in their political establishment.

Kennedy's anti-Communism ran at least as deep as that of Nixon's, and the foreign policy of the nation in the 1960s might not have been very different under the leadership of either man. John Kennedy's father, Joseph P. Kennedy, was a good friend of Sen. Joseph McCarthy and a contributor to his 1952 reelection campaign when the term *McCarthyism* was anathema among liberals and progressives. John Kennedy's younger brother, Robert, had his first Washington, D.C., job as part of the House Un-American Activities Committee (HUAC) investigative staff. President Kennedy had never spoken out against McCarthy and privately approved of most of his less extreme tactics. "It would have been impossible for him (JFK) to maintain his roots in Boston . . . politics . . . without espousing a staunchly anti-Communism line." He ordered the Federal Bureau of Investigation (FBI) to wiretap hundreds of private individuals (including Martin Luther King, Jr.), who were suspected of being Communists. In the 1960s, this brand of "reflexive anti-Communism" was reinforced by the real fear that the Soviet economy would finally live up to its socialistic promise and catch fire.[7]

Three-quarters of Kennedy's budget increases in his first year as president, even in the middle of an ongoing economic recession, were for the military and directed at both Red China and the USSR. Although Kennedy insisted that the Communists were losing their quest for global domination, Soviet Premier Nikita Khrushchev had boasted that "we will bury you" and slammed his shoe on the desk at the United Nations to punctuate his point. It is important to consider the depth of this fear of Communist domination when considering the pattern of events that would lead the nation through its longest war (Vietnam) and the most serious resurgence of war resistance in its history. In fact, Vietnam marked the maturation of the American antiwar movement.[8]

A History of Involvement

Modern pacifist rhetoric commonly calls for talks, negotiations, peace conferences, and compromises to prevent or end a conflict. To further its war resistance arguments, the antiwar message often uses the situation in Vietnam as a counter-example of parties unwilling or incapable of moderation and mediation. Yet a long series of talks, negotiations, conferences, and compromises actually characterized the virtually inevitable spiral of the situation in Vietnam into the longest war in American history. Far more important than any one agreement made during the negotiations surrounding the network that helped produce the war (some more than 100 years old when Kennedy took office) was the inability of the principal players to keep their word. While war was young men fighting and dying, it seemed that diplomacy was old men talking and lying.

As Americans were focusing on their own Civil War in 1862, France was taking steps to tighten its colonial grip on a part of Southeast Asia that included Vietnam. At that time, many Americans were seeking a means to end the bloody internecine conflict that was ripping their own nation apart and had never heard of the place. Ironically, a war in Vietnam would spark the strongest and most widespread anti-war protests of any in U.S. history.

Since the mid-19th century—while Americans were focused on expanding their possession of the North American continent as part of their Manifest Destiny—France had been interested in establishing colonies in Southeast Asia because of the region's important natural resources such as rubber, oil, coal, and tin. Louis Napoleon III took the first steps toward that goal by launching a naval expedition in 1858 to punish the Vietnamese for their mistreatment of Catholic missionaries serving in the region. This eventually led to a full invasion in 1861 to force the Vietnamese to accept a French presence in the country. By 1862, the Vietnamese had conceded three provinces to French colonial control centered on the city of Saigon (known as Cochinchina or Cochin China). They opened three ports to French trade and allowed free passage of French warships to Kampuchea (which led to French control of Kampuchea in 1863). French Catholic missionaries were given freedom of action in the region, and the Vietnamese agreed to give France a large indemnity to cover the cost of the war.

France assumed control of much of the wider region known as Indochina in the treaty that ended the Sino-French War in 1885. As suggested by the name Indochina, the native population was heavily influenced by Chinese and Indonesian culture and religion mainly forms of Buddhism, Confucianism, and Daoism. France completed the conquest of the Vietnamese in 1887, and colonial authorities promoted the further occupation and development of the Mekong Delta region as well as a conversion of the population to Catholicism. As the French imperium in Asia grew, a protectorate was established composed of several small kingdoms, including Vietnam, Cambodia, and Laos. French Indochina was extended to several provinces of Siam as a result of the Franco-Siamese War in 1893. The capital of French Indochina was transferred from Saigon to the city of Hanoi in the Vietnamese north. In this manner in just thirty years, the French had established both Saigon and Hanoi as important centers of governance in the region.

In international law a *protectorate* is a political entity or less developed native polity, such as a tribal chieftainship or feudal kingdom, that formally agrees by treaty to enter into an unequal relationship with another, stronger state, called the *protector*, which engages to protect it against third parties. In the 19th century, the Asian region had several protectorates. Recognized by the world community were, besides French Indochina, the British Raj in India, the Dutch East Indies, the German protectorate centered on New Guinea, and ultimately the American protectorate in the Philippines, Guam, and the Marianas. The bureaucracy of these

colonial governments was often split between those who believed in the accultura-
tion of colonial populations to Western Hemisphere rights and values and those
who favored a less ambitious style of indirect rule that minimized changes in the
native social order and culture. In fact, imperial authorities often gathered all the
power in their hands, leaving the local rulers only as figureheads. Transcultural
assimilation was a significant factor. Indigenous peoples adopted European styles
and manners, and Europeans, colonial diplomats, and civil administrators—
surrounded by the fragrance of cloves, tea, and sandalwood in Asian lands—found
native culture stimulating and attractive.

Large segments of the regional population resented the growing influence of the
French in Indochina, especially the spread of Catholicism. The extent of the religious conflict in Vietnam is often overlooked. For decades, Vietnamese soldiers,
sometimes led by Buddhist monks, staged such effective attacks on colonial troops
that their French commanders admitted to having enormous difficulties in enforcing
imperial authority. Initially no indigenous Vietnamese leader was able to organize
an effective coalition to resist French imperialism and win independence. Nationalist sentiments intensified throughout Indochina as the 19th century ended, and it
deepened as France became more deeply embroiled in World War I.

Ho Chi Minh

Ultimately, a well-educated, cosmopolitan, and charismatic Vietnamese named Ho
Chi Minh emerged as a popular resistance leader. In 1918, Ho Chi Minh petitioned
France for Vietnamese independence at the Paris Peace Conference that was determining the shape of the post–World War I world, but his request was rejected.
Rebuffed, Ho began to engage in radical activities while living in Paris and in 1920
was a co-founder of the French Communist Party. In 1923, he was invited to Russia
for training at the Moscow headquarters of the Communist International, an organization created by Soviet leader Vladimir Lenin to promote Communist revolution
throughout the world. In danger of being arrested by the French authorities should
he return to Indochina, Ho decided to live in China along the border with northern
Vietnam. From there he attempted to organize an anti-French Vietnamese revolution. Ho was forced to leave China in 1927 when local authorities cracked down on
Communist activities, and he moved to the British colony of Hong Kong founding
the Indochinese Communist Party (ICP) in 1930. He remained in Hong Kong overseeing the creation of Communist political entities and popular fronts throughout
Southeast Asia. During his exile, Ho came into contact with the ideas of the
Chinese Communist leader Mao Tse Tung and Mao's theory of violent revolution.
Ho Chi Minh generally adopted Mao's radical approach to warfare, which included
waging *asymmetric war* in the jungles and mountains through the action of mobile
guerrilla bands closely supported by the local inhabitants.

Ho Chi Minh had been officially absent from Vietnamese soil for almost two
decades when Japan attacked his country in 1941 (World War II). He organized the
Viet Minh, a domestic defense force commanded by Vo Nguyen Giap that eventually drove the Japanese out of Indochina using tactics similar to those espoused by

Mao. Because of their opposition to the Japanese, the Viet Minh received funding and military aid from both the Americans and the Chinese during World War II. Nonetheless, Chinese Nationalists, led by Chiang Kai Shek imprisoned Ho Chi Minh for more than a year during the fighting simply because Ho was a Communist.

The first post–World War II peace negotiation in the region was attended by both Chiang Kai Shek and Mao Tse Tung in Chongqing in August 1945. Both the Chinese nationalists and the Communists stressed the importance of a peaceful reconstruction of the region. The conference produced no concrete results, and the two factions remained at odds. Meanwhile, Ho Chi Minh declared the independence of the Democratic Republic of Vietnam, an entity that existed only in theory because it effectively controlled no territory. A few months later, Chinese, Vietnamese, and French representatives came to an understanding regarding the region. The French gave up certain rights in China, the Viet Minh agreed to promises of independence within the French protectorate, and the Chinese agreed to leave Vietnam.

It soon became evident, however, that the French Indochinese imperium was on the verge of a collapse, and the negotiated agreement between the French and Viet Minh quickly broke down. In 1949, a united Siam broke free and became Thailand, the "Land of the Free," ruled by a relatively stable constitutional monarchy. Also in that year, Laos wrested a promise of its independence from France, and the Royal Lao Government took control of the country. In the years that followed, three groups contended for power in Laos: the neutralists, the right-wing conservative party, and the Vietnamese-backed Communist Lao Patriotic Front.

In the presence of apparent French weakness, the negotiated peace in Vietnam evaporated. In the 1950s, battles between the French-sponsored government in the Vietnamese south and the Viet Minh operating from Ho's base of power in the north became common. Reports circulated in the 1950s that American military equipment, captured by the Communist Chinese in Korea, was being transferred across China for use by the Viet Minh against the French. Yet in Vietnam all the uprisings and tentative efforts of the freedom fighters failed to obtain any additional concessions from their French overseers. The French requested help from America and its European allies, but only the United States responded, supplying up to 80 percent of the weapons used by French forces and almost all the air transport needed to deliver them to the battle line. President Truman announced that the United States would support the French, and in the summer of 1950, the first elements of the Military Assistance and Advisory Group (MAAG) arrived in Saigon. In 1951, a young congress member from Massachusetts named John F. Kennedy visited the French forces in Vietnam to formalize the U.S. policy of underpinning the last remnants of the French colonial empire in Southeast Asia. Kennedy declared, "I am frankly of the belief that no amount of American military assistance in Indochina can conquer an enemy which is everywhere and at the same time nowhere, an enemy of the people which has the sympathy and covert support of the people."[9] President Kennedy's continuation of Truman's and Eisenhower's policies of giving economic and military aid to the South Vietnamese contributed to a decade of national difficulties and disappointments on the political landscape.

In 1954, the French requested that President Dwight Eisenhower provide American combat air support to their ground forces. Their request was supported by Secretary of State John Foster Dulles and Chairman of the Joint Chiefs of Staff Admiral Arthur W. Radford. Congressional leaders were called in for consultation, and decisive opposition to the deployment came from the Chairman of the Armed Services Committee Richard Russell of Georgia and the Majority Leader of the Senate Lyndon B. Johnson. Ironically, Johnson, who as president would become the focus of antiwar protests within a decade, argued that no vital American interests were at stake regarding the French war in Indochina.[10]

The French continued fighting until March 1954, when the Viet Minh using heavy weapons (artillery and mortars) supplied through China won a shatteringly decisive victory against French forces at Dien Bien Phu. Gen. Vo Nguyen Giap's artillery had pounded the French forces and shut down the only airport runway, forcing the French to rely on inaccurate parachute drops for resupply. French forces were so closely pressed that they could not bury their dead. Viet Minh troops then took out their shovels and began to construct a maze of tunnels and trenches, slowly inching their way toward the main French position, surrounding it, and forcing the surrender. French casualties totaled more than 7,000 men and an additional 11,000 soldiers were taken prisoner.

The Geneva Accords

A group of peace proponents at a conference in Geneva in 1954 determined to use the French setback at Dien Bien Phu as an opportunity to resolve the unstable situation in Southeast Asia. In Laos, tribal disputes, regional conflicts, unrestrained warlords, and other problems (including the armed turmoil supported by secret Communist and American aid) had led to a horrible civil war. Although Cambodia had achieved independence in 1953 under Norodom Sihanouk, its military situation remained unsettled and reliant on French military aid. Non-Communist factions had joined the Sihanouk government, but pro-Communist Viet Minh border incursions increased at the very time French forces were stretched thin elsewhere. In April 1954, timed to coincide with the opening of the Geneva Conference, several Viet Minh battalions from the north of Vietnam crossed the border into Cambodia in an attempt to strengthen their bargaining position in the negotiations.

At Geneva, Vietnamese delegates from the north and the south, and diplomats from the five permanent members of the U.N. Security Council, with observers from Cambodia and Laos in attendance, agreed to divide Vietnam at the 17th parallel. The Geneva Accords—as the agreement became known—declared multilateral support for the territorial integrity and sovereignty of all the nations formerly a part of French Indochina, thereby guaranteeing their independence. The decision to partition Vietnam along the 17th parallel created a separate Communist North Vietnam under Ho Chi Minh and a non-Communist government of South Vietnam under Ngo Dinh Diem. The agreement was similar to the division along the 38th parallel used in the Korean armistice. France promised to pull all its troops from Vietnam by 1956, and the United States promised to give economic aid to the South. These events marked the end of French involvement in the region.

The provisional line of demarcation would temporarily divide Vietnam into two states until free and legitimate elections could be held. The immediate area on either side of the line would come to be known as the demilitarized zone (DMZ). The accords promised elections in 1956 to determine a single national government for a united Vietnam. However, only France and the North Vietnamese government signed on to the idea of elections. The United States and the Diem government in Saigon refused to abide by the agreement, believing that elections at that time would inevitably result in an easy victory for Ho Chi Minh and the Communists. At the time, Ho Chi Minh was generally popular. His Communist forces had been instrumental in the defeat of both the Japanese and the French, and the ideologies of Communism and nationalism were closely linked in Vietnamese thinking. Diem, fearing electoral defeat, refused to hold any elections in the South, and by the end of the decade, the division of the country seemed permanent.

War among the Vietnamese

Once in power in North Vietnam, Ho Chi Minh's government turned more and more to strict Communist principles of governance. This was certainly within the possibilities foreseen by the Geneva Accords, but "[Ho's] government quickly became a dictatorship where people feared for their lives if they went against their leader's wishes," wrote a historian of the period.[11] Under Vietnamese-style Communism, newspapers, magazines, radio, and other forms of communication were not allowed to criticize government policy or its leaders, and only preapproved Communist candidates could run for office. Peasant unrest in North Vietnam resulting from oppressive land reforms was put down brutally by Ho Chi Minh's forces and more than 6,000 persons were killed or deported.

Many Vietnamese, including residents in the South, were well-disposed to Communism. Other Vietnamese, especially among the Catholic elite, were more democratic in their outlook, and a great deal of emigration took place across the 17th parallel in both directions before the outbreak of war. Many of the South Vietnamese considered the corrupt Diem government merely a French colonial surrogate, and later, an American puppet regime. Catholics made up only 15 percent of the population, but they controlled both the government and the economy under French rule. Diem rewarded his Catholic supporters by giving them land seized from the Buddhist peasant majority, arousing their anger and eroding his support among them. He also allowed big landowners and Europeans to retain their holdings, disappointing peasants who hoped for a socialist-style land reform in the wake of French colonial collapse.

The final departure of the French in 1956 was a signal for the North Vietnamese to attempt a reunion of the country through a pro-Communist South Vietnamese *proxy force* known as the Vietcong (VC, or the National Liberation Front, NLF). Ho Chi Minh sent weapons, supplies, and advisors from the North Vietnamese Army (NVA) to the VC insurgents. Before long a civil war was raging in the South and along the DMZ with both Communists and anti-Communists engaging in military buildups fueled by covert foreign aid given contrary to the spirit of the Geneva Accords.

Responding to the defeat of the French by the Viet Minh at Dien Bien Phu in 1954, President Eisenhower had outlined the so-called *domino theory*. He argued that if the first domino in a row was knocked over, then the rest would certainly topple in turn. Applying this to Southeast Asia, Eisenhower argued that if South Vietnam was taken by Communists, then the other countries in the region, such as Burma, Cambodia, Indonesia, Laos, Malaysia, and Thailand, would inevitably follow. The United States was virtually the only available prop for the non-Communist Diem government. In response, Eisenhower raised the annual amount of American financial support to the South from $10 million to $400 million, and sent American military advisors to South Vietnam to help the Army of the Republic of Vietnam (ARVN) plan a way to defeat the NVA and the VC. In July 1958, two U.S. military advisors, Maj. Dale Buis and Sgt. Chester Ovnand, were killed by Viet Minh guerrillas at Bien Hoa, South Vietnam. These were the first of 65,000 American deaths in the Vietnam War.

When Eisenhower left office in 1961 there were only 675 American advisors in the region. Eisenhower, a Republican under pressure from conservative isolationists in his own party, had not foreseen additional U.S. combat forces entering the region. "If we were to put one combat soldier into Indochina," he noted, "then our entire prestige would be at stake, not only in that area but throughout the world."[12] This statement presaged not only the situation in Vietnam for the next decade, but also the effect on a wider U.S. foreign policy for the remainder of the century.

In a preinaugural meeting between Eisenhower and president-elect John F. Kennedy in 1960, the former noted the need to maintain the non-Communist governments in Southeast Asia. "The United States should accept this task with our allies, if we could persuade them, and alone if we could not," noted Eisenhower, but he warned that unilateral intervention would be a "last desperate hope."[13] Conventional wisdom at this stage suggested that the Vietnamese Communists were too determined, the South Vietnamese too weak, and the Diem government too corrupt to allow the Americans to fight the kind of war that would have been necessary to prevail. Many historians agree with this scenario in retrospect. Yet by limiting serious consideration of the military situation in Vietnam to the earliest period of the war (before mid-1968), historians have left Americans with a view of a strategic situation similar to what was known of World War II in 1942 with the enemy in ascendancy almost everywhere. Then, too, all seemed doomed to failure.[14]

When Kennedy took office in 1961, he was concerned with the spread of Communism. Staring down the USSR across the iron curtain in Europe and continuing his predecessor's policy of sending aid and advisors across the bamboo curtain to Southeast Asia consumed Kennedy's foreign policy and interfered with his domestic agenda. Kennedy's purpose in Vietnam was to fight Communism, not to democratize Southeast Asia. Michael V. Forrestal, appointed to the White House staff in 1962, noted, "The president was appalled at the emotions this problem had stirred up and the basic lack of information about Vietnam. . . . He just couldn't understand how so many Americans could divide almost down the middle in their opinions of what was going on in the country [Vietnam] and what should be done about it."[15]

The public opposition to U.S. policy of some peace groups outside the United States, even at this early stage of American involvement in Vietnam, was remarkable and of such potential that Kennedy hesitated to visit some foreign capitals lest he be subject to demonstrations directed against him. He feared that news photos and reports of such protests might embarrass his administration and give the enemy an effective propaganda tool to show that opposition to the war was more serious than it actually was. It was widely held in administration circles that the protests had been contrived by the Communists.[16]

President Ngo Dinh Diem had been chosen to lead the South Vietnamese government because he was considered at the time the only non-Communist leader who could attract the support of the xenophobic Vietnamese peasantry. Yet Diem had several liabilities as a political leader, including a dedication to Catholicism that precluded his cooperation with other religious groups, especially the Buddhists. Diem also had a desire to control Saigon's underground economy—characterized by prostitution, gambling, and a corrupt police force. Added to this was a recent (1960) natural catastrophe—a major flooding of the Mekong Delta resulting in the temporary loss of farm fields, hundreds of thousands of tons of rice, and countless head of livestock—that impoverished a large part of the peasant population and turned them against the government. Although major floods in this region were common occurrences—the previous flood had taken place in 1958—the Diem government seemed particularly incapable of providing effective disaster relief during the latest episode.

Both the substance of the corruption and the governing style of Diem quickly became assets to the anti-Diem forces in the ARVN military and the pro-Communist elements throughout the South. The situation finally exploded into a virulent form of urban warfare. Beginning in May 1963, the Diem government was greeted by massive riots in the capital of Saigon. Buddhist priests set themselves on fire, and shocking photographs and films of the discord filled American newspapers every morning and its television screens every night. In November 1963—just days before Kennedy was assassinated in Dallas, Texas—Ngo Dinh Diem and his brother and leading advisor Ngo Dinh Nhu were arrested and ultimately killed in a coup led by Gen. Duong Van Minh. The coup ultimately initiated a series of weak and short-lived governments (ten in total) headed by South Vietnamese strongmen and ending in the decade-long wartime presidency of anti-Communist Nguyen Van Thieu (1965–1975).

By the end of 1963, almost 16,000 U.S. advisors had been sent to South Vietnam. Many of these were U.S. Army Special Forces—experts in jungle warfare, heavy weapons, and covert operations, which Kennedy had committed to the South Vietnamese before his death. Kennedy, like his predecessor Eisenhower, held profound reservations concerning the commitment of U.S. combat troops to Vietnam. Yet he believed that the security of the United States was profoundly connected to the security of a non-Communist government in Vietnam. Kennedy had used covert operations to support the Vietnamese generals that had overthrown Diem, and his

Buddhist monk Quang Duc, burning himself to death to protest persecution of Buddhists in Vietnam, as other monks look on, Saigon. (AP Photo/Malcolm Browne)

"complicity in the coup" drew America "ever deeper into a long, divisive, and misunderstood war" that the Johnson administration implemented and enlarged beyond anything Kennedy or Eisenhower had ever envisioned.[17]

The Gulf of Tonkin Resolution

Kennedy was followed in office by vice president Lyndon B. Johnson. The death and funeral of Kennedy initially diverted public interest from Vietnam, and Johnson launched his War on Poverty agenda out from under its growing shadow. The public focused on issues like Medicare, Medicaid, and Head Start, as well as the deliberations of the Warren Commission, phantom gunmen on the grassy knoll in Dallas, and civil rights demonstrations in Tuscaloosa, Alabama (June 1964). Johnson might have wanted to keep Vietnam on the political backburner, but the issue could not be ignored for long.

On August 2, 1964, the U.S. destroyer *Maddox* came under attack while patrolling the Gulf of Tonkin along the coast of North Vietnam. Two nights later, in company with the destroyer *C. Turner Joy*, naval commanders again perceived that the ships had been fired upon. Neither vessel was hit, and no one knows the truth of the allegations. If the Gulf of Tonkin incident did not actually happen (and there is evidence that *something* provocative occurred on August 2), the crewmen and officers aboard ship believed they had been attacked. Nonetheless, two days later Johnson appeared on television to inform the American public that he was going to take direct action against the North. "Our response will be limited," said the president. "We seek no wider war." On August 7, Johnson convinced Congress to pass the Gulf of Tonkin Resolution authorizing him to take all necessary measures to prevent further aggression by North Vietnam. The bill passed 416–0 in the House and 88–2 in the Senate with a number of members absent.[18]

The U.S. Constitution requires that Congress, not the president, declare war, and antiwar protestors would term the Gulf of Tonkin incident a lie and the ensuing warfare in Vietnam illegal and extraconstitutional. This is only partially true. Setting policy under a misapprehension is quite different from staging a provocation to create an excuse for going to war. Moreover, under the Constitution, war powers are divided. Congress has the power to declare war and raise and support the armed forces (Article I, Section 8), while the president as commander-in-chief (Article II, Section 2) is empowered to wage war. Ever since the Korean War, Article II, Section 2 of the Constitution has been interpreted to mean that the president may act with an essentially free hand in foreign military affairs, or at the very least that he may send men into battle without consulting Congress. As a straightforward matter of constitutional law, Congress may not by statute purport to take any action displacing the president's constitutional power as commander-in-chief. The Constitution withholds from the executive only the power to "declare" war, not to "make" war.

The criteria for presidential compliance with the Constitution include prior consultation with Congress, fulfillment of the reporting requirements, congressional authorization for funds expended, and continued consultation as long as troops remain in theater. If the Congress does not agree with the president's decision to make war, it has ways to deal with the situation, generally through the mechanism of denying finances. As a long-time leader in the Senate, Johnson was determined that his actions with respect to the Gulf of Tonkin Resolution fit these requirements. This is not to say that there was no duplicity involved in the passage of the bill, but the Congress and Senate were fully aware of what was going on at the time. Sen. William Fulbright, the bill's floor manager, publicly admitted that "the resolution gave the President power to expand the war and carry it to the enemy virtually wherever and whenever and as much as he pleased." If a number of liberal policymakers, journalists, congress members, and intellectuals chose later to delude themselves about the resolution, or the war, "it was their own delusion, and one virtually endemic among the liberal establishment of the day."[19]

Every president since Johnson has taken the position that it is an unconstitutional infringement by the Congress on the president's authority as commander-in-chief to limit his war powers. The typical response of the administration to this argument is to claim that the three branches of government are equal, and the president, under his war powers, has sent troops into battle hundreds of times in the past without congressional authorization. The Supreme Court—always loathe to insert itself between the other two branches with respect to war-making—has not directly addressed this question, leaving the right or wrong of the assertion in dispute.

Abraham Lincoln had relied on the precedent of his executive prerogative in prosecuting the Civil War and had explained the principle of presidential war powers this way:

> Allow the President to invade a neighboring nation, whenever *he* shall deem it necessary to repel an invasion, and you allow him to do so, *whenever he may choose to say* he deems it necessary for such purpose—and you allow him to make war at pleasure. . . . Study to see if you can fix *any limit* to his power in this respect, after you have given him so much as you propose. If, to-day, he should choose to say he thinks it necessary to invade Canada, to prevent the British from invading us, how could you stop him? You may say to him, "I see no probability of the British invading us" but he will say to you "be silent; I see it [the necessity], if you don't."[20]

The Gulf of Tonkin incident was more a half-truth than a half-lie because Johnson based his request for war on the questionable August 4 attack rather than the better-documented attacks two days earlier. There was no question that the *Maddox* was attacked by three North Vietnamese P-4 patrol torpedo boats in international waters on August 2. There is compelling photographic evidence. The *Maddox* claimed to have evaded a torpedo attack and opened fire with its five-inch (127 mm) guns, forcing the patrol craft away. U.S. aircraft launched from the aircraft carrier *Ticonderoga* then attacked the retiring P-4s, claiming one sunk and one heavily damaged. Two days later, the destroyers received radar and radio signals that led them to believe another attack by the North Vietnamese Navy was imminent. For some two hours the ships fired on radar targets and maneuvered vigorously amid electronic and visual reports of enemy vessels. Capt. John J. Herrick, who commanded the *Maddox* on both occasions, said that the entire incident left many doubts *except* for the apparent ambush on August 2 of which he had no doubt.

Antiwar activists, and historians to this day, focus on the "doubts" part of this statement and ignore the *exception* end of it for which there is ample photographic evidence. Nonetheless, when looking into the incidents, the National Security Agency (NSA) found that rather than being on a routine patrol on August 2, the *Maddox* was actually engaged in intelligence-gathering maneuvers coordinated with attacks on North Vietnam by the South Vietnamese Navy and the Laotian Air Forces. These assaults were part of a campaign of increasing military pressure on the North that the United States had been pursuing since early 1964. The NSA admitted after an investigation in 2005 that four decades earlier the agency had "deliberately distorted the intelligence reports that it had passed on to policymakers regarding the 4 August incident," but it reached no such damning conclusion concerning the August 2 attack.[21] No such conclusion could be made. The series of photographs taken from the *Maddox* during its engagement on August 2 clearly show all three of the enemy boats speeding in attack formation towards the ship and the subsequent exchange of gunfire. Yet the U.S. Navy had been part of the aggressor force in the Gulf on August 2 as an observer and intelligence gatherer.

Virtually the only voices in Washington in opposition to the Gulf of Tonkin Resolution at the time of its passage were those of Senators Wayne Morse (D-Ore.) and Ernest Gruening (D-Alaska). Morse noted, "History will record that we have made a great mistake . . . by means of this resolution."[22] In explaining his vote, Gruening said, "All Vietnam is not worth the life of a single American boy."[23] Gruening was defeated for re-election in 1968 by fellow Democrat Mike Gravel. Morse remained one of the country's most outspoken critics of the war. As early as 1966 he told a student antiwar group that he would like to see "protests such as these multiply by the hundreds" across the country. He got his wish. Also in 1966, he angered many in his own party for supporting Oregon's antiwar Republican governor over the pro-war Democratic nominee in that year's senatorial election. The prowar candidate won the race, and partly as a result, Morse lost his seat in the 1968 general election.[24]

Many historians of the period have forgotten, or have failed to report, just how popular involvement in the war in Vietnam was in 1964. This circumstance may be due to changes in the way journalists came to view the executive office in the decade to follow. Nevertheless, the *New Republic*, the *Washington Post*, and the *New York Times* supported the war through 1966. When Johnson decided to escalate the war, his positive poll numbers jumped up 10 percent, and the vast majority agreed with the increased level of his bombing campaign. Twenty percent called for more bombing. The professionals in government in 1964 had seen within their careers the fall of China and Eastern Europe to Communism and the sad results of the Korean War. To these men, to whom Munich in 1938 had been a "formative experience," the necessity of containment, the logic of the domino theory, and the danger of aggressive Communism in Asia did not seem such idle concerns, regardless of the opinions of the drug-numbed, pot-smoking protestors on American campuses.[25]

The initial decision to send additional advisors into Vietnam was viewed by the public "as a modest increase of the noncombatant American force, signifying no significant change in American policy."[26] President Johnson and his closest advisors in the Cabinet believed that the addition of 15,000 advisors would stabilize the situation. In retrospect, the move seemed like willful deception with one modest increase leading to another in an unending escalation. During World War II and the Korean War, journalists and reporters, trained to be "silent observers" of world affairs, would have withheld their journalistic fire in deference to the executive branch, but during the Vietnam war, a new generation of correspondents had become more involved in the situation and less discreet in their reports. Some became "skeptical" of the government's policy or even "impertinent" in their dealings with military and government officials. What had been considered journalistic responsibility in the 1940s and 1950s gave way to a pitiless quest for publicity, scandal, and scapegoats. The general view of public officials held by journalists was that "they were probably up to something bad, which the Founding Fathers had somehow appointed [them] personally to expose."[27]

Johnson ran for reelection to the Oval Office in 1964 as a peace candidate, who wanted to end American involvement in Vietnam quickly. He ran against arch-conservative Sen. Barry Goldwater of Arizona, a former major general in the U.S. Air Force Reserves. Goldwater believed that aggressive tactics were needed to prevent the spread of Communism in Asia. He charged that Johnson's policy of limited response was devoid of "goal, course, or purpose," leaving only "sudden death in the jungles and the slow strangulation of freedom." Johnson countered by claiming that Goldwater would bring on a nuclear war with the Soviets, and won the election in a landslide. It is ironic that Johnson would expand the war far beyond any of the proposals set forth by Goldwater.[28]

Beginning in January 1965, VC forces mounted a series of attacks across South Vietnam. They briefly seized control of Binh Gia, a village only forty miles from Saigon. Two hundred South Vietnamese troops (ARVN) were killed near Binh Gia, along with five American advisors. In February 1965, just eighteen days after Johnson's inauguration, VC troops made a surprise attack on an American helicopter base and advisor's compound in the central highlands of Vietnam. Eight U.S. soldiers were killed, 109 wounded, and ten aircraft lost. President Johnson immediately ordered U.S. Navy fighter-bombers to attack military targets just inside North Vietnam to cut the VC and NVA supply lines known as the "Ho Chi Minh Trail." This was later expanded to a more general bombing of the North called Operation Rolling Thunder. This bombing strategy generally failed, lasting three years with the loss of 818 U.S. airmen killed and 918 aircraft shot down at a cost of $6 billion. Strategic bombing of the North also catalyzed the growth of the antiwar movement.

The war swelled in 1966. By the end of the year, American forces in Vietnam reached 385,000 men, plus an additional 60,000 sailors stationed offshore. More than 6,000 Americans had been killed in 1966, and 30,000 had been wounded. The American public viewed an average of 500 body bags and flag-draped coffins on their television screens every month. In comparison, an estimated 61,000 VC had been killed in 1966, but their troop strength numbers were estimated to have grown to more than 280,000. Nearly 120 Vietnamese planes had been destroyed in air combat or on the ground. According to U.S. estimates, 182,000 North Vietnamese civilians had been killed in the bombings, along with 20,000 Chinese support personnel in the North. Nonetheless, three-fifths of the supporters of antiwar candidate Eugene McCarthy in the New Hampshire primary of 1968 thought that Johnson's prosecution of the war had been insufficiently aggressive.[29]

While the raw numbers favored the administration, by summer 1967, the relationship between the president and the Washington press corps had "settled into a pattern of chronic disbelief."[30] Vietnam was the first war to be so heavily covered by the media, especially television. When Americans watched the evening news, instead of seeing a carefully managed compilation of administration-friendly war news as they had in World War II, they heard a far different story than was being claimed by their president. Johnson was not lying, but the news reports focused on the ever-increasing number of American soldiers being killed. Some television stations actually kept daily running totals of killed in action (KIA) on the screen during the news hour. Nonetheless, many antiwar activists did not think that television and other media went far enough in exposing the true horror of the war. Partially for this reason, some antiwar leaders tried to make their demonstrations exciting enough to catch the attention of the media.[31]

The Tet Offensive

Tet was the Vietnamese New Year holiday, and it was the North Vietnamese Tet Offensive of January 1968 that drove Johnson to decline a renomination for the presidency. Yet Tet was a military failure for the VC and NVA, if not a propaganda one. During the offensive, 80,000 Communist troops (NVA) and guerilla fighters (VC) attacked the South in a well-planned concerted effort. More than 150 towns and villages were attacked almost simultaneously. One group of VC was able to force its way briefly into the U.S. Embassy compound in Saigon. The offensive was a complete surprise to the Americans, and an embarrassment to the Johnson administration.

Up to this point, the U.S. and ARVN forces seemed to be winning the war or at least holding their own. Yet in a war of attrition, the VC could afford losses that the Americans could not. In 1967, NVA Gen. Vo Nguyen Giap attempted to invest the U.S. Marine outpost at Khe Sanh using large-scale attacks supported by modern weapons as he had at Dien Bien Phu. His stand-and-fight tactics, however, were wholly inappropriate against the Americans, who had an immense advantage in firepower and air mobility. Before Tet, Giap had largely controlled his losses by deciding when to fight, where to fight, and when to melt back into the hinterland. The United States possessed no such tactical advantage. Every strategic withdrawal by American forces was portrayed as a failure in the press emphasizing the lack of military sophistication among the news media. Nonetheless, Giap's troops suffered appalling losses before they withdrew from their objectives during Tet. If the attack on Khe Sanh was a diversion to set the stage for Tet, as some observers have claimed, it was an expensive one. Yet the war proved one of willpower and confidence rather than of manpower and supplies, and this war of attrition was being won by the VC on TV every night in America's living rooms.

By the end of the Tet Offensive, 37,000 VC and NVA troops deployed for the offensive had been killed (46 percent). Many more had been wounded or captured, and the fighting had created more than a half million civilian refugees. Casualties (killed, wounded, missing) may have approached an amazing 75 percent including most of the VC's best irregular fighters, political officers, and secret organizers. During the 1968 Tet Offensive, the Communists attacked 155 cities, towns, and hamlets in South Vietnam. In not one instance did the residents rise up to support the Communists. At the end of thirty days of fighting, not one Communist flag was flying over any of those cities, towns, or hamlets. Had the news media desired to do so, Tet could have been justly portrayed as a disaster for the North. The alternative storyline pressed by the media that Tet represented a general anti-American uprising of the Vietnamese people was a complete illusion, yet for the Americans, who lost 2,500 men in just one month, it was a serious blow to public support at

This photo taken by Associated Press journalist Eddie Adams was among several disturbing images that came out of the Vietnam War. The execution was also captured on video tape. Lt. Col. Nguyen Ngoc Loan is on the left. The unidentified victim was captured in civilian clothing after killing the family of one of Loan's soldiers. (AP Photo/Eddie Adams)

home. After Tet, Johnson became concerned that his generals were dutifully requesting more troops with no underlying hope of success, and ultimately he became convinced that the war at home for the good will of Americans had been lost and decided not to run for reelection.

With respect to U.S. casualties, 1968 was the worst year of the war with 14,594 men killed and 87,388 wounded. One-quarter of all the young soldiers killed in the entire Vietnam War were lost in that year—the fourth official year of the conflict. "To most Americans," wrote one historian of the period, "Tet confirmed what they already expected, that the Johnson administration had not been telling the truth, that America had become involved in an endless war that was consuming ever-increasing numbers of lives and dollars."[32] The war had taken on all the negative aspects that Americans had traditionally been unwilling to tolerate. It was bloody, long, indecisive, and expensive.

A photograph taken by Associated Press photographer Eddie Adams of a bound prisoner being executed in the street by a Saigon police chief (Lt. Col. Nguyen Ngoc Loan) exposed a "frozen moment" during the Tet Offensive of what were becoming uncomfortably common events. The photo would become representative of the brutality of the Vietnam War. Adams, a former Marine combat photographer in Korea, later lamented the picture's notoriety wishing that his images of VC and

NVA brutality on South Vietnamese refugees had been as widely circulated. The photo, which won a Pulitzer Prize in 1969, may have done more than the Tet Offensive to shift public opinion against the war. The photo (and subsequent National Broadcasting Company [NBC] news film of the incident) stirred sentiment against the war to the point that only two months later President Johnson announced he would not seek a second term.

Adams later apologized in person to Nguyen Ngoc Loan and his family for the irreparable damage the image did to Nguyen's honor. "He was fighting our war, not their war," claimed Adams during a National Public Radio (NPR) interview. "Just moments before that photo had been taken, several of his [Nguyen's] men had been gunned down [by the VC]. One of his soldiers had been at home, [killed] along with the man's wife and children." While these facts do not excuse the barbarity of the event, they do help explain why it occurred. Adams noted that Nguyen was a beloved hero in the South, both to his troops and to the citizens, and had fought for the construction of hospitals and other civil improvements. Moreover, Adams claimed that unlike the popular myths about the war, Nguyen had demonstrated the fact that at least some South Vietnamese soldiers really did want to fight for their country and way of life. When Nguyen died, Adams praised him as the "hero" of a "just cause."[33]

The My Lai Massacre

In March 1968, a group of U.S. soldiers led by Second Lt. William Calley was alleged to have been given an order to kill everyone in the village of My Lai in South Vietnam. Approximately 400 men, women, and children were killed. Reportedly many of the victims were beaten, tortured, or maimed, and some of the bodies were found to be mutilated. Only the arrival of a second group of American soldiers stopped the killing. Military officials tried to cover up the incident, and were able to do so for almost a year. The first reports claimed that 128 Vietcong and 22 civilians were killed in the village during a fierce fire fight. When the true story broke many Americans were shocked.

Eventually, Calley was charged with several counts of premeditated murder, and twenty-five other officers and enlisted men were later charged with related crimes. Most of these charges were later dropped. Brigade Commander Oran K. Henderson, charged with the suppression of VC activity in the area surrounding My Lai, had urged his subordinate officers to go in aggressively, close with the enemy, and wipe them out for good. Henderson was the only officer above platoon commander who stood trial on charges relating to the cover-up. He was acquitted in December 1971. Second Lieutenant Calley was sentenced to life in prison, but ultimately served only three and a half years of house arrest in his quarters at Fort Benning pending appeal. Thereafter, Calley had been paroled from confinement by the U.S. Army. This leniency was protested by Secretary of Defense Melvin Laird. In 1974, President Nixon notified the secretary that he had reviewed the case and determined he would take no further action in the matter.

Peace with Honor

The election of Richard M. Nixon as president in 1968 and his adoption of a policy to win the war in Vietnam in 1969 seemingly reversed the political polarity of anti-war sentiment in the country. It did so at a head-spinning speed from a politically conservative position to a largely liberal one and from a Republican Party talking point to a Democratic one. The rapidity of the change suggests that at some level many opponents of the war were insincere and were using the war as a lightning rod to gather support for underlying issues.

With regard to the future conduct of the war in Vietnam, Nixon promised to achieve *peace with honor*. His aim was to negotiate a settlement with the North that would allow the half million U.S. troops in Vietnam to be withdrawn, while still allowing the government of South Vietnam to survive. In spite of congressional restrictions on his war powers, President Nixon authorized Operation Menu, the bombing of North Vietnamese and VC bases within Cambodia. The American Left did not trust Nixon largely because of his involvement in the HUAC in 1947 and 1948, and his administration faced unparalleled domestic resistance to this phase of the war.

Opposition to the War

As U.S. involvement in Vietnam increased, antiwar protests spread across America in the form of marches, sit-ins, and draft resistance. Although professors, business people, religious leaders, and other older adults took part, the majority of the protesters were draft-age college students. These students closed down campuses, locked the doors of buildings with bicycle chains, and occasionally did serious damage to university property. Nonetheless, many of the strategies used by antiwar demonstrators in the Vietnam period were borrowed from the civil rights movement of an earlier decade, including marches, sit-ins, and teach-ins. Despite opposition from law enforcement, peaceful protest had gained the attention of the news media, especially that of television. The nightly news portrayed the situation as if all academia was on the march. It was not. The vast majority of college students were more interested in attending classes than attending protests, but successively larger protests invited media coverage.

The antiwar movement in the Vietnam period was not a single organization, but a combination of hundreds of groups and thousands of individuals. The antiwar groups of this period were almost uncountable, and a sea of alliterative abbreviations filled the signs and posters of protestors: ADA, BEM, CALC, SDA, TTP, VMC, WILPF, and WSP, among others. High-sounding and active names were given to maximum effort events: Assembly to Save the Peace Agreement, International Days of Protest, Second International Days of Protest, March on the Pentagon, March on Washington, Mobilization against the War, Spring Mobilization to End the War in Vietnam, and so on.

Humanitarian groups voicing concern over the deaths of civilians were responsible for the earliest antiwar protests in the Vietnam era. As early as September

Leading the march against the Vietnam conflict are Dr. Benjamin Spock, the tall man with glasses, and Dr. Martin Luther King Jr., third from right, in a parade in Chicago, March 1967. Dr. Spock served as co-chairman of the National Committee for Sane Nuclear Policy. (AP Photo)

1963, the National Committee for a Sane Nuclear Policy (SANE) had called for an end to U.S. involvement in Vietnam. In April 1965, the first major antiwar march on Washington, D.C., took place organized by the Students for a Democratic Society (SDS). At least 25,000 people attended. One hundred war veterans took part. Even Johnson's close advisors were realizing that the American public was unhappy with the course of the war. By 1967, with a half million American soldiers—many unwilling draftees—serving in Southeast Asia, Secretary of Defense Robert McNamara noted, "The Vietnam War is unpopular. . . . All want the war ended and expect their president [Johnson] to end it."[34] In that year, 50,000 antiwar protestor appeared in the national capital. Many of the participants in these marches were college students, and a number of clergy—including priests, ministers, and nuns—associated themselves with the protests.

The antiwar movement had many different branches and some shared little in the way of common interests beyond their antiwar sentiment. The natural mood of rebellion common among college-age students made them particularly susceptible to being motivated by the promise of change. Some protestors (overwhelmingly among the young) were into creating a novel culture based on the promises of acid dreams and pot-induced deliriums, and others (primarily older folk) simply wanted to end the war by the old-fashioned means of protest and war resistance. Some protest was of the old-form religious pacifism.

The New Left

The well-known antiwar leaders of earlier decades seemed mired in the old debates and the narrow thinking of the past. New Left groups were building their radical form of protest from the bottom up, reinventing the tools of pacifism, and were not interested in attracting adults to their movement. It was commonly said among war protestors that no one over the age of thirty was to be trusted. "Adherents of the different forms and forces of social change in the 1960s carried with them different logics, different priorities, different trajectories . . . different frames of reference onto one movement to end the war."[35] Building a coalition among these disparate groups was no easy task.

The 1967 Spring Mobilization against the War originally was conceived as a means to weld the separate antiwar groups into a movement comparable to the 1963 civil rights march on Washington. The plan was impeded, however, by differences in emphasis among the leaders of the movement: A. J. Muste, veteran leader of the liberal-left antiwar coalition; Sid Peck proponent of a broad-based Left-wing political movement; and Dave Dellinger, the radical pacifist who wanted to move beyond protest to actually stopping the war. These leaders simply could not agree on a concerted set of objectives for the Spring Mobilization. Organizers kept referring to it as a new center for the peace movement, but several antiwar groups including WSP, FOR, and SANE refused to endorse the project.

Muste wrote, "It seems to me . . . that such forces . . . are not saying or doing anything of real significance in relation to the problem [of the war]. I have the feeling they are simply marking time . . . which is so widespread and, in my view, so dangerous."[36] Sid Peck, a middle-aged professor of sociology, and several other protest organizers feared that the inclusion of pot-smoking counterculture hippies "would turn off the middle-class types so necessary to give credibility to any antiwar action."[37] Dave Dellinger was not sure that the inclusion of young people with their outlandish clothing, wreaths of flowers in their hair, and loud music would harm the movement, yet the media response to huge turnouts of young energetic activists seemed a good idea. Abbie Hoffman and Jerry Rubin (described as self-appointed political radicals without a constituency and two of the Chicago Eight) had dreams of politicizing the youth counterculture and using the attention of the mass media as a recruiting device. Although some of those who followed the campus-based movement were skeptical, it was the older antiwar organizers who found the inclusion of the college-aged protestors intrusive or even counterproductive. Certain organizations like WSP, SWP (Socialist Workers Party), and other less radical protest groups feared that drugs, hippie dress, and acid-rock music would cut down on the number of "traditional people, the people who had been in the longest."[38]

The problem of creating cohesion and consensus among the disparate factions of the antiwar movement was exacerbated when mobilization director Rev. James Bevel, a top aide to Rev. Martin Luther King, Jr., related the antiwar goals of the project to the civil rights protests of American blacks calling the war "genocide" and making comments on the *NBC Evening News* that could be construed as "anti-American." When questioned by the press, King refused to distance himself from the remarks, and sources in the administration suggested that King had "thrown in with the commies."[39] Former ambassador Ralph Bunche, a more conservative African American, warned King against confusing the just objectives of the civil rights movement with the "malicious antiwar rantings of the hate-America left."[40] Roy Wilkins, director of the National Association for the Advancement of Colored People (NAACP), also disputed King's allegations that the war in Vietnam was inhibiting black civil rights. Much of the internal criticism within the civil right movement was unfair. King, the Nobel Peace Prize recipient of 1964, was a figure of mystic proportions and a key figure in his own right in the antiwar movement in 1967. His own position on the war was as a moderate calling for a bombing halt, a unilateral cease fire, and negotiations with the VC. He explicitly rejected mass civil disobedience, confrontational rhetoric, the carrying of VC flags during demonstrations, and organized draft evasion. "I oppose the war in Vietnam," King said, "because I love America, I speak out against it not in anger but with anxiety and sorrow in my heart."[41]

Extreme radicals talked of ending the war and racism by organizing urban guerilla groups on the model of their new hero, Argentine-born revolutionary Ernesto "Ché" Guevara. As a young medical student, Guevara traveled throughout Latin America and was horrified by the endemic poverty he witnessed. He concluded that the region's ingrained economic inequalities were an intrinsic result of capitalism, colonialism, and imperialism. The only remedy Guevara recognized was a world Communist revolution. He soon rose to prominence among Latin American insurgents and played a pivotal role in the successful two-year guerrilla campaign that deposed Batista in Cuba. Guevara became a prolific writer and diarist, composing a seminal manual on the theory and practice of guerrilla warfare, and a best-selling memoir about his motorcycle journey across South America. He left Cuba in 1965 to incite revolutions first in the Congo and later in Bolivia, where he was captured by Bolivian forces assisted by the American Central Intelligence Agency (CIA) and executed at age thirty-nine in 1967. Guevara evolved into a quintessential icon of the New Left, and his reconstituted visage was used as a global emblem of protest and an insignia for the radical Left.

A small minority of protest groups took up the banner of radical revolution. A group of heavily armed African Americans calling themselves the Black Panther Party marched on the California state legislature and warned that they would resist arrest by the Oakland police. In Nashville, black students at Fisk University fought a pitched battle with police for two days. Similar forms of unrest took place in Cleveland and San Francisco. Antiwar was quickly beginning to look like anti-American on the nightly news. Nonetheless many antiwar activists believed that the protest had to remain focused on appearing anti-administration. Nonetheless, when the Spring Mobilization took place on April 15, 1967, more than 50,000 protestors marched in San Francisco, and more than 200,000 marched in New York. "The participants included blacks and whites, hippies and church members, children and grandparents, military veterans and Vietcong sympathizers." A few examples like these were enough to give "truth to the lie."[42]

Reservists and GIs in uniform had been spit on and had eggs and garbage thrown at them on many American streets and campuses. The public burning of the American flag, and the carrying of VC flags helped the administration to tinge anti-war proponents with the color of treason. Conservative Democratic Gov. George Wallace called for the jailing of all VC supporters as traitors, and Congress was urged to fashion penalties for those giving aid and comfort to the enemy or encouraging the enemy to fight on. The government resurrected the old claim that Communists were at the center of the popular dissent. Gen. William Westmoreland reopened the old standard charge that antiwar demonstrations gave the enemy hope that it might win in America what it could not win on the battlefields of Southeast Asia.

Most of the news media followed this lead. *Time* called the marchers "Vietniks and Peaceniks, Trotskyites and *pot*-skyites" warning that the marijuana-smoking protestors were simply prolonging the war.[43] The *Denver Post* printed an argument suggesting a difference between the "responsible" protests of the past and the "irresponsible" protests of the present, and the *Christian Science Monitor* pointed out that demonstrating against the inhumanity of the bombing was acceptable, but demanding "an early and sharp end [to the war] by America's one-sided withdrawal" was quite another thing.[44] The administration's effort to portray all war protesters as radicals on the political fringe of America was working. Surveys indicated that the public rejected the idea that the war was a mistake (49 to 40 percent by Harris), but that increased troop deployments in theater was also unpopular (61 to 29 percent by Gallop). The internals of a Gallop poll in late 1967 showed that it was the "prospect of endless inconclusive fighting" rather than the fact of the war itself that was the main cause of domestic disquiet.[45] In other words, the majority of Americans were willing to fight the war as long as they were winning it.

The Johnson administration was quick to attack the protestors as un-American. Public opinion polls seemed to show a distaste for "violent doves" like those who espoused the ideas of Che Guevara, the Black Panthers, or the Weather Underground Organization (WUO), but prowar enthusiasm also was absent. The FBI had been engaged in surveillance of dissidents for two years, and the CIA had begun to place undercover operatives inside certain peace groups. An analysis by these agencies in late 1967 showed that there were "many close communist associations" within the majority of antiwar groups, but no overall Communist control or direction of the antiwar protests was indicated. The CIA concluded, "Most of the Vietnam protest activity would be there with or without the Communist element."[46] This antiwar movement, like many in America's past, was fundamentally homegrown. The CIA finding undermined the public relations strategy of the administration, which had hoped to build a backing for continuing the war on the foundation of an anti-Communist boogieman. The administration now had to turn to a "light at the end of the tunnel strategy" that held out the hope of winning the war in the near future.[47]

Chicago: 1968

While most marches were peaceful, the news media was quick to publicize any large crowd with signs and chants, especially if they became unruly or clashed with police. The 1968 Democratic Convention in Chicago featured widespread protests against the Vietnam War, and the convention achieved notoriety because of physical conflict between protesters and police, and the generally chaotic atmosphere of the event. Antiwar delegates supporting Rep. Eugene McCarthy and Sen. George McGovern opposed the controlling faction supporting the presumptive nominee Vice President Hubert Humphrey, not just over the nomination, but in virtually every aspect of the convention and the framing of a party platform.

Debate over the inclusion of an anti–Vietnam War plank in the platform lasted two days. Self-identified conservatives have always outnumbered self-identified liberals among the American electorate, and Democratic Party bosses felt that they had more to lose from the conservative electorate if Vietnam was abandoned than from the radical Left if they pursued the war. In their rush to distance themselves from Johnson's war policies, the liberals in the party failed to recognize that Ho Chi Minh's unwillingness to come to the bargaining table was the greatest obstacle to peace. "Almost to a man, the same liberals insisted on negotiations as a prerequisite to a settlement."[48] Political critics from the Democratic Left, like Eugene McCarthy, Robert Kennedy, and even George McGovern, never proposed that the United States simply leave Vietnam and declare the war finished. They always insisted that the United States negotiate. The strongest attacks on Vietnam policy, including that of Foreign Relations Committee members like William Fulbright, Frank Church, and Joseph Clark, "always presupposed that Ho would negotiate if only Johnson asked him to."[49] The assumption by the antiwar liberals that the North Vietnamese wanted to bargain infuriated the secretary of state under Nixon, Henry Kissinger, who argued, with some justification, that in his secret talks with the North he had offered every possible incentive that any "leftist antiwar proponent" had ever proposed, all to no avail.[50]

Nonetheless, the country had reached the boiling point in 1968. Every day, young American boys were being slaughtered in a war that for many had lost its meaning. Tensions increased and turned into violence in the streets of Chicago when police refused to allow the protestors near the main hotels and the convention hall. As the riots escalated, Democratic Mayor Richard J. Daley called in the troops. In total, 11,900 Chicago police, 7,500 Army regulars, 7,500 Illinois National Guardsmen, and 1,000 FBI and Secret Service agents were stationed in the city. At the end of convention week, police announced that 589 persons had been arrested and 119 police and more than 100 demonstrators injured. Television viewers throughout the country witnessed Mayor Daley's furious response in their living rooms. The immediacy of the violence was unprecedented.

By the end of the 1960s, only ugliness was left. Three American icons, King, John F. Kennedy, and Robert Kennedy (former attorney general and John F. Kennedy's brother), had been assassinated. The opposition protests and sit-ins had become "tawdry and, even worse, boring" requiring larger demonstrations and more outrageous tactics to keep the attention of the media.[51] Government response to protest had become vindictive. The peaceful, pot-induced charm of the musical get-together at Woodstock, New York, had degenerated into street violence on both sides. Black leader Malcolm X had been killed by one of his own followers.

Chicago police had riddled the body of Black Panther Fred Hampton with bullets, although there was some less-than-compelling evidence that he was sleeping when they raided his apartment. It was more certain that Ohio National Guardsmen had fired into a crowd of student protestors at Kent State University, killing four students. Prominent Black Panthers had tortured and killed a disgruntled camp follower in New Haven, Connecticut, and the president of Yale University had proclaimed his doubts that they would receive a fair trial. Student protest leader Tom Hayden had asked if "there [was] anything left in America worth defending," and Abbie Hoffman had brandished a broomstick on the Columbia University campus yelling, "I want to kill a pig [policeman]. I want to kill a pig."[52] Moreover, the once-young student protestors of the 1950s were facing their thirties, and the radical youngsters of the 1960s were entering a more sober adulthood. After two decades of protest, racial inequality and the war were still raging, and much of America was tiring of the time-worn antics of protesters. In fact, one of the achievements of the continued storm of radicalism was to ensure the election of Richard Nixon to two terms in the White House.[53]

The Draft: Evasion and Resistance

On reaching the age of eighteen, all males resident in the United States were required to register for the draft (Selective Service). They were to fill out an "application" and carry their draft card with them at all times. Many looked forward to having a draft card as it served as positive identification with regard to being served alcoholic beverages in an era when the drinking age was eighteen almost everywhere—old enough to die for one's country, old enough to drink in it. Yet the draft card smacked of Nazi requests for "papers" during World War II, and of the Soviet secret police state, not of a nation founded on individual civil liberties.

To show their feeling against the war, many young men burned their draft cards, tore them up, or mailed them back to their local draft boards. Many destroyed fake or duplicate draft cards. The WE WON'T GO! group began at Cornell University and quickly spread to more than two dozen colleges. Antiwar activist Martin Jezer noted, "Once imprisonment becomes an honorable alternative to the military [military service], something to be sought rather than avoided, resistance to the draft can become massive. In order to strike at this fear, some of us will have to face imprisonment with joyous defiance."[54]

David Paul O'Brien, one of the first to burn his draft card in public—a crime under the law—was successfully prosecuted in Massachusetts and spent two years in jail. Chief Justice Warren's decision for the Supreme Court in reviewing the case rejected O'Brien's argument that the 1965 amendment to the Selective Service Act making destruction of the draft card illegal had been passed only to stifle the free speech of antiwar protestors. According to the Court, the law was unquestionably within constitutional powers of the Congress to raise and support armies by classifying and conscripting manpower for military service.

Although singing sensation Elvis Presley had quietly allowed himself to be inducted into the Army as many other stars had in previous wars, champion

Table 17.1 Number of Draftees in U.S. Conflicts

Conflict (dates)	Number of draftees
World War I (Sept. 1917–Nov. 1918)	2,810,296
World War II (Nov. 1940–Oct. 1946)	10,110,104
Korea (June 1950–June 1953)	1,529,539
Vietnam (Aug. 1964–Feb. 1973)	1,857,304

Source: U.S. Selective Service System.

heavyweight boxer Muhammad Ali (Cassius Clay) made news across the nation when he refused to be drafted. Ali believed that he should be exempt from service because he was a black Muslim minister and a conscientious objector. Barring these exemptions, he also purposely failed the army intelligence (IQ) test. Democratic Rep. L. Mendel River of South Carolina was especially angered at the news of Ali's refusal: "[It was] an insult to every mother's son serving in Vietnam. Here he is, smart enough to finish high school, write his kind of poetry, promote himself all over the world, make a million a year, drive around in red Cadillacs—and they say he's too dumb to tote a gun. Who's dumb enough to believe that?"[55] While Ali was waiting for his case to be heard, the World Boxing Association and the New York State Athletic Commission stripped him of his boxing titles and revoked his boxing license. In June 1967 a judge found him guilty of evading the draft and sentenced him to five years in prison and a fine of $10,000. An appeal overturned the lower court three and a half years later, and the Supreme Court ruled that Ali was entitled to exemption as a legitimate religious minister. Thereafter Ali resumed his boxing career.

Draft protestors prominently burned their draft cards at public demonstrations and for the cameras on demand. The act was technically illegal and dramatic, and sometimes the same unscrupulous person did so more than once on the same day. In fact, the number of young Americans that illegally evaded the draft has been greatly overestimated by commentators as evidenced by the large number of men (1.8 million in Vietnam alone) who served and the small number of men (approximately 9,000) who were prosecuted. This is just 0.5 percent of those eligible and does not include the approximately 5 million men who served in the United States, Europe, or on other posts around the world as volunteers. In fact, Vietnam, a ten-year-long war, required the service of only 19 percent of the number of men who had served during the four years of World War II, and only 327,000 more draftees than had served in the two and a half years of the Korean conflict.

As in other U.S. wars, there were less dramatic and more effect ways of avoiding the draft than fleeing to Canada or going to jail. Education deferments required not only full-time school attendance but also a maintenance of passing grades. Medical and religious exemptions were allowed, and family distress and occupational exemptions (police, firemen, inner-city teachers, and so on) were recognized. Many young men joined the Army Reserves or the National Guard, a tiny minority of them to avoid deployment to Vietnam as draftees. More than 170,000 young men were able to gain conscientious objector status through their draft boards. There were, nonetheless, more than 500,000 draft irregularities recorded during the period of the war, but many of these involved temporary failure to apply for reclassification when personal situations—such as graduation from college, change of employment, or change in residence—altered men's deferment status. The Selective Service was almost draconian in its follow-up of terminated deferments.

Nonetheless, the draft had the potential to stifle dissent. In October 1965, U.S. Attorney General Nicholas Katzenbach promised to investigate the antiwar movement and reclassify those found to be active in protests should they have deferments, and in December, the Selective Service Director Lewis B. Hershey bluntly threatened college protestors with reclassification. Since conscription was monitored and controlled on the local level, these were little more than idle threats. Nonetheless, in Michigan, the local Selective Service boards revoked the deferment status of thirty-one students arrested in draft office sit-ins. Meanwhile, the monthly call of draftees for the last month of 1965 rose to 36,000 men, the largest call-up since 1952.[56]

Critics of the war feared the apathy of the political center more than hostility from the government. Draft resistance and inequalities in issuing deferments raised problems for the Selective Service System to a level that had not been seen since the American Civil War. It was "a ready-made issue for radicals eager to stress the way in which the war touches people personally and unjustly."[57] Nothing was more damaging for the government than the growth after 1969 of hundreds of draft counseling centers and legal advisory groups. The Selective Service System, based on local draft boards in every community, was swamped with protests and appeals.

The residents of Middle America (today's so-called Red States) cared little about the bombings of Hanoi or the survival of the government in Saigon, and they expressed almost universal contempt for draft card and flag burners, street demonstrations, marches, hippies, sit-ins, or "love" children. These Americans, however, were not beyond having their own sons find some way around the draft—usually through enlistment in the reserves, the National Guard, or some branch of the service like the Navy or Coast Guard that were believed to be "safer" than deployment to the Army. Yet each of these required a three- or four-year active service commitment (rather than two for draftees), and none of these services guaranteed that personnel would not be deployed to Vietnam. As with World War II, many young men were looking for alternatives to Army life, including an escape from marching, muddy foxholes, cold rations, and sleeping in tents.

The draft was the one issue that most Americans feared more than the spread of Communism or the loss of a war—educations interrupted, employment curtailed, and marriages postponed. It was mostly through the mechanism of the draft that an increasing numbers of Americans (up to 61 percent in a Harris poll) came to feel that the war was affecting them personally. In recent years, with ongoing wars in both Iraq and Afghanistan, a number of antiwar politicians have proposed the reinstitution of the draft, not because they really want to draft young persons into service but because they wish to resurrect the issue as a tool of war resistance. With a draft in place, antiwar and antimilitarist voices might gain the support of a wider portion of the American electorate than they can attract when U.S. fighting forces are composed of volunteers only.

The Nixon administration finally attempted to take some of the fuel out of the antiwar fire by establishing a draft lottery that all but exempt the lower third (random by date of birth) of draft-age Americans and made the drafting of the middle third highly unlikely. Each man called from the upper third of the lottery remained eligible for medical, religious, and hardship deferments. Much of America breathed a deep sigh of relief as this virtual sword of Damocles was removed from over their heads. With the lottery, much of the air was suddenly let out of the antiwar balloon as many mildly committed draft-age protestors suddenly sought the sidelines. The largest number of those in the lottery (of a possible 365) who were called by Selective Service in 1969 was 195 (53 percent); in 1970 it was 125 (34 percent); and in 1971 it was 95 (26 percent). A final lottery was conducted in 1972, but by then the draft had ended.[58]

The idea of an all-volunteer force, while not new, was born amid the withdrawal of American forces from South Vietnam in the summer of 1969. President Nixon, who had called for an end to the draft during the 1968 presidential campaign, instructed the Army chief of staff, Gen. William C. Westmoreland, to determine the feasibility of ending the Army's reliance on selective service to fill the ranks.[59]

By the end of the 1980s, senior military leaders could point to success. By the 20th anniversary of the force, the all-volunteer concept had undergone perhaps its most arduous test, operations Desert Shield and Desert Storm. U.S. and coalition forces had defeated and evicted a battle hardened Iraqi army from Kuwait in just four days. Regular Army, Army National Guard, and Army Reserve Soldiers carried forth the all-volunteer tradition as they patrolled Baghdad, Sadr City, and the mountains of Afghanistan. As of the early 21st century, recruiters continue to meet or exceed volunteer recruiting objectives, a tribute to the founders of the all-volunteer concept. "Today's Soldier is a standard bearer of one of the Army's greatest success stories—the all-volunteer force."[60]

The advent of mechanized and robotic warfare and of long-term strategic planning made a great amount of individual training necessary, which virtually eliminated the utility of untrained and unenthusiastic draftees. Modern tactics and sophisticated equipment operations take time to learn well, making the old-fashioned draftee, who in the past stood as cannon fodder, of little use in a modern force. Given the high level of technological training and the great amount of time needed to give modern soldiers, airmen, and seamen (male and female) a proper level of professional expertise with advanced weapon systems, short-term conscription simply no longer makes sense.

The Men Who Fought

A number of myths were circulated by protesters of the Vietnam War concerning the draft—especially that poor minority men were carrying the weight of the war. Statistical evidence suggests that these observations, if not purposeful lies, were at least overstated. The U.S. military in Vietnam was the best-educated, best-trained, best-disciplined, and most successful force ever fielded in the history of American arms up to that time.[61]

A U.S. medic protects a wounded paratrooper from Vietcong sniper fire in the jungle. The medic crawled forward under fire to treat his comrade. (AP Photo/Horst Faas)

Approximately 8.7 million men were on active duty during the war (August 1964–March 1973), and of these, 2.6 million were assigned to the Southeast Asian command. One million of these men saw no combat whatsoever, being posted to garrisons in Japan and other places. One million additional men served as flight crews and support personnel based in Thailand and in adjacent areas of Southeast Asia or as sailors and Coast Guardsmen in the waters of the South China Sea. In addition, approximately 7,500 women served in theater in noncombat roles—6,200 of which were nurses. The largest number of men on the ground in Vietnam in any one year (1969) was just over 540,000. In the prewar period from 1960 to 1964 almost 50,000 men were in theater serving as advisors and support personnel.[62]

Of all the personnel serving on the ground in Vietnam, only 25 percent were draftees, but of these, 30 percent (17,725) were killed—a significant difference statistically with the losses of volunteers and long-term professionals that may be related to the poor quality of short-term inductee training before deployment. Herein the two-year service requirement under Selective Service was showing the intrinsic flaw that proponents of a professional standing army had long suspected and warned against. The remaining 75 percent who served were three-year volunteers, activated reservists, or National Guardsmen. More than 6,000 National Guardsmen served on the ground and 1.7 percent (101) of these were killed. Of the black minorities that served in Vietnam, 34 percent volunteered for combat assignments.[63]

The American soldier in Vietnam was young, averaging a mere nineteen years of age as compared with an average age of twenty-six for World War II and for the American Civil War a century earlier. The average age of the men who died in Vietnam was 22.8 years. Almost 80 percent of men serving in Vietnam had a high school education or better and were from middle-class and working-class families. Almost 23 percent had fathers who were professionals, managers, or technicians.[64]

Of the men who actually served, 88 percent were Caucasian (including 170,000 Hispanics), 11 percent were black, and 1 percent belonged to other races. Of the men who died in Vietnam, 86 percent were Caucasian, 13 percent (7,241) were black, and 1.2 percent belonged to other races. Of the 170,000 Hispanics serving in Vietnam, 5 percent (3,070) died there. Blacks accounted for 10.5 percent of the combat deaths. Overall, blacks suffered 12.5 percent of deaths from all causes in Vietnam, while the percentage of blacks in the U.S. military was 13.5 percent of the population.[65]

More than 54 percent of all combat casualties took place in the four northern-most provinces of South Vietnam. All four shared a border with Laos. Of these, the one province that claimed the most American lives was Quang Tri, which bordered on both North Vietnam and Laos. More than 19 percent of the deaths in Vietnam were accidental rather than combat related. By way of comparison, helicopter crews accounted for 10 percent of all Vietnam War deaths, making it one of the most dangerous occupations in the theater.[66]

Kent State

The expansion of the war into Cambodia by air and land in 1970 to disrupt the so-called North Vietnamese staging areas somewhat reinvigorated the antiwar radicals somewhat. The subsequent killing of four students during an antiwar protest at Kent State University in Ohio, provoked a national student strike that involved more than 1 million young persons at 450 universities, colleges, and high schools. Violent incidents occurred at about 4 percent of these schools, but one-fifth of the nation's campuses were closed from one day to the rest of the semester. Two protestors were killed by police at Jackson State University in Mississippi and one young man, George Winne, Jr., set himself afire at the University of Southern California–San Diego. In Washington, D.C., 100,000 protestors rallied at the Lincoln Memorial. The Kent State crisis set off a new round of official intimidations and harassments. A federal grand jury absolved the Ohio State Guard for its role in the shootings, but charged twenty-five student activists and the president of the student body with crimes related to the spring disorders. Many of those charged were off-campus antiwar agitators.

The Justice Department opened hearings on the antiwar movement that ulti-mately subpoenaed nearly 2,000 witnesses before 100 separate grand juries in eighty-four cities in thirty-six states. The FBI launched probes into SDS, SANE, and certain antiwar journalists, intellectuals, authors, and civil rights leaders. The CIA began to monitor and infiltrate a wide range of antiwar groups. Many protest-ers and organizers considered this a serious threat to the movement. Although it was not clear at the time, the radical antiwar movement was becoming fragmented. Perhaps the number of individual antiwar groups vying for membership and promi-nence had grown too large. Perhaps some of the protesters were reaching too far in the eyes of the general public in their quest to end the war. For many moderates the

Ohio National Guardsmen throw tear gas at students across the campus lawn at Kent State University during an anti–Vietnam War demonstration at the university on May 7, 1970. Ultimately, the Guard opened fire on the protesters killing four and wounding nine. (AP Photo)

tangible violence and disruption at home had become more disturbing than a remote shooting war half a world away.[67]

The Chicago Eight were eight protestors charged with conspiracy, inciting to riot, and other charges related to the violent protests that took place at the 1968 Democratic National Convention. Early in the course of their trial, Black Panther activist Bobby Seale hurled bitter verbal attacks at the court, calling the judge names and refusing to be silent, among other things. The outraged judge ordered Seale bound and gagged in the courtroom. Ultimately, the judge severed Seale from the case and sentenced him to four years in prison for contempt. The trial lasted for months, with many celebrated figures from the American Left and counterculture called to testify, including folksinger Arlo Guthrie, writer Norman Mailer, LSD (acid) advocate Dr. Timothy Leary, and civil rights activist Rev. Jesse Jackson. In February 1970, all seven remaining defendants (Abbie Hoffman, Jerry Rubin, David Dellinger, Tom Hayden, Rennie Davis, John Froines, and Lee Weiner) were found not guilty on the conspiracy charges, but five were convicted of inciting to riot. Two (Froines and Weiner) were acquitted. The convictions were all overturned on appeal.

The WUO (and its Weathermen) issued a "Declaration of a State of War" against the U.S. government in 1970, and they used the trial of the Chicago Eight as a springboard for additional antiwar, antigovernment protest. During the so-called Days of Rage, up to 200 militants in makeshift battle gear vandalized the city's Haymarket Square and fought hand to hand with police, leaving fifty people injured, twenty-eight policemen injured, six Weathermen shot by police, and 103 protesters arrested. Thereafter, the WUO carried out a campaign consisting of bombings, jailbreaks, and riots. Their bombings were mostly of government buildings, along with several banks, police department headquarters and precincts, state and federal courthouses, and state prison administrative offices. The Weathermen organization largely disintegrated shortly after the United States reached a peace accord in Vietnam.

The origins of the Weathermen can be traced to the collapse and fragmentation of the SDS. The split between the mainstream antiwar followers of SDS and those members more closely aligned with the Progressive Labor Party pushed SDS as a whole further to the left. SDS leaders such as Bernardine Dohrn and Mike Klonsky announced an emerging revolutionary perspective by publishing a document entitled "Toward a Revolutionary Youth Movement" (RYM). The RYM promoted the philosophy that young workers possessed the potential to overthrow capitalism, if not by themselves then by transmitting radical ideas to the working class. The WUO's ideology changed direction in the early 1970s. With help from former Progressive Labor member, Clayton Van Lydegraf, the WUO sought a more Marxist-Leninist approach. The leading members of the WUO collaborated on ideas and published their manifesto: "Prairie Fire: The Politics of Revolutionary Anti-Imperialism."

The WUO generally eschewed organized protests, pursuing only their own covertly planned activities. They threw gasoline-filled Molotov cocktails at the home of a New York State Supreme Court Justice, at a police station in Manhattan, and at two military recruiting stations in Brooklyn. Today they would be classified as domestic terrorists. Widely known members of the WUO included Kathy Boudin, Mark Rudd, David Gilbert, and the still-married couple Bernardine Dohrn and Bill Ayers.[68] Most former Weathermen have successfully reintegrated into mainstream society, without necessarily repudiating their original revolutionary intent.

The convention riots and the tactics of groups like the Weathermen and the Black Panthers led many absolute pacifists to realize that sustained antiwar momentum was leading not to conversion of the government to the ways of peace, but rather to an increasingly violent and self-indulgent confrontation with it. Some clergy and Quaker pacifists openly condemned any appearance of violence on the part of ending the war. One antiwar theologian called the continuation of the violent response "too apocalyptic."[69]

By the last weeks of 1970, enthusiasm for the antiwar movement was flagging. The college freshman of 1966 were graduating and many were more interested in beginning careers than in ending wars. Accelerated troop withdrawals frustrated many antiwar organizers as they took away a fundamental issue around which to rally popular support. Large numbers of antiwar supporters, less committed perhaps than the organizers, faded into other pursuits or transferred their activism to alternate reform crusades (particularly civil rights). This lethargy was especially evident between autumn 1970 and spring 1972. In November 1972, Nixon was reelected in one of the biggest landslide election victories in U.S. political history. While the Watergate Scandal filled the news cycle and left the administration reeling domestically, Nixon quietly resumed the bombing and mining of North Vietnamese harbors, which brought the North Vietnamese back to the peace table.

Nixon's initial proposals to the North Vietnamese in Paris for a peaceful resolution of the war were rejected, but the move encouraged moderate critics of the

Table 17.2 Military Casualties for the Vietnam War

	Killed in action	Wounded	Missing	Captive
U.S. forces				
Combat	47,378	304,704[a]	2,338	766
Noncombat	10,824	n/a	n/a	n/a
Total	58,202	n/a	n/a	n/a
ARVN	223,748	1,169,763	n/a	n/a
NVA/VC[b]	1,100,000	600,000	n/a	26,000

[a]153,329 required hospitalization.
[b]Estimates.
Source: Compiled by author.
Note: n/a = not available.

administration. The *New York Times* praised the president's offer as fair and equitable. The *Christian Century* termed the move "a major propaganda victory." Nonetheless, "the great majority of leading antiwar dissidents were appalled at the ease with which Nixon outflanked his critics."[70] They seemed more interested in scoring points against the administration than ending the war. The message sent to the North Vietnamese by the general approval of Nixon's proposals was that they could not wait for a flagging political dissent in America to win the war for them.[71] In January 1973, North Vietnam and U.S. peace talks in Paris resulted in an agreement on January 27 that all warring parties would cease fire. Secretary of State Henry Kissinger signed the Paris Peace Accords, and major American involvement in the Vietnam War ended.

Vietnam had been devastated. Up to 400,000 South Vietnamese civilians had been killed, 900,000 were wounded, and 6.5 million had become refugees. Almost a quarter-million South Vietnamese soldiers gave their lives and more than a million were wounded. Exact data for the NVA is not available, and only estimates are extent.

The Fall of Vietnam

By March 1973, the last American combat soldiers had left South Vietnam, although a few military advisors and Marines, who were protecting U.S. installations and the embassy, remained. Of the almost 2 million Americans who had served in the war, almost 58,000 were dead, 300,000 were wounded (half of whom required hospitalization), and more than 1,000 were missing or captured in action. For the United States, the war was officially over, but on June 19, 1973 (three months after the fact) Congress—reacting to continued antiwar protests—passed the Case-Church Amendment, which called for a halt to all military activities in Southeast Asia by August 15, thereby ending more than a dozen years of direct U.S. military involvement in the region.

Because of the continuing scandal brought on by Watergate in June 1972, Nixon was forced to resign his office in August 1974 under threat of impeachment—one of the most disliked presidents in American history. His successor, Gerald R. Ford, constrained by congressional action, defaulted on U.S. promises to respond with force to any North Vietnamese violations of the peace terms. In the following fiscal year—in an act that still shames the United States—Congress cut off military and economic assistance to South Vietnam, leaving Americans with newsreel films of diplomats and their Marine guards scrambling onto helicopters to escape from the courtyard and roof of the U.S. Embassy in Saigon. Most historians directly attribute the fall of South Vietnam to the cessation of American aid. Without the necessary funds, South Vietnam found it logistically and financially impossible to fend off the North Vietnamese army. Historian Lewis Fanning went so far as to say that "it was not the Hanoi communists who won the war, but rather the American Congress that lost it."[72]

Ironically, under Nixon, the United States had followed a foreign policy marked by many of the favorite strategies of the pacifists of former times: negotiations to end the war with the North Vietnamese, détente with the Soviet Union, and the opening of diplomatic relations with China. Although he had ended the longest war in American history, Nixon's unorthodox use of executive powers in the interim was considered as a possible article of impeachment by his enemies in Congress. The charge was dropped as his methods were ultimately deemed not a violation of the executive's constitutional powers.

In 1977, President Jimmy Carter granted a pardon to all Vietnam-era draft evaders and called for the Defense Department to reevaluate the case of 420,000 servicemen who had been given less than honorable discharges during the conflict. Many Americans cheered these decisions as attempts to heal the rift between Americans left over from the war. In 1982, the Vietnam Veterans Memorial was dedicated to those who served. The blood shed by government in the name of war had been replaced by the determination of a new generation to have peace.

Notes

1. Charles R. Morris, *A Time of Passion: America, 1960–1980* (New York: Harper & Row, 1984), 98.

2. Morris, 98–99.

3. Morris, 98–99.

4. Morris, 2.

5. Morris, 3.

6. Morris, 3.

7. Morris, 18–19.

8. Morris, 18–19.

9. William J. Rust, *Kennedy in Vietnam: American Vietnam Policy, 1960–1963* (New York: Da Capo Press, 1985), xv.

10. James Reston, *The Artillery of the Press: Its Influence on American Foreign Policy* (New York: Harper and Row, 1966), 27.

11. Anita Lousie McCormick, *The Vietnam Antiwar Movement in American History* (Berkeley Heights, NJ: Enslow Publishers, 2000), 17.

12. McCormick, 19.

13. Rust, 30.

14. Mackubin T. Owens, "The Vietnam War: Winnable After All," editorial, December 1999, Ashbrook Center for Public Affairs at Ashbrook University, http://www.ashbrook.org/publicat/oped/owens/99/vietnamwar.html (accessed June 5, 2008).

15. Rust, 123.

16. Reston, 29.

17. Rust, xii.

18. Rust, xii

19. Morris, 102–103.

20. Thomas E. Woods, Jr. "Presidential War Powers," LewRockwell.com: Anti-state, Anti-war, Pro-market, http://www.lewrockwell.com/woods/woods45.html (accessed June 7, 2008).

21. Robert J. Hanyok, "Skunks, Bogies, Silent Hounds, and the Flying Fish: The Gulf of Tonkin Mystery, 2–4 August 1964," *Cryptologic Quarterly* 19, no. 4 (Winter 2000); 20, no. 1 (Spring 2001).

22. Morris, 101–102.

23. Morris, 101–102.

24. Morris, 101–102.

25. Morris, 101–102.

26. Reston, 7.

27. Reston, 7.

28. Jeffrey J. Matthews, "To Defeat a Maverick: The Goldwater Candidacy Revisited, 1963–1964," *Presidential Studies Quarterly* 27, no. 1 (1997): 662.

29. Morris, 101–102.

30. McCormick, 51.

31. McCormick, 53.

32. McCormick, 30.

33. Jonah Goldberg, "There Are Tears in My Eyes: Eddie Adams and the Most Famous Photo of the Vietnam War," National Review Online, http://article.nationalreview.com/?q=M2QxNWY0N2ZkY2IxMWJhZGQ4MTU3ZjhlZjg3NTk0NzE= (accessed June 6, 2008).

34. McCormick, 34.

35. David Farber, "The Counterculture and the Antiwar Movement," in *Give Peace a Chance: Exploring the Vietnam Antiwar Movement*, ed. Melvin Small and William D. Hoover (Syracuse, NY: Syracuse University Press, 1992), 8.

36. Mitchell K. Hall, "CALCAV and the Religious Opposition to the Vietnam War," in *Give Peace a Chance: Exploring the Vietnam Antiwar Movement*, ed. Melvin Small and William D. Hoover (Syracuse, NY: Syracuse University Press, 1992), 38.

37. Farber, 16.

38. Farber, 17–18.

39. Charles DeBenedetti, *An American Ordeal: The Antiwar Movement of the Vietnam Era* (Syracuse, NY: Syracuse University Press, 1990), 173.

40. DeBenedetti, 173.

41. DeBenedetti, 173.

42. DeBenedetti, 175.

43. DeBenedetti, 177–178.

44. DeBenedetti, 177–178.

45. DeBenedetti, 177–178.

46. DeBenedetti, 205.

47. DeBenedetti, 205.

48. Morris, 100.

49. Morris, 100.

50. Morris, 100.

51. Morris, 128.

52. Morris, 128.

53. Morris, 128.

54. McCormick, 40–41.

55. McCormick, 61.

56. DeBenedetti, 128.

57. DeBenedetti, 128.

58. The author's date of birth in the 1969 lottery came out 273rd, and his mother wept for joy that he would be able to complete college.

59. Leo J. Daugherty, "All-Volunteer Force: Success Story at 35," *Soldiers Magazine*, http://www.army.mil/-news/2008/06/26/10385-all-volunteer-force-success-story-at-35/ (accessed June 2009).

60. Daugherty.

61. Tom Holmann, "Vietnam War Statistics," Vietnam Veterans of America, California State Council, http://capmarine.com/cap/statistics.htm (accessed June 2009).

62. Holmann.

63. Holmann.

64. Holmann.

65. Holmann.

66. Holmann.

67. DeBenedetti, 177.

68. Ayers was a recent associate of Barack Obama, and Ayers's membership in the WUO was made an issue in the 2008 presidential election.

69. DeBenedetti, 254–255.

70. DeBenedetti, 292.

71. DeBenedetti, 292.

72. Lauren Zanolli, "What Happened When Democrats in Congress Cut Off Funding for the Vietnam War?" *George Mason University's History News Network*, http://hnn.us/articles/31400.html (accessed June 2009).

Epilogue

The American ruling class faces a difficulty in fighting a war and implementing an imperialist foreign policy right in front of the American [people]. Today they must fight their wars on TV. They must fight their wars in the newspapers, They must fight their wars with whole layers of their intelligentsia divided and exposing their aims and methods. We . . . have made war more real for them.

—Jack Barnes, war resister, 1976

[M]ake no mistake: evil does exist in the world. A nonviolent movement could not have halted Hitler's armies. Negotiations cannot convince al-Qaeda's leaders to lay down their arms. To say that force is sometimes necessary is not a call to cynicism—it is a recognition of history, the imperfections of man and the limits of reason. . . . So yes, the instruments of war do have a role to play in preserving the peace. And yet this truth must coexist with another—that no matter how justified, war promises human tragedy.

—Barack Obama, on accepting the Nobel Peace Prize, 2009

Hijacking the Antiwar Movement

American social reformers consistently have drawn on the energy of war resistance to promote their agendas. Throughout U.S. history, the American people have largely resisted the expansion of the reach of the federal government in peacetime. Popular acceptance of an extensive regulation of the engines of American production as practiced by the various U.S. governments in wartime—expressed in the term *war socialism*—has raised hope among socialists and liberal progressives in the United States that the electorate might be receptive to a wider government-controlled reform of the U.S. economy and culture in peacetime.

At the close of the Vietnam War, a group of erstwhile American antiwar protestors and self-proclaimed supporters of the Socialist Workers Party advanced a series of ideas and proposals by which they might utilize the antiwar sentiment raised by Vietnam to better promulgate socialism in the United States and thereby eliminate the evils of both the "imperial war machine" and the "capitalist regime" in America.[1] The candor of these self-proclaimed radicals (Jack Barnes, Mary Alice Waters, Tony Thomas, Barry Sheppard, and Betsey Stone) as they published their plans for "hijacking" the antiwar movement was remarkable. They explicitly proposed opening a "new stage" in the crusade toward American socialism by taking advantage of the residual outrage fostered by America's longest and least successful war to expand war resistance into a more far-reaching social protest. With the war in Southeast Asia ended, they hoped to use the damage inflicted on the integrity of the federal government during the Vietnam era to dissemble the "benighted outlooks and institutions upholding capitalism."[2]

In *Prospects for Socialism in America* (1976) they wrote:

> The experience of the Vietnam War produced . . . reassessments of Washington's role and designs in the origins of the cold war, the Korean War, and even World War II [that] are gaining a wider audience. There is more awareness that increasing escalation of the military budget brings something besides jobs for those employed in the war industries—it brings death, destruction, senseless maiming and killing, and misery to the world, to American GIs, and to workers' families here at home.[3]

Among the capitalist "institutions" targeted by these socialists for "deinstitutionalization" in America were the dominant religions, the work ethic, the long-established forms of education, hierarchical authority, traditional marriage, and the nuclear family.[4] These important and historical characteristics of American life were thought to "isolate" the United States from the other "more enlightened" industrial nations of Europe that had rejected the use of warfare as a policy and had adopted a number of socialist doctrines as part of their institutional structure.[5] In this regard, the authors viewed strict construction of the Constitution as a particular obstacle to their plans to overturn Americanism, and they noted that the crisis for capitalism that they envisioned did not favor an "extensive and effective . . . reform" but rather the "development of the prerequisites for a revolution."[6]

By vilifying those tenets underpinning traditional religious practice and industrial capitalism, post–World War II European intellectuals had invented a form of "enlightened socialism" largely to explain the failure of revolutionary Communism to bring about significant social and economic benefits for the common people. Moreover, even generally unbiased academic observers have agonized over the failure of these paradigms to deliver on their promises, and they have been unwilling to admit that the populace has garnered some obvious benefits under a better-regulated form of free market capitalism than that which existed at the beginning of the century. American trade unions, in particular, have found that they can be more effective negotiating with employers as individual entities rather than as part of a nationalized collective labor movement.

Modern political socialism—as opposed to the wildly utopian communitarianism of earlier decades—has had a long and uneven history in the United States since its first appearance as a movement near the turn of the 20th century. Emulating Woodrow Wilson's Nobel Peace Prize–winning "Fourteen Points" doctrine for international peace, in 1920 the Farmer-Labor Party (headed by Utah's Parley Parker Christensen) combined fourteen points of liberal-progressive and socialist-labor demands in its national platform, and in the same year the Socialist Workers Party (headed once again by Eugene V. Debs) ran on a more narrowly focused agenda designed to attract labor and trade unionists. Combined, these two candidates received less than 6 percent of the national vote total. In 1924 the American Federation of Labor (AFL) actively supported the Progressive Party candidacy of Robert LaFollette for president. LaFollette—a third-party candidate—received 16 percent of the vote by supporting the AFL's progressive Bill of Grievances, but he carried only one state, Wisconsin. Nonetheless, LaFollette had received the largest progressive-socialist vote in U.S. history. These attempts at electoral success failed to disrupt the dominant capitalism-based two-party system of the Republicans and Democrats and strongly suggested that the American electorate was generally unsympathetic to socialist and progressive third-party points of view. Moreover, the most successful third-party candidate in modern electoral history (since Teddy Roosevelt in 1912) was H. Ross Perot (19 percent in 1992), founder of the fiscally conservative (some say reactionary) Reform Party that was remarkable for the absence of policy positions regarding social reforms in its 1992 and 1996 platforms.[7]

Early in the 20th century, socialists realized that they would need to co-opt one of the two major parties to be successful on the national level, yet they seemingly missed their best opportunity following the stock market crash in 1929. The widespread economic crisis engendered by the Great Depression of the 1930s had offered socialists their last best chance to make inroads among the poor and unemployed in the United States during the 20th century. In this they were largely frustrated by Franklin D. Roosevelt, who subsumed a number of progressive and prolabor proposals as part of the Democratic Party response to the Depression. Many of the most egregious violations of worker and human rights were addressed through the use of legislation without overturning the free market system, thereby taking much of the vitality from the socialist argument for more drastic changes. It has been pointed out that "Roosevelt played a unique role in keeping the country politically stable during its greatest economic crisis, [and] he did so in a classic and traditional fashion."[8]

Roosevelt established himself as a progressive governor in New York by advocating tax relief and farm price supports for farmers and by supporting inexpensive electric power through the Tennessee Valley Authority (TVA). As president, he became a strong advocate of government intervention establishing relief programs for the unemployed, including the Civilian Conservation Corps (CCC) and Works Progress Administration (WPA) programs that put workers into the forests and parks planting trees, building roads, trails, and park buildings, and taking measures to prevent erosion. In 1935, Congress passed, and Roosevelt signed, the Social Security Act, possibly the most enduring piece of New Deal progressivism. Yet several key pieces of New Deal legislation, notably the National Recovery Act (NRA), were repeatedly struck down as unconstitutional by the Supreme Court, preventing some of its most progressive programs from taking effect. For the dedicated socialist critics of Roosevelt in the 1940s, however, the president had transformed the progressive promise of a New Deal into a War Deal by entering a European conflict that rescued the capitalist system from the crisis, helped to establish a vibrant military-industrial complex, and suggested that war worked as an agent of change.[9]

Nonetheless, socialist-inspired antiwar organizations like the Nonpartisan League, led by otherwise-opportunistic activists in the 1930s, in the 1940s "refrained from engaging in provocative acts or speeches that might [have] set off patriotic violence or governmental repression" once the United States entered World War II.[10] Socialist organizations like the Nonpartisan League were often accused of being dominated by "a small coterie of red-tide fanatics [Communists] who were not farmers, not workers, not property-holders, not tax payers, not homeowners, not producers in any sense." These charges—flourishing through mid-century and especially during the McCarthy era—had some foundation in truth because many social activists, like many of their antiwar counterparts in the 1960s and 1970s, served as full-time agents provocateur among labor unions, college students, and the poor having no obvious livelihood or source of income outside their politics.[11]

Although accepting of clearly progressive programs like Social Security, Medicare, and tax-supported low-income housing and public education, the U.S. population—almost alone among industrial societies—has resisted more dogmatic forms of socialism for more than a century, and the lack of a widespread working-class radicalism in the United States has bedeviled proponents of the socialist movement. Although the United States is arguably the most capitalistic and militarily aggressive of modern industrial nations, it has never had a viable ultra-left-wing political party. The progressive intellectual elite have been hard-pressed to explain the weakness of the movement among a population that has been otherwise so willingly to vocally protest the policies of its various governments in times of crisis.

Many socialist icons—directly addressing this inconsistency and including Lenin, Trotsky, Engels, and Marx in their day—have focused on the relatively high levels of social egalitarianism, economic productivity, and social mobility in America to explain it. Of course, these were the very qualities that supposedly would be enhanced by the introduction of socialist principles into the United States. In analyzing the future prospects for socialism in the United States, many observers have concluded that Americans differ sociologically from their European antecedents and even from those like their Canadian neighbors to the north who have similar demographic backgrounds and standards of living. They have termed this difference "American exceptionalism." It seems that the dominant spirit behind the U.S. antiwar electorate in the 20th century was rooted neither in social justice-progressivism, nor in Socialist-Communism, but seemingly owed more to its "contempt for authority" traditions and "Libertarian leave me alone" attitudes.[12]

To better prepare the soil of America for the extension of their brand of social justice-progressivism in the second half-century, the New Left—led by 1960s pundits like Saul Alinsky author of *Rules for Radicals: A Pragmatic Primer for*

Realistic Radicals (1971)—openly admitted to a policy of engendering artificial and self-serving crises "in education, public facilities, health care, and housing," and of using the threat of "pollution in the environment" as means to "break down" the American economy through the imposition of increased taxation, and expanded regulation and governmental intrusion into the free market system.[13] Through "flood the system" strategies like those of George Wiley's National Welfare Rights Organization of the 1970s,[14] they sought to overburden the existing social security and social welfare networks and to induce "combinations of breakdowns and shortages, slumps and inflation, the degradation of labor, . . . and *new wars* [italics added]" that would accelerate the "inevitable" capitalist decline and trigger a revitalized set of social and antiwar protests that activists might exploit to make significant gains among a jaded electorate. Wiley's group targeted the welfare system of New York City in the 1970s and was a major factor in driving the city into bankruptcy.[15]

The importance of war resistance in engendering widespread social protest cannot be overstated.[16] The post-Vietnam period saw a major economic crisis with high interest rates, spiraling inflation, and long gasoline lines, yet the period from approximately 1984 to recent times (2009) has been one of relatively widespread prosperity. Even the dire economic dislocations under the Carter administration (1976–1980) with double-digit inflation and unemployment proved insufficient to make socialism attractive to most Americans. Moreover, the conflicts in which the United States has become embroiled since Vietnam have not produced similar levels of antiwar activism. Military operations undertaken in Grenada, Panama, Bosnia, Iraq, and Afghanistan have seen war protestors turn out in disappointingly anemic numbers when contrasted with the Vietnam era's tens of thousands—essentially mirroring the small number of war resisters in historical terms from the American past.

Throughout its history, the United States has been a self-interested and self-reliant society—but also a self-indulgent and self-righteous one—in which popular distrust of political authority, a diversity of religious organizations, fiscal conservatism, and distinctly traditional modes of social interaction have provided the foundations of individual civil liberties, an unapologetic patriotism, and a security against tyranny. Both radical populism and governmental authoritarianism in America, as evidenced by their own historical experiences, have been constrained largely by a strict adherence to constitutionalism, judicial review, and the innate moderation of the American people. Many academics, intellectuals, and reformers reveal an underlying belief among themselves in a widespread "ignorance" among Americans concerning the subject of social justice simply because they can accept the idea of waging a "just" war.[17] Irving Howe, a leading socialist intellectual of the late 20th century noted of the essence of "American exceptionalism" that "it can veer toward an American version of anarchism, suspicious of all laws, forms, and regulations." Tilt "exceptionalism" to the right politically "and you have the worship of a free market." Tilt it to the left "and you have the moralism of American reformers."[18]

War resistance as practiced by Americans has had a long tradition largely separate from radical ideals and divorced from convenient sociopolitical labels. As has been shown in this volume, it has taken many forms and has evolved from a predominantly religion-based absolute pacifism toward a war resistance based on a panoply of fundamentally nonsectarian sources: policy, politics, intellectualism, isolationism, constitutionalism, ethnophobia, xenophobia, emotion, and bouts with economic and social engineering. It has been a sometimes unfortunate evolution during which uninformed beliefs have been conflated with uncontested truths on all sides. Paraphrasing Sun Tzu, a fifth century B.C.E. Chinese observer, all wars and all diplomacies are based on deception. Nonetheless, war-making and peace-seeking have joined to form the cross-fibers of the fabric of U.S. history and inevitably have affected both the will and the willfulness of the American people.

Notes

1. Jack Barnes, Mary Alice Waters, Tony Thomas, Barry Sheppard, and Betsey Stone, *Prospectus for Socialism in America* (New York: Pathfinder Press, 1976), 104.

2. Barnes et al., 24–25.

3. Barnes et al., 25.

4. Barnes et al., 24–25.

5. Seymour Martin Lipset and Gary Marks, *It Didn't Happen Here: Why Socialism Failed in the United States* (New York: W. W. Norton, 2000), 15.

6. Barnes et al., 29.

7. Perot's candidacy took votes from the Republicans and essentially guaranteed the election of Bill Clinton in both election years.

8. Lipset and Marks, 72.

9. Barnes et al., 28.

10. Lipset and Marks, 257.

11. Lipset and Marks, 255.

12. Barnes et al., 23.

13. Saul Alinsky, *Rules for Radicals: A Practical Primer for Realistic Radicals* (New York: Random House, 1989), 24–25.

14. Wiley's name was prominently listed on Nixon's so-called enemies list.

15. Barnes et al., 24–25.

16. Communism gained its foothold among Bolsheviks largely as a response to war weariness during World War I.

17. See Robert Stark, *God's Battalions: The Case for the Crusades* (New York: HarperCollins, 2009), 8.

18. Barnes et al., 24–25.

Appendix: Major Peace Organizations, 1960s and 1970s

Absent without Leave

American Friends Service Committee

Americans for Democratic Action

Campaign for Nuclear Disarmament

Campaign to Stop Funding the War

Catholic Peace Fellowship

Catholic Workers Movement

Central Committee for Conscientious Objectors

Committee for Non-Violent Action

Fellowship of Reconciliation

Friends Committee on National Legislation

Indochina Peace Campaign

League for Industrial Democracy

March on the Pentagon

March on Washington

May Second Movement

Movement for a New Congress

National Action Group

National Action/Research on the Military-Industrial Complex

National Coalition Against War, Racism, and Repression

National Committee for a Sane Nuclear Policy

National Conference for a New Politics

National Coordinating Committee to End the War in Vietnam

National Liberation Front

National Mobilization to End War in Vietnam

National Peace Action Coalition

National Student Association

New American Movement

People's Coalition for Peace and Justice

Revolutionary Youth Movement II

Set the Date Now

SLATE

Student League for Industrial Democracy

Student Mobilization Committee to End the War in Vietnam

Student Non-Violent Coordinating Committee

Student Peace Union

Students for a Democratic Society

Summer of Support

Turn Toward Peace

United World Federalists

Vietnam Day Committee

Vietnam Moratorium Committee

Vietnam Veterans against the War

War Resisters League

Women Strike for Peace

Women's International League for Peace and Freedom

Worker Student Alliance

Young People's Socialist League

Young Socialist Alliance

Selected Sources

Works and Articles

Alden, Carroll S., and Allan Westcott, *The United States Navy*. New York: J. B. Lippincott Company, 1945.

Anderson, Fred W. *A People's Army: Massachusetts Soldiers and Society in the Seven Years' War*. Chapel Hill: University of North Carolina Press, 1984.

Bennett, Ralph, ed. *Settlements in the Americas: Cross-Cultural Perspectives*. Newark: University of Delaware Press, 1993.

Boyne, Walter J. *Clash of Titans: World War II at Sea*. New York: Simon & Schuster, 1995.

Brown, Richard D. *Major Problems in the Era of the American Revolution, 1760–1791*. New York: Houghton Mifflin, 2000.

Brown, Seyom. *The Causes and Prevention of War*. New York: St. Martin's Press, 1994.

Bull, Stephen, and Gordon L. Rottman. *Infantry Tactics of the Second World War*. Westminster, MD: Osprey Publishing, 2008.

Burns, James MacGregor. *The Vineyard of Liberty*. New York: Alfred A. Knopf, 1982.

Byrd, Robert C. *The Senate, 1789–1989: Classic Speeches, 1830–1993*. Washington, DC: Government Printing Office, 1994.

Callahan, North. *Royal Raiders: The Tories of the American Revolution*. New York: Bobbs-Merrill, 1963.

Calloway, Colin G. *The Shawnees and the War for America*. New York: Viking, 2007.

Canby, Henry Seidel. *Prefaces to Peace: A Symposium*. New York: Columbia University Press, 1943.

Canney, Donald L. *The Old Steam Navy: Frigates, Sloops, and Gunboats, 1815–1885*, Vol. I. Annapolis, MD: Naval Institute Press, 1990.

DeBenedetti, Charles. *An American Ordeal: The Antiwar Movement of the Vietnam Era*. Syracuse, NY: Syracuse University Press, 1990.

DeVoto, Bernard. *The Year of Decision, 1846*. Boston: Little, Brown, 1943.

Dew, Thomas R. "Dissertation on the Characteristic Differences between the Sexes, and on the Position and Influence of Women in Society (1835)." In *Documenting America: A Reader in*

United States History from Colonial Times to 1877, ed. Leonard Pitt. Dubuque, IA: Kendall/ Hunt, 1989.

Doleac, Charles B. "On the 100th Anniversary of Theodore Roosevelt's Nobel Peace Prize." *Union Leader*, December 10, 2006.

Dull, Jonathan. *The French Navy and American Independence: A Study of Arms and Diplomacy, 1774–1787.* Princeton, NJ: Princeton University Press, 1975.

Eggleston, George C. *A Rebel's Recollections.* 1874; rpt., Bloomington: Indiana University Press, 1959.

Farber, David. "The Counterculture and the Antiwar Movement." In *Give Peace a Chance: Exploring the Vietnam Antiwar Movement,* ed. Melvin Small and William D. Hoover. Syracuse, NY: Syracuse University Press, 1992.

Fischer, David Hackett. *Albion's Seed: Four British Folkways in America.* New York: Oxford University Press, 1989.

Forester, C. S. *The Age of Fighting Sail: The Story of the Naval War of 1812.* Sandwich, MA: Chapman Billies, 1956.

Freehling, William W. *The South vs. the South: How Anti-Confederate Southerners Shaped the Course of the Civil War.* New York: Oxford University Press, 2001.

Gabriel, Richard A. *The Military History of Ancient Israel.* Westport, CT: Praeger, 2003.

Garten, Jeffrey E. *A Cold Peace: America, Japan, Germany, and the Struggle for Supremacy.* New York: Random House, 1993.

Gatewood, Willard B. Jr. *Black Americans and the White Man's Burden, 1898–1903.* Urbana: University of Illinois Press, 1975.

Gavin, John R. *The Minute Men: The First Fight: Myths and Realities of the American Revolution.* Washington, DC: Brassey's, 1996.

George, Alexander. *Forceful Persuasion: Coercive Diplomacy as an Alternative to War.* Washington, DC: United States Institute of Peace Press, 1991.

George, Henry. *Protection or Free Trade: An Examination of the Tariff Question with Especial Regard to the Interests of Labor.* New York: Henry George and Co., 1886.

Gilje, Paul A. *Liberty on the Waterfront: American Maritime Culture in the Age of Revolution.* Philadelphia: University of Pennsylvania Press, 2004.

Griess, Thomas E., ed. *Definitions and Doctrine of the Military Art: The West Point Military History Series.* Wayne, NJ: Avery, 1985.

Herring, George C. *From Colony to Superpower: U.S. Foreign Relations Since 1776.* New York: Oxford University Press, 2008.

Hess, Earl J. *The Rifle Musket on Civil War Combat: Reality and Myth.* Lawrence: University Press of Kansas, 2008.

Holt, Michael F. *The Rise and Fall of the American Whig Party: Jacksonian Politics and the Onset of the Civil War.* New York: Oxford University Press, 1999.

Howarth, Stephen. *To Shining Sea: A History of the Unites States Navy, 1775–1991.* New York: Random House, 1991.

Howe, Daniel Walker. *What God Hath Wrought: The Transformation of America, 1815–1848.* New York: Oxford University Press, 2007.

Kaufman, Bill. *Ain't My America: The Long, Noble History of Antiwar Conservatism and Middle-American Anti-Imperialism.* New York: Henry Holt, 2008.

Kelsey, Rayner Wickersham. *Friends and the Indians, 1655–1917.* Philadelphia: Associated Executive Committee of Friends on Indian Affairs, 1917.

Kennedy, James R. and Walter D. Kennedy, *The South Was Right.* Gretna, LA: Pelican, 1995.

Ketchum, Ralph, ed. *The Anti-Federalist Papers and the Constitutional Convention Debates.* New York: New American Library, 1986.

Leiner, Frederick C. *Millions for Defense: The Subscription Warships of 1798.* Annapolis, MD: Naval Institute Press, 2000.

Levy, Peter B. *Encyclopedia of the Reagan-Bush Years.* Westport, CT: Greenwood Press, 1996.

Lewis, David Levering. *God's Crucible: Islam and the Making of Europe, 570–1215.* New York: W. W. Norton, 2008.

Lundstrom, John B. *The First Team.* Annapolis, MD: Naval Institute Press, 1984.

MacDonnell, Francis. *Insidious Foes: The Axis Fifth Column and the American Home Front.* New York: Oxford University Press, 1995.

Mahan, Alfred Thayer. *The Influence of Sea Power upon History, 1660–1783.* New York: Dover Publications, 1987.

Marcy, Randolph B. *The Prairie Traveler: A Hand-book for Overland Expeditions.* 1859; rpt., Bedford, MA: Applewood Books, 1993.

Martin, James Kirby, and Mark Edward Lender. *A Respectable Army: The Military Origins of the Republic, 1763–1789.* Arlington Heights, IL: Harlan Davidson, 1982.

McCormick, Anita Louise. *The Vietnam Antiwar Movement in American History.* Berkeley Heights, NJ: Enslow, 2000.

Merrell, James H. *Into the American Woods: Negotiators on the American Frontier.* New York: Norton & Company, 1999.

Miller, Nathan. *Sea of Glory: A Naval History of the American Revolution.* Annapolis, MD: Naval Institute Press, 1974.

Millett, Allan R., and Peter Maslowski. *For the Common Defense: A Military History of the United States of America.* New York: Free Press, 1984.

Millis, Walter. *Arms and Men: A Study of American Military History.* New York: A Mentor Book, 1956.

Milner, Clyde A., II. *With Good Intentions: Quaker Work Among the Pawnees, Otos, and Omahas in the 1870s.* Lincoln: University of Nebraska Press, 1982.

Mitchell, Thomas. *Indian Fighters Turned American Politicians: From Military Service to Public Office.* Westport, CT: Greenwood Press, 2003.

Morgan, T. *Reds: McCarthyism in Twentieth-century America.* New York: Random House, 2003.

Morison, Samuel Eliot. *Sources and Documents Illustrating the American Revolution 1764–1788 and the Formation of the Federal Constitution.* New York: Oxford University Press, 1965.

Morris, Charles R. *A Time of Passion: America, 1960–1980.* New York: Harper & Row, 1984.

Nitze, Paul H. "Assuring Strategic Stability in an Era of Détente." In *Arms Control and Security: Current Issues,* ed. Wolfram H. Hanrieder. Boulder, CO: Westview Press, 1979.

Peyer, Bernd C. *The Tutor'd Mind: Indian Missionary-Writers in Antebellum America.* Amherst: University of Massachusetts Press, 1997.

Rehnquist, William H. *All the Laws But One: Civil Liberties in Wartime.* New York: Vintage Books, 1998.

Reynolds, Clark G. *The Carrier War.* Alexandria, VA: Time-Life Books, 1982.

Richards, Caroline C. *Village Life in America, 1852–1872.* Gansevoort, NY: Corner House, 1997.

Richter, Daniel K. *Facing East from Indian Country: A Native History of Early America.* Cambridge, MA: Harvard University Press, 2001.

Robotti, Frances D., and James Vescovi. *The USS Essex and the Birth of the American Navy.* Holbrook, MA: Adams Media, 1999.

Rosenberg, Norman L., and Emily S. Rosenberg. *In Our Times: America Since World War II.* Englewood Cliffs, NJ: Simon & Schuster, 1987.

Rossiter, Clinton, ed. *The Federalist Papers.* New York: New American Library, 1961.

Rowland, K. T. *Steam at Sea: The History of Steam Navigation.* New York: Praeger, 1970.

Rust, William J. *Kennedy in Vietnam: American Vietnam Policy, 1960–1963.* New York: Da Capo Press, 1985.

Sanger, S. F., and D. Hays. *The Olive Branch of Peace and Good Will to Men: The Antiwar History of the Brethren and Mennonites, the People of the South during the Civil War, 1861–1865.* Elgin, IL: Brethren Publishing House, 1907.

Silver, Peter. *Our Savage Neighbors: How the Indian War Transformed Early America.* New York: W. W. Norton, 2008.

Stoessinger, John G. *Why Nations Go to War.* New York: St. Martin's Press, 1993.

Toll, Ian W. *Six Frigates: The Epic History of the Founding of the U.S. Navy.* New York: W. W. Norton, 2006.

Trofimenko, Henry. "The Theology of Strategy." In *Arms Control and Security: Current Issues,* ed. Wolfram F. Hanrieder. Boulder, CO: Westview Press, 1979.

Van Buskirk, Judith L. *Generous Enemies: Patriots and Loyalists in Revolutionary New York.* Philadelphia: University of Pennsylvania Press, 2002.

Van Tyne, Claude Halstead. *Loyalists in the American Revolution.* Ganesvoort, NY: Corner House Historical Publications, 1999.

Volo, Dorothy Denneen, and James M. Volo. *Daily Life during the American Revolution.* Westport, CT: Greenwood Press, 2003.

Volo, Dorothy Denneen, and James M. Volo. *Daily Life in Civil War America.* Westport, CT: Greenwood Press, 1998.

Volo, Dorothy Denneen, and James M. Volo. *Daily Life on the Old Colonial Frontier.* Westport, CT: Greenwood Press, 2002.

Volo, James M. *Blue Water Patriots: The American Revolution Afloat.* Westport, CT: Greenwood Press, 2007.

Walling, Michael G. *Bloodstained Sea: The U.S. Coast Guard in the Battle of the Atlantic, 1941–1945.* New York: McGraw Hill, 2004.

Weber, Jennifer L. *Copperheads: The Rise and Fall of Lincoln's Opponents in the North.* Oxford: Oxford University Press, 2006.

Weigley, Russell F. *History of the Unites States Army.* New York: Macmillan, 1967.

Weisberger, Bernard A. *America Afire: Jefferson, Adams, and the Revolutionary Election of 1800.* New York: HarperCollins, 2000.

Wheelan, Joseph. *Invading Mexico: America's Continental Dream and the Mexican War, 1846–1848.* New York: Carroll & Graf, 2007.

Wisan, Joseph E. *The Cuban Crisis as Reflected in the New York Press, 1895–1898.* 1934; rpt., New York: Octagon Books, 1965.

Internet Sources

Acheson, Dean G. "National Press Club Speech," January 12, 1950. http://www.j-bradford-delong.net/TCEH/Acheson_Korea.html (accessed October 2008).

Bernstein, Eduard. "John Bellers, Champion of the Poor and Advocate of a League of Nations." In *Cromwell and Communism Socialism And Democracy in the Great English Revolution.*

London: George Allen & Unwin, 1895. http://www.marxists.org/reference/archive/bernstein/works/1895/cromwell/17-bellers.htm#top (accessed July 2008).

Borah, William E. "The League of Nations," November 19, 1919. http://www.senate.gov/artand-history/history/resources/pdf/BorahLeague.pdf (accessed October 2008).

Chamberlain, Neville. "Chamberlain's radio broadcast before 10 Downing Street (transcription)," September 30, 1938. http://eudocs.lib.byu.edu/index.php/Neville_Chamberlain%27s_%22Peace_For_Our_Time%22_speech (accessed October 2008).

Cordesman, Anthony H., and William D. Sullivan. "US Defense Planning, The Challenge of Resources," pp. ii–iii. http://www.csis.org/media/csis/pubs/060707_defense_resource_challenges.pdf (accessed March 2009).

Currie, David P. "The Civil War Congress." *University of Chicago Law Review* 73: 1131–1226, 1139. http://lawreview.uchicago.edu/issues/archive/v73/fall/Currie.pdf (accessed June 2008).

Dylan, Bob. "Masters of War." http://www.bobdylan.com/songs/masters.html (accessed October 2008).

Eisenhower, Dwight David. *Farewell Speech to the Nation*, January 17, 1961. http://mcadams.posc.mu.edu/ike.htm (accessed October 2008).

Keil, Amanda. "The Peaceful People And the First Nations: A Brief History Of Friends and Native Americans." American Friends Service Committee. http://www.afsc.org/nymetro/specialprojects/resources/SPpeacefulPeopleAndFirstNations.pdf (accessed June 2008).

King, Martin Luther, Jr. *Autobiography of Martin Luther King, Jr.* http://www.stanford.edu/group/King//publications/autobiography/chp_2.htm (accessed October 2008).

Lodge, Henry Cabot, Sr. "Speech Against the League of Nations," August 12, 1919. http://www2.volstate.edu/socialscience/FinalDocs/WWI-20s/lodgeagainst.htm (accessed October 2008).

Müller, Harald. "Multinational Security Cooperation and Military Doctrines in the OSCE Area." *Disarmament Diplomacy* no. 60 (September 2001). http://www.acronym.org.uk/dd/dd60/60op2.htm (accessed July 2008).

Russell, Bertrand. "The Russell-Einstein Manifesto." http://www.pugwash.org/about/manifesto.htm (accessed July 2008).

Stanton, Gregory H. "How We Can Prevent Genocide: Building an International Campaign to End Genocide." http://www.genocidewatch.org/HOWWECANPREVENTGENOCIDE.htm (accessed February 2009).

Stromberg, Joseph R. "The Old Cause: A Lost Episode of the Old Right: The 'Great Debate,' 1950–1951." http://www.antiwar.com/stromberg/pf/p-s022100.html (accessed October 2008).

Venditta, David. "We Are Now the Frontier." *The Morning Call*. http://www.mcall.com/all-fi_mayhemnov26,0,579176.story?page=2 (accessed September 2008).

Washington, George. *Washington's Farewell Address of 1796*. http://www.yale.edu/lawweb/avalon/washing.htm (accessed October 2008).

Wolkins, Lyra Trueblood. "The American Peace Society." *Swarthmore College Peace Collection*. http://www.swarthmore.edu/Library/peace/DG001-025/DG003APS.html (accessed July 2008).

Index

About the Author

Trained as a scientist, educator, and historian, DR. JAMES M. VOLO brings a unique perspective to his subjects. He is the author or coauthor of more than a dozen historical reference works dealing with American history including *Blue Water Patriots: The American Revolution Afloat* (Praeger, 2007), *Daily Life in Civil War America* (Greenwood, 1998), *Daily Life during the American Revolution* (Greenwood, 2003), and *Daily Life on the Old Colonial Frontier* (Greenwood, 2002). He has also served as a consultant for documentary television and movie projects dealing with the American Revolution and the Civil War. Dr. Volo presently teaches physics at Sacred Heart University in Fairfield, Connecticut.